CW01018897

Introducing

Delphi Programming
Theory through practice

Introducing

Delphi Programming
Theory through practice

FOURTH EDITION

John Barrow

Linda Miller

Katherine Malan

Helene Gelderblom

OXFORD
UNIVERSITY PRESS

Great Clarendon Street, Oxford OX2 6DP

Oxford University Press is a department of the University of Oxford.
It furthers the University's objective of excellence in research, scholarship,
and education by publishing worldwide in

Oxford New York

Auckland Cape Town Dar es Salaam Hong Kong Karachi
Kuala Lumpur Madrid Melbourne Mexico City Nairobi
New Delhi Shanghai Taipei Toronto

with offices in
Argentina Austria Brazil Chile Czech Republic France Greece
Guatemala Hungary Italy Japan Poland Portugal Singapore
South Korea Switzerland Thailand Turkey Ukraine Vietnam

Oxford is a registered trade mark of Oxford University Press
in the UK and certain other countries

Published in South Africa
by Oxford University Press Southern Africa, Cape Town

Introducing Delphi Programming: Theory through practice
Fourth edition
ISBN 019 578911 3

© Oxford University Press Southern Africa 2005

Publishing manager: Marian Griffin
Editor: Lydia Wilson
Design and cover design: Brigitte Rouillard
Indexer: Jeanne Cope
Cover photograph: Great Stock!/Lightscapes

Published by Oxford University Press Southern Africa
PO Box 12119, N1 City, 7463, Cape Town, South Africa

Set in Minion 10.5 on 12.5pt by Global Graphics
Reproduction by The Image Bureau
Cover reproduction by The Image Bureau
Imagesetting by Castle Graphics
Printed and bound by ABC Press, Cape Town

PREFACE

Welcome to the fourth edition of *Introducing Delphi Programming: Theory through practice*. Although there are many books on Delphi, none that we have seen covers all the aspects we feel are important for our students - so we have written this introductory book to teach both the practical side of programming and important programming theory. After working through it you should be able to write simple Delphi programs easily and should be well set to develop your skills further, whether in Delphi, in other programming languages, or in system analysis and design. Since this is an introductory book, little previous experience with computers is necessary. If you enjoy surfing the Internet or understand the basics of spreadsheets and now want to learn about programming, this is the book for you!

What does this book cover? And with all the programming languages and environments now available, what are the important facets a beginning programmer needs to learn about? Several aspects stand out:

o *Visual user interface design.* Many current programming languages support the visual development of graphical user interfaces (GUIs) under operating systems such as Windows. Visual user interface development is an integral part of this book from the first chapter, giving a beginning programmer a sense of achievement and motivation from writing good-looking programs. At the same time, this easy development of a user interface allows a beginning programmer to come to grips early on with the principles and programming that support the user interface.

o *Event-driven programming.* For a large number of GUI applications, event-driven programming provides a natural and congruent design approach. This book introduces simple event handling from the start, giving the programmer a familiarity and ease with event-driven concepts.

o *Procedural and object-oriented programming.* There is a great deal of value in both structured programming and object-oriented programming. Which is best? Many programming fundamentals remain essential irrespective of the approach one adopts. In this book we introduce the learner to valuable aspects from both since knowledge of both will be important for many years to come.

o *Principles and skills.* Computer technology develops at an alarming rate. While learning practical programming skills it is even more important to develop a sound theoretical understanding of programming in general and so to prepare for future languages and environments. This book provides many worked examples to develop programming skills and explains the principles underlying these to provide a foundation for long-term growth.

o *RAD (rapid application development) programming.* While this book emphasizes programming fundamentals, it also covers some RAD aspects since these are an important factor in commercial software development.

We have revised the entire text of the third edition to produce this fourth edition. Some of the more important goals of the revisions are:

o *Incorporate feedback from students and instructors.* Other instructors and our students have commented on what they have experienced as the strengths and weaknesses of the earlier editions. This has helped us include many changes that we hope our readers will find helpful.

o *Incorporate newer versions of Delphi.* This edition also covers Delphi versions 7 and 8. Delphi 8 has several major differences from earlier versions, and the text now gives parallel instructions for the different versions of Delphi where needed.

o *Maintain compatibility with the previous edition.* Since there will be situations where the third and fourth editions will be used together in the same learning situation we have tried where possible to retain the same numbering for examples and figures. For backward compatibility we use Delphi 8 with the VCL Forms library and do not cover its full .NET capability.

o *Use an open source SQL database.* The database chapters, chapters 15 to 17, are completely new and use MySQL as the database with Delphi versions 6 to 8. (Reporting is introduced through Rave Reports, which is packaged with Delphi.)

o *Increase the emphasis on user interface design.* Comments on user interface design principles have been added to the existing examples.

An important aspect is that this book is written for *independent learning*. Our students are distance learning students and so do not have the benefit of face-to-face classes and laboratory sessions. Instead, they must learn an extremely practical subject like programming on their own. This is different to a more conventional learning situation, and the book makes special provision for independent learning while still being well-suited to a conventional classroom situation.

To achieve this we use an experiential approach. We typically introduce a new concept through a worked example that the reader can enter into the computer, in the process seeing and experimenting with the concepts involved. Some of these worked examples proceed in stages to encourage a 'divide-and-conquer' approach to programming. After setting the context in this tangible way, we typically then explain the theory underlying the example. To help emphasise important concepts, each chapter ends with a review section summarising the chapter followed by a section tabulating the new Delphi concepts that have been introduced. This, together with a detailed index and table of contents, simplifies the process of locating the presentation of specific concepts and implementations.

Normal, good learning techniques will make learning from *Introducing Delphi Programming: Theory through practice* much more effective. It may help to scan a chapter before starting on it in earnest. Use this book in front of a computer. Enter each example and engage with it in an interested way, penetrating to the important concepts. Tackle all the problems at the end of each chapter. When you cannot understand or do something, try paging backwards through the book to see whether some concept has slipped your mind. If the difficulty continues, try putting the problem to one side for the moment and going on to the next part. Often experience with a later section will help in solving something you had to skip over. If you are really stuck, it may be best to start the chapter over. Learning is a strange and unpredictable process, so be flexible. Registered Unisa students receive solutions to the problems at the end of each chapter during the course of their studies and they can contact their lecturers to help sort out difficulties. Instructors at other institutions who adopt this book are also entitled to the solutions to the problems. Additional material will become available on the website www.oup.com/za.

One of the original authors, Helene Gelderblom, could not participate in this revision and we'd like to thank Katherine Malan for joining the writing team and for contributing her experience and enthusiasm. We'd also like to acknowledge the contribution of some of our colleagues. Ken Halland has made many valuable comments from the inception of the first edition and has been a helpful sounding board over the years as this book has grown. Patricia Gouws and Bob Jolliffe provided important support in developing the new database chapters for this edition. We'd like to acknowledge the feedback on the previous editions of this book from both students and instructors – we hope you can see how your comments and criticisms have helped to shape this edition. The editorial team at Oxford University Press SA has been flexible and supportive in the difficult production schedule needed for this revision. Without their support this edition would have taken much longer to complete. And finally, without the support of our respective families we could never have done this. Thanks!

John Barrow
Linda Miller
Katherine Malan
Helene Gelderblom

Pretoria
November 2004

CONTENTS

12 Procedures and parameters

CHAPTER 1

Introduction to visual programming

PURPOSE OF THIS CHAPTER

This book introduces computer programming in an easy, informal style. It introduces important concepts and gives you practice through Delphi, a versatile and sophisticated programming environment that allows you to develop Windows and Linux* programs with relative ease.

Delphi has many important features:

o It enables us to create a user interface 'visually' by dropping, dragging and resizing components with a mouse.

o It is fully object-oriented, making it easier to re-use parts of one program in another program and so reduce the costs of program development.

o It has good database facilities, which allow you to explore typical business applications.

o It is rich in rapid application development (RAD) facilities.

The base language for Delphi is 'Object Pascal', sometimes known as 'Delphi Pascal'. Like earlier versions of Pascal, Delphi Pascal is an excellent language for learning to program. It is also a powerful general-purpose programming language widely used for commercial program development. Delphi combines these different aspects very elegantly, and so, once you have completed this book, you will have made a good start in learning to program. You should also be able to adapt readily to other common programming languages and environments.

Since this book is only an introduction to programming and to Delphi, we cannot deal with all their facets in detail. We hope, however, to cover the basics of Delphi in a way that is both interesting and useful. One of the best ways to learn to program is by trying out many examples directly on the computer and to develop programming theory from this practical experience.

So, if you are not already at a computer, sit down in front of one, switch it on, and load Delphi. (We assume that you have already installed Delphi. If not, see Appendix 4.)

* This book concentrates on Win32 programming, but much also applies to .Net (with Delphi 8) and Linux (with Kylix)

Delphi's Integrated Development Environment

When you launch the Delphi program you are taken into Delphi's *Integrated Development Environment* or IDE. Delphi versions 4 to 7 start up with a new application open on the screen. Figure 1.1.a shows the opening screen for Delphi 7, and Delphi versions 4 to 6 are similar. If any of the windows shown in figure 1.1.a are not on your screen, use the View command on the menu bar at the top of the screen to display the Form, the Object Inspector or, in Delphi 6 or 7, the Object TreeView. (The equivalent keystrokes are <Shift+F12>†, <F11> or <Shift+Alt+F11> respectively.)

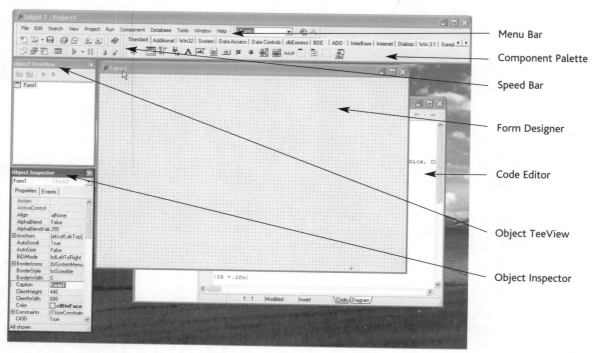

Figure 1.1.a Delphi 7's Integrated Development Environment

Figure 1.1.b shows the opening screen for Delphi 8.

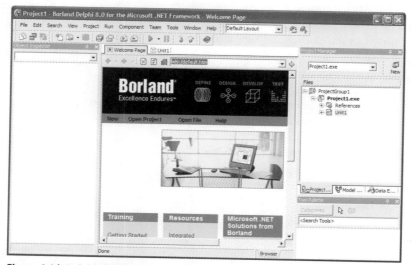

Figure 1.1.b Delphi 8's opening screen

† The notation <Shift+F12> means that you must press the <Shift> key and, while holding it down, press <F12>. Afterwards, release <F12> and then release <Shift>.

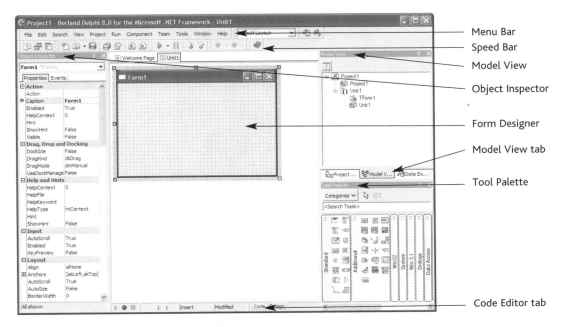

Figure 1.1.c Starting a new VCL Forms Application in Delphi 8

Since Delphi 8 offers the choice of VCL Forms, Windows Forms and ASP .NET applications it does not open with a new application on the screen. VCL Forms is closest to the previous versions of Delphi and so we will use it in this book.

- In Delphi 8 use the menu sequence File | New | VCL Forms Application to start a new application (figure 1.1.c).

The Form Designer

In Delphi we use the Form Designer (labelled in figures 1.1.a and 1.1.c) to design the user interface for the program we are writing. Forms are among the most important objects in Delphi since they are the background on which we place all the other components we use in developing a Delphi program. While we are working with the Form Designer we are in 'design mode'. Once we have written a program, we then compile the program into executable form and go into 'run mode'.

The Object Inspector

The Object Inspector (labelled in figures 1.1.a and 1.1.c) allows us to set the initial properties of all the components we use in the user interface and, as we'll soon see, is an important part of program design in Delphi.

In Delphi 8 the Object Inspector can be arranged by Category or by Name. To select between these, click the right mouse button within the Object Inspector window to bring up a context sensitive pop-up menu (figure 1.2). We have chosen to arrange the Object Inspector by Name since this is how it is arranged in earlier versions of Delphi.

Immediately below the title is a box showing Form1 TForm1 (figures 1.3a or 1.3b). This tells us that the object we are currently inspecting with the Object Inspector is called 'Form1'. Below that is a long list of object properties. Near the top are two tabs, labelled 'Properties' and 'Events'.

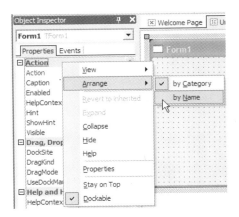

Figure 1.2 Arranging the Object Inspector by Name in Delphi 8

- Click on the Events tab to see the list of the events associated with the form.
- We'll introduce events a little later in this chapter, so for now click on the Properties tab to display the properties.
- Look down the list of properties until you find 'Caption'. (You may have to scroll down – use either the slider of the scroll bar or the up and down arrows on the right edge of the Object Inspector.) Alongside Caption you will see the entry 'Form1'.
- Using your mouse, click in the box and change the Caption to 'First Form'. Notice that, as you type, the title of the form alongside changes too.

Just a few lines below the Caption property is the 'Color' property (notice the American spelling!).
- Click on 'Color'. To the right is a small down arrow. Click on this to display all the different values the Form's Color property can take (figure 1.3.a or 1.3b).
- Using the mouse, scroll up or down through the list by clicking on the arrows at either end of the scroll bar or by dragging the slider, then select 'clAqua'. The form's colour now changes to light blue-green. (If you prefer, you can also type in 'clAqua' directly, without selecting it from the drop-down box.)

Figure 1.3.a Using the Object Inspector to set the Color property in Delphi 6 or 7

Properties

We have now seen our first Delphi object, a form object. From the Object Inspector we see that a whole range of properties is associated with a form object. Soon we'll look at other objects too, and see that each object has its own set of properties.

In Delphi and in some other languages, properties are a sophisticated form of *attribute*. The concept of attributes is very important in object orientation and is central to object-oriented programming. All object-oriented programming languages (not just Delphi) associate a particular set of attributes with an object and the values of the attributes define the object's state.

When we changed the values of the Caption and Color properties, we saw that we can change property values to suit our requirements by using the Object Inspector while we are in design mode.

Soon we'll see that we can also change properties through program statements. Setting properties programmatically is a common part of object-oriented programming.

The Component palette or Tool palette

Figure 1.4.a The Standard tab of Delphi 6's Component palette

Delphi provides a large library of standard user interface components. In Delphi versions 1 to 7 these appear on the Component palette (labelled in figure 1.1.a and shown in greater detail in figure 1.4.a).
- If the component palette does not look like the figure 1.4.a, click on the Standard tab to display the standard components.

Delphi 8 shows the components on the Tool palette (labelled in figure 1.1.c and repeated in figure 1.4.b). Like the Object Inspector, it can be configured. We

Figure 1.3.b Using the Object Inspector to set the Color property in Delphi 8

chose to deselect the Vertical Flow Layout (figure 1.4.c) to get a horizontal layout (figure 1.4.b).

- Move the mouse over the Component / Tool palette and, without clicking, let the pointer rest on the various symbols. After a little wait on the big 'A' symbol in Delphi 1–7, the word 'Label' appears in a small, yellow Hint box. Move the pointer one space to the right and the 'Edit' hint appears. Each symbol represents a standard Delphi component that you can use in your program. Some of the symbols in Delphi 8 differ from the earlier versions, but it too displays the hints to identify each component. In Delphi 8 all component names start with a 'T', and Label appears as TLabel, Edit as TEdit and so on.

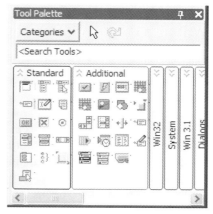

Figure 1.4.b Delphi 8's Tool palette

The Object TreeView or Model View

Delphi 6 and 7 have a window entitled 'Object TreeView' (labelled in fig 1.1.a). Delphi 8 has the Model View, which is a similar though more detailed diagram (to the right of the Form Designer on the Model View tab, labelled in figure 1.1.c). As we shall see, these diagrams display the objects contained on the Form. (Delphi 5 and earlier do not have this facility.)

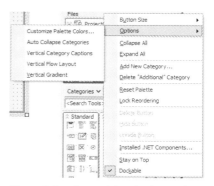

Figure 1.4.c Customising the layout for Delphi 8's Tool palette

EXAMPLE 1.1 A simple program

We'll see how to use these features we have been discussing by writing a simple program. It will have a single button on a form. Clicking on this button will change the form's colour from a blue-green to purple.

- Move the mouse pointer over the standard tab of the Component/Tool palette until it is resting on the OK symbol and the Button hint (Delphi 4 to 7) or TButton hint (Delphi 8) is displayed.
- Click the left mouse button once. The button symbol becomes dimmer.
- Now move the pointer to somewhere in the centre of the form – the exact position is not important for now – and click the left mouse button again. A silvery shape with the Caption Button1 appears on the form (figure 1.5). You have now 'placed a button on the form.' The ease of placing components on a form with a mouse like this is part of Delphi's RAD capability. It speeds up the development of a graphical user interface (GUI) significantly, and is often referred to as *visual GUI development*.
- Move to the Object Inspector at the left of the screen. Click the drop-down arrow near the top and select Button1 TButton (figure 1.6).
- Move down to the Caption property and change the Caption to Colour. Notice that the Caption on the button changes too, as you can see in the screen display of the form.

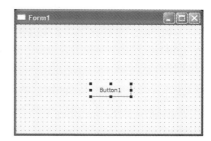

Figure 1.5 A button with the Caption Colour on a form in Delphi 6

Figure 1.6 Inspecting the Button component

Writing a program statement

Delphi has a variety of objects, such as the form and the button, and these objects have properties, such as Caption and Color, that we can set at design time. We do this to set up a program's user interface. To make our program actually do something, we must now write program statements linked to the user interface, and here specifically to the button we have just placed on the form. To keep it simple for our first program, we will write just one line.

- To write the program, move the mouse pointer over the form and onto the Colour button you have just created, then double-click. A new window, the *program editor*, opens over the Form Designer. This window, entitled 'Unit1.pas', contains the following text:

```
procedure TForm1.Button1Click(Sender: TObject);
begin

end;
end.
```

This is an *event-handler skeleton* that Delphi has created automatically for us. Later in this book we'll see what each part of this skeleton means and we'll create similar procedures for ourselves without using Delphi's automatic support. But for now we'll concentrate on how to use this skeleton.

The cursor should be flashing between the begin and end;, and this is where we insert our program code.

Press the space-bar twice to insert two spaces, and type in the line Form1.Color := clPurple; to get the following event handler:

```
procedure TForm1.Button1Click(Sender: TObject);
begin
  Form1.Color := clPurple;
end;
end.
```

Make sure you type the line in exactly as shown! Be particularly careful to distinguish the number 1 (in Form1) from the letter l (in clPurple). Computers are extremely fussy and if the line is wrong, you will get an error message when you try to run your program.

Why do we insert two spaces before typing in the line? As programs become longer and more complicated, the layout of the code becomes very important and inserting spaces to show the program structure makes it neater and therefore easier to read than an untidy or unstructured program. So, from the start, get into the habit of adding extra spaces to group the lines of code between the begin and end statements of the procedure as an indented block.

The Speed bar

We are now ready to run our program. But before we can do that, we must investigate the Speed bar.

The Speed bar is on the upper left side of the screen (figures 1.7.a or 1.7.b).

Figure 1.7.a Delphi 6's Speed bar

Figure 1.7.b Delphi 8's Speed bar

- If you move the pointer over the different buttons on the Speed bar, you will find that these also give pop-up hints.
- Using these hints, find the Run button. As you will see, it is the large green arrow. The hint also shows that the keyboard shortcut for Run is <F9>

Running the program

- Click once on the Run button to compile the program and to move from design mode to run mode. If all is well, the screen flickers briefly, the Object Inspector and the Object TreeView/Model View disappear, and the form we have designed appears. It has a light blue-green (Aqua) background and a button in the middle labelled 'Colour'.
- Move the pointer over this button and then click. As you press the mouse button, the Colour button seems to move into the screen. As you release the mouse button, the button on the screen also returns and the colour of the form changes from light blue-green to a deep purple. By clicking on the button, you initiated the button's OnClick event. This in turn caused the event handler we have just written to execute.

Congratulations! You have just created and run your first Delphi program. (If this did not work, keep reading. We will talk about dealing with common errors in the next example.)

Exiting the program

- To exit the program, click on the Close button (the box with a cross in it in the top right-hand corner) of your *program form*. When you close this program window, Delphi returns to design mode: the Object Inspector and the Object TreeView/Model View should reappear.

Typically (but depending on how Delphi is configured), the IDE remains visible when you run a program. The IDE also has a Close button at the extreme top-right corner of the screen. Don't click on the IDE Close button – that will close Delphi. Click on your own program's Close button. However, should you close Delphi by mistake, it's not a disaster – you can load Delphi again and start over.

An event handler

The program procedure you have just completed is an example of an event handler (sometimes called an 'event-handling procedure' or an 'event procedure'). Events are an important part of Delphi programming, so the following paragraphs give some background. If this does not all quite make sense right now, don't worry, since we use events and event handlers frequently throughout the book and you'll soon become familiar with them.

When you wrote the program procedure above, you were in design mode. You double-clicked on Button1 and Delphi automatically generated the skeleton of Button1's OnClick event handler. The first line of the code that Delphi generated is:

```
procedure TForm1.Button1Click(Sender: TObject);
```

In Delphi Pascal, this line of code refers to the 'procedure that responds to the OnClick event on the Button1 which is part of Form1'. This program procedure is linked to the Button1 object on the user interface and it will run whenever the user clicks on Button1.

As we have just seen, when the program is running and the user clicks on Button1, Delphi automatically runs this event handler and then executes any program code that we as programmers have placed in the event handler. (In this case, the code that ran was `Form1.Color := clPurple;`)

Just as an object can have many properties, so too can an object respond to many different events. You can see this by going to the Object Inspector and clicking on the Events tab (figure 1.8.a or 1.8.b). All the events that the object can respond to appear down the left-hand side (eg ..., OnClick, ..., OnDragDrop, ..., OnKeyPress, ...). Any event handlers we link to these events appear on the right-hand side. Here, the only event handler we have written is the Button1Click event handler and so that is the only one that appears on the right-hand side of the list. We create as many or as few event handlers as we need for the program we are writing.

A little later in this book, once we have become more familiar with Delphi programming, we spend an entire chapter looking at events (Chapter 10). After that, the whole concept of events will become much clearer. For now, the important thing to remember is that an event handler is a piece of program code that runs whenever the associated event occurs. When a user of the program interacts with objects in the GUI (graphical user interface), these objects (eg a button) generate events, such as the button's OnClick event handler. Programmers control how a program responds to these user events by inserting the necessary code into the associated event handlers.

The next line of the event handler is:

```
begin
```

This line marks the beginning of the program statements that make up the event handler. It indicates that the program statements for this event handler commence on the next line. In this example we wrote a program statement to change the colour of the form to purple:

```
Form1.Color := clPurple;
```

When we wanted to change Form1's colour at design time earlier in this chapter, we looked for the Color property in the Object Inspector and changed that to

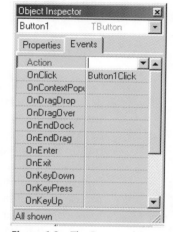

Figure 1.8.a The Events tab in Delphi 6's Object Inspector

Figure 1.8.b The Events tab in Delphi 8's Object Inspector

clAqua. We can also change an object's property at run time by using an *assignment statement* as shown here. This assigns the clPurple value to the Color property of the Form1 object. In Delphi we call the compound symbol `:=` the *assignment operator*. We use the *dot operator* '.' to associate a property with an object. This will become more familiar as we go further. For now, note that the form of the assignment statement to set a property is:

```
ObjectName.PropertyName := Value;
```

In this program we want only to change the Color property of the Form1 object to clPurple. We have written the necessary program statement, and so now we can end the procedure. Sensibly enough, we tell the computer that this is the end of the TForm1.ButtonClick procedure by using:

end;

We do not want to write any other procedures, so the entire program now also comes to an end. There is a second **end** to indicate the end of the entire program, but this time it is followed by a full stop rather than by a semicolon:

end.

As we saw, Delphi created the OnClick programming structure for us after we double-clicked on the button on the form. It inserted the header, the `begin` and both **ends**. All we had to do was to enter the single program statement assigning the colour.

Setting a property in the Object Inspector and in the program

In example 1.1 we initially set the form's Color property in the Object Inspector. This is the value the property will have when the program starts running. We also wrote code in an event handler that could change the Color property, and this took effect once the program was running and the event was generated.

So, we can set property values in two different ways: either in the Object Inspector or programmatically through code in an event handler. How do we decide which way to set a property?

o   If we want a property to have a particular value when the program starts, we use the Object Inspector. In this case we set the colour to be clAqua at startup.

o   If we want to set a property while the program is running, we use a program statement in an event handler. Here we used `Form1.Color :=  clPurple;` in Button1's event handler.

How do we know which properties we can set in a program and what values we can set these properties to?

We can answer these questions by using the Object Inspector, since it lists an object's properties down the left-hand side of the Properties tab and valid values for these properties on the right-hand side (figure 1.9). (Use the scroll bar on the right edge of the Object Inspector to see all the available properties.)

Let's say that we want to be able to set a button's Enabled property in a program. We search for the property we need and then click on the box to the right of that property. This brings up a small downward-pointing arrow. If we click on this arrow, we can see the values that Delphi will recognize in the drop-down box.

In figure 1.9 we see that the Enabled property can be either False or True. This means that, for example, the program statement `Button1.Enabled := False;` is valid.

However, the statement `Button1.Enable := No;` is not valid, for two reasons. First, this statement gives the property as `Enable` (without the 'd' at the end), whereas the Object Inspector shows the property as 'Enabled' (with the 'd'). Second, the Object Inspector shows that the allowed values for Enabled are False or True, and so using 'No' in our program statement is wrong.

As we saw in figures 1.3.a or 1.3.b, some properties, such as a form's Color property, have so many possible values that we may need to scroll through the list to find the value we are looking for.

Figure 1.9 Listing an object's properties and their allowed values

Naming and saving projects

While working through this book, we will be writing many programs and saving them to disk. Keeping track of all the files could become quite difficult, so we use a naming convention that specifies the chapter number, whether it is an example or a problem, a sequence number for that type of category, and an indication of whether it is the unit file or the project file. (We will discuss unit and project files in a little while.) Typical names are:

	Unit name	Project name
Example 1.3	C01e03u.pas	C01e03p.dpr or C01e03p.bdsproj
Problem 7.11	C07p11u.pas	C07p11p.dpr or C07p11p.bdsproj

The naming follows a set of rules:

```
C or A (for Chapter or Appendix)
   01 to 18 (the chapter number)
     e or p (example or problem)
       01 to 99 (number of example or problem)
         p or u (project or unit file)
            dpr/bdsproj or pas (project or unit file respectively)
```

So `C01e01u.pas` means the unit file for chapter 1 example 1.

- We wrote the program above as part of example 1.1, so, using the menu sequence File | Save All or the Save All button on the Speed bar, save the file as C01e01u.pas. Save the project file as C01e01p.dpr (up to Delphi 7) or as C01e01p.bdsproj for Delphi 8. We can also save the files independently, using the menu sequence File | Save As... to save the file (C01e01u.pas) and File | Save Project As... for the project file (C01e01p.dpr or C01e01p.bdsproj).

Unlike some of the earlier programming languages, Delphi programs consist of several different files. The direct programming we do in this book all occurs in one or more unit files with the extension '.pas'. From the unit files and from the form layout, Delphi then automatically generates several other files such as the project file, with the .dpr or .bdsproj extension, and the form description file, with the .dfm or .nfm extension.

Until we begin writing large complicated programs, these different files need not bother us much, since Delphi mostly takes care of them. The important thing to remember is that we must always save the unit files first and then save the associated project file. Save All automatically saves files in the correct sequence. The sequence is important because the project file is the master file that keeps track of the unit file(s) for the project. If at any stage we change the name of a unit file by saving it with a new name, the project file records the new name and so must be saved after the unit file has been saved.

Saving a Delphi program involves two steps: saving the unit file and saving the project file. Using the Save All button as just described saves both files. If you want to make a copy of your program, save both the unit and the project files separately under different names using the File | Save As... and File | Save Project As... menu sequences. When you want to re-open a Delphi program, make sure you open the .dpr or .bdsproj project file and not the .pas file. (We illustrate this process in example 1.3 step 1.) In versions up to Delphi 7, if you open the .pas file, the project file will not open. You will not be able to run the program and the green run button will be disabled ('greyed out'). The Save all button will also be disabled if you open the .pas file instead of the .dpr file. In Delphi 8, if you open the .pas file, the file will be displayed but will not be added to the existing project file and the user interface form will not be opened.

For further information, Appendix 2 lists the common file types found in Delphi projects.

EXAMPLE 1.2) Dealing with errors

Perhaps something went wrong and your program did not work. Since programming mistakes crop up quite often, we must learn how to fix them early on. One way to do this is to make some mistakes on purpose and to see what Delphi does as a result. So, whether your program worked or not, make sure that you are in design mode. If the edit window is not visible on the screen but is covered by the form, double-click on Button1 (the one whose caption you changed to Colour) to bring up the event handler in the editor, as described earlier.

Now, positioning the cursor on the program statement you wrote previously, type in a second 'F' to change Form1 to FForm1. (Remember to distinguish between the number 1 and the letter l.)

```
FForm1.Color := clPurple;
```

Now try running the program again by clicking on the Run arrow on the Speed bar.

What happens? A bar appears over the program line, the cursor is flashing at the error, and an error message appears at the bottom of the window stating that FForm1 is an undeclared identifier.‡ This message means that Delphi does not recognize the object FForm1. So it has picked up the deliberate error we made. Change FForm1 back to Form1.

‡ Different versions of Delphi may give slightly different codes and/or messages for errors. The principle, though, remains the same, irrespective of the version.

Making more errors

Now make the following errors one by one, each time in the same program statement that we used above:

- Change `Color` to `Colour`. Click on the Run arrow on the Speed bar again. Delphi again flashes up a bar on the program statement. It positions the cursor just after `Colour`, and again gives an undeclared identifier message. Change `Colour` back to `Color`.
- Now change `:=` to `=`. Click on the Run arrow, and this time the error message states that Delphi expects `:=` but found `=`. Change `=` back to `:=`.
- Change `clPurple` to `clrPurple`. Click on the Run arrow, and this time the error message once again refers to an undeclared identifier. Change `clrPurple` back to `clPurple`.
- Click on the Run arrow again. This time the program should run perfectly. If not, check the program statement carefully to make sure that it reads

```
Form1.Color := clPurple;
```

All these errors have been *syntax errors*, meaning that they do not obey the rules of the programming language.

Diagnosing errors

Computers and human beings often understand programs in very different ways! Sometimes the error messages the computer gives can be quite helpful, at other times they can be quite confusing. When there is an error in a program, there are two things to bear in mind. First, the computer gives an error message in the way that it understands the error. If the error message makes sense to you, that's great. If it does not make sense, ignore the message and concentrate on the code you have written. Second, the computer places the cursor at the point where it realizes that an error has occurred. Often this points out the error exactly. At other times, the error may have occurred previously. So, if you can't find the error at the position that the computer indicates, go through the previous one or two lines too. The error may have occurred a little earlier, since the error will always be *at the cursor or before it*.

EXAMPLE 1.3) Another button, another colour

Let's extend the program we have just written. This time we'll have a clAqua-coloured form with two buttons on it. One button's Caption is Purple, the other's is Yellow. When the user clicks on the Yellow button, three things must happen:

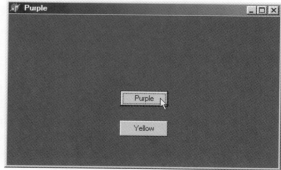

- the form colour must change to clYellow;
- the form's Caption must change to Yellow, and
- the Yellow button must be disabled.

Similarly, when the user clicks the Purple button, the form's colour must change to clPurple, its Caption must change to Purple, and the Purple button must be disabled.

As a final touch, it would be nice if, instead of having to click on the buttons, the user could press the accelerator keys <Alt+Y> or <Alt+P> for yellow or purple respectively.

Figure 1.10 Using two buttons to set the form colour

EX 1.3   Planning

Usually, before starting to write a program, it is a good idea first to think about how best to solve the problem. For selected examples throughout this book there is a planning section to provide guidance in writing the necessary program and to help develop the habit of planning a program before starting to write it.

When faced with a big, difficult-to-solve problem, it is often helpful to work in smaller steps. So a common problem-solving method among programmers is to break a large problem into a series of smaller problems and then to solve each of the smaller problems. If each of the smaller problems is solved correctly, and if these problem solutions are combined correctly, the large problem will then also be solved. Regularly, throughout this book, we use this method of breaking up a large problem into a series of smaller solution steps.

So, to solve this example, the question is: how can we break it into a series of simpler steps? Before reading any further, reread the problem given in example 1.3 and see if you can divide it into a series of smaller problems. Then continue reading here to see how we decided to break the problem down into several simpler subproblems.

Our sequence of subproblems to solve the overall problem is:
1   Start with the program from example 1.1 and add another button to it.
2   Create the code (ie the event handlers) for each button to change the form's Color and Caption properties.
3   Now add the code to enable and disable the buttons.
4   Set up the accelerator keys.

Compare these steps with the original problem statement in example 1.3 and confirm that they will lead to its solution.

EX 1.3   Testing

After writing a program, it is tempting to assume that it works correctly. But this assumption can be dangerous! We have sections throughout the book on points to keep in mind when testing a specific program. For instance, if we have written a program to meet the requirements of this example, we can test it as follows:
1   Does it start up with two buttons, one labelled 'Purple' and the other labelled 'Yellow', on a light blue-green (Aqua) background?
2   When we click on button Purple, does the background change to purple, the form title change to the word Purple, and is the Purple button disabled and the Yellow one enabled?
3   When we click on button Yellow, does the background change to yellow, the form title change to the word Yellow, and is the Yellow button disabled and the Purple one enabled?
4   When we press <Alt+Y> or <Alt +P>, do we get the same effect as if we had clicked on the Yellow or Purple buttons?

In the next few sections of this chapter we explain how to program and test each of the steps we have planned. If you have done some programming before, you may be able to write some, or all, of this program. In that case, why not do one or more of these steps now, without our help, before reading any further?

However, most people who are new to programming will find this a difficult program to write. Do as much as you can of it, even if you don't get it all right. If your program does not do everything we ask for, don't worry. Go carefully through the steps that follow. Most programs are easier to write in stages, and the steps below will take you stage-by-stage through the process of building a program like this.

(Programming hints: 1 – When disabling the Yellow button, remember to enable the Purple one, and *vice versa*; 2 – To create an accelerator key for a button, place an ampersand (&) in front of the first letter when setting the caption in the Object Inspector.)

EX 1.3 STEP 1 Adding another button

It makes sense to write this program by extending the program we did in the example above.
- If the previous program is not still on the screen, go to the menu bar and open the previous example by using File | Open Project and open C01e01p.dpr. (In Delphi 8 you can also open C01e01p.bdsproj, but be sure not to open C01e01u.pas.)

We would like to make a copy of this program that we can modify without affecting the original version.
- To do this, create the copy by using the menu sequence File | Save as ..., and give the unit the name C01e03u.pas.
- Then use File | Save Project As ... and give the project the name C01e03p.dpr (Delphi 4 to 7) or C01e03p.bdsproj (Delphi 8). Note that we *cannot* use the File | Save All sequence when making copies since File | Save All keeps the existing names of the files.

By saving it under a different name like this, we are creating a copy that we can change without affecting the original version. We will modify existing programs often, so this is a useful technique to learn. Note that when renaming a project like this, you must *always save the unit file(s) first and then the project*. If you do it in any other order, the linkage between the project file and the unit file(s) will be set incorrectly.
- If the form is not visible, go to the menu bar at the top of the screen and select the menu sequence View | Forms | Form1 | OK.
- If the Object Inspector is not visible, select View | Object Inspector.

To complete this step, add a second button below the first button to give the layout shown in figure 1.10.
- Do this by selecting the button symbol on the Component/Tool palette and then clicking on the form to place a second button on the form at the required position. The Object Inspector now shows Button2's properties.
- Click once on Button1. The Object Inspector displays Button1's properties.
- Similarly, click once on Form1 (ie, the area of the form that does not have a button on it) and Form1's properties are displayed. Clicking on each object in turn, use the Object Inspector to set the following design-time properties (this will mean changing some existing properties):

Object	Property	Value
Form1	Caption	Colour Demo
	Color	ClAqua
Button1	Caption	Purple
Button2	Caption	Yellow

- To test this step, click on the green Run arrow on the Speed bar to compile and run the version of the program so far. It should look similar to the display shown in (figure 1.10).

Because we started from the program we developed in the example earlier in this chapter, there is still program code connected to button Purple through its OnClick event handler. (In the previous version, the button's caption was Colour but in this version we have changed `Button1`'s Caption property to Purple.)

- Check that the event handler is still working by clicking on button Purple. The form's background should change to deep purple. Of course, we have not yet written an event handler for button Yellow, and so no program action happens when we click on Yellow. We will do this in the next step.
- Close the program by clicking on the Close button in the top-right corner *of the form*. As you return to design mode, the Form Designer and the Object Inspector should reappear. (If not, display them as described above.)

EX 1.3 STEP 2 More program statements

Our next step is to write the event handler that colours the form yellow when we click on the Yellow button, and that changes the form title to state what colour is on display. Can you write the program code to do this before reading any further?

- The first step in writing the code is to double-click on the Yellow button in the Form Designer. This displays the `TForm1.Button2Click` procedure (ie the event handler).
- Edit this by adding two programming statements to match the following. Press the <Enter> key each time you need to create a new line.

```
procedure TForm1.Button2Click(Sender: TObject);
begin
  Form1.Color := clYellow;
  Form1.Caption := 'Yellow';
end;
```

When we work with text in a program, that text is in single quotes, as with `'Yellow'` above (or `'Purple'` in the next event handler).

We now need similar program statements for the Purple button. Scroll up using the arrow button on the scroll bar on the right side of the editor window to find the `TForm1.Button1Click` procedure. Edit this by adding an extra line to assign the word 'Purple' to the form's Caption, matching the following:

```
procedure TForm1.Button1Click(Sender: TObject);
begin
  Form1.Color := clPurple;
  Form1.Caption := 'Purple';
end;
```

- Run the program. If you entered the text exactly as shown, the run-time version of the form with the Aqua background should appear, and the form's colour and title should change when you click the appropriate button. (Of course, if you click the same button again, no further changes happen until the other button is clicked.)
- Once you have tested it enough to convince yourself that it works, close the program to return to design mode.

- If the program does not run and you get an error message instead, compare your code carefully against the code given here to check for errors. Remember that Delphi helps us as much as it can in locating errors. Any error will be either at the cursor or before it. Correct any errors as we showed you earlier in this chapter. There may be more than one, so persevere until the program works.

Understanding event driven programming

We now have a program with two different event handlers, one to respond to a click on Button1 and the other to respond to a click on Button2. Each event handler or procedure stands on its own and within each event handler the computer executes each program statement in the order that it appears. So a click on Button2 will first set the form's colour to yellow and then change the form's caption to 'Yellow'.

So, within each event handler the statements execute in sequence. However the event handlers themselves execute in the order that the events occur. If the user clicks on Button1, Button1's event handler executes. If the user clicks on Button2, Button2's event handler executes, and so on. This style of programming is called *event driven programming* because the program responds to user events such as a click on a button. This means that the order in which the event handlers run and the way in which the program behaves depends on the order in which the events occur.

We write the programs with event handlers because we are working with graphical user interface (GUI) programs. Behind the scenes, GUI programs are waiting to respond to any event that occurs. Once the event happens, Delphi calls the appropriate event handler.

This may sound a bit complicated right now but it becomes completely natural as we write more programs. For now the important point to understand is that each event handler is separate and self-contained. The program statements within an event handler execute in the order in which they occur. However the event handlers themselves do not execute in the order in which they are written. Instead, they execute in the order that their associated events occur.

EX 1.3 STEP 3 Enabling and disabling buttons

Our next step is to disable and enable the buttons as appropriate. In other words, if we click on the Yellow button, the form colour and title must change to Yellow (as already happens) and, in addition, the Yellow button must be disabled so that we cannot press it again. The Purple button must be enabled (figure 1.11).
Now, when we click the Purple button, the Form colour becomes purple, its caption changes to Purple and the Purple button becomes disabled so that we cannot click it again. The Yellow button must be enabled.

- See whether you can modify the two existing event handlers (procedures) to produce the required program.

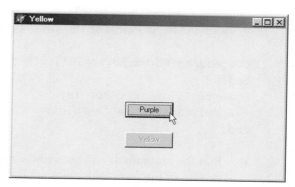

Figure 1.11 The Purple button is enabled and the Yellow button is disabled

To enable and disable the buttons we need to add two more lines of program code to each OnClick event handler. If the Form Designer rather than the editor window is visible, there are several ways to display the editor. On the Speed Bar you can use the Toggle Form/Unit button (Delphi 4 to 7) or Show Code button (Delphi 8) (use the pop-up hints to find the correct button). You can also use the <F12> key or the menu sequence View | Toggle Form/Unit (Delphi 4 to 7) or View | Show Code (Delphi 8). The new versions of the procedures look like this:

```
procedure TForm1.Button1Click(Sender: TObject);
begin
  Form1.Color := clPurple;
  Form1.Caption := 'Purple';
  Button2.Enabled := True;
  Button1.Enabled := False;
end;

procedure TForm1.Button2Click(Sender: TObject);
begin
  Form1.Color := clYellow;
  Form1.Caption := 'Yellow';
  Button1.Enabled := True;
  Button2.Enabled := False;
end;
```

Do you understand how the buttons are enabled and disabled? When a button is clicked, it must enable the other button (ie set the *other* button's Enabled property to True) and it must disable *itself*. So, Button1's OnClick event handler enables Button2 (`Button2.Enabled := True;`) and disables Button1 (`Button1.Enabled := False;`). By contrast, Button2's OnClick event handler enables Button1 and disables Button2.

- Run the program and test it. Notice the differences between when a button is enabled (the Caption is clear and it responds when you click on it) and when a button is disabled (the Caption becomes faint, and clicking on it gives no response).
- When you are satisfied that the program works, close it and return to design mode to tackle the last step.

Making life easier for the user

The reason we enable and disable buttons like this is to help the user. In step 2, if the colour is already yellow and we click the Yellow button again, nothing appears to happen. This can be confusing to the user: why have an active button that seems to do nothing? With this new version (step 3), if the colour is purple and the user clicks the Yellow button, the colour and title change, and the Yellow button becomes disabled (ie it looks dull and 'greyed out'), so that the user can easily see that the appropriate button to press next is the Purple button, and so on.

Enabling and disabling buttons can make a user interface more predictable to the end user. *Predictability* is one of the principles of user interface design that we should aim for when we are developing applications. A button which is enabled, but seems to do nothing when it is pressed, is an example of unpredictable behaviour. It is therefore better to disable a button when pressing it would result in no apparent action. Later we will come across other principles of user interface design, such as economy, compatibility and consistency.

EX 1.3 STEP 4 Accelerator (or hot) keys

An accelerator key, sometimes also called a 'hot key', allows the user to operate the program buttons from the keyboard as well as with the mouse. As we indicated previously, we must insert an ampersand (&) in front of the appropriate letter of the Caption to allow keyboard operation. Try to do this now, before reading further.

- Go to the Object Inspector and change the two buttons' Captions by inserting '&' as follows (leave the other properties unchanged):

Object	Property	Value
Button1	Caption	&Purple
Button2	Caption	&Yellow

Because we added & before the P and the Y on the button Caption properties, there should now be an underline under the P of Purple and under the Y of Yellow on the buttons themselves. Run the program by clicking on the green arrow on the Speed bar as previously. Press <Alt+P> and then <Alt+Y>. These should now have the same effect as clicking on the buttons with the mouse.

If you would like to test the program thoroughly, do all the tests on it that we mention in the Test section above. Use both the keyboard and the mouse. Once you have tested it, exit the program and use File | Save All to save the unit under the previous name, in this way storing all your changes.

Fig 1.12.a Graphical display of the objects in the Object TreeView in Delphi 6 and 7

The interaction between the Form Designer, the Object Inspector, and the Object TreeView or Model View

The Form Designer, the Object Inspector and the Object TreeView (in Delphi 6 and 7) or the Model View (Delphi 8) are interrelated. As we added the Buttons to the Form they appeared in the Object TreeView (fig 1.12.a) or the Model View (figure 1.12.b). As you can demonstrate for yourself, when you select an object in either the Form Designer or the Object Inspector it is then automatically selected in the other. In Delphi 6 or 7 this applies to the Object TreeView too, but not to Delphi 8's Model View.

A note for experienced programmers

Delphi's RAD characteristics simplify many of the mundane tasks in GUI programming. However, a programmer experienced in another language may feel a loss of control. A very positive aspect of Delphi is that none of the 'magic' is hidden. One can access all the code that Delphi generates automatically and modify it as needed. One can, for instance, create and initialize the interface objects at run time, should one need to, instead of using the visual programming ability described in this chapter. One can even set up a 'console application' without any GUI aspects at all.

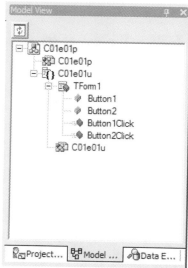

Figure 1.12.b Graphical display of the objects and event handlers in the Model View in Delphi 8

REVIEW

This chapter introduces us to the Delphi Integrated Development Environment (or IDE). We have seen the Form Designer, the Object Inspector, the Component or Tool palette, the Speed bar and the Object TreeView or ModelView. We have placed buttons on a form, modified the buttons' and form's properties and written OnClick event handlers. We have saved programs to disk, run them, seen how they responded to our programming when we operated the buttons, and learnt how to close programs. Properties we changed, either statically in the Object Inspector, or dynamically through program lines, are the form's Color and Caption properties, and the buttons' Caption and Enabled properties. We also created accelerator keys by placing '&' in front of a letter in a Caption.

To become familiar with how Delphi responds to programming mistakes we made some deliberate errors.

We can set properties at design time: we call this the static design. Dynamic design occurs when we alter the value of these properties at run time by writing program assignment statements in the event handlers. For example, to instruct Form1 to change its colour to clYellow we use the assignment statement `Form1.Color := clYellow`.

IMPORTANT CONCEPTS*

In this section we review the concepts covered in this chapter under the headings Programming environment, Fundamental programming concepts, Writing a program, Visual GUI development, and User interface factors. These concepts may not all make sense right now. Don't worry too much about this. We have covered a lot in this chapter and we will return to these concepts again later in the book once you have gained more experience in using Delphi.

Programming environment

Component palette (Delphi 4 to Delphi 7): On the right below the menu bar is the Component palette. Double-clicking on a component icon on the Component palette places the selected object in the middle of the Form. The Component palette is the earlier version of Delphi 8's Tool palette.

Copying an existing program: Open an existing program and save the files under different names. First save the unit file(s) using File | Save As... and then save the project file using File | Save Project As.... In order to keep the correct linkage between the project file and the unit file, don't save the project file until the unit file(s) have been renamed and don't simply copy the files with new names using Windows Explorer.

Design time or *design mode*: Placing objects on a form, setting properties through the Object Inspector and writing the program (event handlers).

Exiting a program: Click on the cross at the top right-hand corner of the *program's* form.

Exiting the IDE: Click on the cross in the top right-hand corner of Delphi's IDE, to the right of the menu bar.

Form Designer and editor: In Delphi 4 to Delphi 7 the Form Designer and the Editor are overlapping windows on the right side of the screen. In Delphi 8 the Form Designer and the Editor are alternate windows at the centre of the screen selected by the appropriate tabs. The Form Designer and the Editor allow the programmer to design the visual layout of the user interface and to

* Each chapter has an 'Important concepts' section. This often describes the concepts already demonstrated in the chapter from a slightly different perspective. It is more than just a summary or a review and so is an integral part of getting to know the concepts that each chapter covers.

write the program code (typically the event handlers) that provide the program's functionality.

Integrated Development Environment (IDE): Delphi, like some other modern programming languages, has an IDE which allows for programming, compiling and testing of programs.

Menu bar: A menu bar runs across the top of the screen, providing access to the IDE operations.

Model View (Delphi 8): The Model View, which shows a tree diagram displaying the logical relationships between the objects on the form, appears at the top right of the screen on the Model tab. (Experienced programmers will notice that the Model View shows a containment hierarchy for the GUI and not an inheritance hierarchy between classes.) The Model View is Delphi 8's version of the Object TreeView (Delphi 6 and 7).

Object Inspector: Down the left side of the screen is the Object Inspector, giving access to the static (design time) properties and events of each object on the form.

Object TreeView (Delphi 6 and 7): The Object TreeView, which shows a tree diagram displaying the logical relationships between the objects on the form appears at the top left of the screen. (Experienced programmers will notice that the Object TreeView (Delphi 6 and 7) or the Model View (Delphi 8) shows a containment hierarchy for the GUI and not an inheritance hierarchy between classes.) The Object TreeView is the earlier version of Delphi 8's Model View.

Opening an existing program: Use the menu sequence File | Open Project.

Run-time or *run mode*: The program is executing, carrying out the programming statements.

Saving a program: Use the menu sequence File | Save All.

Speed bar: On the left below the menu bar is the Speed bar with shortcut buttons to some of the more common commands.

Starting a new application: In Delphi 4 to Delphi 7 start a new application with the menu sequence File | New Application. In Delphi 8 select File | New | VCL Forms Application.

Tool palette (Delphi 8): On the lower right section of the screen is the Tool palette. Double-clicking on a component icon on the Tool palette places the selected object in the middle of the Form. The sections in the Tool palette can be shown vertically or horizontally, and each individual section can be collapsed to show just the section heading or expanded to show the components available under that heading. The Tool palette is Delphi 8's version of the Component palette (Delphi 4 to Delphi 7).

Fundamental programming concepts

Assignment statement: The value of a property can be set by a program using an assignment statement. The assignment operator is :=.

Event handler: A block of program code that runs in response to an event.

Program statements: Programs consist of a series of statements executed one after another in order when the program is running (executing).

Writing a program

Building on previous work: Re-using existing portions of program code can reduce both program development time and the number of errors present in a program.

Incremental development: It is often helpful to develop a program in stages, testing each stage in turn before moving on to the next one. Sometimes this is called the 'divide and conquer' approach to program development.

Planning: Before writing a program we should plan how to write it, thinking about the components it will need, which properties must be set and which event handlers must be written.

Syntax errors: Errors in using the programming language correctly.

Testing: When a program is first written, it is quite likely that it will contain errors. These could be quite subtle, so it is important to test a program thoroughly before deciding it is complete.

Visual GUI development

GUI: stands for 'graphical user interface'. Modern operating systems such as Windows are often GUI-based.

Linking between windows: The Form Designer and the Object Inspector are linked so that selecting an object in one of these windows automatically selects it in the other. In Delphi 6 and 7 the Object TreeView is also linked.

Placing a component: The simplest way to add an object to a form is to click on the icon on the Component/Tool palette and then to click again with the mouse pointer at the required position on the form.

RAD: RAD stands for 'rapid application development'. Among its various strengths, Delphi is a RAD development tool. Examples of this so far are Delphi's ability to create and configure a form and associated objects automatically and to create the skeleton for an event handler. In a 'non-RAD' environment a programmer would have to create each object at run time using program code and would have to enter all the skeleton code. (We can do both these operations manually in Delphi, if necessary.)

Setting properties dynamically: The properties that can be set statically through the Object Inspector can also be set in the program through assignment statements.

Setting properties statically: The Object Inspector allows the programmer to set the properties that each object will have when the program starts.

User interface factors

Accelerator keys: Accelerator keys allow the user to activate a button using a keyboard combination as an alternative to clicking with the mouse.

Enabling and disabling controls: Should there be certain times when a particular control on the screen is not relevant, we can make this clear to the user by disabling it. We subsequently enable the control when it becomes relevant.

Predictability: The user interface should respond to user actions in a way that the user expects. This design principle is called 'predictability'. Disabling and enabling controls as demonstrated above is one way of ensuring that a user interface is more predictable.

NEW DELPHI FEATURES

TForm		
Properties	Caption	The text that appears across the top of a form to identify it to the user.
	Color	Specifies the background colour of the form.
Use		The form provides the basis for the program's user interface. All the other user interface components, eg buttons, appear on a form.

TButton

Properties	Caption	The text that appears on the button to identify it to the user.
	Enabled	Determines whether the button responds to mouse (or keyboard) events. To disable a button, set Enabled to False. The button appears dimmed and it ignores mouse and keyboard events. To enable a button, set Enabled to True. The button is not dimmed, and the user can click on it.
Events	OnClick	Occurs when the user clicks on a button.
Use		The button is a push-button control the user can use to initiate predetermined actions.

Keyboard commands

<F11>	Display the Object Inspector
<F12>	Toggle Form/Unit
<Shift+F12>	Display the form
<Shift+Alt+F11>	Display the Object Tree View (Delphi 6 and 7)
<Ctrl+Alt+P>	Display the Tool Palette (Delphi 8)

PROBLEMS

To be a good programmer, it is important actually to be able to *write* programs. Simply reading about programming theory is not sufficient. So, to complete this chapter, attempt the problems given below. Whether they seem to you to be too difficult or too easy, it would be very valuable to try to write each one of these programs before going on to the next chapter.

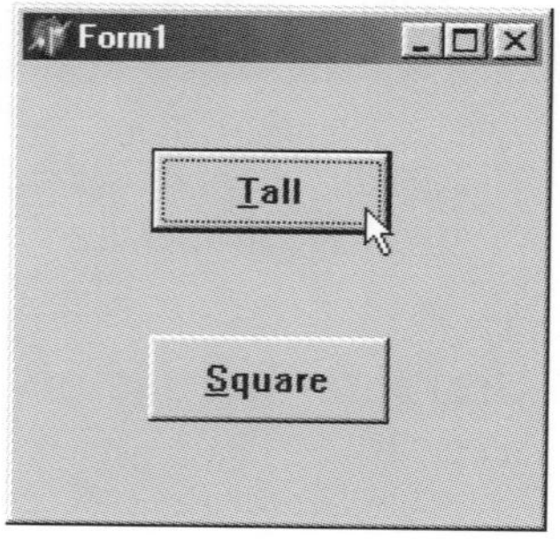

Figure 1.13 The 'square' version of the form

PROBLEM 1.1   Changing the form size with a program

- Start a new application.
- Using the Object Inspector, change the form height to 200 and the form width also to 200 (figure 1.13).
- Place two buttons on the form and call one 'Tall' and the other 'Square'. The accelerator keys for these buttons should be T and S respectively.
- For each of these buttons, write an OnClick event handler.
- For the Tall button, the event handler must change the form's height to 300 (figure 1.14).
- For the Square button, the event handler must change the form's height back to 200 (figure 1.13).
- Save the file and project as C01p01u.pas and the project as C01p01p.dpr (Delphi 4 to 7) or C01p01p.bdsproj (Delphi 8) then run and test the program.

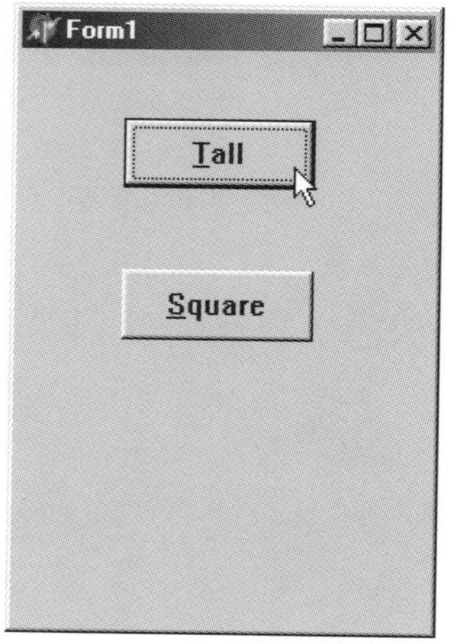

PROBLEM 1.2   Changing button dimensions

This problem extends the concepts of the previous one:
- Start a new Delphi application.

Figure 1.14 The 'tall' version of the form

- Using the Object Inspector, change the form height to 200 and the form width to 130.
- Now place two buttons on the form. Call the one 'Small' and the other 'Big'.
- The height of each button should be 30, their widths should be 60 and their Left properties should be 30.
- The Top property for 'Small' should be 30 and for 'Big', Top should be 100.
- The accelerator keys for these buttons should be S and B respectively.
- For each of these buttons, write an OnClick event handler. For the Big button, the event handler must change the form's height to 300 and its width to 400 (figure 1.16). It should also change the height of each button to 60 and its width to 120. For the Small button, the event handler must change the form and button dimensions back to the initial values given above (figure 1.15).
- Save the file as C01p02u.pas and the project as C01p02p.dpr (Delphi 4 to 7) or C01p02p.bdsproj (Delphi 8), then run and test the program.

Figure 1.15 The 'small' version

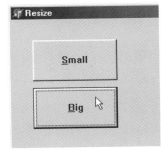

Figure 1.16 The 'big' version

PROBLEM 1.3) Changing a button's Caption in a program

- Create an application with two buttons with the Captions 'First' and 'Second'.
- Clicking on button First should change the Caption on button Second to Close.
- Clicking on button Close should end the program. (Hint: Use Delphi's 'Close;' program statement.)

PROBLEM 1.4) Enabling and disabling buttons

The program we gave for the previous problem works, but can be a bit confusing to the user. If you start by clicking button First, the program works as expected. But if you click button First again, nothing further happens. Also, if you start by clicking button Second, the program closes immediately, while its caption still reads 'Second' instead of 'Close'. To prevent this unpredictable behaviour, change the program as follows:

- When the program first runs, button First should be *enabled* and button Second should be *disabled* (figure 1.17).
- After clicking on First, three things should happen (figure 1.18):
  1 Button Second is *enabled*;
  2 Button First is *disabled*, and
  3 The Caption of button Second changes to Close.
- Now, after clicking on Close, the program must close.

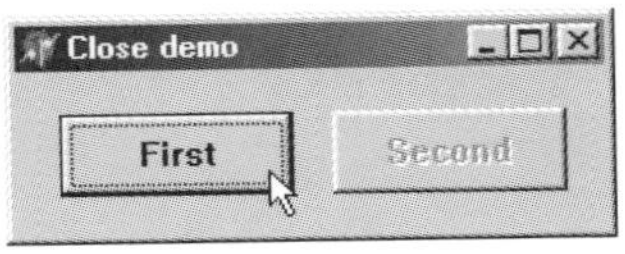

Figure 1.17 The initial display

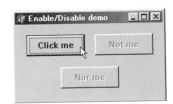

Figure 1.18 After clicking the First button

PROBLEM 1.5) Another Enable/Disable problem

- Create a program with three buttons initially captioned 'Click me', 'Not me' and 'Nor me'.
- This program must alternate between two states, changing the button captions and their Enabled status, as shown in figures 1.19 and 1.20 and in the table below, in response to the user's actions.
- The program starts up in state 1.

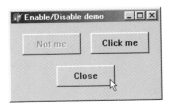

Figure 1.19 State 1

Figure 1.20 State 2

State	Button	Caption	Enabled	Operation
1	Button1	Click me	True	Change to state 2
	Button2	Not me	False	–
	Button3	Nor me	False	–
2	Button1	Not me	False	–
	Button2	Click me	True	Change to state 1
	Button3	Close	True	Exit the program

PROBLEM 1.6 Changing the WindowState property

- Start a new application.
- Using the Object Inspector, change the Caption of the form to Changing WindowState.
- Now place three buttons on the form, captioned 'Minimize', 'Normal' and 'Maximize'. The accelerator keys for these buttons should be M, N and X.
- For each of these buttons write an OnClick event handler. For the Minimize button the event handler must minimize the form, for the Maximize button the event handler must maximize the form, and for the Normal button the form should return to its original size. (Hint: The Caption of the form indicates the correct form property to change.)

PROBLEM 1.7 Reading a program

a   Simply by reading the following two event handlers (ie without entering them into the computer) describe what the program does:

```
procedure TForm1.Button1Click(Sender: TObject);
begin
  Form1.Width := 203;
  Form1.Height := 87;
  Button2.Top := 16;
  Button2.Left := 104;
end;

procedure TForm1.Button2Click(Sender: TObject);
begin
  Form1.Width := 120;
  Form1.Height := 144;
  Button2.Top := 73;
  Button2.Left := 16;
end;
```

b   Once you have worked out this program's operation, enter it into Delphi. Run it and test it. Does it perform as you expected in the previous point? How predictable is the user interface to the user?

CHAPTER 2

Programming with visual components

PURPOSE OF THIS CHAPTER

Delphi has many different components, and in this chapter we introduce several of the more useful ones. This will consolidate the ideas covered in Chapter 1 and increase your confidence to experiment with other components that we do not describe in detail.

As in the first chapter, we concentrate on becoming more familiar with using Delphi, and so it is important that you sit down in front of a computer and try out what we describe.

Many programs deal with what human beings call 'text' and what computers call 'strings'. Our first example in this chapter deals with simple input and output of text. To read text in from the user, we will use the *Edit* component. To display text to the user, we will use the *Label* component. (We look at more detailed text handling in Chapter 3.) We will then look at *BitmapButtons* (or BitBtns), which are like ordinary buttons but they also display a symbol on them, and *RadioButtons*, which offer a convenient way of selecting one out of a number of alternatives. Working with these components will help you to become familiar with positioning, sizing and selecting components.

EXAMPLE 2.1 Simple text output

- Go to the menu bar and select File | New Application to begin a new application.
- Give the form a Name and a Caption and make it smaller (figure 2.1) by setting the following properties in the Object Inspector:

Component	Property	Value
Form1	Name	frmTextDemo
	Caption	Text Demo
	Height	217
	Width	228

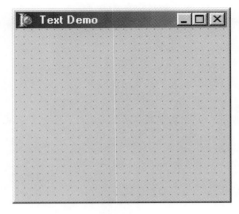

Figure 2.1 Form for example 2.1

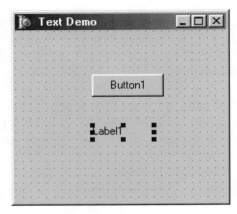

Figure 2.2 A button and a Label

- Using the button symbol on the Component/Tool palette as before, place a button in the middle of the form. Now, move back to the Component/Tool palette with the mouse and select the large 'A'. As the pop-up hint shows, this is the Label/TLabel component.
- Click on this, then place a Label on the form below the button (figure 2.2).
- By clicking once on each object in turn and then using the Object Inspector, set the following static properties:

Component	Property	Value
Button1	Name	btnTransfer
	Caption	Transfer
Label1	Name	lblText
	Caption	Starting Text

Notice that we have changed the names of the components. From now on we will always give each component a descriptive name to replace names such as Form1, Button1 and Label1 that Delphi gives automatically. We use a special style of name that starts with a three-letter prefix to show what kind of component we are using. As you can see from the names above, we use the prefixes frm... to indicate a form, btn... for a button, and lbl... for a Label. We follow this prefix with a descriptive name that describes what the component does. Then when we read a program and see a name like btnTransfer we know immediately that this is a button that has to do with transferring something. Similarly, we can see that lblText is a Label that will display some or other text. (Appendix 3 lists all the prefixes that appear in this book.)

It is important to get into the habit of using a naming convention such as this. When your programs become longer and more complicated it helps to be able to deduce the purpose of a component/variable from its name. Imagine a page of printed Delphi code. The component names that you choose should allow you to read the page of code and understand what the code does without having to look in the object inspector to figure out which component is which.

- Once you have set the properties, double-click on the Transfer button to create the following event handler:

```
procedure TfrmTextDemo.btnTransferClick(Sender: TObject);
begin
  lblText.Caption := 'New Text';
end;
```

By looking at this program, can you guess what the event handler will do? You can probably see right away – by clicking on btnTransfer, the Caption of lblText will become New Text. Or that is what we hope!

Let's see what actually happens by running the program. But first save the program, as in Chapter 1, calling the unit file C02e01u.pas and the project file C02e01p.dpr (Delphi 7) or C02e01p.bdsproj (Delphi 8).

- Now click the Run arrow on the Speed bar. You should see the screen shown here (figure 2.3).

Figure 2.3 Start-up screen of 'Text Demo'

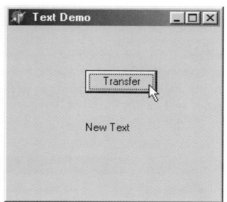

Figure 2.4 After clicking the Transfer button

- Click on the Transfer button. As we expected from the program we have just written, the button's OnClick event handler writes the text New Text to the Label's Caption (figure 2.4), replacing the Label's original Caption that we set in the Object Inspector.
- Close the program by clicking once on the Close box at the top right-hand corner of the form.

What have we achieved in this first example? We have seen that we can use the Label component to display text to the user by changing its Caption property through an assignment statement in the program code. In the next example we introduce the Edit component. This allows the user to enter text from the keyboard. We will then use the Transfer button's OnClick event handler to transfer this text to the Label component.

EXAMPLE 2.2 Reading text in from the user

For this example, we will adapt the program from the previous example.
- If it is not on the screen at the moment, use File | Open Project to open project C02e01p.dpr, which you saved as part of the previous example. (Opening the project file opens the unit file also.)
- Go to the Standard tab on the Component / Tool palette and, using the pop-up hints, locate the Edit / TEdit component. Up until Delphi 7 this is the symbol with the small 'ab' on it. Delphi 8 uses the symbol of a pencil writing on a white background.
- Place the Edit component just above the Transfer button (figure 2.5). Leave the existing properties for Button1 (ie btnTransfer) and Label1 (ie lblText) as they are, and set the following static properties for the new component:

Component	Property	Value
Edit1	Name	edtText
	Text	<Blank>

Notice that we use the naming convention edt... for Edit components.
- Delete the default text in the Text property and leave it blank. The user will enter text when the program runs.
- Now, by double-clicking on the Transfer button, go to the Transfer button's OnClick event handler and change the existing program statement so that it will transfer whatever the user types into the Edit component to the Label's Caption. Try this now for yourself, before looking at our solution. (Hint: You can use the Object Inspector to look at the list of the Edit component's properties and see whether any would be useful to you in this program.)
- We can write this program in different ways, but the easiest is simply to change the existing line of code to the following:

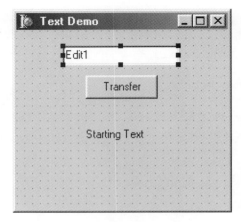

Figure 2.5 Adding an Edit component

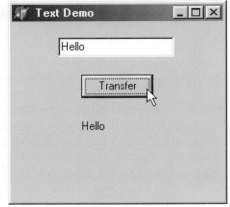

Figure 2.6 Transferring text from an Edit component to a Label

```
procedure TfrmTextDemo.btnTransferClick(Sender: TObject);
begin
  lblText.Caption := edtText.Text;
end;
```

- To give the application a different name, click File | Save As… to save the unit file as C02e02u.pas and File | Save Project As…, to save the project as C02e02p.dpr (Delphi 7) or C02e02p.bdsproj (Delphi 8).
- Click on the green Run arrow on the Speed bar. The opening screen shows a blank Edit component above the Transfer button.
- Click the mouse in the Edit component and type in some text such as 'Hello'.
- Now click the Transfer button, and the text you entered appears as the Caption of the Label (figure 2.6).
- Click the mouse inside the Edit component again, delete the text that is there, and enter something else, such as: 'Welcome to Delphi'.
- Now when you click the Transfer button, this new text appears below, over-writing the text that was there.
- Click on the Edit component again, and this time enter: 'A biif mistake'.
- Use the arrow keys or mouse to move the cursor back along the text to delete the 'if' characters and type in 'g' instead.
- Now click the Transfer button. The corrected text appears as the Label's Caption.

In the previous example, we changed the Name and *Caption* properties of the Button and Label components. In this example, we change the Name and *Text* properties of the Edit component. Notice that an Edit component has no Caption property. The Caption and the Text properties fulfil almost the same purpose since they both specify what text should be displayed to the user when the program is run. However, the Text property can accept input from the user when the program is running, while the Caption property cannot.

It is important also to understand the difference between the Name and the Caption or Text properties of a component. The purpose of the Name property (eg lblText or edtText) is so that the programmer can refer to the component in Delphi code (in an event handler for example). The user, however, sees the text displayed on the Caption or Text property and is not aware of the Name property of a component.

As you can see from this example, the components in a visual development environment such as Delphi can be very powerful. In a traditional language such as Pascal or C it takes a lot of programming to allow the user to edit input text like this.

Assignment statement

In the program statement above we *assign* the value of edtText's Text property to lblText's Caption property. We often use the assignment operator := to transfer a value to an object's property. We call a statement using this operator an *assignment statement*, and will use it regularly from now on.

An assignment statement can take on several different forms. Earlier in this chapter we assigned a specified string to an object's property:

```
lblText.Caption := 'New Text';
```

In the previous chapter we assigned particular values to different objects' properties:

```
Form1.Color := clPurple;
Button2.Enabled := True;
```

In example 2.2 above, an assignment statement transfers the value of one object's property (`edtText.Text`) to a property of another object (`lblText.Caption`).

The assignment statement is a basic form of programming statement; we will see many more examples as we progress through this book.

Reading in text from the keyboard

In the example we have just done we use the Edit component to read in text that the user types at the keyboard, and we see that the user can edit this text. The text that the user enters is available to the program as the value of the Edit component's Text property.

We use a programming *assignment statement* to transfer the value of this Text property to another object (in this case, to the Label's Caption property).

EXAMPLE 2.3) The 'Close' bitmap button

- If the Text Demo program from example 2.2 is not still on the screen, use File | Open Project to open project C02e02p.dpr, which you saved as part of the previous example.
- In Delphi 4 to 7, move the mouse pointer up to the Component palette and click on the Additional tab to select an alternative range of components. The first component from the left, shown selected in figure 2.7.a, has a little tick mark and 'OK' on it. The hint that pops up tells you that it is a BitBtn. In Delphi 8, the TBitBtn is also the first component on the Additional tab of the Tool palette. Delphi 8 also shows the TBitBtn with a tick but without the 'OK' (figure 2.7.b). BitBtn is short for 'BitmapButton'. A BitBtn is similar to a normal button except that it can have an icon, such as a tick, on it as well as a Caption.

Figure 2.7.a The Additional components on Delphi's Component palette

- Place this BitBtn below the Label at the bottom of the screen. Without changing the properties of the components we used previously, set the following static properties for the BitBtn in the Object Inspector:

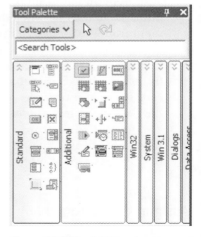

Component	Property	Value
BitBtn1	Name	bmbClose
	Kind	bkClose

Figure 2.7.b The Additional components on Delphi 8's Tool palette

Notice that we use bmb... for BitBtns.

We set the Kind property to bkClose in the same way that we set the Color property in Chapter 1.

- Go to the Object Inspector and click on the little down arrow alongside Kind in the list of properties. You will see a list of the different kinds of standard BitBtns that Delphi provides.
- From this list, select bkClose. (You can also type it in directly if you prefer.) Notice that when you change the Kind property to bkClose, Delphi automatically changes the Caption to '&Close' and puts a picture and the Caption 'Close' on the button.

When the Kind is set to bkClose, a click on the BitBtn will automatically close the form without the need for a special event-handler.

- Since there is no further programming to do, click File | Save As… to save the unit file as C02e03u and File | Save project as… to save the project as C02e03p. Delphi will automatically add the extension of .pas to the unit file and .dpr or .bdsproj to the project file. Click on the Run arrow.

The screen that comes up looks just like the previous one, except that now there is an extra button at the bottom with a little picture on it and the Caption 'Close'.
- Test it by clicking the mouse in the blank Edit component, and typing in something like 'Nice demo'.
- Click on the Transfer button (figure 2.8). The text is transferred to the Label.
- Now click on the Close button. Not surprisingly, the program closes.

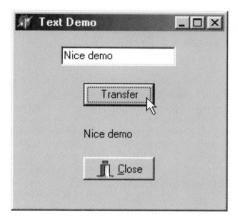

Figure 2.8 Adding the Close BitBtn

Using a BitBtn of kind bkClose is very easy and convenient, and we can use this for all our future programs if we want to. However, it is not essential since the user of the program can click on the Close box at the top of the window, as we have been doing up until now.

EXAMPLE 2.4) Setting focus and clearing text

The program we have developed can be made more user-friendly. As it is at the moment, to enter new text the user must first click in the Edit component with the mouse and then delete the existing text before entering new text. Would it not be nicer to find a way of moving the cursor to the Edit component and clearing the text automatically?

First, when this program runs the first time, we can have the cursor ready and waiting in the Edit component by changing its TabOrder property to 0. In the Form Designer, click on the Edit component, then set the TabOrder property. Delphi automatically adjusts the TabOrder of the other components:

Component	Property	Value
edtText	TabOrder	0

We can Clear many components. We can also program many components to be active by 'giving them the focus'. We can do both of these with Edit components.
- To do this now, add two lines to the OnClick event handler:

```
procedure TfrmTextDemo.btnTransferClick(Sender: TObject);
begin
  lblText.Caption := edtText.Text;
  edtText.Clear;
  edtText.SetFocus;
end;
```

- Click on File | Save As... to save the unit file as C02e04u and on File | Save Project As... to save the project as C02e04p.
- Run and test this final version of the program. Do you notice the differences? Because the Edit component's TabOrder is 0, when the program starts up the cursor is flashing in it. You can type text in directly without first selecting it with the mouse. When you click on the Transfer button, three things happen:
  - the program line `lblText.Caption := edtText.Text;` is an assignment statement that causes the text from the Edit component to appear in the label as before,
  - the program line `edtText.Clear;` is a method call that calls the Clear method to clear the text in the Edit component,
  - the program line `edtText.SetFocus;` is a method call that calls the SetFocus method to set the cursor back in the Edit component once again.

Economy: Making life easier for the user

Setting the focus and clearing the text through program code, as in this example, helps the user to achieve the same task (entering further text) in a fewer number of steps. By clearing the text in the edit component, we save users the step of selecting and deleting the existing text themselves. By setting the focus, we save users the step of clicking on the edit box before typing in the new text.

In Chapter 1 we introduced the user interface design principle called predictability. We now add a second principle called *economy*. This states that the user should be able to achieve a task with the fewest possible steps. Setting the focus and clearing text as we have done in this example is just one way in which we can make our user interfaces more economical.

Method calls

Until now all our programming statements have been assignment statements. The program above introduces a new form of programming statement called a *method call*. This has the form:

`ObjectName.MethodName;`

A method is a set of programming instructions attached to an object that tells that object how to perform a particular operation such as Clear or SetFocus. For now, just use the different methods as we come across them in the chapters that follow. (In Chapters 11 and 12 we look specifically at methods.)

Selecting components on a form

So far, when we have wanted to select a component, possibly to set some of its properties in the Object Inspector, we have clicked on it in the Form Designer. But there is another way to select a component. Notice that just below the title of the Object Inspector there is a drop-down box. If you click on the down-pointing arrow at the right-hand side, a box opens with an alphabetic list of the components on the form (figure 2.9). If you select one of the components on the list, it will be highlighted on the form and its properties displayed in the Object Inspector. It also provides a useful list of all the components on the form.

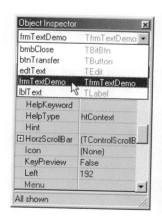

Figure 2.9 Listing the components on the form

EXAMPLE 2.5 Positioning and sizing components

Until now, we have been placing components on the form by single-clicking on the Component/Tool palette and then single-clicking on the form to position the top left-hand corner of the component. Delphi offers more flexibility than this.

- To explore these other ways, start a new application. From the menu select File | New | Application for Delphi 7 and File | New | VCL Forms Application for Delphi 8.
- *Double-click* on the BitBtn symbol in the Component / Tool palette, Additional tab (as located in the previous example). BitBtn1 appears on the Form.
- Go to the Object Inspector and, by scrolling if necessary, find the value of BitBtn1's Left property. On our computer this had the value 169, but it may be different on yours.
- Change this to 200, say, and press <Enter>. The button jumps to the right.

The button has a Top property too. Increase the value to move the button down. So, we can position the button where we want it by modifying the values of Left and Top as needed. (Position 0, 0 is the top left corner of the form.)
  We can also move the button by *dragging* it with the mouse.

- Move the mouse pointer to within BitBtn1, press and hold down the left-hand mouse button and then, still holding the mouse button down, move the cursor towards the bottom left corner of the form. A rectangle is now attached to the mouse pointer (figure 2.10). When the rectangle is in the required position, release the mouse button to reposition BitBtn1. Look now at the values of Top and Left, and you will see that they have changed to reflect the new position of BitBtn1.

We can change the size of a component by modifying the values of its Height and Width properties or by dragging with a mouse.

- First note the current values of the Height and Width properties. Now click once on BitBtn1. Eight small black squares (or sizing handles) are visible around the edges of BitBtn1, as in figure 2.11.
- Move the mouse cursor over the middle handle on the right-hand side. The cursor becomes a double-headed arrow.
- Press the left-hand mouse button down and, keeping it down, move the cursor to the right, almost to the edge of the frame, and then let go. As you move the mouse, you stretch BitBtn1 until you release the mouse button

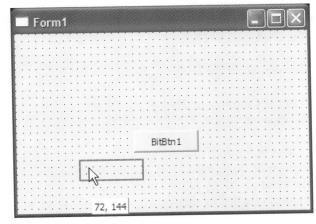

Figure 2.10 Using the mouse, drag BitBtn1 towards the lower left-hand corner

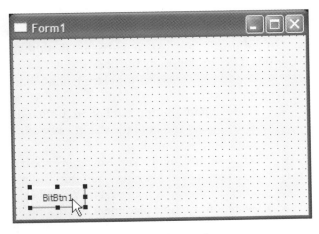

Figure 2.11 Sizing handles around BitBtn1

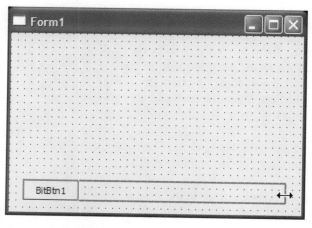

Figure 2.12 Stretching BitBtn1

(figure 2.12). As the button elongates, the value of Width in the Object Inspector increases.

- Single-clicking on most components brings up sizing handles, and by dragging these handles you can make the components wider or narrower, shorter or taller. By dragging from inside a component you can reposition it. In this way, you can judge visually the position and size of the components that make up the user interface, and this is sometimes easier than setting the Height, Left, Top or Width property values.

EXAMPLE 2.6 GroupBox and RadioButton components

- Working from the form developed in the example above, position and size a GroupBox component above BitBtn1, as shown in the screen (figure 2.13). (You may want to try this now on your own, before reading any further.)

We can find the GroupBox component on the Standard tab of the Component/Tool palette using the pop-up hints. Like other components, it can be placed on the form by double-clicking on the icon or by clicking once on the icon and then a second time at the required position on the form.

It can be positioned and sized either by dragging with the mouse, or by setting its Height, Left, Top or Width property values in the Object Inspector.

Until now, we have selected and placed components one by one on the form. We are now going to put six RadioButtons on the form but *inside* the GroupBox (figure 2.14), so make sure that the GroupBox is selected by clicking inside it before going any further.

Delphi has a shortcut for placing more than one component of the same type on a form:

- Find the RadioButton symbol on the Standard tab of the Component/Tool palette, press and hold the <Shift> key down, and click once on the RadioButton symbol.
- Let go of the <Shift> key. Now move the cursor inside GroupBox1 and click six times to place six RadioButtons in two columns of three, more or less as shown in figure 2.14. (We will sort out the exact positions a little later.)
- Switch off multiple placement by clicking on the arrow at the left of the Component/Tool palette (figure 2.7a or 2.7b). If you accidentally place down more than six RadioButtons, press the <Del> key to delete any extras. You may need to select the component first.

Figure 2.13 Sizing a GroupBox

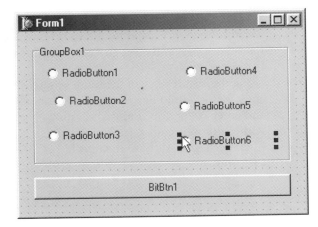

Figure 2.14 Initial layout for example 2.6

The GroupBox differs from the components we have looked at previously because its purpose is to group other components together. This type of component is called a *container component*. Once a component has been placed within a container, it cannot be dragged out of that container. Taking each RadioButton in turn, try dragging it out of the GroupBox with the mouse. If you can, that RadioButton is not within the GroupBox and will not function in synchronism with any other RadioButtons in the GroupBox. Another check is if you move the GroupBox, either by dragging or by changing its Top or Left properties in the Object Inspector, the RadioButtons will move with it. Any RadioButtons contained in that do not move are not contained in the GroupBox.

If by mistake you create a RadioButton that is not within the GroupBox, you can do one of two things. You can delete that RadioButton, click within the GroupBox away from any other component so that the GroupBox's sizing handles appear, and then add a new RadioButton from the Component / Tool palette to the GroupBox. Alternatively, select the RadioButton that you can drag out of the GroupBox, click on Edit | Cut, click within the GroupBox away from any other component, click on Edit | Paste and then position the RadioButton as required.

- To see how RadioButtons work, click on the green 'Run' arrow in the SpeedBar. On the running form, click on RadioButton1. A black 'dot' appears in the small white space alongside RadioButton1 (similar to figure 2.15).
- Now click on RadioButton5. A black dot appears next to RadioButton5, indicating that it is now selected, and the dot disappears from RadioButton1, indicating that it is no longer selected.

Each time you click on a RadioButton that RadioButton is selected and all the other RadioButtons in that GroupBox are automatically deselected. This makes RadioButtons particularly useful where a user must select only one value out of a list of possibilities. If you need two groups of RadioButtons you can place each group in a separate GroupBox.

- When you have finished experimenting with these RadioButtons, end the program by clicking in the Close box in the top corner of the Window and return to the design environment.

Selecting multiple components

- Click on RadioButton1.
- Now, press and hold the <Shift> key down, and then click once each on RadioButton2 and RadioButton3 before releasing the <Shift> key. Small dark grey squares appear at the corners of each selected component.
- Move to the Object Inspector, and enter 50 as the value in the Left property. All three components line up on the left side, 50 pixels from the edge of the GroupBox.

- Similarly, to line up RadioButtons 4, 5 and 6 vertically, click on RadioButton4, press and hold <Shift> down, click once each on RadioButtons 5 and 6, let go <Shift> and then enter a value of 200 for the Left property.
- Using the <Shift> key in the same way, select RadioButtons 1 and 4, and enter 40 for Top to line them up horizontally, select RadioButtons 2 and 5, and enter 70 for Top, and RadioButtons 3 and 6, and enter 100 for Top. The RadioButtons are now neatly lined up.
- Click File | Save All. Save the unit file as C02e06u and the project file as C02e06p.

EXAMPLE 2.7) Setting form colours with RadioButtons

- Write a program, with six RadioButtons in a GroupBox, that switches the form's colour between Blue, Red, Green, Yellow, Fuchsia and Silver using either the RadioButtons or accelerator keys. Also have an elongated Close Bitmap button at the bottom of the screen.

EX 2.7 Planning

In example 1.2 we programmed two buttons to change the form's colour between purple and yellow.
- Combine the principles we used there with the user interface layout of the previous example.

Accelerator keys were discussed in Chapter 1.

EX 2.7 Testing

If you have written a program, it is a good idea to test it carefully. In this case, testing is reasonably simple.
- First, when you run your program, it should give a screen display much like figure 2.15.
- If your program does that, the next stage is to click on each RadioButton in turn, and to check that the form takes on the required colour.
- Check that the first letter of each colour Caption is underlined to indicate the accelerator keys. You should also test that the accelerator keys, <Alt+B> for Blue, <Alr+R> for Red, and so on, actually work.
- Now, click on the Close button or press <Alt+C>.

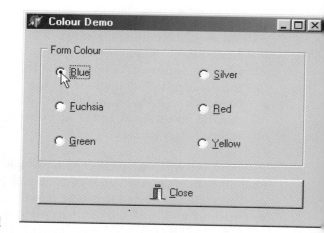

Figure 2.15 Setting a form's colour by means of RadioButtons

EX 2.7 Solution

- Start with the program written in example 2.6. (You can open C02e06.dpr using File | Open if it is not on your screen any more.)
- Modify the property values as follows:

Component	Property	Value
Form1	Name	frmColourDemo
	Caption	Colour Demo
GroupBox1	Name	gpbFormColour
	Caption	Form Colour
RadioButton1	Name	radBlue
	Caption	&Blue
RadioButton2	Name	radFuchsia
	Caption	&Fuchsia
RadioButton3	Name	radGreen
	Caption	&Green
RadioButton4	Name	radSilver
	Caption	&Silver
RadioButton5	Name	radRed
	Caption	&Red
RadioButton6	Name	radYellow
	Caption	&Yellow
BitBtn	Name	bmbClose
	Kind	bkClose

The new naming conventions we introduce here are gpb... and rad... for GroupBox and RadioButton respectively.

In example 2.1 we changed the form size by setting values for Height and Width in the Object Inspector. We can also change the form size by dragging with a mouse.

- Rest the mouse pointer on any edge of the form. The pointer changes to a double-headed arrow.
- Hold down the left mouse button and move the mouse to make the form larger or smaller.

Now, write an appropriate event handler for each of these RadioButtons.
- Double-click on the Blue RadioButton.
- Modify radBlue's OnClick event handler skeleton to:

```
procedure TfrmColourDemo.radBlueClick(Sender: TObject);
begin
  frmColourDemo.Color := clBlue;
end;
```

- Now, if you can see any part of the Form Designer that is not hidden by the editing window, click once on it to show the Form Designer once more (Delphi 4 to 7). Alternatively, you can press <F12> or use the menu sequence View | Toggle Form/Unit (Delphi 4 to 7) or View | ShowCode (Delphi 8).
- Double-click the Fuchsia RadioButton and create the following event handler:

```
procedure TfrmColourDemo.radFuchsiaClick(Sender: TObject);
begin
  frmColourDemo.Color := clFuchsia;
end;
```

- By continuing to move backwards and forwards ('toggling') between the Form Designer and the editor window, enter the remaining event handlers:

```
procedure TfrmColourDemo.radGreenClick(Sender: TObject);
begin
  frmColourDemo.Color := clGreen;
end;

procedure TfrmColourDemo.radSilverClick(Sender: TObject);
begin
  frmColourDemo.Color := clSilver;
end;

procedure TfrmColourDemo.radRedClick(Sender: TObject);
begin
  frmColourDemo.Color := clRed;
end;

procedure TfrmColourDemo.radYellowClick(Sender: TObject);
begin
  frmColourDemo.Color := clYellow;
end;
```

- Save the unit and project files as C02e07u and C02e07p respectively, and then run and test this program as described earlier.

When to use RadioButtons

As you can see from this example, RadioButtons are very useful when we want to *select only one out of a number of different possibilities*. For instance, a form can be only one colour at a time. Since only one RadioButton in a group can be active at a time, this is a typical case of where to use RadioButtons.

As so often happens with programming, using RadioButtons was not the only possibility. We could also have used six ordinary buttons instead of the RadioButtons to change the colour.

User interface design principles can help programmers decide which components best suit a particular situation. So far we have introduced the principles of predictability and economy. Another important user interface principle is *compatibility*. A user interface should (as far as possible) conform to users' previous experience with other packages. To be compatible with other Windows applications we should use RadioButtons when we want the user to select one of several (two to seven) mutually exclusive options. An alternative component to a group of RadioButtons is a ComboBox (introduced in Chapter 8), which is a useful component to use when there is not enough screen space to display all options as RadioButtons. A set of RadioButtons and a ComboBox both have the advantage of showing what the current selection is from the available options.

EXAMPLE 2.8) Two groups of RadioButtons

If we want more than one group of RadioButtons, each group must be in a separate container to allow us to select one RadioButton from each group. A form is a container and so is a GroupBox. For two groups, we can have one group directly on the form and the other in a GroupBox. Alternatively we can have each group in its own GroupBox. In this example we have four RadioButtons directly on the form and another two in a GroupBox.

- Start a new application, set up the screen as shown in figure 2.16 and set the properties according to the following table.
- Make sure that four of the RadioButtons are directly on the form and that the other two are in the GroupBox.

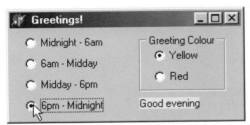

Figure 2.16 Two groups of RadioButtons

Component	Property	Value
Form1	Name	frmGreeting
	Caption	Greetings!
Label1	Name	lblGreeting
	Caption	Hello there
RadioButton1	Name	radNight
	Caption	Midnight – 6am
RadioButton2	Name	radMorning
	Caption	6am – Midday
RadioButton3	Name	radAfternoon
	Caption	Midday – 6pm
RadioButton4	Name	radEvening
	Caption	6pm – Midnight
GroupBox1	Name	gpbColour
	Caption	Greeting Colour
RadioButton5	Name	radYellow
(in gpbColour)	Caption	Yellow
RadioButton6	Name	radRed
(in gpbColour)	Caption	Red

- By double-clicking on each component in turn (except the form and the Label), create the following event handlers (the procedure header for each procedure shows the related component):

```
procedure TfrmGreeting.radNightClick(Sender: TObject);
begin
  lblGreeting.Caption := 'Sleep well!';
end;


procedure TfrmGreeting.radMorningClick(Sender: TObject);
begin
  lblGreeting.Caption := 'Good morning';
end;


procedure TfrmGreeting.radAfternoonClick(Sender: TObject);
begin
  lblGreeting.Caption := 'Good afternoon';
end;


procedure TfrmGreeting.radEveningClick(Sender: TObject);
begin
  lblGreeting.Caption := 'Good evening';
end;


procedure TfrmGreeting.radYellowClick(Sender: TObject);
begin
  lblGreeting.Color := clYellow;
end;


procedure TfrmGreeting.radRedClick(Sender: TObject);
begin
  lblGreeting.Color := clRed;
end;
```

- Save the unit and project files as C02e08u and C02e08p respectively, and then run and test this program.
- Notice that one of the four RadioButtons on the form and one of the two RadioButtons in the GroupBox can be selected at a time.

Listing valid methods and properties through Code Completion

Edit components have a Clear method, while Label components do not. The Object Inspector shows a component's properties and events but not its methods. So how do we know whether a method can be used for a given component? One way is to use Delphi's Code Completion facility. As soon as you type a full stop after a valid component name, Delphi displays a list of the available methods (ie functions and procedures) and properties. As you type in the letters of the name, the pop-up Code Completion box lists only the appropriate ones. So an Edit component has four methods starting with Cle... (figure 2.17). You can either type in the complete method name or select it from the pop-up with the mouse or arrow key. (If the code completion box does not pop up automatically, it can be called up through <Ctrl-Space>.)

Attempting the same thing with a Label component will show that it has no Clear method.

One can also find a list of the available methods and a description of each method through the online Help facility.

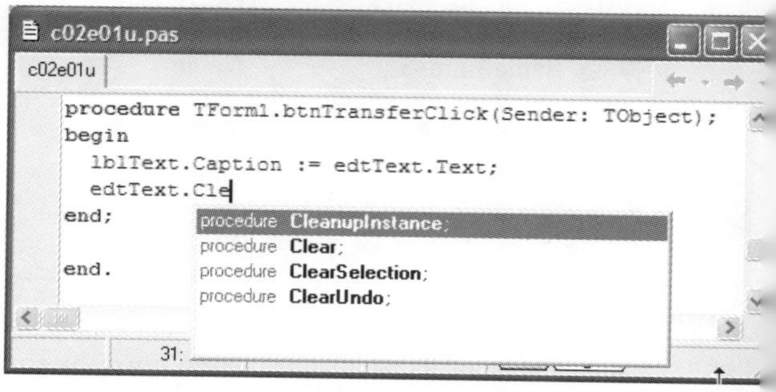

Figure 2.17 Delphi's Code Completion pop-up

A comment on the examples in this chapter

We've used colours a lot in this chapter. Setting colours is not that important and we don't often do it in 'real' programs. However, using colours is a very convenient way of making small, self-contained examples to illustrate other concepts.

REVIEW

We briefly covered several concepts in this chapter. We looked at the Label and Edit components. We display text to the user through the Label's Caption property. We can set this at design time in the Object Inspector or at run time through an assignment statement. Then we read text in from the user through the Edit component. The text the user enters is available as the Edit component's Text property, and we can use it by, for instance, assigning it to a Label's Caption property in an assignment statement.

We looked at BitBtns. These are like ordinary buttons except that they can also display a small diagram. Delphi comes with several ready-programmed BitBtns, and we used the bkClose kind to close the program.

There are several ways of making a program more user-friendly, and in this chapter we looked at the user interface factors of *economy* (reducing the number of steps required to achieve a task) and *compatibility* (conforming to users' previous experience with other packages). For economy, we used the SetFocus method to move the cursor to the Edit component and the Clear method to clear the text in it. For compatibility we used a set of RadioButtons to enable one choice from a set of alternatives.

In Chapter 1 we changed the position and size of components by changing properties such as Top and Left. In this chapter, we saw that we can also use the mouse to drag and resize components.

The other new components we used in this chapter were the GroupBox and RadioButton. RadioButtons work in a group, since only one can be selected at a time, and the GroupBox is a very useful container to group them together. We also saw that the form itself groups RadioButtons which are not inside a Groupbox.We use RadioButtons when the user can select only one possibility at a time out of a number of different ones.

In the process of using RadioButtons, we saw how to use the <Shift> key in two different ways with multiple components: 1) to place multiple components of the same type on the form without having to select them from the Componen/Tool palette each time, and 2) to select a group of components and then set common values for them through the Object Inspector.

IMPORTANT CONCEPTS

Programming environment

Finding the methods available for a particular component: Delphi's Code Completion lists the available methods and properties for a particular object after typing the object's name followed by a full stop.

Fundamental programming concepts

Method: A method is a set of programming instructions attached to an object that tells that object how to perform a particular operation (such as Clear or SetFocus).

Method call: A method call differs from the assignment statements we have seen previously. It invokes an object's method and has the form

```
ObjectName.MethodName;
```

Program statements: Programs consist of a series of statements that are executed one after another in order.

Writing a program

Naming convention: For each component we use a three-letter prefix followed by a descriptive name that describes what the component does so that one knows from the program code (1) what the component is, and (2) what it does. The list of standard prefixes used in this book appears in Appendix 3.

Visual GUI development

Adding an object to the user interface: Double-clicking on the Component / Tool palette places a component on the Form. Single-clicking on the Component / Tool palette allows a component to be selected and placed at a particular position on the form.

Creating multiple objects: Shift-click allows multiple components of the same type to be placed on the form.

Positioning and resizing a component: A visual component's position and size can be changed at design time in two ways, either by dragging with the mouse or by changing the Height, Left, Top or Width properties in the Object Inspector. (These properties can also be changed programmatically.)

User interface factors

Clear: At times a component needs to be cleared (eg the text removed from an Edit). Clear it programmatically so that the user does not need to clear it manually before providing the next set of input.

Compatibility: The user interface design principle of compatibility states that an interface should conform to users' previous experience with other packages.

Displaying text: A Label's Caption is a useful way to display text to the user, though it cannot be used for input. The text displayed can be set at design time in the Object Inspector or programmatically at run time.

Economy: The user interface design principle of economy states that the user should be able to achieve a task with as few steps as are reasonably possible.

Entering text: The Edit component's Text property provides a useful way of reading in a single line of text. It has automatic editing facilities, so that the user can make corrections, it can be read by the program and it can display a particular text string under program control.

Grouping components: Some components act as containers for others. A Form, for example, contains all the components on it. There are also other containers, such as GroupBoxes, that can provide groupings either to facilitate use (to simplify comprehension and/or input by the user) or to group components that interact (eg RadioButtons).

Selecting one from several alternatives: RadioButtons provide a way of allowing the user only one choice out of several. (In Chapter 8 we see ComboBoxes, which provide an alternative to RadioButtons. ComboBoxes are particularly useful when there is a large number of mutually exclusive alternatives. In Chapter 6 we see CheckBoxes, which do not restrict the user to only one choice out of several options.)

Set focus: At times, after a particular action has been performed, there is a particular component that the user will use next. Set the focus on this component programmatically so that the user does not need to select it with the mouse.

TabOrder: Often there is an obvious or preferable sequence to operate the components on a form. If the TabOrder is set to this sequence the user can move between components in this sequence simply by pressing the <Tab> key rather than having to select them using the mouse. Setting a component's TabOrder to 0 in the Object Inspector means that it will have the focus when the program starts. When the programmer sets a particular component's TabOrder, Delphi automatically adjusts the TabOrders of any other components as needed.

NEW DELPHI FEATURES

Many components have similar properties and events. Instead of repeating these for each component, we give a list of properties and events introduced in the chapter that apply to several different types of component. So, if a property does not appear under a specific component, it may be in the following table:

Common component properties and events		
Properties	Caption	Specifies a text string that identifies the component to the user. To underline a character in a Caption for a component like a button include an ampersand (&) before the character. This creates an accelerator character so that the user can select the component by pressing Alt while typing the underlined character. To display an ampersand character in the Caption, use two ampersands (&&).
	Name	Program code refers to a component by its name. Change the Name property at design time only. If the component's Caption is not modified, the Caption changes to match the new name.
	TabOrder	TabOrder is the order in which components receive focus when the user presses the <Tab> key. The component with the TabOrder value of 0 is the component that has the focus when the form first appears. Initially, the TabOrder is the order in which the components were added to the form. The first component added to the form has a TabOrder value of 0, the second is 1, and so on. Change this by changing the TabOrder property.
	Left	Determines the left side of the component or moves the left side of the component if Left is changed in program code. If the component is on a form, the Left property is relative to the left edge of the form (in pixels). If the component is in a container, Left is relative to the container.
	Height	Specifies the vertical size of the component in pixels. Use the Height property to read or change the height of the component.
	Top	Specifies the vertical position of the top-left corner of a component in pixels, relative to its parent or container component.
	Width	Specifies the horizontal size of the component in pixels.
Events	OnClick	Occurs when the user clicks the component. Use the OnClick event handler to write code that responds when the user clicks the component.

TBitBtn (Bitmap Button)		
Properties	Kind	Determines the kind of BitBtn. Refer to online Help for an explanation of the different kinds of BitBtn.
Prefix	bmb...	
Use		Creates a button component that can display a bitmap image on its face. BitBtns behave in the same way as buttons. Use them to initiate actions.

TButton

Prefix	btn...	
Use	See Chapter 1.	

TEdit

Properties	Text	Contains a text string associated with the component. Use the text property to read the text of the component or to specify a new string for the Text value. By default, Text is the component name.
Methods	Clear	The Clear method deletes the text displayed in the Edit component. Use Clear to set the value of the Text property to an empty string.
	SetFocus	The SetFocus method gives the input focus to the Edit component. When an Edit component has focus, it receives keyboard events such as character input. Use SetFocus to force the input focus to the Edit component.
Prefix	edt...	
Use	Displays an editing area where the user can enter or modify a single line of text. Edit components can also display text to the user.	

TForm

Prefix	frm...	
Use	See Chapter 1.	

TGroupBox

Prefix	gpb...
Use	Provides a container to group related options on a form by arranging related components (typically RadioButtons). After placing a GroupBox on a form, select components from the Component palette and place them in the GroupBox. When a component is placed within a GroupBox, the GroupBox becomes the parent of that component.

TLabel

Prefix	lbl...
Use	Labels display text that the user cannot select or manipulate and are usually placed next to other components.

TRadioButton

Prefix	rad...
Use	Presents an option that a user can toggle between Yes/No or True/False. Use RadioButtons to display a group of choices that are mutually exclusive. Users can select only one RadioButton in a group at a time. When the user selects a RadioButton, the previously selected RadioButton becomes unselected. Add the GroupBox to the form first, then place the RadioButtons into the GroupBox. Two RadioButtons on a form can be checked at the same time only if they are in separate containers, such as two different GroupBoxes.

PROBLEMS

PROBLEM 2.1) True or False?

- Complete the table below by indicating with a ✓ in the appropriate column whether each statement is True or False.

Statement	True	False
1 To read text in from the keyboard, you can use the Label component.		
2 To read text in from the keyboard, you can use the Edit component.		
3 To display text on the screen, you can use the Label component.		
4 To display text on the screen, you can use the Edit component.		
5 A Button component has a picture on it.		
6 The Button component appears on the Standard tab of the Component/Tool palette.		
7 You can find the text entered by the user in the Caption property of an Edit component.		

PROBLEM 2.2) Multiple text displays

- Working along the lines used in the examples in this chapter, write a program such as that shown in the startup screen in figure 2.18.

Figure 2.18 Start-up screen for problem 2.2

The program will need an Edit component for text entry, three buttons with the Captions 'Name', 'Department' and 'Birth Date', and, next to each button, a Label. The user will enter text in the Edit component and then click on one of the three buttons. This text must then be transferred from the Edit component to the Label alongside the button that was clicked. Clicking the button must also return the focus to the Edit component and clear it.

Figure 2.19 shows the program after the user has entered the word 'George' and pressed the Name button, entered the word 'Finance' and clicked the Department button, and entered the date '10/12/69' but not yet clicked the Birth Date button.

As you can see, the program also contains a Clear All button. When the user clicks it, all three entries alongside the Name, Department and Birth Date buttons are cleared.

PROBLEM 2.3) Sixpence Joe's Family Supermarket

'Sixpence Joe', the owner of a local supermarket, believes that by using computer technology sensibly he can improve his customer service. As a start, he wants to create a 'Value for Money' Calculator that shows customers what some of his more popular products cost.

- Write a program with four RadioButtons within a GroupBox, as shown in figure 2.20.

Figure 2.19 Problem 2.2 after data entry of name and department.

When a customer clicks on a particular product, the calculator must display its price per kilogram. The four products and the prices he wants to display are Flour at R12.99, Rice at R4.39, Sugar at R4.10 and Mealie Meal at R2.16.

Figure 2.20 Interface for Sixpence Joe's Family Supermarket 'Value for Money' Calculator

PROBLEM 2.4) Delivery charges

Jolly Joe's Family Supermarket will take phone orders and then deliver your purchases for a small fee. The costs are as follows:

Distance	Delivery charge
5 km or less	R7.50
5–10 km	R12.50
10–20 km	R17.50
More than 20 km	Ask Jolly Joe

- Write a Delphi program so that the person taking the order can simply select one of four RadioButtons (depending on the distance) and see the appropriate delivery charge.

CHAPTER 3

....

String variables

PURPOSE OF THIS CHAPTER

In the previous two chapters we saw the basic features of Delphi's IDE
(Integrated Development Environment). In this chapter, we begin to look more
closely at Delphi Pascal, the programming language that is the foundation of all
we do in Delphi. In some ways, using a computer to do an information-
processing task is more difficult than doing it by hand because we must be much
more precise in deciding what actions are required to process the data. We then
have to adhere to the rules of the programming language in writing the program
so that the computer can execute it correctly. It's like learning a whole new
language.

In this chapter we discuss the *rules for manipulating string data*. In Chapter 4
we look at whole numbers (ie numbers such as 137) and numbers with fractions
(ie numbers such as 8.55).

The notion of a variable

Programs manipulate data such as numbers and characters. To name and process data during computation, Delphi Pascal and other programming languages use things called variables. Variables are crucial to programming.

Variables can hold numbers or other types of data. They are rather like small blackboards on which something can be written. Just as something written on a blackboard can be changed, so too can the data held in a variable be changed. The words 'hold' and 'contain', when applied to variables, mean the same thing and, if you think in terms of the blackboard analogy, refer to the item written on the blackboard. The number or character string held in a variable is called its 'value'.

To gain full advantage from this chapter, follow the examples by doing them on the computer.

EXAMPLE 3.1) Text input and output using a variable

Here we demonstrate the use of a variable. Remember example 2.2 in Chapter 2? In that example we allowed the user to type something in an Edit component and transfer it with a button click to the caption of a Label component. In this example, we are going to adapt example 2.2 to use a variable.

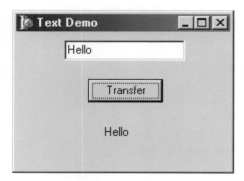

Figure 3.1 Transferring text from an Edit component to a Label

- Begin by opening the program C02e02p.dpr that you saved previously. Figure 3.1 shows the screen after the user entered 'Hello' in the Edit component and clicked on the Transfer button.
- To change the event handler connected to the Transfer button, double-click on the Transfer button on the form, then edit the code to match the following:

```
1 procedure TfrmTextDemo.btnTransferClick(Sender: TObject);
2 var NewText: string;
3 begin
4   NewText := edtText.Text;
5   edtText.Clear;                    //Clearing the Edit box
6   lblText.Caption := NewText;
7   edtText.SetFocus;
8 end;
```

- Save the unit and project files as C03e01u and C03e01p respectively.
- Now run this program. Enter any text in the box provided, click on the Transfer button, and see what happens.

To the user this version of the program appears the same as example 2.2. However, the program now uses a variable. Programs can often be written differently yet behave the same.

Programming instructions versus program comments

Let's take a closer look at our program above. Lines 4 to 7 contain instructions to the computer. These programming instructions are called *statements*. The semicolons at the ends of the statements separate the statements and, strictly speaking, are not part of the statements themselves. The sentence:

```
//Clearing the Edit box
```

in line 5 is a *comment*. Comments are ignored by the compiler and are used to improve the readability of programs. There are several ways to construct comments:

- `{ Text between a left brace and a right brace constitutes a comment. }`
- `(* Text between a left-parenthesis-plus-asterisk and an asterisk-plus-right-parenthesis also constitutes a comment. *)`
- `// Any text between a double-slash and the end of the line`
  `// constitutes a comment.`

Associating values with variable names

We adapted the program to use a variable called `NewText`. With the simple statement

```
NewText := edtText.Text;
```

in line 4 we put the text entered by the user into variable `NewText`. As we saw in Chapter 1, the symbol ':=' is the *assignment operator*, and statements like this are *assignment statements*. The := instructs the computer to change the value of the variable on the left-hand side of it to the value given on the right-hand side.

Variable `NewText` can hold any text. It can hold your age, your birth date, your name, but it can hold only one of these values at a time. If you use it first to hold your name and then later use it to hold your address, your name is gone. For example, if you enter the text 'I can program!' first, transfer it, and then enter 'Hello there!', the statement

```
NewText := edtText.Text;
```

will overwrite 'I can program!' with 'Hello there!'. The variable `NewText` will now contain a new value. Try it out.

Think of a variable as an area of the computer's memory to which you assign a name. You do this by declaring the variable in a declaration statement. In line 2,

```
var NewText: string;
```

we declare variable `NewText` to be of type `string`.

As you can see, a variable declaration has three parts: the reserved word `var`, a name (in this case `NewText`) and a type (in this case `string`). We first discuss the type part and afterwards we will discuss the name part.

The *type* part of a variable declaration

A *data value* is a single piece of information used in a program, such as the single character 'Z' or the single string 'I can program!' or the single number 17. A *data type* is a particular kind of data, such as the data type `string` that we used for our variable `NewText` in the declaration statement

```
var NewText: string;
```

This statement tells the computer to set aside space in memory for storing a string value. We also indicate with this statement that we are going to refer to that space in memory by the name `NewText`. The abbreviation `var` is a reserved word in Delphi Pascal referring to the word 'variable' and `string` is the type of the variable `NewText`. In other words, the declaration statement creates a variable called `NewText` that we can use later in our program to store any string values such as 'I enjoy programming', 'Enter name:' or 'W'. (Chapter 4 deals with numbers.)

An action in the program can change the data value stored in a data variable, but the data type associated with the variable cannot change.

We can use variables in a program only if they have been declared, as you will see for yourself in the next example.

EXAMPLE 3.2 What happens if we don't declare a variable?

- Still working with the same example, delete the declaration statement (line 2)

```
var NewText: string;
```

- Now run the program.

It gives an error message indicating that `NewText` is an *undeclared identifier* with the line `NewText := edtText.Text;` highlighted and the cursor positioned after `NewText` in the assignment statement.

Undeclared identifiers

Whenever the computer gives this message, what is it saying? It is saying: 'I don't know about this variable called `NewText`. We have not been introduced yet.' This problem of an unknown identifier is dealt with by declaring every variable used in a procedure in the *declaration section* of that procedure. That part of any event handler between the procedure header and the `begin` of the procedure body is called the *declaration section* of the event handler.

```
procedure Header
   Declaration Section
begin
   Procedure Body
end
```

As we saw in example 3.1 above, the declaration section starts with the abbreviation var, followed by a list of the variables we will use in our event handler, and their types. When Delphi starts compiling a program and comes across a variable declaration statement, it sets aside memory for each variable in the list. We specify the type of each variable, so that the computer knows how much memory to set aside. The type of the variable NewText in our program is string. Other variable types include double, integer, char and Boolean. We will discuss them later.

EXAMPLE 3.3) Experimenting with incompatible types

We mentioned before that, because of the way NewText is declared, it can be used only to hold string values. Let's see what happens if we try to put a number in it.

• Change the assignment statement in line 4 to match the following:

```
NewText := 5;
```

• Run the program and see what happens.

It gives an error message indicating that types 'string' and 'integer' are incompatible. The line NewText := 5; is highlighted and the cursor is positioned after the assignment statement. When the computer gives this message, it is saying: 'In the declaration section, you have specified that NewText will hold only string values, and now you are trying to store a number in it! I'm sorry, it can't be done!'

The *name* part of a variable declaration

Let's now look at the name part of a variable declaration. Variable names can be any length (but Delphi will use only the first 255 characters), so you can (and should) give your variables descriptive names. For example, if you want to keep track of the current balance in a cheque book program, you can create a variable called ChequebookBalance or Balance.

Choosing meaningful names for the variables you use in your programs is an important part of skillful programming. A meaningful variable name should tell someone reading the code exactly what the variable represents.

We have been using a convention for choosing names for the components in our programs. This is good programming style and we do it consistently throughout the book. The convention is as follows: for every component available on the Component palette we have a standard abbreviation which we attach to the front of a descriptive name that starts with an uppercase letter. For example, the abbreviation for a button is `btn`, so if we use a button that transfers something, we call it `btnTransfer`. An Edit component in which we expect the user to enter the name of a city we call `edtCity`, and so on. We suggest that you get into the habit of using this convention for all the programs you write. A list of all the components used in this book with their associated three-letter prefixes is given in Appendix 3.

Delphi has some rules for any variable or component name:

o   The name can be any length but Delphi will use only the first 255 characters.

o   The first character of the name must be a letter or an underscore. For example: `EmployeeName1` or `_Employee1` are valid variable names but not `1EmployeeName`.

o   The characters that follow the first one can be only letters, digits or underscores.
    For example: `Person3` and `Person_3` are valid but not `Person?`.

o   No spaces are allowed in a name. For example: `Longest_Sentence` is valid but not `Longest Sentence`.

o   Delphi reserved words may not be used as names. Reserved words are those that mean something to the Delphi compiler and cannot be used in any way other than the Delphi compiler expects. Examples of reserved words are: `begin`, `end`, `string`, `program`, `if`, `var`.

o   Since Delphi Pascal is case insensitive, an identifier such as `TheAnswer` could be written in any of these ways (but should be consistent):

```
TheAnswer
theAnswer
theanswer
THEANSWER
```

These rules apply to any name used in Delphi, such as component or variable names.

EXAMPLE 3.4) Trying out a few names for components

- Start a new application in Delphi.
- Put a Label, a button and an Edit component anywhere on the form. In this example we determine whether the following names are valid:

Component	Names to try
Label1	Text Label
	lblText
Button1	?Button
	btnQuestion
Edit1	1st_editbox
	edt1st

- In the Object Inspector, locate the Label's Name property and type the name 'Text Label' (with a space and without quotes), then press <Enter>. You will see that Delphi warns you if you use an invalid name (figure 3.2). No spaces are allowed in a component name.
- Click on OK and try 'lblText' (without the quotes). Delphi accepts it.

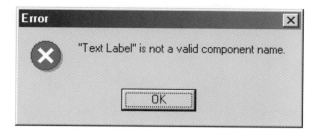

Figure 3.2 Error dialog box

- Select the button on the form and find its Name property in the Object Inspector. Type the name '?Button', then press <Enter>. An error dialog box appears again.
- Click on OK and try btnQuestion. This name is accepted.
- Similarly, select the Edit component on the form and locate its Name property in the Object Inspector. Try out the name '1st_editbox' (starting with the number 1). The error dialog box appears again because a name cannot start with a number.
- Click on OK and try the name 'edt1st'. This name is accepted.

Character strings

A string is any series of characters one after the other enclosed in single quotes. In Delphi, the string type is called `string`. In fact, any series of characters is called a string . If we look at the string 'Bafana Bafana!', we see that it has 14 characters (don't forget to count the space in the middle), and therefore its length is 14. Notice that even though a variable name cannot contain any spaces, spaces are quite acceptable in a string. We can also get a null or empty string. This is a string of length 0 and it has nothing between the single quotes, not even blanks.

In the next example, we continue using string variables and we introduce a new component, the ListBox.

EXAMPLE 3.5) Using string variables and a ListBox

In this example we see how to add character strings to Delphi's ListBox component using variables of type string. We need to write a program that will allow the *Bumble Bee Crèche* to enter the name of each child into one of two lists according to the child's gender. The names of the boys are added to the list of boys and the names of the girls are added to the list of girls. The form should look like the display in figure 3.3, representing the screen after some names have been added.

Figure 3.3 Adding names to lists according to gender

- Start a new application and create this form by adding the components in the table below:

Component	Property	Value
Form1	Name	frmSchool
	Caption	Bumble Bee Creche
Button1	Name	btnAddBoy
	Caption	Add boy
Button2	Name	btnAddGirl
	Caption	Add girl
Edit1	Name	edtChildName
	Text	<Blank>
Label1	Name	lblPrompt
	Caption	Enter child name:
ListBox1	Name	lstBoys
ListBox2	Name	lstGirls

- The next step is to enter the program code. The code we need for this program is connected to the Add boy and Add girl buttons through their OnClick event handlers. Edit the handlers by adding code to match the following (without the line numbers):

```
1 procedure TfrmSchool.btnAddBoyClick(Sender: TObject);
2 var Boy: string;
3 begin
4   Boy := edtChildName.Text;
5   lstBoys.Items.Add(Boy);
6   edtChildName.Clear;
7   edtChildName.SetFocus;
8 end;
```

```
 9 procedure TfrmSchool.btnAddGirlClick(Sender: TObject);
10 var Girl: string;
11 begin
12    Girl:= edtChildName.Text;
13    lstGirls.Items.Add(Girl);
14    edtChildName.Clear;
15    edtChildName.SetFocus;
16 end;
```

- Save the program as C03e05u and C03e05p for the unit and project files respectively. Run the program.
- If you typed in the program exactly as shown, it allows you to enter a name in the space provided on the screen and, when you click one of the Add buttons, adds the name to the appropriate list.
- When you have tested it enough to convince yourself that it works, close the form and return to the design environment.

String variables

Let's see what happened in this program. We explain it by discussing the event handler connected to the Add boy button. (The handler connected to the Add girl button is similar, though it uses a different ListBox.) In line 2 the statement

```
var Boy: string;
```

introduces a variable called Boy and tells the computer to set aside memory space for a string value. We could have specified a maximum length for variable Boy with

```
var Boy: string[15];
```

which will set aside memory space for a string value containing a maximum of 15 characters. But we keep it simple by using type string without the bracketed number after it, and allow Delphi to handle it. The first statement inside the body of the handler (line 4) is

```
Boy := edtChildName.Text;
```

This puts the text that the user entered into the variable Boy.

The ListBox component

The Items property of the ListBox contains all the character strings displayed in the ListBox. Strings can be added, removed or selected. The statement

```
lstBoys.Items.Add(Boy);
```

in line 5 adds the value in the string variable Boy to the list of items in the boys ListBox. A ListBox displays a list of string values from which users can select one or more items. For now, we only add items to the list.

This statement uses some concepts which we have not covered yet, so do not be concerned if you do not understand the details of this statement – it is sufficient to understand broadly what the statement does. The concepts which will be covered include indexed lists (the Items property of a list box is an indexed list), in Chapter 8, and methods with parameters, in Chapter 11.

The last two lines, `edtChildName.Clear;` and `edtChildName.SetFocus;` clear the edit box and make it active again.

Before we move on to the next example, we need to introduce the concept of 'string concatenation'.

String concatenation

Like all computer languages, Delphi has *operators*. An operator acts on one or more variables (or fixed values) and results in a new value . You can concatenate one string onto the end of another string by using the string concatenation operator, the + sign. If you have the following:

```
ThisString := 'Sugar';
ThatString := ' and Spice';
```

then the statement

```
TheOtherString := ThisString + ThatString;
```

sets the variable `TheOtherString` to have the value `'Sugar and Spice'`.

EXAMPLE 3.6) A program using string concatenation

Figure 3.4 Adding couples to a ListBox

In this example, we write a program that concatenates character strings before adding them to a ListBox. The *Bumble Bee Crèche* now needs a program that will allow it to choose couples to dance together in the school concert. The staff want to enter the names of children two at a time – a boy and a girl. The couple must then be added, with ' and ' in between, to the list of couples (figure 3.4). Can you help them?

• Write this program.
• If you do not get the program to work, work through the steps below, then write a correct version of the program and test it thoroughly.

EX 3.6 Planning

This program is similar to the previous one in that a character string must be added to a ListBox. However, we first have to construct the new string using concatenation.

EX 3.6   Testing

- If you have written a program, test it carefully.
- When you run your program, it should give a screen display much like that in figure 3.4.
- If your program does that, the next stage is to enter the boy and girl names and click on the Add couple button.
- Check that the character string consisting of the two names concatenated with ' and ' is added to the ListBox.

EX 3.6   STEP 1   Creating the screen layout

- Start a new application and add the components to the form, as in the table below:

Component	Property	Value
Form1	Name	frmConcert
	Caption	Concatenation demo
Label1	Name	lblBoy
	Caption	Enter boy:
Label2	Name	lblGirl
	Caption	Enter girl:
Edit1	Name	edtBoy
	Text	\<Blank\>
Edit2	Name	edtGirl
	Text	\<Blank\>
ListBox1	Name	lstCouples
Button1	Name	btnAddCouple
	Caption	Add couple

EX 3.6   STEP 2   The variables

- Double-click on the Add couple button to create its OnClick event handler.
- Start writing this event handler by declaring the variables that we need: one for the boy's name (we call it Boy), one for the girl's name (we call it Girl) and another one for the concatenated string containing the two names joined by ' and ' (we call it Couple). We declare these variables by editing the event handler to match the following:

```
procedure TfrmConcert.btnAddCoupleClick(Sender: TObject);
var Boy, Girl, Couple: string;
begin

end;
```

Alternatively we can declare each as a string on its own line, as below:

```
var   Boy: string;
      Girl: string;
      Couple: string;
```

● Save the unit and project files in C03e06u and C03e06p respectively.

EX 3.6 STEP 3   Doing the concatenation

The names entered by the user must now be stored in the variables Boy and Girl respectively. These two values must then be joined by ' and ' and stored in variable Couple. Edit the event handler to match the following:

```
1 procedure TfrmConcert.btnAddCoupleClick(Sender: TObject);
2 var Boy, Girl, Couple: string;
3 begin
4    Boy := edtBoy.Text;
5    Girl := edtGirl.Text;
6    Couple := Boy + ' and ' + Girl;
7 end;
```

In lines 4 and 5, the names of the boy and the girl are stored in variables Boy and Girl respectively. The concatenation is done in line 6 and the result assigned to variable Couple.

EX 3.6 STEP 4   Adding the couple to the ListBox

All that is left to do is to add the value in Couple to the ListBox, clear the Edit component and make edtBoy the active component again.
● The complete event handler connected to the Add couple button is:

```
 1 procedure TfrmConcert.btnAddCoupleClick(Sender: TObject);
 2 var Boy, Girl, Couple: string;
 3 begin
 4    Boy := edtBoy.Text;
 5    Girl := edtGirl.Text;
 6    Couple := Boy + ' and ' + Girl;
 7    lstCouples.Items.Add(Couple);
 8    edtBoy.Clear;
 9    edtGirl.Clear;
10    edtBoy.SetFocus;
11 end;
```

● Save this program before testing it with several different sets of names.

The number of variables used

The solution provided here uses three variables: `Boy`, `Girl` and `Couple`. It is possible to write the event handler with only one variable (`Couple`) or even with no variables (see the alternative solutions below). The question of when to use variables and how many to use is a subjective one. One solution is not more correct than another. The issue is more one of readability. Which solution do you think is easier to read?

Alternative 1:
```
procedure TfrmConcert.btnAddCoupleClick(Sender: TObject);
var Couple: string;
begin
  Couple := edtBoy.Text + ' and ' + edtGirl.Text;
  lstCouples.Items.Add(Couple);
  edtBoy.Clear;
  edtGirl.Clear;
  edtBoy.SetFocus;
end;
```

Alternative 2:
```
procedure TfrmConcert.btnAddCoupleClick(Sender: TObject);
begin
  lstCouples.Items.Add(edtBoy.Text + ' and ' +
                       edtGirl.Text);
  edtBoy.Clear;
  edtGirl.Clear;
  edtBoy.SetFocus;
end;
```

Variable scope: subroutine level and unit level

We declared the variables that we used in this chapter in the `var` section of the respective event handlers (subroutines) between the `procedure` header and `begin`. Such variables are called *subroutine level variables* or *local variables*. That means that each time the event handler subroutine is executed, it creates the variables by allocating memory for them. When the subroutine exits, these variables are no longer used and are disposed of (their memory is freed) and they don't exist anymore.

There is also another kind of variable that we can use: *unit level variables*. Unit level variables are declared separately in the unit and persist for the duration of the program. While a subroutine level variable can only be used inside the subroutine in which it is declared, a unit level variable can be used by all the subroutines in the unit where it is declared. We will use unit level variables later in Chapter 8.

EXAMPLE 3.7 When is a variable necessary?

In this example we write a program that consists of two Edit components and a 'Swap' button. The user enters any two strings into the edit boxes and when they click on the 'Swap' button the contents of the two edit boxes are swapped. Figure 3.5 shows the user interface where the user has typed in two strings. Figure 3.6 shows the result after the user clicked the button.

Figure 3.5 Before clicking the button   Figure 3.6 After clicking the button

EX 3.7 STEP 1 Creating the screen layout

- Open a new application and create the user interface in figures 3.5 and 3.6 using the following property values.

Component	Property	Value
Form1	Name	frmSwap
	Caption	Swap
Label1	Name	lblPrompt
	Caption	Enter any two strings:
Edit1	Name	edtInput1
	Text	<Blank>
Edit2	Name	edtInput2
	Text	<Blank>
Button1	Name	btnSwap
	Caption	&Swap

- Save the unit file as C03e07u and the project file as C03e07p.

EX 3.7 STEP 2 First attempt at the event handler

We are going to try to write the event handler without using variables to see what happens.
- Double-click on the Swap button and type the following event handler:

```
procedure TfrmSwap.btnSwapClick(Sender: TObject);
begin
  edtInput1.Text := edtInput2.Text;
  edtInput2.Text := edtInput1.Text;
end;
```

- Save the unit file again and run the program.
- Type in any two strings and click on the Swap button. What happens?

If you type in 'apple' and 'beetroot' as in figure 3.5 and click on the Swap button, both edit boxes will contain 'beetroot'. The string 'apple' has disappeared. Why does this happen?

The first line of the event handler is

```
edtInput1.Text := edtInput2.Text;
```

This statement takes the contents of the Text property of the second edit box ('beetroot') and stores it in the Text property of the first edit box. This means that the original value of edtInput1's Text field ('apple') has been overwritten by the new value and is lost. In the second statement of the event handler (line 4), the value of edtInput1.Text is therefore 'beetroot', so this is what is stored in edtInput2.Text, which is not what we want. We want the *original* contents of edtInput1.Text to be stored in edtInput2.Text.

We need some way of saving the original contents of the first edit box so that it is not lost when the value of edtInput1.Text is changed. We do this in the next step by introducing a variable.

EX 3.7 STEP 3 Second attempt at the event handler using a variable

- Edit the event handler for btnSwap so that it matches the following:

```
1 procedure TfrmSwap.btnSwapClick(Sender: TObject);
2 var
3   FirstText: string;
4 begin
5   FirstText := edtInput1.Text;  // save the first string
6   edtInput1.Text := edtInput2.Text;
7   edtInput2.Text := FirstText;  // retrieve the original string
8 end;
```

- Save the unit file and run the program to see that it works correctly this time.

In our modified event handler above we declare a variable FirstText of type string in line 3. This variable is used to save a copy of the original contents of edtInput1.Text (line 5), so that this string is not lost when the value of edtInput1.Text is overwritten (line 6). In line 7 the variable FirstText is assigned to edtInput2.Text so that the original contents of edtInput1.Text are stored in edtInput2.Text.

In this example we see that it is sometimes necessary to use a variable as a temporary store to save a value that would otherwise get lost in the program.

REVIEW

In this chapter we have used variables in our programs. We have learned that each variable we use needs to be declared to be of a specific type, here, type string. We also looked at how to concatenate strings with the + operator.

We used ListBox to display a scrollable list of items and we programatically added strings to the ListBox using items. As we shall see later, it is also possible to select or delete from a ListBox.

Finally we saw that it is sometimes necessary to use a variable as a temporary store to save a value that would otherwise get lost in a program.

IMPORTANT CONCEPTS

Programming principles

Assignment operator: The symbol ':=' is the assignment operator, and statements with this symbol are assignment statements. The := instructs the computer to change the value of the variable on the left-hand side to the value given by the right-hand side.

Character string: A string is any series of characters one after another enclosed in single quotes. In Delphi, the string type is `string`. The string 'Bafana Bafana!' has 14 characters and therefore its length is 14. We can also get a null or empty string. This is a string of length 0 and has nothing between the quotes, not even blanks.

Comment: Text in a program that the compiler ignores but that improves the understandability and readability of the program for human readers. In Delphi Pascal the symbols for comments are {}, (**) or //.

Data type: A data type is a particular kind of data, such as the string data type that we used for variable `Newtext` in the declaration statement `var Newtext: string;`.

Data value: A data value is a single piece of information used in a program, for example a single character such as 'Z' or a single string such as 'I can program!' or a single number such as 17.

Declaration section: That part of any procedure between the procedure header and the `begin` of the procedure body is called the variable declaration section of the procedure.

Reserved words: Words that mean something specific to the Delphi compiler and therefore cannot be used in any other way than the Delphi compiler expects. For example `var`, `begin` and `end`.

String concatenation: A string can be concatenated to the end of another string through the string concatenation operator, the + sign.

Variables: Variables have names and can hold numbers or other types of data. We declare them in the variable declaration section. They are rather like small blackboards on which something can be written. Just as something written in a blackboard can be changed, so too the data held by a variable can be changed. The number or character string held in a variable is called its 'value'.

Variable declaration: Each variable declaration in a program reserves a location in the computer's memory for storing the value of the variable. Associated with each variable is a name and a type denoting the type of values that the variable can store and governing how the variable may be used. Variables of type string store a series of characters.

Variable scope: Variables that are declared in an event handler (subroutine) are called subroutine level variables or local variables. That means that each time the event handler subroutine is executed, it creates the variables and when the subroutine exits, these variables are no longer used and they don't exist anymore. Unit level variables are declared separately in the unit and persist for the duration of the program. While a subroutine level variable can only be used inside the subroutine in which it is declared, a unit level variable can be used by all the subroutines in the unit where it is declared.

NEW DELPHI FEATURES

TListBox		
Property	Items	Items represents a list of strings. Use Items to add items (as in this chapter) or to insert, delete or move items (as in later chapters).
Methods	Items.Add	Adds a string to the end of the list.
Prefix	lst...	
Use		We use a ListBox to display a scrollable list of items that users can select, delete from or add to.

PROBLEMS

PROBLEM 3.1) Valid Delphi variable names

- Complete the table below by stating whether or not each name is a valid component or variable name and if not, a reason.

Component/variable name	Valid/not valid	Reason
birth-date		
Who?		
employee_name		
ending		
_Name		
Person_3		
Candidate 10		
End		

PROBLEM 3.2) Finding the mistakes

The following is an event handler written by an inexperienced programmer.
- Complete the table below and help him or her by stating for each line of code whether it is correct or not. If it's not correct, give the reason. Assume one of the components on the form is an Edit component with the name edtChild. This program is only a way of testing the principles and does not do anything useful.

```
 1 procedure Tform1.Button1Click(Sender:Tobject);
 2 var ThisSt, AStr: string;
 3   AName: string;
 4   Emp no: string;
 5 begin
 6   AName := edtChild;
 7   MyStr:= 'The name is ' + AName;
 8   Astr := I can program!;
 9   AName := AName + 'van der Merwe';
10   One_hundred := 100;
11   AName := '30' + '40';
12   ThisStr := AName;
13 end;
```

Program line	Correct	Wrong	Reason for being wrong
1	✓		
2			
3			
4			
5			
6			
7			
8			
9			
10			
11			
12			
13			

PROBLEM 3.3) Variable values

- Complete the table below by giving the value of each variable after execution of the following statements:

```
var X, Y, Z: string;
begin
  X := 'ABCDE';
  Y := '012345';
  Z := Y + Y;
  X := X + Z;
  Y := Y + X;
end;
```

Variable	Value
X	
Y	
Z	

PROBLEM 3.4) Example 3.6 redone

- Redo example 3.6 but with separate ListBoxes for boy names, girl names and couples.
- Change the Caption of the Add couple button to Add.
- With each click on the Add button, the boy name, girl name and couple should be added to the respective ListBoxes.

PROBLEM 3.5) Concatenating title, initials and surname

- Write a program that gets a title, initials and surname from the user in three respective Edit components.
- The program must then join these values and display them in a Label component in the order surname, initials, title.
- There must be a comma after the surname and the title must be in brackets. For example, if the title is 'Ms', the initials are 'TA' and the surname is 'Molefe', then the program must display 'Molefe, TA (Ms)'.

PROBLEM 3.6) Displaying captions

Write a program that displays the value of a RadioButton's Caption property when the RadioButton is clicked. The user interface and Object TreeView are shown in figures 3.7 and 3.8 respectively. The program should work for any captions, ie do not assume that the caption of the first RadioButton will always be 'Button1'.

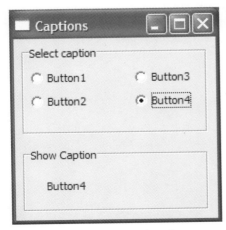

Figure 3.7 Displaying the value of a RadioButton's Caption property

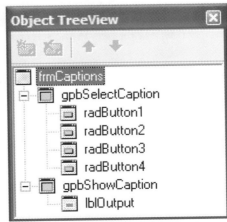

Figure 3.8 The components on the Display Captions user interface

CHAPTER 4

Using numbers

PURPOSE OF THIS CHAPTER

In the previous chapter we considered string variables. String variables contain text. Of course, computers can work with much more than just text, and one of the things they are very good at is working with numbers. In this chapter, we will start looking at how computers handle numbers.

As far as we are concerned in this book, there are two main kinds of numbers. First, there are whole numbers (or integers). We use *integers* when we do not need to talk about fractions. So, if you say 'I have 2 dogs at home', that '2' is an integer. Similarly, if you go to a shop to buy some clothes, you will buy 1 or 2 or 3 shirts, but not half a shirt, or 2.34 shirts. (Note that when we work with computers we use decimal points and not decimal commas.)

Often, though, we need to talk about fractions also, and then we use *real numbers*. For example, cents are fractions of a Rand, and we use real numbers with a decimal point to show this. Someone might put 43.2 litres of petrol into their car. If petrol costs R3.85 per litre, filling the tank will cost 43.2 × R3.85 = R166.32. All three of these numbers are real numbers, because they include fractions of a Rand or a litre.

In this chapter we start with programs using integers and then move on to real numbers. These programs will read numbers from the keyboard, do calculations with them, and write numbers to the screen.

EXAMPLE 4.1 A simple calculator (integer addition)

To familiarize ourselves with arithmetic on a computer, we begin with a very simple calculator that does only integer addition. We will introduce the SpinEdit component and will show you how to display a number in an Edit component (figure 4.1).

- Start a new application and place two SpinEdits, three Labels, an EditBox and a button on the form, as in figure 4.1. (If you are using Delphi 8, you need to install the Samples tab in the Tool Palette before you can use the SpinEdit component. The procedure for this appears in Appendix 4.)

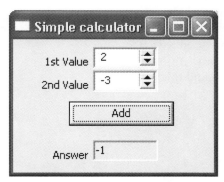

Figure 4.1 Integer adder

Finding the SpinEdit component

- If the Samples tab is not visible on the Component/Tool palette, either click on the right-pointing arrow on the right-hand side of the palette (Delphi 7) or move the slider of the scroll bar (Delphi 8) until the Samples tab appears.
- Now click on the Samples tab to see all its components. Move your mouse over each component, using the pop-up hints to find the SpinEdit.
- When you have placed the components on the form, set the property values as shown below:

Component	Property	Value
Form1	Name	frmSimpleCalculator
	Caption	Simple calculator
SpinEdit1	Name	sed1stValue
SpinEdit2	Name	sed2ndValue
Label1	Name	lbl1stValue
	Caption	1st Value
Label2	Name	lbl2ndValue
	Caption	2nd Value
Label3	Name	lblAnswer
	Caption	Answer
Edit1	Name	edtAnswer
	Text	<Blank>
	ReadOnly	True
	Color	clBtnFace
Button1	Name	btnAdd
	Caption	Add

Consistent user interfaces

Notice that we set the ReadOnly property of edtAnswer to True and the Color property to clBtnFace. The effect of setting the ReadOnly property to True is that it prevents the user from being able to type anything into the Answer box and changing the colour makes the box look different from normal input boxes. Why do we do this?

We change the behaviour and appearance of the Answer box to prevent an *inconsistent* user interface. The design principle of *consistency* states that a user interface should behave similarly throughout the application. In our simple calculator application (figure 4.1) the two SpinEdit components are places for input, while the Answer box is a place for output. If the Answer box looked and behaved like a normal Edit component (ie a white box which can be edited), it would create the incorrect impression that all three boxes were places for input. To be consistent, all input boxes should look and behave similarly and this behaviour should be different from output boxes.

EX 4.1 Adding the numbers

There is only one event handler for this example:

```
1 procedure TfrmSimpleCalculator.btnAddClick(Sender: TObject);
2 var Answer: integer;
3 begin
4   Answer := sed1stValue.Value + sed2ndValue.Value;
5   edtAnswer.Text := IntToStr (Answer);
6   sed1stValue.SetFocus;
7 end;
```

- Enter this program and save the unit and project files as C04e01u and C04e01p respectively.
- Run it and test it with several different sample values. To enter 1st Value and 2nd Value, click on the up and down arrows of the SpinEdit components or type the values in directly.

Declaring an integer

As we saw in the previous chapter, we need to declare all the variables that we use in the declaration section of the event handler. In this example we need a place to hold the result of the addition. So we declare a variable called Answer in line 2.

The type integer is a reserved word in Delphi and refers to a whole number. In other words, Answer is declared a variable that is able to hold only integer values. (We used string variables in Chapter 3.)

The SpinEdit component

The SpinEdits, sed1stValue and sed2ndValue, are components that we have not used before. They are similar to the Edit component, since they get input from the user. The difference is in the type of value. The SpinEdit holds an integer value (a whole number) while the Edit component holds a string. So, when we need to get whole numbers from the user, we can use SpinEdit components. In line 4, the statement

```
Answer := sed1stValue.Value + sed2ndValue.Value;
```

uses the values returned by the SpinEdit components. Note that we get the value entered by the user in the Value property of a SpinEdit component and not in the Text property as we do when we use an Edit component. How do we know that?

We can check the Object Inspector. It lists an object's properties down the left side of the Properties tab and valid values for these properties are on the right side. You will see that the SpinEdit component has a Value property but not a Text property.

Assignment and arithmetic expressions

The assignment statement

```
Answer := sed1stValue.Value + sed2ndValue.Value;
```

is similar to the assignment statements that we have used previously with string variables. A value on the right side of the := is put into the variable on the left of it. This assignment statement adds two values together and puts the result of the addition in the integer variable called Answer. Note that the type of the variable on the left-hand side (Answer) and the type of the value on the right-hand side (sed1stValue.Value + sed2ndValue.Value) must match. Here, they are all integers.

An assignment statement always consists of a variable on the left side of the assignment operator and an *expression* on the right side. The expression may be another variable, a number, or a more complicated arithmetic expression made up of variables, numbers, and arithmetic operators such as plus and minus signs. So this statement instructs the computer to evaluate the expression on the right-hand side of the assignment operator and to set the value of the variable on the left of the := equal to that. A few more examples may help to clarify the way these statements work.

Delphi, like most other programming languages, does not use the traditional multiplication sign. Multiplication is represented by an *asterisk*, as in the following assignment statement:

```
Answer := Number1 * Number2;
```

This statement is just like the assignment statement in our sample program above, except that it performs multiplication rather than addition. The statement changes the value of Answer to the product of the values in Number1 and Number2.

The expression on the right-hand side of an assignment statement can simply be another variable. The statement Number1 := Number2; changes the value of the variable Number1 to that of the value in variable Number2. Note that the value of Number2 is not affected.

An expression can also involve a specific value, ie a fixed value. The statement Number2 := 45; changes the value of Number2 to 45.

Because variables can change in value over time, and because the assignment operator is a way of changing their values, an element of time is involved in the meaning of an assignment statement. First, the expression on the right-hand side of the assignment operator is evaluated. After that, the value of the variable on the left-hand side of the assignment operator is changed to the value obtained from that expression. This means that the same variable name can occur on both sides of an assignment operator. As an example consider:

```
Number1 := Number1 + 1;
```

This statement will increase the value of `Number1` by 1. Thus, the new value of `Number1` becomes its old value + 1. As another example, say we have variables `Sum` and `NewValue` (both of type integer) that have values 10 and 13 respectively. The statement `Sum := Sum + NewValue;` increases the value of `Sum` by the value of `NewValue`. In other words, after execution of this statement, `Sum` has a value of 23. `NewValue` retains the value 13.

Converting an integer to a string

Let's go back to our simple integer calculator program. Line 4 of btnAdd's OnClick event handler is:

```
Answer := sed1stValue.Value + sed2ndValue.Value;
```

This adds two integer values and puts the result into an integer variable called `Answer`. We want to display this answer now by putting it into the Text property of the Edit component. Can we simply use the statement

```
edtAnswer.Text := Answer;?
```

Doing this will result in a compiler error because 'String' and 'Integer' are incompatible types. Do you know why?

If you think back to the previous chapter, you will remember that we used the Text property of the Edit component for holding *string values*. (We also used it for obtaining string values from the user.) So if you have an Edit component, as we have in this example, we can use a statement such as

```
edtAnswer.Text := '50';
```

This puts a string value in the Text property of the Edit component. However, in the statement `edtAnswer.Text := Answer;` we are trying to assign an integer value, `Answer`, to a property that accepts only strings (`edtAnswer.Text`), and this is illegal. We are not allowed to mix types like this. So we need to convert our integer answer to a string value before we do the assignment. We do this in the statement

```
edtAnswer.Text := IntToStr(Answer);
```

`IntToStr(N)` converts the integer value N to the string containing the value of N. Say we were adding values 50 and 40. 50 + 40 gives the answer 90. But we are not allowed to say `edtAnswer.Text := 90;` because 90 is an integer value and the Text property takes only string values. So we use `IntToStr(90)` to convert 90 to '90', and then the assignment can take place.

Numbers in strings

We can also have numbers in quotes, for example '550'. To Delphi a value such as '550' is a string value and we cannot do any arithmetic calculations with it. If we have a variable declared as below

```
var Ninety: string;
```

and we have an assignment statement somewhere in a program that says

```
Ninety := '50' + '40';
```

what would the value in Ninety be after the execution of the statement above? Will Ninety have the value 90? Or '90'?

As we saw in Chapter 3, when we work with strings, the + operator means concatenation, ie joining strings to each other. '50' and '40' are two string values and '50' + '40' has the effect of joining '40' to the end of '50'. So, the answer is '5040'.

Integer arithmetic

The arithmetic operations available for integer values in Delphi appear in the following table:

Operator	Meaning
+	Addition
−	Subtraction
*	Multiplication
DIV	Division producing an integer quotient (no remainder)
MOD	Integer remainder after division of integers

If we have two numbers, say 10 and 3, addition, subtraction and multiplication of these two numbers are each possible with a single statement. So, if we have integer variables Sum, Difference and Product, then in Delphi we can write

```
Sum := 10 + 3;
Difference := 10 - 3;
Product := 10 * 3;
```

In the section that follows, we will see that integer division needs more than one division statement.

Integer division: MOD and DIV

There is a type of division that applies only to integers. For example, with integer division, 19 divided by 5 gives 3 (the quotient) with a remainder of 4.

The two numbers obtained in this way can be produced with the two operators DIV and MOD. The DIV operation gives the number of times one number goes into another and the MOD operation gives the remainder. The operator MOD is short for 'modulo'. In both cases the divisor is given second. For example, if we have integer variables `IntDivide` and `Remainder`, then after execution of the statements

```
IntDivide := 19 DIV 5;
Remainder := 19 MOD 5;
```

`IntDivide` has the value 3 and `Remainder` has the value 4.

The MOD operator can become confusing when used with negative numbers or when the first value is smaller than the 2nd value. Here are some more examples:

10 MOD 3 = 1   (10 DIV 3 = 3;   3 * 3 = 9, which leaves a remainder of 1)
−10 MOD 3 = -1   (−10 DIV 3 = −3; 3 * −3 = −9, which leaves a remainder of −1)
10 MOD −3 = 1   (10 DIV −3 = −3; −3 * −3 = 9, which leaves a remainder of 1)
3 MOD 10 = 3   (3 DIV 10 = 0; 10 * 0 = 0, which leaves a remainder of 3)
−3 MOD 10 = −3   (−3 DIV 10 = 0; 10 * 0 = 0, which leaves a remainder of −3)
3 MOD −10 = 3   (3 DIV −10 = 0; −10 * 0 = 0, which leaves a remainder of 3)

SpinEdit and Samples tab

At the start of example 4.1 we explain that to find the SpinEdit component, you have to scroll to the Samples tab on the Component/Tool Palette. Since we will be using SpinEdits quite often, you may want to move the Samples tab to the left, so that you can find it more easily in future.

• To do this in Delphi 6/7, right-click on the Component palette and select properties. A window called Palette Properties appears. In the list box on the left, select Samples and drag it upwards so that it is closer to Standard. Click OK and the Samples tab will move to the left.
• In Delphi 8, drag the Sample tab towards the left to be closer to the Standard tab.

EXAMPLE 4.2) Extended calculator (integer arithmetic)

We have just seen the special operations for integer division. In this example, apply these concepts by extending example 4.1 to provide a calculator that will perform all five integer operations as in the screen in figure 4.2.

We will create additional buttons for subtract, multiply, integer divide, and modulo. To avoid confusion we will change the Caption of the answer Label to show the function that has just been performed. We will also reorganize the screen layout from that used in the example above.

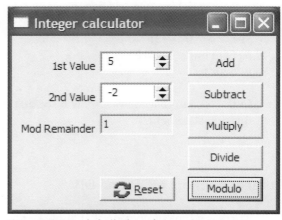

Figure 4.2 Extended calculator for integer arithmetic

For the convenience of the user, we will add a Reset button that sets all the number values to zero, changes the title of the answer Label back to 'Answer', and gives the focus to the first SpinEdit component.

EX 4.2   Planning

This program differs from the one in example 4.1 since we here have five event handlers performing the respective integer operations on 1st Value and 2nd Value. This program also needs a Reset button.

EX 4.2   Testing

- After we have written this program, we should test it to ensure that it works correctly. For example, work out manually the answers that the calculator should give for the values as in the table below and then test the calculator against this table.

1st value	2nd value	Add	Subtract	Multiply	Divide	Modulus
10	4	14	6	40	2	2
25	5	30	20	125	5	0
30	37	67	−7	1110	0	30
5	−10	−5	15	−50	0	5

EX 4.2   STEP 1   Creating the screen layout

- Place the components on the screen roughly as shown in figure 4.2 and then change the property values to match the table below:

Component	Property	Value
Form1	Name	frmIntegerCalculator
	Caption	Integer calculator
All the labels	Alignment	taRightJustify
	Autosize	False
Label1	Name	lbl1stValue
	Caption	1st Value
Label2	Name	lbl2ndValue
	Caption	2nd Value
Label3	Name	lblAnswer
	Caption	Answer
Button1	Name	btnAdd
	Caption	Add
Button2	Name	btnSubtract
	Caption	Subtract
Button3	Name	btnMultiply
	Caption	Multiply

Button4	Name	btnDivide	
	Caption	Divide	
Button5	Name	btnMod	
	Caption	Modulo	
BitBtn1	Name	bmbReset	
	Kind	bkRetry	{set first}
	Caption	&Reset	{set second}
SpinEdit1	Name	sed1stValue	
SpinEdit2	Name	sed2ndValue	
Edit1	Name	edtAnswer	
	Text	<Blank>	
	ReadOnly	True	
	Color	clBtnFace	

How do we get the components neatly aligned and spaced as in the required user interface? Do you remember how we selected multiple components and aligned them in Chapter 2?

- Select the Add button and then, holding down the <Shift> key, select the Subtract, Multiply, Divide and Modulus buttons and change their Left properties. Similarly, set the Left and/or Width properties of the SpinEdits, the Edit and the BitBtn.
- Save the unit and project files as C04e02u and C04e02p respectively.

EX 4.2 STEP 2   Doing the arithmetic

Now it is time to write the event handlers to do the arithmetic. For each operation, we need to keep the answer somewhere. We are doing integer operations, so the answer for each operation will also be an integer value. So we need a variable of type integer for keeping the answer for each respective operation. Then we need to display the answer on the screen. We want to display the answer (integer value) in an Edit component called edtAnswer which takes only string values.

We need five event handlers, one connected to each of the operator buttons. Double-click on the Add button to create a skeleton for the event handler connected to it. Change the event handler to match the following:

```
1 procedure TfrmIntegerCalculator.btnAddClick(Sender: TObject);
2 var Answer: integer;
3 begin
4   Answer := sed1stValue.Value + sed2ndValue.Value;
5   edtAnswer.Text := IntToStr (Answer);
6   lblAnswer.Caption := 'Integer Add';
7 end;
```

The remaining four event handlers also each use a procedure-level variable (local variable) which is declared as an integer – that is, a place in memory that can hold only integer numbers (whole numbers). This is necessary because the result of any integer operation (+, −, * , DIV , or MOD) is also an integer value. It is easy to see this in the table that we used in the *Testing* part above.

The event handlers differ only in the operator that they use. For example, event handler btnAddClick uses the + operator in line 4. Event handler `btnDivideClick` must use the DIV operator and so on. Each event handler must store the result in an integer variable. If we use a variable called `Answer` in each of the event handlers, they must all have the statement in line 5:

```
edtAnswer.Text := IntToStr (Answer);
```

In this statement, the value in `Answer`, which is an integer value, is converted to a string value by `IntToStr` so that it can be placed in the Text property of the Edit component called `edtAnswer`. This has to be done as the Text property of the Edit component can hold only string values.

The last statement (line 6) changes the caption of the answer to the corresponding operation selected.

EX 4.2 STEP 3   The remaining four operator buttons

- Type in the event handlers of the remaining four operator buttons as they appear below:

```
procedure TfrmIntegerCalculator.btnDivideClick(Sender: TObject);
var Answer: integer;
begin
  Answer:= sed1stValue.Value DIV sed2ndValue.Value;
  edtAnswer.Text := IntToStr (Answer);
  lblAnswer.Caption := 'Integer Divide';
end;


procedure TfrmIntegerCalculator.btnMultiplyClick(Sender: TObject);
var Answer: integer;
begin
  Answer := sed1stValue.Value * sed2ndValue.Value;
  edtAnswer.Text := IntToStr (Answer);
  lblAnswer.Caption := 'Integer Multiply';
end;
procedure TfrmIntegerCalculator.btnSubtractClick(Sender: TObject);
var Answer: integer;
begin
  Answer := sed1stValue.Value – sed2ndValue.Value;
  edtAnswer.Text := IntToStr (Answer);
  lblAnswer.Caption := 'Integer Subtract';
end;


procedure TfrmIntegerCalculator.btnModClick(Sender: TObject);
var Answer: integer;
begin
  Answer := sed1stValue.Value MOD sed2ndValue.Value;
  edtAnswer.Text := IntToStr (Answer);
  lblAnswer.Caption := 'Mod Remainder';
end;
```

Why do we declare Answer in each event handler?

Each event handler needs a place in memory to keep the answer of its calculated value. A variable like Answer (declared in the declaration section of a procedure) is a *procedure-level variable* and disappears at the end of each procedure.

EX 4.2 STEP 4   Resetting values

After execution of each operation, the user might want to reset all the values on the screen to 0. The focus also needs to be placed on the SpinEdit at the top for the user to start entering values again. All this will happen in an OnClick event handler connected to the Reset button.

- Double-click on the Reset button and then enter the code for the event handler as follows: (Unlike the Close BitBtn, this one has no default code attached to it.)

```
1 procedure TfrmIntegerCalculator.bmbResetClick(Sender: TObject);
2 begin
3    sed1stValue.Value := 0;          //SpinEdit takes an integer
4    sed2ndValue.Value := 0;
5    edtAnswer.Text := '0';               //EditBox takes a string
6    lblAnswer.Caption := 'Answer';
7    sed1stValue.SetFocus;
8 end;
```

- Save the unit file again.

In the OnClick event handler connected to the Reset button above, the values on the screen are reset to display 0 in lines 3 to 5. Note that the Value property of each SpinEdit is reset by assigning the integer 0 to it, but the Text property of the Edit needs to be reset to the string '0' as it takes only string values.

Lines 6 and 7 in this event handler respectively change the answer Label to 'Answer' again and set the focus on the first SpinEdit component.

That concludes this example. In the examples that follow, we will use numbers with fractions.

Floating point (real) numbers

The data type used by computers to represent quantities with fractional parts is called the *floating point* or *real data type*. Examples of real numbers are prices, weights, measures and decimal fractions. This is in contrast to the integer numbers (discussed up to now), which are used mostly for counting and labelling.

We know that between the numbers 1 and 3 there is exactly one integer number, the number 2. How many real numbers are there between 1 and 3? It varies, and depends on how precisely the computer and software we are using can represent real numbers.

In the remainder of this chapter we will write programs using real numbers. These programs will read real numbers from the keyboard, do calculations with them, and write numbers to the screen.

Within the real data category, Delphi supports various types with different ranges and which use different storage sizes. These are, among others, the Single, Double, Extended and Currency data types. The ranges and storage sizes of these types are shown in the table below:

Real data type	Range	Size in bytes
Single	$1.5 \times 10^{-45} \ldots 3.4 \times 10^{38}$	4
Double	$5.0 \times 10^{-324} \ldots 1.7 \times 10^{308}$	8
Extended	$3.6 \times 10^{-4951} \ldots 1.1 \times 10^{4932}$	10
Currency	$-922337203685477.5808 \ldots$ 922337203685477.5807	8

Generally the examples in this book use the Double type, since this makes very efficient use of the computer.

Run-time errors

- Try entering any number as the first value and zero as the second value. If you press the Divide button an exception is generated and a Delphi error message box like the one in figure 4.3 appears.

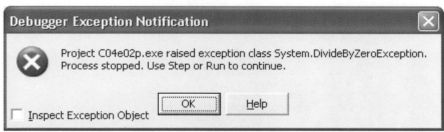

Figure 4.3 Run time error message

This is called a *run-time error*. The program compiles without any errors, but when it is busy running, something goes wrong, and so Delphi raises an exception and activates the debugger (see the title bar of the window in figure 4.3). In the next section, we change the settings of Delphi so that the program does not go into the Debugger, but continues (after a suitable error message) so that you can try other numbers.

- In Delphi 8, uncheck the Inspect Exception Object CheckBox (figure 4.3) if it is checked.
- Click OK, whatever the version of Delphi.
- In Delphi 8, select Run | Program Reset to stop the program.
- Run the program again.

Disabling debugger exception handling

For most of the programs we write in this book it is more convenient to bypass the debugger for exceptions. We do this in the following step:

- If the program is still running, close it.
- Select Tools | Debugger Options (Delphi 6/7) or Tools | Options (Delphi 8).
- For Delphi 6/7, on the Language Exceptions tab, deselect the 'Stop on Delphi Exceptions' checkbox (if it is checked) as shown in figure 4.4a.
- For Delphi 8, select 'Language Exceptions' (under 'Debugger Options' and 'Borland.NET Debugger') and uncheck the box 'Stop on Language Exceptions' as in figure 4.4b.
- Then click the OK button. This will prevent Delphi from breaking into the debugger as in figure 4.3.

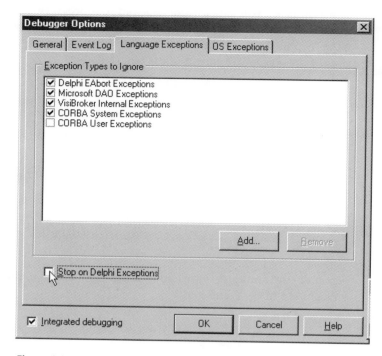

Figure 4.4a Bypassing Debugger exception handling (Delphi 6/7)

We have to do this only once – keep the Language Exceptions setting like this for all the programs in the book.

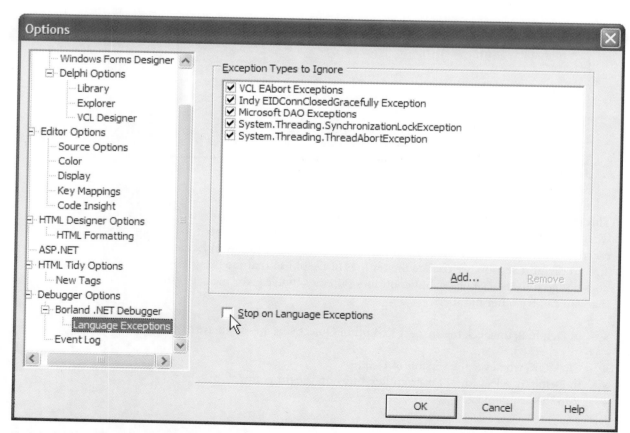

Figure 4.4b Bypassing Debugger exception handling (Delphi 8)

Typing a real number into a SpinEdit

A further way of generating a run-time error is to type a real number (such as 2.5) into one of the SpinEdits and then to perform a calculation. If you have not changed your Delphi settings (as explained in the previous section) you should see a message box something like the box in figure 4.3 but with a different message. However, if you have changed your Delphi settings so that it does not stop on Delphi exceptions, then no error message will be displayed and the program continues. This can lead to confusing results. For example, if you enter 2.5 into 1st value and 3 into 2nd value, the result of adding the two numbers will be 3 and the result of multiplying the numbers will be zero! This is because the SpinEdit component expects only integer values and automatically converts a real number to zero.

Many Delphi operations and functions generate exceptions. There is a lot more to exception handling and we return to it in later chapters in this book.

EXAMPLE 4.3) Rand to Euro calculator (version 1)

Here we demonstrate how to use and display a real number. An airline service between South Africa and Europe needs a program to help them give their passengers an idea of what their money will be worth in Europe. The program needs to accept Rand values (only whole Rands) and then convert them to Euro values. The screen layout appears below:

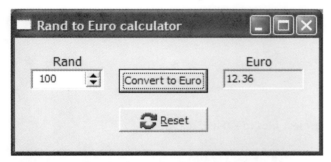

Figure 4.5 Interface for the Rand to Euro calculator

- Start a new application and place the following components on the form: a SpinEdit (on the Samples tab of the Component/Tool palette), an Edit component, two Labels, a Button and a BitBtn.
- Now set each component's property values as shown in the table below:

Component	Property	Value
Form1	Name	frmRandEuro
	Caption	Rand to Euro calculator
Label1	Name	lblRand
	Caption	Rand

Label2	Name	lblEuro	
	Caption	Euro	
SpinEdit1	Name	sedRand	
Edit1	Name	edtEuro	
	Text	<Blank>	
	ReadOnly	True	
	Color	clBtnFace	
Button1	Name	btnToEuro	
	Caption	Convert to Euro	
BitBtn1	Name	bmbReset	
	Kind	bkRetry	{set first}
	Caption	&Reset	{set next}

The event handlers connected to the Convert to Euro and Reset buttons are as follows:

```
1  procedure TfrmRandToEuro.btnToEuroClick(Sender: TObject);
2  var Euro: double;
3  begin
4    Euro := 0.1236 * sedRand.Value;
5    edtEuro.Text := FloatToStrF(Euro,ffFixed,15,2);
6    btnToEuro.Enabled := False;
7  end;


8  procedure TfrmRandToEuro.bmbResetClick(Sender: TObject);
9  begin
10   sedRand.Value := 0;
11   edtEuro.Clear;
12   btnToEuro.Enabled := True;
13   sedRand.SetFocus;
14 end;
```

- Enter this program and then save the unit and project files in C04e03u and C04e03p respectively.
- Make a table with your own set of test cases. Then run and test the program to make sure it works as expected.

We explain these event handlers in the following sections.

Floating point (real) data types

In the previous example we saw how to get integer values from the screen using the SpinEdit component. For this example we need to convert an integer number to a currency value (Euro). Currency values are numbers with fractions (two digits after the decimal point). We use the single, double, extended or currency data types to represent numbers with fractions, such as the ones below:

3.167

0.007

−15.8

1000075.99

80 INTRODUCING DELPHI PROGRAMMING: THEORY THROUGH PRACTICE

So, in the event handler above, the declaration statement in line 2 declares a variable called `Euro` of type `double` because we are working with numbers with fractions. We can also use any of the other real data types here. (We do not use the currency data type in this book, because, although the currency data type minimizes rounding errors in monetary calculations, it has limited conversion capabilities.)

The exchange rate at the time of writing this chapter was 0.1236 Euro to the Rand. So in the statement (line 4)

```
Euro := 0.1236 * sedRand.Value;
```

we multiply the Rand value that the user entered by the exchange rate (which is a fixed value in the program) to get a currency value in `Euro`. So even though `sedRand.Value` is an integer, the multiplication produces a `double` value (a value with fractions) and the result of the multiplication is put in the variable called `Euro`. If any of the values involved in a multiplication is a floating point value, the result is always a floating point value.

Converting a real number to a string with FloatToStrF

Let's return to the rest of the coding in the event handler connected to the Convert to Euro button. In line 4 we calculate the `Euro` amount for the Rand value specified by the user. It is a value of type `double` (a real data type). Now it is time for us to display it in the space provided by the Edit component.

We get a compilation error if we just use the statement `edtEuro.Text := Euro;` because we cannot assign a real value to `edtEuro`'s Text property – the types are incompatible. We have to convert the real value to a string first. Just as we used IntToStr to convert an integer to a string, we use FloatToStrF to convert a float value to a string as in the statement (line 5):

```
edtEuro.Text := FloatToStrF(Euro,ffFixed,15,2);
```

`FloatToStrF` converts a floating point (real) value to a string using a specified format, precision, and number of digits. We can say generally that

```
FloatToStrF(Value,Format,Precision,Digits);
```

converts the floating-point value given by `Value` to its string representation according to the `Format`, `Precision` and `Digits` formatting parameters. Because a float number has a decimal part, FloatToStrF is more complicated than IntToStr.

The `Precision` parameter must be an integer value and specifies the precision of the given value, and is usually 15 for values of type `Double`.

The `Digits` and `Format` parameters together control how the value is formatted into a string. In the program above, we set the `Format` parameter to `ffFixed`, indicating a *fixed point format*. The value is converted to a string of the form '–ddd.ddd...'. The resulting string starts with a minus sign if the number is negative, and at least one digit always precedes the decimal point. The number of digits after the decimal point is given by the `Digits` parameter – it must be between 0 and 18 (we used 2 in the program above because we are working with currencies).

Other values available for the `Format` parameter are `ffGeneral` (general

number format), ffExponent (scientific format),
ffNumber (number format) and ffCurrency
(currency format). (For the purpose of the programs
that we write in this book they are not important and
so we do not discuss them here except for briefly
explaining ffCurrency below.)

Why did we not use ffCurrency? With
ffCurrency, the value is converted to a string that
represents a currency amount, including the currency
symbol specified in the Regional Settings on your
computer. On my computer, the currency symbol is
'R', indicating Rand. If I replace the conversion
statement in the program with

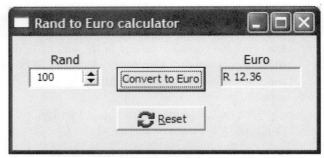

Figure 4.6 Output produced with ffCurrency format

```
edtEuro.Text := FloatToStrF(Euro,ffCurrency,15,2);
```

it will incorrectly produce the screen in figure 4.6.

More examples of FloatToStrF conversions

Below are three conversion statements with their results, using string variable S.
An explanation of each statement is given underneath.

A) `S := FloatToStrF(1234.567,ffFixed,15,2);`   Result in S: '1234.57'
B) `S := FloatToStrF(1234.567,ffFixed,2,0);`   Result in S: '1.2E3'
C) `S := FloatToStrF(1234.567,ffFixed,3,0);`   Result in S: '1.23E3'

In A) we use a large value for Precision (15) and a value of 2 for Digits. The
result is a number which is rounded off to 2 digits after the decimal point.

In B) we use a small value for Precision (2). The result is 1.2E3, which is
equivalent to 1.2 * 10^3 or 1200.

In C) a Precision of 3 results in the number 1.23E3 (equivalent to 1230). Can
you see how the Precision parameter affects how numbers are rounded off? A
low precision can result in an imprecise number. For this reason we usually use a
large number (15 for Double numbers) for Precision. The Digits parameter
influences the number of digits that appear after the decimal.

FloatToStrF versus FloatToStr

We have used the FloatToStrF method above. There is another method,
FloatToStr, which also converts a floating-point value to its string representation.
It gives 15 significant digits and does not have parameters for specifying how the
number should be formatted. For example, after execution of the statement

```
edtEuro.Text := FloatToStr (1388.4523432234123);
```

edtEuro.Text will have the value '1388.45234322341', using 15 digits to
represent the number. Currency values have two digits after the decimal point,

and therefore we need greater control over the formatting of the string. Using FloatToStrF in the statement

```
edtEuro.Text := FloatToStrF(1388.4523432234123,ffFixed,15,2);
```

results in `edtEuro.Text` having the value '1388.45'.

Using a constant for the exchange rate

There are two problems with fixed values (eg 0.1236 in line 4 on page 76) in a computer program. The first is that they carry no mnemonic value. For example, when you see the number 0.1236 in a program, the number itself gives no hint of its significance. To understand any program, you need to know the significance of each fixed value. The second problem is that, when you need to change a program, changing fixed values often introduces errors. Suppose that 0.1236 occurs 12 times in a program: four times it represents the exchange rate between two specific currencies and eight times it represents the exchange rate between two other currencies. When one of the exchange rates needs to be updated, there is a good chance that some of the 0.1236s that should be changed will not be, or that some that should not be changed will be changed. Like many other programming languages, Delphi provides a mechanism to deal with these problems.

You can assign a name to a fixed value and then use the name in place of the fixed value. This is done with a constant declaration. Constant declarations are placed between the procedure heading and the variable declarations. To use a meaningful name rather than a fixed value for the exchange rate, change the event handler for the Convert to Euro button to the following:

```
1 procedure TfrmRandToEuro.btnToEuroClick(Sender: TObject);
2 const ExchangeRate = 0.1236;
3 var Euro: currency;
4 begin
5   Euro := ExchangeRate * sedRand.Value;
6   edtEuro.Text := FloatToStrF(Euro,ffFixed,15,2);
7   btnToEuro.Enabled := False; //Reset before using button again
8 end;
```

Do you see the effect this has? First, when you read the first assignment statement, you see ExchangeRate instead of 0.1236, and so it is clear what the statement does. Second, if the exchange rate changes, you need make only one change (substituting the new value in the constant declaration at the start of the procedure) and the procedure will automatically use this value whenever the name ExchangeRate appears.

- Save your application and then run and test it with some of the values you used previously.

To the user the program works the same way as before on the screen, but behind the scenes we have a program written with better style. It is easier to understand and more resistant to errors when changes are necessary.

Constants

A constant declaration consists of the reserved word `const` followed by the identifier that is to be the name of the constant, followed by the equals sign and then the constant value. The following gives the value 0.1236 to the name `ExchangeRate`:

```
const ExchangeRate = 0.1236;
```

To declare more than one constant, simply list them all, separated by semicolons:

```
const Greeting = 'Hello There';                    //string
  DaysInWeek = 7;                                  //integer
  InchToCm = 2.54;                                 //real value
```

Any word that is not a reserved word can be used as a name for a constant. To change the value of a named constant, you need only change the constant declaration. The value of all occurrences of `ExchangeRate` can be changed from 0.1236 to 0.1399 simply by changing the 0.1236 to 0.1399 in the constant declaration.

To improve readability and reduce the chance of future errors, we use the constant in the statement

```
Euro := ExchangeRate * sedRand.Value;
```

To Delphi, this statement is the same as:

```
Euro := 0.1236 * sedRand.Value;
```

EXAMPLE 4.4) Rand to Euro calculator (version 2)

In the examples in this chapter up to now, we used the SpinEdit component for the user to enter an integer value. In this example we show how to use Edit components for the user to enter floating point values.

As we have seen before, the Text property of an Edit component holds a string value. We cannot use a string value in arithmetic calculations and therefore need a conversion routine to convert the string to a floating point number.

The airline between South Africa and Europe wants an improved program that allows the user to enter Rands and cents and that also converts from Euro to Rands. In addition, they want to subtract a conversion fee of 0.2% and they need a Reset button to set all the number values to zero. The program should also be user friendly. It must display Hints to guide the user through the program and provide accelerator keys on all buttons. Can you write a program to meet their new needs?

The interface is shown in figure 4.7. Remember that the Reset button can be derived from the Retry BitBtn.

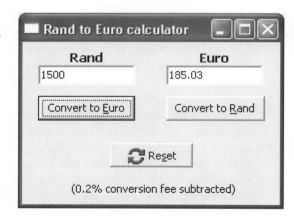

Figure 4.7 User interface for the currency converter

EX 4.4   Planning

To convert the Rand value to Euro, we need to do the following:
- ○   Take the text in the Rand Edit component and convert it to a number.
- ○   Do the calculation using the exchange rate and subtracting the conversion percentage.
- ○   Convert the calculated amount to a string value and put it in the Euro Edit component.
- ○   Converting Euro to Rand will be similar, but here we have to divide by the exchange rate.

EX 4.4   Testing

If we have written a program to do this, we should test it to ensure that it works correctly.
- •   Work out with a pocket calculator the answers that the program should give for the values in the table below.

Rand	Euro
100	
1500.50	
	3500.80
	5

We calculated values of 12.34 and 185.09 Euro and 28266.98 and 40.37 Rand respectively.

- •   If you have programmed a solution, test your program against the values you have calculated, and then check against our solution. Test the accelerator keys, the Hints and the Reset button.

EX 4.4   STEP 1   Creating the screen layout

- •   Start by opening project C04e03p that you saved in example 4.3. We need to reorganize the screen layout.
- •   First replace the SpinEdit component with an Edit component, so that the program can accept Rands and cents (figure 4.7). We will convert this to a real value to be used as Rands and cents.
- •   We also need to add an extra convert button to convert the Euro values to Rand and a Reset button to clear the values on the screen. The changed properties appear in the following table:

Component	Property	Value
Label1	Name	lblFee
	Caption	(0.2% Conversion fee subtracted)
Edit1	Name	edtRand
	Hint	Enter Rand value
	ShowHint	True
edtEuro	Hint	Enter Euro value
	ShowHint	True
	ReadOnly	False
	Color	clWhite
btnToEuro	Caption	Convert to &Euro
	Hint	Click here to convert to Euro
	ShowHint	True
Button1	Name	btnToRand
	Caption	Convert to &Rand
	Hint	Click here to convert to Rand
	ShowHint	True
bmbReset	Name	bmbReset
	Hint	Click here to reset values
	ShowHint	True

- To avoid compilation errors, delete the code and the declarations in btnToEuro's OnClick event handler to leave only the skeleton:

```
procedure TfrmRandToEuro.btnToEuroClick (Sender: TObject);
begin

end;
```

- Save your application in unit and project files C04e04u and C04e04p respectively. Delphi will automatically delete the event handler skeleton.
- Now run the program and move the mouse slowly over the Edit and Button components and see what happens.

Giving the user hints

By changing the Hint and ShowHint properties of any visible component, as we did in the Edit and Button components in the table above, we can display useful messages to the user as he or she moves the mouse over different components. Using Hints on the components helps to increase the predictability of a user interface. Through hints, the user will have a better idea of what to expect before he or she performs an action (such as a button click). Figure 4.8 shows the Hint connected to component btnToEuro.

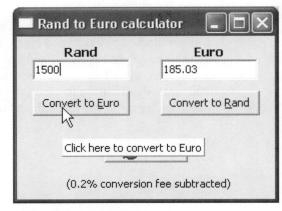

Figure 4.8 Giving the user Hints

EX 4.4 STEP 2 Using constants

As in example 4.3, we define the exchange rate as a constant value. In this example we subtract a conversion fee, which is a percentage of the amount we want to convert. It is a good idea also to have the conversion percentage defined as a constant value.

- Create the `btnToEuroClick` event handler by double-clicking on the Convert to Euro button on the form.
- Type in the following constant declarations:

```
const ExchangeRate = 0.1236;
      ConPercentage = 0.2;          //Conversion fee percentage
```

EX 4.4 STEP 3 The variables needed

Do we need variables? The Edit component returns a string value entered by the user in its Text property. We cannot use string values in arithmetic expressions, so we need to convert the value entered by the user to a real value. So, for the Convert to Euro event handler, we need a variable to keep the number equivalent of `edtRand.Text` – we will call it `Rand`. We also need a variable to keep the calculated Euro value – we will call it `Euro`.

- Type in the following variable declarations in the event handler connected to the Convert to Euro button just below the const declaration:

```
var Euro,              //For the result of the calculation
    Rand: double;      //For the conversion of edtRand.Text
```

EX 4.4 STEP 4 Converting the user's input to a floating-point number

The value that the user enters in the `edtRand` Edit component is returned as a string in `edtRand.Text`. We know now that we have to convert it to a real number before we can use it in calculations. How do we go about it?

- Change the `btnToEuroClick` event handler to have the following statement as the first statement after `begin`:

```
Rand := StrToFloat(edtRand.Text);
```

We cannot use the string value entered by the user in arithmetic calculations, so we convert it to a number first. Just as we used FloatToStrF to convert a floating-point number to a string, we use StrToFloat to convert a string value to a floating-point number.

Later we will see what happens when we try to convert a string value containing alphabetical characters to a number.

EX 4.4 STEP 5 Doing the calculation

- Now that the value entered by the user has been converted to a number, we can use it to calculate the Euro amount. Build the Rand to Euro conversion as well as the computation of the fee into your program by adding the following two lines of code:

```
Euro := ExchangeRate * Rand;
Euro := Euro - ConPercentage/100*Euro;
```

Real division

The first statement is exactly the same as the one used in example 4.3 for calculating the Euro amount. In the second statement we subtract the conversion fee from the Euro amount. The amount of the conversion fee is calculated by

```
ConPercentage/100*Euro
```

and then the result of this, as you can see, is subtracted from the value in `Euro`. / is the real division operator for Delphi. When we use real division, the result of the operation is a real value and includes the decimal fraction.

The table below contrasts the integer operators DIV and MOD and the real operator / .

Operation	Answer
5/2	2.5
5 DIV 2	2
5 MOD 2	1

Operator precedence

The statement `Euro := Euro - ConPercentage/100*Euro;` contains three different operations: subtraction (−), real division (/) and multiplication (*). To work out the value of such an expression (for given values of the variables involved) we need to know the order in which Delphi evaluates the various operations. For example, if `Euro` has value 200 and `ConPercentage` has the value 0.2, then we have:

```
Euro := 200 - 0.2 / 100 * 200;
```

In this expression we need to know whether the subtract, division or multiplication operation occurs first. Is it (200 − 0.2) / 100*200), which evaluates to 399.60, or 200 − (0.2 / 100) * 200, which evaluates to 39999.6, or 200 − 0.2 / (100 * 200) which evaluates to 199.99.

The rules for determining the order of evaluation of operations in a Delphi expression generally match the familiar rules of arithmetic:

Rule 1   *Parenthesized sub-expressions first.* Any sub-expression in parentheses is evaluated before the larger expression. If there are several levels of nested parentheses, then you work outwards from the innermost level. For example, in evaluating the assignment

```
Price := (bValue + 2 * aValue) / (2 * cValue);
```

the two parenthesized sub-expressions are evaluated first, before the division / is performed.

Rule 2 *Multiplication and division before addition and subtraction.* If there are several arithmetic operations, with no parentheses to indicate the order of evaluation (as in rule 1 above), then the order of evaluation is:

Multiplication and division first (ie *, /, DIV, MOD).
Addition and subtraction last (ie +, −).

Therefore the expression 200 − 0.2/100 is evaluated as if it were written:

```
200 − (0.2 / 100).
```

This ordering is called the 'precedence order of the arithmetic operations' – it specifies which operation precedes another in an expression when no parentheses are used.

Rule 3 *Left-to-right associativity of operations of the same precedence.* If several multiplication and division operators appear with no parentheses to indicate the order of evaluation, they are evaluated across the expression from left to right. The same rule applies if there are several addition and subtraction operations with no parentheses.

Therefore the expression A + B − C / D * E is grouped as if it were written:

```
(A + B) − ((C / D) * E).
```

Data type of the result of an expression

We need to know the type of data value that results when an expression is evaluated – is the result of type integer or real (double, single or extended)? We had to know beforehand that the Euro variable would be real in order to declare it type double in our program. In arithmetic operations the data type of the result depends on the types of the operands, as given in the table below. (If we have X + Y, then X and Y are called 'operands'.) Notice in particular that / always gives a real result, even if both operands are type integer. (Wherever the real data type appears in the table, it can be any data type in the real category of data types, for example single, double or extended.)

Left Operand	Operation	Right Operand	Result Type
integer	+ − * DIV MOD	integer	integer
integer	/	integer	real
real or integer	+ − * /	real	real
real	+ − * /	real or integer	real
real or integer	DIV MOD	real	illegal
real	DIV MOD	real or integer	illegal

Within the real category of data types all types are compatible with each other. You can assign a value of one type to a variable of a different type within the same category. For example, a value of type `single` can be assigned to a variable of type `double` because they are both real numbers. A value of type `double` can also be assigned to a variable of type `single`, but this will cause loss of accuracy because of the limit on significant digits.

EX 4.4 STEP 6 Displaying the answer

All that is left to do in this event handler is to display the Euro value we have calculated in the appropriate Edit component. Can we just put the value in `edtEuro.Text`?

The Text property of an Edit component can hold only string values, so before we can display the calculated `Euro` value, which is of type `double`, we have to convert it to a string. We do this with the statement

```
edtEuro.Text := FloatToStrF(Euro,ffFixed,15,2);
```

EX 4.4 STEP 7 Clearing values

We now need to improve the application's user interface by introducing a Reset button that the user can click on to reset all the values on the screen. This is the event handler connected to the Reset button:

```
procedure TfrmRandEuro.bmbResetClick(Sender: TObject);
begin
  edtRand.Clear;
  edtEuro.Clear;
end;
```

Both conversion event handlers

This concludes our discussion of the event handler connected to the Convert to Euro button. The event handler connected to the Convert to Rand button is similar, except that to convert the Euro value to a Rand value, we need to divide the Euro value by the exchange rate. Both event handlers appear below. Work through them to make sure you understand the reason for each program statement and to consolidate the discussion of the previous few pages. Then enter these event handlers.

```
procedure TfrmRandToEuro.btnToEuroClick(Sender: TObject);
const ExchangeRate = 0.1236;
      ConPercentage = 0.2;
var Euro, Rand: double;
begin
  Rand := StrToFloat(edtRand.Text);
  Euro := ExchangeRate * Rand;
  Euro := Euro - ConPercentage/100*Euro;
  edtEuro.Text := FloatToStrF(Euro,ffFixed,15,2);
end;
```

```
procedure TfrmRandToEuro.btnToRandClick(Sender: TObject);
const  ExchangeRate = 0.1236;
       ConPercentage = 0.2;
var Euro, Rand: double;
begin
  Euro := StrToFloat(edtEuro.Text);
  Rand := Euro / ExchangeRate;
  Rand := Rand - ConPercentage/100*Rand;
  edtRand.Text := FloatToStrF(Rand,ffFixed,15,2);
end;
```

- Run and test the program against the criteria given at the beginning of this example.

Attempting to convert alphabetical characters to a number

We used StrToFloat to convert the Rand or Euro value in a text box to a floating point number. It will only be able to convert strings which contain digits and a single decimal point. A number which contains other characters, such as a space, the 'R' symbol or a comma will be invalid. The following are examples of valid and invalid input values:

Valid input values	Invalid input values
345.80	R23.50
3000	4,56
80000	80 000
4.5689	

- Still in run mode, type a value containing an alphabetical character (eg R100) in the Rand Edit component and click the Convert to Euro button. The error message that appears is shown in figure 4.9.

What has happened? Because the user entered an invalid value, the StrToFloat function raised an exception and displayed an appropriate error message.

Figure 4.9 Error message generated by Delphi

- Clicking on OK will enable the user to continue the program and enter another value.

Summary of example 4.4: This example has introduced hints to improve the usability of the user interface and constants to improve the readability of a program. It also considered more complicated arithmetic expressions and described the concept of operator precedence and the data type that results when using mixed operands. Finally we look at the exception StrToFloat generates when given an invalid value to convert.

REVIEW

In this chapter we have used two kinds of numbers: whole numbers and numbers with fractions. For whole numbers we used variables of type integer and for numbers with fractions we used variables of type double.

We can assign a name to a constant value and then use the name in place of the constant value. This is done with a constant declaration between the procedure handler heading and the variable declarations.

The SpinEdit component is used exclusively for the input of integer numbers. With an Edit component we read or display any number by using conversion functions, since the Text property of the Edit component contains only strings. We use the following conversion functions: IntToStr, StrToInt, FloatToStrF, FloatToStr and StrToFloat.

We used hints to display useful messages to the user as he or she moves the mouse over different components.

We used the following arithmetic operations: addition, subtraction, multiplication, division (/) and integer division (MOD and DIV). We discussed the order of precedence of these operations.

We saw that a program might compile without any errors but when it runs things can still go wrong. Attempting to devide by zero, converting a string containing a non-digit to a number or typing a real number in SpinEdit will cause a run-time error and by default Delphi will break into the debugger. Delphi has the option to disable this.

IMPORTANT CONCEPTS

Programming principles

Compatible data types: In any assignment statement, the variable on the left-hand side must be of the same type as the value of the variable or expression on the right-hand side.

Constants: You can assign a name to a constant value and then use the name in place of the constant value. Unlike the value of a variable, the value of a constant cannot be changed by the program itself.

Exceptions: An exception is raised when a run-time error interrupts normal execution of a program.

Floating point or real numbers: Numbers with fractions such as 1.0, −13.678 and 12.00. We declare variables for holding such numbers of type double, single, extended or currency.

Integer arithmetic operations: The arithmetic operations available for integer values in Delphi are + (addition), − (subtraction), * (multiplication), DIV (division producing an integer quotient with no remainder) and MOD (modulus, the remainder of integer division). For example, 12 DIV 3 gives the value 4 and 12 MOD 3 gives the value 0.

Integer numbers: Whole numbers such as 1, −501 and 137. We declare variables for holding such numbers of type integer.

Operator precedence: To work out the value of an arithmetic expression, we need to know the order in which the various operations are evaluated. If parentheses are present, Delphi starts with them after the parentheses, multiplication and division operations are evaluated next, before addition and subtraction operations. If there is still a question of which operation to perform first, the competing operations are performed from left to right.

Real/floating point arithmetic operations: The arithmetic operations available for real values are +, −, * and / . The / operator refers to real division where the result contains a decimal fraction.

User interface factors

Consistency: The user interface design principle of consistency states that the user interface should behave similarly throughout the application. Displaying output to the user in a component that has the same behaviour and appearance as an input box is an example of an inconsistent user interface.

User hints: Hints can be used to give additional help to the user about components which appear on the user interface. Hints are programmed in Delphi by changing the Hint and ShowHint properties of visible components. Adding hints to an application can increase the predictability of the user interface.

NEW DELPHI FEATURES

TSpinEdit		
Property	Value	Specifies the integer value currently entered in the SpinEdit.
Prefix	sed...	
Use	SpinEdits are similar to the Edit component since they get input from the user. The SpinEdit holds an integer value (a whole number) and the Edit component holds a string. So when we need to get whole numbers from the user, we use SpinEdit components.	

Conversion functions	
IntToStr	Converts an integer to a string.
StrToInt	Converts a string to an integer.
StrToFloat	Converts a string to a floating-point number.
FloatToStrF	Converts a floating-point number to a string and formats the string (eg two digits after the decimal point).
FloatToStr	Converts a floating-point number to a string (without any formatting).

Tools | Debugger Options (Delphi 6) or Tools | Options (Delphi 8)

We use the Language Exceptions page of the Debugger Options (Delphi 6/7) or Options (Delphi 8) dialog box to configure how the debugger handles language exceptions when they are raised by the program we are debugging.

We uncheck the Stop On Delphi Exceptions (Delphi 6/7) or Stop on Language Exceptions (Delph 8) checkbox if we want to prevent Delphi from breaking into the debugger of our program when it raises a Delphi exception. By default, this checkbox is checked.

PROBLEMS

PROBLEM 4.1 The declaration section

- Fill in the types of the variables used in the event handler below, so that it executes correctly.

```
1  procedure TForm1.Button1Click(sender : TObject);
2  var
3    V: _____;
4    W: _____;
5    X: _____;
6    Y: _____;
7    Z: _____;
8  begin
9    X := '1020';
10   Y := X + '10';
11   Z := 3;
12   W := Z + 1;
13   V := X;
14   W := W MOD Z;
15 end;
```

PROBLEM 4.2 Jolly Joe's Family Circus admission price calculator (1)

Jolly Joe does not trust his cashiers to calculate admission prices accurately, and so wants to automate his business through a computer-based admission price calculator.

To make it easier for the cashiers, Jolly Joe's admission prices do not include cents. The cost per adult is R10 and per child is R5. The cashier enters the number of adults and the number of children, then clicks the OK button to display the admission price. To clear the values, the cashier can press the Reset button.

- See the user interface in figure 4.10. Can you write a program to meet his needs?
- Use Hints to make the interface more friendly.

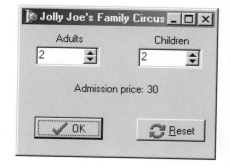

Figure 4.10 User interface for the price calculator

PROBLEM 4.3 Precedence (1)

- Consider the Delphi statement D := B – C / B * C; If B is 4.0 and C is 2.0, calculate the value that will be assigned to D.

PROBLEM 4.4) Precedence (2)

- Consider the assignment statement `D := (B - C / B * C) * (B - C) / C;`
  What will be the value of D if B is 4.0 and C is 2.0?

PROBLEM 4.5) From arithmetic expression to Delphi statement

- Convert the following arithmetic statement to a correct Delphi assignment
  statement, using as few brackets as possible.

$$A = \dfrac{\dfrac{B+C}{D} + \dfrac{2G}{E+F}}{3H^2}$$

PROBLEM 4.6) Determining the type of a result

Say you have the following variables declared in your program:

```
var  R, D, S: double;
     I, J, K: integer;
```

- Complete the table below by filling in the type of the variable Result with
  each Delphi statement.

Delphi Statement	Type of Result
`Result := R + J;`	**var** Result:
`Result := K DIV I;`	**var** Result:
`Result := (K DIV I) / 2;`	**var** Result:
`Result := I / J;`	**var** Result:
`Result := K * K;`	**var** Result:
`Result := R MOD J;`	**var** Result:

PROBLEM 4.7) A faulty program

The following program code is an event handler of a program written by an
inexperienced programmer.
- Complete the table below and help him or her by stating for each line of
  code whether it is correct or not and, if it is not correct, give the reason.
  Assume that one of the components on the form is a SpinEdit component
  with the name `sedNumber`, another component on the form is an Edit
  component with the name `edtNumber`, and that all the declarations are
  correct.

```
 1 procedure TForm1.Button1Click(Sender:TObject);
 2 var
 3   Ten, Answer: string;
 4   Value, Ans: integer;
 5   Price,X: double;
 6 begin
 7   Value := sedNumber.Value;
 8   Price := Value * 2;
 9   Ans := Price / 2;
10   X := 33.456;
11   Ans := FloatToStrF(X,ffFixed,10,2);
12   Answer := FloatToStrF(Price,15,2);
13   edtNumber := Answer;
14 end;
```

Program Line	Correct	Wrong	Reason for being Wrong
6	✓		
7			
8			
10			
11			
12			
13			
14			

PROBLEM 4.8) Rand to Euro calculator (version 3)

- Exchange rates change from day to day. Rewrite example 4.4 to make it more flexible so that the user can enter the exchange rate.

PROBLEM 4.9) Rand to other currencies calculator (version 4)

- Extend example 4.4 to use RadioButtons to accommodate several different currencies.

When the user enters the Rand value and when he or she clicks on one of the RadioButtons, the Rand value is converted to the specified country's currency and displayed in the space provided with the name of the currency on top, as in figure 4.11.

When the user clicks the Reset button, the Edit components are cleared and the label above the foreign Edit component is reset to 'Currency'.

- Use the following exchange rates if you cannot find the current values:

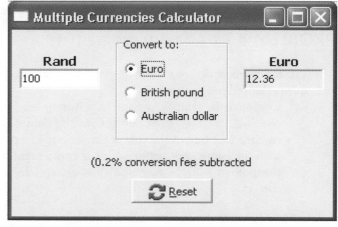

Figure 4.11 User interface for the multiple currencies calculator

Rand	Euro	British pound	Australian dollar
1	0.1236	0.0830	0.2127

PROBLEM 4.10) Jolly Joe's Family Circus admission price calculator (2)

Jolly Joe (problem 4.2) now wants his program to cater for entrance fees including Rands and cents. The cost per adult is R9.90, and per child is R6.60. See the user interface in figure 4.12.

- Alter the program in problem 4.2 to meet Joe's changing needs.

Figure 4.12 User interface for the admission price calculator

PROBLEM 4.11) Calculate room area

- Write a program to read in the length and width of a room in metres and then calculate and display the area of the room with an appropriate heading. The output should be displayed to one decimal place.
- We do not give a sample interface, so before writing the program think about what components you will need to read in the values and then display the output.
- Also, calculate at least three test cases by hand, and then test your program to make sure that it is working correctly. (Formula: Area = Width × Length)

PROBLEM 4.12) Calculate carpeting cost

Sally, of *Sally's Home Furnishing Consultants*, often needs to calculate the cost of carpeting a room.

- Extend the program in the previous problem to allow the user to enter the cost per square metre of carpeting. The program must now display the area of the room and the cost of the carpeting.

CHAPTER 5

Conditional execution

PURPOSE OF THIS CHAPTER

In the programs we have written so far, the program statements included between the begin and end statements of an event handler are executed in sequential order, that is, one after the other. Sometimes, however, a programming problem requires a procedure to include two or more different sets of statements of which only one will be executed, depending on certain conditions. For example, a program that calculates the amount of income tax payable by an employee must take into account the employee's salary. The income tax payable varies according to the size of the income. For each category, different program statements need to be included to calculate the correct tax amount. Depending on the salary, the program should decide which of the different statements it must branch to.

In this chapter we learn how to write programs that include conditional statements which enable a program to decide between different statements to execute. The type of conditional statement we discuss here is the if...then...else statement.

In our discussion of conditional execution we introduce several new programming concepts and Delphi features, including:
o   Boolean expressions;
o   exception handling;
o   the Windows common dialog boxes, and
o   the Memo component.

In order to use an if...then...else statement, we first need to learn how to express a True/False condition in Delphi Pascal. We therefore begin this chapter with a discussion of Boolean expressions.

Boolean expressions

'Conditional execution' implies that some condition must be tested and, depending on whether it is true or not, different statements of the program will be executed. For this we need a programming construct which allows us to include logic of the form: if some condition is true, then do this, otherwise do that. In Delphi, as in most other programming languages, a condition is given in the form of a Boolean expression. A Boolean expression is a statement that can be either True or False. For example, the statement 10 > 1 is a Boolean expression that always evaluates to True, while the statement Value = 0 will evaluate to True only if the variable Value contains the value 0, otherwise it will be False. Boolean expressions often involve relational operators such as =, < and >. The table below summarises the various relational operators, their Delphi form, and what they mean:

Mathematical notation	Delphi notation	Meaning
=	=	equal to
≠	<>	not equal to
<	<	less than
>	>	greater than
≤	<=	less than or equal to
≥	>=	greater than or equal to

Examples of Boolean expressions in Delphi are:

```
Price > 20.00 {True if Price is greater than 20.0, otherwise false}
Value <> 0  {True if Value is not equal to 0, otherwise false}
X >= Y {True if X is greater than or equal to Y, otherwise false}
```

EXAMPLE 5.1) Boolean expressions

This example shows how Delphi evaluates Boolean expressions and, at the same time, introduces the if...then...else statement.
- Open a new application and create the form in figure 5.1 and the table that follows.
- The program will compare the two number values the user supplies for Value 1 and Value 2, and indicate whether each of the listed Boolean expressions is True or False. We will use this program again later in this chapter, so it is important that you write it now.
- Save the unit file as C05e01u and the project as C05e01p.

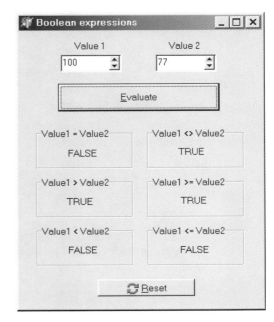

Figure 5.1 Evaluation of Boolean expressions

Component	Property	Value
Form1	Name	frmBoole
	Caption	Boolean expressions
Button1	Name	btnEvaluate
	Caption	&Evaluate
SpinEdit1	Name	sedValue1
	Value	0
SpinEdit2	Name	sedValue2
	Value	0
GroupBox1	Name	gpbEqual
	Caption	Value1 = Value2
GroupBox2	Name	gpbGreater
	Caption	Value1 > Value2
GroupBox3	Name	gpbLess
	Caption	Value1 < Value2
GroupBox4	Name	gpbNotEq
	Caption	Value 1 <> Value 2
GroupBox5	Name	gpbGreaterEq
	Caption	Value1 >= Value2
GroupBox6	Name	gpbLessEq
	Caption	Value1 <= Value2
Label1	Name	lblValue1
	Caption	Value 1
Label2	Name	lblValue2
	Caption	Value 2
Label3 (in GroupBox1)	Name	lblEqual
	Caption	<Blank>
Label4 (in GroupBox2)	Name	lblGreater
	Caption	<Blank>
Label5 (in GroupBox3)	Name	lblLess
	Caption	<Blank>
Label6 (in GroupBox4)	Name	lblNotEq
	Caption	<Blank>
Label7 (in GroupBox5)	Name	lblGreaterEq
	Caption	<Blank>
Label8 (in GroupBox6)	Name	lblLessEq
	Caption	<Blank>
BitBtn1	Name	bmbReset
	Kind	bkRetry
	Caption	&Reset

- Now double-click on the Evaluate button to create the following event handler:

```
procedure TfrmBoole.btnEvaluateClick(Sender: TObject);
var
  Value1, Value2: integer;
begin
  Value1 := sedValue1.Value;
  Value2 := sedValue2.Value;

  if Value1 = Value2 then
    lblEqual.Caption := 'TRUE'
  else
    lblEqual.Caption := 'FALSE';

  if Value1 > Value2 then
    lblGreater.Caption := 'TRUE'
  else
    lblGreater.Caption := 'FALSE';

  if Value1 < Value2 then
    lblLess.Caption := 'TRUE'
  else
    lblLess.Caption := 'FALSE';

  if Value1 <> Value2 then
    lblNotEq.Caption := 'TRUE'
  else
    lblNotEq.Caption := 'FALSE';

  if Value1 >= Value2 then
    lblGreaterEq.Caption := 'TRUE'
  else
    lblGreaterEq.Caption := 'FALSE';

  if Value1 <= Value2 then
    lblLessEq.Caption := 'TRUE'
  else
    lblLessEq.Caption := 'FALSE';

end;
```

Depending on the two values the user enters, this event handler writes either 'TRUE' or 'FALSE' in each of the GroupBoxes that represent the respective Boolean expressions.

To enhance the program we added a Reset button that resets the SpinEdits and the 'TRUE' or 'FALSE' Label Captions, and sets the focus to Value 1's SpinEdit.

```
procedure TfrmBoole.bmbResetClick(Sender: TObject);
begin
  sedValue1.Value := 0;
  sedValue2.Value := 0;
  sedValue1.SetFocus;
  lblEqual.Caption := '';
  lblGreater.Caption := '';
  lblLess.Caption := '';
  lblNotEq.Caption := '';
  lblGreaterEq.Caption := '';
  lblLessEq.Caption := '';
end;
```

- Save the unit and project files again and then run the program. Test it with different input values.
- Make sure your program works correctly for all six types of expression.

The btnEvaluateClick event handler does the important work in this program. It uses two integer variables: `Value1` and `Value2`. The first two statements store the input values in `Value1` and `Value2` respectively.

The if...then...else statements

The rest of the btnEvaluateClick event handler consists of a series of if...then...else statements.

The first one is

```
if Value1 = Value2 then
  lblEqual.Caption := 'TRUE'
else
  lblEqual.Caption := 'FALSE';
```

It works as follows: Delphi evaluates the Boolean expression, `Value1 = Value2`. If it is True, the statement following **then** is executed. If it is False, the statement following **else** is executed. For example, if `Value1` is 100 and `Value2` is 200, then the Boolean expression `Value1 = Value2` is False and the statement `lblEqual.Caption := 'FALSE';` sets the relevant Caption to `'FALSE'`.

The remaining five if...then...else statements are similar.

The difference between = and :=

When used in a Delphi program, there is a big difference between the two statements

```
lblEqual.Caption = 'FALSE'
```

and

```
lblEqual.Caption := 'FALSE'.
```

The first is a Boolean expression which compares the value on the left-hand side of '=' (the equality operator) with the value on the right-hand side of it. It tests whether they are equal and evaluates to either True or False. Thus the expression `lblEqual.Caption = 'FALSE'` tests whether or not the Caption of lblEqual is the text string 'FALSE'. Such an expression will always appear in a program as part of another statement (like an If statement) – we cannot use it as an independent program statement.

The second statement is an assignment statement that assigns the value on the right-hand side of the ':=' (the assignment operator) to the property (or variable) on its left-hand side. The statement `lblEqual.Caption := 'FALSE'` sets the Caption property of lblEqual to the text string 'FALSE'. An assignment statement is always an independent program statement.

Comparing strings

In the same way that we compare numbers with relational operators such as < and >, we can compare alphabetical strings. The string 'A' is less than the string 'B' and 'x' is greater than 'a'. If we compare two letters of similar case, the one that comes first in the alphabet is smaller. With longer strings, the individual letters are compared one-by-one from left to right. For instance, 'adam' is less than 'eve', because 'a' comes before 'e' in the alphabet, and 'apple' is greater than 'adam', because 'p' comes after 'd'. Note, however, that all uppercase letters come before lowercase letters. In other words, 'Z' is smaller than 'a', 'A' is smaller than 'a' and 'Eve' is less than 'adam'.

Let's change the program of example 5.1 so that it compares string values instead of integers.

EXAMPLE 5.2) Comparing strings

- Open the project C05e01p that you saved in example 5.1.
- Replace the two SpinEdit components with two Edit boxes and set their properties as follows:

Component	Property	Value
Edit1	Name	edtValue1
	Text	<Blank>
Edit2	Name	edtValue2
	Text	<Blank>

- Double-click on the Evaluate button and change the first few lines of the btnEvaluateClick event handler to match the following:

```
procedure TfrmBoole.btnEvaluateClick(Sender: TObject);
var
  Value1, Value2: String;
begin
  Value1 := edtValue1.Text;
  Value2 := edtValue2.Text;
  ⋮
```

We changed the variables Value1 and Value2 to string variables and assigned the Text properties (ie string values) of the edit boxes to them.

- Double-click on the Reset button and change the first few lines of the bmbResetClick event handler to match the following:

```
procedure TfrmBoole.bmbResetClick(Sender: TObject);
begin
  edtValue1.Text := '';
  edtValue2.Text := '';
  edtValue1.SetFocus;
  ⋮
```

- Save the unit as C05e02u and the project as C05e02p.
- Before you run the program and test it with the values given in the table below, test your understanding of the Boolean expressions by completing the last two columns of the table by hand (in other words, work out what the values of `Value1 > Value2` and `Value1 < Value2` are).

Value1	Value2	Value1 > Value2	Value1 < Value2
`'hello'`	`'goodbye'`		
`'hello'`	`'Hello'`		
`'BuBbLes'`	`'BubBles'`		
`'JELLY'`	`'JELLYBEANS'`		

- Now run the program entering the above strings for `Value1` and `Value2`. Does it give the answers you expected? The correct answers are:

Value1 > Value2	Value1 < Value2
TRUE	FALSE
TRUE	FALSE
FALSE	TRUE
FALSE	TRUE

Ignoring the case when comparing strings

Suppose we do not want our program to distinguish between upper and lower case letters when comparing two strings. In other words, we want our program to regard the strings 'adam', 'ADAM', 'aDaM' and 'Adam' as equal. We use the UpperCase or LowerCase functions to do this. Say the two strings we want to compare are stored in the string variables `Value1` and `Value2`. Consider the following If statement:

```
if UpperCase(Value1) = UpperCase(Value2) then
   lblEqual.Caption := 'TRUE'
else
   lblEqual.Caption := 'FALSE';
```

`UpperCase(Value1)` and `UpperCase(Value2)` give the values of `Value1` and `Value2` as strings made up of uppercase letters only, so that the case will not affect the result of the comparison. Using the LowerCase function instead of UpperCase will return strings made up of lowercase letters only, and will give the same result in this If statement.

    If the strings to be compared are input from edit boxes, such as `Value1` and `Value2` in this program, there is another way to force upper or lower case on them. An Edit component has a CharCase property which can be set to ecUpperCase, ecLowerCase or ecNormal. If we set the CharCase properties for edtValue1 and edtValue2 to ecUpperCase in the Object Inspector, the user's input will be converted to upper case as he or she types.

- Try this with the program you saved in example 5.2.

The if...then...else statement

In the examples above you have seen the if...then...else statement at work. The general format of this statement is

```
if Condition then
    Statement1
else
    Statement2;
```

Condition is a Boolean expression. If this expression evaluates to True, then *Statement1*, the statement in the **then** part of the if...then...else, is executed. If it evaluates to False, the statement in the **Else** part, *Statement2*, is executed. It is not always necessary to include an **Else** part in an If statement. We may leave out the **Else** part if nothing should happen when the If statement's Boolean condition is False.

Statement1 and *Statement2* can each be a single program statement, as in all the if...then...else statements we have used so far, or a compound statement. A *compound statement* is a group of statements placed between the words **begin** and **end**. We will write a program using an If with compound statements in example 5.4.

It is important that you never use a semicolon after the word **then** or after the word **else**. Also, there should never be a semicolon between *Statement1* and **else**. We'll say more about semicolons in If statements later.

Logical operators in Boolean expressions

In addition to the relational operators (such as <, >, =), Boolean expressions can also include the logical operators **and**, **or**, and **not**. Execution of a program statement can depend on the truth or falseness of more than one condition. We can combine Boolean conditions with the **and** and **or** operations to form compound Boolean expressions. For example, if the condition states that the value of the integer variable Value1 must lie strictly between 10 and 20, the condition will be (Value1 > 10) **and** (Value1 < 20). This condition will be true only if the conditions on both sides of **and** are true.

If we combine two conditions using **or** to get

(Value1 = 10) **or** (Value1 = 20),

the new compound expression will be true if the integer value assigned to Value1 is either 10 or 20. If either (or both) of the constituent conditions is true, the whole expression will be true. The compound expression will be false only if the conditions on both sides of the **or** operator are false.

Note that we should enclose each of the Boolean expressions which make up a compound Boolean expression in brackets.

If we apply the **not** operator to a condition, it returns the negation of the condition's value. In other words, it changes the condition's value from True to

False or from False to True. For example, not(Value1 > 10) will return False if Value1 is greater than 10 and True if Value1 is less than or equal to 10.

The table below shows how we evaluate expressions that contain 'and', 'or' and 'not'.

Value1	Value2	(Value1 and Value2)	(Value1 or Value2)	Not (Value1)
True	True	True	True	False
True	False	False	True	False
False	True	False	True	True
False	False	False	False	True

EXAMPLE 5.3) Ifs, logical operators and Boolean variables

We have written a program that classifies animals as mammals or reptiles based on some basic input from the user. Figure 5.2 illustrates the user interface:

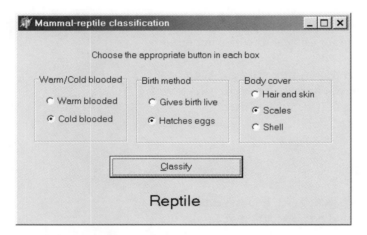

Figure 5.2 Classifying animals

The seven RadioButtons are called radWarm, radCold, radLive, radEggs, radHair, radScales and radShell, whereas the Label at the bottom that displays the classification is called lblClass. The button is called btnClassify.

Note that there are three GroupBoxes containing two or three RadioButtons each. The user has to select one RadioButton from each group. It is therefore important that the RadioButtons are correctly *contained in* the respective GroupBoxes. When you place, for example, radWarm in the left-most GroupBox, that GroupBox must be selected (ie its sizing handles must be visible), otherwise the RadioButton will be contained in the form (even though it appears to be in the GroupBox). If the seven RadioButtons belong to the form and not to the three GroupBoxes, only one of them can be selected at a time. To test whether a RadioButton is contained in a GroupBox try to drag it out of the GroupBox. If this is possible, you have placed it on the form and not in the GroupBox. In this case, delete the RadioButton and place a new one in the GroupBox.

Another way of checking if a RadioButton is contained in a GroupBox is to look in the Object TreeView (Delphi 6 or 7) or the Model... tab of the Model View (Delphi 8). In this view you should be able to expand each GroupBox component to see the RadioButton components contained in that GroupBox.

The event handler below does the classification.

```
1  procedure TfrmClassify.btnClassifyClick(Sender: TObject);
2  var
3    IsMammal, IsReptile: boolean;
4  begin
5    IsMammal := radWarm.Checked and radLive.Checked and
6                radHair.Checked;
7    IsReptile := radCold.Checked and radEggs.Checked and
8                (radScales.Checked or radShell.Checked);
9    if IsMammal then
10     lblClass.Caption := 'Mammal';
11   if IsReptile then
12     lblClass.Caption := 'Reptile';
13   if not(IsMammal) and not(IsReptile) then
14     lblClass.Caption := 'Unknown';
15 end;
```

We work through this code in a little while, but first we discuss some theory on Boolean variables and expressions.

Boolean variables

The data types we have used so far in our programs are Double, Integer, and String. In this example we use the Boolean data type. Like the Boolean expressions we have used in the If conditions so far, a Boolean variable can have the value True or False and we can use it as an If statement's condition.

For example, if we have the variable declarations in lines 2 and 3, we can assign a True or False value to IsMammal (or IsReptile) with an assignment statement of the form

```
IsMammal := SomeBooleanExpression;
```

(as in lines 5 and 6) and then use it in an If statement as follows:

```
if IsMammal = True then ...
```

This is the same as saying `if IsMammal then ...`

Component properties in Boolean expressions

When programming we often want to check the value of a certain component property and act according to that. For example, the Boolean expressions that we assign to IsMammal (lines 5 and 6) and IsReptile (lines 7 and 8) evaluate the Checked properties of selected RadioButtons to determine whether the animal involved is a mammal or a reptile. Checked is a Boolean property (ie it can take the value True or False). In both cases the three Checked properties are connected by and operators because all three RadioButtons must be selected if we want to assign the value True to the particular variable.

EX 5.3   Working through the program code

The table below gives four different combinations of input. The ticks indicate which RadioButtons are selected.

- For each combination, work through the code by hand and write down the expected value of lblClass's Caption.

	Warm/Cold blooded		Birth method		Body cover		
	radWarm	radCold	radEggs	radLive	radHair	radShell	radScales
1	✓		✓		✓		
2		✓	✓			✓	
3	✓			✓	✓		
4		✓	✓		✓		

Note that the first row describes the platypus – a famous Australian egg-laying mammal. Let's do case 1 together.

Evaluating case 1: STEP 1

We must first work out the values for IsMammal and IsReptile respectively. The statement that calculates IsMammal is

```
IsMammal := radWarm.Checked and radLive.Checked and radHair.Checked;
```

Here the three Boolean values associated with the Checked properties are combined with the and operator, meaning that all three of them must be true in order for the whole expression to be true. In case 1, radWarm, radEggs and radHair are selected, which means that two of the three Checked properties in this statement are true. Since radLive.Checked is False, the value False is assigned to IsMammal. We can write the evaluation out as follows:

```
  radWarm.Checked and radLive.Checked and radHair.Checked
= True            and False           and True
= False*
```

Evaluating case 1: STEP 2

The statement to calculate the value for IsReptile is

```
IsReptile := radCold.Checked and radEggs.Checked and
             (radScales.Checked or radShell.Checked);
```

---

* Experienced programmers may know that Delphi uses short circuit evaluation. So in practice Delphi evaluates the expression only up to the point where it determines that radLive.Checked is false, because then it knows that the whole expression is false.

Here we have a combination of ands and an or that combine the Checked properties into a compound Boolean expression. We are still busy with case 1, which has radWarm, radEggs and radHair selected.

Let's write it out:

```
  radCold.Checked and radEggs.Checked and (radScales.Checked or radShell.Checked);
= False           and True            and (False          or False);
= False           and True            and  False
= False
```

So, in case 1, both IsMammal and IsReptile are false.

Evaluating case 1: STEP 3

Now we come to the If statements. Since IsMammal and IsReptile are False, the conditions of the first two If statements (lines 9 and 11) are false and their Then parts (lines 10 and 12) will not be executed. Since they do not have Else parts, we just continue to the next statement. The condition of the third If statement (line 13) evaluates as follows:

```
  not(IsMammal) and not(IsReptile)
= not(False)    and not(False)
= True          and True
= True
```

This means the Then part of the third If statement is executed and lblClass's caption set to 'Unknown'.

This completes case 1. Do cases 2, 3 and 4 yourself. You should get the captions 'Reptile', 'Mammal' and 'Unknown' respectively.

Important comment

In the next chapter we return to this problem. The way we have used the If statements here is not ideal. Once we've learnt how to use nested Ifs, we can write more elegant If statements to solve the problem.

Order of precedence

As with arithmetic expressions, if an expression includes more than one logical and/or relational operator, there must be some order of precedence between operators. Delphi uses the following order of precedence (where operators in an expression have the same precedence the expression is evaluated from left to right):

1 Bracketed expressions
2 The not operator
3 and
4 or
5 relational operators (>, <, =, etc.).

This means that if A and B are False and C is True, then the expression A and B or C evaluates to True, but A and (B or C) evaluates to False. Let's see how we get this:

```
    A    and   B    or   C
= False and False or True    // and has precedence over or ...
=       False      or True   // so evaluate 1st part (gives False)
= True                       // False or True gives result True

    A    and  (B    or   C)
= False and (False or True)  // brackets have precedence ...
= False and           True   // so evaluate 2nd part (gives True)
= False                      // False and True gives result False
```

The relational operators (>, <, =, etc) have the lowest precedence (in other words, they are applied last). So if a condition with logical operators also includes expressions with relational operators, we may need to use brackets to override the order of precedence. For example, let Min, Max and X be integer variables. Given the condition

Min <= X **and** X <= Max,

Delphi will try to evaluate

X **and** X first, because and has higher precedence than <= and >=. Since we can only apply and to Boolean operands, this will result in a compile error. Adding brackets avoids the error. In (Min <= X) **and** (X <= Max) the Boolean expressions on both sides of and are evaluated, and then and is applied to the resulting Boolean values.

EXAMPLE 5.4) Compound statements

This example illustrates the use of an if...then...else statement, which tests the Color property of a form and shows us how to include more than one program statement (in the form of a compound statement) in the If and Else parts of an if...then...else statement.

The program we will write is similar to example 3 of Chapter 1. That example used two buttons to change the form's colour to purple and yellow respectively. In this example we are going to use only one button to change the colour from purple to yellow or from yellow to purple. Initially the button's Caption is 'Purple' and the background colour is set to clYellow (figure 5.3). The form's Caption is 'Yellow' to describe the background colour. A click on the button changes the background colour to purple, the form's Caption to 'Purple' and the button's Caption to 'Yellow' (figure 5.4).

Figure 5.3 The opening form

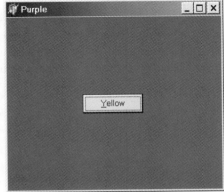

Figure 5.4 After clicking on the Purple button

- Open a new application, add a single button to the form and set the properties as in the table below.

Component	Property	Value
Form1	Name	frmColour
	Caption	Yellow
	Color	clYellow
Button1	Name	btnChangeColour
	Caption	&Purple

- Save the unit file as C05e04u and the project as C05e04p.
- Now double-click on btnChangeColour and write the following event handler:

```
procedure TfrmColour.btnChangeColourClick(Sender: TObject);
begin
  if frmColour.Color = clYellow then
  // Change colour to purple
  begin
    frmColour.Color := clPurple;
    frmColour.Caption := 'Purple';
    btnChangeColour.Caption := '&Yellow';
  end // No semicolon here as it stands directly before else
  else
  // Change colour to yellow
  begin
    frmColour.Color := clYellow;
    frmColour.Caption := 'Yellow';
    btnChangeColour.Caption := '&Purple';
  end;
end;
```

- Save the unit again and run the program.
- Click on the button to see how the background colour, the form's Caption and the button's Caption change.

So far in this chapter both the Then and the Else parts of our If statements have always consisted of a single statement. In this example we do three things in the Then part and three things in the Else part. If the form's colour is yellow (the If condition is True), we change the form's colour to purple, its Caption to 'Purple' and the button's Caption to 'Yellow'. So, if the condition is true, we need three different statements in the Then part:

```
begin
  frmColour.Color := clPurple;
  frmColour.Caption := 'Purple';
  btnChangeColour.Caption := '&Yellow';
end
```

When more than one statement appear in the Then or the Else part of an if...then...else structure, these statements must be enclosed in `begin` and `end` statements as you can see above. We call a group of statements enclosed in `begin` and `end` a *compound statement*. Note that there is no semicolon after `end` as it comes directly before the `else`.

When the If condition is False (in other words, if the form's colour is not yellow), the compound statement in the Else part is executed. The whole compound statement ends with a semicolon as this is the end of the If statement.

Structuring an if...then...else statement

The way you lay out an if...then...else statement is important. Note that in our If statements, `if` and `else` are always aligned, whereas the statements under them are indented. This ensures that anyone who reads the program will immediately see what falls under the Then part, and what falls under the Else part.

To illustrate how important this is, here are two examples of If statements that Delphi will accept and execute correctly, but which are quite difficult to read:

```
if Salary > 70000.00 then Tax := Salary * HighTax else
Tax := Salary * LowTax;
```

and

```
if Salary > 70000.00 then
Tax := Salary * HighTax else
Tax := Salary * LowTax;
```

A good way to structure this If statement is

```
if Salary > 70000.00 then
  Tax := Salary * HighTax
else
  Tax := Salary * LowTax;
```

Semicolons in if...then...else statements

There are three rules to follow when using semicolons in an if...then...else statement:

Rule 1   A semicolon is not used directly after the word `then`.
A semicolon after `then` will be interpreted as the end of the if...then...else statement. For example, if the If statement below appears in a program, a compile error will be reported. The semicolon after `then` is not itself the

syntax error but, because this indicates the end of the if...then...else statement, the else will not be considered as part of the If statement and will cause a syntax error.

```
if X >= 50 then;              // WRONG - semicolon after then
  Result := 'Pass'
else
  Result := 'Fail';
```

If you are using an if...then statement (without an else clause), the compiler will not pick up the error if you place a semicolon after then. Your program will simply not behave as it should. For example, in the case of the following code, the value of result will always be 'Pass', regardless of the value of X. This is because the semicolon after then indicates the end of the if statement, so the second statement has nothing to do with the if statement:

```
if X >= 50 then;     // if x >= 50 then do nothing
  Result := 'Pass'; // this will always be executed
```

Rule 2   A semicolon is not used directly after the word else.
Putting a semicolon after else will not cause a syntax error, but will cause the program to give incorrect results. Consider the following If statement:

```
if X >= 50 then
  Result := 'Pass'
else;                         // else do nothing
  Result := 'Fail';          // always executed
```

Here the If statement ends directly after else (because of the semicolon after else), and the last statement is not seen as part of the if...then...else statement. In other words, this Else part is empty. The statement Result := Fail; will always be executed – when the Boolean condition is false *and* when it is true.

Rule 3   A semicolon directly before else will always be reported as a syntax error.

These rules also apply to compound statements in an if...then...else statement. Never use a semicolon after the end directly preceding the word else. The end of a compound statement in the Else part should, however, end with a semicolon as this indicates the end of the whole If structure (it may be left out if the next statement is end but, to be safe, always include it). Each of the statements inside the compound statement should also end with a semicolon.

Common Windows dialogs in Delphi

A dialog box is a window (or a form in Delphi terms) that appears on top of the existing windows to display information to the user or to get information from the user. The common Windows dialog boxes such as OpenDialog, SaveDialog and PrintDialog appear as components in the Dialogs tab of the Component/Tool palette. We can use them in our Delphi programs to keep our user interfaces consistent with the Windows standards. We see three of them at work in the next example.

Although they are not directly related to conditional execution, we discuss the Windows dialogs in this chapter since using them usually involves conditional statements.

EXAMPLE 5.5) Windows common dialogs

In this example we introduce three of the Windows dialogs, namely the Open, Save and Font dialogs, as well as the Memo component. We also learn how to handle runtime errors in our programs.

Our program will initially display an empty Memo with four buttons (figure 5.5):

o the Load text button will fill the Memo with text from a user-specified file;
o the Save text button will save the text that we have typed into the Memo to a file specified by the user;
o the Set Font button lets the user choose a font for the text in the Memo, and
o the Clear text button clears the Memo.

Let's write the program step-by-step.

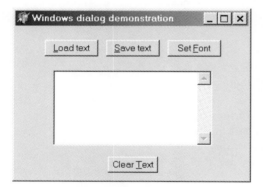

Figure 5.5 The opening form

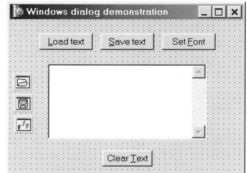

Figure 5.6 The form at design time

EX 5.5 STEP 1 Create the form

• Create the forms in figures 5.5 and 5.6 using the component property values in the table below.

The three icons that appear along the form's left edge (in design view – figure 5.6) are the Dialog components (the OpenDialog, the SaveDialog and the FontDialog) that you can find in the Dialogs tab of the Component/Tool palette.

The Memo component appears on the Standard tab of the Component/Tool palette. It can be seen as a multi-line Edit component for working with text that spans more than one line. The text is stored in the Memo's Lines property, which is very similar to the ListBox's Items property.

Component	Property	Value
Form1	Name	frmDialogDemo
	Caption	Windows dialog demonstration
Button1	Name	btnLoad
	Caption	&Load text
Button2	Name	btnSave
	Caption	&Save text
Button3	Name	btnFont
	Caption	Set &Font
Button4	Name	btnClear
	Caption	Clear &Text
Memo1	Name	memDemo
	Lines	<Blank>
	ScrollBar	ssVertical
OpenDialog1	Name	opdOpenDemo
SaveDialog1	Name	svdSaveDemo
FontDialog1	Name	fodFontDemo

- To clear the Lines property of the Memo, open the Lines property editor in the Object Inspector, delete the text that appears there and click on OK.
- Save the unit file as C05e05u and the project as C05e05p.

Visual versus non-visual components

- Without adding any program code, run the program.

Notice that the three dialog component icons are not visible when you run the program. In Delphi we distinguish between *visual* and *non-visual components*. Buttons, Labels and Memos are examples of visual components. When their Visible property is set to True (which it is by default), we can see them on the form at run time. Non-visual components do not have a Visible property and some of them (like the Timer that we discuss in Chapter 10) will never be visible to the user. A Delphi program uses non-visual components for 'behind the scenes' operations. Although a Dialog component icon is not visible on the form, our program will make the Windows dialog it represents visible when a user action requires that dialog. You'll see how this is done in the next step.

EX 5.5 STEP 2   Loading text from a file

When we have completed this program, clicking on the Load text button at run time should bring up the Windows Open dialog (figure 5.7 – the common dialogs could look slightly different, depending on your version of Windows). The user can then select a folder (directory) and the name of the file from where the text should be loaded. The required folder can be located by clicking on the little down arrow on the right-hand side of the 'Look in' input box. The files that exist in that folder appear in the ListBox from where the user can select one. The user can also type the file name directly into the File name input box.

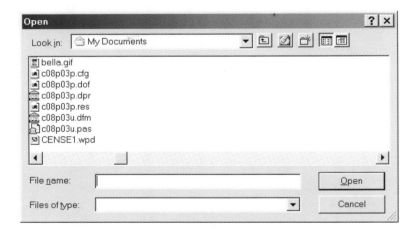

Figure 5.7 The Windows Open dialog

- If you are still in run mode, close the program to return to design mode.
- Create the following OnClick event handler for the Load text button:

```
procedure TfrmDialogDemo.btnLoadClick(Sender: TObject);
begin
  if opdOpenDemo.Execute then
    memDemo.Lines.LoadFromFile(opdOpenDemo.FileName);
end;
```

- And create the following one for the Clear text button:

```
procedure TfrmDialogDemo.btnClearClick(Sender: TObject);
begin
  memDemo.Clear;
end;
```

- Save the unit file again. Run the program and click on the Load text button. The Windows Open dialog as in figure 5.7 appears.

Because you have different files and folders on your computer, the contents of your dialog will be different.
- You can now change the folder in the 'Look in' input box and then, from the list, select a file to load into the Memo. (Click on the down arrow in the Look in input box to select the required folder.)
- Select the folder where you keep your Delphi programs and then pick one of the unit files (in other words, a file with the .pas extension) you created while working through the book. Once the name of that file appears in the File name box, click on Open. The dialog disappears and the selected file should appear in the Memo.

We could have specified c:\My Documents*.txt as the default file name in the OpenDialog's FileName property in the Object Inspector at design time (assuming this folder exists on the specified drive). This will automatically open the folder c:\My Documents\ and list all the files with the .txt extension in the dialog that appears. A default file name c:\My Documents\el*.txt will display those files with the .txt extension whose names start with 'el'. The '*' as used here is called a *wildcard*. When we include a wildcard in a file name, it means that part of the name can have any value.

How did the program activate the Open dialog and how did the contents of the file get into the Memo? Let us explain.

The Execute method

The first statement of the btnLoadClick event handler is

```
if opdOpenDemo.Execute then
```

A common dialog box opens when its Execute method is called. Here, inside the If condition, we call opdOpenDemo's Execute method. Execute returns True if the user chooses the Open button on the dialog, and False if the user chooses Cancel. Since we chose Open, Execute returned True. The dialog's FileName property gets the value that the user typed into the File name input box. Because Execute returns True, the Then part of the If statement is executed, namely

```
memDemo.Lines.LoadFromFile(opdOpenDemo.FileName);
```

The LoadFromFile method loads the contents of the file whose name appears in brackets into the Lines property of memDemo. In this case the required file name is obtained from the FileName property of opdOpenDemo.

Here we see that the If condition can also be a function call, as long as the function returns a Boolean value to the program. (We look at functions and function calls in Chapter 13.)

Should the user select Cancel on the dialog, opdOpenDemo.Execute returns False. The If statement has no Else part and so the event handler takes no action.

EX 5.5 STEP 3 Opening a file that doesn't exist

- Clear the Memo component by clicking on 'Clear text' and then click on the Load text button again.
- Now type a file name that does not exist into the File name input box of the Open dialog (for example, type 'myfile.txt').
- Make sure that the file name you type does not appear in the list of files and then click on 'Open'.
- Depending on whether Delphi is set up to 'Stop on Delphi Exceptions' or not, one of two things will happen now:
  1 A message such as that in figure 5.8 appears and clicking on OK takes you out of the event handler.
  2 If you did not change Delphi's Debugger Options in Chapter 4 to continue when a Delphi exception occurs, a debugger exception notification message such as that in figure 5.9.a or figure 5.9.b appears. (To set up Delphi to continue when an exception occurs in Delphi 4 to Delphi 7, choose Tools | Debugger Options... on the menu and deselect 'Stop on Delphi Exceptions' in the 'Language Exceptions' tab. In Delphi 8, choose Tools | Options... on the menu, select 'Language

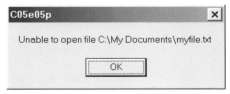

Figure 5.8 Delphi's exception-handling message

Exceptions' (under 'Debugger Options' and 'Borland .NET Debugger') and uncheck the option 'Stop on Language Exceptions'.) Click on OK and then press <F9> to resume program execution.

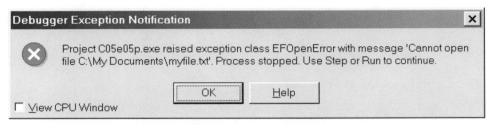

Figure 5.9.a Debugger exception notification message generated by Delphi 6

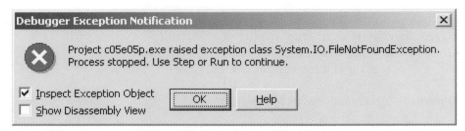

Figure 5.9.b Debugger exception notification message generated by Delphi 8

What happens here? We say that Delphi 'raises an exception'. In other words, an error occurs when Delphi tries to open a file that doesn't exist. When the Debugger Options is set to bypass the debugger, the message in figure 5.8 is displayed and Delphi takes us out of the event handler. Otherwise the message in figure 5.9.a or 5.9.b is displayed first.

EX 5.5   STEP 4   Exception handling

The statement where an exception could occur is in the call to the LoadFromFile method of memDemo.Lines. We can override Delphi's default exception handling by wrapping this statement in a Try block so that our program handles the exception. This would give us the opportunity to display our own error messages and to perform additional operations that might be necessary when an exception has occurred.

- To see how we do this, change the Load text button's event handler to the following:

```
procedure TfrmDialogDemo.btnLoadClick(Sender: TObject);
begin
  if opdOpenDemo.Execute then
    try
      memDemo.Lines.LoadFromFile(opdOpenDemo.FileName);
    except
      ShowMessage('Error loading file ' + opdOpenDemo.FileName);
    end;
end;
```

- Save the unit and project files again and then run the program.
- If you now specify the name of a non-existing file name, a Message box like the one in figure 5.10 appears.
- Clicking OK will end the event handler so that the user can start over. Except for the different wording of the message, our exception handling does exactly what Delphi's built-in exception handling would do.

Figure 5.10 Program-generated error message

The try...except statement

The try...except...end statement works as follows. Delphi executes the statements that follow the `try` keyword. If an exception is raised by one of these statements, Delphi jumps to the statement following the `except` keyword. These statements can then respond appropriately to the exception that occurred. If no exception is raised by the Try block, Delphi skips the Except block and continues with the statement after `end`.

In our event handler there is only one statement in the Try block, namely the call to the LoadFromFile method. If an exception occurs, we know there must have been a problem opening the specified file. Therefore, in the Except block we display a message to the user saying that there was an error loading the file. To do this we call the ShowMessage procedure that displays the string given in brackets in a simple Message dialog box.

Exception handling can become very complex and we return to exception handling in more detail later in this book

EX 5.5 STEP 5 Saving text to a file

When the user clicks on Save text, the Windows Save As dialog should appear in which the user can specify a folder and a file name for storing the text in memDemo.
- Create the following OnClick event handler for the Save text button that does this:

```
procedure TfrmDialogDemo.btnSaveClick(Sender: TObject);
begin
  if svdSaveDemo.Execute then
    memDemo.Lines.SaveToFile(svdSaveDemo.FileName);
end;
```

- Save the unit and project files again and run the program.
- Type any text into the Memo and click on the Save text button. The Windows 'Save As' dialog should appear. In figure 5.11 you can see that we opened the Delphi files folder and typed 'Elephant.txt' in the File name input box.
- When you have typed the name of your choice in the File name box, click on Save. The text in the Memo is now saved on disk.

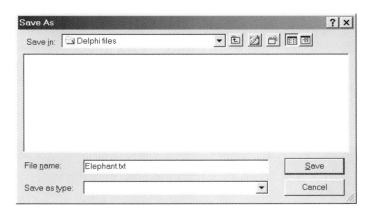

Figure 5.11 The Save As dialog

How did our program make this happen?

The If statement – **if** svdSaveDemo.Execute **then** – opens the Save As dialog and the Execute method waits for the user to click on a button. Execute returns True if the user chooses the Save button on the dialog, and False if the user chooses Cancel. The dialog's FileName property is set according to the user's input (ours is c:\Delphi files\Elephant.txt). When you click on Save, Execute returns True and the Then part of the If statement, namely

```
memDemo.Lines.SaveToFile(svdSaveDemo.FileName);
```

is executed. Using the SaveToFile command, this statement saves the lines in memDemo to the file whose name is specified in brackets – in this case the file specified by svdSaveDemo's FileName property.

What will happen if you specify a file that already exists in the Save As dialog? If you save to a file that already exists, the contents of the file will simply be overwritten by the text you typed in the memo. This will be done without any warning. As an exercise, extend the program to check if the file exists and if it does, display a message informing the user that the file already exists and will be overwritten (Hint: use the FileExists function to see if a given file exists).

EX 5.5 STEP 6   Exception handling in the Save text event handler

What kind of exception can the SaveToFile method raise? When saving text to a file, an exception will be raised if the disk is full or if the file you are trying to write to is currently 'locked' by another application. To show how a file can be locked, open a text file (such as Elephant.txt) in MS Word or any other word processor. While the file is open in Word run the program we are writing and try to save some text to Elephant.txt from this application. An error message will be displayed.

To handle this exception, change the event handler as follows:

```
procedure TfrmDialogDemo.btnSaveClick(Sender: TObject);
begin
  if svdSaveDemo.Execute then
    try
      memDemo.Lines.SaveToFile(svdSaveDemo.FileName);
    except
      ShowMessage ('Error writing to file' + svdSaveDemo.FileName);
    end;
end;
```

With Elephant.txt still open in Word, run the program and try to save some text to Elephant.txt again. The error message 'Error writing to file...' should appear. Click on OK and without exiting your program, switch to Word and close the Elephant.txt file. Return to your program and try to save text to Elephant.txt again. This time it should work. In this way, the Try… Except statement gives the programmer the ability to program appropriate corrective action in the case of an exception.

EX 5.5 STEP 7   Changing the Memo's font

To change the font of the text in the Memo component, we use the Set Font button to display the Windows Font selection dialog (figure 5.12). We do this with the following event handler:

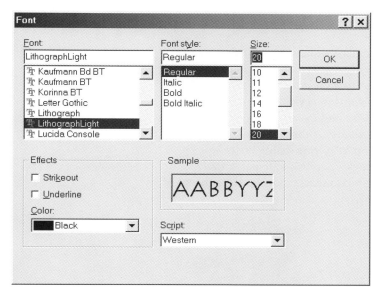

Figure 5.12 The Font dialog

```
procedure TfrmDialogDemo.btnFontClick(Sender: TObject);
begin
  if fodFontDemo.Execute then
    memDemo.Font := fodFontDemo.Font;
end;
```

- Create this event handler, save the program and run it.
- Type some text into the Memo and click on the Set Font button. The Windows Font dialog appears.
- Choose any font that is available in the font list. You can change its style and size and see the result in the Sample window.
- When you are satisfied with your choice, click OK.

This sets the dialog's Font property according to your selections. Here the statement

```
if fodFontDemo.Execute then
  memDemo.Font := fodFontDemo.Font;
```

Figure 5.13 Setting the Memo's font

opens the Font dialog. If we choose OK, the Execute method returns True, otherwise it returns False. If True, memDemo's Font property is set to the dialog's Font property. Setting the font options, as shown in figure 5.12 above, changed the appearance of our text as shown in figure 5.13.

Loading and saving text in Memos and ListBoxes

In this example we used the LoadFromFile and SaveToFile methods to save the contents of the Lines property to a specified file on disk. These methods do not only apply to the Lines property of the Memo component. We can, for example, also use them with the Items property of a ListBox component.

REVIEW

In this chapter we looked at Delphi's If statement which we can use to choose between two possible routes of execution in a program. The If statement tests a condition and based on whether it is True or False, a program branches to one of two sets of program statements. The If condition is written as a Boolean expression that can take the value True or False and usually involves one or more relational and/or logical operators. We also discussed the Boolean data type.

In addition we learned how the common Windows dialog boxes – specifically the Open, Save As and Font dialogs – can be made part of a Delphi program. While looking at the use of dialog boxes we introduced the concept of 'exception handling'.

IMPORTANT CONCEPTS

Fundamental programming concepts

Boolean data type: A variable declared as this data type can take the values True or False.

Boolean expression: An expression that evaluates to True or False. This can be a Boolean variable, a Boolean constant (ie True or False) or any combination of these using relational operators (eg <, >, =) and/or the logical operators (and, or, not).

Comparing strings: We can compare two or more alphabetical strings using the relational operators to determine which comes first (ie is smaller). If we compare two letters of the same case, the one that comes first in the alphabet is smaller. With longer strings, the individual letters are compared one-by-one from left to right. All uppercase letters come before lowercase letters.

Compound statement: A group of statements enclosed in a begin…end block. In this chapter we used compound statements to specify more than one statement in the Then or Else part of an if... then... else statement.

Exception: An error that occurs at run-time. For example, if the user tries to open a file that does exist, Delphi will raise an exception.

Exception handling: Delphi provides default exception handling which includes the printing of an error message. We use the try...except statement to create our own exception handling (see New Delphi features below).

if...then...else statement: This statement directs a program into one of two possible routes. The format is

```
if BooleanExpression then
   Statement1
else
   Statement2;
```

where `Statement1` and `Statement2` represent any simple or compound Delphi statements. If `BooleanExpression` is True, `Statement1` is executed; otherwise `Statement2` is executed.

if...then statement: This statement lets the program execute a part of the program (`Statement1`) only if a certain condition (`BooleanExpression`) is True. Its format is

```
if BooleanExpression then
   Statement1;
```

Logical operators: The three logical operators covered here are and, or and not. We can combine two Boolean expressions with the and operator or the or operator to form a compound Boolean expression.

Order of precedence (in Boolean expressions): If a Boolean expression includes more than one logical and/or relational operator, Delphi uses the following order of precedence when evaluating the expression:

1   Bracketed expressions
2   The not operator
3   and
4   or
5   relational operators (>, <, =, etc).

Relational operators: The relational operators are >, <, =, ≤, ≥ and <>. We use them in a Boolean expression to compare two operands.

Programming environment

CharCase property: We set this property of an Edit or Memo component to ecUpperCase when we require the user's input in uppercase format. Its default value is ecNormal and it can also take the value ecLowerCase.

Visual and non-visual components: We distinguish between visual and non-visual components. Buttons, Labels and Memos are examples of visual components. When their Visible property is set to True (which it is by default), we can see them at run time. Non-visual components do not have a Visible property and are therefore not visible to the user. We use non-visual components for 'behind the scenes' operations. The Timer and the Dialogs are examples of non-visual components.

NEW DELPHI FEATURES

Functions	
LowerCase	A function that converts any string argument consisting of alphabetical characters to the equivalent string consisting only of lowercase characters.
UpperCase	A function that converts any string argument consisting of alphabetical characters to the equivalent string consisting only of uppercase characters.

Delphi Pascal constructs	
try...except	We use the try...except statement to handle exceptions. The code that we want executed appears in the Try block. Any exception that this code raises will cause the execution to jump to the Except block where the code for handling that exception resides. The Except block can consist of any number of Delphi statements.

TMemo

Properties	Lines	Contains the lines of text that are displayed in the Memo.
	ScrollBars	Determines whether the Memo has a vertical and/or a horizontal scrollbar or not. Its possible values are ssVertical, ssHorizontal, ssBoth and ssNone (default).
	WordWrap	If set to True, words will be displayed on the next line if they do not fit into a line.
Methods	Lines. LoadFromFile	The LoadFromFile method loads lines of text from a text file (whose name we specify in brackets) into the Lines property of the Memo. Each line in the file becomes a string displayed in the Memo. For example: `memDemo.Lines.LoadFromFile('c:\myfile.txt');` will load the lines of text in myfile.txt into memDemo's Lines property. Note that the same method can be used to populate a ListBox's Items property.
	Lines. SaveToFile	The SaveToFile method saves the contents of a Memo's Lines property to a specified file on disk. Each string displayed in the Memo becomes a line in the file. For example: `memDemo.Lines.SaveToFile('c:\myfile.txt');` will save the contents of memDemo's Lines property to the file named myfile.txt. Note that the same method can be used to save the contents of a ListBox's Items property to a file.
Prefix	mem...	
Use	Gives the user space to type text of more than one line.	

TOpenDialog

Properties	FileName	Contains the name of the last file selected.
Methods	Execute	Opens the dialog at run time. Execute returns True when the user makes a selection and clicks the Open button. It returns False when the user chooses the Close or Cancel button.
Prefix	opd...	
Use	Displays the Windows common dialog for selecting and opening a file. It appears when the program calls the Execute method. If the user clicks on Open, it returns the selected file name.	

TSaveDialog

Properties	FileName	Contains the name of the last file selected.
Methods	Execute	Opens the dialog at run time. Execute returns True when the user makes a selection and clicks the Save button. It returns False when the user chooses the Close or Cancel button.
Prefix	svd...	
Use	Displays the Windows common dialog for saving a file under a specified name. It appears when the program calls the Execute method. The user clicks on Save to write the file to disk.	

TFontDialog		
Properties	Font	Contains the name of the currently selected font.
Methods	Execute	Opens the dialog at run time. Execute returns True when the user makes a selection and clicks the OK button. It returns False when the user chooses the Close or Cancel button.
Prefix	fod...	
Use		Displays the Windows common dialog for selecting a font type and style. It appears when the program calls the Execute method. When the user clicks OK, it returns the selected font in the Font property.

PROBLEMS

PROBLEM 5.1) If statements

- Write down If statements to do each of the following tasks:
  1 If the variable Age has any value from 13 to 19, set lblMessage's Caption to Teenager!.
  2 If the Boolean variable YearPassed is True, or the integer variable Mileage is greater than or equal to 25 000, set the Boolean variable ServiceDue to True.
  3 If the Boolean variable EatHealthy is False and the Boolean variable Smoker is True, set lblWarning's Caption to High Risk.

PROBLEM 5.2) Evaluating If statements

Suppose we have the following declarations:

```
var
  X, Y   : integer;
  Word   : string;
  Check  : boolean;
```

- Let X have the value 6, Y the value 7, and Word the value 'Squeeky'. Write down the result of each of the following code fragments:

```
1   Check := (Length(Word) = Y);
    if Check then
      lblMessage.Caption := 'Bright lights'
    else
      lblMessage.Caption := 'Big city';

2   Check := (X >= Y) or not(Word = 'Wobble');
    if Check then
      if X = 6 then
        lblMessage.Caption := 'How about that?'
      else
        lblMessage.Caption := 'Bad luck.';

3   Check := (Word <> IntToStr(Y));
    if Check then
      lblMessage.Caption := 'Word is not 7.';
```

PROBLEM 5.3) Calculating maximum heart rate

Many athletes use their maximum heart rate (in beats per minute) to calculate different levels of training. One way of estimating an individual's maximum heart rate is to use the following formulae:
- For males: maximum heart rate = 214 – (0.8 * age)
- For females: maximum heart rate = 209 – (0.7 * age)

Write a program which allows the user to enter their gender (using radio buttons) and their age. Your program should then calculate and display an estimate of the maximum heart rate using the formulae above.

PROBLEM 5.4) Course result

Write a program which reads in from the user a mark obtained for a course (as a percentage) and in response to a button click displays one of the following results:
- *Distinction* for a mark of 75% and above
- *Pass* for a mark from 50% to below 75%
- *Supplementary* for a mark from 45% to below 50%
- *Fail* for a mark below 45%

Your program should also check for invalid input (values below 0 or above 100).

PROBLEM 5.5) Calculating discount

The *SupaDupa* clothing store has a special offer. For any purchase worth R200.00 or more, they give a 50% discount. The discount on all other items is 10%. The discount must be calculated before 14% sales tax is added. Each customer is allowed to buy only one item. The user interface appears in figure 5.14.
- Show the discount amount and the final price with tax added.

Figure 5.14 Calculating the discount on clothing sales

PROBLEM 5.6) Setting colours with the Color dialog

- Add a Color dialog from the Dialogs tab on the Component palette to the program in example 5.5 and name it cdlColourDemo.
- Also add a Colour button (btnColour) and write the event handler for the button so that it opens the Windows Color dialog. The user can select any colour on the dialog and if he or she clicks OK, the form's background must change to that colour.

Although we haven't used this dialog in this chapter, you should be able to do this without difficulty as the Color dialog is used in the same way as the other dialogs that we have discussed.

CHAPTER 6

Nested and multiple conditions

PURPOSE OF THIS CHAPTER

In Chapter 5 we introduced conditional execution with if...then...else statements. So far we have used these statements to choose between two alternative paths in a program. Often, however, the choice lies between more than two alternative sets of code. It can also happen that one or both of the alternatives in an if...then...else statement involve choosing between two further alternatives.

In this chapter we will solve problems such as these using nested if...then...else statements, that is If statements which appear in the Then or Else parts of another if...then...else statement. We will also look at problems with multiple alternative conditions that we can solve with the Case statement – a different Delphi programming construct for handling conditional execution.

While learning to use nested If statements and the Case statement, we'll also look at the Message box and the Input box dialogs, and do some string manipulation.

EXAMPLE 6.1) A nested If statement

In example 5.3 of Chapter 5 we wrote a program for animal classification. The If statements in the OnClick event handler for btnClassify looked as follows:

```
1 if IsMammal then
2   lblClass.Caption := 'Mammal';
3 if IsReptile then
4   lblClass.Caption := 'Reptile';
5 if not(IsMammal) and not(IsReptile) then
6   lblClass.Caption := 'Unknown';
```

This is not the best way to solve the problem. Suppose IsMammal is True, then the condition of the first of the three If statements (line 1) is True and the Caption is set to 'Mammal'. Ideally the program should now just skip over the remaining two If statements in lines 3 to 6 (since only one of the three conditions can be true at a time). As it stands here, however, the program will always test all three conditions. To get rid of this unnecessary processing we replace the three If statements with the following If structure that uses a nested If statement:

```
1 if IsMammal then
2   lblClass.Caption := 'Mammal'
3 else
4   if IsReptile then
5     lblClass.Caption := 'Reptile'
6   else
7     lblClass.Caption := 'Unknown';
```

Now, if IsMammal is True, the first Then part (line 2) is executed and the program jumps out of the If statement without any further testing. If IsMammal is False, the first Else part (lines 4 to 7) is executed. This consists of another if...then...else statement. We say the second if...then...else is nested in the Else part of the first if...then...else. In the nested if...then...else we check whether IsReptile is True. If it is, the Then part (line 5) is executed, otherwise the remaining possibility is covered by the nested Else part (line 7).

- Open the project of example 5.3 and rewrite the btnClassifyClick event handler so that it uses these nested Ifs.
- Save the unit and project files as C06e01u and C06e01p and run the program. It should run exactly as before, but we now have a more efficient program.

The layout of nested If statements

Although the way in which nested If statements are laid out doesn't influence how Delphi interprets them, the layout is important for the readability of the code. Consider the following nested If structure:

```
1 if Condition1 then
2    if Condition2 then
3       Statement1
4    else
5       Statement2
6 else
7    Statement3;
```

The Then part of the first if...then...else statement contains a nested if...then...else statement (lines 2 to 5). The rule for determining which If an Else belongs to is:

an Else belongs to the nearest If preceding it which does not already have an Else part.

There are two If statements and two Else parts in the given statement. The first Else (line 4) belongs to the If directly preceding it, so here it belongs to the If in line 2. The second Else (line 6) belongs to the first If preceding it that does not already have an Else part. The nested If (line 2) already has an Else part, and so the second Else belongs to the If in line 1. Note that `Statement2` is not followed by a semicolon – remember the syntax rule which says that a semicolon may not appear before the word `else`.

The way we laid out the statement reflects its interpretation. Delphi, however, will interpret the following code in exactly the same way:

```
if Condition1 then if Condition2 then Statement1 else Statement2 else Statement3;
```

Consider the following If statement:

```
1 if Condition1 then
2    if Condition2 then
3       Statement1
4    else
5       Statement2;
```

Here we have one Else part. Applying the rule tells us that it goes with the first If preceding it, which here is in line 2. Therefore the If statement in line 1 has only a Then part with an if...then...else statement nested in it. The way we laid out the statement emphasizes that the Else belongs to the inner If statement.

If we want the Else part to belong to the outer If, we must place the nested if...then statement between `begin` and `end`:

```
1 if Condition1 then
2 begin
3    if Condition2 then
4       Statement1;
5 end
6 else
7    Statement2;
```

Now the `Then` part of the first If consists only of the compound statement between `begin` and `end` (lines 2 to 5). Why couldn't we just put a semicolon after `Statement1` (in the previous If structure) to indicate that the second If ends there? The Delphi syntax rule that says we may never use a semicolon in front of Else since it will cause a compile error.

The rules for using semicolons in nested If statements are the same as for simple If statements:

Rule 1   Do not use a semicolon after the word Then.

Rule 2   Do not use a semicolon directly before the word Else (in other words, do not end the statement in the Then part of the If statement with a semicolon).

Rule 3   Do not use a semicolon after the word Else.

There is no restriction on the depth to which If statements may be nested, but the depth of nesting should not make the code difficult to read.

Sometimes we get a series of nested If statements where every Else part consists of a nested if...then...else statement. We can then use the following layout:

```
if Condition1 then
   Statement1
else if Condition2 then
   Statement2
else if Condition3 then
   Statement3
else
   Statement4;
```

We call this type of nested If structure a *multiple alternative If statement*.

EXAMPLE 6.2 Calculating commission on sales

CyberSales software distributors have come up with a scheme to motivate their sales representatives. We must write a program which calculates the commission that a sales representative earns on her monthly sales. The form layout is given in figure 6.1 and the commission is calculated according to the following rates:

Monthly sales (S)	Commission
S > R80 000	40%
R40 000 < S <= R 80 000	20%
S <= R40 000	10%

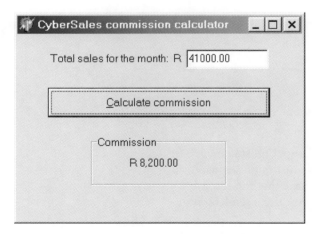

Figure 6.1 Form layout for the CyberSales program

A first attempt

Without looking further, try to program a solution to this problem on your own. It is through practise that you will gain the experience and confidence to tackle new problems. When you run the program, jot down any errors that you made. Even with years of programming experience, every programmer still makes mistakes. What you should gain through experience is the skill of how to approach problems and the ability to fix errors more quickly. When you are happy that your program works as it should, compare your answer to the answer given and see if there are any improvements that you would like to make. If you get stuck, do not be despondent. The process of trying to do something and getting stuck is a more valuable learning experience than simply looking at the answer.

EX 6.2   Planning

Our program should do the following:
o   Get the user's input (the sales amount) from the Edit box and convert it to a real value.
o   Calculate the commission on the sales amount.
   There are three categories here:
   - sales of more than R80 000,
   - sales of R40 000 and less, and
   - sales over R40 000 up to R80 000.
o   Convert the commission amount to a string value and display it in the Label's Caption.

In the second step above a simple if...then...else statement will not be adequate. We will need more than one If statement where one will probably be nested in the other. In designing this If structure we have to be careful that we cover all the cases in a way that will ensure correct calculation of the commission. As you will see in step 3 of the solution below, it is quite easy to write nested If statements that seem correct but which give incorrect results in some cases.

EX 6.2   Testing

The following are sample test cases which we can use to test our final program:

Input Value (Sales)	Expected output (Commission earned)
80000.00	R16 000.00
81000.00	R32 400.00
40000.00	R4 000.00
41000.00	R8 200.00
99000.00	R39 600.00
55o00.oo	Error: invalid input

The last test case has the letter o instead of the number 0 so that we can see how our program behaves when given invalid input.

EX 6.2 STEP 1 Creating the form

- Create the form using the following components and properties:

Component	Property	Value
Form1	Name	frmCommission
	Caption	CyberSales commission calculator
Button1	Name	btnCalculate
	Caption	&Calculate commission
Edit1	Name	edtSales
	Text	\<Blank>
GroupBox	Name	gpbCommission
	Caption	Commission
Label1	Name	lblSales
	Caption	Total sales for the month: R
Label2	Name	lblCommission
	Caption	\<Blank>

- Save the unit file and the project as C06e02u and C06e02p respectively.

EX 6.2 STEP 2 Converting the input to a real value

The user supplies the sales amount in the edtSales Edit box which will give us the amount in string format. Before we can use this input as a double value, we have to convert it to a number of type double. Working on paper away from the computer, write down the statement that stores this converted value in the double variable Sales. This statement is

```
Sales := StrToFloat(edtSales.Text);
```

We use the StrToFloat function to convert the string to a double value.

EX 6.2 STEP 3 A nested If statement

Now assume the sales amount is known and stored in a double variable Sales. Still working on paper, write down the If statement to calculate the correct value for Commission (a double variable) according to the table given in the problem description. We have three cases to test for: Sales greater than R80 000.00, Sales greater than R40 000.00 but less than or equal to R80 000.00, and Sales less than or equal to R40 000.00. The If statement looks as follows:

```
if Sales > 80000.00 then
   Commission := Sales * 0.40
else if Sales > 40000.00 then
   Commission := Sales * 0.20
else
   Commission := Sales * 0.10;
```

If the sales are greater than R80 000.00, we calculate the commission at 40%. If not, we must still decide between the remaining two possibilities. For this we include a nested If in the Else part of the outer If statement. This nested If tests whether the sales are greater than R40 000.00 and acts accordingly. Working through the code by hand, we get the results displayed in the third column of the following table:

Input (Sales)	Expected output	Value of Commission (calculated by hand)
80000.00	R16 000.00	R16 000.00
81000.00	R32 400.00	R32 400.00
40000.00	R4 000.00	R4 000.00
41000.00	R8 200.00	R8 200.00
99000.00	R39 600.00	R39 600.00
55ooo.oo	Error: invalid input	Should produce an error message because we are comparing a string with a number and we are using the string in an arithmetic calculation.

Are the Else parts important? For example, would the following series of non-nested If statements be an acceptable alternative to the above If structure?

```
1 if Sales > 80000.00 then
2    Commission := Sales * 0.40;
3 if Sales > 40000.00 then
4    Commission := Sales * 0.20;
5 if Sales <= 40000.00 then
6    Commission := Sales * 0.10;
```

• Let's work out the answers for our test cases using these If statements.

Input (Sales)	Expected output	Output produced by the series of If statements
80000.00	R16 000.00	R16 000.00 ✓
81000.00	R32 400.00	R16 200.00 ✗
40000.00	R4 000.00	R4 000.00 ✓
41000.00	R8 200.00	R8 200.00 ✓
99000.00	R39 600.00	R19 800.00 ✗
55ooo.oo	Error: invalid input	Should produce an error message.

Why do R81 000.00 and R99 000.00 give wrong answers? Let's go through the If statements for the sales value of 81 000.00:

- ○ `Sales > 80000.00` (line 1) is True and therefore the first If statement calculates the commission as 32 400.00 (which is correct).
- ○ Then the second If condition (`Sales > 40000.00` in line 3) is evaluated and is also True, since 81 000.00 is greater than 40 000.00.
- ○ Now line 4 calculates the commission as 16 200.00 and this value overwrites the previous (correct) value of `Commission`. Any value greater than 80 000.00 is also greater than 40 000.00, so all input greater than 80 000.00 will give the wrong result. Since the second and third If statements are not nested in the Else part of the first If statement, Delphi will always test them as well.

This shows how important it is to test a program with a complete set of test data that tests every possible route the program may follow.

The order of conditions

How about the following alternative? Will it work correctly?

```
1 if Sales > 40000.00 then
2    Commission := Sales * 0.20
3 else if Sales > 80000.00 then
4    Commission := Sales * 0.40
5 else
6    Commission := Sales * 0.10;
```

Applying this If structure to our test data will show that it gives the wrong output for 81 000.00 and 99 000.00. If the sales are less than R80 000.00, it works fine; but if the sales are higher than R80 000.00, the If condition in line 1 (`Sales > 40000.00`) will be True and the commission will be calculated at 20% instead of 40%. If `Sales` is greater than R80 000.00, processing will never branch to the Else If part in lines 3 and 4. This shows that the order in which you place your conditions in a nested If structure is very important.

EX 6.2 STEP 4 Displaying the output

To display the commission we have to convert it to string format. Write down the statement that converts `Commission` to a string and assigns it to the Label's Caption property. The statement is

```
lblCommission.Caption := FloatToStrF(Commission, ffCurrency, 10, 2);
```

Here we use the ffCurrency format. This will automatically place the currency symbol that appears on the Currency page of your computer's Regional Settings in front of the converted number. You can check (and change) the currency symbol by selecting Start | Settings | Control Panel | Regional Settings in Windows or Regional and Language settings in Windows XP. Since we use 'R' for Rand, this is the currency symbol that you will see on our forms.

EX 6.2 STEP 5 Creating the event handler

The user will enter the monthly sales and then click on the Calculate button to see the commission earned. The only event handler needed in this program is therefore the btnCalculateClick event handler.

- Complete this event handler now using the results of steps 2, 3 and 4. For now you may assume that the user will always enter valid input. Here is our solution:

```
procedure TfrmCommission.btnCalculateClick(Sender: TObject);
var
  Sales, Commission: double;
begin
  Sales := StrToFloat(edtSales.Text);
  if Sales > 80000.00 then
    Commission := Sales * 0.40
  else if Sales > 40000.00 then
    Commission := Sales * 0.20
  else
    Commission := Sales * 0.10;
  lblCommission.Caption := FloatToStrF(Commission, ffCurrency, 10, 2);
end;
```

- Save the unit file again and test this against the table of test data. All output values should be as required.

Notice what happens when you enter an invalid number (such as 50ooo or 50 000). Delphi displays an error message box with an OK button. If you click on OK, Delphi returns to the main form and you are able to correct the input value and try again. Later in this chapter we will intercept this exception (using a try...catch) to provide our own error recovery.

EXAMPLE 6.3) Improving nested Ifs

SafeSure Security Services want to recruit young single people who are between and including the ages of 18 and 26 years and who have passed grade 12. Write a program that obtains the relevant information from a candidate. If the person fulfils the requirements, the program must display the message 'Good candidate'. Otherwise it must display 'Not suitable'.

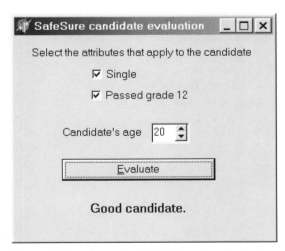

Figure 6.2 Form layout for the SafeSure Security Services program

- Create the form using the following component properties:

Component	Property	Value
Form1	Name	frmEvaluate
	Caption	SafeSure candidate evaluation
Button1	Name	btnEvaluate
	Caption	&Evaluate
Checkbox1	Name	chkSingle
	Caption	Single
Checkbox2	Name	chkGrade12
	Caption	Passed grade 12
SpinEdit1	Name	sedAge
	Value	20
	MaxValue	100
	MinValue	15
Label1	Name	lblSelect
	Caption	Select the attributes that apply to the candidate
Label2	Name	lblAge
	Caption	Candidate's age
Label3	Name	lblEvaluate
	Caption	<Blank>

The CheckBox component

In this program we use CheckBoxes to determine whether the candidate has passed grade 12 and is single. Since you are already familiar with RadioButtons, you should find this easy. We use the CheckBox component to present a Yes/No or True/False option to the user, particularly where more than one choice at a time is available from a group of choices. For example, in the figure above, 'Single' and 'Passed matric' are both selected at the same time. You will remember that you can select only one of a set of RadioButtons grouped together at a time. As with the RadioButton component, a CheckBox component has a Checked property which is True if the box is selected; otherwise it is False.

If the user clicks on the Evaluate button, the program must check whether the candidate is suitable and display an appropriate message. To do this the btnEvaluateClick event handler includes nested If statements. Three attributes must be tested of which the user indicates two with CheckBoxes. There are two ways to test the status of a CheckBox in an If statement. Using chkSingle as an example, you can either have

```
if chkSingle.Checked = True then ...
```

or

```
if chkSingle.Checked then ...
```

Since the Checked property has a Boolean value, the second condition is a valid Boolean expression. We use the shorter option.

- Create the event handler for btnEvaluateClick so that it matches the following:

```
procedure TfrmEvaluate.btnEvaluateClick(Sender: TObject);
var
  Age: integer;
begin
  Age := sedAge.Value;
  if chkSingle.Checked then
    if chkGrade12.Checked then
      if (Age >= 18) and (Age <= 26) then
        lblEvaluate.Caption := 'Good candidate.'
      else
        lblEvaluate.Caption := 'Not suitable.'
    else
      lblEvaluate.Caption := 'Not suitable.'
  else
    lblEvaluate.Caption := 'Not suitable.';
end;
```

- Save the unit file as C06e03u and the project as C06e03p and run the program.

A better solution

Although this works, it is not a very good solution. Looking at the three Else parts, we see they are identical. Here is one way to get rid of this duplication of code:

```
procedure TfrmEvaluate.btnEvaluateClick(Sender: TObject);
var
  Age: Integer;
begin
  Age := sedAge.Value;
  lblEvaluate.Caption := 'Not suitable.';
  if chkSingle.Checked then
    if chkGrade12.Checked then
      if (Age >= 18) and (Age <= 26) then
        lblEvaluate.Caption := 'Good candidate.';
end;
```

We start by setting lblEvaluate's Caption to 'Not suitable.'. Its value will change to 'Good candidate.' only if all the If conditions are True, so we can safely omit the Else parts.

Further improvement

Nested If statements with this format (where each Then part consists of an If statement and either there are no Else parts, or all the Else parts are the same) can be simplified using the logical operators we introduced in Chapter 5. We can rewrite the If structure as follows:

```
if chkSingle.Checked and chkGrade12.Checked and (Age >= 18)
                                            and (Age <= 26) then
  lblEvaluate.Caption := 'Good candidate.'
else
  lblEvaluate.Caption := 'Not suitable.';
```

Yet another alternative is to use a Boolean variable to store the suitability and then use this variable in the If statement. This improves the readability of the If statement.

```
Suitable := chkSingle.Checked and chkGrade12.Checked and (Age >= 18)
                                            and (Age <= 26);
if Suitable then
  lblEvaluate.Caption := 'Good candidate.'
else
  lblEvaluate.Caption := 'Not suitable.';
```

The complete event handler including these changes is then:

```
procedure TfrmEvaluate.btnEvaluateClick(Sender: TObject);
var
  Age: integer;
  Suitable: boolean;
begin
  Age := sedAge.Value;
  Suitable := chkSingle.Checked and chkGrade12.Checked
              and (Age >= 18) and (Age <= 26);
  if Suitable then
    lblEvaluate.Caption := 'Good candidate.'
  else
    lblEvaluate.Caption := 'Not suitable.';
end;
```

- Save the unit file again and test the program with different input values.

The Case statement

The second type of decision structure used in Delphi is the Case statement. Although we can solve any decision problem in a program with an If structure, Case statements provide a tidy way of dealing with certain multiple alternative structures.

In a multiple alternative If structure only one of a number of alternative options is chosen according to the evaluation of one or more Boolean expressions. When the Boolean expressions in all of the If statements test the value of the same variable (or component property) and the variable is of ordinal type (such as an integer or a character), a Case statement is a more suitable structure for solving the problem. Let's look at an example of a Case statement.

EXAMPLE 6.4) A bursary scheme

Gauteng Virtual University has a bursary scheme for first year BCom students. It works as follows. If a student obtained 90% or higher in the final school examination, she gets R10 000.00. If she obtained from 75% to 89%, and she passed either Accounting or Economics, she gets R8 000.00. If she obtained more than 74% but passed neither Accounting nor Economics, she gets R5 000.00. If she obtained less than 75%, but her mark is 60% or more, and she passed Accounting, she gets R3 000.00. Otherwise no bursary is awarded.

• Write a program that reads the student's average mark (an integer), determines whether or not she passed Accounting and/or Economics and then displays a message showing the bursary amount.

• Use the screen layout given in figure 6.3.

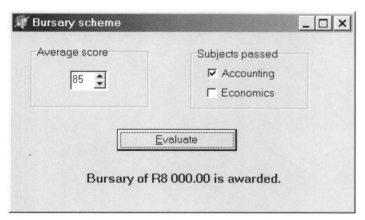

Figure 6.3 After the user has supplied input and clicked the Evaluate button

EX 6.4   Planning

By summarizing how the bursaries are awarded we can get a good idea of what the solution should look like:

o   If mark ≥ 90% award R10 000.00.
o   If mark is 75% to 89% and passed Accounting or Economics, award R8 000.00.
o   If mark is 75% to 89% and passed neither Accounting nor Economics, award R5 000.00.
o   If mark is 60% to 74% and passed Accounting, award R3 000.00.
o   Anything else gets nothing.

We can implement these conditions with a series of If statements that looks something like

```
if (Mark >= 90) then
  Amount := 'R 10 000.00'
else if (Mark >= 75) and (Mark <= 89) and (PassedAcc or PassedEcon)
then
  :
  :
else
  Amount := 'R 0.00';
```

The conditions all depend on the value of Mark and Mark is an integer (an ordinal type). We therefore rather solve this problem with a Case statement.

EX 6.4   Testing

After completing the program, we have to make sure our program gives the right answer for any possible input. We've set up the following test cases against which to test the program:

Score	Accounting	Economics	Expected output
95%	✓		R10 000.00 is awarded
58%	✓	✓	No bursary awarded
80%	✓	✓	R8 000.00 is awarded
80%			R5 000.00 is awarded
63%	✓		R3 000.00 is awarded
63%			No bursary awarded

EX 6.4 STEP 1   Creating the form

- Create the form using the following table:

Component	Property	Value
Form1	Name Caption	frmBursary Bursary scheme
Button1	Name Caption	btnEvaluate &Evaluate
GroupBox1	Name Caption	gpbScore Average score
GroupBox2	Name Caption	gpbSubjects Subjects passed
SpinEdit1 (in gpbScore)	Name Value	sedAverage 0
CheckBox1 (in gpbSubjects)	Name Caption	chkAccounting Accounting
CheckBox2 (in gpbSubjects)	Name Caption	chkEconomics Economics
Label1	Name Caption	lblAmount <Blank>

- Save the unit file and the project in C06e04u and C06e04p respectively.

EX 6.4 STEP 2   A simplified version using a Case statement

Let's first simplify the problem and assume the bursary is awarded based on only the average mark. In other words, the subjects passed do not play a role (so, for now, we ignore the Subjects passed GroupBox and its contents). Now, 90% and higher earns R10 000, 75% – 89% earns R8 000, 60% – 74% earns R5 000, less than 60% earns nothing. The btnEvaluateClick event handler below uses a Case statement to assign the correct value to `Amount`. Note that `Amount` is a string variable, therefore the bursary amount we assign to it appears in quotes. Note also that there are no spaces between the double dots which indicate the ranges in the Case statement (eg `90..100`).

```
procedure TfrmBursary.btnEvaluateClick(Sender: TObject);
var
  Amount: String;
begin
  case sedAverage.Value of
    90..100 : Amount := 'R10 000.00';
    75..89  : Amount := 'R8 000.00';
    60..74  : Amount := 'R5 000.00';
  else
    Amount := 'R 0.00';
  end;
  lblAmount.Caption := 'Bursary of ' + Amount + 'is awarded.'
end;
```

This Case statement first checks whether the value of `Average` is in the number range 90 to 100. If it is, Delphi executes the statement

```
Amount := 'R10 000.00';
```

If not, it checks whether `Average` falls in the range 75 to 89, and so on.

Note that a Case statement is appropriate only when the variable or property tested – for example, `Average` above – is of the integer, Char (a single character) or Boolean data type (the collective name for these data types is the *ordinal data type*). If it is a string variable or any of the real type variables, such as single, double and real, we have to use the multiple alternative If statement.

EX 6.4 STEP 3 Including the subject requirements

Now let us rewrite the Case structure to include the subject requirements. In the two cases where the subjects are also taken into account we include If statements inside the Case options.

```
procedure TfrmBursary.btnEvaluateClick(Sender: TObject);
var
  Amount: String;
begin
  case sedAverage.Value of
    90..100 : Amount := 'R10 000.00';
    75..89  : if chkAccounting.Checked or chkEconomics.Checked then
                Amount := 'R8 000.00'
              else
                Amount := 'R5 000.00';
    60..74  : if chkAccounting.Checked then
                Amount := 'R3 000.00'
              else
                Amount := 'R 0.00';
```

```
    else
      Amount := 'R 0.00';
    end;
    lblAmount.Caption := 'Bursary of ' + Amount + ' is awarded.'
end;
```

- Create this event handler, save the unit file again and then run the program using the following test cases.
- Complete the last column of the table below and then compare your program's output with the expected output given in the 'Testing' section of this example:

Score	Accounting	Economics	Program output
95%	✓		
58%	✓	✓	
80%	✓	✓	
80%			
63%	✓		
63%			

The structure of a Case statement

The general format of a Case statement is

```
case Selector of
  Option1 : Statement1;
  Option2 : Statement2;
      .
      .
      .
  OptionN : StatementN
else
  StatementE
end;
```

The Else part is optional. The Selector is a variable, expression or component property of Char, Boolean* or any integer data type. We call these the *ordinal* data types. Selector may not be of any real data type or a string.

Option1, Option2, ... and OptionN may each take one of four forms:

1   A constant of the same type as Selector.
2   A list of values of the same type as Selector. The values must be separated by commas, for example, 1, 2, 3. If the value of Selector is equal to any one of these, this alternative is chosen.
3   A range of values of the same type as Selector, for example, 1..10. If the value of Selector falls within this range, this alternative is chosen. Example 6.4 uses this format option.
4   A combination of 1, 2 or 3 above.
    The following code illustrates these four forms of option:

*   Although Delphi will accept a Boolean selector, it wouldn't be sensible to use one, because doing so will allow only two options – True and False. A simple If statement would be more appropriate in this case.

```
const MyValue = 100;
var
  SelectValue: integer;
begin
  SelectValue := sedDemo.Value;
  case SelectValue of
    MyValue             : lblDemo.Caption := 'Option type 1';
    40, 50, 60          : lblDemo.Caption := 'Option type 2';
    70..99              : lblDemo.Caption := 'Option type 3';
    1..39, 41..49, 51   : lblDemo.Caption := 'Option type 4';
  else
    lblDemo.Caption := 'Not in one of the options';
  end;
end;
```

The same value may not occur in more than one of the options.

A Case statement works as follows. Delphi searches for the value of `Selector` in the Options (see the general format of a Case statement above). If the value of `Selector` occurs in *Option3, Statement3* will be executed. If the value of `Selector` does not occur in any of the options, *StatementE* is executed (if there is no Else part, no statement will be executed). Only one of the options in a Case statement is executed. After this, Delphi continues with the first statement following the **end** of the Case statement.

`Statement1, Statement2,` ... are any Delphi statements. They can also be compound statements. In other words, if any option requires more than one statement, those statements are enclosed within begin … end.

When is a Case statement preferable to an If statement?

When it can be used, a Case statement is generally preferable to a multiple alternative If because it is easier for a programmer to read and understand. A Case statement can be used only if all the alternative options depend on the value of the same ordinal variable (or expression or Component property). If the choice depends on different variables, or on a real or string variable, nested If statements must be used. Any Case statement can be replaced with a multiple alternative If structure, but not all multiple alternative Ifs can be replaced with a Case.

EX 6.4 STEP 4 Using RadioButtons to get the score

Suppose that, in example 6.4, the user selected a RadioButton to show in which range the average falls (figure 6.4). Could we then still solve the problem with a Case statement?

The solution could now use the RadioButtons' Checked properties to determine in which range the average falls. The different conditions therefore involve different components:

```
if rad90.Checked then
  ⋮
else if rad75.Checked and ...
  ⋮
```

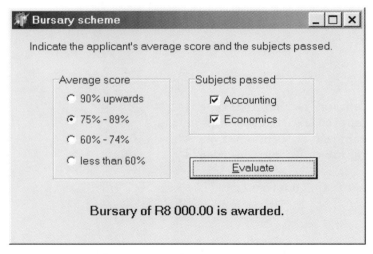

Figure 6.4 Using RadioButtons to indicate the average score

We've said that the Case statement can only test a single variable or component property for the different alternatives, and therefore we cannot use a Case statement here. Writing the complete program using this form layout is set as one of the problems at the end of the chapter. (We'll return to this program in Chapter 8.)

EXAMPLE 6.5) Generating words from characters

In this example we introduce a new data type called Char. In Chapter 3 we introduced the concepts of a variable and a data type and we declared and used variables of type String. In Chapter 4 we worked with variables of type Integer (for storing whole numbers) and of type Double (for storing floating point or real numbers). In Chapter 5 we introduced yet another data type, Boolean, for storing the value True or False.

The type Char stands for 'character' and a variable declared of this type can store only a single character as a value. In Delphi, a character is written in single quotes, just like a string, except that it can only ever contain one character. The following are examples of valid characters in Delphi:

'a'   'A'   'n'   '9'   '0'   '*'   ','   ' '

The last character is the single space character. The following are examples of strings, and are not valid characters:

```
'ab'    // a string which contains two characters
'b '    // this is a string of 2 characters: 'b' and a space
''      // this is the empty string which contains no characters
```

The relationship between characters and strings

Although a character can usually be treated as a string, the reverse is not true. Consider the following portion of code:

```
var
  Ch: char;
  Str: string;
begin
  Ch := 'a';
  Str := Ch;   // the character 'a' is converted into a string
  Ch := Str;   // error: incompatible types
```

In the first statement after begin, variable Ch is initialised to the character 'a'. In the second statement the String variable Str is assigned the value stored in the character Ch. This produces no error as the character is automatically converted into a string. The third statement, however, does produce an error. Even though Str contains a string with only one character, Delphi reports an error that the types are incompatible because a string may contain several characters. To access a specific character inside a string we need to specify an index in square brackets, which we do in the program below.

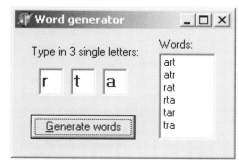

Figure 6.5 Form layout for the Word generator program

EX 6.5 STEP 1 Creating the form

In this program the user enters any three letters. The program then generates all possible combinations of these three letters to form six 'words', which are displayed in a ListBox (figure 6.5).

- Create the form using the interface in figure 6.5 and the property table below:

Component	Property	Value
Form1	Name	frmWords
	Caption	Word generator
Label1	Name	lblPrompt
	Caption	Type in 3 single letters:
Edit1...Edit3	Name	edtChar1...edtChar3
	Text	<Blank>
Button1	Name	btnGenerate
	Caption	&Generate words
Label2	Name	lblWords
	Caption	Words:
ListBox1	Name	lstWords
	Items	<Blank>
	Sort	True

The Sort property of lstWords is set to True, so that the words generated are listed in alphabetical order.

EX 6.5 STEP 2   Writing the event handler

• Double click on the button and type in the following event handler:

```
procedure TfrmWords.btnGenerateClick(Sender: TObject);
var
  Char1, Char2, Char3: char;
begin
  // extract the characters from the strings:
  Char1 := edtChar1.Text[1]; // extract first character
  Char2 := edtChar2.Text[1];
  Char3 := edtChar3.Text[1];
  lstWords.Clear;         // clear any previous entries
  lstWords.Items.Add(Char1 + Char2 + Char3);
  lstWords.Items.Add(Char1 + Char3 + Char2);
  lstWords.Items.Add(Char2 + Char1 + Char3);
  lstWords.Items.Add(Char2 + Char3 + Char1);
  lstWords.Items.Add(Char3 + Char1 + Char2);
  lstWords.Items.Add(Char3 + Char2 + Char1);
end;
```

Although the user only enters single characters into the EditBoxes, the type of the Text property of any EditBox is always a String. To extract it as a character, we use the number 1 in square brackets after the string to specify that we want the first character in the string. Notice how we can concatenate three characters to form a string using the '+' operator.

In the following example we show how a character variable can be used as the selector in a Case statement.

EXAMPLE 6.6) Classifying names with a Case statement

We want to write a program that divides a class of students alphabetically into study groups using their surnames. There are four groups to which we will allocate students using the following table*:

Group	Surname starts with
1	A to H
2	I to P (but not M)
3	Q to Z (but not V)
4	M or V

The program gets a surname from the user using an Input dialog box. It then reports in which group that student falls.

• Create the following user interface using the component properties in the table below. The opening screen is figure 6.6. To start reading in the names the user clicks on the 'Next name' button. This causes a Delphi Input dialog box to appear in which the user can type the surname (figure 6.8). On entering a surname and clicking OK, the relevant group is displayed (figure 6.7).

* In South Africa, surnames starting with M or V are very common

Component	Property	Value
Form1	Name	frmStudyGroups
	Caption	Study groups
Button1	Name	btnNextName
	Caption	&Next name
GroupBox	Name	gpbGroup
	Caption	Which group
Label1	Name	lblGroup
	Caption	<Blank>

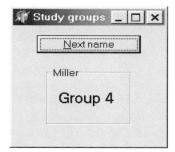

Figure 6.6 Opening form

Figure 6.7 After assigning a name to a group

Input dialog boxes

Like the Message box, the Input box is a standard Delphi dialog box. It includes space for the user to type an input value in string format and always has an OK and a Cancel button. For example, the statement

```
Surname := InputBox('User input', 'Enter a surname', '');
```

will open an Input dialog box with the caption 'User input', the prompt 'Enter a surname', and the empty string as default input value. The user can type any input string in the space provided (figure 6.8).

When the user clicks on OK, the InputBox statement returns the string to the program where it is assigned to the variable Surname. If the user clicks the Cancel button, the default string is returned (in this case the empty string).

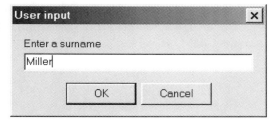

Figure 6.8 The Input box

• Create the following event handler for the Next name button:

```
1  procedure TfrmStudyGroups.btnNextNameClick(Sender: TObject);
2  var
3    FirstLetter, Group: char;
4    Surname: String;
5  begin
6    Surname := InputBox('User input', 'Enter a surname', '');
7    if Surname <> '' then                  // Input box not empty
8    begin
9      FirstLetter := UpCase(Surname[1]);  // Change to upper case
10     case FirstLetter of
11       'A'..'H'            : Group := '1';
12       'I'..'L', 'N'..'P'  : Group := '2';
13       'Q'..'U', 'W'..'Z'  : Group := '3';
14       'M','V'             : Group := '4';
15     else // First letter not alphabetical
16       Group := '?';
17     end; //case

18     if Group = '?' then
19       ShowMessage('Invalid surname entered')
20     else
```

```
21      begin
22        lblGroup.Caption := 'Group ' + Group;
23        gpbGroup.Caption := Surname;
24      end;
25    end //if Surname ...
26    else // User pressed Cancel or left input box blank
27      ShowMessage('No surname provided');
28 end;
```

- Save the unit file as C06e06u and the project as C06e06p.

In the program above we use an InputBox to read in a surname from the user. The result from the InputBox is stored in the variable Surname (line 6). To test whether the user pressed Cancel on the InputBox, we check that the value inside Surname is not the empty string (line 7). If it is empty, then the Else part of the If executes (line 27) and a message is displayed.

If the user entered a character and pressed OK, the statements inside the If execute (lines 8 – 25). We start by extracting the first letter of the surname using square brackets and the number 1 (Surname[1] in line 9). We then use a new function called UpCase to convert this character into a capital letter (UpCase(Surname[1]) before storing it in the char variable FirstLetter. Why do we change the letter to upper case? If the user types 'miller' in the InputBox, we would still want that surname to be allocated to group 4. Instead of later having to check for both characters 'm' and 'M', we convert the character into upper case, so that we only have to check for the relevant capital letters. In Chapter 5 we used the UpperCase function to convert a string to upper case. When working with data of the Char type, we use the UpCase function instead.

In the Case statement, we use the character FirstLetter as the selector (line 10). Remember that we said the selector of the Case statement may only be of an ordinal data type. This includes integer and char, but not string or any of the real types. We can use the double dot range symbol (..) with characters, just as we used them with integers. In line 11 of the Case statement, the range 'A'..'H' therefore covers all letters of the alphabet from 'A' to 'H'. In the Case statement, the variable Group is assigned to the relevant numeric character value depending on the first letter of the surname. We declared Group as a char (rather than an integer) so that it can be conveniently concatenated with a string in line 22.

Our programs should always be able to handle invalid input. In this program an input value that doesn't start with a letter of the alphabet will be invalid. The Else part of our Case statement will pick this up (lines 15 and 16) and set Group to the character '?'. Then in line 18 we check whether the input was invalid (by checking if Group has the value '?'), If so, an error message is displayed (line 19), otherwise the result is displayed (lines 22 and 23). Note that we set the GroupBox's Caption to the surname to make it clear which surname has been allocated.

In Chapter 12 we return to this example and create an alternative solution to the problem.

String processing

The next program we write gives us some exercise in using nested Ifs and the InputBox we learned to use in this chapter. It also does some string processing. In Delphi we can do several things with string data besides concatenating two strings (as we have done in Chapter 3). We can

- delete a specified section of a string;
- insert a substring into a string at a given location;

o get the length of a string;
o find the position of a substring in a string, and
o extract part of a string.

We'll do all but the last of these string operations in the following example.

EXAMPLE 6.7 String manipulation

In this example we write a program that searches for the first occurrence of a specified string in the text of a Memo component. It then replaces this string with a different string, as specified by the user.

• Open a new application and create the following form. The Lines property of the Memo is blank initially.

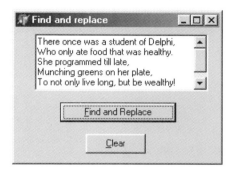

Figure 6.9 The form after typing text into the Memo

Component	Property	Value
Form1	Name	frmFindReplace
	Caption	Find and replace
Button1	Name	btnFindReplace
	Caption	&Find and Replace
Button2	Name	btnClear
	Caption	&Clear
Memo1	Name	memText
	Lines	<Blank>
	ScrollBars	ssVertical

EX 6.7 Planning

What would you expect from this program? We propose the following steps:
1 An Input box appears where the user types the string to search for.
2 The program searches for the string in the Memo's text.
3 If the string is found the following happens:
  a Another Input box appears where the user gives the replacement string.
  b The search string is deleted from the Memo's text.
  c The replacement string is inserted at that same location.
4 If the string is not found a Message box appears to notify the user of this and nothing else happens.

EX 6.7 STEP 1 The event handlers

To implement this we wrote the following event handler. It is quite a mouthful, but we explain it in detail below:

```
1  procedure TfrmFindReplace.btnFindReplaceClick(Sender: TObject);
2  var TextToSearch, StrToFind, ReplaceStr: string;
3     Position: integer;
4  begin
5     TextToSearch := memText.Text;

6     // Get the string to search for
7     StrToFind := InputBox('Find','Enter the string to find','');

8     if StrToFind <> '' then // If the user provided a string
9     begin
10      // Get the position of the string to find in the text
11      Position := Pos(StrToFind,TextToSearch);

12      if Position > 0 then  // If the string was found
13      begin
14        // Get the replacement string
15        ReplaceStr := InputBox('Replace with',
16                              'Enter replacement string','');
17        // Delete the string searched for
18        Delete(TextToSearch, Position, Length(StrToFind));

19        // Insert the replacement string at that position
20        Insert(ReplaceStr,TextToSearch,Position);

21        memText.Text := TextToSearch;
22        ShowMessage('String replaced');
23      end // if Position > 0
24      else
25        ShowMessage(StrToFind + ' does not appear in text');
26    end // if StrToFind <> ''
27    else
28      ShowMessage('No search string provided');
29 end;
```

The btnClearClick event handler looks like this:

```
procedure TfrmFindReplace.btnClearClick(Sender: TObject);
begin
  memText.Clear;
  memText.SetFocus;
end;
```

- Save the unit file as C06e07u and the project as C06e07p and then run the program. Type in some text, and click on the Find and Replace button to see how the program works.
- If your program doesn't run correctly, make sure you've named the components exactly as we did and that every bit of the code looks like ours. Below we explain the event handler line by line.

The Memo's Text property

Line 5 assigns the Text property of the Memo component to a variable. If you look at the properties of a Memo component in the Object Inspector, the Text property does not appear there. Instead it has a Lines property where we type any text we want to include at design time as individual lines. In this program we want to work with the text as a whole. Delphi makes this possible through the Text property which we can change through program code. How does one know about properties that do not appear in the Object Inspector? Delphi's Help and the code completion facility lists them all.

Line 7 displays an Input box (Figure 6.10) and assigns the user's input to StrToFind. This is the string that we will search for in the text.

If the user clicks the Cancel key, or clicks on OK without supplying any input, the search string will be empty. In this case we don't want to continue with the 'find and replace' process. The If statement in line 8 checks for an empty input string. If it is empty the Else part in lines 27 to 28 displays a Message box with a message that no string was provided.

If the user did supply an input string, Delphi executes the Then part in lines 9 to 26.

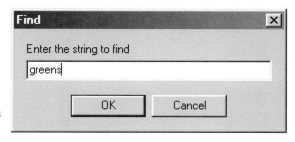

Figure 6.10 Input box for the string to find

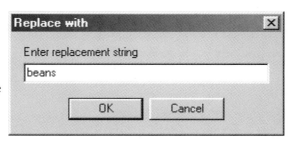

Figure 6.11 Input box for the replace string

EX 6.7 STEP 2 Finding a substring in a string

The next step of our solution is to locate StrToFind in the text. For that we use the statement

```
Position := Pos(StrToFind, TextToSearch);
```

in line 11. The Pos function searches for the first string given in brackets (here StrToFind) in the second string (TextToSearch) and returns the position where it is located. Here that position is assigned to the variable Position. If the string does not appear in the text, Pos returns 0. For example,

```
Position := Pos('is', 'This is it!');
```

stores the integer value 3 in variable Position, because the first occurrence of 'is' is in 'This'.

If the string was found (as checked with the If statement in line 12) the first thing to happen is that another Input box appears where the user types the string to replace the first input string (figure 6.11). The string is assigned to ReplaceStr. Here we allow the empty string.

EX 6.7 STEP 3 Deleting a substring from a string

Our next step is to delete the search string from the text with the statement

```
Delete(TextToSearch, Position, Length(StrToFind));
```

in line 18. This statement works as follows: In `TextToSearch`, starting at position `Position`, it deletes the number of characters given by the third value in brackets. Here that number of characters is the length of `StrToFind` which we get with the statement `Length(StrToFind)`. As a simple example of the Delete statement, consider the statements:

```
Sentence := 'What will be deleted?';
Delete(Sentence, 1, 4);
```

This deletes 4 characters from `Sentence`, starting at position 1. In other words, `Sentence` becomes `' will be deleted?'` (the first character is a space).

EX 6.7 STEP 4 Inserting a substring into a string

The next thing to do is to insert the replacement string, `ReplaceStr`, into the text at the same position where `StrToFind` was deleted. This we do in line 20 with

```
Insert(ReplaceStr, TextToSearch, Position);
```

This just says: insert `ReplaceStr` into `TextToSearch` at position `Position`. For example, the statements

```
Sentence := 'What inserted?';
Insert('is ', Sentence, 6);
```

change the value of `Sentence` to `'What is inserted?'`.

`TextToSearch` now contains the text with the replacement string, but this will only show in the Memo on the form if we assign it to the Memo's Text property as in line 21. To keep the user informed of the progress we then display a Message box which states that the process is complete.

If the If statement in line 12 finds that the search string does not appear in the text, its Else part in lines 24 to 25 reports this in a Message box.

Study the program carefully and make sure you understand the nesting of the If statements. This is probably the most complicated program we've written so far, so don't worry if you don't understand all the code immediately. You will probably need to read through the code and the explanation several times before everything is crystal clear.

Copying part of a string

One string processing function that we haven't used in this program is the Copy function that copies a substring from a string. We use the Copy function as follows:

```
SubStr := Copy(TheString, BeginPosition, Len);
```

It copies a substring in `TheString` from the character in `BeginPosition` and containing `Len` characters to variable `SubStr`. `TheString` must be a character string while `BeginPosition` and `Len` must be integers. If `BeginPosition` is greater than the length of `TheString`, an empty string is returned. If `Len` specifies more characters than remain from position `BeginPosition`, whatever is there is returned. An example is

```
Word := Copy('This is copied', 1, 4);
```

that assigns the string `'This'` to `Word`.

EXAMPLE 6.8) Message dialog boxes

In this section we look at dialog boxes in more detail. We have come across a number of different types of dialog boxes so far which we have used in different ways:

o   We used the ShowMessage procedure to display a simple message to the user with an OK button. For example:
```
ShowMessage('Invalid number');
```
o   We used the InputBox function to display a dialog box that allows the user to enter a String. InputBox is a function (as opposed to a procedure such as ShowMessage). This means that it returns an answer (the string that the user typed into the input box), so we usually use it as part of an assignment statement. For example:
```
Surname := InputBox('User Input', 'Enter a surname', '');
```
o   We also used OpenDialog, SaveDialog and FontDialog components to display common Windows dialogs. To use these, we placed them as non-visual components on the form and to display them we called the Execute method of the relevant component (see Chapter 5).

The MessageDlg function provides another way of displaying dialog boxes. The purpose of MessageDlg is to display a message and obtain a response from the user through button clicks. One advantage of the MessageDlg function is that it is very flexible – the same function can be used to display many different types of message to the user. The following section gives examples of Delphi statements to display dialogs and the corresponding boxes that will be displayed.

Dialog box examples

```
// A simple ShowMessage dialog

ShowMessage(
  'Simple show message example');
```

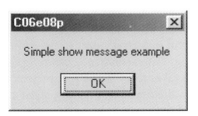

```
// An InputBox dialog
// Note: UserInput is of type string

UserInput := InputBox('The Caption',
  'Please enter something:',
  'Something');
```

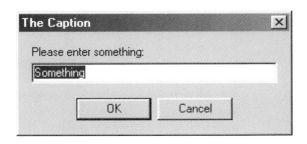

```
// A warning dialog with OK button:

MessageDlg('This is a warning',
  mtWarning,[mbOK],0);
```

```
// An information dialog with OK:

MessageDlg(
  'This is some information',
  mtInformation,[mbOK],0);
```

```
// An error dialog with OK and Abort:

if MessageDlg(
  'This is an error',mtError,
  [mbOK, mbAbort],0) = mrOK then
  // executed if user clicks OK
else
  // executed if user clicks Abort
```

```
// A confirmation dialog with Yes/No

if MessageDlg(
  'Are you sure you want to exit?',
  mtConfirmation,
  [mbYes, mbNo],0) = mrYes then
  // executed if user clicks Yes
else
  // executed if user clicks No
```

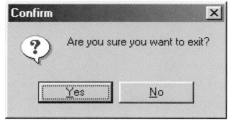

The first code example shows a simple ShowMessage statement. Notice that the user only has the option of clicking OK and that the name of the application (which defaults to the project file name) appears as the caption of the dialog. The second code example shows the InputBox function. This function takes three string parameters: the first is the caption of the box, the second is the message to be displayed and the third is the string that should be displayed in the input box before the user does anything (ie the default string). The user has the option of clicking on either OK or Cancel. If Cancel is clicked, the function returns the default string, otherwise it returns the string that is entered by the user. To use this string later in our program, we have to store it in a variable.

The next four examples above show some different ways of using the MessageDlg function. Notice that each dialog contains a different icon that represents the purpose of the message. An exclamation mark indicates a warning, an 'i' symbol indicates information, a cross indicates an error and a question mark indicates a question.

The general format of the MessageDlg function is as follows:

```
MessageDlg(StringToDisplay, TypeOfMessage, WhichButtons, HelpTopic);
```

- o `StringToDisplay` is the message displayed inside the dialog;
- o `TypeOfMessage` is a Delphi constant (e.g. `mtWarning` or `mtError`) that determines the icon and the box's caption.
- o `WhichButtons` is a set of Delphi constants that represent a selection of standard buttons. Notice in the examples above that for the first two examples we only specify the OK button (`[mbOK]`), while the last two examples have two buttons each (`[mbOK, mbAbort]` and `[mbYes, mbNo]`).
- o `HelpTopic` is an integer value that we will not use in our programs and therefore we always use 0. (Refer to online Help for more information on HelpTopic).

In the last two examples we use the MessageDlg statement as part of an If statement, while in the first two examples the statement stands on its own. Why is this? In the first two cases, the user is only presented with an OK button. The user therefore has no choice other than to click on OK. These two examples are equivalent to ShowMessage statements, except that they include icons and sensible captions.

The Error and Confirm boxes, however, present the user with a choice of two buttons. In our program we should therefore do something different depending on which button was pressed. If the user clicks on Abort, for example, the program should exit, but not if the user clicks on OK. How do we know which button the user clicked? MessageDlg returns the value of the button the user selected, so we can check this value using an If statement. For example, if a Yes button is selected, the value `mrYes` is returned.

At the end of this chapter we give a list of the values MessageDlg's different parameters can take.

EX 6.8 Handling exceptions using message dialogs

In example 6.2 we wrote a program to calculate commission on sales. In this example we see how to use message dialogs when handling exceptions.

The original event handler for btnCalculate looked as follows:

```
1 procedure TfrmCommission.btnCalculateClick(Sender: TObject);
2 var
3     Sales, Commission: double;
4 begin
5     Sales := StrToFloat(edtSales.Text);
6     if Sales > 80000.00 then
7         Commission := Sales * 0.40
8     else if Sales > 40000.00 then
9         Commission := Sales * 0.20
10    else
11        Commission := Sales * 0.10;
12    lblCommission.Caption := FloatToStrF(Commission,ffCurrency,10,2);
13 end;
```

If the user types in an invalid number for the sales (such as 50 000), an exception will be raised in the StrToFloat function. This means that the statement in line 5 of our event handler will fail. Since we have no error handling programmed into our event handler (in the form of a try...except), Delphi performs its default exception handling operation, which is to exit the event handler and display the error message shown in Figure 6.12 (this assumes that you have set Delphi's debugger options to not stop on exceptions as explained previously).

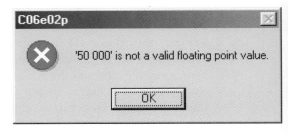

Figure 6.12 Delphi's default error message

We will now program our own exception handler as part of the event handler:

• Open C06e02p and change the code of the btnCalculate event handler as follows:

```
 1 procedure TfrmCommission.btnCalculateClick(Sender: TObject);
 2 var
 3   Sales, Commission: double;
 4 begin
 5   try
 6     Sales := StrToFloat(edtSales.Text);
 7   except
 8     if MessageDlg('Unable to process sales value ' +
 9                   edtSales.Text, mtError, [mbOK, mbAbort],0)
10                = mrOK then
11     begin      // The user clicked OK
12       edtSales.SetFocus;
13       Exit;    // Jump out of the event handler here
14     end
15     else       // The user clicked Abort
16       Close;   // End the program
17   end;    // end of try ... except

18   if Sales > 80000.00 then
19     Commission := Sales * 0.40
20   else if Sales > 40000.00 then
21     Commission := Sales * 0.20
22   else
23     Commission := Sales * 0.10;

24   lblCommission.Caption := FloatToStrF(Commission,ffCurrency,10,2);
25 end;
```

• Save the unit file and run the program. Enter the value 50 000 for sales and click on Calculate commission. The error message shown in Figure 6.13 appears. If you click OK, the program returns to the main form and you can correct the input value. If you click Abort, the program exits.

To handle the exception, we insert a Try statement just before the statement where things could go wrong (the call to StrToFloat). If something does go wrong, execution continues at the first line inside the Except block (line 8). If nothing goes wrong (the input is valid), Delphi skips the Except block and continues with the rest of the event handler (lines 18 to 24).

Inside the Except block we give the user the choice to continue or abort. If they choose to continue, we set the focus on the Edit box and jump out of the event handler. If they choose to Abort we exit the program. There is an important

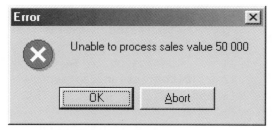

Figure 6.13 Message displayed by our own exception handler

difference between the Exit statement in line 13 and the Close statement in line 16. The Exit procedure only exits the event handler. This means that the program jumps out of the event handler (ignoring lines 14 to 24) and returns to the main form. Remember that the event handler is called by Delphi every time the relevant button (btnCalculate) is pressed. If the user therefore clicks on button btnCalculate again, the event handler will be called again. That way, the user is given repeated chances to enter different values.

In contrast, the Close statement closes the main form of the application, which terminates the program.

REVIEW

In this chapter we looked at nested if...then...else statements. These allow us to use an If statement inside the Then or Else parts of another If statement. We saw that one should take care in structuring a nested If structure, so that each Else part is paired with the intended If statement.

If the Else part of every If statement (except the last one) in a series of nested Ifs contains a nested if...then...else statement, we call it a multiple alternative If structure. In this case we align all the Else's to the left for readability.

We also looked at the Case statement which can be used instead of a multiple alternative If statement when all the conditions involved test the value of the same variable or component property that is of an ordinal data type.

While introducing the nested If and Case statements we discussed several new Delphi concepts. We saw how we can use Delphi's *Message box* to display information to the user and get user input through button clicks and how we can use the *Input box* to get input strings from the user. We learned to use the *CheckBox* component and we did some string manipulation which included (amongst other things) finding a particular string in another string, deleting part of a string and determining the length of a string.

IMPORTANT CONCEPTS

Fundamental programming concepts

Char data type: A variable declared of this ordinal type can take only a single character as a value. In Delphi, a char constant is written in single quotes.

Data validation: This is the process of checking input data for possible errors. For example, if the user has to enter a person's age, the program should check whether the input falls within a sensible range. If not it should report an error and ask the user to correct it.

Nested If statement: A nested If statement appears in the Then or the Else part of another If statement.

Ordinal data types: Char, Boolean and all the integer types are ordinal data types. The values that variables of these types can take are discrete (meaning the values can be counted) and follow in a specific sequence. The real data types and String are *not* ordinal types.

User interface factors

Selecting any number of several choices: CheckBoxes provide a way of allowing the user to select any number of options out of several choices. In contrast, RadioButtons in a group allow the user to select only one option from a number of choices.

NEW DELPHI FEATURES

String manipulation

[]	To access a single character from a string we specify the position of the character to be extracted in square brackets after the string. For example, if `Str` has the value `'potato'`, then the statement `Ch := Str[4];` will assign the character `'a'` to `Ch`.
Copy function	Copies a substring from a string. The format of the Copy function is `SubStr := Copy(TheString,BeginPosition,Len);` It copies a substring from `TheString` that starts at the character in `BeginPosition` and contains `Len` characters. The resulting substring is assigned to variable `SubStr`. `TheString` is a character string while `BeginPosition` and `Len` are integers. If `BeginPosition` is greater than the length of `TheString`, an empty string is returned. If `Len` specifies more characters than remain from position `BeginPosition`, whatever is there is returned.
Delete procedure	We use this procedure to remove part of a string. Its format is `Delete(OriginalString, Position, NoOfChars);` Here, in `OriginalString`, starting at position `Position`, delete the number of characters given by `NoOfChars`..
Insert procedure	We use this to insert one string in another string at a specified position. A call to the procedure has the format `Insert(InsertStr, OtherString, Position);` This just says: insert `InsertStr` into `OtherString` at position `Position`.
Length function	This returns the number of characters in a string. For example, `Len := Length('Delphi');` assigns the value 6 to the variable `Len`.
Pos function	Searches for the first occurrence of one string in another string. The format is `Position := Pos(StrToFind, TextToSearch);` It returns the position (an integer) in `TextToSearch` (a string) where `StrToFind` (a string) occurs for the first time. If the string does not appear in the text, the function returns 0.

Other methods, functions and procedures

Close method	This is a method of TForm. When used from inside an event-handler, it closes the form which contains the component of that event-handler. If this form is the main form, it terminates the program.
Exit procedure	The Exit procedure immediately ends the current subroutine and causes the calling procedure to continue with the statement after the point at which the subroutine was called.
InputBox function	Displays an Input box (window) to get a single input string from the user. It contains a prompt, an input field and two buttons (OK and Cancel). We activate it with a function call as in the following statement: `InputVal := InputBox(WindowCaption, Prompt, DefaultVal);`

WindowCaption is a string that will appear as the box's Caption. Prompt is a string that contains a prompt like 'Enter a surname' which is displayed inside the dialog, and DefaultVal is a string that will appear in the input field as a default input value. The user types any input string in the input field and clicks on the OK button. The InputBox function returns the string to the program where it is assigned to the variable InputVal. If the user clicks the Cancel button, the default string is returned.

MessageDlg function	See below.
ShowMessage procedure	Provides the simplest way to create a Message box. It has the following form: `ShowMessage(StringToDisplay);` StringToDisplay is the message that will appear in the box. The box's Caption is by default the name of the project file linked to the unit file that includes the statement. An OK button appears in the box and execution of the program will continue when the user clicks on this button.
UpCase function	We use this function to change the value of a variable of the Char type to upper case. For example, `UpLetter := UpCase(AnyLetter);` where UpLetter and AnyLetter are of type Char. To change a string variable to upper case, use the UpperCase function instead.

Message dialog

A Message dialog box is a simple Delphi form that appears on top of a running application and usually contains an icon that represents the purpose of the message, the user-defined message and one or more buttons that the user can select in response to the message. We use the MessageDlg function to activate a Message dialog box. One way to call it is:

`MessageDlg(StringToDisplay, TypeOfMessage, WhichButtons, HelpTopic);`

where StringToDisplay is the message, TypeOfMessage is a Delphi constant that determines the icon and the box's Caption, WhichButtons is a list of Delphi constants that represent a selection of standard buttons and HelpTopic is an integer value that we will not use in our programs and therefore always set it to 0. We can also call the function as part of an If statement.

The MessageDlg function returns a value depending on the button that the user selects. Here is an example of a function call where TypeOfMessage is mtError, WhichButtons contains an OK and an Abort button, and one of the values mrOK or mrAbort is returned:

`if MessageDlg('Invalid input', mtError, [mbOK, mbAbort], 0) = mrOK then ...`

Below we give a table with the possible values that TypeOfMessage can take. Below that we describe each of the button types that can be included in WhichButtons.

TypeOfMessage (in MessageDlg)	Displays
mtWarning	A Message box containing a yellow exclamation mark.
mtError	A Message box containing a red stop sign.
mtInformation	A Message box containing a blue 'i'.
mtConfirmation	A Message box containing a green question mark.
mtCustom	A Message box containing no bitmap. The Caption of the Message box is the name of the application.

WhichButtons is a set of zero or more button types that appear in square brackets and are separated by commas. The possible button types include mbYes, mbNo, mbOK, mbCancel, mbHelp, mbAbort, mbRetry, mbIgnore, mbAll. In addition to the individual values, three constants exist which are predefined sets that include common button combinations. These are:

Type of button (in MessageDlg)	In the Message box the button appears ...
mbYesNoCancel	A set that puts the Yes, No, and Cancel buttons in the Message box.
mbOkCancel	A set that puts the OK and Cancel buttons in the Message box.
mbAbortRetryIgnore	A set that puts the Abort, Retry, and Ignore buttons in the Message box.

When using these constants, remember not to add the brackets [ ] to define the set. These constants are already predefined sets.

Delphi Pascal constructs

Case statement

We use a Case statement where the program must branch to one of several possible statements depending on the value of an ordinal variable, expression or component property. The general format of a Case statement is

```
case Selector of
   Option1 : Statement1;
   Option2 : Statement2;
      .
      .
   OptionN : StatementN
else
   StatementE
end;
```

The Else part is optional. The `Selector` is a variable, expression or Component property of the Integer or Char data type. The Options can take different forms and list the possible values of the `Selector`. The same value may not occur in more than one of the Options. Delphi searches for the value of Selector in the Options and, if found, executes the `Statement` associated with that Option. If not found, the Else part is executed (if there is one). The `Statements` can be compound statements.

Multiple alternative If statement

If the Else part of every If statement (except the last one) in a nested If structure contains a nested if...then...else statement, we have a multiple alternative If statement. All the Elses are aligned to the left as follows:

```
if Condition1 then
   Statement1
else if Condition2 then
   Statement2
   .
   .
else if ConditionM then
   StatementM
else
   StatementN;
```

Nested If statement

A nested If statement appears in the Then or the Else part of another If statement. For example:

```
if Value1 > 20 then
   if Value2 > 20 then // nested If
      Answer := Value1 * Value2
   else
      Answer := Value * 20
else
   Answer := 20;
```

TCheckBox		
Properties	Checked	If True a tick (✓) appears in the box; if False the box is empty.
Prefix	chk...	
Use	To give the user a True/False (or Yes/No) choice which can be made by checking or unchecking the box. Often used in a group to give the user a list of True/False choices from which one or more can be selected.	

PROBLEMS

PROBLEM 6.1) Who is older?

- Write a program that gets the names and ages of two people from the user and then displays a message to report who is older, or whether they have the same age.
- Use a Message box to display the result and include data validation on the ages (ie check that the ages fall in a sensible range).

PROBLEM 6.2) Book classification

The *Putsonderwater Public Library* classifies its books using three-digit numbers (ie integers from 100 to 999). The table below shows the location of the books according to their classification numbers.
- Write a program that requests the classification number of a book and displays the location of the book.

Number	Location
100 to 199	Basement
200 to 500 and over 900	Ground floor
501 to 900 except 700 to 750	First floor
700 to 750	Annexe

PROBLEM 6.3) The bursary scheme again

a Consider the problem described in example 6.4 step 4 with the modified interface shown in figure 6.4. Does the following multiple alternative If structure calculate the bursary amount correctly? Explain your answer.

```
if rad90.Checked then
   Amount := ' R 10 000.00'
else if rad75.Checked then
   Amount := ' R 5 000.00'
else if rad75.Checked and (chkAccounting.Checked or
                           chkEconomics.Checked) then
   Amount := 'R 8 000.00'
```

```
else if rad60.Checked and chkAccounting.Checked then
  Amount := 'R 3 000.00'
else
  Amount := 'R 0.00';
```

b   Write the complete program using the user interface given in figure 6.4, making any changes that may be needed to this multiple alternative If.

c   Check your program against the test cases in example 6.4, step 3.

PROBLEM 6.4 Number of days in a month

- Write a program that reads the number of a month of the year (1–12) and displays the number of days in that month. If the user enters 2, the program must ask the user whether this is a leap year and give the correct number of days for February if it is. (In a leap year February has 29 days.) If the user enters an invalid month, display an error message. Here are two example screens from test runs of the program:

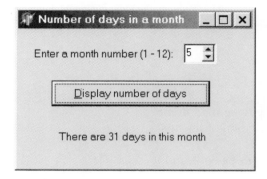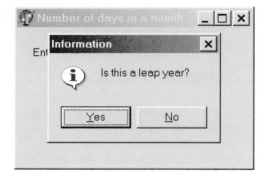

Figure 6.14 The form layout for a month other than February

Figure 6.15 The result if the month is February

PROBLEM 6.5 MarsSpeak translator

- Write a program that requests a word (in lowercase letters) as input and translates the word into code called MarsSpeak. The rules for translation are:
  1   If the word begins with a vowel (a, e, i, o, u), add 'way' to the end of the word. For example, 'else' becomes 'elseway'.
  2   If the word begins with a consonant, move the first letter to the end of the word and add 'ay'. For example, 'chip' becomes 'hipcay'.

- Display the converted string in the same Edit box as the user typed the original string.

PROBLEM 6.6 Checking English grammar

The general rule for using the indefinite article 'an' instead of 'a' in English is to replace 'a' with 'an' whenever it appears before a word starting with a vowel (a, e, i, o, u). There are exceptions to this rule, but for this problem we assume it always applies.

- Write a program which reads a simple sentence, searches for the word 'a' or 'an' and checks whether it is used correctly (by checking the first letter of the next word).

- Assume that the sentence contains only one occurrence of either 'a' or 'an'. If 'a' appears before a word that starts with a vowel (figure 6.16), then display the message `Replace 'a' with 'an'`(figure 6.17). If it is used correctly, display `'a' used correctly`. If 'a' does not appear in the sentence and 'an' does, display similar messages. If neither of them appears in the sentence, display the message `No indefinite article used`.

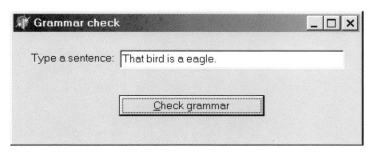

Figure 6.16 The form layout

Figure 6.17 An error message

Hints:

- Use the Pos function to locate the words 'a' and 'an'. In order to distinguish them from similar strings used in other words in the sentence, locate the strings `' a '` and `' an '` (with spaces on both sides). If either is found, use the Copy function to get the first letter of the next word (if `' a '` was found at position x, then the next word will start at position x+3, and if `' an '` was found at position x, then the next word starts at position x+4).
- Use a Message box to display the result. To display a quote inside a character string we use *two consecutive single quotes*, as in the following statement:

```
MessageDlg('Replace ''a'' with ''an''.', mtError, [mbOK], 0);
```

This statement will display the Message box in figure 6.17. Note that a double quote will not work correctly – you must use two single quotes.

CHAPTER 7

Repetition

PURPOSE OF THIS CHAPTER

In an event-driven programming language such as Delphi we often write programs so that the user can execute the same programming tasks repeatedly by clicking on the same button. For example, if we want the user to add names to a ListBox, we will typically have an Edit component, where the user can type a name, and an Add button. By clicking on the Add button every time the user has typed a new name in the Edit box, he or she can add as many names to the list as needed. In this example the *user* controls the repetition. By contrast, this chapter focuses on *program controlled repetition*. Some programming problems require a program to repeat statements automatically in order to reach the desired result. The examples in this chapter solve this kind of problem with 'iteration structures' (also called repetition or loop statements) using For and While loops.

EXAMPLE 7.1) A For loop

We start with a simple program which illustrates the basic structure and use of a For loop by calculating the sum of a series of integers. The program asks the user for two integer values: one is a lower bound and the other an upper bound. When the user clicks on the Calculate sum button, it calculates the sum of all the values from the lower value to the upper value. For example, if the user enters 4 and 6 as the two values, the program will calculate 4 + 5 + 6, and display the result, which, in this case, is 15 (figure 7.1).

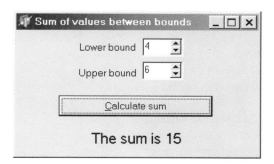

Figure 7.1 Calculating the sum of the values between two bounds

EX 7.1 STEP 1 Creating the form

- Start a new application and create the form according to the table below:

Component	Property	Value
Form1	Name	frmSum
	Caption	Sum of values between bounds
Button1	Name	btnSum
	Caption	&Calculate sum
SpinEdit1	Name	sedLower
	Value	0
SpinEdit2	Name	sedUpper
	Value	0
Label1	Name	lblLower
	Caption	Lower bound
Label2	Name	lblUpper
	Caption	Upper bound
Label3	Name	lblSum
	Caption	<Blank>

EX 7.1 STEP 2 Calculating the sum

- Double-click on the Calculate sum button to open the btnSumClick event handler and change it to the following:

```
1 procedure TfrmSum.btnSumClick(Sender: TObject);
2 var
3   Count, Sum: integer;
4 begin
5   Sum := 0;
6   for Count := sedLower.Value to sedUpper.Value do
7     Sum := Sum + Count;
8   lblSum.Caption := 'The sum is ' + IntToStr(Sum);
9 end;
```

- Save the unit file as C07e01u and the project as C07e01p, and run the program. Test it with different values for the lower and upper bounds.

Let's investigate the code. The first statement assigns the value 0 to the variable Sum. We say that Sum is *initialized* to 0. We discuss the importance of the initialization of variables after this example. The new and important statement here is

```
for Count := sedLower.Value to sedUpper.Value do
```

This For statement causes the next statement (Sum : = Sum + Count) to be executed for each of the integer values from sedLower.Value to sedUpper.Value. To see how this works, let's suppose the lower bound is 4 and the upper bound is 6. The For loop executes as follows:

1   Count initially gets the value sedLower.Value (which is 4). Delphi then compares this value with sedUpper.Value (which is 6). Since 4 is less than or equal to sedUpper.Value, the body of the For loop (in this case only the assignment statement) is executed. So, Sum is 0 + 4 = 4.

2   Delphi then adds 1 to Count (so Count becomes 5) and the new value is compared with sedUpper.Value. If Count is less than or equal to sedUpper.Value, which it is, the assignment statement is executed again. Now Sum is 4 + 5 = 9.

3   Delphi adds 1 to Count (now 6) and compares this value with sedUpper.Value. It is still less than or equal to sedUpper.Value, so the assignment statement is executed once more and Sum is 9 + 6 = 15.

4   Again Delphi adds 1 to Count (now 7) and compares it with sedUpper.Value. Count is now greater than sedUpper.Value and so the loop ends.

5   Delphi leaves the For loop and executes the next statement, which displays the result as lblSum's Caption.

Trace tables

The process of execution of a portion of code can be summarised in a trace table. A *trace table* is a way of keeping track manually of the values of variables as a program progresses and can help in understanding the logic of a program. As above, assuming the user entered a value of 4 in sedLower and a value of 6 in sedUpper, the following trace table shows the sequence of steps involved in executing the event handler.

Line	Count	Sum	Description
5		0	Sum is initialised to 0
6	4	0	Count is initialised to 4. Because Count has not exceeded 6, the statement inside the loop (line 7) is executed next
7	4	4	Sum is set to Sum + Count (0 + 4 = 4).
6	5	4	Count is incremented by 1 to 5. Because Count has not exceeded 6, the statement inside the loop (line 7) is executed next
7	5	9	Sum is set to Sum + Count (4 + 5 = 9).
6	6	9	Count is incremented by 1 to 6. Because Count has not exceeded 6, the statement inside the loop (line 7) is executed next
7	6	15	Sum is set to Sum + Count (6 + 9 = 15).
6	7	15	Count is incremented by 1 to 7. Because Count has exceeded 6, the statement inside the loop (line 7) is skipped and the next statement after the loop (line 8) is executed next
8	7	15	The value of Sum is displayed on the interface.

The first column lists the line number of the code in the event handler (we only list the line numbers which are relevant). Notice how lines 6 and 7 are repeated three times, because the loop executes three times. The second and third columns give the values of the variables Count and Sum respectively. The value of Count is initialised to 4 in line 6 and stays as 4, until it increases to 5 in the second iteration of line 6. Make sure you understand how each step in the trace table works. To test yourself, block out the rows and see if you can insert the line numbers and values of variables yourself.

In this example the For loop repeats a single program statement. A For loop can also repeat more than one statement by using begin and end to group them as a compound statement under the For statement.

Initializing variables

When you have finished programming this example and have checked that it works properly, comment out line 5 and run it again. What happens? With lower bound of 4 and an upper bound of 6, a sample run of the program produced a sum of 12402407! How does this happen?

In the program we use the statement Sum := Sum + Count; in the For loop. Sum appears on both sides of the assignment statement. This means a new value is assigned to Sum by adding Count to the last value stored in Sum. The old value of Sum is overwritten with the new value. When this statement is encountered the first time, it is important that Sum has the value 0, otherwise some random number will be added to Count and the end result will be incorrect. That is why we get a nonsense value for our final sum. We must therefore initialize Sum to 0 before we enter the loop. Remove the comment in front of line 5 and run the program to see that it is working correctly again.

If we wanted to calculate the *product* of the values between the two bounds instead of their sum, we would include the statement Product := Product *

`Count;` in the loop. Again the value of `Product` must be initialized before the loop, but this time to 1. If we initialize it to 0 the value of `Product` will remain 0, because any value multiplied by 0 gives 0.

The For loop

The For loop has the following structure:

```
for CounterVariable := LowValue to HighValue do
    Statement;
```

`CounterVariable` is the loop control variable that the For statement automatically initializes to `LowValue`, and then automatically increases by 1 with each iteration, until its value is greater than `HighValue`. For each value of `CounterVariable`, `Statement` (ie the loop body) is executed. `Statement` can either be a single statement or a compound statement enclosed within `begin` and `end` statements.

`CounterVariable` must be an ordinal variable. In other words, it may not be of one of the real data types, or of the string data type, but must be declared as an Integer or Char variable (Delphi will also allow a Boolean variable, but since there are only two Boolean values, namely True and False, it wouldn't make sense to use such a counter variable.) `LowValue` and `HighValue` are variables, constants, or expressions of the same data type as `CounterVariable`. If `LowValue` is greater than `HighValue` initially, the loop will never execute. If the two values are equal, the loop will execute once.

The formats of the following For statements are valid. Suppose X and Y are integers and that C is a Char variable.

```
for X := 10 to (Y*10-30) do...
```

The expression (Y*10-30) is evaluated and the upper bound set to that value. The number of times the statement is executed is determined by the value of Y. If (Y*10-30) is less than 10 the statement will never be executed.

```
for X := 100 to 50 do...
```

The statement in this loop is never executed since the lower bound is greater than the upper bound.

```
for C := 'a' to 'z' do...
```

The statement will be executed 26 times.

```
for C := 'a' to 'a' do...
```

The statement will be executed exactly once.

An important characteristic of the For loop (as opposed to other kinds of loop) is that before the looping starts the exact number of iterations that will take place is known. All For loops are 'counter-driven'. This means a counter variable is assigned an initial value and the iterations are 'counted' so that the exact predetermined number of them occurs.

As with the if...then...else statement, we use indentation to format the For loop neatly. We indent the statement that forms the body of the For loop two spaces to the right so that a reader can clearly see which part of the program is repeated by the loop.

Counting downwards with For

It is also possible to use a For loop with the counter variable going from a high value down to a lower value. Just replace the word **to** with **downto** in the For statement, and place the higher value first. The structure then looks as follows:

```
for CounterVariable := HighValue downto LowValue do
  Statement;
```

Now `CounterVariable` starts at `HighValue` and is *decreased* by 1 after every iteration. If you use `downto` and `HighValue` is less than `LowValue`, the loop will never execute.

Compound statements with For

A For loop can repeat more than one statement by using Begin and End to group them as a compound statement. The following program takes an initial balance and an interest rate and displays how this investment grows for 4 years. The interface is shown in figure 7.2 and the event handler for the 'Grow for 4 years' button is listed here:

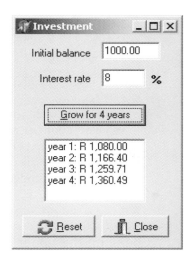

Figure 7.2 Growing an investment for 4 years

```
 1 procedure TfrmInvestment.btnGrowClick(Sender: TObject);
 2 var
 3   Counter: integer;
 4   Balance, Rate, Interest: double;
 5 begin
 6   Balance := StrToFloat(edtBalance.Text);
 7   Rate := StrToFloat(edtRate.Text) / 100;
 8   {Grow investment for 4 years at the given interest rate: }
 9   for Counter := 1 to 4 do
10   begin
11     Interest := Balance * Rate; // calculate the interest
12     Balance := Balance + Interest; // add interest to Balance
13     {Display the year and the new balance in the list box: }
14     lstGrowth.Items.Add('year ' + IntToStr(Counter) + ': ' +
15                 FloatToStrF(Balance,ffCurrency,10,2));
16   end;
17 end;
```

The For loop iterates 4 times and contains a compound statement (3 statements within a Begin...End block). This means that all 3 statements (lines 11 - 15) are repeated 4 times. Assume the user enters 1000 for the initial balance and 8 for the interest rate (variable `Rate` is therefore initialised to 0.08 in line 7), the following trace table shows how the variables change from line 9 onwards. See if you can draw the table yourself before looking.

Line	Counter	Balance	Interest	Description
9	1	1000.00		Counter initialised
11	1	1000.00	80	Calculate interest for that year
12	1	1080.00	80	Update balance with interest
14–15	1	1080.00	80	'year 1: R 1,080.00' added to listbox
9	2	1080.00	80	Counter incremented
11	2	1080.00	86.4	Calculate interest for that year
12	2	1166.40	86.4	Update balance with interest
14–15	2	1166.40	86.4	'year 2: R 1,166.40' added to listbox
9	3	1166.40	86.4	Counter incremented
11	3	1166.40	93.312	Calculate interest for that year
12	3	1259.712	93.312	Update balance with interest
14–15	3	1259.712	93.312	'year 3: R 1,259.71' added to listbox
9	4	1259.712	93.312	Counter incremented
11	4	1259.712	100.77696	Calculate interest for that year
12	4	1360.48896	100.77696	Update balance with interest
14–15	4	1360.48896	100.77696	'year 4: R 1,360.49' added to listbox
9	5	1360.48896	100.77696	Counter incremented and loop ends
17	5	1360.48896	100.77696	End of event handler

In the trace table you can see how lines 9 - 15 are repeated 4 times and how the value of Counter matches these 4 iterations. Notice how we write the values of Balance and Interest in precise form (eg 1360.48896). These precise values are used in the calculations. Only when a double is converted to a string (as in line 15) is it rounded off for display purposes.

Changing the upper bound inside the loop

Look at the following simple code:

```
1 High := 5;
2 Sum := 0;
3 for Count := 1 to High do
4 begin
5    Sum := Sum + Count;
6    High := High - 1;
7 end;
```

The For loop's counter goes from 1 to 5 since High is initialized to 5 (line 1). In line 5 the value of Count is added to the current value of Sum. Sum was initialized to 0 (line 2) so after repeating the loop body the required five times Sum's value will be 1 + 2 + 3 + 4 + 5 = 15. But what about the statement in line 6 that subtracts 1 from the upper bound (ie the variable High) with each iteration? Will that not influence the number of iterations? The answer is 'no'. The beginning and end values of the counter variable are set *before* the repetition starts, when the loop is encountered for the first time. If the lower bound or the upper bound (or both) are variables, changing the values of these variables inside the loop will not influence the number of times the loop executes. So, here the loop is executed five times despite the fact that High's value is decreased inside the loop.

A second principle regarding the For loop is that the value of the counter variable may not be changed inside the loop. In the example above we *use* the variable Count within the loop's compound statement. We are allowed to do this, but any attempt to *change* the value will be reported as a syntax error. So, for example, if line 5 were Count := Sum + 3;, Delphi would reject it.

EXAMPLE 7.2) A raffle competition

A school needs a Delphi program to select randomly a number of prize winners in a raffle competition. The program receives the number of tickets sold and the number of prizes to be drawn as input, and then randomly selects the required number of tickets as prizes (figure 7.3). The tickets are numbered from 1 upwards. The same ticket can win more than one prize.

The OnClick event handler for the Select winners button selects the winning numbers and adds them to a ListBox.

The Random function

To solve this problem we need to generate some random numbers to decide who the winners are. As a different example, say we wanted to simulate the throw of a dice. This would involve generating a random number from 1 to 6. Delphi has a function called Random that can do this for us. If Throw is an integer variable, the statement:

```
Throw := Random(6) + 1;
```

assigns any number from 1 to 6 to the variable Throw. (We add 1 because Random(6) generates a number from 0 to 5.) After executing this statement, Throw could contain the value 1 or 2 or 3 or 4 or 5 or 6 – we don't know which, because it is random.

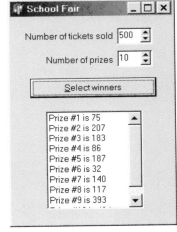

Figure 7.3 Form for selecting winners in a raffle competition

EX 7.2   Planning

To solve our raffle competition program we need to generate a few random numbers (this depends on the number of prizes to be allocated) and the range of these random numbers depends on the number of tickets sold. Say we sold 120 tickets. This means that there are 120 possible winners. To generate a single random number from 1 - 120, we use:

```
Winner := Random(120) + 1;
```

The problem with this is that the number of tickets is not set at 120. How do we know how many tickets were sold? The number is specified by the user in the first SpinEdit. Our general random winner is therefore:

```
Winner := Random(sedTickets.Value) + 1;
```

Adding 1 ensures that 0 is not one of the random values and that `sedTickets.Value` is also included in the range.

Note that before we can use the Random function in a program, we have to initialise Delphi's random number generator with the `Randomize;` statement (more on this later).

The OnClick event handler for the 'Select winners' button has to generate the required number of random numbers. Say it has to generate 10 numbers. This means we must call the Random function 10 times. For each random number generated the program must add an item to a ListBox. We need a repetition structure that implements the following logic:

o   Repeat the following steps as many times as there are prizes:
   o   Get a random number (say y) between (and including) 1 and the number of tickets sold.
   o   Create a string of the form 'Prize #x is y' (where x starts at 1 and goes up to the required number of prizes).
   o   Add the string to the Winners ListBox.

EX 7.2 STEP 1   The user interface

- Create the user interface using the following components and properties:

Component	Property	Value
Form1	Name	frmSchoolFair
	Caption	School Fair
Button1	Name	btnSelectWinners
	Caption	&Select winners
SpinEdit1	Name	sedTickets
	Value	0
SpinEdit2	Name	sedPrizes
	Value	0
Label1	Name	lblTickets
	Caption	Number of tickets sold
Label2	Name	lblPrizes
	Caption	Number of prizes
ListBox1	Name	lstWinners
	Items	<Blank>

- Save the unit file as C07e02u and the project as C07e02p.

EX 7.2 STEP 2   The For statement

We can implement the repetition structure of our solution plan using a For loop. Write down the first line of the For statement that implements the instruction 'Repeat the following steps as many times as there are prizes:'. The general structure of a For statement is

```
for CounterVariable := LowValue to HighValue do
```

Let's use the variable Count for CounterVariable. What should the values of LowValue and HighValue respectively be? LowValue will be 1 and HighValue will depend on the value the user entered into the 'Number of prizes' SpinEdit. In other words, HighValue will be sedPrizes.Value. The required statement is then

```
for Count := 1 to sedPrizes.Value do
```

EX 7.2 STEP 3 The loop's body

Now write down the statements that form the body of the For loop. There will be one statement for each of the following steps:

o   Get a random number (say y) between 1 and the number of tickets sold.
o   Create a string of the form 'Prize #x is y' (where x starts at 1 and goes up to the required number of prizes).
o   Add the string to the Winners ListBox.

The three Delphi statements are:

```
Winner := Random(sedTickets.Value) + 1;
ListItem := 'Prize #' + IntToStr(Count) + ' is ' + IntToStr(Winner);
lstWinners.Items.Add (ListItem);
```

EX 7.2 STEP 4 The complete For loop

We can now write down the complete For loop. The three statements that form the body must be enclosed in begin and end to form a compound statement.

```
for Count := 1 to sedPrizes.Value do  // for each prize do ...
begin
   {Generate a random winner}
   Winner := Random(sedTickets.Value) + 1;
   {Display prize number and winner number in list box}
   ListItem := 'Prize #' + IntToStr(Count) + ' is ' +
               IntToStr(Winner);
   lstWinners.Items.Add(ListItem);
end; // end of for each prize
```

Is this all that we need to include in the Select winners button's event handler? Remember when we discussed the Random function above we said that before we can use it we must call Delphi's Randomize procedure. So, above the For loop we need to include the statement Randomize;. This statement should not appear inside the For loop. We must only call it once before the first time we use the Random function.

We also need to clear the ListBox before we start adding items to it in the For loop (to clear any results from a previous competition), therefore we include the statement

```
lstWinners.Clear;
```

at the beginning of the event handler.

EX 7.2 STEP 5 The event handler

The complete event handler for the Select winners button is:

```
procedure TfrmSchoolFair.btnSelectWinnersClick(Sender: TObject);
var
  Count, Winner: integer;
  ListItem: string;
begin
  lstWinners.Clear; // clear previous results
  Randomize;        // initialise random number generator
  for Count := 1 to sedPrizes.value do  // for each prize do ...
  begin
    {Generate a random winner}
    Winner := Random(sedTickets.Value) + 1;
    {Display prize number and winner number in list box}
    ListItem := 'Prize #' + IntToStr(Count) + ' is ' +
                IntToStr(Winner);
    lstWinners.Items.Add(ListItem);
  end  // end of for each prize
end;
```

- Save the unit file again and run the program with different input values to make sure it works correctly.

The Randomize procedure

In this example we use Delphi's Random function. What happens if we do not initialize the random number generator with the Randomize statement? To see what happens, comment out the Randomize statement from your final program. Run the program with input values of 100 tickets and 3 prizes. Who were the winners? Close the program and run it again with the same input values. Who were the winners? No matter how many times you close the program and run it again, you will get the same three winners the first time you click on the button.

Therefore, if you do not initialise the random number generator, the numbers are not random from one run to the next. Delete the comment in front of Randomize and run the program again to see that the starting values are different for different runs.

We have seen that it is critical to call the Randomize procedure before calling the Random function. It is, however, only necessary to do this once. In our program the Randomize statement appears in the btnSelectWinners event handler. This means that Randomize is called every time the button is clicked, which is unnecessary. We will see in Chapter 8 that we can place such code in the form's OnCreate event handler, so that it is only executed once the form is created.

Commenting code effectively

In Chapter 3 we introduced program comments and the different ways of writing comments. In this section we look at how to write comments that are useful and what sort of comments to avoid.

Look back at the event handler for btnSelectWinners in example 7.2 Step 5. Ignoring the code and only looking at the comments, we have:

```
// clear previous results
// initialise random number generator
// for each prize do ...
   {Generate a random winner}
   {Display prize number and winner number in list box}
// end of for each prize
```

Even without seeing a single Delphi statement, you can understand more-or-less what the program does by reading these comments. The comments above explain the *intention* of the statements – what the code achieves, rather than the details of how. Commenting the Ends of program blocks (like the final comment above) can be useful in matching Begin statements with End statements.

Although comments make no difference to how your program runs, they are still extremely important. Comments can make your code more readable and understandable to you and other programmers. When code is understandable it is far easier to debug (find and fix errors) or change. In the real world very few programmers work in isolation. As a developer, you will continually have to read and understand other programmers' code (as well as your own code later on).

Not all comments are, however, useful. Consider the following alternative to the comments above:

```
// call lstWinners.Clear
// call Randomize procedure
// for loop
   {Call Random function and store in Winner}
   {Concatenate strings and store in ListItem}
   {add ListItem to lstWinners.Items}
// end of for loop
```

Although there are even more comments than before and all are accurate, these comments are not much use. The problem is that they fail to describe the intention of the code, ie why the statements are there, and simply repeat the program statements.

Here are some general guidelines about commenting:

o   Write comments as you are writing your code, not afterwards. Better still, write comments before writing your code. That way, your plan is in place before you start programming and you can insert the code between the comments.

o   Avoid making obvious comments like:

```
Counter := Counter + 1;   // add one to Counter
```

Rather explain *why* Counter is being incremented. In other words: comments should explain the *intention* of the code.

o   Always comment tricky or confusing code.

o   Don't forget to revise your comments if your code changes significantly. (If your comments explain the intention, these changes should be minimal.)

As a final point, remember that naming conventions and descriptive variable names are also extremely important. Sensible variable names often mean fewer comments are needed.

EXAMPLE 7.3) Nested For loops

This example illustrates how loops, like If statements, can be nested. This means the statement that is repeated by a loop may contain a loop.

Study the following code carefully.

```
1 var
2    OuterChar, InnerChar: char;
3    MyString: string;
4 begin
5    for OuterChar := 'a' to 'e' do
6    begin
7      MyString := '';
8      for InnerChar := 'a' to OuterChar do
9        MyString := MyString + InnerChar;
10     lstStrings.Items.Add(MyString)
11   end;
12 end;
```

The outer loop (starting in line 5) will repeat five times – for each of the values 'a', 'b', 'c', 'd' and 'e'. With each iteration of the outer loop, three statements are executed: the first one (line 7) initializes MyString to the empty string; the second (lines 8 and 9) is a For loop which constructs a new string MyString by adding characters to MyString; and the last statement (line 10) adds MyString to the lstStrings ListBox. Since the outer loop repeats five times, the inner loop is encountered five times. When OuterChar has the value 'a', the inner loop's counter variable, InnerChar, goes from 'a' to 'a', which means it executes once; the second time (when OuterChar has the value 'b') InnerChar goes from 'a' to 'b', so it executes twice. The fifth time (when OuterChar has the value 'e') InnerChar goes from 'a' to 'e', so it executes five times. Starting with an empty string MyString, each iteration of the inner loop adds the current value of InnerChar to it.

The code adds the following five different string values to the lstStrings ListBox:

```
'a'
'ab'
'abc'
'abcd'
'abcde'
```

In example 7.6 we will write a program that uses nested loops.

The While...do statement

So far we have looked only at counter-driven loops, and specifically at the For loop. Not all loops are counter-driven, and we therefore need a loop structure where the number of iterations is not necessarily controlled by a counter variable. The While...do statement that we discuss next is a general-purpose loop which can handle counter-controlled loops as well as 'conditional' loops. In a conditional loop the number of repetitions is determined by some condition (ie a Boolean expression). In the case of a conditional While loop, the loop body repeats as long as a certain condition is True and ends when that condition becomes False.

The structure of a While...do statement looks as follows:

```
while Condition do
  Statement;
```

Statement can be a single Delphi statement, or it can be a compound statement enclosed within begin and end statements. The Condition is tested and if it is True, Statement is executed. Statement is then executed repeatedly until Condition becomes False. If Condition (called the loop condition) initially evaluates to False, Statement is never executed.

The condition of a While...do statement takes the same form as the condition of an If statement – it can be any Boolean expression (including a Boolean variable or a Boolean component property).

EXAMPLE 7.4) A While...do statement

We can replace any For loop with a While loop. In example 7.1 we had the following For loop:

```
Sum := 0;
for Count := sedLower.Value to sedUpper.Value do
  Sum := Sum + Count;
```

A While loop that does exactly the same is

```
1 Sum := 0;
2 Count := sedLower.Value;
3 while Count <= sedUpper.Value do
4 begin
5   Sum := Sum + Count;
6   Count := Count + 1;
7 end;
```

While the For loop automatically sets Count initially to the value in sedLower, when using a While loop we have to include a separate assignment statement (line 2) to do this. We also have to include a statement in the While loop's body that increases Count's value by 1 (line 6).

Two important rules

When using a While...do statement, always keep the following rules in mind:

Rule 1 The variable(s) that appear in the loop condition must be initialized before the While loop is first encountered. These variable(s) are called the loop control variable(s).

Rule 2 Inside the loop body the value of the loop control variable(s) must be modified to ensure that the loop condition becomes False at some stage, otherwise the program will continue forever.

In the While...do statement of the example above, `Count <= sedUpper.Value` is the loop condition and `Count` is the loop control variable. Note how the two rules for While loops have been applied here:

Rule 1 `Count` is initialized to `sedLower.Value` before the loop is encountered (line 2). If we don't do this, `Count` will contain an unknown integer value that may cause the loop to execute incorrectly.

Rule 2 Inside the loop the value of `Count` is modified by adding 1 to it (line 6). If we don't include the statement `Count := Count + 1;` the loop will keep on executing forever, since `Count`'s value will remain 1 and the loop condition will never become False.

EXAMPLE 7.5) Finding a name in a Memo

We are now going to write a program that searches for a particular name in a list of names in a Memo component. The user will type in the list of names and then give a name to search for in the list (figure 7.4).

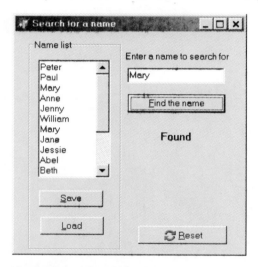

Figure 7.4 Searching for a name in a Memo

EX 7.5 Planning

We will use a While...do statement to compare the name with each name in the list. We will also include a Save button that allows the user to save the list of names to a file called Names.txt in the c:\Delphi files* folder, and a Load button to load those names into the Memo. (This is so that you do not have to retype a whole list of names every time you test the program.)

EX 7.5 Testing

When testing the program, we must make sure it handles each of the following possibilities correctly:

1   The name appears in the list once.
2   The name appears more than once.

* If you want to keep your program exactly like ours, you should create a directory called 'Delphi files' on the C:\ drive. Use Windows Explorer to do this.

3   The name is the first item in the list.
4   The name is the last item in the list.
5   The name does not appear in the list.

EX 7.5 STEP 1 Creating the form

- Start a new project and create a form such as figure 7.4 using the table below. (Recall that the SaveDialog and OpenDialog components are found in the Dialogs tab of the Component/Tool palette)

Component	Property	Value
Form1	Name	frmFindName
	Caption	Search for a name
Button1	Name	btnSave
	Caption	&Save
Button2	Name	btnLoad
	Caption	&Load
Button3	Name	btnFind
	Caption	&Find the name
SaveDialog1	Name	dlgSave
	FileName	c:\Delphi files\Names.txt†
OpenDialog1	Name	dlgOpen
	FileName	c:\Delphi files\Names.txt
Edit1	Name	edtName
	Text	<Blank>
GroupBox1	Name	gpbNames
	Caption	Name list
Label1	Name	lblPrompt
	Caption	Enter a name to search for
Label2	Name	lblResult
	Caption	<Blank>
Memo1	Name	memNames
	Lines	<Blank>
	ScrollBars	ssVertical
BitBtn1	Name	bmbReset
	Kind	bkRetry
	Caption	&Reset

- Save the unit file as C07e05u and the project as C07e05p.

EX 7.5 STEP 2 Saving names to and loading names from a file on disk

- To simplify future testing, create the event handlers for the Save and Load buttons first. Use the Open and Save dialogs as we did in example 5.5 of Chapter 5.

† If you want to use this as the default file name, the C:\Delphi files directory must exist.

```
procedure TfrmFindName.btnSaveClick(Sender: TObject);
begin
  if dlgSave.Execute then
    memNames.Lines.SaveToFile(dlgSave.FileName);
end;

procedure TfrmFindName.btnLoadClick(Sender: TObject);
begin
  if dlgOpen.Execute then
    memNames.Lines.LoadFromFile(dlgOpen.FileName);
end;
```

- In the next chapter, example 8.5 will also use the Names file you save here, so do not delete it once you have completed this example.

EX 7.5 STEP 3 Finding the name

- Double-click on btnFind and create the following event handler:

```
1  procedure TfrmFindName.btnFindClick(Sender: TObject);
2  var
3    NameToFind: string;
4    Found: boolean;
5    LineCount, Index: integer;
6  begin
7    {Initialise variables before starting search}
8    NameToFind := UpperCase(edtName.Text);
9    Index := 0;
10   Found := False;
11   LineCount := memNames.Lines.Count; // number of names in list

12   {Traverse the list to the end to find the name}
13   while Index <= LineCount - 1 do
14   begin
15     if UpperCase(memNames.Lines[Index]) = NameToFind then
16        Found := True;
17     Index := Index + 1;   // go to the next line in the list
18   end; // end of while

19   {Report if the name was found or not}
20   if Found = True then
21     lblResult.Caption := 'Found'
22   else
23     lblResult.Caption := 'Not Found';
24 end;
```

- Save the unit file again, run the program and do the following:
  - Type a list of names into the Memo component, each on a separate line (include some names more than once).
  - Click on Save and save the names in a file called Names.txt.
  - Type a name that appears in the list into the Edit box and click the Find the name button. Does the program correctly report that it has been found?

- Type a name that does not appear in the list and see whether the program gives the correct result.

Numbering and counting the lines in a Memo

In our program we have to compare NameToFind with each line in the Memo component. To refer to a specific line in the memo we give the number of the line in square brackets as follows: memNames.Lines[LineNo]. The lines are numbered from 0 upwards, so the first line is memNames.Lines[0] and memNames.Lines[5] refers to the 6th line. (We'll say more about this in Chapter 8.)

To get the total number of lines in a Memo we use the Lines.Count property. In this program we have, for example

```
LineCount := memNames.Lines.Count;
```

If there are 5 lines in the Memo, LineCount will be 5. Note, however, that to refer to the last line using LineCount we say memNames.Lines[LineCount – 1]. We have to subtract 1 from LineCount because Delphi numbers the lines in a Memo from 0 upwards and not from 1.

The counter-driven While loop in our event handler works as follows: Index is initialized to 0 (line 9) and at the end of each iteration of the loop it is increased by 1 (line 17) until it reaches LineCount – 1. For each value of Index, line 15 compares the upper case form of memNames.Lines[Index] to NameToFind (converted to uppercase in line 8). If they are equal, Found is set to True. (Note that line 17 is not part of the If statement, so Index is incremented whether or not they are equal.)

Why do we not have an Else part that assigns False to Found if the names are not equal? Well, if NameToFind is 'Mary' and 'Mary' is not the last name in the list, the name(s) that come after 'Mary' in the list will cause the Else part to be executed. This will set Found to False. This will give the wrong answer, because Mary did appear earlier in the list. Once Found has the value True (ie Mary has been found), we don't want it to change back to False.

To ensure that Found will have the value False if the name is not in the list, we must initialize Found to False *before* the loop (line 10).

Problems with the solution

Although this program works correctly, there are some problems with the code. First, if we want to use a counter-driven loop like this one, it would be better to use the following For loop:

```
Found := False;
for Count := 0 to LineCount – 1 do
  if UpperCase(memNames.Lines[Index]) = NameToFind then
    Found := True;
```

However, whether we use the While loop or the For loop, this is not a very efficient way to solve the problem. Assume 'Mary' appears five times in our list of names. Both the given loops will compare all the names in the list before giving the result. By that time Found will have been assigned the value True five times (for every time 'Mary' was found). All the program actually needs to do is to find the *first* occurrence of the name, set Found to True and then stop. This means we could use `Found` as our loop control variable and end the loop as soon as it becomes True. Here is a new version of the While loop:

```
1 Index := 0;
2 Found := False;
3 while not(Found) do
4 begin
5   if UpperCase(memNames.Lines[Index]) = NameToFind then
6     Found := True;
7   Index := Index + 1;
8 end;
```

Now, if a name is found, `Found` becomes True (line 6) and the loop ends the next time the loop condition is tested (line 3). This will work well if we search for a name that is in the list, but what will happen if we search for a name that does not appear in the list? In this case the While condition will always remain True, since `Found` will always be False, and the loop will not terminate normally. Consequently `Index` will continue increasing even when all the lines in the Memo have been checked and will result in an exception when we try to access lines which do not exist in the Memo. To solve this problem we expand the loop condition to

```
while (not Found) and (Index <= LineCount - 1) do
```

Now, if the name doesn't appear in the list, the loop will end when `Index` becomes equal to `LineCount`. Because it is also controlled by the Boolean variable `Found`, this While loop is not a counter-driven loop any more. We cannot find an equivalent For loop to replace it. However, the two rules for While loops that we mentioned before still apply: the loop control variables (in this case `Found` and `Index`) are initialized before the loop (lines 1 and 2), and the values of one or both of these variables change inside the loop to ensure that the loop will terminate (lines 6 and 7).

EX 7.5 STEP 4 An improved version of the event handler

To make sure there is no confusion, we give the complete improved version of the btnFindClick event handler:

```
1 procedure TfrmFindName.btnFindClick(Sender: TObject);
2 var
3   NameToFind: string;
4   Found: boolean;
5   LineCount, Index: integer;
6 begin
7   {Initialise variables before starting search}
8   NameToFind := UpperCase(edtName.Text);
9   Index := 0;
10  Found := False;
11  LineCount := memNames.Lines.Count; // number of names in list
```

```
12   {Traverse list until name is found or reaches end of list}
13   while not(Found) and (Index <= LineCount - 1) do
14   begin
15     if UpperCase(memNames.Lines[Index]) = NameToFind then
16        Found := True;
17     Index := Index + 1;   // go to the next line in the list
18   end; // end of while

19   {Report if the name was found or not}
20   if Found = True then
21     lblResult.Caption := 'Found'
22   else
23     lblResult.Caption := 'Not Found';
24 end;
```

To clarify how the code works, we trace the event handler using a trace table. Assume that we have the same input as before (figure 7.4). We start with the While loop in line 13. At this point, NameToFind is 'MARY' and, assuming there are 15 names in the list, LineCount is 15.

Line	Index	Found	Description
13	0	False	**not**(Found) **and** (Index <= 14) evaluates to True, so body of While loop is executed
15	0	False	UpperCase(memNames.Lines[0]) evaluates to 'PETER', so If condition fails and line 16 is ignored
17	1	False	Increment Index
13	1	False	**not**(Found) **and** (Index <= 14) evaluates to True, so body of While loop is executed
15	1	False	UpperCase(memNames.Lines[1]) evaluates to 'PAUL', so If condition fails and line 16 is ignored
17	2	False	Increment Index
13	2	False	**not**(Found) **and** (Index <= 14) evaluates to True, so body of While loop is executed
15	2	False	UpperCase(memNames.Lines[2]) evaluates to 'MARY', so If condition succeeds
16	2	True	Found := True
17	3	True	Increment Index
13	3	True	**not**(Found) **and** (Index <= 14) evaluates to False, so body of While loop is ignored
20	3	True	Found = True evaluates to True, so line 21 executes. The text 'Found' is displayed on lblResult's Caption and then the event handler ends.

EX 7.5 STEP 5 Resetting the input fields

The Reset button clears the Memo and the Edit box.
- Create its OnClick event handler and change it as follows:

```
procedure TfrmFindName.bmbResetClick(Sender: TObject);
begin
  memNames.Clear;
  edtName.Clear;
  memNames.SetFocus;
end;
```

- Save this final version of the program.

Choosing between For and While

Any For loop can be replaced with an equivalent While loop, but the opposite is
not true. If a loop is counter-driven, and if we know the number of times the
loop should execute, then a For loop is appropriate. (Note that in these cases we
can still solve the problem with a While loop, but it is simpler to use the For
loop.) In all other cases we have to use a While loop. In other words, if the loop
is not controlled by a counter and you do not know beforehand how many times
the loop will repeat, use a While loop.

EXAMPLE 7.6) Nested loops

In this example we illustrate the use of nested loops. We write a program
that simulates the following game: a coin is tossed *repeatedly* until the first
head appears. Suppose it takes N tosses to get the first head. A payout of
R5 × N is then made. For example: Tail, Tail, Head pays R5 × 3 = R15. The
program should play the game *repeatedly*, and should display the payout
for the consecutive games in a ListBox. It should also display the average
of all the payouts. The user must indicate how many times he or she
wants to play the game. Use the form layout shown in Figure 7.5.

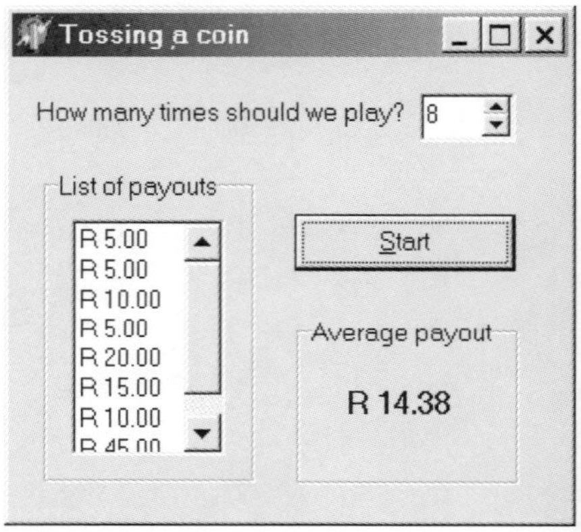

Figure 7.5 A sample run of 8 games

EX 7.6 Planning

The word 'repeatedly' appears twice in the problem statement. This indicates
that we should use two loop structures: one to repeat the tossing of the coin until
a head appears, and one to repeat the entire game as many times as the user
requested. Because the user tells us how many times to play the game we can
implement the latter loop as a For loop. We cannot predict how many tosses it
will take to get a Head, so we must implement the loop for that as a While loop.

How can we 'toss a coin' programmatically? What we need is a function that
returns one of two possible values, say 0 and 1. Let 0 represent Head and 1
represent Tail. In example 7.2 we used the Random function to return a random
integer. How can we use that function to return 0 or 1 randomly? With the
statement `Toss := Random(2);`.

The loops

As we've said, the outer loop which repeats the complete game is a For loop. If
the number of games is stored in the integer variable NoOfGames, we'll have

```
NoOfGames := sedNoOfGames.Value;
TotalPayout := 0;
for Count := 1 to NoOfGames do  // for each game do ...
begin
  :
  :
end;
```

Inside this loop the following must happen:

1   Toss the coin until we get a Head. (Count the number of tosses.)
2   Calculate the payout.
3   Add the payout to the ListBox of payouts.
4   The payout amount must be added to the total payouts made so far (so that we can calculate the average payout after the loop has ended).

EX 7.6 STEP 1   The body of the outer loop

In the planning section above we listed four steps that should take place inside the For loop that repeats the game as many times as the user requested. The first of these steps involves a While loop:

```
NoOfTosses := 1;
Toss := Random(2); // Randomly toss a coin (1st toss of game)
while Toss = 1 do  // while it is tails, do ...
begin
  Toss := Random(2); // toss the coin again
  NoOfTosses := NoOfTosses + 1;
end;
```

To calculate the payout we must multiply the number of tosses (NoOfTosses) by 5. Hence,

```
Payout := NoOfTosses * 5;  // payout is R5 for each toss
```

Then add the string form of this to the ListBox with

```
PayStr := FloatToStrF(Payout, ffCurrency, 10, 2);
lstPayOffs.Items.Add (PayStr);
```

And finally add the new payout to the current total payouts with

```
TotalPayout := TotalPayout + Payout;
```

When the outer loop has ended, the final step of the program will be to calculate the average payout and display it in the relevant Label Caption.

EX 7.6 STEP 2   The program

•   Let's write the program now. The form contains the following components:

Component	Property	Value
Form1	Name	frmTossCoin
	Caption	Tossing a coin
Button1	Name	btnStart
	Caption	&Start
GroupBox1	Name	gpbPayouts
	Caption	List of payouts
GroupBox2	Name	gpbAverage
	Caption	Average payout
Label1	Name	lblHowMany
	Caption	How many times should we play?
Label2 (in GroupBox2)	Name	lblAverage
	Caption	<Blank>
ListBox1 (in GroupBox1)	Name	lstPayouts
	Items	<Blank>
SpinEdit1	Name	sedNoOfGames
	Value	1

The btnStartClick event handler looks as follows:

```
procedure TfrmTossCoin.btnStartClick(Sender: TObject);
var
  NoOfTosses, Count, NoOfGames, Toss: integer;
  Payout, TotalPayout, AveragePayout: double;
begin
  lstPayouts.Clear;  // clear any previous payouts
  NoOfGames := sedNoOfGames.Value;
  TotalPayout := 0;
  Randomize;
  for Count := 1 to NoOfGames do  // for each game do ...
  begin
    NoOfTosses := 1;
    Toss := Random(2); // Randomly toss a coin (1st toss of game)
    while Toss = 1 do  // while it is tails, do ...
    begin
      Toss := Random(2);  // toss the coin again
      NoOfTosses := NoOfTosses + 1;
    end;
    Payout := NoOfTosses * 5;  // payout is R5 for teach toss
    lstPayouts.Items.Add(FloatToStrF(Payout,ffCurrency,10,2));
    TotalPayout := TotalPayout + Payout;
  end;  // end of for each game
  {All games now complete, so display average}
  AveragePayout := TotalPayout / NoOfGames;
  lblAverage.Caption := FloatToStrF(AveragePayout,ffCurrency,10,2);
end;
```

- Save the unit file as C07e06u and the project as C07e06p.
- Run it and test it a few times with different input values.

The Repeat...until loop

Delphi also has a Repeat loop, which is very similar to the While loop. It has the following structure:

```
repeat
    Loop body
until Condition;
```

The loop body consists of one or more Delphi statements. If there is more than one statement in the loop body, we need *not* enclose them in `begin` and `end` statements the way we have to with the While...do statement. The statements in the loop body are executed repeatedly until `Condition`, a Boolean expression, evaluates to True. This means that the condition is tested only *after* the loop body has been executed. In a While...do statement the loop condition is tested *before* the loop body is executed. As a consequence, the loop body of a Repeat...until loop will always be executed at least once (even if the condition is True right from the start). With a While...do statement it is possible that the loop body never executes (if its loop condition is False when tested the first time).

Any Repeat...until loop can also be implemented as a While...do statement, but the opposite is not true. Some While...do statements may never execute and we cannot write a Repeat loop that never executes. We will not discuss the Repeat loop in any more detail – if you can use the While...do statement correctly, you will not find it difficult to learn how to use a Repeat loop.

REVIEW

In this chapter we discussed two iteration structures, namely the For loop and the While loop. Iteration structures are used in a program when a part of the code needs to be executed repeatedly. The For loop is a counter-driven loop that is executed a predetermined number of times. We use it in a program only when we know exactly how many times the loop should repeat before entering the loop.

The While...do statement, on the other hand, is suitable where statements must be repeated while some condition is True. In such cases the number of repetitions may not be known before starting the loop. The Repeat...until loop is similar to the While...do loop, but the condition is tested after the loop body has been executed and so will always execute at least once. We've seen how loops can be nested, and how we can avoid infinite loops.

We also introduced the trace table, which is a technique for manually keeping track of the values of variables as a program executes. We looked at comments in more depth, in particular at how useful comments describe the *intention* of the code.

IMPORTANT CONCEPTS

Fundamental programming concepts

Commenting code: You should use comments so that your code is understandable to yourself and to other programmers. Comments should explain the intention of the code (ie what the code achieves, rather than the intricate details of how it does it).

Conditional loop: A loop where the number of iterations depends on the truth or falsity of the loop condition (a Boolean expression). One or more statements in the loop body influence the value of the condition, so that at some point it will cause the repetition to stop. While loops and Repeat loops can function as conditional loops, but not For loops.

Counter-driven loop: The number of iterations in a counter-driven loop is determined by the value of a variable that counts the number of times the loop executes. All For loops are counter-driven. While loops may be counter driven if there is a variable that is incremented inside the While loop's body and this variable is a loop control variable.

Infinite loop: A loop where the loop condition never reaches the value that makes the repetition end. To avoid an infinite loop the programmer must make sure that the loop control variable is updated inside the body of the loop in such a manner that it will eventually cause the loop to end.

Initialization (of variables): Assigning initial values to variables. When we declare a variable, Delphi assigns a memory location to the variable where its value will be kept. We do not know what value that particular memory location contains. Therefore, in programs where the initial value of a variable might influence the working of our program, we have to assign the correct initial value to that variable.

Nested loop: A loop that appears inside the body of another loop.

Random number generation: Programs frequently need to generate random numbers to simulate a chance outcome such as the throw of a dice or a lottery win.

Trace table: A trace table is a way of manually keeping track of the values of variables as a program progresses and can help in finding errors and understanding the logic of a program. Each line of code is represented as a line in the table and the order in which lines appear match the order of execution of the program. Important variables form the columns of the trace table.

NEW DELPHI FEATURES

Procedures and functions	
Random function	A function that returns an integer value in a specified range. For example, Random (10) returns a value from 0 to 9.
Randomize procedure	This procedure must be called before the Random function is used in a program. It initializes Delphi's random number generator.

New properties	Lines.Count	Gives the number of lines of text in the Memo component
	Lines[n]	The (n+1)th line of text in the Memo (a string). The lines are numbered from 0 upwards (unlike the characters in strings, which are numbered from 1 upwards). For example, the first line of text in a Memo memNames is memNames.Lines[0] and the last line is memNames.Lines[memNames.Lines.Count - 1].

Delphi Pascal commands

For statement	Implements counter-driven loops where the number of iterations is known. The structure of a For loop is

	```for CounterVariable := LowerBound to UpperBound do```
	    ```Statement;```
	or
	```for CounterVariable := UpperBound downto LowerBound do```
	    ```Statement;```
	
	where CounterVariable, LowerBound and UpperBound are of the same ordinal data type, and Statement is any Delphi statement.

Repeat...until statement	Implements an iteration structure of which the body is always executed at least once. Its format is:
	
	```repeat```
	    ```Statement sequence (loop body)```
	```until Condition;```
	
	Statement sequence (any sequence of Delphi statements) is repeated until Condition (a Boolean expression) has the value True.

While...do statement	Implements an iteration structure that repeats a Delphi statement while some condition is True. Its structure is:
	
	```while Condition do```
	    ```Statement;```
	
	Statement (a single Delphi statement or a compound statement between begin and end) is repeatedly executed while Condition (a Boolean expression) has the value True.

PROBLEMS

PROBLEM 7.1 Predicting population growth

- Write a program that reads the population of a city in 2003 as well as the annual population growth rate. It then displays the projected population of that city until the year 2020. Each year with its expected population must be shown in a ListBox. Your program should be well commented (as should all your programs from now onwards).
- When you have finished programming the solution, draw up a trace table to show how the variables change after each statement in your program. You can stop the trace when the year reaches 2007. Check the values in your table against the values printed in the ListBox when your program runs.

PROBLEM 7.2) Counting a character in a string

- Write a program that inputs a string and a character from the user and then counts the number of times the character appears in the string (figure 7.6).

Remember: we refer to a specific character in a string by specifying its position in square brackets. For example, word[1] is the first character of word. In general word[Index] is the character at position Index in word, where Index is an integer ranging from 1 to Length(word).

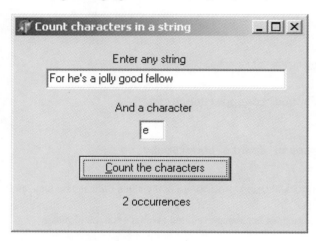

Figure 7.6 Counting the occurrences of a letter in a sentence

PROBLEM 7.3) A savings account

- Write a program that reads an amount deposited into a savings account that pays 5% interest (figure 7.7). The deposit amount may not exceed R15 000.00. If R1 000.00 is withdrawn every year and nothing more is deposited, the program must calculate how many years it will take for the account to be depleted. Use a loop and not a formula to answer this question.

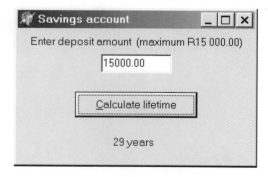

Figure 7.7 The Savings account form

PROBLEM 7.4) Counting the number of words in a sentence

- Write a program that uses a While...do statement to count the number of words in a sentence supplied by the user. The program must also work if one word is given, or no words at all.

- To keep the program simple, you may assume that the user will not type more than one space between the words.

PROBLEM 7.5) Nested loops

a   Work through the For loop below (by hand) and write down the contents of the lstShape ListBox after execution of the code (if necessary, draw a trace table to figure it out). Assume that the variables have all been declared correctly.

```
1 for I := 1 to 4 do
2 begin
3    Line := '';
4    for J := 1 to 3 do
5       Line := Line + '@ ';
6    lstShape.Items.Add(Line);
7 end;
```

b   How would the final contents of the ListBox change if the upper bound of the outer For loop changed to 10 as follows?

```
1 for I := 1 to 10 do
2 ...
```

c   How would the final contents of the ListBox change if the upper bound of the inner For loop changed to 10 as follows?

```
1 for I := 1 to 4 do
2 begin
3    Line := '';
4    for J := 1 to 10 do
5    ...
```

d   How would the final contents of the ListBox change if the upper bound of the inner For loop changed to be the variable I as follows?

```
1 for I := 1 to 4 do
2 begin
3    Line := '';
4    for J := 1 to I do
5    ...
```

PROBLEM 7.6) The repeat ... until loop

- Change example 7.6 so that it uses a Repeat loop in place of the While loop.

CHAPTER 8

Arrays and indexes

PURPOSE OF THIS CHAPTER

The programs we write often need to access and manipulate individual items in a collection of related data items. Like any other programming language, Delphi Pascal includes features that make it easy to work with groups (or lists) of data items. The array data structure allows us to store a group of elements of the same type under one name. Similarly the ListBox and Memo components allow us to store lists of string items. To access a specific item in an array or string list we need a way of specifying which item we want. For this we use an *index*, which is usually an integer number that indicates the position of a data item relative to the beginning of the list or array.

In this chapter we look at string lists, and how we use indexes to access the characters of a string. We introduce arrays, how to declare, initialise and manipulate arrays, including dynamic arrays, two-dimensional arrays and array constants. We see how we can use indexing to manipulate and query components such as ComboBoxes, ListBoxes and RadioGroups. Finally we look at how we can manipulate groups of components in the same way using loops with component arrays.

In our discussion of indexing and arrays we introduce several new Delphi components and programming concepts. These include the *RadioGroup*, the *ComboBox*, the notion of *scope* and *unit-level declarations* and *typecasting*.

Strings and indexes

To get a copy of the first letter of a string named `Surname` we use the statement

```
FirstLetter := Surname[1];
```

The number that appears in square brackets after a string variable is the index to a specific character in that string. `Surname[1]` is the first character, `Surname[2]` is the second character, and so on. A string is therefore a list of characters that we can access individually using an index in square brackets after the variable name. Note that the index to the first character of a string is 1. As you will see, the first element of some other kinds of list (such as the items in a ListBox) has the index 0.

EXAMPLE 8.1 Reversing a string

This example reverses the letters of a word that the user supplies to illustrate how we can manipulate the individual characters in a string using an index. To do this the program builds a new word where the first letter is equal to the last letter of the original word, the second letter is equal to the second last letter of the original word, and so on. So, to solve this problem our program must traverse the input string backwards starting from the last letter, and add the individual letters to a new string.

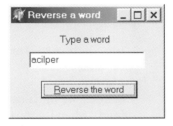

Figure 8.1 After clicking the Reverse button

EX 8.1 Planning

What is the index to the last letter of String variable `word`, if we do not know what the value of `word` is? Indexing of a string starts at 1, so the index of the last letter is equal to the length of the string. This we can get with the Length function. `Length(word)` returns an integer value that is equal to the length of `word`, and so `Length(word)` is also the index to the last letter of `word`. In our solution we will use a For loop where the counter variable's value starts at `Length(word)` and goes down to 1. This counter variable will act as an index to the individual letters. Inside the For loop we will then build up the new (reversed) word, letter by letter.

EX 8.1 STEP 1 Creating the form

- Open a new application and create the user interface with the following property values:

Component	Property	Value
Form1	Name	frmReverseWord
	Caption	Reverse a word
Button1	Name	btnReverse
	Caption	&Reverse the word

Edit1	Name	edtWord
	Text	<Blank>
Label1	Name	lblPrompt
	Caption	Type a word

The button's OnClick event handler looks like this:

```
 1 procedure TfrmReverseWord.btnReverseClick(Sender: TObject);
 2 var
 3   Word, NewWord: String;
 4   Index: Integer;
 5 begin
 6   Word := edtWord.Text;        // Copy the input string to a variable
 7   NewWord := '';               // Initialize NewWord to the empty string

 8   for Index := Length(Word) downto 1 do  // working from end of Word...
 9     NewWord := NewWord + Word[Index]; // append each char to NewWord

10   edtWord.Text := NewWord;
11 end;
```

In line 7 we initialize NewWord to the empty string. This is to make sure that it is empty when we start to build up the string in line 9. In the For loop (lines 8 and 9), the value of Index goes from the length of the word down to 1. Suppose the word is 'abc'. Its length is 3, so Index starts at 3. Word[Index] (in other words, Word[3]) is then 'c'. This 'c' is concatenated with NewWord, which is initially empty (line 9). So, NewWord is now equal to 'c'. Next, Index becomes 2 (line 8) and Word[2] (ie 'b') is concatenated with NewWord to get 'cb'. Then Index becomes 1 and Word[1] (ie 'a') is concatenated with NewWord to get 'cba'. The loop ends and NewWord is assigned to the edit box's Text property in line 10.

Replacing the For loop (lines 8 and 9) with the following one will also solve the problem correctly:

```
for Index := 1 to Length(Word) do
  NewWord := Word[Index] + NewWord;
```

Here Index goes from 1 up to Length(Word), but now each letter is added to the front of the current NewWord.

- Work through this alternative For loop with the word 'abc' to convince yourself that the result will again be the reversed word.

Arrays

An *array* is a data structure that allows us to store a set of data items of the same type under a single name. So far we've used variable names for single data items only. Using an array variable, we can, for example, store a whole list of names under the same variable name and then refer to the different items in the list through an index value. One can compare an array with the Items property of a ListBox (or Memo), which also provides a way to store a list of data items in one structure. One difference between the Items property of a ListBox and an array is that the elements of an array can be of any Delphi data type – not just strings (though all elements must be of the same type).

If we want to store 20 names in an array called NamesArray, we can declare it as follows:

```
var NamesArray: array[1..20] of String;
```

and refer to the individual elements with NamesArray[1], NamesArray[2], and so on, or with NamesArray[Index] where Index is an integer with a value from 1 to 20.

The lower bound of the index range need not be 1. For example,

```
var TotalRainfall: array[1990..1999] of double;
```

declares an array that holds the total rainfall figures for the years 1990 to 1999 (ie 10 rainfall figures). The index to the first element of this array is 1990. In this case using the relevant year as index is more meaningful than using 1 to 10.

We can assign a value to an array element with an assignment statement. For example:

```
TotalRainfall[1990] := StrToFloat(edtInput.Text);
```

or

```
NamesArray[1] := 'James';
```

When programming with arrays, be careful to keep the value of the index within the declared bounds. Using index values outside the specified range will cause a run-time error.

EXAMPLE 8.2) Reversing five strings

In this example the user enters five words and the program forms a nonsense sentence by reversing these words (figure 8.2 and 8.3). While the first button reverses the characters in the words before forming a sentence, the second button reverses the actual words in the sentence. In figure 8.2, the user typed in five words and clicked on the 'Reverse and form sentence' button. Figure 8.3 shows the result after the user clicked on the 'Reverse Words in sentence' button. Notice how the first word in the final sentence in figure 8.2 ('elbmuj') is the last word in figure 8.3.

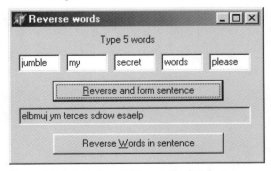

Figure 8.2 Result after clicking on the first button

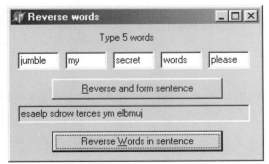

Figure 8.3 Result after clicking on the second button

EX 8.2 Planning

We start by tackling the first button only. In the previous example we wrote code to reverse a single string. We can use the same approach except that we do it five times for each word. Rather than using five separate variables, we store the five words in an array of strings. We can then use a For loop to loop through this array and reverse each string. Our array declaration will look like this:

```
var Words: array[1..5] of String;
```

For convenience we index the array from 1 to 5. We can represent this array graphically as follows:

1	2	3	4	5

We show the index values (1..5) at the top. The open boxes below each index represent the space for the strings. Since the array has not yet been initialised with string values, the boxes are shown as empty.

EX 8.2 STEP 1   Creating the form

- Open a new application and create the user interface in figure 8.2 using the following property values.

Component	Property	Value
Form1	Name	frmReverseAll
	Caption	Reverse words
Label1	Name	lblPrompt
	Caption	Type 5 words
Edit1…Edit5	Name	edtWord1…edtWord5
	Text	<Blank>
Button1	Name	btnReverse
	Caption	&Reverse and form sentence
Edit6	Name	edtSentence
	Text	<Blank>
	ReadOnly	True
	Color	clBtnFace
Button2	Name	btnReverseWords
	Caption	Reverse &Words in sentence

- Save the unit file as C08e02u and the project file as C08e02p.

EX 8.2 STEP 2   Creating the event handler

- Double-click on the button and type the following event handler

```
 1 procedure TfrmReverseWord.btnReverseClick(Sender: TObject);
 2 var
 3   Words: array[1..5] of string;
 4   Word, NewWord, Sentence: string;
 5   Index, Counter: integer;
 6 begin
 7   {copy the input to the array of words}
 8   Words[1] := edtWord1.Text;
 9   Words[2] := edtWord2.Text;
10   Words[3] := edtWord3.Text;
11   Words[4] := edtWord4.Text;
12   Words[5] := edtWord5.Text;

13   {for each word in Words array: reverse it}
14   for Counter := 1 to 5 do
15   begin
16     NewWord := '';   // Initialize NewWord to the empty string
17     Word := Words[Counter];

18     {for each char in Word (from the end) concatenate to NewWord}
19     for Index := Length(Word) downto 1 do
20       NewWord := NewWord + Word[Index];

21     Words[Counter] := NewWord; // store reversed word in array
22   end; // end of for each word in the array

23   {form a sentence from the reversed words}
24   Sentence := '';
25   for Counter := 1 to 5 do
26     Sentence := Sentence + Words[Counter] + ' ';
27   edtSentence.Text := Sentence;   // display the sentence
28 end;
```

- Save the unit file again and run the program to see that it is working correctly.

In the event handler we start by initialising the elements of the Words array (lines 8 to 12). Each element is initialised with the value of the corresponding EditBox's Text property. At this point the array can be represented graphically as follows (assuming the user input values as in figure 8.2):

1	2	3	4	5
jumble	my	secret	words	please

We then use a For loop to iterate through the array (line 14 to 21). For each element, the string is reversed (lines 19 to 20) and stored back in the array (line 21). At the end of the loop (after line 22) the contents of the array can be represented as follows:

1	2	3	4	5
elbmuj	ym	terces	sdrow	esaelp

In the final part of the event handler we use another For loop to form the Sentence string by concatenating each element in the array to Sentence with a space between (lines 25 to 26). The final sentence is then displayed (line 27).

Looping through an array

For loops are very useful for accessing and manipulating arrays. In the event handler above, the For loop starts at 1 (the index of the first element of the array) and ends at 5 (the index of the last element of the array). By using such a For loop, we can perform the same task (in this case reversing the string) on each element of the array. Inside the loop, we refer to the particular element in the array by using the For loop counter (Words[Counter]).

Let's consider a different example. Assume we have an array of 10 rainfall figures declared as follows:

```
var TotalRainfall: array[1990..1999] of double;
```

Assuming the array above has been initialised (ie it contains rainfall figures), we can use the following For loop to calculate the total rainfall for all 10 years from 1990 to 1999:

```
Sum := 0;
for Counter := 1990 to 1999 do
  Sum := Sum + TotalRainfall[Counter];
```

We will see many more examples of For loops and arrays in the remaining examples of this chapter.

EX 8.2 STEP 3 Programming the second button

In this step we write the event handler for the second button. While the first button reversed the characters in the words before forming a sentence, the second button needs to reverse the actual words in the sentence.

- Double click on button btnReverseWords and type the following event handler:

```
1 procedure TfrmReverseWord.btnReverseWordsClick(Sender: TObject);
2 var
3   Counter: integer;
4   RevSentence: string;
5 begin
6   RevSentence := '';
7   for Counter := 5 downto 1 do
8     RevSentence := RevSentence + Words[Counter] + ' ';
9   edtSentence.Text := RevSentence;
10 end;
```

- Run the program. You should get the following error message on line 8:
  `Undeclared identifier: 'words'.`

Why do we get this error? The problem relates to where the variable words has been declared and is an issue of *scope*.

Scope and unit-level declarations

A variable can be used only within the *scope* of its declaration. The scope of a variable is defined by the block in which it is declared. For example, if a variable is declared inside a procedure, that variable has a scope limited to that procedure. This means that it can only be used inside the Begin...End block of that procedure. We say the variable is *local* to that procedure.

In our example above, the words array is declared in the var section of the btnReverseClick event handler (step 2, line 3). This means that the scope of the words array is local to the btnReverseClick event handler (step 2 lines 1 – 28) and cannot be used outside that procedure. Another way of saying this is that the words array only exists inside the event handler and when the event handler ends, the variable no longer exists. Trying to use the words array from inside the btnReverseWords event handler (a different procedure) therefore generates an 'undeclared identifier' error.

A solution to this problem is to give the words array a larger scope by declaring it inside a bigger code block that includes both the event handler procedures. We do this by moving the declaration of the array out of the event handler and placing it in the unit's declaration section (see step below).

EX 8.2 STEP 4 Declaring array Words as a unit-level variable

To change the scope of the Words array from local to unit-level scope, do the following:
- In the code of C08e02u, scroll up to above the first procedure until you see the implementation keyword. It is below this keyword that we declare unit-level variables.
- Move the declaration of the words array so that the code looks as follows (note: the line *{$R *.dfm}* is an instruction to the compiler and should not be deleted):

```
1  implementation

2  {$R  *.dfm}

3  var
4    Words: array[1..5] of string;

5  procedure TfrmReverseWord.btnReverseClick(Sender: TObject);
6  var
7    Word, NewWord, Sentence: string;
8    Index, Counter: integer;
9  begin
10   {copy the input to the array of words}
11   :
```

The unit-level declaration appears in lines 3 to 4 above. The Words array can therefore be used from inside any procedure within the unit. In contrast, the local variables declared in lines 6 to 8 can only be used from within the btnReverseClick event handler.

- Save the unit file and run the program. An error message no longer appears and the program works as it should.

Dynamic arrays

In example 8.2 above we knew beforehand that there would be five strings, so we could declare the array using an appropriate index range [1..5]. What do we do if we know we need to store a number of elements in an array, but we don't know how many elements there will be? The solution is to use a *dynamic array*. When we declare a dynamic array, we leave out the index range. For example

```
var
  ManyWords: array of string;
```

In the above declaration, the variable ManyWords is declared as an array, but the number of elements is unknown. Before using the array, the size must be set by calling the SetLength procedure. For example, to store 10 strings in the ManyWords array, set its length as follows:

```
SetLength(ManyWords, 10);
```

The first parameter is the name of the array and the second parameter indicates the number of elements that the array can now store.

A dynamic array is indexed from 0 to the number of elements − 1. In our example, ManyWords[0] is therefore the first element and ManyWords[9] is the last element.

EXAMPLE 8.3) Test results

In this example we illustrate a dynamic array of integers. The user can enter the test results of any number of students as well as the total for that test (figure 8.4). The program then calculates and prints a summary of the test marks: the highest percentage obtained in the test, the average percentage for the test and the number of students who passed (ie obtained 50% or more).

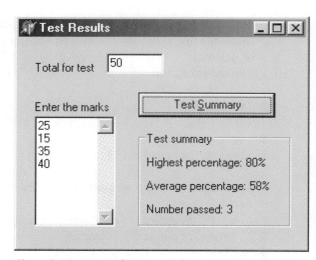

Figure 8.4 Summary of test results for any number of marks

EX 8.3   Planning

Since we do not know how many marks will be entered, we use a dynamic array of integers to store the marks. The marks will be typed in a Memo component, so we can find out how many marks have been entered by using the `Lines.Count` property of the Memo. We can write the overall plan of the event handler in the form of comments as follows:

```
{set the length of the array based on the number of marks entered}

{store the marks in the array as percentages}

{for all of the marks,
 calculate the total and keep track of the highest mark}

{calculate the average and display the summary figures}
```

When we are ready to write the code, we can type these comments directly into the event handler and use them as a guide for writing the actual code.

EX 8.3   Testing

After coding the program, we have to make sure it is working correctly. The input to the program is the total for the test and a list of marks. The output is three values: the highest percentage, the average percentage and the number

Test case	Input		Expected output		
	Test Total	Marks	Highest	Average	Number passed
1	50	25	80%	58%	3
		15			
		35			
		40			
2	120	120	100%	100%	1
3	80	39	49%	25%	0
		0			
		21			

These test cases cover three different scenarios. The first test case is a normal case where the test is out of 50, 4 students write and 3 pass. The second scenario is where only one student writes the test and gets 100%. In the third scenario, no students pass and one student gets zero.

EX 8.3 STEP 1   Creating the form

- Open a new application and create the user interface in figure 8.4 using the following property values:

Component	Property	Value
Form1	Name	frmTestResults
	Caption	Test Results
Label1	Name	lblTotal
	Caption	Total for test
Edit1	Name	edtTotal
	Text	<Blank>
Label2	Name	lblMarks
	Caption	Enter the marks
Memo1	Name	memMarks
	Lines	<Blank>
	ScrollBars	ssVertical
Button1	Name	btnSummary
	Caption	Test &Summary
GroupBox1	Name	gpbSummary
	Caption	Test summary
Label3	Name	lblHighest
	Caption	Highest percentage:
Label4	Name	lblAverage
	Caption	Average percentage:
Label5	Name	lblPassed
	Caption	Number passed:

- Save the unit file as C08e03u and the project file as C08e03p.

EX 8.3 STEP 2   Creating the event handler

- Double click on the button and create the following event handler:

```
1 procedure TfrmTestResults.btnSummaryClick(Sender: TObject);
2 var
3   Percentages: array of double;      // dynamic array
4   I, NoOfMarks, TestTotal, NumPassed: integer;
5   Sum, Highest, Average: double;
6 begin
7   {set the length of the array based on the number of marks entered}
8   NoOfMarks := memMarks.Lines.Count;
9   SetLength(Percentages, NoOfMarks);
```

```
10    {store the marks in the array as percentages}
11    TestTotal := StrToInt(edtTotal.Text); // read in total of test
12    for I := 0 to NoOfMarks-1 do
13       Percentages[I] := StrToInt(memMarks.Lines[I]) / TestTotal * 100;

14    {for all of the marks, calculate the total and keep track of
15     the highest mark}
16    Sum := 0;
17    Highest := 0;
18    NumPassed := 0;
19    for I:= 0 to NoOfMarks-1 do
20    begin
21       Sum := Sum + Percentages[I];
22       if (Percentages[I] > Highest) then
23          Highest := Percentages[I];
24       if (Percentages[I] >= 50) then
25          NumPassed := NumPassed + 1;
26    end;

27    {calculate the average and display the summary figures}
28    Average := Sum / NoOfMarks;
29    lblHighest.Caption := 'Highest percentage: ' +
30                          FloatToStrF(Highest,ffFixed,12,0) + '%';
31    lblAverage.Caption := 'Average percentage: ' +
32                          FloatToStrF(Average,ffFixed,12,0) + '%';
33    lblPassed.Caption := 'Number passed: ' + IntToStr(NumPassed);
34 end;
```

- Save the unit file again.
- Run the program using the test cases given before to check that the program gives the expected output values for each test case. When you type in the marks, make sure you do not enter an empty line after the last mark, otherwise Delphi will try to convert an empty line to an integer and an exception will occur.

In line 3 we declare the array Percentages for storing the individual marks as percentages. We declare the array as a dynamic array since we do not know beforehand how many marks need to be stored. The number of marks will only become clear at run-time when the user has entered the marks. In line 8 we determine this value by accessing the Lines.Count property of memMarks and we set the length of the array accordingly (line 9).

To store the marks in the array, we use a For loop (lines 12 to 13) that starts at 0 (dynamic arrays are always indexed from 0) and ends at NoOfMarks - 1 (the last element). Each mark is converted from a string to an integer, divided by the test total and multiplied by 100 to be stored as a mark out of 100 in the array.

We then iterate through the array again (lines 19 to 26), to calculate the sum of all marks (line 21), determine the highest mark (lines 22 to 23) and count the number of students who passed (lines 24 to 25).

Finally, we calculate the average (line 28) and display the mark summary figures on the user interface (lines 29 to 33).

Notice how every variable is initialised before it is used. The array Percentages is initialised in the For loop (line 13); loop counter I is initialised to 0 in the For statement (line 12 and again in line 19); NoOfMarks is initialised to the number of lines in the Memo (line 8); TestTotal is initialised to the value typed in by the user (line 11); NumPassed, Sum and Highest are initialised to 0 (lines 16 to 18) and Average is initialised to the result of Sum divided by NoOfMarks. Initialising variables to sensible values is a critical part of a working program.

Initialising arrays and array constants

In example 8.2 we declared an array of strings called Words. In the event handler we initialised the array by assigning each element a value in separate statements:

```
Words[1] := edtWord1.Text;
Words[2] := edtWord2.Text;
Words[3] := edtWord3.Text;
Words[4] := edtWord4.Text;
Words[5] := edtWord5.Text;
```

In example 8.3 we initialised the Percentages array using a For loop:

```
for I := 0 to NoOfMarks-1 do
  Percentages[I] := StrToInt(memMarks.Lines[I]) / TestTotal * 100;
```

Another way of initialising an array is to give it values when it is declared as shown in the examples below. This notation is used for array constants. Array constants are simply arrays which do not change.

```
const
  BoxingWeightLimits: array[1..10] of integer = (48,51,54,57,60,
                                                  64,69,75,81,91);
  BoxingWeightCategories: array[1..11] of String =
            ('Light Fly','Fly','Bantam','Feather','Light',
             'Light Welter','Welter','Middle','Light Heavy',
             'Heavy','Super Heavy');
```

The two array constants above store the names of the men's boxing weight limits with their associated weight categories. For example, a boxer with a weight of 48kg and less would be in the 'Light Fly' weight category, while a boxer weighing over 91kg would fall into the 'Super Heavy' weight category.

Array constants are indexed just like normal arrays, except that the values inside array constants cannot be re-assigned (changed). In the following code segment, we print the category of a boxer, depending on their weight:

```
var
  BoxerWeight: double;
  I: integer;
begin
  BoxerWeight := StrToFloat(edtWeight.Text);
  I := 1;
  {check which weight category the boxer falls into}
  while (BoxerWeight > BoxingWeightLimits[I]) and (I <= 10) do
    I := I + 1; {go on to the next weight category}
  lblCategory.Caption := BoxingWeightCategories[I] + ' Weight';
end;
```

The While loop consists of two conditions which must both be True for the loop to continue. The first condition checks if the given weight is greater than one of the set limits (stored in array `BoxingWeightLimits`). If not, the loop stops because we have found the category that applies to that boxer. The second condition (`I <= 10`) makes sure that the index does not go over the limit of the `BoxingWeightLimits` array. This will happen in the case where the given weight is greater than 91. In this case, the value of `I` will be incremented all the way to 11, the loop will stop (because of the second condition) and the category displayed will be 'Super Heavy Weight'.

We use other examples of array constants in our next example.

Two-dimensional arrays

The arrays we have described so far all contain a single list of elements. We can also declare multi-dimensional arrays that store tables with several rows and columns. For example

```
var Rainfall : array[1995..1999, 1..12] of double;
```

declares a two-dimensional array with 5 rows (indexed 1995 to 1999) and 12 columns (indexed 1 to 12). In each row we can store the 12 monthly rainfall figures for the relevant year. We can represent this graphically as follows:

	1	2	3	4	5	6	7	8	9	10	11	12
1995												
1996				A								
1997												
1998									B			
1999												

We refer to the cell marked A as `Rainfall[1996, 4]` and to the cell marked B as `Rainfall[1998, 9]`. So now we have to give a row index and a column index when accessing an array element. The row index always comes first.

In example 8.4 you will get some practice in using two-dimensional arrays.

The ComboBox component

The next example introduces the ComboBox component, which appears in the Standard tab of the Component/Tool palette. When placed on a form, it looks like an edit box with a little down arrow on the right-hand side (figure 8.5). Clicking on the down arrow displays a list of options from which the user can choose. These options are specified in the ComboBox's Items property. When the user clicks on an item in the list, that item is placed in the text box and the list disappears. The items in a ComboBox's list are indexed from 0 upwards. The ItemIndex property gives the index of the currently selected item in the list. If ItemIndex has the value -1, it means that no element in the list is selected. The ItemIndex property can only be set programmatically (ie we cannot set it in the Object Inspector).

EXAMPLE 8.4 ComboBoxes and two-dimensional arrays

This example illustrates the use of ComboBoxes and a two-dimensional array. The program prompts the user to enter two names from a list of South African cities. Clicking on the Show distance button displays the road distance (in kilometres) between the two cities (figure 8.5).

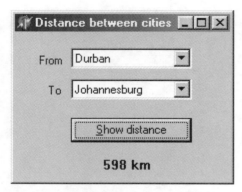

Figure 8.5 Distance between two selected cities

EX 8.4 Planning

We'll store the distance information in a two-dimensional array called Distances. It contains the integer values given in the table below.

	Durban	Cape Town	Johannesburg
Durban	0	1660	598
Cape Town	1660	0	1405
Johannesburg	598	1405	0

To make it easier to add more cities later, we declare a constant for the number of cities (3 to start with) and we store the names of cities in an array constant of strings called Cities. In a problem at the end of the chapter you will be able to add other South African cities.

To make it easy for the user to choose two cities, we use two ComboBoxes — one for the 'from' city and one for the 'to' city. We populate the ComboBoxes with the names of the cities in the Cities array in the form's OnCreate event handler.

EX 8.4 STEP 1 Create the form

- Start a new application and create a form with the following components and properties:

Component	Property	Value
Form1	Name	frmDistance
	Caption	Distance between cities
ComboBox1	Name	cboFrom
	Style	csDropDownList
ComboBox2	Name	cboTo
	Style	csDropDownList
Button1	Name	btnShowDistance
	Caption	&Show distance
Label1	Name	lblFrom
	Caption	From
Label2	Name	lblTo
	Caption	To
Label3	Name	lblDistance
	Caption	<Blank>

The Style property of the ComboBoxes is set to csDropDownList, so that the user cannot type directly into the ComboBox's input box – they have to select a city from the list. When you want to allow users to type a value into that box, keep the default style, namely csDropDown.

- Save the unit and project files as C08e04u and C08e04p respectively.

EX 8.4 STEP 2 Defining the array constants

We define the Cities and Distances arrays as constants in the declaration section of the unit so that we can use them in more than one event handler in the unit. The unit's constant declaration section (just below the implementation keyword) should look like this:

implementation

```
{$R *.dfm}
const
  NoOfCities = 3;
  Cities: array[1..NoOfCities] of String
        = ('Durban','Cape Town','Johannesburg');
  Distances: array[1..NoOfCities, 1..NoOfCities] of integer
        = ((   0, 1660,  598), // Durban to ...
           (1660,   0, 1405), // Cape Town to ...
           ( 598, 1405,    0)); // Joburg to ...
```

Each row of values inside the the two-dimensional Distances array is written as a list of three values separated by commas inside brackets. These three brackets of values (each representing a row in the table) are separated by commas in another set of brackets to form the whole array.

EX 8.4 STEP 3 Loading the ComboBoxes with values

Before the form appears we should load the ComboBoxes with the names of the cities as they appear in the `Cities` array constant defined above.

- In design view, double-click anywhere on the form background (ie not on any of the components on the form). This creates the skeleton for the Form's OnCreate event handler.
- Type the following event handler.

```
1 procedure TfrmDistance.FormCreate(Sender: TObject);
2 var
3   I: integer;
4 begin
5   {add the cities to both ComboBoxes:}
6   for I := 1 to NoOfCities do
7   begin
8     cboFrom.Items.Add(Cities[I]);
9     cboTo.Items.Add(Cities[I]);
10   end;
11   {set defaults in ComboBoxes to 1st city:}
12   cboFrom.ItemIndex := 0;
13   cboTo.ItemIndex := 0;
14 end;
```

- Save the unit file and run the program. Notice how both ComboBoxes contain the city names as they appear in our `Cities` string array constant and both show Durban as the default value.

The Form's OnCreate event is called when the form is created, so the OnCreate event handler is a useful place to put code that you need to be executed before the form is displayed to the user for the first time.

To add the city names to our ComboBoxes, we loop from 1 to `NoOfCities` (line 6) and we use the loop variable (`I`) to access each city name in the `Cities` array. As with a ListBox component, we add entries to a ComboBox component by calling the `Add` method of the `Items` property (lines 8 and 9).

The ItemIndex property

The ComboBox's ItemIndex property contains the index to the currently selected item. If none is selected, its value is −1. In this example, Durban is the first item in both ComboBoxes, so setting the ItemIndex properties to 0 (lines 12 and 13) displays Durban as the selected value. If we leave out these statements, the form is displayed with no selection in either of the ComboBoxes, because the default ItemIndex value is −1.

EX 8.4 STEP 4 Showing the distances

Type the btnShowDistanceClick event handler as follows:

```
 1 procedure TfrmDistance.btnShowDistanceClick(Sender: TObject);
 2 var
 3   FromCity, ToCity: integer;
 4 begin
 5   {get the selected from and to cities}
 6   FromCity := cboFrom.ItemIndex + 1; // add 1 to correspond to
 7   ToCity := cboTo.ItemIndex + 1;    // ..indices of Distance array
 8   {display the relevant distance}
 9   lblDistance.Caption := IntToStr(Distances[FromCity,ToCity]) + 'km';
10 end;
```

- Save the unit file again and run the program. Select any two cities and click on the button to display the relevant distance.

When the user selects an item from the ComboBox's drop-down list, the ItemIndex property takes on the index value of the selected item in the list. So, the statements in lines 6 and 7 get the indexes of the two selected items through the ItemIndex properties of the two ComboBoxes. Since the ComboBox's items have indexes 0 to 2, and our Distances array has indexes 1 to 3, we add one to both indexes before storing them in variables FromCity and ToCity. Distances[FromCity, ToCity] now refers to the relevant distance and the statement in line 9 displays the string form of the required distance in the Label.

EXAMPLE 8.5) ListBoxes

Although we had not specifically discussed 'indexes' at that stage, in Chapter 7 (example 7.5) we used an index to access the individual lines of a Memo component. There we saw that the index to the first line is 0 and the index to the last line is one less than the number of lines in the Memo. The same applies to the items in a ListBox. Suppose we have a ListBox called lstNames, then lstNames.Items[0] is the first item and lstNames.Items[NoOfItems - 1] is the last item, where NoOfItems is the number of items in the ListBox and is given by the property lstNames.Items.Count.

In this example we are going to change the program written in example 7.5. We replace the Memo with a ListBox and instead of finding the first occurrence of a given name in the list of names, we delete all occurrences of the name from the list. So, while we are moving through the list (using a While loop), the number of items in the list may change. You will see how this affects the way we use the index to the ListBox items as well as the format of the While condition.

We will also count the number of items that we delete and report this when the delete process is completed.

EX 8.5 STEP 1   The interface

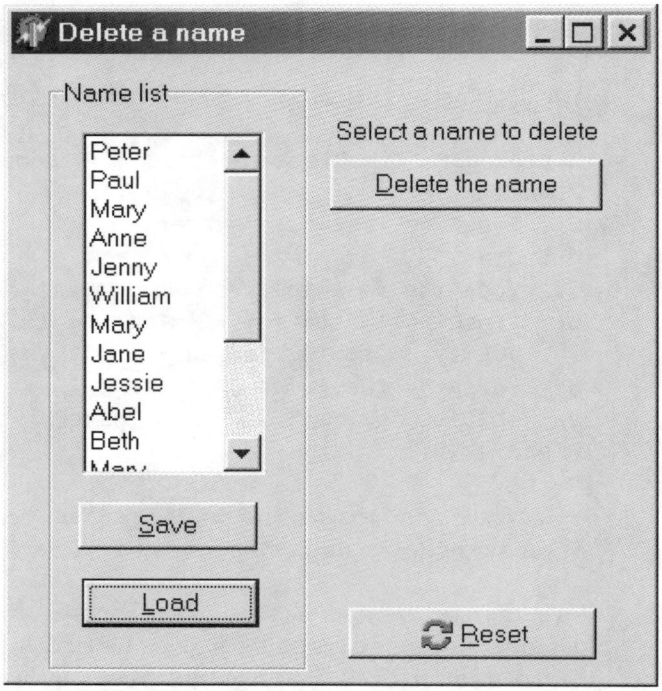

In example 7.5 we used a Memo component for typing in names. We programmed Save and Load buttons which used SaveDialog and OpenDialog non-visual components to save the list of names to a text file or load a list from a text file. In this example we use a ListBox instead of a Memo (figure 8.6). The purpose of a ListBox is different from a Memo. In the case of a Memo, the user can type in multiple lines of text, whereas with a ListBox, the user cannot type in text, but can select items in the list.

In example 7.5, we typed in a number of names and saved the names to a file Names.txt. Since we cannot type these names into the ListBox, we will use the Load button to load the names from Names.txt. If you do not have a file Names.txt, run example 7.5 again to create one before continuing with the steps below.

- Open the project C07e05p.dpr.
- Save the unit and the project files as C08e05u and C08e05p respectively.

Figure 8.6 Deleting a name from a list

- Remove lblResults, edtName and memNames from the form.
- Add a ListBox where the Memo was and then change the properties of the components as follows:

Component	Property	Value
Form1 (frmFindName)	Name	frmDeleteName
	Caption	Delete a name
Button3 (btnFind)	Name	btnDelete
	Caption	&Delete the name
Label1	Name	lblPrompt
	Caption	Select a name to delete
ListBox1	Name	lstNames
	Items	<Blank>

- Edit the btnSaveClick and btnLoadClick event handlers to refer to lstNames.Items instead of memNames.Lines as follows:

```
procedure TfrmDeleteName.btnSaveClick(Sender: TObject);
begin
  if dlgSave.Execute then
    lstNames.Items.SaveToFile(dlgSave.FileName)
  else
    ShowMessage('Invalid file name');
end;
```

```
procedure TfrmDeleteName.btnLoadClick(Sender: TObject);
begin
  if dlgLoad.Execute then
    lstNames.Items.LoadFromFile(dlgLoad.FileName)
  else
    ShowMessage('Invalid file name');
end;
```

- Change the bmbResetClick event handler as follows:

```
procedure TfrmDeleteName.bmbResetClick(Sender: TObject);
begin
  lstNames.Clear;
  lstNames.SetFocus;
end;
```

Before the program will compile, we need to program the btnDeleteClick event handler which we do below.

EX 8.5 STEP 2 Deleting names from the list

The user selects the name to delete from the list by selecting it in the list and clicking on the 'Delete the name' button. Although the user only selects a single name in the list, the program should delete all occurrences of this name from the list.

- Change btnDelete's OnClick event handler as follows (this was btnFind in example 7.5 and therefore the event handler still contains the code we wrote for that example):

```
1  procedure TfrmDeleteName.btnDeleteClick(Sender: TObject);
2  var
3    NameToDelete: string;
4    LineCount, Index, ListIndex, NumDeleted: integer;
5  begin
6    {Get the index of the selected name}
7    ListIndex := lstNames.ItemIndex;
8    {Use index to get name, store uppercase form in NameToDelete}
9    NameToDelete := UpperCase(lstNames.Items[ListIndex]);
10   NumDeleted := 0;   // initialise counter for deleted items
11   Index := 0;   // initialise index for traversing list
12   LineCount := lstNames.Items.Count;   // total number of names

13   {Traverse the list and delete all occurrences of Name}
14   while Index <= LineCount - 1 do
15   begin
16     if UpperCase(lstNames.Items[Index]) = NameToDelete then
17     begin
18       lstNames.Items.Delete(Index);
19       LineCount := lstNames.Items.Count; // adjust line count
20       NumDeleted := NumDeleted + 1;
21     end
```

```
22        else // this item is not the name, so move on ...
23           Index := Index + 1;
24      end;
25   ShowMessage(IntToStr(NumDeleted) + ' occurrences deleted.');
26 end;
```

- Save the unit file again and run the program. Click on the Load button to load the names stored in Names.txt into the ListBox. Then select any name and click on the Delete button to see that it is working correctly.

The While statement (line 14) is similar to that of example 7.5, but it doesn't end when the name is found the first time. It repeats as many times as there are items in the list. Note, however, that the number of items may decrease as the loop progresses. (For this reason we cannot use a For loop here.) We make sure that the While condition handles the changing length of the list correctly by adjusting the value of LineCount every time we delete a line (line 19). If we don't do this, the value of Index may become larger than the number of items in the list and the loop will repeat too many times. If this happens, the statement in line 16 will cause a run-time error when it attempts to access an item that does not exist and generate an exception.

The Delete method

We use

```
if UpperCase(lstNames.Items[Index]) = NameToDelete then
```

to determine whether the current line contains the required name. If it does, we delete that name in the Then part of the If statement. To delete an item from the ListBox component we use

```
lstNames.Items.Delete(Index);
```

where Index is the index to the current item. Note that here the index appears in *round* brackets. This is because Delete is a method of the Items property and Index is a *parameter* (not an index) that is passed to that method. (You will learn about methods and parameters in Chapter 11.) When a value in *square* brackets follows a reference to a list (eg lstNames.Items[Index], where lstNames.Items refers to a list), that value is an *index* to a specific value in the list.

Every time we delete an item, we add 1 to the Deleted variable to keep count of the number of items we have deleted (line 20).

Initialization of variables

In lines 7 to 12 we initialize the variables we use inside the While loop. ListIndex is assigned the index of the name the user selected (line 7). We get this index from the ListBox's ItemIndex property. For example, if the user selects the third name in lstNames, ItemIndex has the value 2. In line 9 we get the selected name from the list with lstNames.Items[Index], change it to uppercase letters only with the UpperCase function and assign the result to the variable NameToDelete. We want to count how many items we delete from the list and for that we use the counter variable `NumDeleted`. We initialize `NumDeleted` to 0 in line 10. `Index`, the loop control variable, is set to 0 (line 11), since that is the index to the first name in the ListBox (where we want to start searching for the selected name). The variable `LineCount` represents the number of items in the list. We use the Count property to get this number and assign it to `LineCount` in line 12.

EX 8.5 STEP 3   A problem with the solution

- Run the program and click on the Delete button without selecting a name from the list. An error message 'Array index out of bounds' (or something similar) is displayed.

If we click on Delete without selecting a Name, `lstNames.ItemIndex` has the value −1. `ListIndex` (line 7) will therefore also be −1. Line 9 will try to retrieve the name with index −1 and this causes the error mentioned above.

One way to solve this problem is to include an If statement after line 7 which tests whether `ListIndex` is greater than −1. The rest of the event handler then forms the Then part of the If statement, and in the Else part we prompt the user to select a name before trying to delete.

Alternatively, we can set the Delete button's Enabled property to False initially and then include the following OnClick event handler for the ListBox:

```
procedure TfrmDeleteName.lstNamesClick(Sender: TObject);
begin
  btnDelete.Enabled := True;
end;
```

Then we should also include the statement

```
btnDelete.Enabled := False;
```

in the btnDeleteClick event handler. The Delete button will become enabled only when the user selects a name in the ListBox.

- Make the second change, save the unit file and run the program to test whether the problem has been solved.

RadioGroups

Up to now we have used RadioButtons in our programs by grouping them in a GroupBox. Delphi provides a component called the RadioGroup, which is a special GroupBox that contains only RadioButtons. To add RadioButtons to a RadioGroup we edit its Items property in the Object Inspector. Each string in Items represents the Caption of a RadioButton in the RadioGroup. So, the number of strings you type into the Items property determines the number of RadioButtons in the group.

Like the Listbox, the RadioGroup has an ItemIndex property (an integer) that indicates which RadioButton in the group is currently selected. If its value is

0 the first button is selected, if it is 1, the second button is selected, and so on. If no button is selected, ItemIndex is equal to –1.

The RadioButtons in a RadioGroup will be placed in one column below one another by default. If we want to divide them into more than one column, we can set the RadioGroup's Columns property in the Object Inspector to the required number of columns.

Using a RadioGroup instead of a GroupBox with RadioButton components can simplify program code considerably. We show how in the next two examples.

EXAMPLE 8.6 Using a RadioGroup

In example 6.4 step 4 the user interface included a GroupBox with four RadioButtons (figure 8.7). In problem 6.3(b) you were asked to write the program attached to this interface that assigns bursaries to students based on the following criteria:
- If the score is greater than or equal to 90%, the bursary amount is R10 000.00.
- If the score is 75% to 89% and passed Accounting or Economics, it is R8 000.00.
- If the score is 75% to 89% and passed neither Accounting nor Economics, it is R5 000.00.
- If the score is 60% to 74% and passed Accounting, it is R3 000.00.
- Otherwise no bursary is awarded.

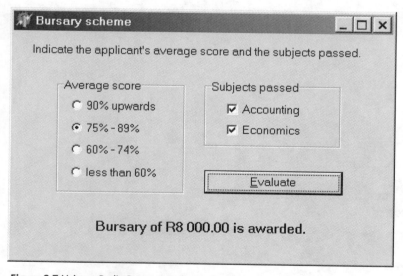

Figure 8.7 Using a RadioGroup to indicate the average score

To solve the problem you probably used a multiple alternative If structure. The Evaluate button's OnClick event handler could then look something like this:

```
procedure TfrmEvaluate.btnEvaluateClick(Sender: TObject);
var
  Amount: String;
begin
  if rad90.Checked then
    Amount := 'R10 000.00'
```

```
else if rad75.Checked and (chkAccounting.Checked or
                          chkEconomics.Checked) then
  Amount := 'R8 000.00'
else if rad75.Checked then
  Amount := 'R5 000.00'
else if rad60.Checked and chkAccounting.Checked then
  Amount := 'R3 000.00'
else
  Amount := 'R 0.00';
lblAmount.Caption := 'Bursary of ' + Amount + ' is awarded.'
end;
```

We are now going to rewrite the program using a RadioGroup instead of the GroupBox with RadioButtons. The RadioGroup identifies its individual RadioButtons through an index rather than as separate components, as you'll see in step 3 below.

EX 8.6 STEP 1   Open the project

- If you wrote that program in Chapter 6, open the project (which should be called C06p04p.dpr) and start by saving the unit file as C08e06u and the project file as C08e06p.
- If you didn't write that program, do it now (btnEvaluate's OnClick event handler appears above).

EX 8.6 STEP 2   The interface

- Delete the GroupBox and put a RadioGroup in its place. The RadioGroup icon appears near the GroupBox in the Standard tab of the Component/ Tool palette.
- Change its Name, Caption and Items properties as follows:

Component	Property	Value
RadioGroup1	Name	rgpAverage
	Caption	Average score
	Items	90% upwards
		75% – 89%
		60% – 74%
		Less than 60%

- To specify the Items, go to the Items property in the Object Inspector and click on the dots to open the String list editor. Type the four lines shown in figure 8.8, then click OK.

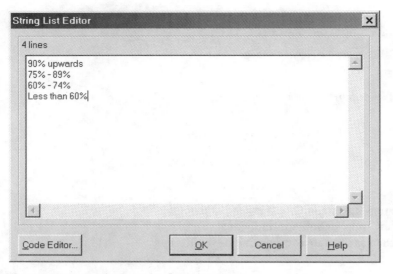

Figure 8.8 Entering the items for the RadioGroup

The RadioGroup now looks like the GroupBox we had before.

EX 8.6 STEP 3   The code

- Change the Evaluate button's OnClick event handler as follows:

```
1 procedure TfrmBursary.btnEvaluateClick(Sender: TObject);
2 var
3   Amount: String;
4 begin
5   case rgpAverage.ItemIndex of
6    -1 : begin                                    // None selected
7           MessageDlg('Indicate the average score.',
8                      mtWarning, [mbOK], 0);
9           Amount := 'R0.00';
10          end;
11     0 : Amount := 'R10 000.00';
12     1 : if chkAccounting.Checked or chkEconomics.Checked then
13           Amount := 'R8 000.00'
14         else
15           Amount := 'R5 000.00';
16     2 : if chkAccounting.Checked then
17           Amount := 'R3 000.00'
18         else
19           Amount := 'R0.00';
20     3 : Amount := 'R0.00';
21   end;
22   lblAmount.Caption := 'Bursary of ' + Amount + ' is awarded.'
23 end;
```

- Save the files as C08e06u and C08e06p.

Using a Case statement with the RadioGroup

The user will typically click on one of the RadioButtons in rgpAverage and then choose none, one or both the CheckBoxes in the Subjects GroupBox before clicking on the Evaluate button. When any of the RadioButtons are clicked, rgpAverage's ItemIndex property gets a value (0, 1, 2 or 3) depending on the chosen button. If none is selected, its value remains –1. The Evaluate button's OnClick event handler begins with a Case statement with ItemIndex as selector (line 5). Depending on this value it branches to one of the options. The first option (–1, in line 6) is executed when the user does not select a RadioButton before clicking on Evaluate. It displays a Message box prompting the user to do so. It then sets Amount to 'R0.00', since line 22 (which uses the value of Amount to report the result) will always be executed and needs a value for Amount. The other three options assign the appropriate value to Amount.

Compare this version, using a RadioGroup, with the version earlier in this example that uses RadioButtons in a GroupBox. When we used RadioButtons in a GroupBox we couldn't use a Case statement to solve this problem, since every 'case' depended on the status of a different RadioButton. (Remember: the selector of a Case statement can only be an integer, a Boolean value or a Char value.) Now, with the RadioGroup, every case depends on the value of the integer ItemIndex, so we can use a Case statement.

An alternative solution

The statement Amount := 'R0.00'; appears three times in the event handler. We can get rid of this duplication by taking R0.00 as the default value for Amount and change it only when necessary. The solution then looks like this:

```
procedure TfrmBursary.btnEvaluateClick(Sender: TObject);
var
  Amount: String;
begin
  Amount := 'R0.00';                              // Default amount
  case rgpAverage.ItemIndex of
   -1 : MessageDlg('Indicate the average score.',
                 mtWarning, [mbOK], 0);           // None selected
    0 : Amount := 'R10 000.00';
    1 : if chkAccounting.Checked or chkEconomics.Checked then
           Amount := 'R8 000.00'
         else
           Amount := 'R5 000.00';
    2 : if chkAccounting.Checked then
           Amount := 'R3 000.00';
  end;
  lblAmount.Caption := 'Bursary of ' + Amount + ' is awarded.'
end;
```

In this way we can leave out the assignment statement in option –1, the else part of option 2 and the whole of option 3, because Amount is 'R0.00' by default.

EXAMPLE 8.7) Sixpence Joe (a short version)

In problem 2.3 we wrote the first Sixpence Joe program, which involved a separate event handler for each of the RadioButtons. If we use a RadioGroup instead, we can identify the selected RadioButton through the ItemIndex and so need only one event handler, the RadioGroup's OnClick event handler. Suppose we replace the GroupBox with a RadioGroup called rgpProducts. Then we can remove the existing four event handlers attached to the RadioButtons and replace them with the OnClick event handler for the RadioGroup given in step 4 below. We'll see how using the index makes the program much simpler.

EX 8.7 STEP 1   Open the Sixpence Joe program

• Open the project C02p03p.dpr. If you haven't written that program, do it now.

EX 8.7 STEP 2   Remove the event handlers from the program

Removing an existing event handler from a Delphi program does *not* mean that you merely block the code and delete it. This may cause all kinds of problems, since Delphi still expects that event handler to be there. The right way to remove an event handler is to remove all the code inside it. In other words, delete everything between the event handler's begin and end and all the declarations you've added before begin. When you save or compile the file again, Delphi automatically removes the empty event handler, along with the internal references to it.

• Do this now with each of the four event handlers. For example, change radRice's OnClick event handler to look like this:

```
procedure TfrmSixpenceJoe.radRiceClick(Sender: TObject);
begin

end;
```

• Save the unit file as C08e07u and the project as C08e07p. If you look at the code in the file now, you will notice that Delphi has removed the event handler skeletons.

EX 8.7 STEP 3   The RadioGroup

• Remove the GroupBox from the form and put a RadioGroup in its place. Set its properties as follows:

Component	Property	Value
RadioGroup1	Name	rgpProducts
	Columns	4
	Items	Flour
		Rice
		Sugar
		Mealie meal

We've set the Columns property to 4 to place the four RadioButtons horizontally next to each other. The default value for Columns is 1 and, if left like that, the RadioButtons will appear below one another.

- Adjust the size of the RadioGroup so that your form looks the way it did previously with the GroupBox.
- Save the program again.

EX 8.7 STEP 4   The RadioGroup's event handler

- Double-click anywhere in the RadioGroup to open the group's OnClick event handler. The required event handler is

```
procedure TfrmSixpenceJoe.rgpProductsClick(Sender: TObject);
begin
  case rgpProducts.ItemIndex of
    0 : lblCostText.Caption := 'Flour costs R12.99 per kilogram';
    1 : lblCostText.Caption := 'Rice costs R4.39 per kilogram';
    2 : lblCostText.Caption := 'Sugar costs R4.10 per kilogram';
    3 : lblCostText.Caption := 'Mealie meal costs R2.16 per kilogram';
  end;
end;
```

- Save the file again, then run and test this version of the program.

Clicking on any of the RadioButtons in the RadioGroup activates this event handler. (Clicking anywhere else in the RadioGroup will have no effect.) Delphi sets the value of the ItemIndex property accordingly. Using this value as selector, the Case statement displays the appropriate message.

This shows how the same problem can be solved in different ways and clearly demonstrates how using a RadioGroup along with its ItemIndex property can reduce the amount of code needed in a program. Indexes can be very useful!

EXAMPLE 8.8 The Controls and ControlCount properties

When you visit a doctor for the first time, you fill in a form with your personal details, information about your medical aid and your medical history. A technologically inclined medical doctor wants a program that allows patients to fill in this form directly on a computer. The user interface for the program is shown in figure 8.9.

The program should ideally store the patients' information in a patient database, but we will not attempt to write that part of the program. All we'll do is write event handlers for the Reset and Submit buttons.

The Reset button must clear all the Edits and the Memo and uncheck all the CheckBoxes. There are nine Edits and a Memo to clear with the Clear method, and we must set the Checked property for nine CheckBoxes to False. All of this can easily be done with 19 simple Delphi statements such as edtFullName.Clear; and chkMeasles.Checked = False;. But suppose there were 40 Edits and 30 CheckBoxes. This would require 70 simple Delphi statements, which would not be fun to type. The question that arises is: 'How can we easily clear all the CheckBoxes on a form without having to set each one's Checked property to False, or all the edit boxes without having to call the Clear

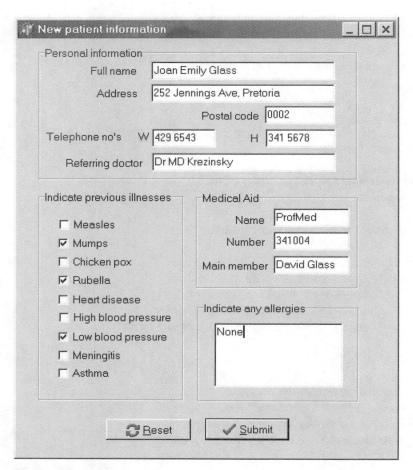

Figure 8.9 Interface for entering patient information

method for each one?' We do this by using the *Controls* and *ControlCount* properties of the GroupBox component.

For our purposes, the Submit button will do only the following:

1. Check whether all the personal information fields have values.
2. Check whether all the medical aid fields have values.
3. Count the number of previous illnesses checked and display a message if it is five or more.
4. Display a warning message if the patient has a history of both heart disease and high blood pressure.

Steps 1, 2 and 3 also use the Controls property to avoid having to write separate statements to check every field individually.

EX 8.8 STEP 1 Creating the interface

- Create the interface shown in figure 8.9. The components and properties appear in the table below. We do not list all the Edits, Labels and CheckBoxes. Using the figure, you should be able to assign the correct property values where we have left them out.

Component	Property	Value
Form1	Name	frmNewPatient
	Caption	New patient information
GroupBox1	Name	gpbPatientInfo
	Caption	Personal information
GroupBox2	Name	gpbMedicalAid
	Caption	Medical Aid
GroupBox3	Name	gpbIllnesses
	Caption	Indicate previous illnesses
GroupBox4	Name	gpbAllergies
	Caption	Indicate any allergies
Edit1 – Edit6	Name	edtFullName, edtAddress, edtPostalCode …
(in GroupBox1)	Text	<Blank>
Edit7 – Edit9	Name	edtMedAidName, edtMedAidNo, edtMainMember
(in GroupBox2)	Text	<Blank>
CheckBox1 –	Name	chkMeasles, chkMumps, chkChickenPox …
CheckBox9	Caption	Measles, Mumps, Chicken pox, …
(in GroupBox3)		
Label1 – Label7	Name	lblFullName, lblAddress, lblPostalCode …
(in GroupBox1)	Caption	Full name, Address, Postal code …
Label8 – Label10	Name	lblMedAidName, lblMedAidNo, lblMainMember
(in GroupBox2)	Caption	Name, Number, Main member
Memo1	Name	memAllergies
(in GroupBox4)	Lines	<Blank>
BitBtn1	Name	bmbReset
	Kind	bkRetry
	Caption	&Reset
BitBtn2	Name	bmbSubmit
	Kind	bkOK
	Caption	&Submit

EX 8.8 STEP 2 Resetting the components

- Create the following event handler for the Reset button:

```
procedure TfrmNewPatient.bmbResetClick(Sender: TObject);
var
  I: integer; // Index to controls array
begin
  // Clear Illness check boxes
  for I := 0 to gpbIllnesses.ControlCount - 1 do
    if gpbIllnesses.Controls[I] is TCheckBox then
      TCheckBox(gpbIllnesses.Controls[I]).Checked := False;
```

```
// Clear Patient info
for I := 0 to gpbPatientInfo.ControlCount - 1 do
  if gpbPatientInfo.Controls[I] is TEdit then
    TEdit(gpbPatientInfo.Controls[I]).Clear;

// Clear Medical aid info
for I := 0 to gpbMedicalAid.ControlCount - 1 do
  if gpbMedicalAid.Controls[I] is TEdit then
    TEdit(gpbMedicalAid.Controls[I]).Clear;

// Clear allergies
memAllergies.Clear;
end;
```

- Save the unit and the project as C08e08u and C08e08p respectively.

The Controls and ControlCount properties

A *windowed control* is a component, such as a form or a GroupBox, that can act as container of other components. Any windowed control has a Controls and a ControlCount property. The Controls property is an array of the windowed control's child components (ie the components it contains). The elements in this array are of type TControl. Many visual components are of this type, including the Edit, Memo and CheckBox components. Since Controls is an array, its elements are indexed. The first component placed in a container component such as the GroupBox will have the index 0 in that GroupBox's Controls property. The second component's index is 1, and so on.

The Controls array may be used to perform the same operation on all the children of the windowed control. To do this we use a loop with a counter variable that acts as the index to Controls. This counter goes from 0 to one less than the number of components in Controls as the loop progresses.

A windowed control's ControlCount property indicates the number of components that are children of the windowed control. The value of ControlCount is always 1 greater than the highest Controls index, because the first index to Controls is 0.

How did we use the Controls and ControlCount properties in our program above? Let's first consider the GroupBox, gpbIllnesses, that contains nine CheckBoxes. This GroupBox has a Controls property that is an array of nine CheckBoxes. This means `gpbIllnesses.Controls[0]` contains chkMeasles (which is the first CheckBox we placed in the GroupBox) and `gpbIllnesses.Controls[8]` contains chkAsthma (the last CheckBox we placed in the GroupBox). The `gpbIllnesses.ControlCount` is 9, since the index runs from 0 to 8.

Typecasting

If we try to set the Checked property of one of the CheckBoxes in the Controls array to False with a statement such as:

```
gpbIllnesses.Controls[0].Checked := False;
```

(which seems like the right thing to do), Delphi will report an error such as 'Undeclared identifier: Checked'. Since the elements of gpbIllnesses.Controls are of type TControl and not specifically of type TCheckBox, Delphi doesn't recognize Checked as a property of its elements. Not all components that are TControls have a Checked property. We therefore need to *typecast* the relevant elements of Controls as CheckBoxes when using their Checked property in a program. This means we specify which type of Control (lower down in the class hierarchy) we are working with. (We will return to component types and their hierarchical relationships in Chapter 18.) For example, if we want to uncheck the first CheckBox in the list, we use

```
TCheckBox(gpbIllnesses.Controls[0]).Checked := False;
```

To typecast an expression in Delphi, you give the type followed (in brackets) by the expression you want to typecast. Read more about *Typecasts* in Delphi's Help.

Unchecking the CheckBoxes

We could now use the following simple For loop to uncheck all the CheckBoxes:

```
for I := 0 to gpbIllnesses.ControlCount - 1 do
   TCheckBox(gpbIllnesses.Controls[I]).Checked := False;
```

Whether the GroupBox contains two, nine or 30 CheckBoxes, only these two lines of code are necessary to uncheck them all. Of course, this will work only if the GroupBox contains nothing but CheckBoxes. To avoid problems when other types of components are added to the GroupBox we include an If statement that ensures that we change only the Checked property of CheckBoxes:

```
for I := 0 to gpbIllnesses.ControlCount - 1 do
   if gpbIllnesses.Controls[I] is TCheckBox then
      TCheckBox(gpbIllnesses.Controls[I]).Checked := False;
```

To check whether a component is of a certain type, we use **is**. An expression of the form ObjectReference **is** Type returns True if the object's value is of type Type.

To clear the Edits we use similar For loops for each of the gpbPatientInfo and gpbMedicalAid GroupBoxes. Here it is essential that we check whether the component is of type TEdit before we try to typecast and clear it, since both these GroupBoxes also contain Label components. We typecast the selected component as TEdit in the call to its Clear method.

The Components and ComponentCount properties

Container components also have a Components property and a ComponentCount property that can be used in a similar way to Controls and ControlCount respectively. What is the difference between Components and Controls? We have seen that the Controls property of a container component is an array of all the components that are *child components* of the container. In example 8.7, for example, frmNewPatient.Controls includes four

GroupBoxes and two BitBtns. It does *not* include the components contained in the four GroupBoxes. By contrast, the Components property of a component is an array of all the components it owns. frmNewPatient owns all the components on the form, including the Edits, Labels, CheckBoxes and the Memo that appear inside the GroupBoxes. Therefore `frmNewPatient.Components` includes the GroupBoxes, all the components contained in these GroupBoxes, and the two BitButtons. Whether we use Controls or Components will depend on the program requirements. For example, if the program must perform an action on *every* component on the form, whether it is a child of the form or appears inside a child of the form we'll use the Components property. If the program should perform an action only on the form's child components, we use the Controls property.

Using the Components and ComponentCount properties, we can rewrite the OnClick event handler for the Reset button as follows:

```
procedure TfrmNewPatient.bmbResetClick(Sender: TObject);
var
  I: integer;
begin
  for I := 0 to frmNewPatient.ComponentCount - 1 do
    if frmNewPatient.Components[I] is TCheckBox then
      TCheckBox(frmNewPatient.Components[I]).Checked := False
    else if frmNewPatient.Components[I] is TEdit then
      TEdit(frmNewPatient.Components[I]).Clear
    else if frmNewPatient.Components[I] is TMemo then
      TMemo(frmNewPatient.Components[I]).Clear;
end;
```

The For loop now traverses all the components on the form and uses a multiple alternative If statement to classify them as a CheckBox, an Edit or a Memo component.

In the code above, there are numerous references to `frmNewPatient.Components[I]`. To avoid having to type this expression so many times, we can assign it to a variable of type TComponent as follows:

```
procedure TfrmNewPatient.bmbResetClick(Sender: TObject);
var
  I: integer;
  Comp: TComponent;
begin
  for I := 0 to frmNewPatient.ComponentCount - 1 do
  begin
    Comp := frmNewPatient.Components[I]; // temporary variable
    if Comp is TCheckBox then
      TCheckBox(Comp).Checked := False
    else if Comp is TEdit then
      TEdit(Comp).Clear
    else if Comp is TMemo then
      TMemo(Comp).Clear;
  end;
end;
```

In the code above, we declared two variables: `I` of type integer and `Comp` of type TComponent. There are different categories of types in Delphi. We have come across simple types (such as integer, double or character), strings and structured types (these include arrays). Another kind of structured type is a class. Examples of classes are TComponent, TEdit and TForm (the T at the beginning of each class name stands for Type). When we declare a variable of one of these class types, we call the variable an object, so in the code above, `Comp` is an object of type TComponent.

REVIEW

In this chapter we used indexing to write programs that access or manipulate the elements of arrays and lists of data. We saw that the items in a ListBox and the lines in a Memo are indexed from 0 upwards and that we can use For loops and While loops to traverse the items stored in these components through their indexes. We learned how to define one- and two-dimensional *arrays* of related data elements. We saw how we could declare dynamic arrays by leaving out the index range in the declaration and later setting the number of elements using the SetLength procedure. We learnt more about scope and how, by declaring arrays at unit level, we made them available to all procedures inside the unit.

   We introduced two new Delphi components, the ComboBox and the RadioGroup, and we saw how the Form's OnCreate event can be used to execute code before the form is displayed to the user for the first time. We also saw how the Controls and ControlCount properties (or Components and ComponentCount properties) of windowed controls can be used to perform the same operation on a number of components in the same Form or GroupBox.

IMPORTANT CONCEPTS

Fundamental programming concepts

Array: A data structure for storing related data items of the same type. The data elements are ordered and individual elements are accessed through an index. The following is the Delphi declaration of a one-dimensional array that contains 10 integer values:

```
IntArray: array[1..10] of integer;
```

Its elements can be accessed by using the name followed by an index in square brackets. For example,

```
IntArray[5] := 100;
```

assigns the value 100 to the element in position 5.

Array constant: An array with fixed values. The values are specified when the array is declared. For example, the following is a Delphi declaration of an array constant of the names of important currencies:

```
const Currencies: array[1..4] of string = ('US Dollar', 'Euro', 'Pound', 'Yen');
```

Dynamic array: An array which is declared without specifying the index range (and therefore the number of elements). In Delphi, the size of a dynamic array must be set using the SetLength procedure before the array is used.

Index: An ordinal value (usually an integer) that indicates the position of an item in a list or an element in an array.

Scope: A variable can be used only within the scope of its declaration. The scope of a variable is defined by the block in which it is declared. For example, if a variable is declared inside a procedure, that variable has a scope limited to that procedure.

Two-dimensional array: An array which is declared and accessed using two indexes: a row and column index value.

Typecasting: A way of instructing the compiler to treat a variable or an expression like a given type. For example, in Delphi the Controls array of a GroupBox (say gpbInfo) is declared by Delphi as an array of TControls. If we know that a given element (at position I) is a TEdit, we could typecast it as follows:

```
TEdit(gpbInfo.Controls[I])
```

This prevents compiler errors if we need to refer to properties or methods that apply specifically to TEdit and not to the more general type TControl.

Unit-level scope: When a variable is declared above all procedures in a unit file, below the implementation keyword, it has unit-level scope. This means that the variable can be used by any procedure in that unit.

Visual development

Windowed control: A component, such as a form or a GroupBox, that can act as container of other components.

NEW DELPHI FEATURES

Properties which apply to windowed controls (such as Forms and GroupBoxes)	
ComponentCount	An integer value giving the number of components contained in the windowed control, that is, the number of components in the Components array.
Components	An array of all the components contained in the windowed control (including the components contained in other components). The component placed there first has the index 0 and the one placed there last has the index ComponentCount – 1. We typically use this property when the same operation must be performed on all the components in a windowed control.
ControlCount	An integer value giving the number of child components contained in the windowed control, ie the number of components in the Controls array.
Controls	An array of all the child components contained in the windowed control, but not including components contained in a child component that is also a container. The component that was placed there first has the index 0 and the one that was placed there last has the index ControlCount – 1.

Operators/keywords and procedures

is	A Boolean operator that checks whether a given object is of a certain type. For example: `gpbPersonalInfo.Controls[0] is TEdit` is True if the first element of the GroupBox's Controls array is an Edit; otherwise it is False.
SetLength procedure	Sets the number of elements of a dynamic array. The format of the procedure is `SetLength(theArray, theSize);` where `theArray` is an array which has been declared without specifying an index range and `theSize` is the number of elements which the array should hold.

TComboBox

Properties	Items	Contains the strings that appear in the drop-down list.
	ItemIndex	Gives the index of the currently selected item in the list. Its value is −1 if no item is selected.
	Items.Count	Gives the number of items listed in the ComboBox
	Style	Determines the display style of the ComboBox. Setting this property to csDropDownList results in a ComboBox where the user cannot enter text manually. In contrast, the style csDropDown allows the user to enter text.
Methods	Items.Add	Adds a string to the end of the list of items in the ComboBox
Prefix	cbo...	
Use		It is an edit box with a scrollable drop-down list attached to it. The user can either select an item from the list (by clicking on it) or type directly into the edit box.

TForm

New event	OnCreate	Called when the form is created. The OnCreate event handler is a useful place to put code that needs to be executed before the form is displayed to the user for the first time.

TListBox

New properties	ItemIndex	Gives the index of the currently selected item in the list. Its value is −1 if no item is selected.
	Items.Count	Gives the number of items listed in the ListBox.

TRadioGroup

Properties	Items	Contains the Captions of the RadioButtons that appear in the group.
	ItemIndex	Gives the index of the currently selected RadioButton in the RadioGroup. Its value is −1 if no RadioButton is selected.
	Items.Count	Gives the number of RadioButtons in the RadioGroup.
	Columns	This integer value determines the number of columns in which the RadioButtons are arranged inside the RadioGroup. The default value 1 makes the buttons appear in a single column.

Events	OnClick	This event is activated if the user clicks on any of the RadioButtons in the RadioGroup.
Prefix	rgp...	
Use	A GroupBox that contains only RadioButtons. The number of RadioButtons and their Captions are determined by the strings contained in the Items property.	

PROBLEMS

PROBLEM 8.1) Is it a palindrome?

A palindrome is a word such as 'madam' or 'peep', that is, a word that reads the same forwards and backwards.
- Write a program that inputs a word from the user and checks whether it is a palindrome. Use a message dialog to report the result.

PROBLEM 8.2) Improving example 8.3

In example 8.3 we wrote an application that read in any number of test results from a Memo. The results were stored in a dynamic array and we determined the number of elements to store in the array from the number of lines in the Memo. With this program, if the user enters Return after the last mark, Delphi tries to convert this empty line into a number and an error message is displayed.
- Change the program from example 8.3 so that it checks if the last line is empty and if so, it ignores this line. In this case, the size of the array should therefore be one less than the number of lines in the Memo.

PROBLEM 8.3) Adding cities to example 8.4

- Extend example 8.4 to add Pretoria, Port Elizabeth and Bloemfontein to the two lists of cities. The complete distances table should contain the following information:

	Durban	Cape Town	Johannesburg	Pretoria	Bloemfontein	Port Elizabeth
Durban	0	1660	598	656	667	927
Cape Town	1660	0	1405	1463	998	756
Johannesburg	598	1405	0	56	417	1062
Pretoria	656	1463	56	0	475	1120
Bloemfontein	667	998	417	475	0	635
Port Elizabeth	927	756	1062	1120	635	0

PROBLEM 8.4   A ComboBox of colours

- Write a simple program with a form that contains only a ComboBox and a Label. The label appears above the ComboBox and prompts the user to select one of eight colours in the ComboBox. Depending on the colour selected, the form's background colour changes.
- Do this using the following unit-level array constants:

```
const
  DelphiColours: array[0..7] of Integer = (clMaroon, clGreen,
            clNavy, clPurple, clRed, clBlue, clFuchsia, clAqua);
  ColourNames: array[0..7] of String = ('Maroon', 'Green',
            'Navy', 'Purple', 'Red', 'Blue', 'Fuchsia', 'Aqua');
```

- The ComboBox should be populated with the colours as they appear in the ColourNames array before the form appears to the user for the first time. The corresponding Delphi colour (in the DelphiColours array) should be used to change the colour of the form depending on the user's selection.

PROBLEM 8.5   A RadioGroup of colours

- Modify problem 8.4 so that it uses a RadioGroup instead of a ComboBox. As with the ComboBox, the RadioButtons in the RadioGroup must be initialised with values from the string array. When the user clicks on any of the RadioButtons, the form's colour must change accordingly.

PROBLEM 8.6   Road running history

A friend of yours is a keen road runner. She would like you to write a program for her to keep a record of the races she has run.

- Write a program for keeping a record of road races so that it matches the user interface given in figure 8.10. The user enters race information in a Memo. Each line of the Memo represents information on a single race: the race name, the race distance (in km) and the finishing time (these three entries are separated by commas). The finishing time is written in hours (2 digits) followed by a colon and the minutes (2 digits).
- The application should include Load and Save buttons for loading and storing the race information in a text file. There must also be a Calculate button for determining the best running time (in minutes per kilometre) as well as the name of the race in which this best time was run. The Calculate button should also display the total distance of all races (in kilometres).

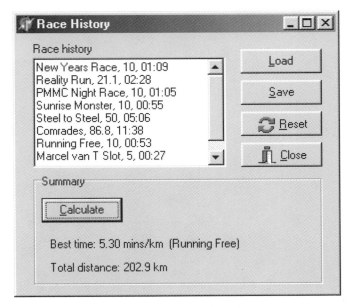

Figure 8.10 Application for recording road race history

PROBLEM 8.7) Lotto game

- Write a program that plays a lotto game. The user selects 6 numbers in the range 1 to 20 (figure 8.11). On pressing the Play Lotto button, the computer generates six random numbers in the same range. These values are displayed in the Results GroupBox. For every match between a user-selected number and a computer generated number, R2.50 is paid out. The total payout is displayed in the GroupBox.
- Include a Reset button which sets all the SpinEdit values to 1 and clears the labels in the GroupBox.

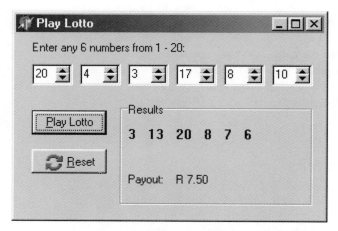

Figure 8.11 Lotto game application. The user selects six numbers from 1–20 and the computer generates six random numbers. Every match pays R2.50.

CHAPTER 9

··

Menus and actions

PURPOSE OF THIS CHAPTER

Menus provide lists of items on which the user can click to invoke different program operations. They are usually displayed only at the user's request and therefore help to simplify user interfaces which, without menus, would be cluttered with buttons and other components needed to trigger the different operations. In this way, menus provide a concise way to give the user access to a large number of operations.

Since menus are a standard part of the Windows user interface, Delphi provides the necessary tools to include them easily in our interfaces.

In this chapter we:

o   learn how to create a main menu bar with drop-down and cascading menus attached to it;

o   learn how to create pop-up menus that the user can invoke by right-clicking on designated user-interface components, and

o   demonstrate three different ways of associating code with the items on a menu, gradually working towards the most effective method where the program code and component properties are maintained centrally in Action lists.

Menus

The main menu bar is a special area displayed across the top of a form directly below the caption (or title) bar. It includes a set of choices called 'menu titles'. Figure 9.1 illustrates Delphi 6's menu bar.

Figure 9.1 The Delphi 6 menu bar

Each menu title provides access to a drop-down menu comprising a collection of menu items. The content of the menu bar and its drop-down menus depends on the functionality of the application and the user's interaction with it.

Figure 9.2 is an example of a drop-down menu. This particular menu drops down when we select the File menu title in Delphi 6.

In the example that follows you will learn how to use the following aspects of menus in your applications:

Menu items can include an underscored character (an *accelerator key*) that gives you access to the menu items through the keyboard, using the Alt key plus the underscored character (eg <Alt+O> to Open a file).

Some menu items have *shortcuts* that we can use to activate a menu option without having the menu visible on the form. For example, the shortcut key for Save is <Ctrl+S>, which allows you to save your file directly without working via the menu.

When we select a menu item that has an ellipsis (three dots) next to it (as Save As... in figure 9.2), a dialog box appears on the screen to get additional information from the user.

A menu item can also have a little right-pointing arrow next to it, eg Reopen in the menu in figure 9.2, indicating that it has a *cascading submenu* connected to it (see eg figure 9.10).

A menu item can be dimmed, as with Save All in figure 9.2. This means that the option is currently unavailable.

Groups of options on a drop-down menu can be separated with horizontal lines called *separator lines*.

Figure 9.2 A drop-down menu

EXAMPLE 9.1) Drop-down, cascading and pop-up menus

We explore the ins and outs of menus by creating a simple form that allows the user to change its colour at run time. Besides menus, the form contains only a Label. All user actions will involve selecting commands from either a main menu, a drop-down menu or a pop-up menu.

The user interface appears in figure 9.3.

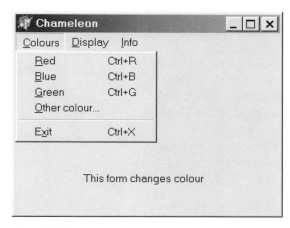

Figure 9.3 The user interface

EX 9.1 STEP 1   Adding a menu to the form

- Start a new application and place a MainMenu component from the Standard tab of the Component/Tool palette on the form. The MainMenu icon appears on the form, but it does not display a menu bar because we haven't defined any items for it yet.

- Put a Label on the form and change the component properties as in the table below:

Component	Property	Value
Form1	Name	frmChameleon
	Caption	Chameleon
Label1	Name	lblChameleon
	Caption	This form changes colour
MainMenu1	Name	mnuChameleon

- To define items for the menu, double-click on the mnuChameleon icon to open the Menu editor. Initially, the menu bar inside the Menu editor is empty, as shown in figure 9.4.

Figure 9.4 The Menu editor

- With the Menu editor open, type &Colours, then press <Enter>. The text you entered appears inside the Caption property of a newly created MenuItem. A MenuItem is a Delphi component representing a single choice on a menu. It can be a title for a drop-down menu or a particular menu option invoking a program's command. Here, Colours will be a title for a drop-down menu. Note that Delphi automatically assigns an intelligible name to your menu item's Name property, based on the Caption you have given it – in this case Colours1.
- After you press <Enter>, the highlight bar of the Menu editor moves to below the Colours item. Complete the Colours drop-down menu by typing:
&Red<Enter>
&Blue<Enter>
&Green<Enter>.
Delphi assigns the names Red1, Blue1 and Green1 to these new MenuItems. So far the Menu editor should look like the one in figure 9.5.

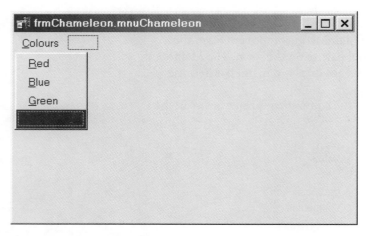

Figure 9.5 Using the Menu editor

- Now type a single hyphen (-), then press <Enter>. This inserts a separator line.
- We now add our last item in this drop-down menu, namely Exit, by typing E&xit and then pressing <Enter>. Close the Menu editor by clicking on the little cross in the top right-hand side of the Menu editor window.
- Save the unit and project files as C09e01u and C09e01p respectively and run the program to see what your menu looks like.
- When you click on the Colours MenuItem, the drop-down menu (figure 9.6) should be displayed. Clicking on the items in the drop-down menu will have no effect because we haven't attached any code to them yet.

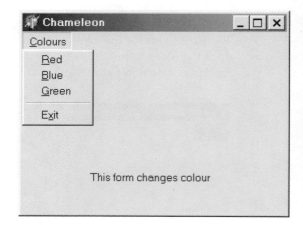

Figure 9.6 The running program

- When you are satisfied with your program thus far, close it to return to the design environment.

What should the program do? If the user selects the Red MenuItem, the colour of the form must change to red. A click on the Blue item should make the form blue and a click on Green should make the form green. Choosing Exit should close the program.

To add this functionality to the program we are going to write OnClick event handlers for each of the drop-down menu items.

EX 9.1 STEP 2   Associating events and shortcuts with the MenuItems

- Double-click on the MainMenu component mnuChameleon to open the Menu editor.
- Double-click on the Exit item from the drop-down menu. Delphi responds by opening an empty event handler connected to the Exit item.
- Now change the handler so that it contains the code that should be executed when the user chooses Exit from the Colours menu. Your code should match the following:

```
procedure TfrmChameleon.Exit1Click(Sender: TObject);
begin
  Close;
end;
```

- Switch to Form/Designer view and make sure Exit1 is selected in the Object Inspector.
- To create a shortcut to the Exit MenuItem, select its Shortcut property in the Object Inspector.
- Click once on the down arrow next to the Shortcut property to see the drop-down list of possibilities. Use the arrow to go down, then select Ctrl+X by clicking on it.
- The shortcut to the Exit MenuItem has been added, as can be seen in figure 9.7.
- Save the unit file and run the program several times, each time testing it either by selecting Exit from the menu or by using <Ctrl+X> directly.

Next we create event handlers and shortcuts for the Red, Blue and Green MenuItems respectively. The shortcuts to the MenuItems must be <Ctrl+R>, <Ctrl+B> and <Ctrl+G> respectively. Can you write the event handlers and create the shortcuts?

- Open the Menu editor and double-click on Red. Type the Red MenuItem event handler so that it looks as follows:

```
procedure TfrmChameleon.Red1Click(Sender: TObject);
begin
  frmChameleon.Color := clRed;
end;
```

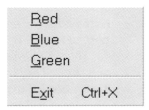

Figure 9.7 New Colours menu

- Similarly, type in the event handlers connected to the Blue and Green MenuItems to match the following:

```
procedure TfrmChameleon.Blue1Click(Sender: TObject);
begin
   frmChameleon.Color := clBlue;
end;

procedure TfrmChameleon.Green1Click(Sender: TObject);
begin
   frmChameleon.Color := clGreen;
end;
```

- Set the Shortcut property of each of the MenuItems to the corresponding key sequence. With the help of the drop-down list of shortcut possibilities, select <Ctrl+R>, <Ctrl+B> and <Ctrl+G> respectively.
- Save the unit and run the program to test the new event handlers. Check that you can change each colour either by using the menu and the mouse or by using the shortcut keys.

Shortcuts versus accelerator keys

In our menu so far we have five accelerator keys and four shortcuts. What is the difference between an accelerator key and a shortcut? Both allow the user to invoke an action using the keyboard instead of a mouse.

- Run the program again and invoke the Exit action using accelerator keys only. What keys did you have to press?

To exit the program using accelerator keys you hold down the <Alt> key and press <C> to display the Colours menu. Then, still holding down the <Alt> key, you press <X> to invoke the Exit menu item. In contrast, to exit the program using the shortcut, you simply press <Ctrl+X>. To use accelerator keys to invoke menu items, the relevant menu item must be visible for it to work. In the case of shortcut keys, this is not necessary.

Shortcut keys are a positive feature of a user interface because they can save users' time. They increase the economy of the interface by reducing the number of steps needed to perform a task, without compromising on the ease of use (since users still have the option of navigating the menu in the traditional way).

Editing a menu

We can delete a MenuItem by selecting the item inside the Menu editor and pressing the <Del> key. To insert a MenuItem, we select the item in front of which we want to insert it (again in the Menu editor) and press <Ins>. We can expand a menu in two directions:
○ by extending its main menu bar, or
○ by adding items for the drop-down menus.

EX 9.1 STEP 3   Adding a main MenuItem

We now extend our form's main menu bar with an Info menu title.
- If it is not still open, open project C09e01p.dpr and double-click on the mnuChameleon icon to open the Menu editor.
- Position the menu's highlight bar in the blank spot next to the Colours main menu title, type the Caption &Info, then press <Enter>.
- When the user clicks on the Info option, we want a dialog box to appear displaying some text. To create an event handler for the Info menu title, double-click on it in the Menu editor and edit the event handler to match the following:

```
procedure TfrmChameleon.Info1Click(Sender: TObject);
var Msg: string;
begin
  Msg := 'A chameleon is a small reptile with the ability' + #13
       + 'to change colour according to its surroundings' + #13
       + 'and to live for a long time without food.';
  MessageDlg(Msg, mtInformation, [mbOK],0);
end;
```

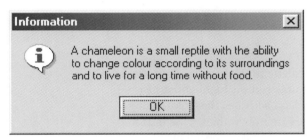

Figure 9.8 The result when choosing the Info MenuItem

- Save the unit file and run the program. Select the Info menu title to display the message dialog shown in figure 9.8.

In the code above, #13 is a special character code representing a carriage return. It is a way of telling Delphi to put text onto a new line.

EX 9.1 STEP 4   Adding an item to a drop-down menu

Here we expand the menu by extending its Colours drop-down menu. We are going to insert a new item to allow the user to select any colour from the Windows colour palette.
- Switch to Form/Designer view and double-click on the mnuChameleon icon to open up the Menu editor again.
- Click on the Colours MenuItem, position the editor's highlight on the separator line and press <Ins>. This opens up space for a new item.
- Type '&Other colour...', then press <Enter>. Close the Menu editor.
- To make the Other colour... MenuItem functional, add a ColorDialog component to frmChameleon. (Find it on the Dialogs tab of the Component/Tool palette.) A small icon representing the ColorDialog component appears on the form. Change its Name property to cdlChameleon.

- In the Menu editor, double-click on 'Other colour...' to open up the event handler connected to it. Change the event handler to the following:

```
1 procedure TfrmChameleon.Othercolour1Click(Sender: TObject);
2 begin
3   cdlChameleon.Color := frmChameleon.Color;
4   if cdlChameleon.Execute then
5     frmChameleon.Color := cdlChameleon.Color;
6 end;
```

- Save the unit file, run the program and select the Other colour... option on the drop-down menu to see what the Color dialog looks like.

You can now change the form's colour by choosing any colour on the display and pressing OK.

The ColorDialog component

The ColorDialog allows the user to select any of the colours available in the Windows environment. The statement

```
cdlChameleon.Color := frmChameleon.Color;
```

(line 3) sets the colour highlighted on the colour palette to the form's colour. (In figure 9.9, the colour in the bottom row third from the right is highlighted.) In line 4, the call to the Execute method of cdlChameleon activates the ColorDialog component for the user to select a colour. The program now waits for the user to press OK or Cancel before it continues. If he or she clicks OK, the Execute function returns True and the Then part of the If statement is executed (line 5). This changes the form's colour to the user's selection. If the user clicks Cancel, the form's colour remains unchanged.

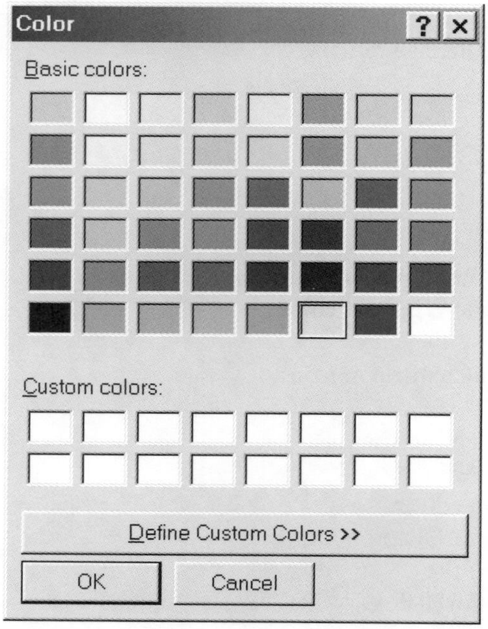

Figure 9.9 Color dialog

EX 9.1 STEP 5 Adding a cascading submenu

We want to allow the user to change the style and the font of the sentence 'This form changes colour', that is the Label's Caption.

- Switch to Form/Designer view.
- Insert a new menu title in the menu bar by opening the Menu editor, selecting the Info menu title and pressing <Ins>. This inserts space for a new menu title between the Colours and Info menu titles.
- Type in '&Display' and complete the drop-down menu with the items &Font and &Style (figure 9.10).
- To create a cascading submenu attached to the right-hand side of the Style MenuItem, do the following: with the Style MenuItem highlighted, right-click and select 'Create Submenu' (alternatively press <Ctrl> and hold it down while pressing the right-arrow key). This enables you to define the submenu.
- Complete the submenu with the items Bo&ld, &Italic and &Underline as in figure 9.10. (Note that 'l' is the accelerator key we chose for Bold because we already have a 'B' accelerator key for Blue and an 'O' for Other colour....)
- For now, we do not want any functionality associated with the Font MenuItem, so disable the Font MenuItem by setting its Enabled property to False.

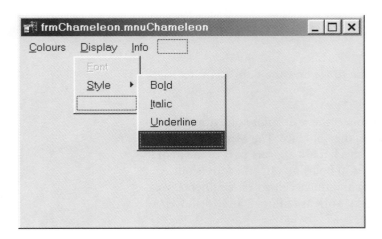

Figure 9.10 Completing the cascading submenu

Cascading submenus

A cascading menu can be opened from a drop-down menu item (such as the Style menu in figure 9.10), a pop-up menu item or another cascading menu item. Menu items that lead to cascading submenus are marked with a right-pointing triangle at run time to indicate that the menu item opens another submenu instead of executing a command. Although there is no limit to the depth of nesting of cascading menus (in other words, the number of cascading menus opened from higher level cascading menus), the use of deeply nested cascading menus is not recommended, for several reasons:

o   Multi-level cascading menus are very difficult for the user to manipulate, because every time an item is chosen from the bottom-level menu, the entire cascade disappears.

- The user must then navigate explicitly all the way down through the cascade to restore his or her context in the menu.
- It is also very easy to issue a wrong, unintended command when in a cascading menu.

EX 9.1 STEP 6 Changing the font using checkmarked menu items

- In the Menu editor, select the Bold MenuItem and edit the event handler to match the following:

```
1  procedure TfrmChameleon.Bold1Click(Sender: TObject);
2  begin
3    if Bold1.Checked then     // If the Bold item is already checked
4    begin
5      lblChameleon.Font.Style := lblChameleon.Font.Style - [fsBold];
6      Bold1.Checked := False; // Remove Bold check mark
7    end
8    else      // The Bold item is not checked
9    begin
10     lblChameleon.Font.Style := lblChameleon.Font.Style + [fsBold];
11     Bold1.Checked := True;  // Display Bold check mark
12   end;
13 end;
```

- Save the unit file and run the program to see how the Bold MenuItem works.

The Bold MenuItem acts as a toggle button. If the text is not bold, it makes it bold. If the text is already bold, it removes the bold face. The MenuItem's Checked property determines whether a check mark appears next to the item to indicate whether it is 'on' (the font appears in bold) or 'off' (the font is not bold). We start by discussing the checking and unchecking of menu items. We will later discuss how the font style changes work as in lines 5 and 10 above.

Checking and unchecking menu items

In our program Bold1 is called a *checkmarked menu item*. The value of the Checked property of such a menu item is set dynamically at run time to reflect the value of the corresponding setting. The statements

```
Bold1.Checked := False;
Bold1.Checked := True;
```

(lines 6 and 11) ensure that the Bold MenuItem is appropriately checked or unchecked. These two statements can be combined into a single statement outside of the If statement:

```
Bold1.Checked := not (Bold1.Checked);
```

The effect of this single statement is to set the Checked property to the opposite of what it was before. In this way we can simplify our event handler as follows:

```
1 procedure TfrmChameleon.Bold1Click(Sender: TObject);
2 begin
3   if Bold1.Checked then  // If the Bold item is already checked
4     lblChameleon.Font.Style := lblChameleon.Font.Style - [fsBold]
5   else   // The Bold item is not checked
6     lblChameleon.Font.Style := lblChameleon.Font.Style + [fsBold];

7   Bold1.Checked := not (Bold1.Checked); // toggle Bold check mark
8 end;
```

- Select the Italic MenuItem and edit the event handler to match the following:

```
procedure TfrmChameleon.Italic1Click(Sender: TObject);
begin
  if Italic1.Checked then  // If the Italics item is already checked
    lblChameleon.Font.Style := lblChameleon.Font.Style - [fsItalic]
  else   // The Italics item is not checked
    lblChameleon.Font.Style := lblChameleon.Font.Style + [fsItalic];

  Italic1.Checked := not (Italic1.Checked); // toggle Italics check mark
end;
```

Here we toggle between 'italics on' and 'italics off' in the same way we toggled between 'bold' and 'not bold',

- Select the Underline MenuItem and edit the event handler to match the following:

```
procedure TfrmChameleon.Underline1Click(Sender: TObject);
begin
  if Underline1.Checked then  // If Underline item is already checked
    lblChameleon.Font.Style := lblChameleon.Font.Style - [fsUnderline]
  else   // Underline item is not checked
    lblChameleon.Font.Style := lblChameleon.Font.Style + [fsUnderline];

  Underline1.Checked := not (Underline1.Checked); // toggle check mark
end;
```

- Save the unit file again. Run the program and see what happens when you change the font style.

Sets

Like an array, a *set* is a collection of data elements of the same type. While array elements are ordered and we can access the individual elements through an index, a set's elements are not ordered and we cannot access the individual elements. We can only check whether a given element appears in a set. Also, the same element cannot appear in a set more than once, whereas an array can contain duplicates. In Delphi we write a set as a list of values (called 'elements') separated by commas and enclosed in square brackets, for example [1, 2, 3], which is a set containing three integer elements.

In the three event handlers that change the font, we use the Font.Style property, which is a set that contains elements of type TFontStyle. Delphi's TFontStyle type consists of the values fsBold, fsItalic, fsUnderline and fsStrikeOut. This means the Font.Style property takes values such as [fsBold], [fsItalic], [fsBold, fsItalic] and []. If the Font.Style property of a Label component is equal to [fsBold], it means the Caption is displayed in bold face. If it is [fsBold, fsItalic], then the Caption is displayed in bold italics. The value [] (the empty set) means that the Caption appears in a regular font style.

The statement

```
lblChameleon.Font.Style := lblChameleon.Font.Style - [fsBold];
```

removes the element fsBold from the set lblChameleon.Font.Style, thereby removing the bold face of the lblChameleon's Caption. The statement

```
lblChameleon.Font.Style := lblChameleon.Font.Style + [fsBold];
```

adds fsBold to that set and so changes the Caption to bold.

We can also define our own set variables to use in a program. Examples of set declarations are

```
var
  Digits: set of 0..9;
  Letters1, Letters2, Letters3: set of 'a'..'z';
```

With these declarations we can include assignment statements such as the following in a program:

```
Digits := [1, 3, 5, 7, 9];
Letters1 := ['a', 'b', 'c'];
Letters2 := ['x', 'y'];
```

The values on the left- and right-hand sides of the assignment operator must be of compatible types. This means the elements listed in square brackets (on the right-hand side of :=) must fall in the range of elements specified in the declaration of the variable on the left-hand side of :=. For example, Digits is declared as a set containing digits from 0 to 9. All the elements in the set that is assigned to Digits must fall within this range.

Using the in operator we can test whether a given element appears in a set with a statement such as:

```
if sedInput.Value in Digits then ...
```

This checks whether the SpinEdit's value is one of 1, 3, 5, 7 or 9.

We can combine two sets with the + operator, as in the following statements:

```
Letters3 := Letters1 + Letters2;    // Gives a set with 5 elements
Letters1 := Letters1 + ['d'];       // Adds the letter d to Letters1
```

To remove an element from a set we use the – (minus) operator:

```
Letters2 := Letters2 - ['x'];                 // Removes x from Letters2
```

Note that both operands of the + and − operators are sets, and specifically sets of
the same element type.

EX 9.1 STEP 7   Adding a pop-up menu

If you click with the right mouse button on a Delphi form in design mode, a
menu appears that gives you all the functions you can perform in relation to the
form (eg figure 9.11). This is a *pop-up menu*. Pop-up menus appear only upon
user request and are not attached to the application's menu bar.

Figure 9.11 A pop-up menu

The items that appear on the menu depend on where the cursor is when the
user presses the button. Pop-up menus can be programmed to provide only
those choices that are relevant to the object that was clicked. We can add pop-up
menus to our applications too.

In the Chameleon example we are now going to add a pop-up menu as an
alternative to invoking the commands via the Colours item on the main menu
bar.

- Open the project if you closed it, switch to Form/Designer view and put a
  PopupMenu component from the Standard tab of the Component/Tool
  palette on the form.
- Change its Name property to pumChameleon in the Object Inspector.
- Double-click the pumChameleon icon to open the Menu editor.
- Now enter the MenuItems as before, defining the contents of the pop-up
  menu, as shown in figure 9.12. (Remember: to enter a separator line, you
  enter a single hyphen (-) as the Caption of the MenuItem component.)
  Delphi automatically assigns the names Red2, Blue2, Green2, Othercolour2
  and Exit2 to these MenuItems.

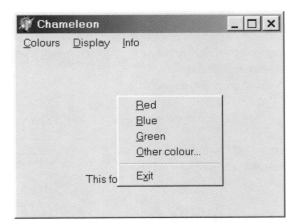

Figure 9.12 The contents of a pop-up menu

- Close the Menu editor window.
- Click the form to make it the active component, then find its PopupMenu
  property in the Object Inspector.
- Open the drop-down list of the available pop-up menus and associate
  pumChameleon with this property.
- Save and run the program.

Now, when you click the right mouse button on the form, a pop-up menu
appears from which you can select commands.

Of course, as it is, the pop-up menu doesn't yet cause any actions, so the next step is to associate events with the pop-up menu items.

EX 9.1 STEP 8 Associating events with the pop-up menu items

- Open the Menu editor by double-clicking on the pumChameleon component on the form.
- Double-click on the Red MenuItem to open the Red2Click event handler. Change it to look as follows:

```
procedure TfrmChameleon.Red2Click(Sender: TObject);
begin
  frmChameleon.Color := clRed;
end;
```

- Save the program and run it.
- Right click on the form to bring up the pop-up menu and click on Red. The form should turn red.

We can now go on to create similar event handlers for the other pop-up menu items. However, a problem with this is that we are duplicating code that we have written before. Identical event handlers already exist for the items of the Colours drop-down menu. Could we possibly use those event handlers instead of duplicating them? The answer is 'yes' – we can direct the pop-up menu's OnClick events to execute the existing event handlers associated with the corresponding drop-down menu items.

Using existing event handlers

- Remove the Red2Click event handler from your program by deleting the single program line that you've added to it, and then saving the file.
- Switch to Form/Designer view and double-click on the PopupMenu icon to open the Menu editor.
- Click on the Red item and then on the Events tab in the Object Inspector. This opens the list of possible events for the MenuItem.
- Find the OnClick event and click on the little down arrow next to it to see a drop-down list of all the existing event handlers in the application (figure 9.13).
- Select Red1Click. By doing this we tell Delphi to execute Red1Click whenever the user clicks on Red2.
- Now click on the Blue MenuItem, the Events tab and then, next to the OnClick event, select Blue1Click from the drop-down list.
- Similarly, select event handlers Green1Click, Othercolours1Click and Exit1Click for the Green, Other colours... and Exit pop-up MenuItems respectively.
- Save the file and run the program to test that all the pop-up menu items work correctly.

Figure 9.13 Selecting an existing event handler

We saw above that if we want to execute the same event handler through different events, we connect both events to a single event handler. For example, we can activate Red1Click via the Red item on the drop-down menu connected to the Colours menu title, and via the Red item on the pop-up menu.

EXAMPLE 9.2 Action lists

In this example we redo example 5.5 from Chapter 5 to get more practice in using menus and, more importantly, to introduce Action lists. In that program we created the form shown in figure 9.14.

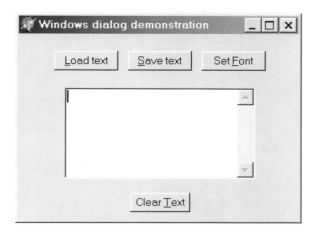

Figure 9.14 The form in example 5.5

We are going to add a menu and a pop-up menu that offer alternative ways to perform the different actions here available only through button clicks.

At the end of example 9.1 we saw how an event handler associated with one component (eg a main menu item) can be called by another component (eg a pop-up menu item), so doing away with unnecessary duplication of code. Here you will learn about another way to avoid duplication. Instead of associating event handlers with each individual button or MenuItem, this example will use an Action list that centralizes the procedures (or event handlers) in one place from where they can be triggered by different user events. In other words, the same actions will be initiated via different routes and have exactly the same effect.

Also, by setting certain property values in the Action list rather than for the individual components, we will synchronize the corresponding properties of two or more different components. For example, when the 'Save text' operation should be disabled, it means the button, the drop-down MenuItem and the PopupMenu item which perform that operation must all be disabled. Instead of setting the Enabled property to False three times (once for each of these components) we can set it once for an Action in the Action list. Linking the Action with the three components will ensure that their Enabled properties are always synchronized. Properties such as the Caption and accelerator keys can also be set centrally in this way, thereby introducing uniformity into the user interface.

How we achieve all of this will become clear as you work through the steps below.

EX 9.2 Planning

What we are aiming at in this example is to write a program with the functionality of example 5.5, but which also uses a drop-down menu and a pop-up menu to perform the different actions. The new interface will look like this:

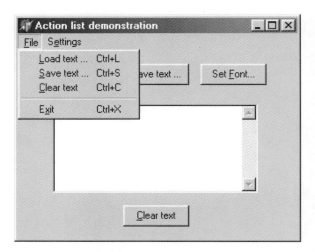

Figure 9.15 Interface displaying a drop-down menu

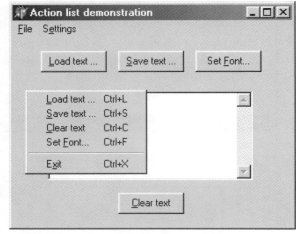

Figure 9.16 Showing the form's pop-up menu

Instead of creating an event handler for each of the MenuItems or the buttons, we create an Action for each of the tasks the user can perform. These will be contained in an ActionList component. Each MenuItem and button will then be linked to the appropriate Action, thereby giving it the necessary functionality and shared property values.

EX 9.2 STEP 1   Creating the form

To make sure you understand the use of Action lists correctly it is important that you start with a program that contains no code.

- We recommend that you open a new application to create a completely new form for this example based on the properties table below. If you prefer to work from the existing project (C05e05p.dpr), remove all the event handlers before you continue to write this program. Do that by deleting all (and only) the code that you added to the event handlers and then saving the unit and project files under the new names C09e02u and C09e02p respectively. Delphi will delete the empty event handlers.

The component properties should have the values listed below.

- If you are working from project C05e05p.dpr, change the Name and Caption properties of the form.
- We don't give the button's Caption properties because it doesn't matter at this point what the Captions are. You will see later how they are set automatically when we use Actions.

Component	Property	Value
Form1	Name	frmActionListDemo
	Caption	Action list demonstration
Button1	Name	btnLoad
Button2	Name	btnSave
Button3	Name	btnFont
Button4	Name	btnClear

Memo1	Name	memDemo
	Lines	<Blank>
	Scrollbar	ssVertical
OpenDialog1	Name	opdOpen
SaveDialog1	Name	svdSave
FontDialog	Name	fodFont

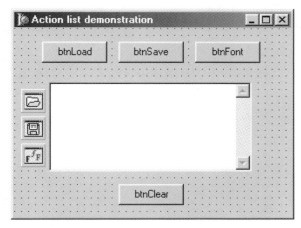

Figure 9.17 The form in design view after step 1

Note that we do not add any menu components at this stage. The form should look like figure 9.17.

• Save the unit as C09e02u and the project as C09e02p.

EX 9.2 STEP 2   Creating an Action list

An Action list contains a list of actions that can take place during execution of a program. Before we can create an Action list we have to determine which actions are involved in this program. Here is a list of operations that we think the user should be able to perform:

1 Type text into the Memo.
2 Load the text into the Memo from a file on disk.
3 Save the text in the Memo to a file on disk.
4 Change the font of the text in the Memo.
5 Clear the Memo.
6 Exit the program.

To achieve the first action in the list we needn't add any program code because the Memo already provides that functionality. All the other actions require some program code. The user will perform action number 2 (loading the text) by clicking the Load text button. We also plan to include a Load text... MenuItem on a drop-down menu to perform the same action, and right-clicking on the form component will display a pop-up menu that contains a similar MenuItem. The same applies to actions 3, 4 and 5 in the list. Both the File drop-down menu and the form's pop-up menu will include Exit items to perform the last action on the list (of course, we can also exit the program with the Windows Close button on the form, but for that we do not need any program code).

Instead of creating event handlers for the buttons, we now create an Action list that will contain the code for user actions 2 to 6 in the list above. The Action list will include a separate Action (in the form of a procedure) for each of these operations. Once we have all the procedures in place we'll link the buttons to their corresponding Actions.

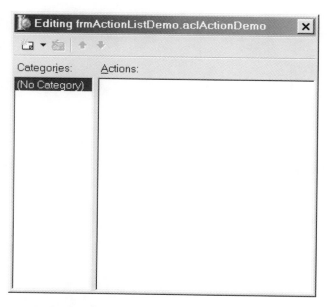

Figure 9.18 The Action list editor

- Find the ActionList component on the Standard tab of the Component/Tool palette and double-click on it to place an Action list on the form.
- Change its name property in the Object Inspector to aclActionDemo and then double-click on it to open the Action list editor (figure 9.18).
- In the editor, click on the New Action icon (the only active icon to the far left) on the toolbar to add an Action to the list. The default name for this Action is Action1.
- In the Object Inspector, change the Name to actSave and its Caption to '&Save text...'.
- Now double-click on actSave in the Action list editor to open the actSave event handler. Change it so that it looks like this:

```
procedure TfrmActionListDemo.actSaveExecute (Sender: TObject);
begin
  if svdSave.Execute then
    memDemo.Lines.SaveToFile (svdSave.FileName);
end;
```

- Switch to Form/Designer view, go back to the Action list editor and add another Action list with the New Action icon.
- Change its name to actLoad, its Caption to '&Load text...', then double-click on this new item in the list to open the actLoadExecute event handler. Change it to:

```
procedure TfrmActionListDemo.actLoadExecute (Sender: TObject);
begin
  if opdOpen.Execute then
```

```
      try
        memDemo.Lines.LoadFromFile(opdOpen.FileName);
      except
        ShowMessage ('Unable to open file ' + opdOpen.FileName);
      end;
end;
```

- Now create the actSetFont, actClear and actExit Actions, set their Captions and create their associated event handlers in the same way (use the Captions given in the properties table below). The three event handlers should look like these:

```
procedure TfrmActionListDemo.actSetFontExecute (Sender: TObject);
begin
  if fodFont.Execute then
    memDemo.Font := fodFont.Font;
end;

procedure TfrmActionListDemo.actClearExecute (Sender: TObject);
begin
  memDemo.Clear;
  memDemo.SetFocus;
end;

procedure TfrmActionListDEmo.actExitExecute (Sender: TObject);
begin
  Close;
end;
```

The table below summarizes the relevant property values for the ActionList and its Actions.

Component	Property	Value
ActionList1	Name	aclActionDemo
Action1	Name	actSave
	Caption	&Save text...
Action2	Name	actLoad
	Caption	&Load text...
Action3	Name	actSetFont
	Caption	Set &Font
Action4	Name	actClear
	Caption	&Clear text
Action5	Name	actExit
	Caption	E&xit

- Close the Action list editor by clicking in the Close button in the top right-hand corner.
- Save the unit file again.

If you run the program now, clicking on any of the buttons will still have no effect. This is because we haven't linked the buttons to their associated Actions yet.

EX 9.2 STEP 3   Linking buttons to the Actions

- Select the btnSave button on the form and find its Action property in the Object Inspector.
- Click on the down arrow to open the drop-down list. The names of all the Actions we created in step 2 appear in the list (figure 9.19).
- Select actSave.

We have now associated the actSave Action with the btnSave button. Note that the button's Caption has changed to 'Save text…'.

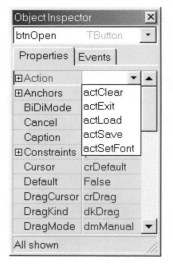

Figure 9.19 Selecting a value for the Action property

Action properties

As with any component, an Action has properties such as Caption, Enabled and Visible. This seems strange, since an Action is not a visible component. But although they are not visible, Actions can be associated with visible components such as buttons and MenuItems. An Action's property values will always be carried over to the corresponding properties of any component that is linked to the Action. For example, when we set btnSave's Action property to actSave, the button's Caption property takes on the value of the Action's Caption, namely 'Save text…'. So, if the Caption of your btnSave did not change to 'Save text…', it means that you did not give actSave's Caption property that value. If this is the case, go back to the Action list editor and change the Caption of the actSave to '&Save text…'. If you now return to the form, btnSave's Caption should be correct.

- Save the program again. If we now run the program and click on the Save text button, the Save As dialog should appear.
- For now, just click on Cancel in the Save As dialog and close the program.
- In design mode, set the Action properties of the remaining buttons as follows:

Button	Action
btnLoad	actLoad
btnFont	actSetFont
btnClear	actClear

- Make sure that the buttons have the correct Captions after you have set their Action properties. Then save the program and run it.
- A click on each of the buttons should now trigger the appropriate Action.

EX 9.2 STEP 4   Adding a main menu

Add a MainMenu component (Standard tab) to the form and change its Name property to mnuMain:

- Double-click in the mnuMain icon to open the Menu editor, then type '&File' as the title of the first drop-down menu.
- Now click in the empty item that appears below the File option (this is the first item in the File drop-down list). Do not type anything in its Caption property.

- Find its Action property in the Object Inspector and select actLoad from the list of Actions. The Caption '&Load text…' should appear in the MenuItem.
- Click once on the next new item that is displayed and set its Action property to actSave. The next item's Action property gets the value actClear.
- Now add a separator bar by clicking in the next new item, typing a hyphen in its Caption property and pressing the <Enter> key.
- Create the last item on this drop-down menu by setting its Action property to actExit.

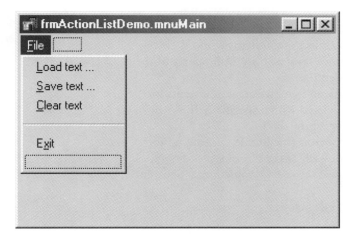

Figure 9.20 The File drop-down menu

The menu should now look as shown in figure 9.20. Each MenuItem here has been linked to an Action and, as a result, has taken on the properties of that Action (eg the Caption).

- Now add a Settings main menu item by clicking on the space to the right of the File Menu title and typing 'S&ettings' into the Caption property in the Object Inspector. Then press <Enter>. An empty item appears for which you can set the Action property to actSetFont (figure 9.21).

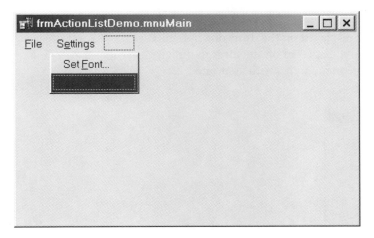

Figure 9.21 The Settings drop-down menu

Our Main menu is now complete with all its functionality. We did not create event handlers for the menu items, but associated a procedure with each menu item through its Action property.

- Save the file and run the program to test whether all the menu items perform the correct operations.

EX 9.2 STEP 5 Creating shortcuts for all the menu items

When we set the Caption property of the Actions, we included accelerator keys by placing an ampersand ('&') before the designated letter in the Caption. When setting the component's Action properties, these Captions appear on the components with their accelerator keys underlined. In our example all the Actions, and therefore all the buttons and MenuItems, have accelerator keys. We can also provide shortcut keys for the user to select menu items without having the menu displayed on the form. In this step we set the Shortcut property of the Action, which will then be reflected in the MenuItems.

Instead of creating a shortcut for each menu item, we create shortcuts for each of the Actions. A menu item that is associated with a specific Action will then take on the value of that Action's Shortcut property.

- To create shortcuts, open the Action list editor (by double-clicking on the ActionList component on the form). For each of the Actions click on its name in the list, then, in the Object Inspector, select a value for its Shortcut property from the drop-down list.
- Choose the shortcuts according to the table below:

Action	Shortcut
actSave	Ctrl+S
actLoad	Ctrl+L
actSetFont	Ctrl+F
actClear	Ctrl+C
actExit	Ctrl+X

- Close the Action list editor to return to the form and select the File MenuItem. The shortcuts should be displayed on the drop-down menus, as in figure 9.22. (If the drop-down is not displayed on the form in design view, open the Menu editor to see the menu items with associated shortcuts.)

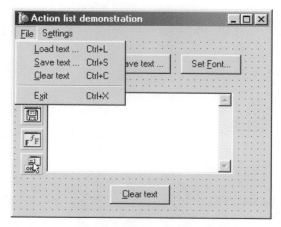

Figure 9.22 The File menu with shortcuts in design view

- If you have added the shortcuts, save the unit and run the program. Check that you can perform each action by using the buttons, the menu, the accelerator and the shortcut keys.

EX 9.2 STEP 6 Adding a pop-up menu

- Add a PopupMenu component to the form and change its name to pumMemoActions.
- Double-click on the icon to open the Menu editor. An empty MenuItem appears highlighted in the editor.
- Find its Action property in the Object Inspector and select actLoad from the list. The Caption Load text... together with the shortcut <Ctrl+L> appears on the MenuItem.
- Continue to add items in this way until your pop-up menu looks like that in figure 9.23. For each of the items (except the separator bar) you only need to set its Action property. For the separator, type a hyphen in the Caption property.

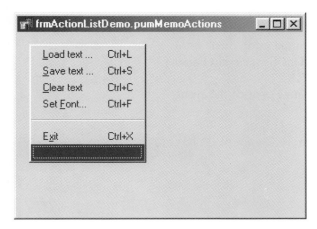

Figure 9.23 The pop-up menu at design time

- Close the Menu editor and click anywhere on the form to make it the active component. Find its PopupMenu property in the Object Inspector and select pumMemoActions from the drop-down list so that this menu will appear when the user right clicks on the form.
- Save the unit file again. Run the program to make sure the pop-up menu appears when you right click on the form.
- Clicking on any of the menu items or using shortcuts should trigger the appropriate action.

EX 9.2 STEP 7 Enabling/disabling the Actions

As a final step in this example we change the user interface so that the Save text and Clear text buttons, MenuItems and PopupMenu items are initially disabled. The user should not try to save or clear the contents of the Memo if it doesn't contain any text. Only after the user has either loaded text into the Memo or started typing text into the Memo component should these operations become available.

To disable the relevant buttons, MenuItems and PopupMenu items involved we could change each of their Enabled properties to False in the Object Inspector. However, changing the Enabled properties of only the actSave and actClear Actions to False will have the same effect, with less likelihood of making a mistake in the settings.

- Open the Action list editor and make the following changes:

Action	Property	Value
actSave	Enabled	False
actClear	Enabled	False

- Save the unit file. If you run the program now, the Save text and Clear text buttons are disabled. If you open the File menu or the pop-up menu, these menu items are also dimmed.

We want to enable these buttons and MenuItems when text is loaded into the Memo or when the user types in it. The event that will pick this up is the Memo's OnChange event.

- To open this event handler, select the Memo on the form, then, in the Object Inspector, click on the Events tab. The OnChange event handler appears at the top of the Events list (figure 9.24).
- Double-click in the blank space next to OnChange to open the event handler. Change it as follows:

Figure 9.24 Creating the Memo's OnChange event

```
procedure TfrmActionListDemo.memDemoChange (Sender: TObject);
begin
  actSave.Enabled := True;
  actClear.Enabled := True;
end;
```

- Also change the actClear Action's event handler, so that after clearing the text, these buttons and MenuItems are again disabled (open this event handler in the Action list editor by double-clicking on actClear in the list). It should change as follows:

```
procedure TfrmActionListDemo.actClearExecute (Sender: TObject);
begin
  memDemo.Clear;
  memDemo.SetFocus;
  actsave.Enabled := False;
  actClear.Enabled := False;
end;
```

- Save the file and run the program. Make sure the enabling and disabling works correctly.

This last step illustrates how we can change the properties of an Action at run time under program control, thereby making synchronized changes to the components that share that Action.

When different sources trigger the same operation

In example 9.1 we added functionality to the menu items in two different ways. First, we created a separate event handler for the Red1 and Red2 MenuItems, although they performed the same operation. All property values were set for each individual menu item.

Figure 9.25 Duplication of identical procedures

Second, we created event handlers for the drop-down menu items only and then rerouted the OnClick events of the pop-up menu items to the existing OnClick event handlers. Here, however, the property values were set separately for each individual component.

Figure 9.26 One-way centralization through one component's event handler

Finally, in example 9.2, we centralized the code as well as some property values by defining them in an Action list. The buttons and menuItems are linked to Actions and then react to OnClick events by executing the Execute procedure of the associated Action. The centralization works in two directions, seeing that changes made to an Action's property value (eg the Enabled property) are immediately taken on by all the buttons and MenuItems linked to that Action.

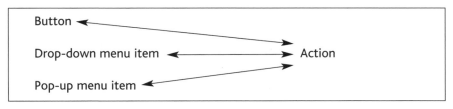

Figure 9.27 Two-way centralization through an Action

Using ActionLists helps us to avoid duplication and redundancy. It improves the reliability and maintainability of a program in which the same operation can be activated by different components, and where corresponding properties of different components must be synchronized.

REVIEW

In this chapter we saw how to include menus in our Delphi applications. We created main menus which included drop-down menus as well as cascading submenus, and we included pop-up menus attached to the forms. Other menu-related concepts we dealt with were shortcuts and checkmarked menu items. We explored different ways of linking event handlers to the menu items and saw that more than one event can be linked to the same event handler. From this we moved on to the concept of Action lists.

We saw that Action lists provide a way to centralize our program code. Sometimes a user interface gives the user different ways to accomplish the same task. We saw in this chapter that if we want to trigger the same action through different components, we just specify the same Action in their respective Action properties. The OnClick event for any of these components will then be routed to the corresponding Action's OnExecute event handler. All components linked to an Action will also take on the property values of the Action. For example, when we want to disable all components that trigger a particular action, we need only to set the Enabled property of the associated Action to False.

IMPORTANT CONCEPTS

Fundamental programming concepts

Set: An unordered collection of related data elements of the same type. The individual elements cannot be accessed (they are not indexed) and a set cannot contain duplicate elements. We can test whether a given element appears in a list. In Delphi we represent a set by listing its elements in square brackets separated by commas. For example,

```
Vowels := ['a', 'e', 'i', 'o', 'u'];
```

The variable Vowels has to be declared as a set before we can use it like this. The declaration will typically be

```
var
  Vowels: set of 'a'..'z';
```

meaning any set consisting of lowercase alphabetical characters can be assigned to Vowels. To check whether an element appears in a set, we use the in command.

Although arrays and sets are both collections of data of the same type, there are some fundamental differences which are summarised in the table below:

Arrays	Sets
Elements are ordered	There is no order (it does not matter what the order is)
Individual elements can be accessed through an index	Cannot access individual elements (can only test if a given element exists in the set)
Can store duplicates	Cannot store duplicates

User interface elements

Accelerator key: Accelerator keys allow the user to activate a button or menu item using a keyboard combination as an alternative to clicking with the mouse. In contrast to a shortcut, an accelerator key is active only when its associated menu item is displayed on the screen.

Cascading menu: A submenu that can be opened by clicking on (or pointing to) an item on a drop-down menu or a pop-up menu that has a right-pointing arrow as indication.

Checkmarked menu items: When a menu item toggles between two states (eg Bold/Not bold), we can use its Checked property to indicate the current state. If the Checked property is True a ✓ appears in front of the item.

Drop-down menu: Choosing a menu title on the main menu bar can open up a list of related options. This list is a drop-down menu (also referred to as a pull-down menu).

Main menu bar: A list of menu titles that have drop-down menus associated with them. It is usually placed horizontally across the top of a window.

Pop-up menu: A menu that appears when the user clicks on a control with the right mouse button. To associate a pop-up menu with a specific component, we assign the name of the PopupMenu to the component's PopupMenu property.

Separator lines: Groups of options on a drop-down or pop-up menu can be separated with horizontal lines called separator lines. In Delphi a separator line is created by setting the caption of a MenuItem to a single hyphen.

Shortcut: We use shortcuts to allow the user to type a key combination to invoke a menu option instead of selecting the item from the menu. To assign a shortcut key combination to a menu item, we specify it in the item's shortcut property in the Object Inspector. This key combination is displayed to the right of the menu item in the menu. Shortcuts increase the economy of a user interface without compromising its ease of use.

NEW DELPHI FEATURES

New common property

Action	Some Delphi components, such as Buttons and MenuItems, have an Action property where we can specify the name of an associated Action (see TAction below). A click on the component invokes the Action's OnExecute event. The values of the associated Action's properties are taken on by the corresponding properties of the component.

Operators/keywords and special characters

#13	Special character code representing a carriage return. To place text onto a new line, concatenate #13 with a string using the + operator. For example: `ShowMessage('line 1' + #13 + 'line 2');`
+	When used with sets, this operator combines the contents of two sets into one set (union operator).
–	When used with sets, this operator forms a set from the contents of one set minus the contents of another set (difference operator).

[]		Notation for an empty set, ie a set containing no elements.
[mem1, mem2, ...]		Notation for a set containing members mem1, mem2, ...
in statement		Checks whether an element appears in a set. For example, the expression, 'a' in Vowels, returns True if element 'a' appears in the set Vowels.

TAction

Properties	Caption	Text that will be linked to the client component's Caption property.
	Enabled	Determines whether the client component is enabled or disabled.
	Shortcut	If the client component is a menu item, the key combination specified here will appear to the right of the menu item. The user can use this key combination to execute the operation instead of selecting the menu item from the menu.
Event	OnExecute	OnExecute is triggered by a client component's default event (typically an OnClick event).
Prefix	act...	
Use		Centralises code and property values so that multiple components (such as Buttons or MenuItems) can be linked to these properties and code through their Action properties. When the name of an Action appears in a component's Action property, clicking on that component (assuming a click is the default event for that component) invokes the Action's OnExecute event handler.

TActionList

Properties	Actions	Contains an indexed list of the Actions in the ActionList object.
Prefix	acl...	
Use		An ActionList coordinates Actions. We place an ActionList component on a form and use the Action list editor to maintain the list of Actions contained in it. We can add an Action to the list, delete an Action from the list and rearrange the Actions.

TColorDialog

Properties	Color	Contains the currently selected colour.
Methods	Execute	A call to this method opens the Color dialog. Execute returns True if the user clicks OK or False if the user clicks Cancel or closes the dialog.
Prefix	cdl...	
Use		Displays the Windows common dialog for selecting a Colour. It appears when the program calls the Execute method. When the user clicks OK, it returns the selected colour in the Color property.

TMainMenu

Property	Items	Defines the items (of type TMenuItem) that are displayed in the menu.
Prefix	mnu...	
Use		Maintains a menu bar with its associated drop-down menus.

TMenuItem		
Properties	Action	Contains the name of the Action associated with the menu item. When the user selects a menu item, the OnExecute event of the Action specified here is triggered.
	Caption	Contains the string that will be displayed as the menu item.
Events	OnClick	Is triggered when the user clicks the menu item or uses the relevant accelerator or shortcut.
Use		Determines the appearance and behaviour of an item in a menu.

TPopupMenu		
Property	Items	Defines the items (of type TMenuItem) that are displayed in the menu.
Prefix	pum…	
Use		Defines a pop-up menu that is displayed when the user right clicks on a component. The pop-up menu associated with a component is specified in the component's PopupMenu property.

PROBLEMS

PROBLEM 9.1) Deleting names using a menu

In example 8.5 we wrote a program to delete all occurrences of a given name from a ListBox of names.
- Add the following main menu to the program from example 8.5: The first main menu item is File, which has a drop-down menu with the items Load, Save, Reset and Exit. There should be a separator between Save and Reset. The second main menu item is Name with a single drop-down item, Delete.
- Each menu item should have a suitable accelerator key and shortcut and should execute the relevant action.

PROBLEM 9.2) A font menu item

- Alter the application in example 9.1 so that the Font MenuItem is enabled and brings up the Font dialog form where the user can choose a font for the Label.

PROBLEM 9.3) Addition tester

A young nephew wants a program for practising addition.
- Write a program which tests addition. The user interface is shown in figure 9.28. The program generates two random numbers and the user must type in the sum of these two numbers. If the user clicks on the Check button, the program displays a message stating whether the answer is correct or not. If the user clicks on 'New Sum' a new random sum is generated.
- The program includes a set of radio buttons where the user can select the difficulty level of the sum. If '1 digit' is selected, the numbers for the next sum will be generated from the numbers 1..9; if '2 digits' is selected, the numbers for the next sum will be generated from the numbers 10..99; and so on.

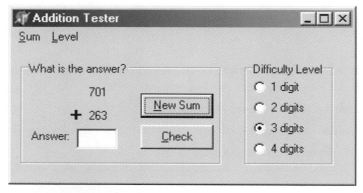

Figure 9.28 Application for testing addition

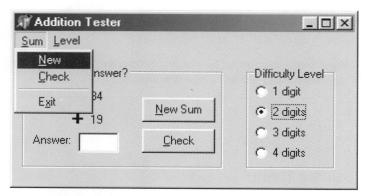

Figure 9.29 Drop-down list for the first main menu item

- Add a main menu to the program. The menu has two main items, Sum and Level. The drop-down items under Sum are: New, Check and Exit (figure 9.29). The New and Check menu items correspond to the actions of the two buttons. The drop-down items under Level are: 'Increase difficulty' and 'Decrease difficulty'. These menu items should result in the level increasing or decreasing by 1 digit and this change should be reflected on the radio buttons on the form as well. When the level is on '1 digit' the 'Decrease difficulty' menu item should be disabled and when the level is on '4 digits', the 'Increase difficulty' menu item should be disabled.

Hints:
- Declare the values of the two random numbers and the level (1 – 4) as unit-level variables.
- In the FormCreate event handler, set a default level and generate the first two random numbers.
- To generate a 1-digit random number, use the statement: `Random(9) + 1`; to generate a 2-digit random number, use the statement: `Random(90) + 10`; and so on. Remember to call the Randomize procedure once before calling Random for the first time (this is best done in the FormCreate event handler).

PROBLEM 9.4 Action lists (1)

- Add a menu to the program we wrote in example 1.3. The only main menu item is Colour, which has a drop-down menu with the items Purple and

Yellow attached to it. These have shortcuts <Ctrl+P> and <Ctrl+Y> respectively (figure 9.30). The form also has a pop-up menu with the same menu items.

- Remove the existing OnClick event handlers for the two buttons and instead use an ActionList to give the buttons and menu items functionality.
- Enable and disable the buttons and menu items appropriately to make the interface user friendly.

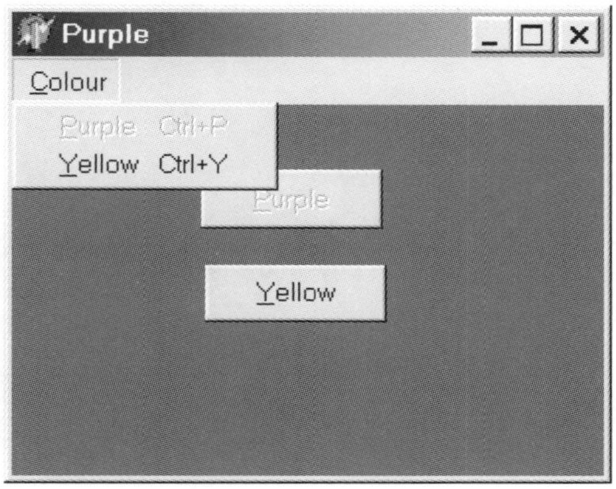

Figure 9.30 The new interface

PROBLEM 9.5) Action lists (2)

- Redo example 9.1 using an ActionList.

PROBLEM 9.6) Action lists (3)

- Modify problem 9.3 to use an ActionList, with Actions replacing the event handlers.

CHAPTER 10

Events and parameters

PURPOSE OF THIS CHAPTER

So far, all our programming has been in small chunks we have called 'event handlers'. An event handler is a particular form of a more general programming structure called a 'procedure' and is generally attached to either a user event or a system event.

In this chapter we start by looking at some other events in addition to the OnClick user events we have used almost exclusively until now. At times data must pass from an event to its event handler. This happens through the use of parameters. Parameters are a thread running through this and the next two chapters.

Event handlers are special procedures attached to events. Other kinds of procedure, such as Clear and SetFocus, are attached to components. These procedures are called 'methods', and we look at Delphi's standard methods in Chapter 11.

In Chapter 12 we look at writing procedures and methods ourselves. Then we deal with functions, which are closely related to procedures, in Chapter 13. Taken together, procedures and functions are often called 'subroutines' or 'subprograms'. Subroutines in their various forms are a crucial part of programming. This chapter forms the basis for understanding subroutines and introduces a whole new way of viewing programs.

In the process of looking at the various types of subroutine in these four chapters we also cover many other fascinating aspects of programming with Delphi, so there is a lot to keep you going and to think about. You may find it helps to tackle these chapters in several comfortable stages. Give yourself time to think about what you are reading and doing, and possibly to page backwards every now and then to remind yourself about what we have covered, rather than rushing ahead. And don't worry if you don't understand all the finer details first time through! As you become more familiar with these ideas, you'll find that it all becomes more obvious and easier to understand.

Event-driven programming

Thinking about the programs we have written so far, we see that the program often cannot work out in advance what the next event will be. Because of the GUI, the user is in control and may, for example, click on any one of the buttons displayed or enter text into any of the Edit components. This means that the program must be ready at any time to respond to any event that may occur. Between events, it is simply waiting for something to happen.

In most older programming languages it is difficult to write a program that can accept any event. Fortunately for us, Delphi and Windows together do the hard work in event handling. All we have to do is to write the event handlers we need in the program.

There are three stages to the event-processing sequence:

1   Some action (or 'event') occurs.
2   Windows detects this event and sends an event message to Delphi.
3   If the programmer has created an event handler, Delphi initiates the event handler. If there is no linked event handler, Delphi discards the event message from Windows.

To summarize, because of the GUI, most Delphi programs are event-driven. This means that much of our programming is in the form of event handlers. An event handler is a group of program statements, or a 'mini-program', attached to an event, that runs whenever that event occurs.

EXAMPLE 10.1   OnMouseMove event handlers

The mouse-click, which we have used extensively so far, is a common user event. However, there are many other types of event too, and we will start this chapter with an example based on the MouseMove event.

You may have seen some Internet applications where an area of the screen changes colour or the caption of a button becomes bold when the mouse pointer moves over it. We'll use similar techniques in this example.

- Open a new application and give the following values to the component properties. The Panel is a new component which we have not used previously. It closely resembles the GroupBox and is next to it on the Standard tab of the Component/Tool palette.

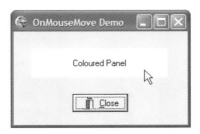

Figure 10.1 Demonstrating the OnMouseMove event

Component	Property	Value
Form1	Name	frmShow
	Caption	OnMouseMove Demo
Panel1	Name	pnlShow
	Caption	Coloured Panel
	BevelOuter	bvNone
BitBtn1	Name	bmbClose
	Kind	bkClose

- The next step is to create the event handlers. Up to now, we have mostly used the OnClick event handler. To see which other event handlers are available, click *once* on the Close BitBtn to select it. Move over to the Object

Inspector, which currently shows all the available properties and their values. Click the Events tab in the Object Inspector, and the list of events that a BitBtn can respond to appears on the left-hand side.

'OnClick' is the first event listed but there are various others including the groups of events starting with OnDrag... , OnKey... and OnMouse... (figure 10.2). We cannot go into all of these events here, but we can look at their descriptions in Delphi's online Help.

Accessing context-sensitive online Help

Like many Windows systems, Delphi has an online Help facility. Let's use this to find out about the OnMouseMove event.
- Click *once* on an event so that it is highlighted in the Object Inspector and then press <F1>.
- We selected OnMouseMove (figure 10.2) and got the following text. (Delphi 8 has similar help text.)

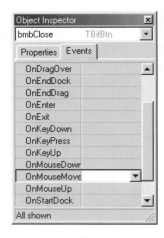

Figure 10.2 Delphi's Object Inspector

TControl.OnMouseMove

Occurs when the user moves the mouse pointer while the mouse pointer is over a control.

type
```
TMouseMoveEvent = procedure(Sender: TObject; Shift: TShiftState;
  X, Y: Integer) of object;
property OnMouseMove: TMouseMoveEvent;
```

Description

Use the OnMouseMove event handler to make something happen when the mouse pointer moves within the control.

Use the Shift parameter of the OnMouseDown event handler to respond to the state of the shift keys and mouse buttons. Shift keys are the Shift, Ctrl, and Alt keys or shift key-mouse button combinations. X and Y are pixel* coordinates of the new location of the mouse pointer in the client area of the Sender.

This description may not make complete sense right now, but it seems at least that this event handler will be called whenever the user moves the mouse pointer over the Panel or the BitBtn.
- Let's test this by writing OnMouseMove event handlers that highlight the BitBtn or the Panel when the mouse pointer moves over either of them. (Like the BitBtn, the Panel and the form also have OnMouseMove events.)

Writing the event handlers

- First close the Help display.
- Now create the OnMouseMove event handlers for the Panel, the BitBtn and the form as shown below. To do this:
- Select the required component by single-clicking on it in the Form Designer, by selecting it from the Object TreeView (Delphi 6 or 7), or by selecting it from the drop-down box at the top of the Object Inspector;

---

* The screen is made up of hundreds of little dots. Each dot is called a 'pixel'.

- Click on the Events tab in the Object Inspector, and
- Double-click on the space alongside OnMouseMove in the list of events.

For each in turn, Delphi brings the Code editor window to the top and inserts the code for the skeleton of the event allowing you to type in the program statements shown below:

```
procedure TfrmShow.pnlShowMouseMove(Sender: TObject;
  Shift: TShiftState; X, Y: Integer);
begin
  pnlShow.Color := clAqua;
end; // end TfrmShow.pnlShowMouseMove


procedure TfrmShow.bmbCloseMouseMove(Sender: TObject;
  Shift: TShiftState; X, Y: Integer);
begin
  bmbClose.Font.Style := [fsBold, fsUnderline];
end; // end TfrmShow.bmbCloseMouseMove


procedure TfrmShow.FormMouseMove(Sender: TObject;
  Shift: TShiftState; X, Y: Integer);
begin
  pnlShow.Color := clBtnFace;
  bmbClose.Font.Style := [];
end; // end TfrmShow.FormMouseMove
```

- Save the file as C10e01u and the project as C10e01p. Run the program. Initially you can see the BitBtn and the Caption of the Panel but not the Panel itself, because the Panel's BevelOuter property is set to bvNone.

Move the mouse towards the Panel's Caption. As the mouse pointer crosses the edge of the Panel, the Panel changes colour to Aqua. Move the pointer over the BitBtn: its Caption becomes bold and underlined. Move the pointer over the form away from either the Panel or the BitBtn: the Panel's colour and the button's Font.Style properties change back.

Do you understand how this program works?

The computer monitors the mouse every time it moves. This causes the OnMouseMove event that fires one of the form, Panel or BitBtn OnMouseMove event handlers, depending on the mouse's position.

The statement in bmbClose's OnMouseMove event handler is:

```
bmbClose.Font.Style := [fsBold, fsUnderline];
```

Notice that Style is a property of Font, which is a property of bmbClose. We extend the standard dot notation to connect these three. On the right of the assignment operator appear two constant names enclosed in *square* brackets and separated by a comma. As we saw in exercise 9.1 step 6, this notation means a *set* that contains two members, fsBold and fsUnderline. The final program statement of the form's MouseMove event handler contains the empty set, meaning that bmbClose's font has no special style.

Exercise 10.1 Summary: In addition to the common OnClick event attached to many components, there are also a variety of other events. These are available through the Events tab on the Object Inspector. In this example we have seen several components' OnMouseMove events. We also saw how to call up the online Help through the <F1> key and how to set and clear the fsBold and fsUnderline styles programmatically for a button's Caption through the Font.Style property.

User events and system events

OnClick and OnMouseMove are events initiated by the user. Consequently, we call them 'user events'. There is also a class of events, called 'system events', that respond to something happening in the computer without any direct action by the user. In this chapter we look at two examples of system events from the many that are available in Delphi. The computer has an internal clock which can trigger Delphi's Timer component and its event handler. We explore the OnTimer event in the next two examples. Delphi also initiates a whole lot of system events, such as OnCreate and OnShow, in its form management and we look briefly at the OnShow event after that.

EXAMPLE 10.2) Generating system events through the Timer

To demonstrate a system event based on the computer's internal clock, we will display the current time using a system event handler. This will be linked to the Timer component and to Delphi's built-in Time function:

- Start a new application.
- On the form place a Label component (Standard tab of the Component/Tool palette) and a Timer (System tab) to match figure 10.3.
- Set the property values as follows:

Figure 10.3 Form design to display system time

Component	Property	Value
Form1	Name	frmSystemTime
	Caption	System Time
Label1	Name	lblSysTime
Timer1	Name	tmrSysTime

- Double-click the Timer component to create the handler for the OnTimer event. (For most components we have used until now, double-clicking on the component during design time takes us to the OnClick event handler. However, the Timer is a non-visual component – see Visual and non-visual components below – and does not have an OnClick event. Double-clicking on it creates the OnTimer handler.)

```
procedure TfrmSystemTime.tmrSysTimeTimer(Sender: TObject);
begin
  lblSysTime.Caption := TimeToStr (Time);
end;
```

- Save the unit file as C10e02u and the project file as C10e02p. When you run the program, you get the display shown in figure 10.4. The time of day, as determined by the computer, ticks up second by second in the window you have just programmed without any further action on your part. This continues until you click the Close box at the top right of your program's window and return to Delphi's design environment.

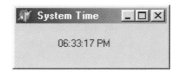

Figure 10.4 Running the system time program

Can you see how the event handler that we have just programmed for the Timer works? Because it is linked to the Timer, it runs periodically (here, once per second). In the program statement above, `Time` is a function call that returns the 'system time', based on the computer's built-in clock. (We look at functions in Chapter 13.) `TimeToStr` is a function that converts a Time data type variable to a string. The assignment operator `:=` assigns this string to the Caption of the Label and so displays the updated time once a second. Pretty good for a single program statement!

Visual and non-visual components

Have you noticed that, unlike the components we used previously, such as buttons and Labels, the Timer component is not visible when the program runs? It is simply working in the background, and so is called a *non-visual* component. There are various other non-visual components too, such as the Dialog components we saw in Chapter 5. Since non-visual components are not visible at run time, they can be placed anywhere on the form that is convenient.

The user interacts directly with most of the other components we have used until now. Consequently, they must be visible on the form and are called *visual* components.

The Timer

If you use the Object Inspector to look at the Timer's properties and their values, you will see that there are not many, only four (figure 10.5). What do you think the Interval property does? Change it to 5000, and run the program again. Did you guess correctly? The time now updates only once every five seconds. An interval of 5000 tells the Timer's event handler to trigger every five seconds, an interval of 1000 triggers every second, an interval of 200 triggers every 0.2 seconds, and so on.

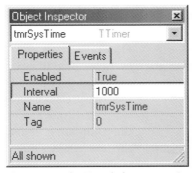

Figure 10.5 The Timer's four properties

The programmer allows the Timer to run by setting its Enabled property to True and stops it running by setting Enabled to False through program code. When the Timer is disabled (ie Enabled is False), its OnTimer event handler does not fire, and so it does not perform any of the operations in its OnTimer event handler.

- Click the Events tab in the Object Inspector (figure 10.6).

The OnTimer event is the only event the Timer responds to, and this is triggered by the computer, not the user. This is why we refer to it as a 'system event'. When the preset interval expires, any Delphi program code in the OnTimer event handler will execute and the interval starts all over again. So, if we want anything to happen repeatedly at a specific time interval, we put that program code into an OnTimer event handler and adjust the value of the interval as needed.

Figure 10.6 The Timer's only event

Once we have enabled the Timer, it runs on its own and we can carry on with other activities in the program if necessary. When the Timer expires the OnTimer event fires and this will be handled like any other event.

If you have programmed before, perhaps in Pascal or C, and have used a loop to create a delay timer, note that Delphi's Timer is different. Enabling the Timer does not introduce a delay in the entire program the way a delay loop does. You can start a Delphi Timer and then continue doing something else in your program. You can even have several Timers running at the same time. Any action needed at the end of the interval must therefore be in the OnTimer event handler and *not* in the program immediately after enabling the Timer.

EXAMPLE 10.3) Combining system and user events

- Extend the program written above so that the time changes every second except while either the left or the right mouse button is held down anywhere on the form, when the time display should stop at the current value. When the mouse button is released, the time once again updates every second. The time display should appear only after the user has clicked on the form for the first time.

EX 10.3   Planning

Before reading further, reflect for yourself on how to write this program.

In the previous program the Timer ran continuously. We can use this program as a starting point, modifying it so that the Timer is disabled when either mouse button is down. So, how do we know when the mouse button is down and when it is up, and how do we switch the Timer on and off?

Looking at the form's events (figure 10.7), we see that it has OnMouseDown and OnMouseUp events in addition to the OnMouseMove event we used in example 10.1. Click on OnMouseDown and then press <F1> to call up the online Help. We see that the OnMouseDown event 'occurs when the user presses a mouse button with the mouse pointer over a control': in other words, it fires when the user presses the mouse button down and is directed to the component under the mouse pointer. Similarly, OnMouseUp occurs when the user releases the mouse button. Just what we need! (Note that OnMouseDown and OnMouseUp do *not* refer to moving the mouse down or up but to pressing the mouse button down or releasing it.)

In the description above of the Timer, we say that the Timer runs when its Enabled property is True, and stops when Enabled is set to False. So, in the MouseDown event handler we must set Enabled to False and set it to True in the MouseUp handler.

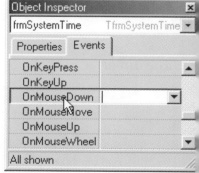

Figure 10.7 Locating the form's OnMouseDown event

EX 10.3   Testing

When the program is running, the time display must freeze whenever the mouse button is pressed anywhere on the form and start updating again when the button is released. On startup the time display should not appear until after the first mouse click.

EX 10.3 STEP 1 Enabling the Timer programmatically

- Working from the program in the previous example, change the value of the Timer's Interval property back to 1000. Although the OnTimer event handler can stay as it is, we now need to enable and disable it through OnMouseDown and OnMouseUp handlers.
- Click on the form and then select the Events tab in the Object Inspector.
- Scroll down until you see the OnMouseDown event and double-click opposite it to create the form's OnMouseDown event handler as follows:

```
procedure TfrmSystemTime.FormMouseDown(Sender: TObject;
        Button: TMouseButton; Shift: TShiftState; X, Y: Integer);
begin
  tmrSysTime.Enabled := False;
end;
```

Because of this event handler, the Timer will be disabled and the OnTimer event handler will not run when either mouse button is pressed down. The display will therefore no longer update.

- Now double-click opposite OnMouseUp in the Object Inspector to create an event handler to enable the Timer:

```
procedure TfrmSystemTime.FormMouseUp(Sender: TObject; Button:
        TMouseButton; Shift: TShiftState; X, Y: Integer);
begin
  lblSysTime.Caption := TimeToStr (Time);
  tmrSysTime.Enabled := True;
end;
```

This procedure is triggered as soon as a mouse button is released anywhere on the form (except over another component). The first program line updates the time immediately so that there is not a one second delay before the time appears. The second line enables the Timer. As a result, while the mouse button is released, the time display will update each time Interval elapses.

- Save the unit file as C10e03u and the project file as C10e03p.
- Run and test the program by clicking a mouse button. According to our test criteria, the system time should freeze at the current value for as long as you hold the button down anywhere on the form. When you release the mouse button, the time display should appear, updating once every second until you again press a button down.

If you test this program carefully, you will notice that it works well *unless* the mouse pointer is over the Label when you press the button down. This is because the time display is controlled by mouse clicks on the form, and any mouse clicks on the Label go to lblSysTime's event handlers and *not* to the form's handlers.

This is an example of an inconsistent user interface: the same action (pressing down a mouse button) unexpectedly produces a different reaction depending on where the mouse pointer is on the form. In Chapter 4 we introduced the user interface design principle of consistency, which states that the user interface should behave similarly throughout the application. To ensure that our application is consistent, we need the OnMouseDown event of the Label to give the same behaviour as the OnMouseDown event of the form.

There are several ways to correct this. We could, for example, take the program code that controls the Timer in the FormMouseDown and FormMouseUp event handlers and repeat this in the lblSysTimeMouseDown and lblSysTimeMouseUp event handlers. This would be quite tedious, though, and Delphi provides a more elegant solution.

EX 10.3 STEP 2   Routing events

- If the program is still running, close it and then click on the Label in the Form Designer.
- Go to the Object Inspector and select the Events tab.
- Click once opposite the OnMouseDown field, then click again on the downward-pointing arrow to bring up a ListBox. A list of the available event handlers appears. Select FormMouseDown (figure 10.8). By doing this, we are routing the *Label's* OnMouseDown event to the *form's* MouseDown event handler. Similarly, with OnMouseUp, select FormMouseUp to route the Label's OnMouseUp event to the form's MouseUp event handler.

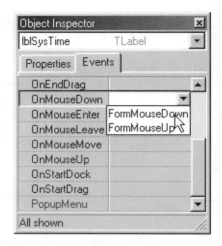

Figure 10.8 Linking the Label's event to the form's event handler

Now, whenever there is a down or up click on the Label, Delphi will route the Label's event to the matching Form event handler.

- Save the unit again under the same name (C10e03u given in step 1), and then run the program.
- Test it carefully. It should respond to MouseDown and MouseUp events anywhere on the form or Label by starting and stopping the time display.

Routing several events to the same handler when appropriate is a useful way of reducing the amount of code one has to write and of simplifying future maintenance and evolution of the program. If future changes become necessary, one makes the change once in the shared handler and all the events using this handler will use the updated code.

EX 10.3 STEP 3   Renaming event handlers

There is, however, one confusing thing about sharing the handler as we have just done: both the form's OnMouseDown and the Label's OnMouseDown go to the handler called FormMouseDown. Perhaps we need a different name? Delphi accommodates this neatly.

- Simply go to the Events tab in the Object Inspector for either the form or the Label and then change the handler's name to StopTimer (figure 10.9).

Delphi changes the name of the procedure in the program code and links both the form's OnMouseDown and the Label's OnMouseDown events to this new name. Similarly, using the Object Inspector, change the name FormMouseUp to StartTimer. These new names no longer signify a specific component and clarify the operation of the program. Because Delphi maintains the links between the event and the event handler, it is important to change the name *only* in the Object Inspector and *not* directly in the program code.

Figure 10.9 Changing the name FormMouseDown to StopTimer

EX 10.3 STEP 4   Some final touches

The program is still not quite correct. When we start the program, the time display should not begin until we click on the form for the first time. So on startup we want the Timer to be disabled. It would also be helpful if the Label showed a useful message. Change the properties as below. This final step emphasizes that many properties, in this case the Timer's Enabled property and the Label's Caption, can be manipulated both statically through the Object Inspector and dynamically through the program.

Component	Property	Value
lblSysTime	Caption	Click to show the time
tmrSysTime	Enabled	False

EXAMPLE 10.4 The 'form' system events

There are many system events besides OnTimer and this example looks briefly at the form's OnShow event:
- Start a new application and, without adding any components to the form, select the form's Events tab in the Object Inspector. This shows a long list of events.
- Locate the OnShow event, double-click in the column alongside it, and enter the following OnShow event handler:

```
procedure TfrmFormEvents.FormShow(Sender: TObject);
begin
  ShowMessage ('Form about to appear');
end;
```

- Save the unit and project as C10e04u and C10e04p respectively and then run the program.

Instead of the form being displayed as normally happens, the message in figure 10.10 is displayed.

After clicking on the OK button, the form is displayed as expected. Do you understand what has happened? Delphi associates a whole lot of (system) events with creating and displaying, hiding and destroying the form. Among these is the OnShow event. Just before showing the form, Delphi calls the OnShow event handler (if it exists). We placed a ShowMessage statement in this event handler which is why the message appears just before the form does. Delphi waits for us to accept the message before continuing as normal and showing the form.

This is a simple example to illustrate another form of system event in addition to the OnTimer event. If you'd like to learn more about these form events, click alongside the appropriate event in the Events tab of the Object Inspector, then press <F1> for help.

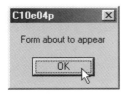

Figure 10.10 ShowMessage output

EXAMPLE 10.5 Parameters in event handlers

You've probably noticed that the header Delphi generates automatically for each event handler contains a list of words in brackets. For instance, in example 10.1, we had three MouseMove event handlers each with a heading that contained a list in brackets:

```
procedure TfrmShow.pnlShowMouseMove (Sender: TObject;
            Shift: TShiftState; X, Y: Integer);

procedure TfrmShow.bmbCloseMouseMove (Sender: TObject;
            Shift: TShiftState; X, Y: Integer);

procedure TfrmShow.FormMouseMove (Sender: TObject;
            Shift: TShiftState; X, Y: Integer);
```

Each list contains three groupings:

```
Sender: TObject;
Shift: TShiftState;
X, Y: Integer
```

In each grouping, the name on the left of the colon (ie Sender, Shift, X and Y) represents a *parameter*. As we'll see in a moment, Delphi makes the parameters available to the programmer in the event handler. The name on the right of the colon (ie TObject, TShiftState or Integer) represents the *data type* of the corresponding parameter. We've seen similar notation previously when declaring variable names.

In this example we'll see how we use the OnMouseDown event's parameters in an event handler:

- Open a new application.
- Call the form 'frmMousePos' and set its Caption to 'Mouse Position' (figure 10.11).

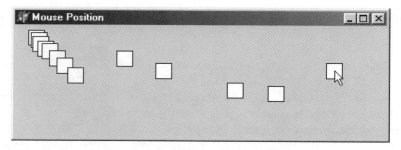

Figure 10.11 A square appears wherever you click the mouse

- Without putting any components on the form, go to the form's Events tab in the Object Inspector, double-click alongside OnMouseDown and write the following event handler:

```
procedure TfrmMousePos.FormMouseDown(Sender: TObject;
        Button: TMouseButton; Shift: TShiftState; X, Y: Integer);
begin
   frmMousePos.Canvas.Rectangle (X-10, Y-10, X+10, Y+10);
end;
```

If you compare this procedure heading to OnMouseMove's procedure heading, you'll notice that OnMouseDown has an additional parameter, Button of type TMouseButton, in its parameter list.

- Save the unit as C10e05u and the project as C10e05p, then run the program.

EX 10.5 STEP 1 Positioning squares

A square appears wherever you click on the form with either the left or the right mouse button (figure 10.11. Depending on the computer setup, the squares may or may not contrast with the background). Had you worked out this would happen? In case you hadn't, let's look at the event handler above line by line.

The header of the event handler is:

```
procedure TfrmMousePos.FormMouseDown(Sender: TObject;
        Button: TMouseButton; Shift: TShiftState; X, Y: Integer);
```

The first word, 'procedure', tells us that this is a procedure definition. (An event handler is a special kind of procedure.) The name, TfrmMousePos.FormMouseDown, tells us that this is the OnMouseDown event handler for frmMousePos. Next we have a parameter list enclosed in parentheses. A parameter list defines the parameters available in the procedure or event handler. Looking at this list, we see that an OnMouseDown event handler has parameters called Sender of type TObject, Button of type TMouseButton, Shift of type TShiftState, and two parameters, X and Y, of type integer. The last two parameters, X and Y of type Integer, give the position of the mouse (in pixels) at the moment that either mouse button is pressed down.

The single program line is:

```
frmMousePos.Canvas.Rectangle (X–10, Y–10, X+10, Y+10);
```

In this statement, the X and Y receive the value of the X and Y parameters. These give the mouse's position at the moment the button was clicked. An important thing to realise with parameters is that when the program is inside the event handler (in this case, when Delphi has called the FormMouseDown procedure) the parameters already have values that the event handler can use. This statement draws a rectangle on the screen. It subtracts 10 from the values of both X and Y for the top left corner of the rectangle and adds 10 to X and Y for the bottom right corner. The result is a rectangle positioned around the mouse pointer at the moment the mouse is clicked. (We return to the Canvas and its methods in Chapter 11, and will explain it more fully then.)

EXAMPLE 10.6) Help for the OnMouseDown event parameters

Using online Help, let's find out the significance of the Button and Shift parameters mentioned in the previous paragraph and the values they can take. (Try looking up the significance of these parameters yourself in Help before reading further.)

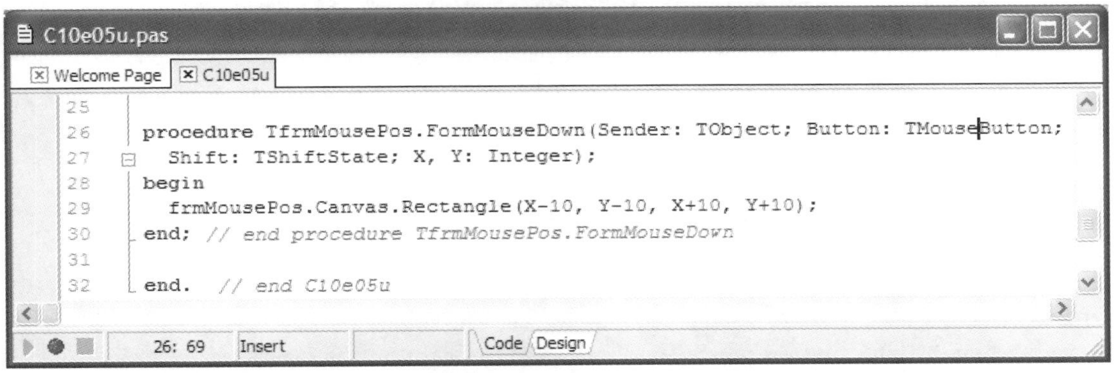

```
25
26      procedure TfrmMousePos.FormMouseDown(Sender: TObject; Button: TMouseButton;
27        Shift: TShiftState; X, Y: Integer);
28      begin
29        frmMousePos.Canvas.Rectangle(X–10, Y–10, X+10, Y+10);
30      end; // end procedure TfrmMousePos.FormMouseDown
31
32      end.  // end C10e05u
```

```
26: 69    Insert                    Code / Design
```

Figure 10.12 Position the mouse pointer over 'TMouseButton' to get online Help in Delphi 8

- Place the cursor over TMouseButton in the event handler's header (figure 10.12), then press <F1> to invoke Help (figure 10.13). (The figures show Delphi 8, but the concepts are similar for earlier versions too.)

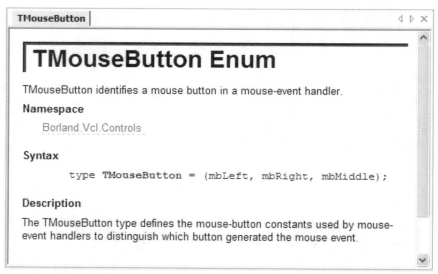

Figure 10.13 The Help display for TMouseButton in Delphi 8

From the Help screen we see that the parameter Button, of type TMouseButton, can take on the values mbLeft, mbRight or mbMiddle. Since nowadays most mouses under Windows have only two buttons, the values that interest us are mbLeft and mbRight.

Similarly, by positioning the cursor over TShiftState in the event handler's parameter list and then pressing <F1>, we see that parameter Shift, of type TShiftState, returns a set of values containing none, one or more of the values: ssShift, ssAlt, ssCtrl, ssLeft, ssRight, ssMiddle, ssDouble. These show whether any of the keyboard's <Shift>, <Alt> or <Ctrl> buttons were held down when the OnMouseDown event occurred and whether the event was initiated by the mouse's left, right or middle button or a double-click.

EXAMPLE 10.7) Detecting the left mouse button

The program in the previous example displays a square when either the left or the right mouse button is pressed down. How can we modify the program so that it ignores the right mouse button and responds only to the left button?

The OnMouseDown event fires when any mouse button is clicked. To work out precisely which action caused the event, we must test the values of either the Button or the Shift parameters. For this example we have two options: we can test whether parameter Button has the value mbLeft or we can test whether the set representing the Shift parameter contains the value ssLeft. First we'll test the value of the Button parameter:

```
procedure TfrmMousePos.FormMouseDown(Sender: TObject;
        Button: TMouseButton; Shift: TShiftState; X, Y: Integer);
begin
  if Button = mbLeft then // Was the left button pressed?
    frmMousePos.Canvas.Rectangle (X-10, Y-10, X+10, Y+10);
end;
```

- Save this as C10e07Au and C10e07Ap, then run and test it. The square should appear only when the left button is pressed and not when the right button is pressed.

As an alternative, we can modify this procedure to use the Shift parameter. Because Shift is a *set of zero or more values*, we must test whether ssLeft is one of the values in the set by using the 'in' keyword when doing the 'if ... then' test. (See the notes after example 9.1 step 6.)

```
procedure TfrmMousePos.FormMouseDown(Sender: TObject;
        Button: TMouseButton; Shift: TShiftState; X, Y: Integer);
begin
  if ssLeft in Shift then // Does the set Shift contain ssLeft?
    frmMousePos.Canvas.Rectangle (X-10, Y-10, X+10, Y+10);
end;
```

- Save this version as C10e07Bu and C10e07Bp, then run and test it. Once again, the square appears only when the left button is pressed and not when the right button is pressed.

REVIEW

Because Delphi runs in a GUI environment, the user is in control of the program, which must be ready at any time to respond to any event that may occur. Many Delphi programs are event-driven and much of our programming is in the form of event handlers. An event handler is a special procedure, attached to either a user event or a system event, that runs whenever such an event occurs. User events are initiated by the user; system events respond to an event in the computer without any direct action by the user. Data passes from an event to its event handler through parameters, allowing us, for example, to determine the type and position of a mouse click. Several events can be redirected to the same handler and the default event-handler names can be changed accordingly.

There are three stages to the event processing sequence:

1   An event occurs.
2   Windows detects this event and sends an event message to Delphi.
3   If the programmer has created an event handler, Delphi initiates the event handler. If there is no linked event handler, Delphi discards the event message from Windows.

A component's event list appears on the Object Inspector's Events tab. Delphi is a large and sophisticated environment and it is not possible to cover all the events here. We investigated the OnMouseMove, OnMouseDown, OnMouseUp, OnTimer and OnShow events specifically in this chapter. Online Help (<Ctrl+F1> or <F1> for context sensitive Help) is an important source of information on the other events.

Previously we explored some user events (eg OnClick), which support the user's interaction with a program. Delphi also has system events such as the timer's OnTimer and the form's OnShow events. Several events can be routed through the same event handler and the event handlers themselves can be renamed through the Object Inspector.

Parameters have an important role in programming because they provide a way of transferring data to and from an event handler, procedure or function. The concept of parameters has been introduced in this chapter by looking at the OnMouseDown event's X and Y, TMouseButton, and TShiftState parameters.

IMPORTANT CONCEPTS

Fundamental programming concepts

Event handler: An event handler is a procedure that responds to the particular event it has been programmed to recognize. Consequently, a programmer should write an event handler for each event that is expected to occur. The parameters passed by the event vary between different types of event. On completion of the event handler, control reverts to the operating system, which is then ready for the next event. An event handler may be attached to either a user event or a system event.

Event routing: Often each event is handled by its own event handler. However, where more than one event requires an identical response, it is possible to route an event generated by one component to the appropriate handler written for another component by changing the linking in the Object Inspector. The Events tab of the Object Inspector shows a list of all the events an object can intercept on the left-hand side. On the right-hand side we make the connection to the required event handler through the drop-down box.

Event renaming: Through the Events tab in the Object Inspector, Delphi allows us to rename event handlers to avoid confusion over names. This is particularly useful when several events share the same event handler. Always rename event handlers through the Object Inspector and not directly in the program code so that Delphi can update the necessary links.

Event-driven programming: When GUIs are programmed, the user and not the program is in charge. A style of programming that accommodates this well is *event-driven programming*. Events are initiated either by the user (such as a mouse-click) or by the computer system itself (such as when showing a form). The program often does not know in advance what the next event will be and so it must be ready at any time to respond to any event that may occur. Between events, it is simply waiting for something to happen. Windows detects these events and notifies Delphi, which then calls the appropriate event handler, if one exists.

Parameters: Parameters transfer data from the initiating event to the event handler, for instance the position of the mouse when either of its buttons is clicked. (Chapters 11–13 deal with parameters in more detail.)

System events: System events (eg Timer's OnTimer, form's OnShow) arise from something happening in the computer without any action by the user. We respond to system events through program statements in an event handler in the same way that we respond to user events. To investigate system events we used the Timer component and looked briefly at the form's OnShow event.

User events: User events (eg OnClick and OnMouseMove) are initiated by the user and cause the matching event handler to run, if it exists. We explored user events by writing a program where a Panel changed colour or the font style of a BitBtn's Caption changed whenever the mouse moved over one or the other.

Visual GUI development

Non-visual components: Non-visual components are not visible on the screen while the program is running. They often deal with system operations (eg Timer) and not directly with the user interface. For the convenience of the programmer, they are visible during design time.

Visual components: Visual components are the user interface components that appear on the screen and allow the user to interact with the program while it's running.

NEW DELPHI FEATURES

OnMouseDown and OnMouseUp event parameters	
Sender	The component initiating the event. (Refer to online Help and chapter 18 for further details).
Button	mbLeft, mbMiddle or mbRight
Shift	A set with members ssShift, ssAlt, ssCtrl, ssLeft, ssRight, ssMiddle, ssDouble
X, Y	Mouse coordinates when event was raised.
Several other mouse events have the same or similar parameters.	

TTimer

Properties	Interval	Determines the period of time between consecutive operations of the OnTimer event handler. A value of 1000 corresponds to 1 second, 5000 to five seconds, and so on.
	Enabled	The OnTimer event handler fires only if Enabled is set to True. If Enabled is set to False, the interval is reset and the Timer is disabled.
Events	OnTimer	Fires every time the Timer interval expires if Enabled is True.
Prefix	tmr...	
Use		If anything must happen after a specific time interval, place that program code into an OnTimer event handler and adjust the value of the interval as needed. Set Enabled to True when the interval must start. Stop the Timer running by setting Enabled to False. If only a single interval is needed, set Enabled to False in the OnTimer event handler. When the Timer is disabled (ie Enabled is False), its OnTimer event handler does not fire, and so it does not perform any operations in its OnTimer event handler.

TButton

New property	Font.Style	A set of styles for the Caption [fsBold, fsItalic, fsStrikeout, fsUnderline]

TPanel

New properties	BevelOuter, BevelInner (see also BevelWidth and BorderWidth)	Determines the appearance of the outer edge of the Panel. Its default value is *bvRaised*, which makes the Panel appear to stand out from the screen. *bvLowered* gives the appearance of sinking into the screen. *bvNone* hides the bevel.
Prefix	pnl...	
Use		As a TGroupBox but with the ability to control its appearance through the bevel.

PROBLEMS

PROBLEM 10.1) Double-clicking

- Write a program that will change the colour of the form to red when *double-clicking* anywhere on the form, and back to its original colour when *clicking* anywhere on the form.

PROBLEM 10.2) Hiding a form

a   Many components, including forms, have Hide and Show methods, as this problem illustrates:
  - Start a new application.
  - On the form place a button with the Caption 'Hide' (figure 10.14) and a Timer.

Figure 10.14 Screen layout to illustrate a form's Hide and Show methods

- Set the properties and write two event handlers so that a click on the Hide button hides the form and starts the Timer.
- When the Timer period of two seconds elapses, the OnTimer event handler shows the form and disables the Timer. In other words, clicking on the Hide button must hide the form for two seconds before it reappears.

b Extend this example to use the form's OnShow event to create an event handler that displays a brief message before the form appears. Similarly, use the OnHide event to display a message before the form disappears.

PROBLEM 10.3) A traffic-light

- Start a new application.
- Place a Timer on the form.
- Set the following properties:

Component	Property	Value
Form1	Name	frmRobot
	Caption	Traffic Light
	Color	clRed
Timer1	Name	tmrRobot
	Enabled	True
	Interval	1000

- Create the following event handler:

```
procedure TfrmRobot.tmrRobotTimer(Sender: TObject);
begin
  if frmRobot.Color = clRed then
    frmRobot.Color := clGreen
  else if frmRobot.Color = clGreen then
    frmRobot.Color := clYellow
  else
    frmRobot.Color := clRed;
end;
```

- Run this program, and the form's colour will cycle red, green, yellow, red, and so on.
- Respond to the following questions and tasks:
  a In this program what, if any, are the system events and what are the user events?
  b In the program above, is Color a method or a property? How do you know?
  c Change the timing for the colours so that red lasts for 4 seconds, green for 3 seconds and yellow for 1 second.
  d Place a Label on the form that displays 'Stop' when it is red, 'Go' when it is green and 'Caution' when it is yellow. The text should be large enough to read easily.
  e When working as programmers, we come across aspects of a language that we have not seen before. As an example of this, change the traffic-light program to have three circular shapes on it and then have these

change red, green, yellow in turn to resemble a normal traffic light. Find the Shape component on the Component/Tool palette or, in Delphi 4 to 7, through the menu sequence View | Component List. Look through Shape's properties in the Object Inspector and use online Help to find out how to set the shape and colour of the Shape component.

PROBLEM 10.4) A simple Status Panel

- Create a new application to match figure 10.15, using the following components and properties:

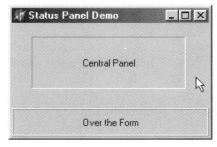

Figure 10.15 Indicating the pointer's position on the Status Panel

Component	Property	Value
Form1	Name	frmDemo
	Caption	Status Panel Demo
Panel1	Name	pnlCentral
	BevelOuter	bvLowered
	Caption	Central Panel
Panel2	Name	pnlStatus
	Align	alBottom
	BevelInner	bvLowered
	Caption	Status panel

- Write an OnMouseMove event handler for each component so that the Caption of the Status Panel indicates whether the mouse pointer is positioned over the form, the Central Panel or the Status Panel. (Setting pnlStatus's Align property, which is different from the Alignment property, stretches the Status Panel across the bottom of the form.)

PROBLEM 10.5) Catch me if you can

Look at the following program and then answer the questions that follow:

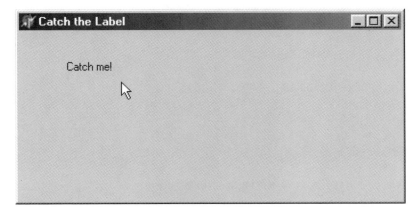

Figure 10.16 The slippery Label – an OnMouseMove demo

Component	Property	Value
Form1	Name	frmCatch
	Caption	Catch the Label
Label1	Name	lblCatch
	Caption	Catch me!

```
1 procedure TfrmCatch.lblCatchMouseMove(Sender: TObject; Shift:
2   TShiftState; X, Y: Integer);
3 begin
4   lblCatch.Top := Random (frmCatch.ClientHeight - 20);
5   lblCatch.Left := Random (frmCatch.ClientWidth - 50);
6 end;
```

- 'Random (X)' is a function call that returns an integer value in the range 0 to (X–1). ClientHeight (line 4) and ClientWidth (line 5) give the inside dimensions of the form. Answer the following questions before writing this program:
  a   What, if any, are the parameters in the function call 'Random (X)'?
  b   Under what condition will the event handler shown above run?
  c   What is the possible range of values of lblCatch.Top after this event handler has run?
  d   What does this program do?
- Now enter this program and test it. If it does not perform as you predicted under question d, study the program again to make sure that you understand it.

PROBLEM 10.6) Drawing ellipses

- Write an event handler that will enable you to draw a series of Aqua-coloured ellipses if the mouse is moved while the <Alt> button is held down and purple ellipses while the <Ctrl> button is held down.

PROBLEM 10.7) Using parameters 1

In example 10.7 the second version of the event handler checks whether the left mouse button was pressed by checking if ssLeft is in the Shift set. What is the effect of the following check?

```
if ssShift in Shift then
  frmMousePos.Canvas.Rectangle (X-10, Y-10, X+10, Y+10);
```

PROBLEM 10.8) Using parameters 2

Modify example 10.3 so that the Timer runs only while the right mouse button is held down.

CHAPTER 11

Methods and parameters

PURPOSE OF THIS CHAPTER

In the previous chapter we looked at event handlers. An event handler consists of program code attached to a particular *event*. Program code can also be attached to an *object* such as a component. We call this code a *method*. Whereas an event handler is activated by the occurrence of an event, a method is activated by a *method call in a program* and it performs some operation related to the object in response to this call. With an event, Delphi automatically supplies the necessary parameters to the event handler. With a method, because we call it through program code, we must supply the necessary parameters.

The standard objects and components in Delphi each have their own methods, and we will look at some of them here. You may have noticed that not all the program statements we have written so far have been assignment statements. As an example, take the OnClick event handler for `btnTransfer` in example 2.4, which we repeat here:

```
procedure TfrmTextDemo.btnTransferClick(Sender: TObject);
begin
  lblText.Caption := edtText.Text;
  edtText.Clear;
  edtText.SetFocus;
end; // end procedure TfrmTextDemo.btnTransferClick
```

Two of these program statements, `edtText.Clear;` and `edtText.SetFocus;` have no assignment operator. As we saw in Chapter 2, these are method calls to the `Clear` and `SetFocus` methods attached in this case to the Edit component called 'edtText'. As we will see as we go through this and the next chapter, many different components have `Clear` and `SetFocus` methods.

As an example of a program that uses only method calls we will look at the Memo component's methods that transfer text between the Memo and the computer's Clipboard and at its `Clear` and `SetFocus` methods.

EXAMPLE 11.1 Methods and the Memo component

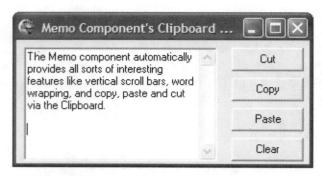

Figure 11.1 Typing some text into the Memo component

When using an editor program such as a word processor or Delphi's Code editor, it is often convenient to be able to move text from one place to another, or to be able to copy some text to a new position. As we saw in examples 5.5 and 6.7, Delphi provides a Memo component that includes simple text editing such as entering and deleting text. As we will see in this example, it also has a set of methods to transfer text to and from the computer's Clipboard. (The Clipboard is a space set aside by Windows that we can use to store text temporarily.)

- To explore the Memo's Clipboard methods, start a new application.
- On the form place a Memo component and four buttons.
- Set the static design as follows:

Component	Property	Value
Form1	Name	frmMemoDemo
	Caption	Memo Component's Clipboard Methods
Memo1	Name	memDemo
	Scrollbar	ssVertical
	WordWrap	True
Button1	Name	btnCut
	Caption	Cut
Button2	Name	btnCopy
	Caption	Copy
Button3	Name	btnPaste
	Caption	Paste
Button4	Name	btnClear
	Caption	Clear

This gives us the static properties of the components.

- Create the run-time behaviour by writing the following event handlers. These are programmed entirely from method calls to the Memo component without a single assignment statement.

```
procedure TfrmMemoDemo.btnClearClick (Sender: TObject);
begin
  memDemo.Clear;
  memDemo.SetFocus;
end; // end procedure TfrmMemoDemo.btnClearClick


procedure TfrmMemoDemo.btnCopyClick (Sender: TObject);
begin
  memDemo.CopyToClipboard;
  memDemo.SetFocus;
end; // end procedure TfrmMemoDemo.btnCopyClick


procedure TfrmMemoDemo.btnPasteClick (Sender: TObject);
begin
  memDemo.PasteFromClipboard;
  memDemo.SetFocus;
end; // end procedure TfrmMemoDemo.btnPasteClick


procedure TfrmMemoDemo.btnClearClick (Sender: TObject);
begin
  memDemo.Clear;
  memDemo.SetFocus;
end; // end procedure TfrmMemoDemo.btnClearClick
```

We see the familiar Clear and SetFocus methods cropping up again – they are very common – and see the new methods CutToClipboard, CopyToClipboard and PasteFromClipboard. Several components, including the Memo and Edit components, have Clipboard methods.

- Save the unit file as C11e01u and the project file as C11e01p. Run the program.
- Click the Clear button to remove the memDemo start-up text that appears.
- Now enter text like that shown in figure 11.1. Notice that, as in a word processor, you do not have to press the <Enter> key at the end of each line, since the Memo component automatically does the word wrapping for you.
- Place the mouse cursor at the start of the word 'like', press down the left-hand mouse button and, keeping it down, move the mouse to the end of the text you have entered, then release the mouse button.
- The text is automatically highlighted.
- Click on the Copy button. This invokes the btnCopyClick event handler, which contains the program line memDemo.CopyToClipboard. The CopyToClipboard method copies the highlighted text in the Memo component to the Windows Clipboard.
- Now click on the Memo component (at the end of the text) to clear the highlighting, and create a blank line, if necessary, by pressing the <Enter> key.
- Click on the Paste button. The text you copied to the Clipboard is pasted to the Memo (so it appears a second time) because of memDemo's PasteFromClipboard method (figure 11.2).

If you have used the same sizes and text as we have done, the complete text is now too long for it all to appear in the Memo at the same time. The top line has scrolled off the top, and the slider in the vertical scroll bar at the right-hand side

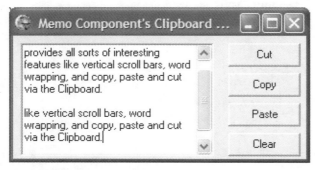

Figure 11.2 Pasting part of the text

of the Memo has moved down a bit (figure 11.2). By moving the slider with the mouse or by clicking on the arrows at each end of the scroll bar or on the scroll bar itself, you can move up and down within the text.

- Experiment with these buttons, remembering to highlight text before trying to copy or cut it.

EXAMPLE 11.2) Methods with constants as parameters

The methods we have just used give a single, direct command: Clear, SetFocus, CutToClipboard, and so on. Sometimes, we need to send additional information to a method. For instance, in the program that follows (figure 11.3) we'll use the Canvas.TextOut method to display text on the form. To do this, we must tell the TextOut method where to display the text by giving it coordinates (eg 40 pixels from the left edge of the form and 15 pixels from the top) and by telling it which text to display (eg `'Two rectangles and two ellipses'`). Similarly, we'll use the Rectangle and Ellipse methods to draw shapes at specific coordinates.

As with event handlers, data is passed to a method through one or more *parameters*. Delphi supplies parameter values automatically when an event occurs. However, a method is initiated through a program statement, so we must ourselves supply the values of the parameters as part of the method call statement.

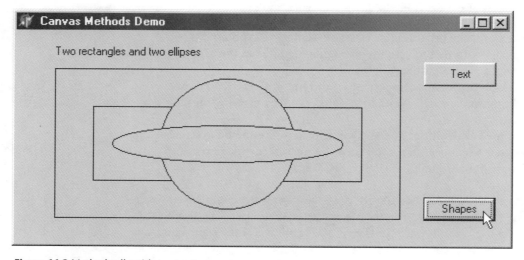

Figure 11.3 Method calls with parameters

- Start a new application and enter the following static design:

Component	Property	Value
Form1	Name	frmCanvasMethods
	Caption	Canvas Methods Demo
Button1	Name	btnText
	Caption	Text
Button2	Name	btnShapes
	Caption	Shapes

- Now enter the following two event handlers. As in the previous example, they contain only *method calls* and no assignments. However, after each method's name is a series of numbers separated by commas and enclosed by round brackets (or parentheses). These values are the parameters we send through to the method in each method call statement:

```
procedure TfrmCanvasMethods.btnTextClick(Sender: TObject);
begin
  Canvas.TextOut (40, 15, 'Two rectangles and two ellipses');
end; // end procedure TfrmCanvasMethods.btnTextClick


procedure TfrmCanvasMethods.btnShapesClick(Sender: TObject);
begin
  Canvas.Rectangle (40, 40, 400, 200); { The larger rectangle }
  Canvas.Rectangle (80, 80, 360, 160); { The smaller rectangle }
  Canvas.Ellipse (150, 50, 290, 190); {A 'square' ellipse = circle}
  Canvas.Ellipse (100, 100, 340, 140); { An ellipse }
end; // end procedure TfrmCanvasMethods.btnShapesClick
```

EX 11.2 STEP 1 The meaning of the parameters

- Before running this program, can you work out the meaning of each parameter in the `Canvas.Rectangle` call? Try this before reading any further.

As a guess, we could say that the series of parameters in each method call determines the position and size of the object being drawn on the Canvas. We have already been told that the 40 and 15 in the TextOut method position the text in 40 pixels and down 15 pixels from the edge of the window. So, in the line

```
Canvas.Rectangle (40, 40, 400, 200); { The larger rectangle }
```

we could guess that the top left corner of the large rectangle is 40 pixels from the left of the window and 40 pixels from the top, whereas the bottom-right corner would be 400 from the left and 200 from the top. This would give a rectangle 360 pixels wide (= 400 − 40) and 160 pixels high (= 200 − 40).

We can check this by using online Help.

- In the editor, place the cursor over `Rectangle` and press <F1>. The Help display confirms that in the call

```
Rectangle(X1, Y1, X2, Y2);
```

the parameters (X1, Y1, X2, Y2) must all be integers and that the rectangle's upper left corner is at (X1, Y1) and its lower right-hand corner at (X2, Y2).

The top left corner of the canvas (the inside of the form) is (0,0). These values count upwards when we move to the right or to the bottom of the canvas. To specify a rectangle, we give four values: top, left, bottom and right. To specify an ellipse we similarly give four values that specify a rectangle. The ellipse is then drawn as the largest ellipse which can fit into that rectangle. We say that we specify the *bounding box* of the ellipse. If we specify a bounding box that is a square, the ellipse becomes a circle.

EX 11.2 STEP 2 Test the program

- Save the unit file as C11e02u and the project file as C11e02p.
- Run the program and click first on the Text button. Did you expect the text to appear as a result of the Canvas.TextOut method call?
- Now click on the Shapes button, and see if you can match each method call in the OnClick event handler for the Shapes button with a shape that appears on the screen.

EXAMPLE 11.3) The order of the parameters

The order of the parameters in the method call is important! We demonstrate this in the following example, where we swap the order of some of the numbers around and so get a program that performs incorrectly.

- In the OnClick event handler of the Shapes button in the program in example 11.2, predict what the effect will be of:
  - swapping the X2 and Y2 parameters in the first call to the Rectangle method, that is, instead of:

    ```
    Canvas.Rectangle (40, 40, 400, 200);
    ```

    what would happen if we used:

    ```
    Canvas.Rectangle (40, 40, 200, 400);?
    ```

  - swapping the X1 and Y1 and the X2 and Y2 parameters in the first call to the Ellipse method?
- Make these changes in the program before reading any further, and see whether your predictions are correct.

Changing parameter order

Swapping these parameters around changes the positions of the large rectangle and the circle.

- Make the changes shown in the event handler below:

```
procedure TfrmCanvasMethods.btnShapesClick(Sender: TObject);
begin
  Canvas.Rectangle (40, 40, 200, 400); { parameter order changed }
  Canvas.Rectangle (80, 80, 360, 160);
  Canvas.Ellipse (50, 150, 190, 290); { parameter order changed }
  Canvas.Ellipse (100, 100, 340, 140);
end; // end procedure TfrmCanvasMethods.btnShapesClick
```

- Save the file as C11e03u and the project as C11e03p, then run and test the program.

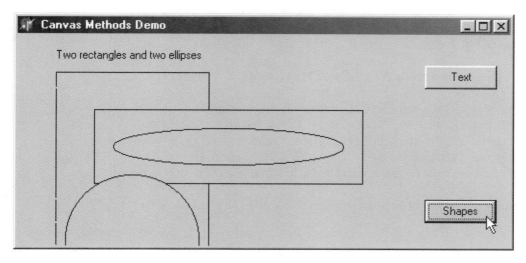

Figure 11.4 Altering parameter sequence affects the method's operation

The changes become clear on the screen, as you can see in figure 11.4. Swapping X2 and Y2 in the first call to the Rectangle method moves the bottom right-hand corner of the larger rectangle, and actually positions it outside the form. Similarly, swapping X1 and Y1, and X2 and Y2 for the first ellipse moves both its top left-hand corner and its bottom right-hand corner.

This shows quite clearly how in Delphi, as in other programming languages, the *order of the parameters* in the method call is important. As the next example shows, the type and number of parameters are also important.

EXAMPLE 11.4) Wrong type or number of parameters

- Undo the changes you have just made so that the program output once again matches figure 11.3.
- Now go to the Text button's event handler. Its only program statement is the call to Canvas's TextOut method. The parameter list consists of two integers and a string, since these are the types and number of parameters that the TextOut method needs.
- To see what happens if you do not send the correct parameter types, change the first integer in the parameter list (ie 40) to a string by placing it between single quote marks (ie '40') as follows:

```
procedure TForm1.btnTextClick(Sender: TObject);
begin
  Canvas.TextOut ('40', 15, 'Two rectangles and two ellipses');
end; // end procedure TForm1.btnTextClick
```

- Run this version of the program. Because you are now trying to use a string where Delphi expects an integer, the program does not compile. Instead, the cursor is positioned at the '40', with the error message:*

```
Incompatible types: 'Integer' and 'String'
```

* If you are using a different version of Delphi, error messages may be worded slightly differently.

We see that Delphi insists that the parameters must be compatible.

- Remove the single quotes around 40 and try running the program again. The program once again works as it did previously.
- To see that we need the right number of parameters, remove the integer 200 from the end of the parameter list in the first call to Canvas's Rectangle method in the btnShapesClick event handler to get the following:

```
procedure TfrmCanvasMethods.btnShapesClick(Sender: TObject);
begin
  Canvas.Rectangle (40, 40, 400); { The larger rectangle }
  Canvas.Rectangle (80, 80, 360, 160); { The smaller rectangle }
  Canvas.Ellipse (150, 50, 290, 190); {A 'square' ellipse = circle}
  Canvas.Ellipse (100, 100, 340, 140); { An ellipse }
end; // end procedure TfrmCanvasMethods.btnShapesClick
```

When you try to run this, the cursor stops just after 400 and gives the error message:

```
Not enough actual parameters
```

- Type the 200 back in and then type in a second 200, so that you now have five parameters:

```
Canvas.Rectangle (40, 40, 400, 200, 200); { The larger rectangle }
```

When you try to run the program this time, the error message is:

```
Too many actual parameters
```

The Rectangle method expects four integer parameters, and Delphi insists that you give it four – no more and no less.

Specifying a method call

For a particular method call how do we know what the number, order and types of parameter should be? In the code editor we can place the cursor on a method call. The pop-up help will then give a list of the parameters. For greater detail we can press <F1> to display the description in Help. The three canvas methods we used are specified as:

```
procedure TextOut (X, Y: Integer; const Text: string);
procedure Rectangle (X1, Y1, X2, Y2: Integer);
procedure Ellipse (X1, Y1, X2, Y2: Integer);
```

(In some versions of Delphi, the type is given separately for each parameter along with the visibility, for example:

```
public procedure TextOut(X: Integer, Y: Integer, const Text: string);
```

However the principle remains the same.)

What do these descriptions mean? Do you see that the parameter lists look a bit like the variable declarations we first saw in Chapter 3? Look at the parameter list for TextOut. It starts with `X, Y: Integer;`, which tells us that the first two parameters must be integers. Then comes `const Text: string`, which tells us that the third parameter is a constant parameter and must be of type string. (We look at constant parameters in Chapter 12.) Similarly, the parameter lists for Rectangle and Ellipse tell us that each of these needs four integers.

The order, the type and the number of parameters in the method call must match the method definition.

REVIEW

In Chapter 10 we looked at event handlers. An event handler consists of program code attached to a particular *event*. Program code can also be attached to an *object* such as a component. We call this code a *method*. Whereas an event handler is activated by the occurrence of an event, a method is activated by a *method call in a program*. A method performs some operation related to the object in response to the call. In Chapter 10 we wrote the actual event handlers which are called by Delphi in response to events. In this chapter we called methods which were written by other programmers.

With an event, Delphi automatically supplies the necessary parameters to the event handler. With a method, because we call it through program code, we must supply any parameters that are needed. The standard objects and components in Delphi each have their own methods. We looked at Clipboard methods, which have no parameters, and Canvas methods, which have parameters. As with events, we saw that parameters are a 'channel' for transferring information to the method, though this time from the method call rather than the event. In a method call it is essential that parameters match in terms of order, type and number.

IMPORTANT CONCEPTS

Fundamental programming concepts

A method: A subroutine (either a procedure or a function – see the next two chapters) attached to an object is called a *method*. It performs some specific operation *related to that object*. Some methods, such as the Clear, SetFocus and Clipboard methods, require no input data. Others require input data in the form of parameters, as with the Canvas methods that draw different shapes on the screen depending on the values of the parameters passed to them. Taken together, all of an object's various methods establish its behaviour, defining the operations it can perform. After completion of the method, control reverts to the calling statement. Here we looked at using the methods that are part of Delphi's standard components. In Chapter 18 on object orientation we will look at writing our own classes and their associated methods.

Calling a method: To call a method, we attach the method name to the object name by a dot. When a method requires parameters, we supply the right number of parameters in the right order and of the right type as a list in parentheses after the method's name. All the programming in example 11.1

consists of calls to various methods without any parameters. The method calls in example 11.2 list the necessary parameters separated by commas. If there are no parameters, a method's call has the form: `ObjectName.MethodName`. If a method has parameters, its call has the form `ObjectName.MethodName (ParameterList);`.

Using parameters: A method accepts parameters in a set order from the method call and uses them internally on the basis of their names. As a result, parameter order is important, parameter types must match, and there must be the right number of parameters. (This applies equally to the procedures and functions we'll look at in Chapters 12 and 13.)

NEW DELPHI FEATURES

TMemo		
Properties	Name, Height, Width	As with previous components
	ScrollBars	Valid values: ssNone, ssHorizontal, ssVertical, ssBoth
	WordWrap	Valid values: True, False. It wraps text at the right margin to improve the visibility of the text but does not insert any additional return characters. If WordWrap is False, a separate line appears only where return characters occur. If WordWrap is True, a horizontal scroll bar is unnecessary.
Methods	Clear, SetFocus	As with previous components
	CopyToClipboard, CutToClipboard	Both copy the selected text to the Clipboard. If no text is selected, the Clipboard contents remain unaltered. CutToClipboard deletes the selection.
	PasteFromClipboard	Pastes the contents of the Clipboard into the Memo, replacing any text that is selected. If the Clipboard is empty, PasteFromClipboard does nothing.
Prefix	mem...	
Use	Allows the user to enter and manipulate more than one line of text and so is useful for representing lengthy text. (See also Chapter 5.)	

TCanvas		
Methods	TextOut (X, Y, Text)	Draws the string contained in Text on the canvas with the upper-left corner of the string at (X, Y).
	Rectangle (X1, Y1, X2, Y2)	Draws a rectangle with its upper-left corner at (X1, Y1) and its lower-right corner at (X2, Y2).
	Ellipse (X1, Y1, X2, Y2)	Draws an ellipse defined by a rectangle on the canvas. The top-left of the rectangle is at (X1, Y1) and the bottom-right is at (X2, Y2). If this rectangle forms a square, a circle results.
Use	The Canvas differs from the other components we have been using. Although it is an object, Canvas is not a standalone component. It is a *property* attached to something else, such as a form, and provides a surface to draw or write on. It has many different methods for displaying text and drawing graphics. Refer to Help for further information.	

PROBLEMS

PROBLEM 11.1 Understanding parameters

- Look at the following event handler:

```
1   procedure TfrmMousePos.FormMouseDown(Sender: TObject; Button:
2           TMouseButton; Shift: TShiftState; X, Y: Integer);
3   var
4     XPos, YPos : String;
5   begin
6     if ssLeft in Shift then
7       Canvas.Ellipse (X-10, Y-10, X+10, Y+10)
8     else
9     begin
10      XPos := IntToStr (X);
11      YPos := IntToStr (Y);
12      Canvas.TextOut (X, Y, 'Right click at ' + XPos + ', ' + YPos);
13    end;
14  end; // end procedure TfrmMousePos.FormMouseDown
```

a   Describe the purpose and operation of lines 1-2 and lines 3-4. What is the difference between the list of names and types in lines 1-2 and the variable names and type in line 4? (We explore this in more detail in Chapters 12 and 13, so working it out for yourself here is a useful preparation.)

b   Describe the purpose and operation of:
- o   Line 10
- o   Line 12
- o   Line 7.

c   What does this event handler do?

d   How can this event handler be changed to use the Button parameter rather than the Shift parameter in the conditional statement?

PROBLEM 11.2 Undoing changes in a Memo

a   Add an Undo button to example 11.1. This must Undo (or cancel) the last change made by the user in the Memo component. Use the Help facility to find out how the Undo and ClearUndo methods of TMemo work.

b   A potential difficulty with this program is that a call to the Clear method cannot be undone using the Undo method. To solve this problem, change the btnClearClick event handler in example 11.1 to select all text in the Memo (using a suitable method) and then cut it to the clipboard, instead of calling memDemo.Clear.

CHAPTER 12

Procedures and parameters

PURPOSE OF THIS CHAPTER

In the previous two chapters we looked at event handlers and at some of the standard methods available in Delphi. An event handler is a procedure attached to an event. It has both a predetermined call (the initiating event) and a predetermined set of parameters. Delphi can thus produce the event handler skeleton, consisting of the header and the parameters, automatically and the programmer must write the event handler body. In contrast to events, each of Delphi's standard methods has a predetermined set of parameters and the programmer must call the method with the matching parameters that the method requires.

Taken together, procedures and functions are called *subroutines*. A method is a subroutine, ie a procedure or a function, that is attached to an object (or, more strictly, to a class). In this chapter and the next we introduce programmer written methods, with procedures in this chapter and functions in the next chapter.

Differently to Delphi's standard events and methods, with a programmer written method the programmer chooses the form of the header and so determines the form of the matching call. In other words, the programmer decides what parameters the method will have, and what their order and type will be.

So in this chapter we build on our knowledge from the previous two chapters to broaden our understanding of subroutines and particularly of methods. We look at

o   how to declare and define methods that are *procedures*;
o   the different types of parameter we can use with a procedure, and
o   the reasons for using procedures.

In the next chapter we look at methods that are *functions*, the other kind of subroutine available in Delphi Pascal.

Previous editions of this book presented subroutines from a traditional Pascal perspective, where subroutines are independent, standalone blocks of code. This edition follows the more modern object-oriented perspective and presents subroutines as *methods*. Methods are subroutines that are attached to a particular class, and we will start by incorporating our procedures and functions into the structure of the form that makes up the user interface. From an initial perspective, the main difference is that to create a method we need to declare it as part of the form's structure while with a stand alone procedure we do not.

The following table may help to clarify some of these different shades of meaning:

Use of subroutines	Subroutine types	
	Procedures	Functions
Event handlers	Yes (In Delphi all event handlers are procedures.)	No (In Delphi event handlers are not functions.)
Standard subroutines and methods	Yes (eg Inc in ex 12.8 step 1; TEdit's Clear method).	Yes (eg StrToInt and MessageDlg in Chapter 13).
Programmer written methods	Yes (Chapter 12.)	Yes (Chapter 13.)
General (or standalone) subroutines	Yes (Possible; not covered here.)	Yes (Possible; not covered here.)

Declaring and defining a method

Up until now we have concentrated our attention on the code defining the event handlers and ignored the block of code that Delphi creates at the start of a unit. Let's go back to example 1.1, but look at the code for the entire unit.

```
1  unit Unit1;

2  interface

3  uses
4    Windows, Messages, SysUtils, Variants, Classes, Graphics,
5    Controls, Forms, Dialogs;

6  type
7    TForm1 = class(TForm)
8      Button1: TButton;
9      procedure Button1Click(Sender: TObject);
10   private
11     { Private declarations }
12   public
13     { Public declarations }
14   end;

15 var
16   Form1: TForm1;

17 implementation

18 {$R *.nfm}

19 procedure TForm1.Button1Click(Sender: TObject);
```

```
20 begin
21   Color := clPurple;
22 end;

23 end.
```

(There are slight differences between different versions of Delphi, but the principles remain the same. This is the Delphi 8 version, and earlier versions may have different lists under the uses clause (lines 4 & 5) and the compile directive in line 18 will differ. Delphi 8, as here, has *{$R *.nfm}* to generate a .NET form module in line 18. Earlier versions have *{$R *.dfm}* to generate a Delphi form module.)

A Delphi unit consists of three parts: a name (line 1), an interface section (lines 2–16) and an implementation section (lines 17–23). Up until now we have always worked in the implementation section. However in declaring a method we are also interested in the type declaration (lines 6–14). Because we have added a TButton to the form in this program, Delphi has declared a component of type TButton called Button1 (line 8) to be part of the TForm1 class (line 7). We have also created an event handler, in this case it's a procedure called Button1Click, and so Delphi has declared this procedure also to be part of the TForm1 class (line 9). This procedure, the event handler, is therefore a method of the TForm1 class. The definition of this method follows in the implementation section, lines 19–22. Notice that the header in the method definition (line 19) combines the class name, TForm1, and the method name, Button1Click and has the same parameter list as the declaration (line 9).

When we create our own methods we will follow Delphi's example closely. We'll declare the method's signature, in the private section of the form's type definition, (lines 10–11 above), and then we'll define the method in the implementation section as we defined the event handler methods earlier in this book.

EXAMPLE 12.1 Procedures and Sixpence Joe

Do you remember example 8.7, which involved a program to display the cost of flour, rice, sugar and mealie meal for *Sixpence Joe's Family Supermarket*? We are going to modify that program to use a method that is a procedure.

- Using File | Open project (or the Open button of the Speed bar), open project C08e07p. Save the file as C12e01u and the project as C12e01p to create a copy of the program to modify without destroying the original one. (If you have not yet done example 8.7, it would be a good idea to do it first, and then to continue with this example.)

- Look at the program code. The statements in the Case construct are all very similar:

```
procedure TfrmSixpenceJoe.rgpProductsClick(Sender: TObject);
begin
  case rgpProducts.ItemIndex of
    0: lblCostText.Caption := 'Flour costs R12.99 per kilogram';
    1: lblCostText.Caption := 'Rice costs R4.39 per kilogram';
    2: lblCostText.Caption := 'Sugar costs R4.10 per kilogram';
    3: lblCostText.Caption := 'Mealie meal costs R2.16 per kilogram';
  end;
end; {procedure TfrmSixpenceJoe.rgpProductsClick}
```

- To avoid this duplication and extra typing we can write our own method procedure. We'll call it DisplayPrice and it will handle all the updating of lblCostText's Caption. Each line of the Case construct then needs only to call DisplayPrice and pass the product name and its price as parameters.

- First we must declare the method. Start by scrolling upwards in the unit file to see the current type definition of the form:

```
type
  TfrmSixpenceJoe = class(TForm)
    lblCostText: TLabel;
    rgpProducts: TRadioGroup;
    procedure rgpProductsClick(Sender: TObject);
  private
    { Private declarations }
  public
    { Public declarations }
  end;
```

- Now, immediately under the private keyword, replace the text *{ Private declarations }* with the method declaration **procedure** DisplayPrice (Product, Price: String);:

```
type
  TfrmSixpenceJoe = class(TForm)
    lblCostText: TLabel;
    rgpProducts: TRadioGroup;
    procedure rgpProductsClick(Sender: TObject);
  private
    procedure DisplayPrice (Product, Price: String);
  public
    { Public declarations }
  end;
```

- Change the program by adding the code defining the new method and by changing the Case statement to call this method. Differently to the event handlers, where Delphi inserts the procedure skeleton for us, we ourselves type in the header and the begin and end statements along with the procedure body. The procedure name and parameter list must correspond between the declaration, as shown above, and the header in the definition (line 3 below) with the addition of the class name.

```
 1 implementation

 2 {$R *.DFM}

 3 procedure TfrmSixpenceJoe.DisplayPrice (Product, Price: String);
 4 begin
 5   lblCostText.Caption := Product + ' costs R' +
 6                               Price + ' per kilogram';
 7 end; {proc TfrmSixpenceJoe.DisplayPrice}

 8 procedure TfrmSixpenceJoe.rgpProductsClick(Sender: TObject);
 9 begin
10   case rgpProducts.ItemIndex of
11     0: DisplayPrice ('Flour', '12.99');
12     1: DisplayPrice ('Rice', '4.39');
```

```
13      2: DisplayPrice ('Sugar', '4.10');
14      3: DisplayPrice ('Mealie meal', '2.16');
15   end;
16 end;  {procedure TfrmSixpenceJoe.rgpProductsClick}

17 end.
```

- Click on File | Save All (or the Save All button or press <Ctrl+S>) to save the changes under the new names we created at the start of this example, then run the program.

Although the screen display and the program behaviour are the same as for example 8.7, the use of a procedure method behind the scenes makes this version decidedly different.

Procedures are very widely used since, among other things, they can reduce the amount of programming needed, they can make changing a program simpler and less likely to cause errors, and they can lead to a library of re-usable procedures that may be useful in future programs. (Because this is a deliberately simple example, these advantages may not seem too obvious right now.)

Calling (invoking) a procedure

In using a procedure we use our existing knowledge from both event handlers and from the standard Delphi methods we saw in the previous chapter. Writing our own procedure is similar to writing an event handler and calling our own procedure is similar to calling a standard method.

In the program above, when the user clicks on a RadioButton, Delphi calls the associated event handler. This event handler code then calls the procedure DisplayPrice, passing the required values for the Product and Price string variables as parameters. A *procedure call* has the form:

```
DisplayPrice ('Flour', '12.99');
```

As with the Memo's Clipboard methods in example 11.1, we can create procedures that don't use parameters at all. But if there are parameters, the call must match the header in the order, number and type of parameters. We saw this in the Canvas methods in Chapter 11.

The structure of a simple procedure

We ourselves typed in the procedure header (line 3). The first word of the header, procedure, tells Delphi that we are about to create a procedure, one of the two main types of subroutine available in Delphi Pascal. Next is the class name, in this case TfrmSixpenceJoe, followed by a fullstop connecting it to the procedure's name, in this case DisplayPrice. After the procedure's name we have a list of the procedure's *parameters* in brackets. Here we have Product and Price, followed by a colon and a type. In this case, both Product and Price are of type string. This is similar to the variable declarations of Chapters 3 and 4. As we shall see, we use parameters in very much the same way that we use variables. When we call (invoke) the procedure in line 11 the parameter Product in the procedure (line 3) receives the value 'Flour' from the call and Price receives the value '12.99'. From the call in line 12, parameter Product receives the value 'Rice' and Price receives the value '4.39', and so on.

The next line we typed in (line 4) is a begin statement to tell Delphi that the program statements for the procedure are about to start. Here we have just one program statement that extends over lines 5 and 6.*

This is an assignment statement that specifies what the procedure must do. On the right-hand side of the statement is a series of four strings that combine to make a new string. The first string is the value of the string parameter `Product` we declared in the procedure header. It acts like a variable, except that *its value comes into the procedure from the calling statement.* Next is the '+' operator, telling Delphi to join on (ie concatenate) the string constant `' costs R'`. There's another concatenation operator followed by the value of the second string parameter `Price` and a final '+' with the string constant `' per kilogram'`.

If parameter `Product` has the value `'Flour'` and parameter `Price` has the value `'12.99'`, the concatenation of the four strings gives the new string `'Flour costs R12.99 per kilogram'`. This new value is now assigned to `lblCostText.Caption`.

The final statement of any procedure is `end;` (line 7), balancing the `begin`. (We also have to type `end;` ourselves.) Here the comment *{proc TfrmSixpenceJoe.DisplayPrice}* follows the `end;` to remind us of which procedure ends here. Because this is such a short procedure, a comment like this is not really necessary here, but it helps considerably with longer procedures.

Reasons for using procedures

An important thing to realise about this example is that the new version of the Sixpence Joe application looks no different from the end user's perspective than the previous version. When we run the program, it appears as if there is no change. The difference is seen only by the programmer and is a change in the structure of the program, but not in its functionality. As programs become more complicated, the structure of the program can have a huge impact on a number of things, including:

1   the time and effort put into programming (a better structure can result in a shorter, 'simpler' program);

2   the number of errors (a better structure can result in less duplication of code, and duplication of code often leads to errors);

3   how understandable the code is to other programmers (a better structure can be easier to understand for other programmers – and for yourself when you have forgotten what you did a few months ago!). Code which is more understandable is easier to modify, and,

4   reusability of code (code that is well structured is easier to use again in different contexts).

General comments on procedures   .

Understanding parameters is crucial to using subroutines effectively. We've introduced parameters bit by bit over the last few chapters to illustrate their

---

* A program statement is terminated by a semicolon (;) so we can split a statement over two lines provided that there is no semicolon at the end of the first line and provided that we don't split the statement in the middle of a string enclosed in single quotes. So Delphi will reject the following line break because it splits the string `'costs R'` across 2 lines:

```
lblCostText.Caption := Product + ' costs
                       R' + Price + ' per kilogram';
```

different uses. Now that we have begun defining our own parameters, perhaps we should ask exactly what parameters are. *Parameters provide the communication between a subroutine and the surrounding program.* Within a subroutine a parameter has a value that we can manipulate much like any other variable. However, unlike local variables that are declared within a subroutine, parameters also have meaning outside the subroutine.

Some important points to remember when using procedures are:

1   For all methods, the parameter lists of the procedure call and procedure definition must match in respect of type, order and number† of parameters.
2   Within a procedure, parameter matching is by name, not by order.
3   Procedures that are methods, as is the case here, must be declared in the class's type declaration.
4   Depending on circumstances, the values sent in a procedure call can either be constants or variables.
5   If a procedure is a method that is part of a class, the procedure is bound to that class (which in this case is a form). When we define the procedure we must therefore explicitly include the class name in the header. In this case the class name is a 'T' followed by the form's name.

These are all important points, but possibly they don't mean much when just listed like this, so the next few examples will illustrate these points to help clarify them.

EXAMPLE 12.2) Parameter list matching

Point 1 in the list above states: 'For all methods, the parameter lists of the procedure call and procedure definition must match in respect of type, order and number of parameters.' We have already seen an example of this in Chapter 11, where changing the type, order or number of parameters led to various errors, either compile errors from Delphi or the incorrect display of the rectangles and ellipses. We'll reinforce these concepts with another short example.

• Reverse the parameter order in the 'Flour' call of the previous example:

```
procedure TfrmSixpenceJoe.rgpProductsClick(Sender: TObject);
begin
  case rgpProducts.ItemIndex of
    0: DisplayPrice ('12.99', 'Flour'); // parameters swopped
    1: DisplayPrice ('Rice', '4.39');
    2: DisplayPrice ('Sugar', '4.10');
    3: DisplayPrice ('Mealie meal', '2.16');
  end;
end; {procedure TfrmSixpenceJoe.rgpProductsClick}
```

What effect do you expect this will have?
• Run the program and see what happens.
• The Rice, Sugar and Mealie meal displays are unaffected, but the Flour display shows the parameters in the wrong order because the order of parameters is incorrect in the call:

```
12.99 costs RFlour per kilogram
```

This shows that parameters are transferred from the call to the procedure on the

† Experienced programmers may know that Delphi Pascal can also have default parameters. These are not covered in this book, and for further information refer to the online Help. Default parameters allow one to send fewer parameters, but those transferred must still correspond in type and order.

basis of their *order*. The parameter order in the procedure call must be the same as the parameter order in the procedure heading.

In this case Delphi can't pick this error up because both parameters are of type `string`. However, if the type is incorrect, Delphi does detect it. Modify the Flour line again, this time leaving the quotes off 12.99, making it a floating point number rather than a string:

```
0: DisplayPrice ('Flour', 12.99);
```

The program does not compile and Delphi displays an error message. Similarly, there are error messages if there are too few or too many parameters:

```
0: DisplayPrice ('Flour');
```

or

```
0: DisplayPrice ('Flour', '12.99', 'Rice');
```

- Restore the procedure call to what it was before, so that the program works correctly again.

EXAMPLE 12.3) Parameter names

Point 2 in the list above is: 'Within a procedure, parameter matching is by name, not by order.'
- Change the assignment statement in the procedure DisplayPrice as follows:

```
3  procedure TfrmSixpenceJoe.DisplayPrice (Product, Price: String);
4  begin
5    lblCostText.Caption := 'ONLY R' + Price +
6      ' per kg for ' + Product;
7  end; {proc TfrmSixpenceJoe.DisplayPrice}
```

Notice that in the procedure *header* (line 3) Product comes first and then Price. The procedure *calls* in the event handler must use *the same order* for the parameters. However, *within* the procedure, reference to the parameters is by *name*. So, within the procedure, parameters can be used *in any order*. In the modified assignment statement above (lines 5-6) we use Price before Product.
- Make this change once, in the procedure, and run the program.
- You'll see that the new form of the text with Price before Product appears for all four products because they all use the same procedure.

This example illustrates another advantage of using procedures. We make the change only once, in the procedure, and this change is then reflected in *all the calls* using this procedure.

EXAMPLE 12.4) Declare the method in the type declaration

Point 3 above states: 'Procedures that are methods must be declared in the class's type declaration.' We can test this. Comment out the method declaration:

```
type
  TfrmSixpenceJoe = class(TForm)
    lblCostText: TLabel;
```

```
  rgpProducts: TRadioGroup;
  procedure rgpProductsClick(Sender: TObject);
private
  //procedure DisplayPrice (Product, Price: String);
public
  { Public declarations }
end;
```

- Try to run this.

Delphi gives an 'undeclared identifier' message with the cursor flashing on the first appearance of DisplayPrice, in the method's header. So, without the method declaration in the TfrmSixpenceJoe type declaration, Delphi cannot recognise the DisplayPrice identifier.

- Uncomment the method declaration to return the type declaration to its previous form. The program compiles successfully, confirming that a method must be declared in the class type declaration.

EXAMPLE 12.5) Variables as parameters

Point 4 in the list of important points about procedures is: 'Depending on circumstances, the values sent in a procedure call can either be constants or variables.' Until now we have used only constants as parameters.

- Load the program from example 12.1 (C12e01p) and modify the event handler to use variables as parameters:

```
 8 procedure TfrmSixpenceJoe.rgpProductsClick(Sender: TObject);
 9 var
10   Product, Price: string;
11 begin
12   {Assign values to variables}
13   case rgpProducts.ItemIndex of
14     0: begin
15          Product := 'Flour';
16          Price := '12.99';
17        end;
18     1: begin
19          Product := 'Rice';
20          Price := '4.39';
21        end;
22     2: begin
23          Product := 'Sugar';
24          Price := '4.10';
25        end;
26     3: begin
27          Product := 'Mealie meal';
28          Price := '2.16';
29        end;
30   end; // end Case statement

31   {Now use variables in procedure call}
32   DisplayPrice (Product, Price);
33 end; {procedure TfrmSixpenceJoe.rgpProductsClick}
```

Here we don't have a procedure call for every case in the Case construct. Instead, we declare two local variables, `Product` and `Price`, both of type `string`. In the Case construct we assign values to these variables. The procedure call, which now comes after the Case construct (line 32), uses the *variables* as parameters rather than the constants we used previously.

EXAMPLE 12.6) A method is part of a class

Point 5 above states that we must include the class name (ie the form's name) in the method's header.

Let's explore this a bit further. You may have noticed that, in their headings, both event handlers‡ and the methods the programmer writes have compound names that include a link to the Form (eg `TfrmSixpenceJoe.rgpProductsClick`, `TfrmSixpenceJoe.DisplayPrice`) because these methods are an integral part of `frmSixpenceJoe`.

To illustrate this, remove the reference to `TfrmSixpenceJoe` from the method's heading (line 3 below):

```
3 procedure DisplayPrice (Product, Price: String);
4 begin
5    lblCostText.Caption := 'ONLY R' + Price  +
6                           ' per kg for ' + Product;
7 end; {proc DisplayPrice}
```

Interestingly, if you run this now, Delphi accepts this procedure header (line 3) on the basis that this could be a standalone procedure. But at line 5 Delphi gives an 'undeclared identifier' message with the cursor positioned on `lblCostText`. Because this version of the `DisplayPrice` procedure does not refer to `TfrmSixpenceJoe` in the header, it knows nothing about the form or any of its components. So, when we write a method, we must include the class in the method's header.

EXAMPLE 12.7) Components as parameters

The method we wrote in the examples above, `DisplayPrice`, has only a single program statement and so while it helps to convey the basic principles, it is almost too simple. Here we'll look at a slightly more complicated example and at the same time extend the concept of parameters to include using *components* as parameters.

As this example demonstrates, there are often several different ways of writing a program to meet a particular set of requirements.

EX 12.7 STEP 1 The program without procedures

- Start with C06e06p. We will change the group assignment, with no special consideration for 'M' or 'V', and add ListBoxes to list the names of each of the three groups as they are created.

‡ Experienced programmers may have noticed that event handlers are actually methods of the associated component's parent form.

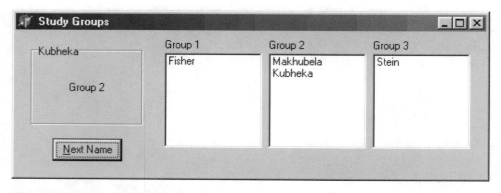

Figure 12.1 Revised study groups program

- Modify the screen layout to match figure 12.1.

Component	Property	Value
ListBox1, ListBox2, ListBox3	Name	lstGroup1, lstGroup2, lstGroup3
Label1, Label2, Label3	Name Caption	lblGroup1, lblGroup2, lblGroup3 Group 1, Group 2, Group 3

- As preparation for looking at components as parameters, modify the event handler as follows:

```
1  procedure TfrmStudyGroups.btnNextNameClick(Sender: TObject);
2  var
3     Surname: string;
4  begin
5    {Get next name}
6    Surname := InputBox ('User input', 'Enter a surname', '');

7    {Input checking}
8    if Surname = '' then
9    begin
10     ShowMessage ('No surname provided');
11     Exit;
12   end;

13   {Assign group}
14   case UpCase (Surname[1]) of
15   'A'..'G': begin
16             lblGroup.Caption := 'Group 1';
17             gpbGroup.Caption := Surname;
18             lstGroup1.Items.Add (Surname);
19           end;
20   'H'..'O': begin
21             lblGroup.Caption := 'Group 2';
22             gpbGroup.Caption := Surname;
23             lstGroup2.Items.Add (Surname);
24           end;
```

```
25   'P'..'Z': begin
26               lblGroup.Caption := 'Group 3';
27               gpbGroup.Caption := Surname;
28               lstGroup3.Items.Add (Surname);
29            end;
30   end;

31 end; // TfrmStudyGroups.btnNextNameClick
```

In example 6.6 we did the input validation within an if...then...else statement. As an alternative here, we first check to see whether the input is the empty string (ie check whether the user has pressed Cancel, clicked the Close box or not entered a name in the Input box) (line 8). If it is the empty string, we issue a warning message as before (line 10) and then exit this event handler without any further processing (line 11). Of course, this is not complete input validation. The user could enter numbers or typographic symbols such as a hash sign (#). If the validation fails, we could also clear the display. However, we'll leave it like this for the sake of simplicity.

The if...then...else (example 6.6) and the early exit (this example) are two common ways of handling errors. Some programmers favour the one approach and others the second approach, so you can choose the way you prefer.

Here, in contrast to example 6.6, we do all the processing within the Case construct as a prelude to introducing a procedure. This means that we use begin...end compound statements for each case. In the options for the Case construct we assume that the input always starts with an alphabetic character. A string starting with any other character is ignored.

- Save the unit and project files as C12e07u and C12e07p, then run and test the program.

Now that we have a framework, we'll introduce procedures in the next few solution steps.

EX 12.7 STEP 2 Introducing a simple method

If we look at the event handler, we'll see that there is a lot of repetition of similar-looking code. Whenever we come across this sort of repetition (lines 16–18, 21–23, 26–28), we should see whether we can use one or more methods to remove the repetition and so make the program easier to understand and maintain. When methods are used like this, they are often called *helper methods*.

Lines 16-17, 21-22 and 26-27 in the event handler above are very similar. Before reading further, see whether you can replace them with a procedure. (Lines 18, 23 and 28 are also similar, but each refers to a *different* component, so we'll leave them for now.)

First we must declare the method under the private section of the form's type declaration:

```
type
  TfrmStudyGroups = class(TForm)
    btnNextName: TButton;
    gpbGroup: TGroupBox;
    lstGroup1: TListBox;
```

```
      lstGroup2: TListBox;
      lstGroup3: TListBox;
      lblGroup1: TLabel;
      lblGroup2: TLabel;
      lblGroup3: TLabel;
      lblGroup: TLabel;
    procedure btnNextNameClick(Sender: TObject);
  private
    procedure ShowGroup (GrpNo, Surname: string);    // new method
  public
    { Public declarations }
  end;
```

The method definition and calling statements are as follows:

```
1  procedure TfrmStudyGroups.ShowGroup (GrpNo, Surname: string);
2  begin
3    lblGroup.Caption := 'Group ' + GrpNo;
4    gpbGroup.Caption := Surname;
5  end; // procedure TfrmStudyGroups.ShowGroup

6  procedure TfrmStudyGroups.btnNextNameClick(Sender: TObject);
7  var
8    Surname: string;
9  begin
10   {Get next name}.
11   Surname := InputBox ('User input', 'Enter a surname', '');

12   {Input checking}
13   if Surname = '' then
14   begin
15     ShowMessage ('No surname provided');
16     Exit;
17   end;

18   {Assign group}
19   case UpCase (Surname[1]) of
20   'A'..'G': begin
21            ShowGroup ('1', Surname);
22            lstGroup1.Items.Add (Surname);
23          end;
24   'H'..'O': begin
25            ShowGroup ('2', Surname);
26            lstGroup2.Items.Add (Surname);
27          end;
28   'P'..'Z': begin
29            ShowGroup ('3', Surname);
30            lstGroup3.Items.Add (Surname);
31          end;
32   end;

33 end; // TfrmStudyGroups.btnNextNameClick
```

If you change your program as above, you'll see that it works well. (We are not going to explain this operation here, since it is similar to what we have already done. Go through it yourself and make sure you understand how the method and the method calls work.)

This version is an improvement but there is still some duplication. Lines 22, 26 and 30 differ only in the component they refer to and in the next step we will pass the relevant ListBox as a parameter to method TfrmStudyGroups.ShowGroup.

EX 12.7 STEP 3 Passing a component as a parameter

Just as we use normal data types like strings and integers as parameters we can also use components.

- First modify procedure ShowGroup's method declaration to include a component of type TListBox:

```
type
  TfrmStudyGroups = class(TForm)
    btnNextName: TButton;
    { … other Delphi generated declarations as before }
    procedure btnNextNameClick(Sender: TObject);
  private
    procedure ShowGroup (GrpNo, Surname: string;
                          GroupList: TListBox);            // changed
  public
    { Public declarations }
  end;
```

- Now modify the method definition and btnNext's OnClick event handler:

```
1  procedure TfrmStudyGroups.ShowGroup (GrpNo, Surname: string;
2                                         GroupList: TListBox);
3  begin
4    lblGroup.Caption := 'Group ' + GrpNo;
5    gpbGroup.Caption := Surname;
6    GroupList.Items.Add (Surname);
7  end; // procedure TfrmStudyGroups.ShowGroup

8  procedure TfrmStudyGroups.btnNextNameClick(Sender: TObject);
9  var
10   Surname: string;
11 begin
12   {Get next name}
13   Surname := InputBox ('User input', 'Enter a surname', '');

14   {Input checking}
15   if Surname = '' then
16   begin
17     Show Message ('No surname provided');
18     Exit;
19   end;

20   {Assign group}
21   case UpCase (Surname[1]) of
22     'A'..'G': ShowGroup ('1', Surname, lstGroup1);
23     'H'..'O': ShowGroup ('2', Surname, lstGroup2);
```

```
24      'P'..'Z': ShowGroup ('3', Surname, lstGroup3);
25    end; // end case UpCase (Surname[1]) of
26 end; // TfrmStudyGroups.btnNextNameClick
```

Run and test this version. To the user it looks the same as before. But now the program has better structure making it easier to read and maintain.

You may be wondering how we knew what type to make the component parameter in the method declaration and heading (eg line 2 above).

- One way is to look at the type listing Delphi declares for the form. We give an example of this under example 12.7 step 2 above, and there we see that lstGroup1, 2 and 3 are all shown as type TListBox.

- Alternatively, we can use the Object Inspector to find out the type of each component on the form (figure 12.2).

Figure 12.2 Determining a component's type

Why and when should we use procedures?

A good use for a method is when we code the same or a similar task more than once. In the example above we repeat the same operation with only slight differences based on the first letter of the surname. So we take the similar code out of each individual case in the Case construct and put it into a separate method. In the event handlers we now just call the method and pass the differences from one call to the next as parameters. We write the method only once to handle the general problem. We then use parameters to accommodate the differences needed under different circumstances. In other words, we can now call the method time and again, changing the parameters to get the behaviour we want. So, using methods can help us to write less code.

Using methods also helps us to consolidate the program statements connected to a particular operation in one place. In the final version of the study groups program, everything to do with displaying the group information happens through procedure ShowGroup. If in the future we need to change the display text we need change only procedure ShowGroup (ex 12.7 step 3). In the initial version of the program (ex 12.7 step 1), control of the screen display is spread over twelve lines of the Case structure. To change the display consistently means making the same changes repeatedly in each of these lines. Making changes in more than one place makes errors more likely and is more work. Using methods reduces the chance that we will introduce errors and inconsistencies into the program and often reduces the effort involved.

Once we have written a method and tested it thoroughly, we then have a piece of code for possible re-use in future programs or by other people. If we have to design and write a big program that several people must work on, we can identify a common set of methods that everyone can use. Some people can write the methods while others can write the sections of the program that will use the methods. This can make it easier for several people to work on a program at the same time and can improve consistency. We give a small example of code re-use in the *Joe's Security Emporium* example in the next chapter.

In terms of programming style, when writing a method it is a good idea to choose a name that describes clearly what the method does. This helps considerably when later we need to re-read the program and understand how it operates and also if the occasion ever arises when the method can be re-used.

Commenting a method

The previous paragraph mentions how much a careful choice of names can contribute to understanding a program. Another important aspect is to comment clearly. One convention that is very valuable with methods is to include a brief comment after the method's header to describe what the method does and the role of each parameter. Here, for example, a helpful comment might be:

```
procedure TfrmStudyGroups.ShowGroup (GrpNo, Surname: String;
                                      GroupList: TListBox);
{This method displays GrpNo as the caption of lblGroup,
 sets the caption of gpbGroup to Surname, and
 adds Surname to the listbox GroupList}
```

EXAMPLE 12.8) Returning values from a procedure

So far, we have only sent values *into* a procedure. From the procedure's perspective, we have used only procedures that *receive* values. For example, the Canvas methods receive integer values for X and Y (example 11.2), the ShowGroup procedure receives string values and the names of components (example 12.7), and the OnMouseDown event handler receives the X and Y coordinates of the mouse (example 10.5). This type of parameter is called a *value* parameter.

We can also write a procedure that sends data in the other direction, *out* of the procedure to the calling statement. As you will see below, to do this we place the reserved word var in the parameter list in front of the parameter whose value we want to calculate and then send out from the procedure to the calling statement. This type of parameter is called a *variable* (or reference) parameter.

EX 12.8 STEP 1   The Inc(x) procedure

As a starting point for exploring variable parameters we'll look at a standard Delphi procedure, Inc (), that uses variable parameters. As you'll see, Inc (x) has the same effect as x := x + 1.

Create a new application, double click on the form to generate the skeleton for the form's OnCreate event handler and type in the code below. What is the result when you run the program?

```
procedure TForm1.FormCreate(Sender: TObject);
var
  x: integer;
begin
  x := 10;
  Inc(x);
  ShowMessage('The value of x is now ' + IntToStr(x));
end;
```

The program displays the value 11 for x. This means that procedure Inc (x) changed the value of the variable x by incrementing it by one. This is what a variable parameter is about – a procedure can change the value of the variable that is passed to it if it is declared as a variable parameter. In step 2 we will write our own procedure that uses a variable parameter.

EX 12.8 STEP 2   A var parameter

Figure 12.3 Calculating the fee for a stall

To raise funds, the local school uses its playground as a flea market on public holidays. Anyone who wants to set up a stall pays a fee of R20.00 plus 7.5% of their takings. Let's write a small program (using a variable parameter) to calculate the fee.

* Start a new application and place a SpinEdit, a button and a Label on the form (figure 12.3).
* The relevant properties are:

Component	Property	Value
Form1	Name	frmFee
	Caption	Flea Market Fee
SpinEdit1	Name	sedTakings
	Increment	10
Label1	Name	lblFee
	Caption	Fee appears here
Button1	Name	btnFee
	Caption	Fee

Setting sedTakings' increment property to 10 means that the value in the SpinEdit will change in steps of 10 when the user clicks on the up or down arrows but does not restrict the user from typing in values that are not multiples of 10.

* This program uses a helper method and an event handler. First scroll up towards the start of the unit and add the declaration for method CalcFee to the private section of the form declaration that Delphi has generated:

```
type
  TfrmFee = class(TForm)
    sedTakings: TSpinEdit;
    btnFee: TButton;
    lblFee: TLabel;
    procedure btnFeeClick(Sender: TObject);
  private
    procedure CalcFee (Takings: integer; var FeeStr: string);
  public
    { Public declarations }
  end;  // end TfrmFee = class(TForm)
```

* Now enter the code for the CalcFee method (lines 3 to 9 below) and complete btnFee's OnClick event handler skeleton (lines 10 to 16).

```
1  implementation

2  {$R *.DFM}

3  procedure TfrmFee.CalcFee (Takings: integer; var FeeStr: string);
4  var
5    Fee: double;
6  begin
7    Fee := Takings * 0.075 + 20; // Calculate fee
8    FeeStr := 'The fee is ' + FloatToStrF (Fee, ffCurrency, 15, 2);
9  end; // procedure CalcFee

10 procedure TfrmFee.btnFeeClick(Sender: TObject);
11 var
12   FeeStr: string;
13 begin
14   CalcFee (sedTakings.Value, FeeStr); // Proc call: derive string
15   lblFee.Caption := FeeStr; // Display it
16 end; // procedure TfrmFee.btnFeeClick
```

- Save the unit as C12e08u and the project as C12e08p. When you run the program, the Form appears and waits for an event. When the user enters a value for the earnings and clicks btnFee, the program displays the appropriate fee.

Lines 10 to 16 define btnFeeClick's event handler. Lines 11 and 12 declare a local variable, FeeStr, as a string. Line 14 is a call to the method CalcFee. It transfers the value of the SpinEdit to the method and provides the variable FeeStr, declared locally in line 12, as a *parameter for the method to use to provide the return value.*

The method CalcFee

Lines 3 to 9 above define the method CalcFee. The header, line 3, indicates the start of a method called CalcFee that takes two parameters: Takings, a *value* parameter of type integer, and FeeStr, a *variable* parameter of type string.

How do we know which is a value parameter and which is a variable parameter? The reserved word var comes immediately before FeeStr in the parameter list in line 3, and so FeeStr is a *variable* parameter. In the same parameter list, no reserved word precedes the parameter Takings and so it is a *value* parameter.

Lines 4 & 5 declare that method CalcFee has a local variable called Fee of type double. We see here that we can have both *variable parameters*, declared in the method header (eg FeeStr in line 3), and *local variables*, declared between the method header and the begin (eg Fee in lines 4 & 5). Parameters and local variables have different uses. Parameters provide communication between the calling statement and the procedure and so have a value outside the method. Local variables are available only inside a method. They come into existence at the start of the method and disappear when the method comes to an end and so cannot be used outside of the method.

Execution moves to line 7, the first program line of method CalcFee. The value of the SpinEdit is available in the method as the parameter Takings since the first parameter in the call (ie sedTakings.Value in line 14) matches the first parameter in the method's header (ie Takings in line 3) even though they have different names.

Line 7 calculates 7.5% of Takings, adds 20 and assigns this value to Fee. Line 8 converts the value of Fee to a string with two decimal places, concatenates this to some descriptive text and assigns this to the variable string parameter FeeStr.

Returning to the event handler: using the variable parameter's value

Once the method has finished, execution continues just after the method call and so line 15 is next. Because of the method call and since parameter FeeStr is declared as a *variable parameter* (line 3), the matching parameter in the method call, FeeStr, has the value assigned by the method. So, in line 15, the variable FeeStr has the value assigned to the FeeStr parameter in line 8. Note how important it was to declare this as a variable parameter (line 3). If we had omitted the var in front of FeeStr, it would have been a *value* parameter and then FeeStr would have had a meaningless value in line 15. To sum up, line 15 assigns the string received from procedure CalcFee via parameter FeeStr to the Label's Caption, and the event handler ends.

Error: leaving out the 'var'

To emphasize the importance of choosing the correct parameter type, consider what happens when we leave out the var in the method header. Think through for yourself the kind of error that will occur when the var is missing before going on to the next paragraph where we will do a small experiment to find out.
- Remove the var from the declaration of CalcFee in the form's type declaration:

  ```
  procedure CalcFee (Takings: integer; FeeStr: string);
  ```

- Remove var from the procedure CalcFee header (line 3 above) to get:

  ```
  procedure TfrmFee.CalcFee (Takings: integer; FeeStr: string);
  ```

- Run the program and test it. What difference is there now from before? Can you explain this difference?

The program compiles and runs and so seems to be OK. But, no matter what the input value is, the program does not display an accurate fee. Because FeeStr in method CalcFee is not a variable parameter, the value is not transferred back from the method to the calling statement and so the correct answer cannot be displayed. If you insert the var once more in front of FeeStr in the type declaration and in line 3, the program will again work correctly.

So when a parameter must transfer a value out from a method back to the calling statement to modify the value in the calling statement, it must be declared in the method header with a var. If this var is missing, the method *cannot* modify the value in the calling statement and the program will give strange answers that can be very difficult to track down.

Hiding detail with a method

The method CalcFee is called only once in the program above, so why do we go to the trouble of writing a separate method? If we look at btnFee's OnClick event handler (lines 10 to 16), we can see that because we have used descriptive names and a function call, it's easy to follow. We can guess that line 14 calculates some fee through a method call and that line 15 displays this value as the Caption of a Label. By using a method we have removed all the detailed calculations from the event handler and have made the event handler easier to understand.

Example 12.8 summary: We pass the value of the SpinEdit from event handler btnFeeClick to method CalcFee via the *value* parameter `Takings`. From this the method calculates the fee, converts it to a string and returns it to the event handler via the *variable* parameter `FeeStr`. We denote a variable parameter by placing `var` in front of it in the method header's parameter list (line 3 above). If there is no `var` in front of it, the parameter becomes a value parameter and the method does not return the value to the calling statement.

EXAMPLE 12.9) Sixpence Joe's selling price calculator

Sixpence Joe's Family Supermarket Product Price Indicator (example 12.6) has been so successful that Joe now wants another program. This must help him calculate the price at which he should sell his products. He buys all the products wholesale. Depending on the product, he then calculates the selling price by adding 15%, 20% or 25% to the wholesale price. He wants a computer program where he can enter a wholesale price, select 15%, 20% or 25% markup, and then see the selling price.

EX 12.9   Planning

Now that we know what Joe wants, how do we write the program? Where do we start?

User interface

Program design often starts with the interface, since that gives us a framework of the system's operations. Once we have a suitable interface, we can implement the required operations one by one. Here we need a logical, friendly interface to:
- Enter the wholesale price (we can use an Edit component in a GroupBox);
- Select 15%, 20% or 25% markup (we can use three SpeedButtons in a GroupBox – this gives us a chance to investigate the SpeedButton component);
- Display the selling price (we can use a Label in a GroupBox), and
- Reset the values (we can use a button).

Incremental development

Whenever we have come across complicated problems in this book we have solved them in stages rather than trying to solve the final problem in one go. This is sometimes called *incremental development*. We strongly recommend that whenever you write programs you approach them in a number of smaller steps and check each step as you go, testing out your ideas and getting a feel for the overall program. There are several reasons for taking a step-by-step, or incremental, approach:

- By breaking the problem into smaller steps, and then solving these smaller steps one by one, we deal with smaller, easier-to-write programs.
- As we write each smaller program, we can test it thoroughly. With a small program, the chances of making programming mistakes are less and it is easier to test and to correct the errors than with a big program.
- Once we have tested a program, we extend it in a small step and then retest it. This makes it easier to find errors and reduces the chance of introducing several errors at once.

Calculating the different markups will each require the same kind of calculation, just with different values for the markup percentage. This suggests that we should use one or more helper methods which the markup SpeedButtons' event handlers share rather than repeating all the code separately for each SpeedButton.

Taking all of this into account, we've decided to write the program in five steps:

1 Create and test the user interface (we'll include hints to improve usability);
2 Check that we understand how to do the arithmetic correctly by writing the event handler for the 15% markup;
3 Place the common code from this event handler into one or more methods;
4 Add the 20% and 25% event handlers. These will use the methods developed already, and
5 Modify the program to pass components as parameters and to use a component array.

EX 12.9 Testing

Checking that the program calculates the correct selling price for various different wholesale prices and for markups of 15%, 20% and 25% is relatively easy.

We draw up a table of wholesale prices and then, using a calculator or spreadsheet, calculate what the selling price should be for each markup. We later test that the program we write does actually give these values:

Wholesale Price	15% Markup		20% Markup		25% Markup	
	Expected	Program	Expected	Program	Expected	Program
100.00	115.00		120.00		125.00	
0.00	0.00		0.00		0.00	
12.50	14.38		15.00		15.63	
48.76	56.07		58.51		60.95	

To test for user-friendliness we check that:

1 The layout is logical and easy to understand;
2 The hints pop up, and
3 The Reset button clears the wholesale and selling prices and all the SpeedButtons.

Checking that the program gives the correct answers and that the user interface is friendly are 'external' checks. Many organizations also require 'internal' checks where the program itself is inspected for quality. Internal checks can take many different forms. Here we restrict ourselves to checking that methods have been used to avoid unnecessary program duplication.

EX 12.9 STEP 1 The user interface

We need to design a screen layout that is logical and easy for the user to understand. Our design is in figure 12.4 below.

- Open a new project and place three GroupBoxes on the form. In the first, place an Edit component to enter the wholesale price. In the second place, three SpeedButtons (Additional tab) to choose a markup of 15%, 20% or 25%. In the third, place a Label to display the selling price. Finally, place a BitBtn on the form to reset the prices.

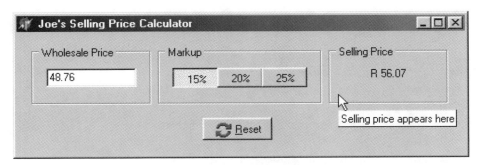

Figure 12.4 Demonstrating parameter flow to and from procedures

- Set the following static properties, sizing components as necessary to match the display.

Component	Property	Value
Form1	Name	frmMarkUp
	Caption	Joe's Selling Price Calculator
GroupBox1	Name	gpbWholesale
	Caption	Wholesale Price
	Hint	Enter wholesale price
GroupBox2	Name	gpbSelling
	Caption	Selling Price
	Hint	Selling price appears here
GroupBox3	Name	gpbMarkUp
	Caption	Markup
	Hint	Select markup percentage

All GroupBoxes	ParentShowHint	False
	ShowHint	True
Edit1 (in GroupBox1)	Name	edtWholesale
Label1 (in GroupBox2)	Name	lblSelling
Previous two components	ParentShowHint	True
	ShowHint	True
SpeedButton1 (in GroupBox3)	Name	spdFifteen
	Caption	15%
	Hint	Click here for a 15% markup
SpeedButton2 (in GroupBox3)	Name	spdTwenty
	Caption	20%
	Hint	Click here for a 20% markup
SpeedButton3 (in GroupBox3)	Name	spdTwentyFive
	Caption	25%
	Hint	Click here for a 25% markup
All SpeedButtons	AllowAllUp	True
	GroupIndex	1
	ParentShowHint	False
	ShowHint	True
	Width	41
BitBtn1	Name	bmbReset
	Kind	bkRetry
	Caption	&Reset
	Hint	Clear old values
	ParentShowHint	False
	ShowHint	True

- Compile the program and test the user interface. It does not 'do anything' yet, but we should check that the interface itself is generally acceptable, which it seems to be!

Notice how the hints work: for both the Wholesale Price and Selling Price GroupBoxes the same hint pops up whether the mouse pointer is on the GroupBox or on the component inside since the ParentShowHint property is true for both the Edit component and the label. However, for the MarkUp GroupBox, different hints appear for the GroupBox on its own and for each SpeedButton, since the SpeedButtons' ParentShowHint properties are False. (A point for experienced OO programmers is that the reference to a Parent here is to the parent container, not the parent class, since this is in the context of a containment hierarchy and not an inheritance hierarchy.)

Notice that only one SpeedButton can be down at a time, similarly to RadioButtons. This is because they all have the same GroupIndex (ie 1) and it is greater than zero. If a SpeedButton's GroupIndex is 0, it acts independently, like a normal button. We can't go into all the SpeedButton's capabilities here, so you may want to refer to the online Help.

EX 12.9 STEP 2 Calculating 15% markup directly

Now that we have a suitable user interface we will write program code to implement these operations one by one. To begin we will calculate only the 15% markup. For now we will do it directly, without any methods. When we have this working correctly, we can move the relevant code into a method.

- Double-click on spdFifteen and bmbReset to create these event handlers:

```
1  procedure TfrmMarkUp.spdFifteenClick(Sender: TObject);
2  var                {Local variables needed only in the event handler}
3    SellStr: string;
4    Wholesale, Selling: double;
5  begin
6    Wholesale := StrToFloat (edtWholesale.Text);
7    Selling := Wholesale + 0.15 * Wholesale;  // add 15% markup to cost
8    SellStr := FloatToStrF (Selling, ffCurrency, 15, 2);
9    lblSelling.Caption := SellStr;
10 end;


11 procedure TfrmMarkUp.bmbResetClick(Sender: TObject);
12 begin
13   edtWholesale.Clear; // clear wholesale price
14   lblSelling.Caption := ''; // clear selling price
15   edtWholesale.SetFocus;
16   spdFifteen.Down := False; // reset 15% button
17 end;
```

Let's look at event handler spdFifteenClick before running the program. We are going to need several temporary (or local) variables to help with performing the operations we require, so we declare these locally just after the procedure header (lines 2 to 4). The first program line of the procedure (event handler) is line 6. This converts the text the user entered into the Edit component to a value for Wholesale of type double using the StrToFloat function, so we declare Wholesale as a double type (line 4).

The second program line, line 7, converts the Wholesale price into the Selling Price by including the 15% markup. (Alternatively, we can also code line 7 as:

```
Selling := 1.15 * Wholesale;)
```

In order to do this calculation we declare Selling as a local variable of type double (line 4). Since Selling is a double value, and we need a string for the display, we convert Selling to string SellStr in line 8 (we declare SellStr as a local string variable in line 3). In the final line of the spdFifteenClick event handler (line 9) we display the value.

bmbResetClick clears the text from the Edit component and the Label and sets the focus on the Edit component (lines 13 to 15), as we have seen in previous programs. It resets spdFifteen through the Down property (line 16). (A SpeedButton's Down property is similar to a RadioButton's Checked property.)

- Save the file as C12e09u and the project as C12e09p, then run the program.
- Test with the different 15% markup values in the table above and check that the Reset button works.

EX 12.9 STEP 3   Creating procedure methods

With the 15% markup working, we have shown that our concept works. We could now go ahead and write the spdTwentyClick and spdTwentyFiveClick event handlers in the same style, except that we would use factors of 20% and 25% instead of 15%. However, this would mean repeating a lot of code and would complicate making changes in the future. So, we will first separate out the common operations into a helper method that will use the values of the cost price and the markup to calculate the selling price. We will need two value parameters (Cost and Markup) to bring these values into the method and a variable parameter (SellStr) to supply the selling price to the calling statement (lines 1 and 2 below).

We first modify spdFifteenClick to use and test this method before doing the 20% and 25% markups. bmbResetClick remains unchanged.

- Start by modifying the form's type declaration to accommodate this new method:

```
type
  TfrmMarkUp = class(TForm)
    gpbWholesale: TGroupBox;
    { … other standard Delphi declarations }
    procedure spdFifteenClick(Sender: TObject);
    procedure bmbResetClick(Sender: TObject);
  private
    procedure SellingPrice (Cost: string; Markup: double;
                              var SellStr: string);    // new method
  public
    { Public declarations }
  end;  // end TfrmMarkUp = class(TForm)
```

- Now define the method and modify the event handler to call it. (Read through this program and see whether you can understand it before reading our description below.)

```
implementation
```

```
{$R *.DFM}
```

```
 1 procedure TfrmMarkUp.SellingPrice (Cost: string; Markup: double;
 2                                           var SellStr: string);
 3 var
 4    Wholesale, Selling: double;
 5 begin
 6    Wholesale := StrToFloat (Cost);
 7    Selling := Wholesale + Markup * Wholesale;    // add markup
 8    SellStr := FloatToStrF (Selling, ffCurrency, 15, 2);
 9 end; // procedure TfrmMarkUp.SellingPrice

10 procedure TfrmMarkUp.spdFifteenClick(Sender: TObject);
11 var
12    SellStr: string;
13 begin
14    SellingPrice (edtWholesale.Text, 0.15, SellStr);
15    lblSelling.Caption := SellStr;
16 end; // procedure TfrmMarkUp.spdFifteenClick
```

The event handler spdFifteenClick is activated when the user clicks on the '15%' SpeedButton. Program operation starts at line 14 with a method call invoking method SellingPrice with three parameters. The first parameter, edtWholesale.Text, is the input value. The second, 0.15, is the markup. The third, SellStr, currently has no value, though it has been declared as a string in line 12. What is the purpose of this parameter? If we look at the header of method SellingPrice (lines 1 and 2), we see that the third parameter is a *variable parameter* (as denoted by the var keyword), so SellStr will carry the value that method SellingPrice derives back to the method call in the event handler.

Having been called by spdFifteenClick, method SellingPrice now runs. The method header (line 1) has three parameters in its parameter list. Neither of the first two parameters, Cost: string or Markup: double, has var in front of it, so they are *value parameters*. They *cannot* send any data back. By contrast, the third, var Sell: string, has a var, so it is a *variable parameter*. Because of this we can, if we need to, use SellStr to send data into the method *and to send data back out to the calling statement*. Here we use it to transfer data back to the calling program.

The parameters, declared in lines 1 and 2, and the locally declared variables, declared in lines 3 and 4, are all available for use within the body of the method SellingPrice. We use a table to highlight the differences between step 2, where the code is in an event handler, and step 3, where the code is in a method. Compare these two sets of code and notice how step 3 uses parameters.

Line no	Step 2: event handler	Step 3: helper method
6	Component property: edtWholesale.Text	Value parameter: Cost
7	Hard coded: 0.15	Value parameter: Markup
8	Local variable: SellStr	Variable parameter: SellStr

In step 3 we still need local variables Wholesale and Selling. But SellStr is now a variable *parameter*, and it is *not* declared as a local variable as in step 2.

When we come to the end of the method (step 3 line 9), the value of the *variable parameter* SellStr is available in the calling statement in event handler spdFifteenClick as *local variable* SellStr (line 14). Now that spdFifteenClick has the selling price, the next line (line 15) displays it by assigning SellStr to the Label's Caption. This is the last statement in event handler spdFifteenClick, so the event that started when the user clicked on the '15%' SpeedButton has come to an end.

- Modify the program from step 2 to look like this, save the new version as C12e03u2 and the project as C12e03p2, and then run it.
- Repeat the 15% markup tests.

EX 12.9 STEP 4 Adding further event handlers

Now that we have done all this preparatory work, implementing the 20% and 25% markups is relatively straightforward.
- Try it now before going any further.

```
17 procedure TfrmMarkUp.spdTwentyClick(Sender: TObject);
18 var
19   SellStr: string;                                {Local variable}
20 begin
21   SellingPrice (edtWholesale.Text, 0.2, SellStr);
22   lblSelling.Caption := SellStr;
23 end; // procedure TfrmMarkUp.spdTwentyClick


24 procedure TfrmMarkUp.spdTwentyFiveClick(Sender: TObject);
25 var
26   SellStr: string;                                {Local variable}
27 begin
28   SellingPrice (edtWholesale.Text, 0.25, SellStr);
29   lblSelling.Caption := SellStr;
30 end; // procedure TfrmMarkUp.spdTwentyFiveClick
```

- One more change is needed – did you remember to extend bmbResetClick to reset spdTwenty and spdTwentyFive?

```
31 procedure TfrmMarkUp.bmbResetClick(Sender: TObject);
32 begin
33   edtWholesale.Clear;
34   lblSelling.Caption := '';
35   edtWholesale.SetFocus;
36   spdFifteen.Down := False;
37   spdTwenty.Down := False;
38   spdTwentyFive.Down := False;
39 end; // procedure TfrmMarkUp.bmbResetClick
```

- Save the file and then run the program.

EX 12.9 STEP 5   Testing the program

A program is not really finished until it has been properly tested, so go through all the checks listed in the Testing section above. When we tested the program, it gave the expected values every time and passed the user interface checks. It also avoids duplication through appropriate use of a method. Since it complies with the test criteria set at the beginning of the example and no unexpected problems have come up, we can now accept this program and show it to the customer.

EX 12.9 STEP 6   Some refinements

Many programmers would feel content that the program given in step 4 is quite satisfactory. However, there are two further developments that would be interesting to look at briefly to reinforce concepts we have already seen. First, we can transfer the names of the relevant components as parameters to the method (example 12.7), and so update the interface directly from this method. Second, we can reset the SpeedButtons by using a control array (Chapter 8). We start by modifying the method declaration to accommodate the new parameters – as we mentioned previously the procedure name and parameter list must correspond exactly between the declaration and the header in the definition:

```
type
   TfrmMarkUp = class(TForm)
      gpbWholesale: TGroupBox;
      { other standard Delphi declarations }
      procedure spdFifteenClick(Sender: TObject);
      procedure bmbResetClick(Sender: TObject);
      procedure spdTwentyClick(Sender: TObject);
      procedure spdTwentyFiveClick(Sender: TObject);
   private
      procedure SellingPrice (Input: TEdit; Markup: double;
                              Output: TLabel);
   public
      { Public declarations }
   end;   // end TfrmMarkUp = class(TForm)
```

We won't comment any further on the coding, which follows below, but it is informative to compare it with the previous versions.

```
 1 procedure TfrmMarkUp.SellingPrice (Input: TEdit; Markup: double;
 2                                    Output: TLabel);
 3 var
 4    Wholesale, Selling: double;
 5 begin
 6    Wholesale := StrToFloat (Input.Text);
 7    Selling := Wholesale + Markup * Wholesale; // add markup
 8    Output.Caption := FloatToStrF (Selling, ffCurrency, 15, 2);
 9 end; // procedure TfrmMarkUp.SellingPrice

10 procedure TfrmMarkUp.spdFifteenClick(Sender: TObject);
11 begin
12    SellingPrice (edtWholesale, 0.15, lblSelling);
13 end; // procedure TfrmMarkUp.spdFifteenClick

14 procedure TfrmMarkUp.spdTwentyClick(Sender: TObject);
15 begin
16    SellingPrice (edtWholesale, 0.2, lblSelling);
17 end; // procedure TfrmMarkUp.spdTwentyClick

18 procedure TfrmMarkUp.spdTwentyFiveClick(Sender: TObject);
19 begin
20    SellingPrice (edtWholesale, 0.25, lblSelling);
21 end; // procedure TfrmMarkUp.spdTwentyFiveClick

22 procedure TfrmMarkUp.bmbResetClick(Sender: TObject);
23 var
24    i: integer;
25 begin
26    edtWholesale.Clear;
27    lblSelling.Caption := '';
28    edtWholesale.SetFocus;
29    for i := 0 to (gpbMarkUp.ControlCount - 1) do
30       TSpeedButton(gpbMarkUp.Controls[i]).Down := False;
31 end; // procedure TfrmMarkUp.bmbResetClick
```

EXAMPLE 12.10 Variable parameters in event handlers

So far in event handlers we have looked only at value parameters. However, Delphi also uses other types of parameter in its event handlers when necessary. As the following example shows, these other types of parameter allow us to change Delphi's default behaviour by intercepting system events.

- Open a new application and place a Memo on the form.

Component	Property	Value
Form1	Name	frmNoCaps
	Caption	No Caps Please!
Memo1	Name	memNoCaps

Figure 12.5 A variable parameter in a user event

- Create two event handler skeletons through the Events tab on the Object Inspector by double-clicking alongside the OnKeyPress event for memNoCaps and alongside OnClose for the form.

```
1  procedure TfrmNoCaps.memNoCapsKeyPress(Sender: TObject;
2                                          var Key: Char);
3  begin
4    if (Key >= 'A') and (Key <= 'Z') then
5      Key := '#';
6  end;

7  procedure TfrmNoCaps.FormClose(Sender: TObject;
8                                 var Action: TCloseAction);
9  begin
10   if MessageDlg('Close Form?', mtConfirmation,
11                 [mbYes, mbNo], 0) = mrYes then
12     Action := caFree
13   else
14     Action := caNone;
15 end;
```

- Save the unit and project files as C12e10u and C12e10p and then run and test the program.
- Type any capital letter into the Memo (figure 12.5).
- It appears on the screen as a hash (#) but lowercase letters are unaffected.

For every normal keystroke in a Memo, Delphi generates the OnKeyDown, OnKeyPress and OnKeyUp events. Usually we don't write event handlers for these events and our program ignores them. Here, however, we have written an OnKeyPress event handler (lines 1 to 6). This has two parameters, the standard Sender: TObject parameter and, on line 2, a *variable* parameter var Key: Char. This means that the key the user has pressed is available inside the event handler as Key. We can manipulate Key within the event handler. Then, *because it is a variable parameter*, when the event handler finishes, Delphi receives this changed value of Key and displays it in the Memo. So, in line 4, we test whether the incoming Key is a capital letter and, if it is we change it to a hash symbol in line 5. There is no Else part to the If statement, so if the incoming Key is not a capital letter, the event handler leaves it unchanged.

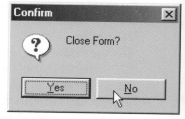

Figure 12.6 Intercepting the OnClose event

- After you've played with this a bit, try closing the form. Instead of simply closing as before, it now displays a MessageDialog (figure 12.6):

Why is this? We have intercepted a system event, the form's OnClose event (lines 7 to 15). When the form receives the Close instruction it generates the OnClose event. This also has two parameters, the standard `Sender: TObject` parameter and, on line 8, a *variable* parameter `var Action: TCloseAction`. This means that the programmer can manipulate the `Action` parameter within the event handler. So in lines 10 and 11 we ask the user if he or she really wants to exit. If the user responds by clicking on the Yes button, the `Action` parameter receives the value `caFree`. If the user clicks on the No button or the Close box, the Else part is executed and `Action` receives the value `caNone`. After the event handler completes, Delphi receives the new value of the variable parameter `Action`. If this has the value `caNone`, Delphi abandons the Close operation and returns to the Memo component.

We can simplify lines 10 to 14 by leaving a Yes response as the default value and changing `Action` only if the user does *not* reply with a Yes:

```
10  if MessageDlg('Close Form?', mtConfirmation,
11              [mbYes, mbNo], 0) <> mrYes then
12    Action := caNone;
```

Delphi's event signatures

Delphi determines the parameters that are available for each event. How does the programmer know what these parameters are and what their significance is? For example, how do we know that the OnClose event we used in this example has two parameters and that caFree and caNone are valid values for the second one? Double-clicking alongside the event's name in the Events tab of the Object Inspector generates the event handler skeleton in the editor, and from this we can see the number and type of parameters, but not their significance or allowed values. One way to find out is to use Help. However, if we place the cursor on either FormClose or TCloseAction and press <F1> we don't get the required information. Another possibility is to position the cursor opposite 'OnClose' in the Events tab of the Object Inspector and then press F1. This brings up Help text that varies between versions but for all versions includes a table showing that the Action parameter can have one of four values:

Value	Meaning
caNone	The form is not allowed to close, so nothing happens.
caHide	The form is not closed, but just hidden. Your application can still access a hidden form.
caFree	The form is closed and all allocated memory for the form is freed.
caMinimize	The form is minimized, rather than closed.

User interface factors: reversibilty vs economy

By intercepting the OnClose event handler and displaying a message box as we have done above, we are giving the user the option of going back on their decision to exit the program. *Reversibility* is a user interface design principle which states that the user should be able to backtrack when choices are made. We would like to build interfaces in such a way that the user feels comfortable to experiment and try out new features without being concerned that they will do something wrong that cannot be undone.

However, is it always a good idea to ask the user if they are sure that they want to do something before it is done? By introducing a Confirm dialog box we are forcing the user to click on 'Yes' before the program exits. This violates the user interface design principle of *economy*: the user has to click twice to achieve a task which could be achieved with one click. Is it better to have an interface that is economical or one that is reversible? As in this case, you may find that two user interface design principles are in conflict with each other and you will have to use your own judgement to decide which is the best strategy to follow.

In this example we have shown you how to intercept the OnClose event. This could be an important feature to use in an application where, for example, the user has not saved a file and you want to check if they want to save before exiting. As a general guideline, however, it is usually best to avoid using dialog boxes which force the user to respond unless it is absolutely necessary.

Delphi's other parameter types

We have looked at only two of Delphi's parameter types here: value and variable parameters. Originally these two were the only types available in Pascal. Delphi Pascal has two further types, *constant* and *out* parameters, which you may come across.

A *constant* parameter is a restricted version of the value parameter since you cannot change its value in the method. Using it where appropriate can limit the chance of changing values by mistake and so of introducing errors. Under certain conditions it produces more efficient code.

An *out* parameter is a restricted version of the variable parameter, since it can only return a value from a method and cannot bring a value into a method the way a variable parameter can.

Often, though not always, one can use constant parameters in the place of value parameters and can use out parameters in the place of variable parameters. This will work with the examples in this chapter. In ex 12.9 step 3, for instance, we could replace the present declaration of SellingPrice in the form's type declaration as follows:

```
procedure SellingPrice (const Cost: string;
        const Markup: double; out SellStr: string);
```

The heading for SellingPrice would have to change to match this declaration:

```
procedure TfrmMarkUp.SellingPrice (const Cost: string;
        const Markup: double; out SellStr: string);
```

We use constant and out parameters in Chapter 13 and Delphi describes them in the online Help.

REVIEW

This chapter extends the concepts of event handlers and standard methods to include the concept of a programmer written method. Methods are used to avoid duplication, to consolidate code, to simplify changes and to ease re-use.

When writing a method, we ourselves type in the header and the `begin` and `end` statements along with the method body. Procedures should have meaningful names and helpful comments.

If necessary, parameters provide the communication between the method and the surrounding program. Unlike events or Delphi's standard methods, with a programmer-written method we define the header and so determine the matching call (ie the parameters, their order and their type). Data is taken into a method through constant, value or variable parameters and brought out of a method through variable or out parameters. Within a method, parameter matching is by name, not by order. A parameter has a value that we can manipulate much like any other variable. We can use normal data types and components (objects) as parameters. Delphi uses variable parameters in some of its system methods, allowing us to influence responses to system events (eg OnClose).

Parameters have meaning both inside and outside a subroutine (whether the subroutine is a procedure or a function). In contrast, *local variables*, which are declared within a subroutine, have meaning only within that subroutine. Parameters and local variables have different uses. Parameters provide communication between the calling statement and the subroutine and so have a value outside the subroutine. Local variables provide temporary storage within a subroutine. They come into existence at the start of the subroutine and disappear when the subroutine comes to an end. They exist inside the subroutine only and so cannot be used outside of it.

When designing a program it is often useful to start with the user interface, plan to implement the operations behind the interface in stages and to work out a set of test cases. Repeated operations are first implemented once in a single event handler. When this has been tested, the code can be moved into a helper method which all the affected event handlers then call. This incremental approach allows a large problem to be divided into a series of smaller problems which are easier to code and test separately before being combined with other parts of the program.

IMPORTANT CONCEPTS

Fundamental programming concepts

Comments: When writing a method it is useful to include a comment that describes briefly what the method does and the role of each parameter.

Constant parameter:
- A constant parameter transfers a value from the calling statement into the method but does not supply a value back to the calling statement.
- Declaring a constant parameter: `ProcName (`**`const`** `Param: type)`
- A constant parameter accepts a constant, a variable or an expression.
- The parameter value cannot be changed in the subroutine (ie the value is constant within the method).
- Constant parameters are typically used as inputs to a calculation the method must perform or as values the method must display.

General procedure: A procedure that stands alone and is not part of a class. General procedures are covered in the third edition of this book but have been replaced here by methods. Also called a standalone procedure.

Helper method: A method that is used only within the class where it is defined. All the methods used in this chapter are helper methods.

Local variables and constants: Local variables (and local constants) are declared in the declarations section of the method, just after the header. Local variables and constants are valid only while the method is running. As soon as the method ends, its local variables and constants disappear. (Local variables were introduced in Chapter 3.)

	Parameters	Local variables and constants
Type	Value, Constant, Variable and Out	Constant and Variable
Scope	Communication between calling statement and method	Exist within the method only
Declaration	Method header's parameter list	Between method's header and begin

Method: A method is a subroutine (either a procedure or a function) that is part of a class. In this chapter all the methods have been part of a form class.

Out parameter:
- An out parameter is only for output from the procedure. Its incoming value is reset. An out parameter is not typically used with a function.
- Declaring an out parameter: `ProcedureName (out Param: type)`
- An out parameter cannot bring a value into a procedure.
- The parameter value must be assigned in the procedure.
- Out parameters are typically used to carry the resulting value from a calculation that a procedure performs.

Parameters: Parameters provide the communication between a method and the surrounding program. We can create methods that don't use parameters at all. But if there are parameters, the call must match the header in the order and number of parameters, and their type. Within a method, parameter matching is by name, not by order, and a parameter has a value that we can manipulate much like any other variable. We can use normal data types and components (objects) as parameters.

Procedure: A procedure is like a 'mini program' that packages a particular action (eg calculating or displaying a value). A procedure can be called as frequently as needed from different parts of the program. Data transfer, if any, between the calling statement and the procedure and back again occurs through parameters.

Procedure call: Procedure calls differ from assignment statements and take the form:

```
ProcedureName (ParameterList);
```

For some operations (eg clearing the screen) no data transfer is needed, so `ParameterList` may be empty (eg ResetUI in example 13.2).

Procedure declaration and definition: To declare a procedure as a method, include the procedure header (without the class name) in the class declaration. Use the following structure to define a procedure that is a method:

```
procedure ClassName.ProcedureName (ParameterList);
Declarations                        {for local variables and constants}
begin
  ProcedureBody
end;
```

A method requires both a declaration and a definition within the appropriate class. A general (or standalone) procedure is declared independently of a class, if at all. It is defined without a ClassName.

Procedure name: When writing a procedure, it is a good idea to choose a name that describes clearly what the procedure does. This helps considerably when later we need to re-read the program and understand how it operates and also if the occasion ever arises when the procedure can be re-used.

Subroutine: Subroutine is the collective name for procedures and functions, whether they are attached to a class, and so become methods, or whether they are standalone, when they are often called general subroutines (or general procedures or general functions depending on the context). Differences between procedures and functions are presented in Chapter 13.

Value parameter: A value parameter is the default type.

- o A value parameter transfers a value from the calling statement into the method but does not supply a value to the calling statement.
- o Declaring a value parameter: `MethodName (Param: type)`
- o A value parameter accepts a constant, a variable or an expression, since any of these can transfer a value into a method and there is no need to receive a value back from the method.
- o Value parameters are typically used as inputs to a calculation the method must perform or as values the method must display.
- o The parameter value can be changed in the method.

Variable (or reference) parameter:

- o A variable parameter transfers a value from a calling statement into a procedure and also transfers a value back to the calling program. A variable parameter is not typically used with a function.
- o Declaring a variable parameter: `ProcedureName (`**`var`**` Param: type)`
- o A variable parameter accepts a variable only, since constants or expressions cannot receive the value back from the procedure.
- o Variable parameters are typically used to carry in a value the procedure may modify and to carry the resulting value from a calculation that a procedure performs.
- o To reduce the chance of error, do not use a variable parameter when a constant, value or out parameter is sufficient.

Common issues when using methods

1. Between method call and definition, parameters must match in type, order and number.
2. If a value is to be returned to the calling statement, it must be a `var` or `out` parameter.
3. When used as a method, a procedure is declared as part of a class.
4. When used as a method, the procedure's name is appended by the dot operator to the class name in the procedure header.
5. Within procedures, parameters are used by name.
6. Use the most restricted parameter type that meets the data transfer needs, working in the order constant, value, out and variable parameters.

Benefits of using methods

We write our own methods for several reasons:

1. If a particular operation must occur several times, we can avoid duplication by writing this operation once as a method.

Each time we need the operation we call the method and pass the parameter values required to accommodate the differences needed under different circumstances. We can call the method time and again, changing the parameters to get the behaviour we want. So, using methods helps us to write less code. This leads to smaller programs and less programming effort.

2   Using methods helps us to consolidate the program statements connected to a particular operation in one place.

3   Methods can make changing a program simpler and less likely to cause errors since we make the change only once, in the method, and this change is then reflected in all the calls using this method. If, instead of a method, the code is repeated, we may miss one of the places where we must make a change, and so introduce strange errors that can be difficult to fix. Using methods therefore reduces the chance that we will introduce errors and inconsistencies into the program.

4   We can test one small, well-defined method more easily than if that code is repeated throughout the program.

5   Once we have written a method and tested it thoroughly, we then have a piece of code for possible re-use in future programs. Over time we can develop a library of re-usable, tested methods that may be useful in future programs, reducing our subsequent programming and testing effort.

6   Using methods encourages teamwork, allowing different people to work on different parts of an overall program.

7   Programs with methods are often easier to design and, if we choose the method names carefully, easier to understand.

Program development

Incremental development: There are several reasons for taking a step-by-step, or incremental, approach (as in example 12.8 and some previous examples):

o   By breaking the problem into smaller steps, and then solving these smaller steps one by one, we deal with smaller, easier-to-write programs.

o   As we write each smaller program, we can test it thoroughly. With a small program, the chances of making programming mistakes are smaller and it is easier to test and to correct the errors than with a big program.

o   Once we have tested a program, we extend it in a small step and then retest it. This makes it easier to find errors and reduces the chances of introducing several errors at once.

Planning based on the user interface: Program design often starts with the interface since it gives us a framework of the system's operations. Once we have a suitable interface, we can implement the required operations one by one (*incremental development*).

Program acceptance: Checking that the program gives the correct answer and that the user interface is friendly are 'external' checks. Many organizations also require 'internal' checks where the program itself is inspected for quality. Internal checks can take many different forms, such as use of meaningful names and comments and the appropriate use of methods.

User interface factors

Reversibility: The user interface design principle of reversibility states that the user should be able to backtrack when choices are made. The user should ideally feel free to experiment with an interface without being concerned that they will do something wrong that cannot be undone.

Conflicting principles: Different user interface design principles may at times be in conflict with each other (eg reversibility and economy). In these cases a programmer will have to use his or her own judgement to decide how to balance the two.

NEW DELPHI FEATURES

TSpeedButton		
Properties	AllowAllUp	If AllowAllUp is True, all of the SpeedButtons in a group can be unselected. If AllowAllUp is False, the group acts like a group of RadioButtons.
	Down	To select a SpeedButton, set the Down property to True, either in the Object Inspector or programmatically. By default, SpeedButtons appear in an up (unselected) state.
	GroupIndex	SpeedButtons can function independently or in groups. If a SpeedButton's GroupIndex is zero, it functions independently. If several SpeedButtons have the same nonzero value for GroupIndex, they function as a group.
Prefix	spd...	
Use	Speed buttons often have images on their faces and are often used with panels to create toolbars. They can function either independently or in groups.	

PROBLEMS

PROBLEM 12.1) Adding method calls

- Modify Sixpence Joe's price indicator (example 12.1) to contain two further products (salt at R22.35, oats porridge at R10.49) with the RadioButtons in a 2×3 matrix.

PROBLEM 12.2 Different parameter types

- Consider this slight modification to example 12.8:

```
1 implementation

2 {$R *.DFM}

3 procedure TfrmFee.CalcFee (Takings: integer; var FeeStr: string);
4 var
5   Fee: double;
6 begin
7   Fee := Takings * 0.1 + 20;                          // Calculate fee
8   FeeStr := 'The fee is ' + FloatToStrF (Fee, ffCurrency, 15, 2);
9 end; // procedure TfrmFee.CalcFee

10 procedure TfrmFee.btnFeeClick(Sender: TObject);
11 var
12   FeeStr: string;
13 begin
14   FeeStr := 'Test string';
15   CalcFee (sedTakings.Value, FeeStr);                 // Derive string
16   lblFee.Caption := FeeStr;                           // Display it
17 end; // procedure TfrmFee.btnFeeClick
```

- Assume that the user enters the value 100 into sedTakings.
  a What will this program display? Why?

- What will this program display with each of the following procedure headers? Why? Assume that each in turn replaces line 3 in the program above. Remember to modify the type declaration as well.
  b **procedure** TfrmFee.CalcFee (Takings: integer; FeeStr: string);
  c **procedure** TfrmFee.CalcFee (Takings: integer; **out** FeeStr: string);
  d **procedure** TfrmFee.CalcFee (Takings: integer; **const** FeeStr: string);

PROBLEM 12.3 Enhancing the admission price calculator

Figure 12.7 Modified admission price calculator

The circus gives a 10% discount on weekdays. Weekend rates are R9.90 for adults and R6.60 for children. It uses a method, called 'AdmissionPrice', to calculate the admission price. The number of adults, number of children and discount rate must be parameters. This means that the WeekDay and Weekend OnClick event handlers are as follows:

```
procedure TfrmJJCircus.btnWeekendClick(Sender: TObject);
var
  PriceStr: string;
begin
  AdmissionPrice (sedAdult.Value, sedChild.Value, 0.0, PriceStr);
  lblPrice.Caption := PriceStr;
  sedAdult.SetFocus;
end; // end procedure TfrmJJCircus.btnWeekendClick


procedure TfrmJJCircus.btnWeekDayClick(Sender: TObject);
var
  PriceStr: string;
begin
  AdmissionPrice (sedAdult.Value, sedChild.Value, 0.1, PriceStr);
  lblPrice.Caption := PriceStr;
  sedAdult.SetFocus;
end; // end procedure TfrmJJCircus.btnWeekDayClick
```

a   Draw up an appropriate set of test cases for this application.
b   Write the AdmissionPrice method.
c   Write the Reset button's event handler.
d   Test the program using your test cases and correct any errors that your testing reveals.

PROBLEM 12.4) Currency converter

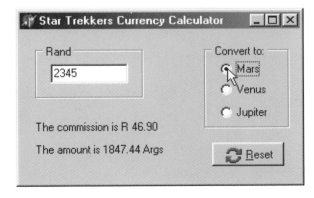

Figure 12.8 Currency conversion using a program

Star Trekkers Inc fly their Star Cruisers between Johannesburg Interplanetary Spaceport and Mars, Venus and Jupiter. We have previously used several currency conversion programs to explore real number concepts. In this version, developed for *Star Trekkers Inc,* we must read the Rand value, calculate and display the commission in Rands (calculated at 2%), convert the remaining amount into the required currency, and display it appropriately. The currency conversions are:

South Africa (Rands)	Mars (Args)	Venus (Amours)	Jupiter (Gargants)
1.00	0.8039	29.889	2.5379

a   Draw up a suitable set of test cases to test the program.

The framework for this program follows. Complete the program as requested in the subquestions below.

As structured, the program places all the 'messy' conversion code into a single method instead of repeating it in each event handler. This makes the event handlers easier to understand. It also concentrates the conversion code in one place, making changes and error control easier.

- Enter the following framework into your computer, remembering to create the event handlers by double-clicking on the appropriate components or through the Object Inspector:

```
procedure TfrmConvert.Convert (RandStr, CurrStr: string; Rate: double;
                               out AmtStr, CommStr : string);
const CommissionRate = 0.02;
var Rand, Currency, Commission: double;
begin
  {Calculate commission string}
  {Write this section of the procedure as part b - see below}

  {Calculate amount string}
  {Write this section of the procedure as part c - see below}
end; {end procedure TfrmConvert.Convert}

procedure TfrmConvert.radMarsClick(Sender: TObject);
var
  AmountStr, CommissionStr: string;
begin
  Convert (edtRand.Text, 'Args', 0.8039, AmountStr, CommissionStr);
  lblCommission.Caption := CommissionStr;
  lblAmount.Caption := AmountStr;
end; // end procedure TfrmConvert.radMarsClick

procedure TfrmConvert.radVenusClick(Sender: TObject);
  {Write this event handler as part d - see below}
end; // end procedure TfrmConvert.radVenusClick

procedure TfrmConvert.radJupiterClick(Sender: TObject);
  {Write this event handler as part d - see below}
end; // end procedure TfrmConvert.radJupiterClick

procedure TfrmConvert.bmbResetClick(Sender: TObject);
begin
  {Write this event handler as part e - see below}
end; // procedure TfrmConvert.bmbResetClick
```

The components referred to in the program are:

Component type	Names
Label	lblAmount, lblCommission
Edit	edtRand
RadioButton	radMars, radVenus, radJupiter
BitBtn	bmbReset

b   Extend the Convert method by writing the first part. Using the parameters and local constants and variables as needed, calculate the commission and return this as a string parameter of the form `'The commission is R 24.68'`.

c   Write the second part of the Convert method. Using the parameters and local constants and variables as needed, calculate the amount left after commission is subtracted, convert this amount to a currency value and return this as a string parameter of the form `'The amount is 972.17 Args'`.

d   Write the radVenus and radJupiter event handlers. These are very similar to the radMars event handler, except that the parameters in the method call differ as necessary.

e   Write the bmbReset event handler to clear all values and reset the RadioButtons.

f   As it stands, this program displays the commission in Rands. Change method Convert so that the commission is displayed instead in the target currency (ie Args, Amours or Gargants). Do this without changing method Convert's header or any of the event handlers.

g   If your testing of the program shows up any problems, make appropriate enhancements to the existing program.

PROBLEM 12.5   Making changes

- Consider making a simple change to example 12.7, swapping the surname and group designation in the Panel. List the line numbers and changes needed in

a   example 12.7 step 1 and

b   example 12.7 step 3.

c   Based on parts a and b, discuss the pros and cons of implementing this program with and without the ShowGroup method.

PROBLEM 12.6   Components as parameters

- Modify example 12.7 step 3 by placing three Labels vertically in the GroupBox. The top Label displays the Surname entered, the middle Label carries the text `'goes to group'` and the bottom one displays the group number. Thus the program no longer changes the Caption of the GroupBox.

PROBLEM 12.7) Introducing a method

Quite often as programmers we must take a program that already exists and modify it in some way. If the documentation for the program being changed is poor, we have to spend time working out the program design before any changes can be made. Sometimes not all the information is available and we must then do the best we can with incomplete knowledge.

- In this problem, you must adapt a given program by taking code out of an event handler and putting it into two methods. The screen display for the program and the original program listing are displayed below.

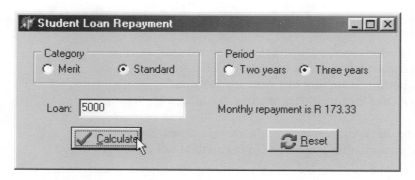

Figure 12.9 A student loan calculator

```
1  procedure TfrmLoan.bmbCalculateClick(Sender: TObject);
2  var NoOfPayments: Integer;
3      Rate, Loan, Repayment: Double;
4      Factor: Double;

5  begin

6    {Get loan details}

7    {Determine rate of loan based on academic performance}
8    if radMerit.Checked then
9      Rate := 0.01
10   else // must be standard student
11     Rate := 0.0125;
12   {Determine no of months for repayment}
13   if radTwo.Checked then
14     NoOfPayments := 24
15   else // must be three years
16     NoOfPayments := 36;
17   {Convert loan entered from string to type double}
18   Loan := StrToFloat (edtLoan.Text);
19   if Loan < 0 then
20   begin
21     Loan := 0;
22     edtLoan.Text := '0.00';
23   end;
```

```
24   {Calculate monthly repayment}
25   Factor := (1 - exp (-NoOfPayments * ln (1.0 + Rate)));
26   Repayment := Loan * Rate / Factor;
27   {Display monthly repayment}
28   lblRepay.Caption := 'Monthly repayment is '
29                             + FloatToStrF (Repayment, ffCurrency, 12, 2);

30 end; {end procedure TfrmLoan.bmbCalculateClick}

31 procedure TfrmLoan.bmbResetClick(Sender: TObject);
32 begin
33   radStandard.Checked := True;
34   radThree.Checked := True;
35   lblRepay.Caption := '';
36   edtLoan.Text      := '0.00';
37   edtLoan.setFocus;
38 end; // end procedure TfrmLoan.bmbResetClick
```

a   Using the screen display and this listing, 'reverse engineer' as much of the Properties Table (ie the static design: component names, Captions, etc) as you can.

b   By reading carefully through the program, work out the interest rates applicable for merit and standard students.

• Now enter the program and get it running. Unless you are pretty good at financial mathematics, you probably won't understand the Calculate Repayments section (lines 25-26). (This entire problem can be done without understanding it, so enter it just as it stands.)

c   Complete the following table of test cases. You will use these test results to test your modified program.

	Merit/2yrs	Merit/3yrs	Standard/2yrs	Standard/3yrs
5000.00				
0.00				
−90				

Having investigated the existing program in some detail, the time has now come to make some changes. We'll restrict the changes to creating two procedures, as in the next two subquestions:

d   Write a method called DetermineDetails, which gathers all the information from the user interface. Replace lines 7-23 above with a call to method DetermineDetails.

e   Write a method called CalcRepay, which calculates the monthly repayment. Replace lines 25-26 above with a call to method CalcRepay.

After these two steps, the new version of the event handler should look like this.

```
procedure TfrmLoan.bmbCalculateClick(Sender: TObject);
var NoOfPayments: Integer;
    Rate, Loan, Repayment: Double;
```

```
begin
  {Get loan details}
  DetermineDetails (Loan, Rate, NoOfPayments);

  {Calculate monthly repayment}
  CalcRepay (Loan, Rate, NoOfPayments, Repayment);

  {Display monthly repayment}
  lblRepay.Caption := 'Monthly repayment is '
                      + FloatToStrF (Repayment, ffCurrency, 12, 2);
end; {end of procedure TfrmLoan.bmbCalculateClick}
```

• Test this new version of the program against the test cases established in (c) above to ensure that no errors have been introduced while making these changes.

PROBLEM 12.8) Salesperson's commission

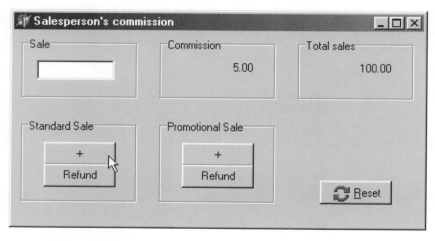

Figure 12.10 The Rave and Save Electrical Appliance Superstore commission

The Rave and Save Electrical Appliance Superstore pays its salespeople 7% commission on standard sales and 10% commission for selling any item on promotion. It also guarantees all its goods, and a customer can return any item undamaged within a week of buying it for a full money-back refund. When an item is returned, the commission is taken back from the salesperson. Based on this screen layout, write a program to total up each salesperson's weekly sales and commission. Clearly, since this problem appears in a chapter on procedures, the program should use appropriate methods.

a   Start by planning how to develop the program using steps similar to those in example 12.9.

b   Then draw up a set of typical test cases covering standard and promotional sales and refunds.

c   Implement this program in the steps you planned, using the test cases you have drawn up to make sure that each step is working correctly.

CHAPTER 13

Functions and exceptions

PURPOSE OF THIS CHAPTER

So far in this book we have looked at several different types of subroutine:

o *Event handlers*, which are a special type of procedure. They are often activated by user-events such as mouse clicks, but they can also be called by system-events such as OnTimer or OnFormShow.

o *Standard methods*, which may be either procedures or functions. They provide the special capabilities of different types of object (eg the Ellipse method of the Canvas object).

o *Standard subroutines*, such as StrToInt and ShowMessage, which may be either procedures or functions

o *Programmer-written methods*, which the programmer writes, such as the SellingPrice procedure we used in Chapter 12.

Delphi Pascal provides two categories of subroutine, procedure and function. We looked at procedures in the previous chapter. Now it is time to turn our attention to *functions*. There are many similarities between functions and procedures, and so the knowledge gained in the previous chapters will be useful in learning how to use functions effectively. There are also important differences: functions are designed particularly for doing arithmetic and mathematical operations and supply a single value without using variable or out parameters.

As with procedures, functions may be written either as methods (and so part of a class) or as standalone functions. In this chapter we look at writing functions that are methods.

Error handling in subroutines is important and we explore exception handling briefly in this chapter too.

Delphi's standard functions

We have already used some of Delphi's standard functions while, for example, doing string handling. Statements such as:

```
NewValue := StrToInt ('2468');
CapitalsStr := UpperCase ('ThIs Is A cRaZy StRiNg');
```

use functions. Message Dialogs also often involve functions:

```
if MessageDlg('Do you want to exit?', mtConfirmation,
                        [mbYes, mbNo], 0) = mrYes then
  // executed if user clicks Yes
else
  // executed if user clicks No
```

Functions are different from procedures because a function's name carries a value. So in these examples StrToInt or UpperCase have values that can be assigned to variables, and MessageDlg has a value that can be tested in an If statement.

Procedure names, on the other hand, do not carry any values, and any values that procedures supply are through the var and out parameters in their parameter lists. In this chapter we'll see how to write our own functions in addition to those that are a standard part of Delphi.

EXAMPLE 13.1 A simple function

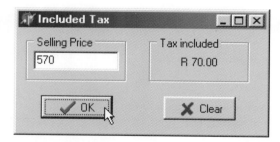

Figure 13.1 Testing the TaxIncl function

Our first example accepts a selling price for an item and then calculates how much tax is included in that price.
- Inside a GroupBox in a new application place an Edit component.
- Inside another place a Label. Add two Bitmap buttons to the form.
- Set the following properties:

Component	Property	Value
Form1	Name	frmTax
	Caption	Included Tax
GroupBox1	Name	gpbSell
	Caption	Selling Price

Edit1	Name	edtSell
GroupBox2	Name	gpbTax
	Caption	Tax included
Label1	Name	lblTax
BitBtn1	Name	bmbOK
	Kind	bkOK
BitBtn2	Name	bmbClear
	Kind	bkCancel
	Caption	Clear

Remember that when you want to change the Caption on a Bitmap button as for bmbClear above, set the Kind first and then the Caption. The program below has a method which is a function and two OnClick event handlers. (This program does not add tax to a price. Instead, it takes a selling price which includes tax and then calculates what portion of this selling price is tax). The formula to calculate the included tax is:

Tax included = (Selling Price * Tax Rate) / (1 + Tax Rate).

Because this program uses a method, the method is declared as part of the structure of the form class under the private section:

```
type
  TfrmTax = class(TForm)
    gpbSell: TGroupBox;
    edtSell: TEdit;
    gpbTax: TGroupBox;
    lblTax: TLabel;
    bmbOK: TBitBtn;
    bmbClear: TBitBtn;
    procedure bmbOKClick(Sender: TObject);
    procedure bmbClearClick(Sender: TObject);
  private
    { function TaxIncl declaration }
    function TaxIncl (Selling, Rate: double): double;   // added
  public
    { Public declarations }
  end;   // end TfrmTax = class(TForm)
```

The program with the method definition to implement the formula above is as follows:

```
1 implementation

2 {$R *.DFM}

3 function TfrmTax.TaxIncl (Selling, Rate: double): double;
4 begin
5   Result := (Selling * Rate) / (1 + Rate);
6 end; // function TfrmTax.TaxIncl

7 procedure TfrmTax.bmbOKClick(Sender: TObject);
8 const
9   Rate = 0.14;
```

```
10 var
11   Selling, Tax: double;
12 begin
13   try
14     Selling := StrToFloat (edtSell.Text); // Convert input to double
15     Tax := TaxIncl (Selling, Rate);   // Calculate tax via function
16     lblTax.Caption := FloatToStrF(Tax, ffCurrency, 15, 2); //Display
17   except
18     ShowMessage ('Invalid Input');
19     bmbClear.Click;          // Reset interface by 'clicking' bmbClear
20   end; // end try .. except block
21 end; // procedure TfrmTax.bmbOKClick

22 procedure TfrmTax.bmbClearClick(Sender: TObject);
23 begin
24   lblTax.Caption := '';
25   edtSell.Clear;
26   edtSell.SetFocus;
27 end; // procedure TfrmTax.bmbClearClick
```

EX 13.1   Testing

Since functions (eg lines 3 to 6 above) are often re-used in different programs (just as procedures are), it is important to test them thoroughly when first written. We can then rely on the functions we have written and subsequent programmers will be able to re-use them with confidence. We create a series of test cases where we list a series of pretax prices (row 1 below) and calculate the tax (at 14% as coded into the program, row 2) and the final selling price (row 3) as follows. To test, enter a value from row 3 and check that the program displays the corresponding value in line 2.

		Case 1	Case 2	Case 3	Case 4	Case 5
1	Pretax price	0.00	1.00	43.22	1342.87	500.00
2	Tax (at 14%)	0.00	0.14	6.05	188.00	70.00
3	Final price	0.00	1.14	49.27	1530.87	570.00

EX 13.1   STEP 1   Run and test the program

- Enter the program above and save it as C13e01u and C13e01p.
- Test it by entering in turn each Final price value (row 3) and checking that it gives the corresponding Tax value (row 2) for each of the five cases in the table above. Figure 13.1 shows test case 5.

EX 13.1   STEP 2   How do we write a function?

As with procedures that are methods, functions that are methods must be declared as part of the class type declaration. A function *declaration*, has the general form:

```
function FunctionName (ParameterList): ReturnType;
```

It is similar to a procedure declaration. The first word, `function`, tells the compiler that this is a function that follows. `FunctionName` in this case is `TaxIncl`. `ParameterList`, here `Selling, Rate: double`, like a procedure's parameter list, contains zero or more parameters. With functions we generally use *only value or constant parameters* to bring values *into* the function. Functions calculate a value of type `ReturnType` that becomes attached to the function's name, and the function's name is in many ways similar to a variable's name. So function TaxIncl in the program above supplies a single value of type double to the calling statement.*

A function *definition*, like a a procedure definition, starts with the header (eg line 3). The header definition is similar to the function declaration except that the class name is attached to the front of the function name by a fullstop. So, for the program given above, the function *declaration* is:

```
function TaxIncl (Selling, Rate: double): double;
```

while the function *header* (line 3) includes the name of the class, TfrmTax:

```
function TfrmTax.TaxIncl (Selling, Rate: double): double;
```

Line 4 of the program, `begin`, shows that the function *body* is about to start. Here there is a single statement, line 5, in the function body. Given the selling price and the tax rate, which come into the function through the value parameters `Selling` and `Rate` in line 3, the statement in line 5 calculates the amount of tax that is included in the selling price. The `end;` in line 6 shows that the function is complete.

EX 13.1 STEP 3 Supplying the function's value to the calling statement

Perhaps, as you entered the program above, you wondered where the `Result` variable (line 5) came from – after all, we don't declare it anywhere. Delphi Pascal creates a temporary `Result` variable automatically whenever a function is called. The programmer can use `Result` to set the value that the calling statement receives when the function ends.

Here, `Result` (line 5) involves an arithmetic expression using the value parameters `Selling` and `Rate` defined in the function header. These parameters bring a selling price and a sales tax rate *into* the function. The procedure then calculates the tax included in the selling price and assigns this to `Result`, giving the value that the function will supply to the calling statement.

An alternative way of supplying the value to the calling statement is to use the *function's name* (`TaxIncl`) instead of `Result`, as in line 5 below:

```
3 function TaxIncl (Selling, Rate: double): double;
4 begin
5   TaxIncl := (Selling * Rate) / (1 + Rate); // Using function name
6 end;
```

If you change `Result` in your program to `TaxIncl` and run it again, you will see that it works as before. So, to supply a value to the calling statement, at least one of the statements in the function body must assign a value either to *Result* or to

---

*   Strictly speaking, we can use variable parameters, as with procedures, but in Delphi Pascal this is generally considered to be poor programming practice. Generally, variable parameters are used with functions only when interfacing to programs written in languages other than Delphi Pascal.

the *function name. Without this assignment in the function body, the calling statement receives no value from the function.*

As a general practice in this book we use the `Result` variable rather than the function's name, since this is a more flexible approach. (For further details, consult Delphi's online Help.)

EX 13.1 STEP 4 How do we use a function?

We use the function in our program through a *function call* (line 15), which here takes the form of an assignment statement. (Procedure calls are always independent program statements, whereas function calls are part of an expression.) A function call can also be used in a conditional statement (example 13.2) or as a parameter in a procedure or function call (example 13.5).

The parameters of the function call in line 15 are `Selling`, declared in line 11 and assigned from the user's input (line 14), and `Rate`, a constant declared in line 9. The function uses these values to calculate the required value (line 5 as already described) and then supplies the value to the calling statement through the `Result` variable. The assignment statement assigns this value to `Tax` in line 15. (`Tax` is declared as double in line 11.)

EX 13.1 STEP 5 Displaying the output

Line 16 converts `Tax` to a currency-type string and assigns it to lblTax's Caption, displaying the final value to the user.

EX 13.1 STEP 6 Soft click

Because of the Try (line 13), an error in the input such as an alphabetic character will cause `StrToFloat` to raise an exception (line 14). Program execution will then jump immediately to the first statement in the Except block, which is an error message (line 18). We then need to clear the user interface. We could now write the specific program statements to do this. However, bmbClear's OnClick event handler (lines 22-27) already does this. So we call this event handler programmatically by 'soft clicking' bmbClear (line 19).

Example 13.1 summary: When we need a single value back from a subroutine, a function is often easier to use than a procedure with an out or a variable parameter. In the function body we assign the return value to the automatic variable `Result` or to the function's name.

EXAMPLE 13.2) Joe's Security Emporium

Professional programmers must often take existing programs and change them to meet new requirements or to fix problems in them. So it's important not only to be able to write new programs but also to be able to read existing programs written by someone else. In this and the next example we start from an existing program and then modify and develop it to meet changing requirements.

In the process of developing these programs we bring together several concepts about subroutines. (Subroutine is the collective name for a procedure or a function.) We start with a program that illustrates when to use a method that is a function and when to use a procedure. We then re-use this basic program structure in the subsequent example to demonstrate how subroutines support re-use.

These examples use constant and out parameters, though they can also use value and/or variable parameters.

Recently Joe hired you as a Delphi programmer to help develop computer-based access control systems. He has just sold a system to control access to the storeroom in Mr Kite's *Toye Shoppe* and wants you to familiarize yourself with the program. The screen layout is shown in figure 13.2. The static properties are:

Figure 13.2 Access control screen

Component	Property	Value
Form1	Name	frmAccess
	Caption	Store Access
Label1	Name	lblStatus
	Caption	Enter Code
SpinEdit1	Name	sed1st
SpinEdit2	Name	sed2nd
SpinEdit3	Name	sed3rd
All SpinEdits	MaxValue	9
	MinValue	0
	MaxLength	1
Button1	Name	bmbOK
	Kind	bkOK
Button2	Name	bmbClear
	Kind	bkCancel
	Caption	&Clear

- We'll improve Joe's program (shown below) in a little while, but for a start just read and understand the program as it stands below.

There are four subroutines declared as methods in the private section of the form's declaration (three procedures and one function):

```
type
  TfrmAccess = class(TForm)
    { standard Delphi generated declarations }
    ...
  private
    procedure ReadCode (out A, B, C: integer);
    function Validate (const a, b, c: integer): boolean;
    procedure ResetUI;
    procedure ShowAccessStatus (const Status: boolean);
  public
    { Public declarations }
  end; // end TfrmAccess = class(TForm)
```

The definitions of these four methods follows in the implementation section. Each method has a brief comment describing its parameters and its operation:

```
1  procedure TfrmAccess.ReadCode (out A, B, C: integer);
2  { Read the values on the three TSpinEdits and
3    return these in the A, B and C parameters }
4  begin
5    A := sed1st.Value;
6    B := sed2nd.Value;
7    C := sed3rd.Value;
8  end; // procedure TfrmAccess.ReadCode

9  function TfrmAccess.Validate (const a, b, c: integer): boolean;
10 { Determine whether incoming values of a, b and c together
11   comprise a valid code, and return a Boolean result }
12 const
13   Key = 10;
14 var
15   Sum, Leftover: Integer;
16 begin
17   Sum := a + b + c;
18   Leftover := Sum mod Key;
19   if (Sum > 0) and (Leftover = 0) then
20     Result := true
21   else
22     Result := false;
23 end; // function TfrmAccess.Validate

24 procedure TfrmAccess.ResetUI;
25 { Reset the user interface }
26 begin
27   sed1st.Value := 0;
28   sed2nd.Value := 0;
29   sed3rd.Value := 0;
30 end; // procedure TfrmAccess.ResetUI

31 procedure TfrmAccess.ShowAccessStatus (const Status: boolean);
32 { Modify the user interface as determined by parameter Status }
33 begin
34   if Status = true then
35   begin
36     frmAccess.Color := clGreen;
37     lblStatus.Caption := 'Proceed';
38   end
39   else
40   begin
41     Color := clYellow;
42     lblStatus.Caption := 'Invalid';
43   end;
44 end; // procedure TfrmAccess.ShowAccessStatus

45 procedure TfrmAccess.bmbOKClick(Sender: TObject);
46 var
47   A, B, C: integer;
```

```
48 begin
49    ReadCode (A, B, C);
50    if Validate (A, B, C) = true then
51      ShowAccessStatus (true)
52    else
53      ShowAccessStatus (false);
54    ResetUI;
55 end; // procedure TfrmAccess.bmbOKClick

56 procedure TfrmAccess.bmbClearClick(Sender: TObject);
57 begin
58    ResetUI;
59    frmAccess.Color := clBtnFace;
60    lblStatus.Caption := 'Enter Code';
61 end; // TfrmAccess.bmbClearClick
```

- You could enter this program now and then play around with it and see if you can work out how it operates. But instead of doing that, why not practise the skill of reading a program by first answering the questions below and working through the accompanying discussion.

EX 13.2 STEP 1 The program operation

Question: Assume the user has entered the numbers 9, 1 and 0 respectively into the three SpinEdits and clicks on the OK button. List in order the program lines that the program will execute and describe the program operation before reading any further.

Discussion: When the user clicks on the OK button, the bmbOKClick event handler fires (line 45). Program execution starts at line 49, which calls the method procedure TfrmAccess.ReadCode with parameters A, B and C. These have been declared as integer variables in lines 46 and 47 but have not been assigned any values yet. If we look at the header for ReadCode (line 1), we see that all three parameters are out parameters, so the parameters in line 49 will *accept* values from procedure ReadCode.

Procedure ReadCode is defined in lines 1 to 8. The actual program lines are lines 5 to 7, which assign respectively the values of the three SpinEdits (given as 9, 1 and 0 in the question) to the *out* parameters A, B and C defined in line 1. When procedure ReadCode ends at line 8 the out parameters have the values 9, 1 and 0. Because these are *out* parameters the values 9, 1 and 0 become available to the calling statement (line 49). In line 1 we could also have declared these as variable parameters and achieved the same effect.

From this we see that ReadCode is a user interface procedure responsible for reading in three values entered by the user. As a result of the call in line 49 it makes these values available to bmbOK's OnClick event handler.

Program execution now moves to line 50 (just after the calling statement). Line 50 is the first line of an If statement. It contains an embedded call to function Validate and so it transfers the values of A, B and C received from procedure ReadCode (9, 1 and 0 in this case) to function Validate as the constant parameters a, b and c defined in line 9. (Lines 9 to 23 define function Validate.)

Program execution continues at line 17, the first line of program code in function Validate. This sums together the three incoming parameters (9, 1 and 0) to assign the value 10 to Sum (declared as a local variable in line 15). Line 18 calculates the remainder after Sum is divided by Key. Key is a constant given the value of 10 in line 13. 10 divided by 10 leaves a remainder of 0, so Leftover (declared in line 15) is assigned the value 0. Line 19 is the first line of an If statement. It checks whether Sum is greater than 0 (it is) and whether Leftover is equal to 0 (it is).

Both conditions are True and so the And is also True. Program execution moves to the Then part, line 20. This assigns the value True to variable Result. The Then part is complete and program execution jumps out of the If statement to come to the end of function Validate (line 23). Validate acts as a decoding function. If the incoming parameters match a certain pattern, Validate gives the value True. If they don't match this pattern, it gives False.

Let's pause for a moment and look at the Result variable. Delphi creates a temporary variable called Result automatically every time a function is called. This variable is of the same type as the function which in this case, as we see from the last keyword in line 9, is Boolean. Delphi supplies the value that the programmer assigns to Result as the value of the function call in the calling statement. In other words, when the program execution now continues at the If statement in line 50, Validate (A, B, C) has the value True.

Since the test in the If statement succeeds, execution moves to the Then part (line 51). This is a call to procedure ShowAccessStatus with the parameter as True, so program execution moves to line 34.

Line 34 is an If statement that evaluates to True in this case. Execution moves to the Then part (lines 36 and 37). The form's colour is set to Green and the Label's Caption to Proceed. Jumping out of the If statement past the Else part brings execution to line 44, the end of procedure ShowAccessStatus. ShowAccessStatus has only a single constant parameter (line 31) and so does not supply any value to the calling statement. We see that its responsibility is to update the user interface.

Since procedure ShowAccessStatus is complete, program execution continues at line 51. This is the only statement in the Then part, so execution jumps past the Else part to line 54, which is a call to procedure ResetUI. ResetUI is also a user interface procedure. It has no parameters and merely resets the values of all the SpinEdits to 0 (lines 24 to 30).

On completion of ResetUI execution returns to line 55 and the event handler is complete. The program returns to a wait mode until another event happens.

Look again briefly at the bmbOKClick event handler, lines 45 to 55. Can you see that even if we ignore the procedures and function for now, we still get a very good idea of the program's operation? By using the names in the subroutine calls we can guess that line 49 reads a code and that line 50 validates it. If it is valid, line 51 displays that access state is True, whereas if it is invalid line 53 displays that access state is False. Finally, line 54 resets the user interface.

The event handler acts as a central control procedure that then calls the other subroutines as they are needed. Just by looking at the code for the event handler (lines 45 to 55) and without understanding the details contained in the subroutines, we can still get a good idea of what the program is about. This illustrates again how subroutines help to keep low-level detail separate from the main program flow. If we had put all the code into the event handler instead we would have been swamped by detail. It would have been far more difficult to understand the overall program operation.

Example 13.2 step 1 summary: The user enters three digits on the SpinEdits and presses the OK BitBtn. If these three digits comply with the pattern that the

Validate function tests for, the form goes green and displays the text 'Proceed'. (Similarly, if the digits do not comply with the pattern, the form goes yellow and displays the text 'Invalid', as one can see from lines 41 and 42.) We use subroutines to perform all the detailed operations (three for user interface operations and one for the validation), while the event handler takes responsibility for high-level coordination of the subroutines.

EX 13.2 STEP 2 Procedures or functions?

Question: Besides the two event handlers, this program has three procedures and one function. For each subroutine explain why it is either a procedure or a function.

Answers:

o Subroutine ReadCode must supply *three* parameters to the calling statement. A function supplies only *one* parameter through its call and so ReadCode should be a *procedure* using either out or variable parameters.

o Subroutine Validate receives three values from the calling statement and supplies one value back. A function receives zero or more parameters and supplies a single value, so Validate fits the pattern of a *function* perfectly. The incoming values must be transferred through either constant or value parameters. (We could also make Validate a procedure but that would make the programming more complicated without gaining any benefits.)

o Subroutine ShowAccessStatus receives a single value and returns no values. It does not fit the pattern of a function and so should be a *procedure* with either a constant or a value parameter.

o Subroutine ResetUI neither receives nor returns any values. It too does not fit the pattern of a function, so it should be a *procedure*. Because it needs no parameters, it has no parameter list or brackets after the procedure name (line 24).

Example 13.2 step 2 summary: If a subroutine must supply only one value it is usually more convenient to use a function. If two or more values come back, one uses a procedure with variable or out parameters. If no values come back, one uses a procedure.

EX 13.2 STEP 3 Enhancing the If statements

Question: Having covered Chapter 5, you may have noticed that each If statement in the program above can be improved in some way. Can you work out how?

Answers:

o Let's first look at lines 34 and 50. Each of these has the form `if X = true then` ... . This is exactly the same as saying `if X then` ... . In other words, line 34 can be replaced by:

```
if Status then
```

while line 50 can be replaced by:

```
if Validate (A, B, C) then
```

o   Now let's look at lines 19 to 22. These have the form:

```
if X then
   Result := true
else
   Result := false;
```

Can you see that an easier way to achieve the same effect is through a statement of the form:

```
Result := X;?
```

So, lines 19 to 22 can be replaced by a single statement:

```
Result := (Sum > 0) and (Leftover = 0);
```

o   Lines 50 to 53 are similar and they can also be replaced by a single statement. The Validate (A, B, C) function call becomes a parameter for the ShowAccessStatus procedure call, giving rise to a nested subroutine call:

```
ShowAccessStatus (Validate (A, B, C));
```

We'll use these alternatives to the If statements in subsequent versions of this program.

EXAMPLE 13.3) Henry's 'Horse Heaven' Farm

Mr Kite's friend Henry has a farm where he breeds horses. He needs an access control program for the farm's storeroom. He likes the program above, except that he does not want the SpinEdit interface. He wants to enter the values into a field and have just stars displayed so that no-one can see the number he enters.

• Take the program above and modify it accordingly. The revised screen should look like figure 13.3.

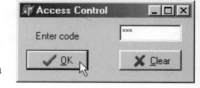

Figure 13.3 Modified input screen

EX 13.3   Planning

What changes must we make to the previous program? We'll have to change the form, replacing the SpinEdits with an Edit component and setting the PasswordChar property. The only parts of the previous program that use the SpinEdits are the ReadCode and ResetUI procedures. So if we can change these procedures to work with an Edit component (without changing either procedure header or the parameters), we should be able to re-use all the other code.

EX 13.3   Testing

Once we have made the program changes, how can we test the modified program?

If we assume that the previous program was thoroughly tested when it was first written and that it works correctly, we can test our new version against the old version.

- Draw up a short table of suitable test values. A sample table could be:

Value entered	First version (example 13.2)	Modified version (example 13.3)
000		
011		
019		
343		
434		
19m		

- Run the above program (example 13.2), enter the values in the left-hand column of this test table and fill in the results in the middle column. Then, when we have modified the program, we have a base to test it against.
- With the changed interface, do we need any additional checks? Well, since we can now enter alphabetic values, which we couldn't with the SpinEdits, we must make sure that the program rejects non-numeric values (the last entry in the table above) and that any input values are shown as stars and not as their actual value. The Reset button must clear the Edit component, the label's caption and the form's colour and give the focus to the Edit.
- See how far you can get with modifying program C13e02.dpr to meet the new set of requirements before reading further.

EX 13.3 STEP 1   Changes to the form

- If it is not loaded into your Delphi editor, open file C13e02p.
- Create a copy to work on by saving the unit as C13e03u and the project file as C13e03p.
- Delete the three SpinEdit components by selecting each in turn and pressing the <Del> key.
- Now add an Edit component to get the screen layout in figure 13.3. The other components and their property values remain unaltered. Set the PasswordChar property value for the Edit component to '*':

Component	Property	Value
Edit1	Name	edtCode
	PasswordChar	*

EX 13.3 STEP 2   Changing the code

- Adapt the existing program to match the following. (Since none of the subroutine headers have changed, the subroutine declarations in the private section of the class declaration remain as in example 13.2.)

```delphi
 1 procedure TfrmAccess.ReadCode (out A, B, C: integer);
 2 { Read the 3 digit value on the TEdit and
 3   return this in the A, B and C parameters }
 4 var
 5   Value: integer;
 6 begin
 7   Value := StrToInt (edtCode.Text);
 8   C := Value mod 10;      // Get rightmost digit
 9   Value := Value div 10;  // Remove rightmost digit
10   B := Value mod 10;      // Get rightmost digit
11   Value := Value div 10;  // Remove rightmost digit
12   A := Value mod 10;      // Get rightmost digit
13 end; // procedure TfrmAccess.ReadCode

14 function TfrmAccess.Validate (const a, b, c: integer): boolean;
15 { Determine whether incoming values of a, b and c together
16   comprise a valid code, and return a Boolean result }
17 var
18   Sum, Leftover: Integer;
19 begin
20   Sum := a + b + c;
21   Leftover := Sum mod 10;          // 0 if divisible by 10
22   Result := (Sum > 0) and (Leftover = 0); // also reject 000
23 end;   // end function TfrmAccess.Validate

24 procedure TfrmAccess.ResetUI;
25 { Reset the user interface }
26 begin
27   edtCode.Clear;
28   edtCode.SetFocus;
29 end; // procedure TfrmAccess.Reset

30 procedure TfrmAccess.ShowAccessStatus (const Status: boolean);
31 { Modify the user interface as determined by parameter Status }
32 begin
33   if Status then
34   begin
35     Color := clGreen;
36     lblStatus.Caption := 'Proceed';
37   end   // end then ..
38   else
39   begin
40     Color := clYellow;
41     lblStatus.Caption := 'Invalid';
42   end;   // end else ..
43 end; // end procedure TfrmAccess.ShowAccessStatus

44 procedure TfrmAccess.bmbOKClick(Sender: TObject);
45 var
46   A, B, C: integer;
47 begin
48   ReadCode (A, B, C);
49   ShowAccessStatus (Validate (A, B, C));
50   ResetUI;
```

```
51 end; // procedure TfrmAccess.bmbOKClick
```

```
52 procedure TfrmAccess.bmbClearClick(Sender: TObject);
53 begin
54    ResetUI;
55    Color := clBtnFace;
56    lblStatus.Caption := 'Enter Code';
57 end;    // TfrmAccess.bmbClearClick
```

- Make these changes, save the program and test it according to the criteria we established earlier.

EX 13.3 STEP 3 Comments on each subroutine

Procedure ReadCode: Compared to the previous version, this procedure retains the *same heading* and so *appears* to be unchanged to any other part of the program. But the code within the procedure changes to read the Edit component. Line 7 uses the StrToInt system function to convert the input text to the integer Value (declared in line 5). Lines 8 to 12 show an interesting use of the *integer division* operations mod and div. An integer cannot have a decimal part so integer division differs from real division. As you may remember from Chapter 4, div divides one number by another and *ignores the remainder* whereas mod divides one number by another and *gives the remainder*. We can illustrate how lines 8 to 12 work by using a trace table as shown below. We assume that the user has entered the value '109':

Line	Value	A	B	C	Comment
	109				
8: C := Value mod 10;	109	?	?	9	// Get remainder = rightmost digit
9: Value := Value div 10;	10	?	?	9	// Remove rightmost digit
10: B := Value mod 10;	10	?	0	9	// Get rightmost digit
11: Value := Value div 10;	1	?	0	9	// Remove rightmost digit
12: A := Value mod 10;	1	1	0	9	// Get rightmost digit

So the succession of mod and div operations splits the number the user entered into three digits as parameters A, B and C.

With SpinEdits we can enter integers only, whereas with Edits we can enter alphanumeric characters. The IntToStr function raises an exception if the user enters an alphabetic character. The exception terminates the ReadCode method and its calling method, and Delphi's default event handler displays an error message. We return briefly to exception handling later in this chapter.

Function Validate: Since it does not interact directly with any input component, Validate remains unaltered. (We have updated line 22 to illustrate the comments in example 13.2 step 3, but this is not essential.)

Procedure ResetUI: ResetUI retains the same header as the previous version for compatibility with the other subroutines, but the body of the procedure changes to accommodate the Edit component.

Procedure ShowAccessStatus: ShowAccessStatus remains unaltered.

Event handlers bmbOKClick and bmbClearClick: Because no subroutine headers were changed, the calls from both event handlers remain unaltered. This means that the event handlers remain the same – all the changes have been accommodated within subroutine bodies, so these changes do not affect any of the other subroutines that interact with them. (We have updated line 49 to illustrate the comments in example 13.2 step 3, but this is not essential.)

EX 13.3 STEP 4 Alternative implementations

As a final example of the 'pluggability' of subroutines, we give an alternative version of the ReadCode procedure. The internal working of this version is very different from that of the previous version but we are keeping the header exactly the same. This means that we can use either version of the procedure in our program without affecting any other part. This version of ReadCode determines the values of A, B and C by string manipulation:

```
procedure TfrmAccess.ReadCode (out A, B, C: integer);
var
   strValue: string;
begin
   strValue := frmAccess.edtCode.Text;
   C := StrToInt (strValue[3]);
   B := StrToInt (strValue[2]);
   A := StrToInt (strValue[1]);
end; // procedure TfrmAccess.ReadCode
```

Example 13.3 summary: This example illustrates how subroutines can allow one to accommodate future changes by 'plugging' in new versions of specific subroutines while leaving the rest of the program unaltered. The exact extent of the change depends on the particular circumstances. Here, a change in the user interface means that we must change procedures ReadCode and ResetUI while the rest of the program remains unchanged.

Differences between functions and procedures

Functions are convenient when one needs a single value back from a subroutine. This is because function calls, like variable or constant names, have a value when used in an expression whereas procedure names do not. This explains several of the differences between the ways we write functions and procedures. We'll illustrate this by assuming that we want a subroutine to accept an integer value called InValue, do some calculation, and then provide the double result called OutValue.

In a *procedure*, we would use two parameters. InValue would be a constant or value parameter, of type Integer, and OutValue would be an out or variable parameter of type Double. If the procedure is called DoCalc, our procedure declaration using constant and out parameters is:

```
procedure DoCalc (const InValue: Integer; out OutValue: Double);
```

With a *function*, `InValue` is also a constant or value parameter of type Integer but the role of the `OutValue` parameter is now achieved through *the function's name*. So we have one parameter fewer. To compensate we must *declare the function's name as type Double*. Consequently, if the function is called `OutValue`, the function declaration is:

```
function OutValue (const InValue: Integer): Double;
```

Using a procedure is different from using a function. To call a *procedure*, we simply use the procedure's name followed by the required number, type and sequence of parameters to match the procedure header. Any values calculated by the procedure become available to the calling program through those parameters declared as out or variable parameters. In the case above, the following call would make the value of `OutValue` calculated by the procedure available to subsequent program steps as variable `OutVal`:

```
DoCalc (InVal, OutVal);
```

Because a function call usually acts like a variable's name, we call a function *in an expression*. The function call matching the procedure call immediately above is:

```
OutVal := OutValue (InVal);
```

If we wanted to add 10, say, to the value calculated by the subroutine and call this value `Final`, using the procedure would require two lines:

```
DoCalc (InVal, OutVal);
Final := OutVal + 10;
```

We can do this in only one line using a function, since a function call can be part of an expression:

```
Final := OutValue (InVal) + 10;
```

As we saw earlier in this chapter, a function call can also act as one of the parameters in a nested subroutine call (eg example 13.3 step 2 line 49) or as part of a conditional evaluation (eg in an If statement, as in example 13.2 line 50).

In a procedure we can send several values back if we declare each one as either an out or a variable parameter. We might not need to send any value back at all, in which case we need no out or variable parameters. In a function, we typically send only one value back, through the function call. Although we can also use variable or out parameters with functions, it is good programming practice not to do so unless there are unusual circumstances that require them.

EXAMPLE 13.4) Nested function calls

One of the advantages of using functions is that a function call is similar to a variable. We have already seen this, but perhaps a specific example would help clarify it. We'll use the user interface shown in figure 13.4.

Using standard system functions, we can read the value in the Edit, convert it to an integer, manipulate this value, convert it back to a string,

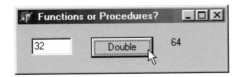

Figure 13.4 Nested function calls

and display it on the Label's Caption in a single statement (line 3 below). Because all of this happens in a single statement, we don't need any local variables to hold intermediate values, which reduces the size and complexity of the event handler.

```
1 procedure TfrmFuncProc.btnDoubleClick(Sender: TObject);
2 begin
3   lblOut.Caption := IntToStr ( StrToInt (edtIn.Text) * 2 );
4 end; // procedure TfrmFuncProc.btnDoubleClick
```

Here we see that using a function's call as though it is a variable can be very useful. First, we use the function call StrToInt(edtIn.Text) to convert the input value to an integer. Because this takes on an integer value, we can then double it. The expression after doubling also has a value, so we can use it as the parameter in the IntToStr function call. This returns a string value which we can assign directly to the Label's Caption.

Although this example uses standard Delphi functions, functions we write can be equally effective. In summary, a function returns a single value. If we require only a single value (whether it is an integer, string or other type) back from a subroutine, using a function is usually a lot more convenient than a corresponding procedure.

EXAMPLE 13.5) Exception handling

Several of the programs in this book do not take any kind of error handling into account, and simply assume that the user will give valid input. If the user does not, that is usually not a disaster because Delphi takes these exceptions into account through its *default exception handling mechanism*.

We have seen exception handling before, most notably in example 6.8 where we used Message Dialogs in the exception handling path. (It may be interesting to read through that example again now.) Mostly, though, we have ignored exceptions. With Delphi's exception handling architecture and its default exception handler, when an exception occurs in a subroutine that does not have a specific exception handler, that subroutine terminates and an exception return occurs to the calling subroutine. If this subroutine has an exception handling path, the exception is steered through it. If not, that subroutine is also abandoned and an exception return happens to its calling subroutine and so on. If the programmer has not included any specific exception handling for a particular exception anywhere in the program, Delphi calls the default exception handler which then displays a message.

To see this for yourself, open the program from example 13.3 step 4. Its ReadCode method looks like this:

```
1 procedure TfrmAccess.ReadCode (out A, B, C: integer);
2 var
3   strValue: string;
4 begin
5   strValue := edtCode.Text;
6   C := StrToInt (strValue[3]);
7   B := StrToInt (strValue[2]);
8   A := StrToInt (strValue[1]);
9 end; // procedure TfrmAccess.ReadCode
```

```
44 procedure TfrmAccess.bmbOKClick(Sender: TObject);
45 var
46    A, B, C: integer;
47 begin
48    ReadCode (A, B, C);
49    ShowAccessStatus (Validate (A, B, C));
50    ResetUI;
51 end; // procedure TfrmAccess.bmbOKClick
```

Let's trace the program's response to an exception. When the user enters an alphabetic string into edtCode, the StrToInt function in line 6 raises an exception. Procedure ReadCode is abandoned and execution returns to the subroutine call (line 48). Because the exception has not yet been handled it is still alive. bmbOKClick does not have any exception handling and so it too is abandoned. There are no higher level calling routines and now Delphi's default exception handler comes into action and displays an exception message (figure 13.5).

This is a very useful ability in a programming language. Before the days of exception handling, one had to include code to handle all possible errors to protect against a program crash. Nowadays we can often leave Delphi's default handler to deal with our program's exceptions. But in this case it is not sufficient, as we see when we test it carefully .

Figure 13.5 Delphi's default exception display with a StrToInt exception

EX 13.5 Testing

Try the following input sequence:

	Code	Status	Input Box	Comments
Step 1	122	Invalid	Cleared	Correct.
Step 2	7122	Proceed	Cleared	Accepted, but should fail the validation (code not 3 characters).
Step 3	abc	No change	Not cleared	Exception message displayed; neither status nor input cleared (figure 13.5).

Both testing steps 2 and 3 point to errors in the program that we'll correct in the remainder of this example.

EX 13.5 STEP 1 Accepting three characters only

Let's deal first with the problem in step 2 above. We could try using an if…then…else construct to test for an invalid length string. But that is quite cumbersome. We are already using an exception handling mechanism, and it would be very neat if we could also use exception handling to deal with an input of fewer or greater than three characters. To do this, we use the `raise` keyword to generate our own exception (lines 6–7 below):

```
1  procedure TfrmAccess.ReadCode (out A, B, C: integer);
2  var
3    strValue: string;
4  begin
5    strValue := edtCode.Text;
6    if length (strValue) <> 3 then
7      raise Exception.Create ('Length Invalid');
8    C := StrToInt (strValue[3]);
9    B := StrToInt (strValue[2]);
10   A := StrToInt (strValue[1]);
11 end; // procedure TfrmAccess.ReadCode
```

Make this change, run the program and repeat the tests. The result is now:

	Code	Status	Input Box	Comments
Step 1	122	Invalid	Cleared	Correct.
Step 2	7122	No change	Not cleared	Exception message displayed; neither status nor input cleared (figure 13.6).
Step 3	abc	No change	Not cleared	Exception message displayed; neither status nor input cleared (figure 13.5).

Figure 13.6 An incorrect length code now generates an exception

Step 2 now gives the same response as step 3, except that we get our own exception message as defined in line 7 (figure 13.6). An incorrect length code now generates an exception, displaying the message we specified in line 7, and no longer generates a valid status. That's a start, but, like the problem with an alphabetic character, it does not generate an Invalid status on the user interface as it should. We'll correct this in step 2.

EX 13.5 STEP 2 Generating an Invalid status

A problem that remains with this program is that when an exception occurs the event handler bmbOKClick does not handle it and so the event handler is abandoned and the display is not updated (ie lines 49 and 50 do not run). We must change bmbOKClick to handle the exception in an orderly way and then update the display accordingly as follows:

```
44  procedure TfrmAccess.bmbOKClick(Sender: TObject);
45  var
46    A, B, C: integer;
47  begin
48    try
49      ReadCode (A, B, C);
50    except
51      A := 0;
52      B := 0;
53      C := 0;
54      ShowMessage ('Recovered from an exception');   // test purposes
55    end;
56    ShowAccessStatus (Validate (A, B, C));
57    ResetUI;
58  end; // procedure TfrmAccess.bmbOKClick
```

We place ReadCode (A, B, C) within a try statement (lines 48–49). If the user enters a 3 digit numerical code there is no exception and execution continues to show the access status and reset the interface (lines 56–57). If, however, the user enters an alphabetic character or a code that is not three digits long an exception occurs in ReadCode, causing an exception return to bmbOKClick. bmbOKClick now has exception handling and so execution is not abandoned but continues in the exception handling path (lines 50–55). Because the parameters could have any values they are all set to zero, which is an invalid code, and then a suitable message is displayed. The end; in line 55 indicates that exception handling is now complete and so normal execution resumes at line 56. The access status is displayed as invalid, because A, B and C now all have the value of zero, and then the interface is reset (line 57). Once an exception has been handled, it is destroyed and so does not invoke Delphi's default exception handler.

An important aspect of exception handling is that an exception can be raised in one place and handled somewhere else. In this version the exceptions are raised either in the StrToInt function or in the ReadCode procedure but are finally handled in the bmbOKClick event handler.

To demonstrate conclusively that the errors we noted above now no longer occur, try the previous tests and then the following sequence:

	Code	Status	Input Box	Comments
Step 1	712	Valid	Cleared	Correct. No default exception handling.
Step 2	7122	Invalid	Cleared	Correct. No default exception handling.
Step 3	712	Valid	Cleared	Correct. No default exception handling.
Step 4	abc	Invalid	Cleared	Correct. No default exception handling.

All correct! Because this is a security application we should remove the error recovery message from the program (line 54 above) before delivering the program to the customer.

EX 13.5 STEP 3 The try...finally construct

We can achieve the same effect as in example 13.5 step 2 in a different way by using the try...finally construct. Try...finally can be used when there is finalisation code that must be executed irrespective of whether or not an exception occurs. In this case, we want ResetUI to run irrespective of whether or not an exception has occurred. So we can wrap a try...finally (lines 48, 55 to 57 below) around a try...except statement (lines 49 to 54) as follows:

```
44 procedure TfrmAccess.bmbOKClick(Sender: TObject);
45 var
46   A, B, C: integer;
47 begin
48   try
49     try
50       ReadCode (A, B, C);
51       ShowAccessStatus (Validate (A, B, C));
52     except
53       ShowAccessStatus (false);  // force error display
```

```
54      end;  // end try...except
55   finally
56      ResetUI;
57   end;  // end try...finally
58 end; // procedure TfrmAccess.bmbOKClick
```

If an exception occurs in the call in line 50 execution continues at line 53, which calls ShowAccessStatus with its parameter set to false. The end; in line 54 terminates the try…except section and the finally in line 55 introduces the code that runs irrespective of whether an exception has occurred or not. This means that Delphi guarantees that ResetUI will always run.

We again give no notification that any exception handling has been performed. Run this program through the test sequences given earlier in this example and verify for yourself that it works correctly.

EX 13.5 STEP 4 Handling the exceptions closer to the source

Returning to example 13.5 step 2, there is only a single statement within the try section (line 49). This coding motif of a single try statement often suggests that we can move the exception handling down into the subroutine called in that single statement, and we can do so here. It's a relatively simple transfer of the exception handling code in bmbOKClick to ReadCode.

```
 1 procedure TfrmAccess.ReadCode (out A, B, C: integer);
 2 { Read the 3 digit value on the TEdit and
 3   return this in the A, B and C parameters }
 4 var
 5    strValue: string;
 6 begin
 7    try
 8       strValue := edtCode.Text;
 9       if length (strValue) <> 3 then
10          raise Exception.Create ('Length Invalid');
11       C := StrToInt (strValue[3]);
12       B := StrToInt (strValue[2]);
13       A := StrToInt (strValue[1]);
14    except
15       A := 0;
16       B := 0;
17       C := 0;
18    end;
19 end; // procedure TfrmAccess.ReadCode

20 ...


44 procedure TfrmAccess.bmbOKClick(Sender: TObject);
45 var
46    A, B, C: integer;
47 begin
48    ReadCode (A, B, C);
49    ShowAccessStatus (Validate (A, B, C));
50    ResetUI;
51 end; // procedure TfrmAccess.bmbOKClick
```

Read Code's exeption handling path, lines 14–18, will handle any exeption that occurs in lines 8 to 13. So by the end of ReadCode all its exceptions have been handled and destroyed. There is no exception return to the calling statement and the rest of the program is unaware that an exception ever occurred.

We again give no notification that any exception handling has been performed. Run this program through the test sequences given earlier in this example and verify for yourself that it works correctly.

This example presents several alternative solutions to the same problem, and the programmer needs to select whichever is best for a particular programming problem.

Exception handling can become considerably more sophisticated. One can raise and test for specific exceptions instead of the general approach we use here. Exception handling may also be spread over several routines in which case it is necessary to reraise an exception after the preliminary handling. (Inserting the statement `raise` between lines 17 and 18 above would reraise the exception and cause an exception return to the calling routine.) Delphi's online Help gives further details on exception handling.

REVIEW

Delphi Pascal has two types of subroutine: procedures and functions. Values are passed from the subroutine call to the subroutine through value, constant or variable parameters. A function returns a single value through the function call, whereas a procedure returns values to the calling statement through variable or out parameters. A function call can therefore appear either in an assignment statement or within an expression. Functions are intended for calculating a single answer, returning this through the call. (A function can also use variable and out parameters, though this often defeats the benefit of using functions.) Since the function call itself carries the return value, the call can participate in expressions (eg example 13.4).

In this chapter we saw how subroutines can allow us to accommodate future changes by 'plugging in' new versions of specific subroutines while leaving the rest of the program unchanged. As long as the headers of the subroutines remain the same the inner workings can change without the calling subroutines needing to change or even being aware that changes have been made.

Subroutines also facilitate re-use, since the existing subroutines can be used as appropriate in new programs, so reducing the development time by providing well-tested software to build on.

Delphi has an exception handling mechanism which we can use to ensure that our programs handle errors, such as invalid input, in sensible ways. Some standard Delphi subroutines, such as `StrToInt`, raise an exception when an error occurs. If our program does not handle these exceptions Delphi's default exception handler will, greatly reducing the chance of the program crashing under error conditions. We can provide our own exception handling through the `try...except` and `try...finally` constructs, and can raise our own exceptions using the `raise` keyword and the `Exception.Create` method call.

IMPORTANT CONCEPTS

Programming fundamentals

Assigning a value to the function call: Within the body of a function either the automatic variable `Result` or the function's name must be assigned a value of the same type as the function's result type. This value will be available to the calling statement. Without this assignment in the function body, the call receives no value from the function.

Function definition: Function definitions have the form:

```
function FunctionName (ParameterList): ResultType;
const
   Constant declarations                {for local constants}
var
   Variable declarations                {for local variables}
begin
   FunctionBody
end;
```

Handling an exception: Any exception that occurs aborts normal processing and diverts to the appropriate exception handling path as programmed through the `try...except` construct in the same routine, or if that does not exist, in successively higher level calling routines. If an exception is not handled it reaches the top calling level and is then handled by Delphi's default exception handler. After an exception is handled, normal processing resumes.

Raising an exception: A programmer can raise an exception under specific conditions through the `raise` keyword.

Receiving values from a subroutine: Use out or variable parameters for a procedure, or the function call for a function. A procedure need not return a value. A function always returns a single value. Both types of subroutine can raise exceptions for error handling while procedures can also provide error codes through out or variable parameters.

Soft clicking: Many components allow the program to call their OnClick event handler through their `Click` method. If there is no matching OnClick event handler but an Action OnExecute event handler exists, it is called.

Subroutine: Any procedure or function, whether or not it is a method.

Subroutines and re-use: Examples 13.2 and 13.3 illustrate how subroutines promote re-use and how there might be unexpected side-effects, such as the need for revised error handling.

Transferring values to a subroutine: Through value, constant and variable parameters, though variable parameters should generally not be used with functions.

Using procedures and functions

Form of header (example with one return value)

Procedure
```
procedure DoCalc (InValue: Double; var OutValue: Double);
```
(using the traditional value and variable parameters)

Function
```
function OutValue (InValue: Double): Double;
```

Form of call (examples with one return value)

1. Procedure
```
DoCalc (InVal, OutVal);
Temp := OutVal + 10;
```

   Function
```
Temp := OutValue (InVal) + 10;
```

2. Procedure
```
DoCalc (InVal, OutVal);
if OutVal = 0.0 then …;
```

   Function
```
if OutValue(InVal) = 0.0 then …;
```

3. Procedure
```
DoCalc (InVal, OutVal);
DisplayValue (OutVal);
```

   Function
```
DisplayValue (OutValue (InVal));
```

Data transfer

Procedure   Use value, constant or variable parameters to transfer values into a procedure. Use out or variable parameters to transfer values from a procedure to a calling statement. Assign values to the out or variable parameters in the body of the procedure.

Function   Use value or constant parameters to transfer values into function. Transfer a single value from the function to the calling statement by assigning a value to the Result variable (created automatically by Delphi) or to the function name. Usually no variable or out parameters are used, although they can be used when needed.

Error checking and validation

Procedure   Use one (or more) parameter to return error code(s) or use exeption-handling principles.

Function   Use exception-handling principles.

Which type of subroutine to use

Procedure   Performing general operations such as user interface operations. Calculating none, two or more values, sometimes one value.

Function   Calculating one value to use in an expression or a conditional evaluation. Generally should not do I/O directly as this restricts re-use.

- To bring together a sequence of operations in one place, and then to call this subroutine whenever the sequence is needed.

- To perform a clearly defined arithmetic operation.

- To separate different types of activity (eg a procedure for a user interface operation or a function to perform an arithmetic or mathematical calculation).

Differences between event handlers, methods and subroutines

	Event handlers	Delphi's methods	Programmer methods	General Subroutines
Type	Procedure	Procedure or function	Procedure or function	Procedure or function
Initiation	Event: fixed format	Program code	Program code	Program code
Action	Program code	Predetermined	Program code	Program code
Status	A method of the Form	Part of a class	Part of a class	Independent

NEW DELPHI FEATURES

Exception handling in Delphi

`raise`
To raise an exception, the programmer creates the exception and supplies an identifying string within a raise statement:

```
raise Exception.Create ('String');
```

`try ...`
`except ...`
`end;`
Exceptions are handled within try...except constructs.

```
try
    StatementBlock
except
    ExceptionBlock
end;
```

A `try...except` construct executes the statements in the StatementBlock. If no exception is raised, the ExceptionBlock is ignored and processing continues after the `try...except` construct.

If an exception is raised in the StatementBlock, either by a raise statement or by a subroutine called within the StatementBlock, processing is interrupted and execution passes to the ExceptionBlock. At the conclusion of the ExceptionBlock the exception is destroyed and normal processing continues after the `try...except` construct.

When an exception occurs outside a try...except construct, processing is interrupted and the exception is passed to the calling routine.

`try ...`
`finally ...`
`end;`
Sometimes specific operations must occur whether or not an exception occurs. In this situation use a `try...finally` statement.

```
try
    StatementBlock
finally
    FinalBlock
end;
```

A try...finally construct executes the statements in the StatementBlock. If no exception is raised processing continues through the FinalBlock.

If an exception is raised in the StatementBlock, either by a raise statement or by a subroutine called within the StatementBlock, the remainder of the StatementBlock is aborted and execution passes to the FinalBlock. At the conclusion of the FinalBlock the most recent exception is not destroyed but passed to the calling routine. If the exception is to be handled locally, use a try...except construct within the StatementBlock of the try...finally construct (eg example 13.5 step 3).

TBitBtn		
Methods	Click	Simulates a mouse click, as if the user had clicked the BitBtn. When Click is called, any code attached to the OnClick event is executed.

PROBLEMS

PROBLEM 13.1) Safe spraying conditions

Figure 13.7 Determining safe crop-spraying conditions

In a certain area of the country crops have been severely infected by a disease. The Department of Agriculture has started spraying the crops from an aeroplane in an attempt to eradicate the disease. For safety and other reasons, this spraying can occur only if the temperature is greater than 20 °C, if the humidity is between 25 and 65 percent, and if the wind speed is at most 15 kph (kilometres per hour). Shown below is a partial program which helps people decide whether weather conditions are suitable for spraying or not. If conditions are not suitable, the text 'DO NOT SPRAY' is displayed in large letters against a red background. If conditions are suitable, the text 'OK to spray' is displayed on a green background.

- How can function TempOK below be simplified?
- Complete this program by filling in the appropriate code for functions WindOK and HumidOK and for the event handler bmbResetClick.

```
function TfrmSpraying.TempOK : Boolean;
begin
  if sedTemp.Value > 20 then
    Result := True
  else
    Result := False;
end; {end function TfrmSpraying.TempOK}

function TfrmSpraying.WindOK : Boolean;
begin
  {.. Insert appropriate code here ..}
end; {end function TfrmSpraying.WindOK}

function TfrmSpraying.HumidOK : Boolean;
begin
  {.. Insert appropriate code here ..}
end; {end function TfrmSpraying.HumidOK}

procedure TfrmSpraying.btnEvaluateClick(Sender: TObject);
begin
  if TempOK and WindOK and HumidOK then
  begin
    lblDecision.Caption := 'OK to spray';
    lblDecision.Color := clGreen;
  end
  else
  begin
    lblDecision.Caption := 'DO NOT SPRAY';
    lblDecision.Color := clRed;
  end;
end;

procedure TfrmSpraying.bmbResetClick(Sender: TObject);
begin
  {.. Insert appropriate code here ..}
end;
```

- Work out a set of test cases that will check each condition for safe spraying.
- Enter the full version of the program and then check that it works correctly by using these test cases.

PROBLEM 13.2) Mortgage bond application

- Write a program for a mass housing development scheme.
- There are two criteria for being accepted into the scheme. First, an applicant's annual income must be R24000 or more and R60000 or less. Second, the applicant must be at least 18 years old.
- Your program should match the screen display in figure 13.8. It must use a function to assess whether the applicant meets the criteria.
- Draw up a set of test cases testing each of the boundary conditions (R23000/R24000, R60000/R61000, 17/18) and check that the program works correctly.

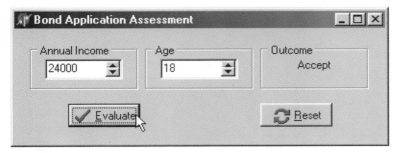

Figure 13.8 Mass housing bond application

PROBLEM 13.3) Converting a procedure to a function

- Convert problem 12.3 to use a function.
- This means that procedure AdmissionPrice needs some changes to the header and to assign the value that goes back to the calling statement.
- The two event handlers will need slight modification to call the function instead of the procedure.

PROBLEM 13.4) Procedure/function criteria (1)

Based on the guidelines given in this chapter for deciding whether a subroutine should be a procedure or a function, explain whether or not procedure Convert in problem 12.4 should be changed to a function.

PROBLEM 13.5) Procedure/function criteria (2)

- Using example 13.2 as a guide, decide which (if any) of the procedures in problem 12.7 should preferably be functions and then modify the program accordingly.
- Use the same test cases to check that the modified version of the program still works correctly.

PROBLEM 13.6) Improved validation for Mr Kite

The Validate code in examples 13.2 and 13.3 is very simple – any three digits that add up to either ten or twenty will work. A friend of Mr Kite's, George Smiley, suggested a more sophisticated validation method. If the expression

$$((103 \times A + 17 \times B + C) \bmod 43) - 19$$

is equal to zero, validation must be True. For all other values, validation must be False. George Smiley has given the following set of test case:

Code	Validate
012	True
123	False
279	False
384	True

a   Starting with the version of the program in example 13.5 step 3, change the Validate function to use this new expression.

b   Will this new function work unchanged in the previous versions of this program? If not, what other changes are needed in the programs to be able to use the new version of Validate? If it will work unchanged, what programming principle does this illustrate?

c   As a further upgrade the interface must be reset automatically after the status display (Proceed or Invalid code) has been on display for two seconds.

d   Extend this program or write a new program to generate all the valid codes that this new Validate method will accept.

PROBLEM 13.7) Convert a procedure to a function

Convert example 12.9 step 4 to use a function rather than a procedure.

CHAPTER 14

Debugging and Testing

PURPOSE OF THIS CHAPTER

When a computer is executing a program, we cannot easily see what it is actually doing inside its little grey box. How does it carry out the programming instructions? What happens as it executes each program statement? We need to find ways of following a program's operation while it is running. This can help us both to gain a better understanding of how the program works and to track down errors. We demonstrate both these aspects in this chapter.

There are several different ways to follow a running program. We can put in special, temporary programming statements that announce what is happening by using a temporary ShowMessage statement or by writing to a Label's or form's Caption.

However, most modern programming languages allow more sophisticated tracing of a program's operation through built-in *debuggers*. Delphi has a particularly good debugger and we look at some of its simpler capabilities in this chapter.

Three concepts are basic to a debugger:
o   breakpoints;
o   controlled execution (eg single-stepping), and
o   variable evaluation.

The programmer places a breakpoint on a particular line of the program. Then, when the running program reaches this breakpoint, the program 'breaks' and displays the source code at the breakpoint. The programmer can then step through the program line by line from there, checking the values of important variables and seeing the route program execution follows.

Talking about debugging leads naturally to a discussion of what kinds of errors are possible and how to test for them, and so this chapter ends by looking at these two aspects.

Preliminary

Delphi uses an 'optimizing compiler'. This means that it sometimes makes slight changes to the executable code to help the program run faster without changing its functionality. However, this also means that program execution (and program tracing) is sometimes slightly different from what we would expect.

For this set of examples it is a good idea to switch the optimization off. Use the menu sequence Project | Options... | Compiler, make sure there is no tick either alongside Optimization in the Code generation section or next to Default at the bottom-left corner (figures 14.1.a and 14.1.b) and then click OK.

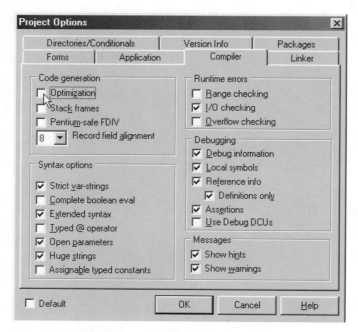

Figure 14.1.a Disabling compiler optimization in Delphi 4 to 7

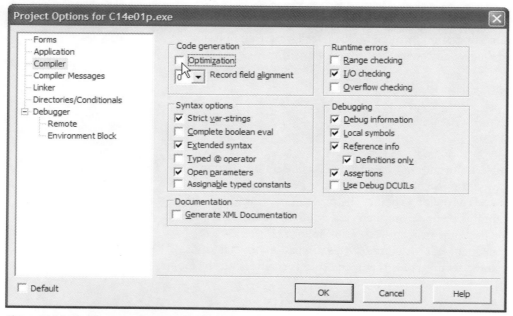

Figure 14.1.b Disabling compiler optimization in Delphi 8

After doing this, you are all set to go.

EXAMPLE 14.1 Breakpoints and tracing

While the general public, when thinking about astronomy, is familiar with the concept of a 'light year', professional astronomers tend to work in terms of 'parsecs'. One parsec is 3.26 light years. We will write a very simple program to convert parsecs to light years and use this to explore Delphi's debugger. (Don't worry if you don't know the relationship between light years and parsecs, it's not important for this example. Just concentrate on the debugger.) The program has the screen layout shown in figure 14.2 and the following Component properties:

Figure 14.2 The test program for debugging

Component	Property	Value
Form1	Name	frmSingleStep
	Caption	Single Step Demo
GroupBox	Name	gpbParSec
	Caption	ParSecs
Edit1	Name	edtParSec
	Text	<Blank>
Button1	Name	btnParSec
	Caption	Convert
Label1	Name	lblLightYr
	Caption	<Blank>

The button has an OnClick event handler to read a value from edtParSec, convert it to light years and display it as lblLightYear's Caption.

- Before reading any further, write this OnClick procedure.

EX 14.1 STEP 1 btnParSec's OnClick handler

- Double-click on btnParSec and enter this event handler:

```
1 procedure TfrmSingleStep.btnParSecClick(Sender: TObject);
2 var
3    ParSecs, LightYears: double;
4    LightYrStr: String;
5 begin
6    ParSecs := StrToFloat(edtParSec.Text);
7    LightYears := 3.26 * ParSecs;
8    LightYrStr := FloatToStrF (LightYears, ffFixed, 15, 2);
9    lblLightYr.Caption := LightYrStr + ' light years';
10   edtParSec.SetFocus;
11 end; // end procedure TFrmSingleStep.btnParSecClick
```

- Save the files as C14e01u and C14e01p. Run the program, check that it works properly and then return to the design-time environment.

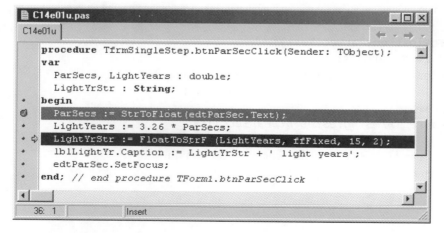

```
C14e01u.pas
C14e01u
procedure TfrmSingleStep.btnParSecClick(Sender: TObject);
var
   ParSecs, LightYears : double;
   LightYrStr : String;
begin
   ParSecs := StrToFloat(edtParSec.Text);
   LightYears := 3.26 * ParSecs;
   LightYrStr := FloatToStrF (LightYears, ffFixed, 15, 2);
   lblLightYr.Caption := LightYrStr + ' light years';
   edtParSec.SetFocus;
end; // end procedure TForm1.btnParSecClick
34: 1                    Insert
```

Figure 14.3 Setting a breakpoint

EX 14.1 STEP 2   Setting breakpoints

You can place a breakpoint on a line in several ways.
- Place the cursor on the first line after `begin`.
- Now either click in the space to the left of the line (the 'gutter', figure 14.3) or select the menu sequence Run | Add Breakpoint. For versions up to Delphi 7, then select New. For Delphi 8 select Source Breakpoint | OK. Otherwise press <F5>. The line with the breakpoint is now highlighted.
- Run the program as before.
- Enter a value, say 2, into the Edit component and click the Convert button. If the breakpoint is set up correctly, control returns to the editor with the cursor on the breakpoint line and a small green arrow to the left of it.
- Press <F7> to single step once. The green arrow jumps to the next line.
- Press <F7> again and the green arrow jumps to the next line. Each time you press <F7> you single step the program to the next line of source code to be executed and so you can go line by line through your program while it is running. (But don't go any further quite yet!)

The little green arrow shows the next line to be executed (figure 14.4). So, at this point in the program, the first two program lines have been executed but the `FloatToStrF` line has not yet been executed. This means that the variables

```
C14e01u.pas
C14e01u
procedure TfrmSingleStep.btnParSecClick(Sender: TObject);
var
   ParSecs, LightYears : double;
   LightYrStr : String;
begin
   ParSecs := StrToFloat(edtParSec.Text);
   LightYears := 3.26 * ParSecs;
   LightYrStr := FloatToStrF (LightYears, ffFixed, 15, 2);
   lblLightYr.Caption := LightYrStr + ' light years';
   edtParSec.SetFocus;
end; // end procedure TForm1.btnParSecClick
36: 1                    Insert
```

Figure 14.4 After single stepping twice

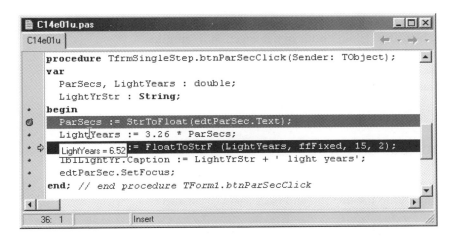

Figure 14.5.a The tool-tip evaluation showing the value of a variable

`Parsecs` and `LightYears` have values but `LightYrStr` and
`lblLightYr.Caption` do not yet have new values because those lines have not
yet been executed.

The debugger allows us to see the value of each variable.

- Run the mouse pointer over one of the variables that have already been
  evaluated and let it rest there. A little yellow box, like that used for Hints
  on the Component/Tool palette, pops up to show the value of the variable
  (figure 14.5.a). This is called 'Tool-tip evaluation'.

Sliding the mouse pointer over each variable name in turn gives us the following
variable values:

```
Text part of edtParSec.Text = '2'
Parsecs = 2
LightYears = 6.52
LightYrStr = ''
Caption part of lblLightYr.Caption = ''
```

Figure 14.5.b Delphi 8's Local
variables window

In addition to the tool-tip evaluation Delphi 8 displays a *Local variables*
window in the middle of the left side of the screen. This shows the values of
all the variables in the event handler (figure 14.5.b).

Notice two things here:

- The value displayed depends on the variable type. `Parsecs` and `LightYears`
  are numbers (integer and double), so they are shown as normal numeric
  values. `edtParSec.Text`, `LightYrStr` and `lblLightYr.Caption` are
  strings, so their values appear within single quotes.
- The first three variables have already been evaluated, so their values are
  available. Program execution has not yet run far enough to assign values to
  `LightYrStr` and `lblLightYr.Caption`, so they are shown as empty
  strings.

- We could continue single stepping through this program, but for now just
  press <F9> to resume normal, full-speed execution. The program form
  comes to the top and displays the converted value.
- Repeat this again with other values until you feel comfortable with these
  debugging concepts.

Example 14.1 summary: In this section we see how to inspect a program's operation while it is running by using Delphi's built-in debugger. At its simplest, a debugger allows the programmer to set a breakpoint. This causes the program to pause at that particular line when the program is running. From there, the programmer can inspect variable values and can single-step the program.

EXAMPLE 14.2) Method calls and watches

We'll modify the previous program to use a simple method. Then we'll trace the program flow from the method call to the method and back again. We'll also monitor values by using a *Watch List*.

Of course, for a typical programming task this is too simple to justify using a separate method. But for now it's just the right size for us to be able to work on the underlying concepts without getting bogged down by excessive programming detail. We'll also use a procedure rather than a function so that we can use the debugger to see the flow of data with the different kinds of parameter, particularly with the out parameter type.

EX 14.2 STEP 1 Introducing a method

We'll modify the previous program to include a method that converts parsecs to light years and then call this method from the event handler.

- Start by declaring the procedure in the private section of the class's declaration:

```
type
  TfrmSingleStep = class(TForm)
    btnParSec: TButton;
    lblLightYr: TLabel;
    gpbParSec: TGroupBox;
    edtParSec: TEdit;
    procedure btnParSecClick(Sender: TObject);
  private
    procedure ConvertProc (const ParSecs: double;
                           out LightYr: double);
  public
    { Public declarations }
  end;  // end TfrmSingleStep = class(TForm)
```

- Now define the method and call it from the event handler:

```
1 procedure TfrmSingleStep.ConvertProc (const ParSecs: double;
2                                       out LightYr: double);
3 begin
4   LightYr := 3.26 * ParSecs;
5 end; // end procedure TfrmSingleStep.ConvertProc

6 procedure TfrmSingleStep.btnParSecClick(Sender: TObject);
7 var
8   ParSecs, LightYears: double;
9   LightYrStr: String;
10 begin
```

```
11    ParSecs := StrToFloat(edtParSec.Text);
12    ConvertProc (ParSecs, LightYears);        // NEW, method call
13    LightYrStr := FloatToStrF (LightYears, ffFixed, 15, 2);
14    lblLightYr.Caption := LightYrStr + ' light years';
15    edtParSec.SetFocus;
16 end; // end procedure TfrmSingleStep.btnParSecClick
```

Since the process of structuring a program by introducing methods can be a bit confusing, let's use this opportunity for a review.

o To create the method (lines 1-5) we have taken existing code – in this case just the single line for calculating LightYears (line 7, example 14.1) – and packaged it in a procedure 'wrapper'. This wrapper consists of the procedure header (the procedure name and a list of parameters, lines 1-2 above) along with begin and end statements.

o We must be careful in creating a procedure's parameter list (lines 1-2):
   In this case, the value of ParSecs must come into the procedure. It does not need to be sent out again. So it must be either a value or a constant parameter. We'll make it a constant parameter. In the list of parameters in the procedure header we write const in front of ParSecs.

   The calling method does not know the value for the equivalent light years. This new method must therefore calculate the value and send it to the calling method. Whenever a method sends a value out it must use either a variable or an out parameter. We'll use an out parameter. That is why there is an out in front of LightYr in the parameter list.

o We have used the variable LightYears in the calling method (ie in btnParSecsClick, line 12) but LightYr in the method itself (line 2). The names do not have to be the same in the calling statement and the called method since parameters are transferred on the basis of their order. The names must, however, be consistent within the calling method and within the called method.

• Run this new version of the program and see that, from the user's perspective, it operates in the same way as example 14.1.

EX 14.2 STEP 2   Tracing flow to a method and back

• Now we can go on to use the debugger to trace the program flow, but first make sure that compiler optimization is switched off as described at the start of this chapter.

• Place a breakpoint on the same statement as in the previous section (ie line 11 above, as shown by the bar in the screen display of figure 14.6).

• Run the program, enter a value for ParSecs (say 2) and click on the Convert button. As before, the program pauses at the breakpoint and displays the code (line 11).

• Press <F7> to step the small green arrow to the next line.

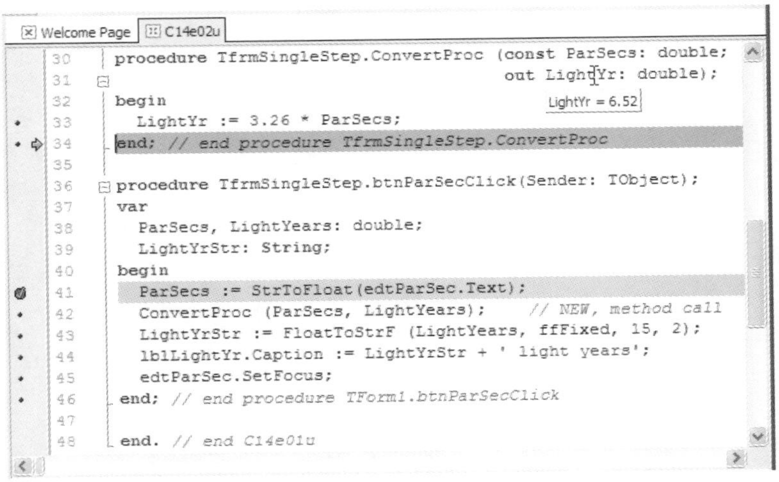

```
    ⌧ Welcome Page    C14e02u
30        procedure TfrmSingleStep.ConvertProc (const ParSecs: double;
31   ⊟                                                out LightYr: double);
32        begin                                       LightYr = 6.52
33           LightYr := 3.26 * ParSecs;
34   ⇨ end; // end procedure TfrmSingleStep.ConvertProc
35
36   ⊟ procedure TfrmSingleStep.btnParSecClick(Sender: TObject);
37        var
38           ParSecs, LightYears: double;
39           LightYrStr: String;
40        begin
41   ⌀       ParSecs := StrToFloat(edtParSec.Text);
42   •       ConvertProc (ParSecs, LightYears);        // NEW, method call
43           LightYrStr := FloatToStrF (LightYears, ffFixed, 15, 2);
44   •       lblLightYr.Caption := LightYrStr + ' light years';
45   •       edtParSec.SetFocus;
46   •    end; // end procedure TForm1.btnParSecClick
47
48        end. // end C14e01u
```

Figure 14.6 Tracing through a procedure (in Delphi 8)

- Press <F7> again. Execution now jumps from the btnParSecsClick procedure (line 12) to the method because of the method call.
- Press <F7> to move to the end; statement (figure 14.6).

Running the mouse pointer over the different variable and parameter names shows their current values as before. In figure 14.6 we see that LightYr has a value of 6.52.

Pressing <F7> again causes execution to jump back to the btnParSecsClick procedure and to continue at the next valid program statement (line 13). Run the mouse pointer over the variables in btnParSecsClick. You'll notice that LightYears has the value 6.52 as shown in figure 14.7. This is the value that was calculated in procedure ConvertProc as LightYr (figure 14.6).

Using the debugger, we have been able to trace the flow of the parameter ParSecs from the btnParSecsClick to the ConvertProc procedures. The ConvertProc procedure used the value of ParSecs to calculate a value for LightYr. This value was then sent to the btnParSecsClick procedure as the parameter LightYears. The arrows overlaid on the screen (figure 14.7) illustrate this flow. The heavy straight arrows show the parameter flow from the call to the method and back again. The light, curved arrows show the flow within the method.

Press <F9> to end single stepping and resume running the program normally.

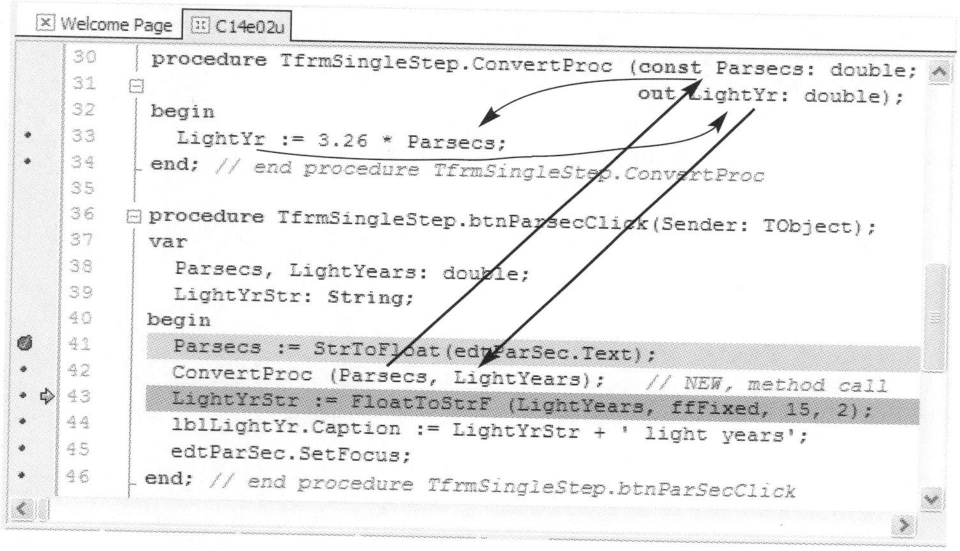

```
  │ ☒ Welcome Page │ ▥ C14e02u │
  │    30  │   procedure TfrmSingleStep.ConvertProc (const Parsecs: double;
  │    31  │ ⊟                                          out LightYr: double);
  │    32  │   begin
• │    33  │     LightYr := 3.26 * Parsecs;
• │    34  └   end; // end procedure TfrmSingleStep.ConvertProc
  │    35  │
  │    36  ⊟ procedure TfrmSingleStep.btnParSecClick(Sender: TObject);
  │    37  │   var
  │    38  │     Parsecs, LightYears: double;
  │    39  │     LightYrStr: String;
  │    40  │   begin
❂ │    41  │     Parsecs := StrToFloat(edtParSec.Text);
• │    42  │     ConvertProc (Parsecs, LightYears);    // NEW, method call
⇨ │    43  │     LightYrStr := FloatToStrF (LightYears, ffFixed, 15, 2);
• │    44  │     lblLightYr.Caption := LightYrStr + ' light years';
• │    45  │     edtParSec.SetFocus;
• │    46  └   end; // end procedure TfrmSingleStep.btnParSecClick
```

Figure 14.7 The flow of parameters

EX 14.2 STEP 3 Setting the Watch List

During a debug session it is sometimes convenient to display the values of selected variables constantly rather than needing to run the mouse pointer over them. Delphi 8 offers the Local variables window (figure 14.5.b) and that is often sufficient. But if you are working in Delphi 7 or earlier or need more control in Delphi 8 one can use the *Watch List*.

- Place the mouse pointer over ParSecs in the code window and press <Ctrl+F5> to enter it into the Watch List. (Alternatively you can right click

on a variable and select Debug | Add Watch at Cursor as in figures 14.10 and 14.11, or use the menu sequence Run | Add Watch.)
- Do the same after placing the pointer over `LightYears` and then over `LightYr`.
- Now run the program, single stepping through it.

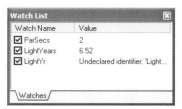

Figure 14.8.a Delphi 7's Watch List after returning from the procedure

The Watch List displays the values of the selected parameters. At first these values are garbage because they have not yet been initialized but the values are updated as we move from line to line. Within the ConvertProc method, `ParSecs` shows the value of the `ParSecs` *parameter*. `LightYears` is shown as being an undeclared identifier, since this name has not been declared in the ConvertProc method (figure 14.8.b). When we return to the event handler, `ParSecs` and `LightYears` show the values of the *local variables* declared for the event handler and parameter `LightYr` appears as an undeclared identifier as we would expect (figure 14.8.a).

Figure 14.8.b Delphi 8's Watch List just before returning from the procedure

EX 14.2 STEP 4 Tracing into, stepping over, and other niceties

So far we have used <F7> to step through our programs. <F7> is the Trace Into command and is also available from the Run menu item on the system menu. As you can see from this menu, there are other tracing options too:
- ○ <F9> Run (ie resume normal operation)
- ○ <F8> Step Over
- ○ <F4> Run to Cursor.

Figure 14.9 Speed bar controls

Trace Into, Step Over and Run are also available from the Speed bar (figure 14.9), as the pop-up hints and the glyphs show.

The arrow icon, equivalent to <F9>, is Run; the next is Pause, followed by Trace Into (<F7>) and then Step Over (<F8>). The Step Over operation ignores procedure and function calls.
- To see this, run the program again if it is not already running, enter a value for `ParSecs` and click on Convert.
- This time, instead of pressing <F7>, press <F8> (or click on the Step Over icon on the Speed bar or use the menu sequence Run | Step Over) to move through the program. You will see that now it steps over the procedure call, going on to the next valid statement in the `btnParSecsClick` procedure.
- Press <F9> or the Run icon to resume normal operation.
- Experiment with <F4> Run to Cursor also.
- Click the right-hand mouse button in the editor window to pop-up a menu (figure 14.10). Select Debug to give yourself convenient access to some of the debug operations (figure 14.11).

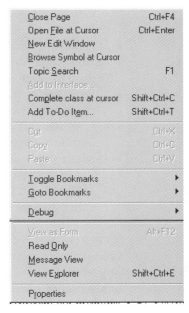

Figure 14.10 Debug options on the Run menu

EX 14.2 STEP 5 Value and variable parameters

In example 12.8 we looked at the differences between value and variable parameters and the confusing errors that can happen if they are not used correctly. Similar comments apply to const and out parameters too.
- To see the effect of not using parameters types properly, remove the `const` and `out` from ConvertProc's parameter list in both the type declaration and the procedure definition header:

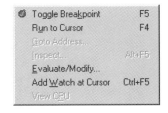

Figure 14.11 The Debug menu

```
type
  TfrmSingleStep = class(TForm)
    btnParSec: TButton;
    lblLightYr: TLabel;
    gpbParSec: TGroupBox;
    edtParSec: TEdit;
    procedure btnParSecClick(Sender: TObject);
  private
    procedure ConvertProc (ParSecs: double;    // remove const
                           LightYr: double);    // remove out
  public
    { Public declarations }
  end;  // end TfrmSingleStep = class(TForm)
...

procedure TfrmSingleStep.ConvertProc (ParSecs: double; LightYr: double);
{no const or out keywords}
begin
  LightYr := 3.26 * ParSecs;
end; // end procedure TfrmSingleStep.ConvertProc
```

- Check that compiler optimisation is still switched off as described at the beginning of this chapter. In Delphi 8, switch off the compiler's compatibility warnings. Use the menu sequence Project | Options | Compiler messages and then uncheck the Platform Unit checkbox. You can leave the Platform Symbol checkbox checked.
- Run the program, enter a value (eg 2) and click on Convert.
- Now single-step using Trace Into (<F7>, the menu sequence or the icon) until the end; statement of procedure ConvertProc.
- From the Watch List or by placing the mouse pointer on top of LightYr check that its value is correct (eg if ParSecs is 2, LightYr should be 6.52).
- Compare this value with the previous run (figure 14.6); you will see that so far it looks fine.
- Single step again to return from the ConvertProc procedure to the next line in the btnParSecsClick procedure. Now check the value of LightYears. Depending on the version of the Delphi compiler the value is either garbage (figure 14.12) or zero.

Figure 14.12 The Watch List after returning from the procedure without the out parameter

If ParSecs was 2, LightYears should of course be 6.52, as was calculated in ConvertProc (figure 14.8). But, because we removed the out from the procedure's parameter list, this value did not pass from ConvertProc to the btnParSecsClick procedure, and so LightYears has an incorrect value.

As you can see from the box below the editor, Delphi let us know that something was wrong.

o It issued the warning that the variable LightYears might not have been initialized. This is because LightYears does not receive any value if it is not linked to an out (or a variable) parameter.

o It also gave us the Hint that the value assigned to LightYr in ConvertProc is never used. Since without the out it is no longer an out parameter, this value is not sent on to the calling procedure, so it simply disappears when the ConvertProc procedure ends.

- Press <F9> or the Run icon to resume normal operation. The value displayed in the label is the same incorrect value that appeared in the Watch List.

- Put the out back into ConvertProc's parameter list in front of LightYr and then run and test the program again. Once again it works correctly. Leaving out either the out or the var keyword for parameters that must supply a value to the calling statement is quite easy to do by mistake. This can lead to errors that can be difficult to track down, so watch out for this in your programming.

EX 14.2 STEP 6 Parameter order

Let's use the debugger to look at the importance of parameter order.
- To do this, make sure that you have corrected the error introduced in step 4 (ie reinsert the const and out parameters in the type declaration and in line 1), then change the parameter order in the method call (line 12):

```
1 procedure TfrmSingleStep.ConvertProc (const ParSecs: double;
2                                         out LightYr: double);
3 begin
4    LightYr := 3.26 * ParSecs;
5 end; // end procedure TfrmSingleStep.ConvertProc


6 procedure TfrmSingleStep.btnParSecClick(Sender: TObject);
7 var
8    ParSecs, LightYears : double;
9    LightYrStr: String;
10 begin
11    ParSecs := StrToFloat(edtParSec.Text);
12    ConvertProc (LightYears, ParSecs); // WRONG ORDER FOR TESTING
13    LightYrStr := FloatToStrF (LightYears, ffFixed, 15, 2);
14    lblLightYr.Caption := LightYrStr + ' light years';
15    edtParSec.SetFocus;
16 end; // end procedure TfrmSingleStep.btnParSecClick
```

Do you see the problem we have just created for ourselves? The situation is like this:
o The procedure header has ParSecs first then LightYr:

```
procedure TfrmSingleStep.ConvertProc (const ParSecs: double;
                                       out LightYr: double);
```

o The procedure call in the btnParSecsClick procedure has LightYears first, then ParSecs:

```
ConvertProc (LightYears, ParSecs);
```

This is wrong! Because Delphi transfers parameters in order, the procedure call transfers LightYears in btnParSecsClick to ParSecs in ConvertProc and receives LightYr from ConvertProc as ParSecs in btnParSecsClick. Since the *parameter order does not match* between the procedure header and the procedure call, the parameters get swopped around and our answer is nonsense.
- Run the program to see this happen for yourself. Single-step through the program and check the values at different stages to see the problems this swapping of the parameter order causes. In this case, the parameters are both of type double, so the compiler can't pick up the error directly.

However, Delphi once again warns that LightYears might not have been initialized.

- Correct this program by changing the parameters in the procedure call so that again they match the order in the procedure header. The call should once again be:

```
ConvertProc (ParSecs, LightYears);  {correct order to match header}
```

Additional Debug features

The Delphi debugger has considerably more power than just these features, and once you are familiar with what we covered, we recommend that you use online Help to discover further possibilities, which are useful in more demanding situations, such as conditional breakpoints (based on counts or specific conditions), viewing the call stack and modifying values while the program is running.

Types of error

Debugging is about tracking down errors in a program. In this section we look at the different kinds of error that occur in programming. In the next section we look at systematic ways to test for these errors.

We can divide errors into four main kinds: compilation errors, run-time errors, errors of logic and rounding errors. To see how these affect us, we'll discuss them in the context of writing a program.

When we have written some code and then press the Run button two things happen:

- Delphi compiles the code we have written. Compilation involves checking for errors (which are reported to the programmer) and, if there are no errors, converting the code into machine code. (This is the .exe file that one can run from outside the IDE.)
- If compilation is successful (ie no errors), Delphi then runs the compiled files (the .exe file) to start the program

Compilation errors are picked up by the compiler at compile-time and occur if we break any of the rules of the language (syntax errors) such as leaving out a semi-colon at the end of a statement or spelling a variable name incorrectly. (These are like the spelling and grammar errors that a word processor can pick up.)

Run-time errors (or exceptions) are errors which occur while the program is running. For example, consider the following statement:

```
x := StrToInt(edtValue.Text);
```

If the user enters a valid integer in edtValue, no error occurs. However, if the user enters an invalid integer (such as 4.5), a run-time error is generated. Many run-time errors can be managed using exception handling.

Here is another example of a run-time error:

```
x := 0;
Ans := 5 DIV x;
```

This will compile without errors, but will generate a 'Division by zero' run-time error.

Errors in logic are not reported either by the compiler or at run-time. The program runs, but gives incorrect results. Errors in logic occur when there is a problem in the meaning of your Delphi code. Using the analogy of a spelling and grammar checker in a word processor, logic errors are like the sentences which pass the tests but do not make sense, such as 'The boy ran the cat.' The word processor will accept this sentence, although a human reader will know that it does not make sense. As an example of a logic error consider the following statements:

```
ans := sqr (x);
ShowMessage ('Square root of x is: ' + IntToStr(ans));
```

The first statement calculates the *square* of a number and then the message claims that it is the *square root*. The compiler will not report any error, but the program produces output that does not make sense.

Consider another example of a logic error. We need to check if a variable x is between 5 and 10. The code below will not report any error, but the program will give the incorrect output.

```
if (x > 5) or (x < 10) then      // should be AND, not OR
```

Logic errors are often difficult to find and fix. If we do not test programs thoroughly (more on this later), we might not even realise that there is an error. If a program produces incorrect results apparently for no reason, a good strategy is to step through it using the debugger while checking the values of variables to see where things are going wrong.

Finally we discuss *rounding errors*. Computers can represent some data types, such as strings, integers and booleans, exactly. However, because computers use binary representation they represent floating point numbers to a certain precision but not exactly. We have used floating point numbers of type double throughout this book but there are several other types too, including the following in Delphi 7:

Type	Size in bytes	Significant digits
Single	4	7-8
Real48	6	11-12
Double	8	15-16
Extended	10	19-20

This means that programs occasionally give different results depending on the precision of the floating point numbers as a result of rounding errors. To see this, start a new application, double click on the form to create the OnFormCreate event handler, and enter the following code where is x declared as Double:

```
 1 procedure TForm1.FormCreate(Sender: TObject);
 2 var
 3   x: double;
 4   TestStr: string;
 5 begin
 6   x := 1.2;
 7   if (x = 1.2) then
 8     ShowMessage('Values are equal')
 9   else
10     ShowMessage('Values are NOT equal');
11   TestStr := FloatToStrF (x, ffFixed, 50, 50);
12   ShowMessage (TestStr);
13 end;
```

The variable x starts off with the value of 1.2. One would then expect the if statement to evaluate to true and the 'Values are equal' message to be displayed. If you run the code in Delphi 7, however, the 'Values are NOT equal' message is displayed. This is because x and the constant 1.2 are represented with different precisions. We can see the discrepancies in the value of x by displaying it with extreme precision and many digits after the decimal as in lines 11 and 12 above. These discrepancies are not always the same in all compilers and it is interesting to change the type of x in line 3 to single, real48, double and extended in turn. We did this in Delphi 7 and Delphi 8 and got the following results:

Type of x	Delphi 7	Delphi 8
single	Not equal	Not equal
real48	Not equal	(Not available)
double	Not equal	Equal
extended	Equal	Equal

What can one do about this? First, one needs to be aware that this is a potential problem. Second, it is usually better to test for a specific range rather than a precise value. In other words, instead of writing:

```
if (x = 1.2) then
```

use:

```
if (x > 1.199999) and (x < 1.200001) then
```

In summary, rounding errors occur because there is limited precision available on a computer and so many real numbers cannot be perfectly represented. These errors are typically extremely small and can be ignored for many purposes. However, in exact comparisons, such as those above, rounding errors may cause unwanted behaviour.

Testing

Testing code carefully is a critical part of being a good programmer. So it is worth developing the habit of testing even simple programs carefully. Many of the examples and problems in the textbook have emphasised test data. They present carefully thought out test cases before coding the solution and then use these test cases to check if the program works correctly.

There are many different ways of testing software and we will cover the question of creating suitable test data. Ideally we should test a program with all possible combinations of input data. That way we would know that the program is working correctly. This is usually not possible, so instead we choose appropriate sample test cases. When deciding on which values to use as test data, we should at least cover each of the following types:

- *Normal test data*: These are the input values that you would expect.
- *Boundary test data*: These are the input values which are valid, but are boundary cases. We specifically test the boundary cases because if a program works correctly on normal cases and boundary cases, then it will probably work correctly for the full range of valid values.
- *Erroneous test data*: These are invalid input values. We test using these values because we should know how the program behaves with invalid data. If the behaviour is not acceptable, we need to program corrective action (by handling exceptions, for example).

To explain these further, consider problem 12.3 in the list of problems at the end of Chapter 12. This involves programming an admission price calculator for a circus. Weekend rates are R9.90 for adults and R6.60 for children. There is a 10% discount on weekdays. Part a of this question asks for an appropriate set of test cases.

When deciding on test cases, the first thing to do is to make sure what the input data is. Often the input data will be entered in some way by the user, but sometimes the input data will come from another source (such as the system clock, a different program, function or procedure, a text file, or a database). In this case our input data is easy: the number of adults and the number of children.

Having clarified the input data we then decide on test cases. Here are some possible test cases with a column indicating the type of test case:

| Type | Input values | | Expected ouput | |
			Weekday	Weekend
Normal	Adults = 1	Children = 1	R 14.85	R 16.50
Normal	Adults = 2	Children = 5	R 47.52	R 52.80
Boundary	Adults = 0	Children = 0	R 0.00	R 0.00
Boundary	Adults = 1	Children = 0	R 8.91	R 9.90
Boundary	Adults = 0	Children = 1	R 5.94	R 6.60
Erroneous	Adults = -2	Children = 0	<invalid>	<invalid>

Normal test cases are those which have some adults and some children.

Boundary test cases are valid, but test boundaries. The boundary cases above test for where there are no adults or children, where there is 1 adult and no children and where there are no adults and 1 child. The erroneous test case gives an invalid (negative number) number of adults. An invalid number of children would also be an erroneous test case. For each case we calculate the expected ouput values so that we can test the actual output against these values.

Let us now look at a completely different example. Problem 10.1 involves changing the colour of a form to red on a double-click and back to the original colour on a single click. What are good examples of normal, boundary and erroneous test data? Try to work these out for yourself before continuing further.

The first step involves determining the input data. In this case the input data consists of two things: an event from the user (a mouse click) and the current state of the form (red or the original grey colour). Our test cases appear below. You may have come up with different cases and different interpretations of what is normal, boundary and erroneous. The purpose of categorizing test cases as normal, boundary and erroneous is to give a wide range of different cases that test the program as thoroughly as possible.

Type	Event	Form's Input State	Expected Result
Normal	Double click	Grey	Form changes to red
	Left single click	Red	Form changes to grey
Boundary	Double click	Red	Form stays red
	Left single click	Grey	Form stays grey
Erroneous	Right single click	Any state	Colour does not change
	<Enter>	Any state	Colour does not change

Different implementations that give the same correct behaviour can have different error characteristics. As a final example consider the different error responses of example 13.3 steps 3 & 4.

Type	Code	Expected Output	Actual Output Step 3	Actual Output Step 4	Comment
Normal	333	Invalid	Invalid	Invalid	Correct operation
Normal	334	Proceed	Proceed	Proceed	Correct operation
Erroneous	3334	Invalid	Proceed	Invalid	Step 3 incorrect
Erroneous	3344	Invalid	Invalid	Proceed	Step 4 incorrect

Example 13.3 step 5 corrects the problem with example 13.3 step 4, and the same approach will also correct the problem with example 13.3 step 3.

In this example it is important to distinguish between an erroneous test case and a normal case that gives 'Invalid' as the correct program output. In the example above the program expects three digit inputs and so an input value of 333 is normal. However, the number 333 does not meet the program's criteria for granting access and so it gives an 'Invalid' output. This is correct behaviour with normal data. However the program does not expect a four digit number and that is why the last two cases are classified as erroneous.

REVIEW

This chapter introduces Delphi's integrated debugger. In essence, we place a breakpoint on a particular line of the program. Then, when the running program reaches this breakpoint, the program breaks and displays the source code at the breakpoint. The programmer can step through the program line by line from there, checking the values of important variables and parameters and seeing the route the program execution follows.

Three concepts are fundamental to a debugger:
o breakpoints;
o controlled execution (eg single-stepping), and
o variable evaluation.

In this chapter we saw how to set a breakpoint, to trace into, to step over, to evaluate variable values and to set a watch. We traced program flow from a calling statement to a subroutine and back again and saw how using parameters incorrectly leads to errors.

We discussed four main kinds of error (compilation errors, run-time errors, errors of logic and rounding errors) and the need to consider normal, boundary and erroneous data when testing a program.

IMPORTANT CONCEPTS

Breakpoint <F5>: A breakpoint marks a line where the program will pause during debugging. When the program is paused, you can examine the state of your program (eg values of variables) at that point.

Error types: Compilation errors, run-time errors, errors of logic and rounding errors.

Execution point: The execution point highlights the next program line to be executed.

Local variables window (Delphi 8): While execution is paused, the local variables window displays the values of all the variables declared locally in the currently active subroutine.

Run to Cursor <F4>: Runs the program at full speed until the line of code containing the cursor, then pauses. From there you can use Step Over or Trace Into to trace individual lines of code or Run to resume normal execution.

Single step: Using the debugger to step through a program one statement at a time. The next line of code will not execute until you tell the debugger to continue. After each step, you can examine the state of the program, view the program output, and modify program data values. Then, when you are ready, you can continue executing the next program statement.

Step Over <F8>: Step Over executes the line currently highlighted by the execution point and moves to the next line in that routine, executing but not tracing any subroutine call. Step Over is useful to skip working through fully tested subroutines.

Test data types: Normal, boundary and erroneous data.

Trace Into <F7>: Trace Into executes the line currently highlighted by the execution point. If this is a subroutine call, the execution point moves to the first line of code in the subroutine being called. When you step past the subroutine `end;` execution continues to the line following the original subroutine call. Use Trace Into when the subroutine is not fully tested.

Watch <Ctrl+F5>: A watch displays the current value of a selected variable while execution is paused. As you step through your program, the value of the watch changes as the variable's value changes.

NEW DELPHI FEATURES

Debug keyboard commands	
\<F4\>	Run to Cursor
\<F5\>	Toggle breakpoint at cursor
\<F7\>	Trace Into
\<F8\>	Step Over
\<F9\>	Run
\<Ctrl+F2\>	Program reset
\<Ctrl+F5\>	Add Watch

PROBLEMS

PROBLEM 14.1

Problem 12.7c provides a set of test cases. Based on this chapter, classify each test case as normal, boundary or erroneous. Do the test cases given provide an adequate test of this program? Would it be worth adding any further test cases?

PROBLEM 14.2

Problem 12.4a asks for a suitable set of test cases for the problem given. In view of the discussion on testing in this chapter, review the answer you gave earlier and add any further test cases that are missing. Consider also whether any of the initial test cases are repetitive and so not strictly necessary.

PROBLEM 14.3

Joe's Airlines makes extensive use of email. Up until now each employee has chosen his or her own email address, but this is now becoming chaotic. So Joe wants a program that will create each employee's email address automatically by combining the first three letters from each employee's surname and the first three letters from his or her first name. If a surname or first name has only two letters, the program must add an 'x' to make up the three letters. The company's email domain is joesair.com.

As an example, Joe's surname is Soape, and so his email address is soajoe@joesair.com.

- Draw up an appropriate set of test cases for this example.
- Now write a suitable program and then test it against these test cases.

CHAPTER 15

Introduction to database programming

PURPOSE OF THIS CHAPTER

Programmers often build programming applications around a large amount of data that can be arranged into one or more tables. These tables (called the *database*) are stored separately from the application. In this chapter we create a MySQL database. We also build simple Delphi applications to store data in the database and to look up and manipulate (add, delete, and change) the data. We'll do all of this with writing very little Delphi code to demonstrate some of Delphi's RAD capabilities.

To discuss database theory fully, we would have to write a complete book on the topic. This chapter (together with the next two), however, gently introduces the most basic database concepts we will need in order to build database applications.

As all the examples in this chapter will be used to put together one bigger application in the next chapter, it is very important that you do each one of them on your computer. Doing only some of them will not work.

What is a database?

A database is an organized collection of related data. Here we will create a relational database† where the data is organized into tables stored in separate files on disk.

To see how the data is arranged in the tables we look at a simple example. Most companies maintain a computer-based personnel system for storing data about their employees. This data typically includes a name, employee number, address, salary, date of employment, leave status, and so on. We store data like this in a table with a row for each employee, and columns for the different data items associated with the employees. The rows are called *records*, and the columns divide the records into *fields*. The following simple database table consists of three records with five fields each.

Number	Name	Address	Date employed	Leave credit
123456	PJ Smith	PO Box 435 Pretoria	1 January 1995	6
234567	F Naidoo	20 John Ave Parktown	1 July 1990	12
345678	G Xulu	PO Box 65 Ifafa	1 January 1997	16

The header (shaded) row contains the five field names: Number, Name, and so on, and is not part of the data inside the table. The fields of each record contain five data values associated with one particular employee.

The simplest type of database is a *local database*. That is a database that resides on a single machine. Any changes made to the database are written directly to the database.

A *client/server database* is stored and maintained on a file server and one or more users (the *clients*) have access to the database. The users of this type of database are usually spread across a network and more than one might attempt to access the database at the same time. The server handles all the problems of simultaneous database access.

A *database application* is a program or collection of programs that manipulates the data in a database. It typically reads the information in the database, adds records, deletes records, or changes existing information. Databases allow data to be shared among different applications. When using a local database, the database and the application reside on the same machine. The users of a client/server database access the database through applications on their local computers. These applications are called client applications and ensure that users do not corrupt the database.

Before we start to create our database, we briefly discuss the alternatives Delphi offers in terms of data access.

Delphi's alternatives in terms of data access

In the first versions of Delphi, the only available technology to access databases was the Borland Database Engine (BDE). The BDE has direct access to a number of database systems including dBASE, Paradox, FoxPro and Microsoft Access as well as ASCII text files. A series of drivers allows access to some SQL servers, including Oracle, Sybase, Microsoft SQLServer, Informix, Interbase and DB2 .

† A relational database is made up of tables consisting of columns (attributes) and rows (records).

If access to a different database is needed, the BDE can also interface with ODBC drivers.

Delphi 5 introduced specific sets of components supporting Microsoft's ActiveX Data Objects (ADO) and InterBase Express (IBX). Delphi 6 added dbExpress, a new cross-platform and database-independent data access technology provided by Borland with Kylix on Linux and Delphi 6 on Windows.

In this book, we use the combination of dbExpress and MySQL.

MySQL database

MySQL is a database that has become well-known and widely used and is included in the list of dbExpress drivers in Delphi. It is free under the GNU General Public License (GPL) model although a commercial license can also be purchased. Running MySQL.exe gives us a command-line interface to MySQL which is a primitive way of using databases. To offer you a more visual interface to MySQL, we use a Windows application called MySQL Control Center which is free software. You can redistribute it and/or modify it under the terms of the GNU General Public License as published by the Free Software Foundation (FSF). You can download MySQL and MySQL Control Center from www.mysql.org. (See Appendix 4 for more information on installing MySQL).

A library database application

The database application that we will create is for a library keeping track of its members, books and loans. Our database will have the following tables:

Table	Purpose
LibraryMember table	For the number, name, telephone number, birth date and email address of each member of the library.
LibraryBook table	For the ISBN number, title, author and category of each book title in the library.
LibraryAcquisition table	For an acquisition number and the ISBN number for each copy of a book title in the library. (We need this table because the library may have more than one copy of a specific book title.)
LibraryLoan table	This table keeps track of book loans, so it stores the acquisition number of the book, the number of the member that has the book and the due date of each book issued.

Figure 15.1 shows the relationships between the tables in the database: For each ISBN (book title) in the LibraryBook table, there can be one or more copies (acquisitions) in the LibraryAcquisition table. Each member can borrow zero (0) or more books. Each acquisition can be borrowed by zero or one person.

In this chapter, we build three different database applications.

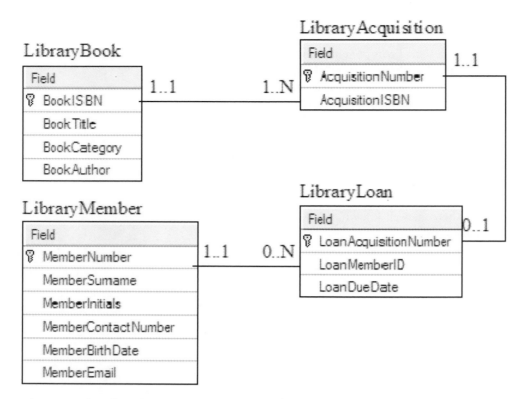

Figure 15.1 The relationships between tables in the database

In example 15.1 we create the database and table LibraryMember. In example 15.2 we create an application that uses table LibraryMember through a DBGrid component. In example 15.3 we create the LibraryBook table and an application that uses the table through DBEdit components. In example 15.4 we change example 15.3 to use a DBComboBox component.

EXAMPLE 15.1) Create the database containing one table

In the real world a database server normally runs on a networked computer and users of the database access the server from different computers over a network. A person called the database administrator is in charge of looking after the database.

In our examples we are going to perform many different roles and do everything on one computer. We run the MySQL server and manage the database using MySQL Control Center (usually done by the database administrator.) On the same computer we write Delphi applications to access the database, which would normally be done on a remote computer.

We start this example by making sure the database server is running in the background. We then connect to this server using MySQL Control Center and we create a database called MyVPLibrary and one table called LibraryMember.

EX 15.1 STEP 1 Make sure the MySQL server is running

- The MySQLAdmin server runs in the background after you have installed MySQL as indicated by the traffic light on the taskbar (figure 15.2). If the traffic light is not present, refer to Appendix 4 for instructions on how to install MySQL.

Figure 15.2 Entering the path to the database

EX 15.1 STEP 2 Connecting to the database server

- Run the MySQL Control Center by executing MySQLcc (the dolphin icon).
- If the Register Server window shown in figure 15.3 is not present, click File | New on the Console Manager. Register a new server and name it VisualProgrammingServer as in figure 15.3. The name 'Visual Programming Server' is simply the name we chose to refer to the connection to the server.
- Type in localhost next to Host Name. This specifies that we wish to connect to the current computer rather than some other computer on the network.
- Click Add.

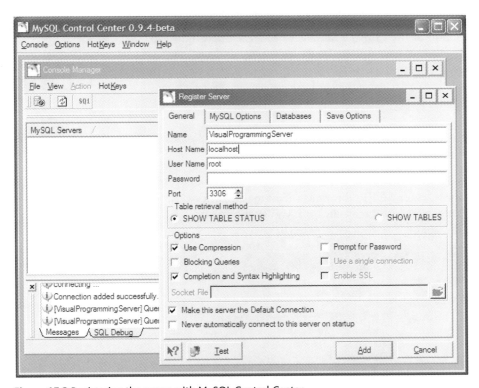

Figure 15.3 Registering the server with MySQL Control Center

- Right-Click on VisualProgrammingServer under MySQL Servers and select Connect as in figure 15.4.

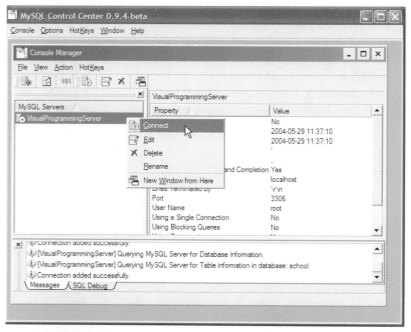

Figure 15.4 Connecting to the server

The MySQL Servers section of the Console Manager now resembles figure 15.5 (expand Databases). The two entries under Databases (mysql and test) are default databases which are created on installation. In the next step we add our own database.

Figure 15.5 Dialog box for creating a table

EX 15.1 STEP 3   Create the database

- Right-click on Databases and select New Database.
- To create the database, enter MyVPLibrary as the name and click OK.
- To connect to the new database, right-click on MyVPLibrary and select Connect as in figure 15.6.

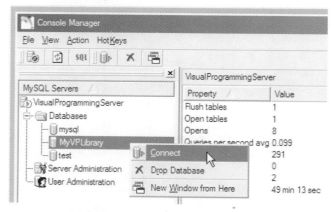

Figure 15.6 Connecting to database MyVPLibrary

Why is it necessary to connect to the database? When we create a database, the files of the database are created on the server which is normally running on a different computer and many other computers can try to use the same database. We connect to the database to notify the server that we want to work with the data in the database. When we have finished working with the data, we disconnect from the database.

EX 15.1 STEP 4   Create table LibraryMember

- To create a new table for the members of the library, right-click on Tables (double-click on MyVPLibrary if Tables is not visible) and select New Table as in figure 15.7.

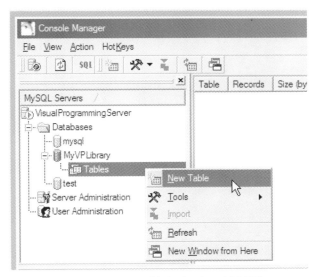

Figure 15.7 Creating a new table in database MyVPLibrary

A window entitled *[VisualProgrammingServer] Creating Table in database 'MyVPLibrary'* opens for us to specify the table structure (the names of the fields in the table). (Figure 15.9 shows the window after the field names, types and sizes have been entered.) The database table that we will create includes the following fields: library member identification number, surname, initials, contact telephone number, birth date and email address.

There are three columns in the window: the first column is used to specify the field names; the second column is used to indicate whether the particular field can be left empty, and the third column is used for the data type of the particular field. These are selected from a drop-down list (figure 15.8). We use *varchar* to indicate a character string type and *date* to indicate that a field will be a date. We can specify the maximum length of each varchar field in the Length edit box at the bottom of the window.

Figure 15.8 Selecting a field type

- Enter the field names as shown in figure 15.9, selecting the field types from the drop-down list as in figure 15.8. Specify the lengths in the table below for the varchar (string) fields. (If we don't specify any lengths, a default length of 100 is used.) Not everybody has an email address so we allow null values in the MemberEmail field

Field name	Allow Null	Length
MemberNumber		13
MemberSurname		20
MemberInitials		4
MemberContactNumber		15
MemberBirthDate		
MemberEmail	✓	50

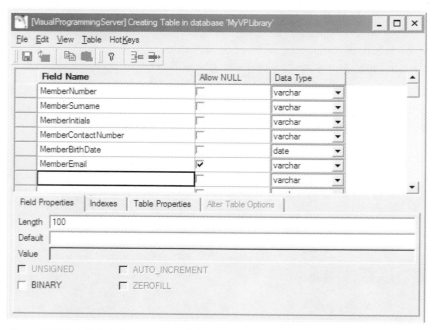

Figure 15.9 Specifying the structure of the new table

- Create the primary key by right-clicking on field MemberNumber and selecting Add Primary Key as in figure 15.10.
- Save the new table with File | Save or click the Save speed button.
- Enter LibraryMember as the name of the new table and click OK.

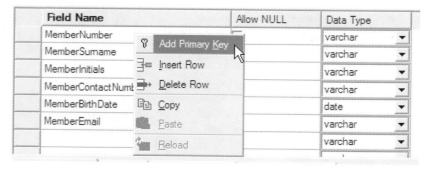

Figure 15.10 Creating a primary key

What is a key?

A key is a field whose value must be unique for each record in the database table. In other words, no two records may have the same value in the data table's MemberNumber field since this field is the key.

Why do we need key fields? A program that accesses a database table must be able to distinguish between the records. The records in a table are automatically indexed according to the values of the key field(s). (The key can consist of more that one field.) Using the key, an application locates any specific record it needs to access. If we define a field as a key, it cannot be allowed null values (every record needs to have a value in this field). In this example, we can allow the MemberEmail field to have null values since it is not a key field.

EX 15.1 STEP 5 Change the structure of the table

What if you've made a mistake setting up the structure of the database table and only realized it after you have saved it? You can always modify it by right-clicking on the table and selecting Edit Table as in figure 15.11.

We can use the MySQL Control Center to enter data into the table, but to get some practice in writing Delphi applications to access a database table, we will write a Delphi application to add data to our table.

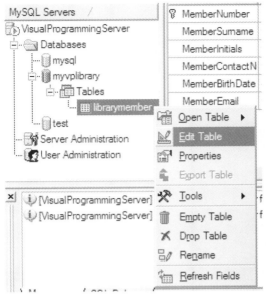

Figure 15.11 Changing the structure of a table

Handling database errors

In the next example we will create a Delphi application to access and manipulate the data in the LibraryMember data table. It will allow the user to add and change data. If the user enters invalid data (for example, of the wrong data type) an exception will occur which needs to be handled. We can handle it in the program, or we can let Delphi show an exception message each time a database error occurs. We will not be doing a lot of programming here, so Delphi will have to 'catch' the exceptions for us. If you have not done it previously in Chapter 4, change the Delphi setup so that it handles the exceptions directly without invoking the debugger.

(If you're not sure whether you did it in Chapter 4, just make sure by going through the steps again.)

EXAMPLE 15.2 Create an application that uses the table through a DBGrid component

In example 15.1 we created a database that consists of a table for the members of a library, table LibraryMember. Now we are going to build a Delphi application to store and manipulate data in this table.

- Select the File | New VCL Forms Application (Delphi 8) or File | New Application (Delphi 6/7) menu sequence to start a new application.

In this application we use some new Delphi components.

EX 15.2 STEP 1 Build the connection to the database

We need a TSQLConnection component to connect to the MyVPLibrary database.
- Find the TSQLConnection/SQLConnection component on the dbExpress tab of the Component/Tool Palette, place it on the form and double-click on it to start the dbExpress Connections Editor. (See figure 15.12.)
- Select MySQL from the Driver Name.
- Select MySQLConnection (MSConnection in Delphi 6) as the connection to work with.
- Once you set either the DriverName or the ConnectionName property value, other properties will automatically get values as well, such as the GetDriverFunc, LibraryName and VendorLib properties.

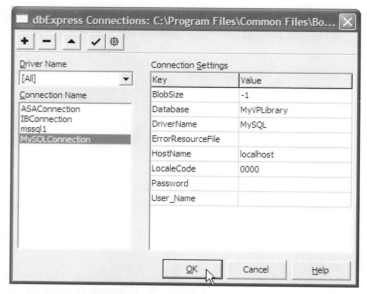

Figure 15.12 SQLConnection's Connection Editor

- Click OK to close the Connections Editor.
- Make sure that the other relevant properties of the SQLConnection component are set as in the table below. (Some of the properties will be correct by default.)

Component	Property	Value
Form1	Name	frmMember
	Caption	Member
SQLConnection1 (dbExpress tab)	Name	scoMyVPLibrary
	ConnectionName	MySQLConnection (MSConnection in Delphi 6)
	DriverName	MySQL
	LibraryName	dbexpmysql.dll
	VendorLib	c:\mysql\bin\LIBMYSQL.dll†
	LoginPrompt	False
	Connected	True

A note for Delphi 6 and 7 users: The default value for LibraryName is dbexpmys.dll. This is the driver for a previous version of MySQL (version 3.22.x). For the connection to work you must explicitly change the property value to dbexpmysql.dll. Delphi 6 has to be upgraded with an update pack to include this driver. (See Appendix 4 for details.)

We did not enter a password in the Connections Editor, meaning that the users of the application need to log in to the database themselves. This is handled by a built-in log in dialogue. In order to disable this dialogue explicitly, we set the LoginPrompt property of the SQLConnection component to False in the table above.

- Save the unit and project or C15e02u and C15e02p.

† Unfortunately, after you install MySQL, this DLL is not added to the search path, so we hardcode the full path here for it to work.

EX 15.2 STEP 2 Add the dbExpress and DataAccess components

- Add the following components to the new form and set the properties *in the order given*. We discuss these components later.

Component	Property	Value
SQLDataSet1 (dbExpress tab)	Name	sdsMember
	SQLConnection	scoMyVPLibrary
	CommandType	ctTable
	CommandText	LibraryMember
	Active	True
DataSetProvider1 (Data Access tab)	Name	dspMember
	DataSet	sdsMember
ClientDataSet (Data Access tab)	Name	cdsMember
	ProviderName	dspMember
DataSource1 (Data Access tab)	Name	datMember
	DataSet	cdsMember
	Active	True
	(Expand the Dataset property in the Object Inspector to see the Active property.)	

EX 15.2 STEP 3 Add the data control components

- Place a DBGrid component from the Data Controls tab of the Component/Tool Palette on the form. A table-like object appears on the form. Set the properties as below. Note that we link the DBGrid to the DataSource component.

Component	Property	Value
DBGrid1 (Data Controls tab)	Name	dbgMember
	DataSource	datMember

If the Active properties of sdsMember and datMember are True, we get live data at design time. The form now looks like figure 15.13. (There are no records yet, however the field names imply live data.)

All the fields may not be visible in the grid. We can specify the display lengths of the fields in the grid so that all of them are visible. We do this in the next step.

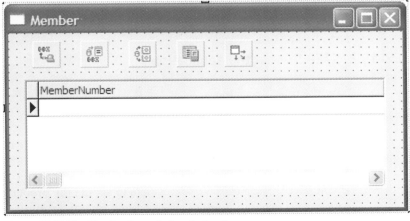

Figure 15.13 The Member form during design time

EX 15.2 STEP 4 Specify the display lengths of the data in the DBGrid

- Double-click on the grid to open the grid column editor (or right-click on DBGrid and select the columns editor) and click the Add All Fields speed button. (See figure 15.14.)
- Click on each field respectively in the column editor and change their Width properties in the Object Inspector as follows:

Field	Width property
MemberNumber	100
MemberSurname	100
MemberInitials	70
MemberContactNumber	100
MemberBirthDate	87
MemberEmail	100

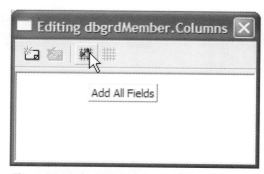

Figure 15.14 The DBGrid Column Editor

- Close the grid column editor.
- Size and reposition the components to resemble the form in figure 15.15 without the data.

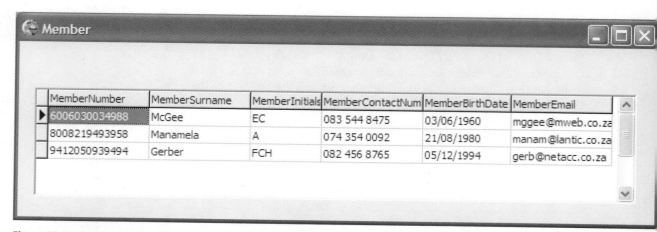

Figure 15.15 The Member form during run time after three records have been added

EX 15.2 STEP 5 Run the application

- Save the unit file again.
- Now run the program and enter data into the table. (If you didn't set the LoginPrompt of the SQLConnection component to False, you may see a login dialogue before seeing your data. If you haven't defined a user name and password (as in figure 15.12) you can just click OK or enter the user name and password that you have defined and click OK.)
- If you have made a mistake somewhere in setting the property values and it causes your program to raise an exception, reset the running program with Run | Program Reset, correct the mistake and run it again.

- Click on the field where you want to start entering data, and type the appropriate value. Use the Tab key to move between fields. You can also use the up arrow and down arrow keys to move between the records in the table. Figure 15.15 shows the form at run time, after we've added three records. You can use the scroll bars to move through the grid.
- A small triangle to the left of a record indicates that it is the current (or active) record.
- Note that the date format depends on the settings in the computer's Regional and Language Settings. We can set it to the format of our choice by clicking the Start button, selecting Settings | Control Panel and double-clicking on the Regional and Language Settings (or Regional Settings) icon. Click the Customise button and then change the format on the tab labelled Date.

If you enter dates in a different format than specified in the Regional and Language Settings, Delphi will handle the exception by displaying an error message, as in figure 15.16, and you can then correct the error. An appropriate error message will also appear if you use the same member number in two different records, because we defined the MemberNumber field as a key and it must be unique.

Notice that all the fields require values except for the MemberEmail field.

- Delphi sorts the records according to the value of the MemberNumber field as you enter them. If you have filled in all the fields of a record and press the Tab key to go to the next line you might end up somewhere in the middle of the table instead of on the next line. This happens when Delphi moves the last record that you have entered to its correct position in the table (according to the key value). In this case, you can use the down arrow key to move down to below the last record.
- You can change any of the values that you have entered. Just move to that field with the arrow keys (or click on it) and edit it. To delete a record completely, move to the field in that record and press <Ctrl+Del>. Delphi will ask for confirmation to delete the record.

Figure 15.16 The error message for entering a date in the wrong format

A local (unidirectional) data set

- When you close the application and start it again, however, you'll find that no changes have been applied to the database; they were only made to the local in-memory ClientDataSet and are now gone.

A dbExpress dataset is provided as a read-only and unidirectional dataset. This means that the application can open the table and walk through it, from the first record to the last, but the application cannot make any permanent changes to it. dbExpress datasets act this way to maximize performance: the resulting data access is fast and requires little overhead.

To apply the updates to the database table, the application must call the *ApplyUpdates method* of the TClientDataSet. This can be programmed to occur automatically when the user closes the application in the OnClose event handler of the form. Before we show how to do this, we explain each component that we have on the form so far.

Bringing the database and the application together

How did we 'link' the database to the application that uses it? Schematically, the relationship between all the components used to get the records from the physical database to the ClientDataSet in the computer's memory, to the data control component (the DBGrid here) on the form, is represented in figure 15.17. We explain each of these in the sections that follow.

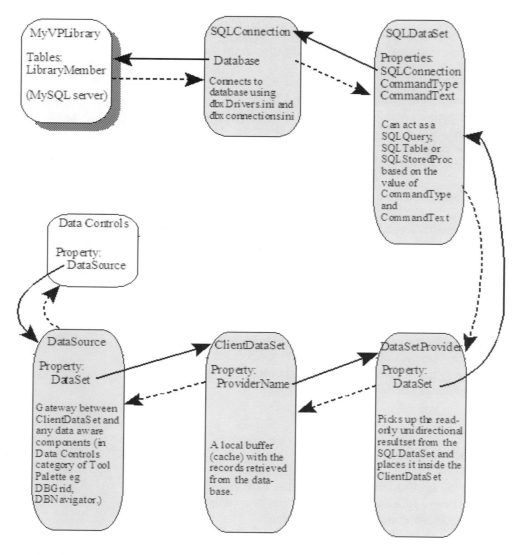

⟶ Indicates the chain of components from the data control to the database.

⇢ Indicates the flow of the selected records from the database to the data control.

Figure 15.17 Schema of the relationships between the components used to get the records from the database to the ClientDataSet, to the data control components of the form

The SQLConnection component

The SQLConnection component is responsible for connecting the application to the database, MyVPLibrary in this application. The SQLConnection component interacts with a dbExpress driver and two files. The first, dbxdrivers.ini, lists the installed driver types (for example Interbase, Oracle, MySQL) and, for each driver, lists the libraries (DLLs or shared objects) and the default settings for all connection parameters required. The second file, dbxconnections.ini on Windows, lists named sets of connection configurations. Each configuration represents a set of settings for the SQLConnection and describes a particular database connection. You can use the SQLConnection component to choose one of the named configurations in dbxconnections.ini and use it to connect to a database or to define new configurations and add them to dbxconnections.ini.

The SQLDataSet component

The SQLDataSet component converts requests from the application for data, into SQL queries to the database. SQL is a computer language with a specific syntax designed to manipulate relational databases. Before we can use an SQLDataSet component, it must be connected to the database server via the SQLConnection component.

The SQLDataSet can perform one of three tasks and switch to the desired behaviour during run time. This behaviour is defined through two properties: CommandType and CommandText. The CommandType property can be set to ctTable, ctQuery or ctStoredProc, while the CommandText property can be a table name, an SQL query or a stored procedure name correspondingly.

The SQLDataSet component uses SQL *query statements* to retrieve records from the database to which it is connected. You can use it to define a database's structure, to modify data and to retrieve data. During run time, the SQLDataSet component generates an SQL query to the database. In example 15.2 it generates the statement : SELECT * FROM LibraryMember. This SQL query is then executed and all the records in table LibraryMember are retrieved. We look at SQL in more detail in the next chapter.

The SQLDataSet can generate SQL queries retrieving data from multiple data tables, producing representations of tables or views from any number of tables. (We do this in Chapter 17.)

The DataSetProvider component

We use a DataSetProvider component to provide data from the SQLDataSet to the ClientDataSet and to resolve updates (to get the changed data back to the physical database). We will show this later. The DataSetProvider packages data from the SQLDataSet and passes it to the ClientDataSet. The ClientDataSet reconstructs the data to create a local, in-memory copy for user access. When user access is complete, the ClientDataSet repackages any changed data and sends the updates back to the provider. The provider applies the updates to the database.

The ClientDataSet component

The ProviderName property of the ClientDataSet must be connected to the DataSetProvider. The effect of this is that the read-only, unidirectional contents of the SQLDataSet (with the resulting records of the SQL statement) will be collected and placed inside the ClientDataSet component. The latter will act as a local in-memory data set that we can use to browse through the resulting records (and make modifications, as you'll see in a moment).

The DataSource component

The DataSet property of this component should point to the ClientDataSet component, and all visual data-aware components (covered in the next section) can connect their DataSource property to the DataSource component in order to get access to the data from the SQL query on the database.

The data control component: DBGrid

The components discussed above are not visible at run time. We need data control components to display the data on the screen. With the DBGrid data control we can display several records of a database table (or the result of an SQL query) simultaneously on a form. A DBGrid component is associated with data through its DataSource property. The value of this property must be the name of a DataSource component on the form, (ie datMember in this example). The table (or query) we specify in the SQLDataSet's CommandText property (LibraryMember here) determines the size of the grid. By default, there will be a column in the DBGrid component for each column in the table. The field names appear in the top row of the grid as column headings, and any data already in the table is displayed.

A small triangle to the left of a record indicates that it is the current or active record in the data set. In figure 15.18, the record for member McGee is the active record.

MemberNumber	MemberSurname	MemberInitials	MemberContactNum	MemberBirthDate	MemberEmail
▶ 6006030034988	McGee	EC	083 544 8475	1960/06/03	mcgee@mweb.co.za
8008219493958	Manamela	A	074 354 0092	1980/08/21	manam@lantic.co.za
9412050939494	Gerber	FCH	082 456 8765	1994/12/05	gerb@netacc.co.za

Figure 15.18 A DBGrid component with live data

When we run an application that includes a DBGrid data control, we can add new records to the table it represents in memory, delete records from the table in memory or edit the fields of existing records. (To apply these changes to the actual database, we need to apply the updates to the database. We will do this in the next step.)

EX 15.2 STEP 6   Apply the updates to the database

To apply the updates to the database table, the application must call the
ApplyUpdates method of the ClientDataSet component (ie cdsMember in this
example). We apply the updates when the user closes the application in the
form's OnClose event handler.

- Enter the code below for the OnClose event handler for frmMember:

```
1  procedure TfrmMember.FormClose(Sender: TObject; var Action: TCloseAction);
2  begin
3    if cdsMember.ChangeCount > 0 then
4      cdsMember.ApplyUpdates(0);                    //MaxErrors parameter: 0
5  end;
```

- Save and run the application. Enter the data again.
- When you close the application and start it again, you'll find that the
  changes have been applied to the database. This is because we have used the
  ApplyUpdates method to update the database table.

The ClientDataSet's ChangeCount property

The ChangeCount property used in line 3 above indicates the number of
changes currently made to the in-memory ClientDataSet that will be applied to
the database. If the value is zero this means that no changes have been made
since the last update. We check the value to avoid unnecessary calls to
ApplyUpdates.

The ClientDataSet's ApplyUpdates method

The changes (updated, inserted, and deleted records) were made to the local in-
memory ClientDataSet, cdsMember and when you closed the form, the updates
were explicitly applied to the database table via the call to the ApplyUpdates
method of the ClientDataSet (line 4 above). The constant parameter (called the
MaxErrors parameter; 0 here) indicates the maximum number of errors that the
provider should allow before prematurely stopping the update operation. –1 is
used to indicate that there is no limit to the number of errors.

EX 15.2 STEP 7   Undo data updates

Since all changes are kept in memory until the moment of applying the update,
it is possible to undo a change before it is made permanent. We provide the user
with an Undo button which will allow the reverse of the last change made. In
Chapter 12 we introduced the user interface design principle of *reversibility*. This
principle is extremely important when working with databases. It is very easy for
a user to delete a record or accidently make some change, so we should provide
support for undoing the last operation. To add an Undo button do the
following:

- Drop a BitBtn component on the form and set its properties as shown below.

Component	Property	Value
BitBtn1	Name	bmbUndoLastChange
	Kind	bkRetry
	Caption	Undo last change

- Enter the code below for the OnClick event handler of bmbUndoLastChange:

```
6  procedure TfrmMember.bmbUndoLastChangeClick(Sender: TObject);
7  begin
8    cdsMember.UndoLastChange(True);
9  end;
```

The ClientDataSet's UndoLastChange method

The ClientDataSet supports Undo using the UndoLastChange method (line 8 above). The UndoLastChange method undoes the last edit, insert, or delete operation to a record in the ClientDataSet. The only argument specifies whether to reposition the cursor on the restored record. If it is true, the cursor is positioned on the restored record. If it is false, the cursor remains on the current active record.

Opening and closing data sets correctly

We set the Connected property of the SQLConnection as well as the Active properties of the SQLDataSet and the DataSource properties to True. We did this so that we can see the live data during design time. It is always important to make sure that all data sets are closed (inactive) at design-time when you finish your project (including the ClientDataSet and SQLDataSet components). Ensure that the SQLConnection component is not connected by setting the Connected property to False. Making sure that nothing is active at design-time prevents run-time errors, but means that you have to open the ClientDataSets explicitly when the form is created. We do this in the OnShow event handler of the main form (we have only one form in this example).

EX 15.2 STEP 8 Open the ClientDataSet when the form is displayed

- Set the Connected property of scoMyVPLibrary and the Active property of sdsMember and cdsMember to False.
- Enter the TfrmMember.FormShow event handler as follows:

```
procedure TfrmMember.FormShow(Sender: TObject);
begin
  scoMyVPLibrary.Connected := True;
  cdsMember.Open;
end;
```

- Change the TfrmMember.FormClose as follows:

```
procedure TfrmMember.FormClose(Sender: TObject; var Action: TCloseAction);
begin
  if cdsMember.ChangeCount > 0 then
    cdsMember.ApplyUpdates(0);              //MaxErrors parameter: 0
  cdsMember.Close;
end;
```

- Save the unit and run it. Check that the program behaves as expected by adding records, making changes or deleting records and undoing changes.

EXAMPLE 15.3) Creating the book data table and using it in an application

In example 15.2 we used the DBGrid component to access the data in the LibraryMember table in database MyVPLibrary. In this example we
o   create the LibraryBook table in database MyVPLibrary and
o   write a new application to use the DBEdit and DBNavigator components to access the data in the LibraryBook table.

EX 15.3 STEP 1   Create the LibraryBook table in database MyVPLibrary

- Run the MySQL Control Center.
- Create a new table for the books in the library, by right-clicking Tables (under myvplibrary) and selecting New Table. (Click on the + to expand the list of tables.)
- Specify the table structure and field lengths as given in figure 15.19.
- Specify field BookISBN as the primary key.
- Save the new table with File | Save or click the Save speed button.
- Enter LibraryBook as the name of the new table and click OK. The Console Manager now shows two tables in database MyVPLibrary as in figure 15.20.
- Close the MySQL Control Center.

Field	Type	Null	Key	Default
⚷ BookISBN	varchar(13)		PRI	
BookTitle	varchar(50)			
BookCategory	varchar(20)			
BookAuthor	varchar(20)			

Figure 15.19 The structure of the LibraryBook table

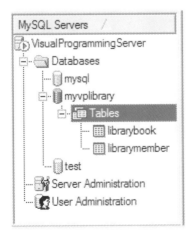

Figure 15.20 The two tables in database MyVPLibrary: LibraryMember and LibraryBook

Creating an application to add data to the LibraryBook table in database MyVPLibrary

In the previous step, we created a table for the books in a library. Now we are going to build a Delphi application to store and manipulate data in this table.
- In Delphi, select File | New VCL Forms Application (Delphi 8) or File | New Application (Delphi 6/7) to start a new application.

EX 15.3 STEP 2 Build the connection to the database

As before, we need a TSQLConnection component to connect to the MyVPLibrary database.

- Find the TSQLConnection component on the dbExpress tab on the Component/Tool Palette, place it on the form and double-click on it to start the dbExpress Connections Editor.
- Set the DriverName to MySQL and the ConnectionName property to MySQLConnection (Delphi 7 or 8) or MSConnection (Delphi 6).
- Make sure the Database is set to MyVPLibrary and the HostName is localhost.
- Test the connection by right-clicking on the connection name, MySQLConnection or MSConnection and selecting Test Connection. (This sets the TSQLComponent's Connected property to True.) If a Database login window appears, type root for the User Name and leave the Password blank.
- When you have verified that the connection can be made successfully, click OK to save the connection settings and to close the Connections Editor.
- Make sure that the other relevant properties of the SQLConnection component are set as in the table below. (Remember to change the VendorLib and LibraryName properties if necessary.)

Component	Property	Value
Form1	Name	frmBook
	Caption	Book
SQLConnection1 (dbExpress tab)	Name	scoMyVPLibrary
	ConnectionName	MySQLConnection (Delphi 7 or 8) or MSConnection (Delphi 6)
	DriverName	MySQL
	LibraryName	dbexpmysql.dl
	VendorLib	c:\mysql\bin\LIBMYSQL.dll
	LoginPrompt	False

EX 15.3 STEP 3 Add the dbExpress and DataAccess components

- Add the following components to the new form.

Component	Property	Value
SQLDataSet1 (dbExpress tab)	Name	sdsBook
	SQLConnection	scoMyVPLibrary
	CommandType	ctTable
	CommandText	LibraryBook
DataSetProvider1 (Data Access tab)	Name	dspBook
	DataSet	sdsBook
	Active	True
ClientDataSet (Data Access tab)	Name	cdsBook
	ProviderName	dspBook
	Active	True

DataSource1	Name	datBook
(Data Access tab)	DataSet	cdsBook

- Save the unit as C15e03u and the project file as C15e03p.

EX 15.3 STEP 4 Add the DBEdit Data Control components

In example 15.2 we used a DBGrid component to display the data from the LibraryMember table in a tabular format. In this example we use different Data Control components to create a form that displays the data one record at a time (see figure 15.21). With this view the user uses navigation buttons to move from one record to the next.

- Drop four DBEdits and a DBNavigator from the Data Controls tab of the Component/Tool Palette, five Labels and a BitButton on the form to resemble figure 15.21 (without the data).
- Use the table below to set the component properties.

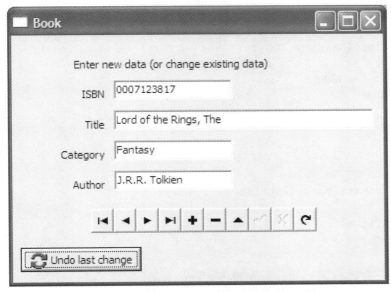

Figure 15.21 The book form during run time after a record is added

Component	Property	Value
Form1	Name	frmBook
	Caption	Book
All DBEdits	DataSource	datBook
Label1	Name	lblMsg
	Caption	Enter new data (or change existing data)
DBEdit1	Name, DataField	dbeISBN, BookISBN
Label2	Name, Caption	lblISBN, ISBN
DBEdit2	Name, DataField	dbeTitle, BookTitle

Label3	Name,Caption	lblTitle, Title
DBEdit3	Name, DataField	dbeCategory, BookCategory
Label4	Name,Caption	lblCategory, Category
DBEdit4	Name, DataField	dbeAuthor, BookAuthor
Label5	Name, Caption	lblAuthor, Author
DBNavigator1	Name	navBook
	DataSource	datBook
	ShowHint	True
BitBtn1	Name	bmbUndoLastChange
	Kind	bkRetry
	Caption	Undo last change

We set the ShowHint property of the DBNavigator to True. This displays helpful hints when the user moves the mouse over the navigation buttons.

EX 15.3 STEP 5   Write the event handlers

- Enter the code below for the OnClose event handler of form frmBook:

```
procedure TfrmBook.FormClose(Sender: TObject; var Action: TCloseAction);
begin
  if cdsBook.ChangeCount > 0 then
    cdsBook.ApplyUpdates(0);
  cdsBook.Close;
end;
```

- Enter the code below for the OnClick event handler of bmbUndoLastChange:

```
procedure TfrmBook.bmbUndoLastChangeClick(Sender: TObject);
begin
  cdsBook.UndoLastChange(True);
end;
```

- Enter the code below for the OnShow event handler of form frmBook:

```
procedure TfrmBook.FormShow(Sender: TObject);
begin
  scoMyVPLibrary.Connected := True;
  cdsBook.Open;
end;
```

EX 15.3 STEP 6   Run the application

- Ensure that scoMyVPLibrary's Connected property and sdsBook's Active property are False, save the application and run it.

You will see that some of the navigation buttons are not active at times. For example, when you are at the first record in the table, the buttons for moving to the first or previous record are inactive. The two rightmost buttons will become active only when you edit the data in the table, as their purpose is either to store or cancel the changes made.

- Play around with the application by adding and deleting records (use the hints for the navigation buttons), making changes which you save and some which you undo without saving, and moving around between the records. Figure 15.22 contains data that you can enter.

	♀ BookISBN	BookTitle	BookCategory	BookAuthor
1	0747551006	Harry Potter and the Order of the Phoenix	Fantasy	J.K. Rowling
2	0140282610	Out of Africa	Drama	K. Blixen
3	0099425238	Seven-Day Weekend, The	Business	R. Semler
4	0007123817	Lord of the Rings, The	Fantasy	J.R.R. Tolkien

Figure 15.22 Data for LibraryBook table

The current record

Each active data set has a cursor, or pointer, to the current row (record) in the data set. The current record in a data set is the one whose field values currently show in the data aware controls on the form, such as DBEdit. If the data set supports editing, the current record contains the values that can be manipulated by edit, insert, and delete methods. You can change the current row (record) to another one by using the navigator buttons to display values from a different record.

The DBEdit data control

Like the DBGrid component, the DBEdit data control component enables us to view the data in a database table. However, where we associate the DBGrid component with a whole data set, the DBEdit component is linked with only one field of a data set. This means we need a DBEdit component for each field of a table that we want to display. We can then view only one record – the currently active record – at a time.

Example 15.3 uses four DBEdit components to display a single record from the LibraryBook data table. Like the DBGrid component, the DBEdit component connects to the ClientDataSet–DataSource chain. It therefore has a DataSource property where we specify the name of the DataSource linked to the data table that we want to access. The field that we want to associate with the DBEdit component is given in its DataField property. Once the DataSource has been specified, a list of available fields appears in the DataField property (it appears when you click on the down arrow) and you can choose the appropriate one by clicking on it.

DBNavigator data control

The DBGrid data control has a built-in navigation mechanism which enables us to move between the records and fields using the Tab key, the arrow keys, or the mouse. We can add new records by moving to a new record after the current last record, and we can delete records with <Ctrl+Del>. How would you do all of this if you used only DBEdit components to view the records? We need a separate navigation component, the DBNavigator data control, to link onto the ClientDataSet–DataSource chain. The DBNavigator consists of a series of buttons that the user can use to move through the records in the database one at a time, insert and delete records, move to the beginning or end of the database, and so on. Figure 15.23 shows the navigation bar and the purpose of each button.

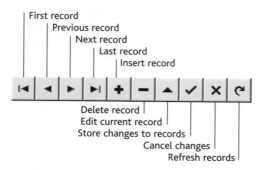

Figure 15.23 The DBNavigator data control

We use the VisibleButtons property of the DBNavigator component to specify which of the buttons should appear in the bar. By default Delphi includes all ten. Records need to be 'refreshed' (the right most button) only if two or more users can access a data table simultaneously. For example, if we used MySQL Control Center to edit the LibraryBook table at the same time we would be regarded as a second user of the data table. When you click on the Refresh button, any changes made by another user will appear on your application.

The DBNavigator component is also linked to the appropriate database through its DataSource property.

EXAMPLE 15.4) Change example 15.3 to use a DBComboBox

It is unwise to add, edit or delete a record without adequate checks of the validity of the data. Will a search for all the books in the library in the category 'Interior decorating' also return all the books in category 'Interior-decorating' (spelt with a hyphen)? The answer is No, because the category is spelt differently and a search for one will not locate the other. Making spelling mistakes is human and our programs need to cater for human error. We know that the category is the same in both instances, but the computer does not.

In this example we limit human error by allowing the user only predefined values for the BookCategory field. We change the user interface of application C15e03p to introduce the DBComboBox. This allows the user to select the value of the BookCategory field from a drop-down list of valid values, as shown in figure 15.24.

Figure 15.24 Selecting a category from the drop-down list

- Open project C15e03p and replace the dbeCategory DBEdit (figure 15.21) with a DBComboBox (Data Controls tab).
- Set the property values as in the table below.

Component	Property	Value
DBComboBox1	Name	dbcCategory
	DataSource	datBook
	DataField	BookCategory
	Style	csDropDownList
	Sorted	True

- Double-click on TStrings next to the Items property in the Object Inspector (or click once on the three dots in the square next to the Items value).
- Enter the valid values in the String List Editor (figure 15.25).
- Save the unit and project files as C15e04u and C15e04p respectively.
- Run the application and see the effect of the change.

Figure 15.25 The String List Editor

The DBComboBox

Like the DBEdit, the DBComboBox links a specific DataField within a specific DatasSource. At run time the DBComboBox displays a drop-down list from which the user can select from a predetermined set of values (in this case, valid book categories) for updating the corresponding data field, BookCategory. The Items property of the component specifies the items contained in the drop-down list. At design time, we use the String List Editor to populate the Items list.

The Style property determines user interaction with the control. We set Style to csDropDownList, which displays a drop-down list and edit box and does not allow the user to enter or change values that are not in the drop-down list at run time.

Setting the Sorted property to True sorts the items in the list in alphabetic order.

When the primary key consists of more than one field: The SQLDataSet component

Often we need the primary key of a database table to consist of more than one field value. For example, in a reservations table for accommodation consisting of the fields ResortName, RoomNumber, Date, GuestName and GuestAddress, the primary key consists of the first three fields: ResortName, RoomNumber, Date. On their own none of these fields identify unambiguously a single record. However a maximum of one record can match a specific combination of values for these fields.

In cases like these we need to specify that the SortFieldNames property of the SQLDataSet component contains all the field values that make up the primary key of the table, delimited by commas (ie ResortName, RoomNumber, Date). The SortFieldNames property has a Sort Field Editor to help us specify these fields.

You need to do this in problem 16.1 in the next chapter.

REVIEW

In this chapter we created a database, data tables for the database and applications to access the tables in the database. We used MySQL Control Centre to create the database and the tables inside the database. To do this, the MyQL database server had to be running in the background.

We wrote Delphi applications to manipulate the data in the database.

We used dbExpress components (SQLConnection, SQLDataSet), Data Access components (DataSetProvider, ClientDataSet and DataSource) and DataControl components (DBGrid, DBNavigator, DBEdit and DBComboBox) to display the contents of the data tables and to navigate through the records.

Along with its other strengths, Delphi is also a good Rapid Application Development (RAD) tool. We saw some of the RAD aspects in this chapter where we were able to move through a database adding, deleting and changing records, all with writing very little program code. We simply had to select components and link them appropriately through their properties.

IMPORTANT CONCEPTS

Databases

Applying updates: The ClientDataSet contains data retrieved from the database. To write all updated, inserted, and deleted records from the local ClientDataSet to the database, they must be applied to the database to have any effect on the database. We do this with the ClientDataSet's ApplyUpdates method.

Database: A collection of data stored in a number of tables.

Database application: A program or collection of programs that manipulates the data in a database.

Data set: Data sets provide database access. Here we used only the ClientDataSet data set representing a specific table in a database, but a data set can also represent the results of a query or stored procedure in a database. All data sets are associated with a DataSource component, a DataSetProvider component, an SQLDataSet component and an SQLConnection component if their data is to be displayed and manipulated in data controls. Unidirectional data sets are data sets that cannot be changed permanently (the ClientDataSet component represents a unidirectional data set).

Key: A key is a field that has a unique value for each record in a data table. For example, no two records may have the same value in the data table's MemberNumber field if this field is the key. A key can also consist of more than one field.

SQL query: An SQL query can be one of the following two types of statement:
- statements that define the fields to include, the tables from which to select those fields, conditions that limit the records that can be included and the order of the resulting data set (SELECT statements);
- statements that manipulate the data in a database table or tables.

Unidirectional data set: This means that the application can open the data set and walk through it but cannot make any changes to it. The behaviour of the data set is like performing an SQL SELECT query and having the ability to view the resulting records but nothing more. dbExpress data sets act this way to maximize performance: The resulting data access is fast and requires little overhead.

User interface factors

Reversibility: To support reversibility in database applications, an Undo button can be programmed to reverse the last change made before the change is made permanent.

NEW DELPHI FEATURES

Data controls

Display data from a database source, such as a Table, outside the application, and can optionally post (save) data changes to a database source. Each data-aware control needs to be associated with a DataSource component in order for the control to receive and manipulate data.

Used here: DBEdit, DBGrid, DBNavigator, DBComboBox.

TClientDataSet (Data Access tab)

Properties	ProviderName	Specifies an external provider object (the DataSetProvider component) that links the ClientDataSet to another source data set (for example the SQLDataSet component). The provider specified by ProviderName can reside in the same application as the ClientDataSet or in an application server running on another system.
	Active	Determines whether the client data set makes its data available. When Active is false, the client data set is closed and it can't manipulate or read the data it represents. When Active is true, data can be read or edited using the ClientDataSet. Setting Active to true fills the ClientDataSet with data.
Methods	ApplyUpdates	Writes all updated, inserted, and deleted records from the client data set to the database.
	UndoLastChange	Undoes the last edit, insert, or delete operation to a record in the client data set.
Prefix	cds	
Use		TClientDataSet represents an in-memory or local data set. We used it as a local in-memory buffer of the records from the data table. It communicates with the data table through a DataSetProvider.

TDBEdit (Data Controls tab)

Properties	DataSource	The link to the data set where the component finds its data.
	DataField	Identifies the field whose value is represented by the DBEdit.
Text		The property representing the contents of the field.
Prefix	dbe	
Use		DBEdit enables users to edit a database field.

TDataSetProvider (Data Access tab)

Properties	DataSet	Links the DataSetProvider to the data set that it represents.
Prefix	dsp	
Use		Used to provide data from a data set to a client data set or to resolve updates from that client data set back to the data set or to its underlying database server. When the provider supplies data to a client data set, the client data set reconstructs the data in the data packet to create a local, in-memory copy for user access. When user access is complete, the client data set repackages any changed data and sends the updates back to the provider. The provider applies the updates to the database or source data set.

TDataSource component (Data Access tab)

Property	DataSet	Specifies the data set (in this chapter we used only ClientDataSets) for which the DataSource component serves as a connector to the data-aware components.
Prefix	dat	
Use		We use a DataSource component to provide a connector between a data set (the ClientDataSet here) and the data controls on a form that enable the display, navigation and editing of the data underlying the data set.

TDBComboBox (Data Controls tab)

Properties	DataField	This property specifies which field is represented by the DBComboBox. (The field into which the selected value is inserted.) The DBComboBox displays the current value of this field and allows the user to set the value of this field on the current record.
	DataSource	This property links the DBComboBox to a data set. Both the DataSource and the DataField properties must be set. The data set containing the field is specified by the DataSource property.
	Items	We use Items to supply the values in the list from which the user can choose.
Prefix	dbc	
Use		We use a DBComboBox to allow the user to change the value of a field in the current record of a data set either by selecting an item from a list or by typing in the edit box part of the component. The selected item or entered text becomes the new value of the field if the DBComboBox's ReadOnly property is False. The DBComboBox can be customized to enable or disable typing in the edit region of the control, to display the list as a drop-down or as a permanently displayed list, to sort the items in the list, and so on.

TDBGrid (Data Controls tab)

Property	DataSource	The link to the data set where the grid finds its data.
Prefix	dbg	
Use		DBGrid displays and manipulates records from a data set in a tabular grid.

TDBNavigator (Data Controls tab)

Properties	DataSource	Specifies the DataSource component which identifies the data set that the navigator manipulates.
	VisibleButtons	We use this property to select the buttons to appear on the navigator. Leave any of the buttons out of the VisibleButtons set to hide them and thereby prevent the user from performing certain operations.
Prefix	nav	
Use		The database navigator is used to move through the data in a data set and to perform operations on the data.

TSQLConnection Component (dbExpress tab)

Property	Connected	Set Connected to true to establish a connection to the database server. When a data set that uses the TSQLConnection object is activated, it automatically sets Connected to true. Set Connected to false to close a connection.
	ConnectionName	Set ConnectionName to use a named connection configuration. Setting ConnectionName automatically sets the DriverName and Params properties to reflect the driver and connection parameters stored under that name in the dbxconnections.ini file. You can define new connection configurations using the Connection Editor. To launch the Connection Editor, double-click on the TSQLConnection component.
	DriverName	If you are not using named connections, set DriverName to the name of an installed dbExpress driver such as INTERBASE, MYSQL, INFORMIX, ORACLE, or DB2. Installed drivers are listed in the dbxdrivers.ini file.
		If you are using named connections, the DriverName property is automatically set when you set the ConnectionName property. When you set DriverName, TSQLConnection automatically sets the LibraryName and VendorLib properties to the names of the libraries (DLLs or shared objects) that implement the specified driver.
	LibraryName	LibraryName is the dbExpress library associated with the driver specified by DriverName. Most applications do not need to use LibraryName directly, because this property is set automatically when the DriverName property is set. The file named by this property is the only dbExpress file that must be deployed with your application.
	VendorLib	VendorLib is the library supplied by the database vendor to support the client-side use of the database. Most applications do not need to use VendorLib directly, because this property is set automatically when the DriverName property is set. The association between a vendor library and a driver name is stored in the dbxdrivers.ini file when you install the associated dbExpress driver. The file named by this property must be running on the same system as your application when it is deployed. Typically, it is installed rather than with your application.
	LoginPrompt	Set LoginPrompt to true to provide login support when establishing a connection. When LoginPrompt is false, the application must supply user name and password values programmatically.
Prefix	sco	
Use		Use TSQLConnection to represent a dbExpress database connection. The connection provided by a single TSQLConnection component can be shared by multiple SQL data set components through their SQLConnection properties.

Property	SQLConnection	Use SQLConnection to specify an SQL connection object that connects the dataset to a database server.
	CommandType	CommandType indicates the type of command that is contained in the CommandText property.
	CommandText	**Command type** — **Corresponding CommandText**

Command type	Corresponding CommandText
ctQuery	An SQL statement that the dataset executes.
ctStoredProc	The name of a stored procedure.
ctTable	The name of a table on the database server. The SQL dataset automatically generates a SELECT statement to fetch all the records on all the fields in this table.

	SortFieldNames	Use SortFieldNames to specify the fields that should be used to order the records in the data set. SortFieldNames is only used when CommandType is ctTable and when the table's primary key consists of more than one field.
Prefix	sds	
Use		TSQLDataSet is a general-purpose unidirectional data set for accessing database information using dbExpress. Use TSQLDataSet to:

a. Represent the records in a database table, the result set of a SELECT query, or the result set returned by a stored procedure.

b. Execute a query or stored procedure that does not return a result set.

Before we can use a TSQLDataSet component, it must be connected to the database server. Therefore, the first step to take when working with TSQLDataSet is to set the SQLConnection property. Once the dataset is connected to a server, we can set the CommandText property if we are using the data set to execute a query. To execute a stored procedure or represent a single database table, set the CommandType property and then choose the table or stored procedure name from a drop-down list on the CommandText property.

PROBLEMS

PROBLEM 15.1) A database of compact discs

A CD shop needs a database to store the following detail about its CDs:

Field	Data type	Length
BarCode (Primary key)	varchar	15
Artist	varchar	30
Title	varchar	30
YearProduced	date	
RecordingCompany	varchar	30
Price	double	

a. Create a database called DBCDShop that has one table called CD with the fields shown above.

b.   Write a Delphi application that uses a DBGrid and a DBNavigator to populate (add, delete and change) the CD data table.
c.   Write a Delphi application that uses DBEdits and a DBNavigator to maintain the CD data table.
d.   Change the application written in 15.1.c above to enable its users to select the bar code of an existing CD from a drop-down list to display the corresponding CD's detail.

PROBLEM 15.2 A telephone directory

We need a database for storing data that would typically appear in a telephone directory. It must include the following fields:

Field	Data type	Length
Surname (Key)	varchar	30
Initials (Key)	varchar	5
Address (Key)	varchar	50
City	varchar	20
Telephone	varchar	15
Fax	varchar	15

a.   Create a database called TelephoneDirecrory, with one table called Person with the above structure. Then write a Delphi application to populate the table using a DBGrid.
b.   Write another Delphi application that displays only the surnames, initials and phone numbers in a DBGrid component, and does not allow the user to modify any of the data in the table.

PROBLEM 15.3 Using a DBComboBox

Modify the application in problem 15.1.c above to allow the user a choice of the following four recording companies only:
Gallo Music Productions
Hoezit Musiek
Maranatha
JNS Music

The four recording companies must be displayed in a drop-down list and the user has to choose one for each record.

CHAPTER 16

Database programming using data modules and multiple forms

PURPOSE OF THIS CHAPTER

In the previous chapter we created Delphi applications that access data tables. We wrote very little program code in order to view the data in a table, add data to a table, or change existing data. Sometimes, however, it is necessary to do things with data that requires more programming. In this chapter, we create an application that includes event handlers that access and manipulate the data in tables using more program code.

This chapter includes detail of how to:

o   use data modules;
o   use more than one form in an application (a Delphi project);
o   use forms from other applications;
o   create new forms for an existing application;
o   add, delete and change records using program code;
o   use SQL queries.

The options and alternatives for Delphi and databases are vast – too vast for a single chapter. By way of introduction, the examples in this chapter will cover a few of the commonly used Delphi commands for accessing a database.

We will create the application with the user interface given in the three figures below. With each example in this chapter, we will add more functionality to the application.

All the examples in this chapter (and the next one) form part of a single application. It is therefore important that you do each one of them on your computer. Doing only some of them will limit your insight into the concepts involved.

In example 16.1, we write that part of the application that will allow the user to maintain the LibraryMember and LibraryBook tables in database MyVPLibrary. We will use the forms and code created in example 15.2 and 15.4 respectively. The Member table..., Book table... and Acquisition table... menu items will be available to the user as in figure 16.1. The Book loans and Reports menu items will initially be disabled.

In example 16.2, we create a new form with code for adding records to the LibraryAcquisition table.

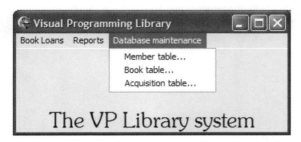

Figure 16.1 The menu items for maintaining the books, members and book acquisitions

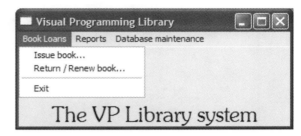

Figure 16.2 The menu items for issuing, returning and renewing a book

In example 16.3, we write the program code for recording a book loan (adding a new record to the loan table) when the user selects the Book Loans | Issue book... menu sequence, (figure 16.2).

In example 16.4, we write the program code for deleting (returning) or changing (renewing) an existing book loan record when the user selects the Book Loans | Return / Renew book... menu sequence. (figure 16.2)

In Chapter 17 we generate reports and will write the program code for the Reports menu sequences (figure 16.3).

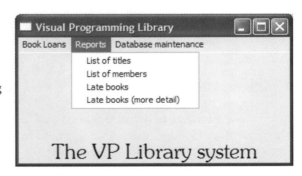

Figure 16.3 The user can generate reports about the titles, the members and the late books

---

EXAMPLE 16.1) Database maintenance | Member table... and Book table...

In this example we start writing the application with the interface shown in figures 16.1, 16.2 and 16.3. Selecting the Database Maintenance | Member table... menu sequence enables the user to maintain the LibraryMember data table using the form in figure 16.4.

Figure 16.4 Maintaining the LibraryMember table

Selecting the Database Maintenance | Book table... menu sequence enables the user to maintain the LibraryBook data table using the form in figure 16.5.

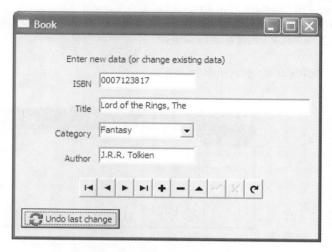

Figure 16.5 Maintaining the Librarybook table

EX 16.1   Planning

We need to create the forms in figures 16.1, 16.4 and 16.5. We then need to link them so that form 16.4 and form 16.5 can be activated from the main form (figure 16.1).

We have already created forms 16.4 and 16.5 in the previous chapter in examples 15.2 and 15.4, so we will not re-create them here, but rather reuse the existing ones in this new application.

Something that we need to think about is: on which of the two forms do we put the SQLConnection component? It needs to be accessed from the forms in both figure 16.4 and figure 16.5. We will introduce a data module to keep all the database components in one place to be accessed from all the forms in the application.

EX 16.1   Testing

Our program should behave as follows:
o   When the user selects the Database Maintenance | Member table... menu sequence, the form in figure 16.4 must appear for maintenance of the LibraryMember table.
o   When the user selects the Database Maintenance | Book table... menu sequence, the form in figure 16.5 must appear for maintenance of the LibraryBook table.
o   The changes must actually appear in the database.

EX 16.1 STEP 1   Create the main form of the application

• Start a new application and create the user interface by adding a MainMenu component to the form.
• Use the menu editor to add the menu items as shown in figures 16.1, 16.2 and 16.3.
• Add a Label.

- Set the properties as in the table below:

Component	Property	Value	
Form1	Name	frmLibrary	
	Caption	Visual Programming Library	
Label1	Name	lblLibrary	
	Caption	The VP Library system	
	Alignment	taCenter	
	Font	Times New Roman size = 20	
Bookloans1	Enabled	False	{Book loans menu item}
Reports1	Enabled	False	{Reports menu item}

- Save the project and unit files as C16e01u and C16e01p respectively.

EX 16.1 STEP 2 Add the Member and Book forms to the project

- With menu sequence Project | Add to Project, select C15e02u and click the Open button (or just double-click on C15e02u).
- With menu sequence File | Save As..., save the unit as Memberu.
- With menu sequence Project | Add to Project, select C15e04u and click the Open button (or just double-click on C15e04u).
- With menu sequence File | Save As..., save the unit as Booku.

Multiple forms and units in an application

Our application now consists of three forms and the top part of the Code Editor now looks like the one in figure 16.6.

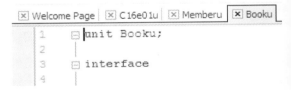

Figure 16.6 The Code Editor with three forms in Delphi 8

- To work in a specific unit or form, click the corresponding tab and use the Toggle Form/Unit (Delphi 6 or 7) or Show Designer/Show Code (Delphi 8) SpeedButton or <F12> to switch between the program code and the form.
- If at any time during this example (or any other application you work on) any of the tabs are not visible, it means that the specific unit is not open. When you open a project, it opens only the main unit and form (the one that is visible when your program starts (C16e01u and frmLibrary here).
- We will see later that you can run the application without any other open units; but if you want to change code, you have to open them with the View form SpeedButton (or <Shift+F12> or View | Forms or View | Units) which offers all the forms or units in the current application for you to choose one to open.

At this stage our application consists of the main form frmLibrary and its unit (C16e01u), frmMember and its unit (Memberu) and frmBook and its unit (Booku). The two units that we have added (Memberu and Booku) are part of this project, but at the moment they are unrelated to each other and to the main unit.

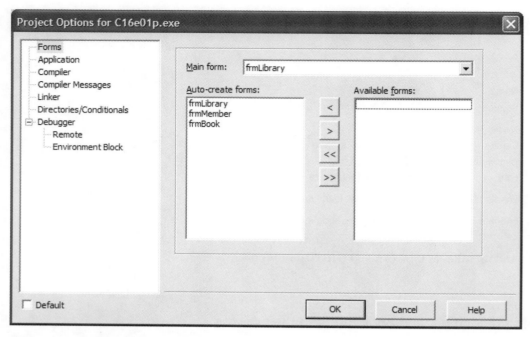

Figure 16.7 Project Option for C16e01p in Delphi 8

The Project Options

- Selecting the menu sequence Project | Options shows all the forms currently in the project and allows us to select another form as the main form if we need to (figure 16.7). (The Project Options screen looks slightly different in Delphi 6/7.)

The forms are currently auto-create forms. For a more efficient application, they can be created programmatically. However, this is beyond the scope of this book.

- We do not want to change any of the project options so close this window.

EX 16.1 STEP 3 Add code to activate frmMember from the main form

- Go to form frmLibrary and double-click the MainMenu component to open the Menu Editor.
- Double-click on the Member table item in the Database Maintenance menu to generate the skeleton for the TfrmLibrary.Membertable1Click event handler.
- Change the code as shown below:

```
procedure TfrmLibrary.Membertable1Click(Sender: TObject);
begin
  frmMember.Show;
end;
```

- Save the unit with File | Save or use the Save SpeedButton or <Ctrl+S>.

EX 16.1 STEP 4 Make unit Memberu accessible from the main form

With the statement `frmMember.Show;` in event handler `TfrmLibrary.Membertable1Click` in unit C16e01u, unit C16e01u refers to unit Memberu (where frmMember is declared), but it does not have access to that unit. We create that access by including unit Memberu in unit C16e01u's uses clause as follows:

- Click on the C16e01u tab in the designer or CodeEditor to make it the active unit.
- Using File | Use Unit, select unit Memberu as in figure 16.8. Click OK.

This adds Memberu to the uses clause in C16e01u. (See figure 16.9.)

- Save the application using File | Save All.
- Run the application.

You should now be able to maintain the LibraryMember data table by using the menu sequence Database Maintenance | Member table....

Figure 16.8 Making C15e02u accessible from C16e01u

```
17    var
18      frmLibrary: TfrmLibrary;
19
20  ⊟ implementation
21
22    uses Memberu;
23
24    {$R *.nfm}
25
```

Figure 16.9 Memberu added to the uses clause C16e01u

EX 16.1 STEP 5 Adding code to activate frmBook from the main form

- Go to form frmLibrary and double-click the MainMenu component to open the Menu Editor.
- Double-click on the Book table... item in the Database Maintenance menu to generate the skeleton for the TfrmLibrary.Booktable1Click event handler.
- Change the code as shown below:

```
procedure TfrmLibrary.Booktable1Click(Sender: TObject);
begin
  frmBook.Show;
end;
```

EX 16.1 STEP 6 Running the application without making unit Booku accessible to the main form

If we do not add the uses clause (with File | Use Unit), but still attempt to show or refer to objects on another form when we run the program, Delphi will pick up what we are trying to do and will display a dialog (as in figure 16.10) to ask whether the clause must be added. Clicking Yes will result in the clause being added. The next time you run the program it will run.

- Run the application.
- Click Yes to add Booku to the uses clause in C16e01u.
- Save the unit with File | Save or using the Save SpeedButton or <Ctrl+S>.
- Run the program, use the menu sequence, see that we've linked the two forms from Chapter 15 to frmLibrary.

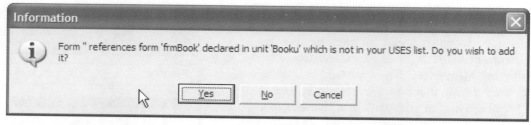

Figure 16.10 The dialog when we attempt to show a form that we do not have access to

Showing forms: modal and modeless

In the two event handlers connected to the Member table... and Book table... menu items, we show forms frmMember (step 3) and frmBook (step 5). There are two styles in which a form can be shown: *modal* and *modeless*. We display a modeless form with the Show method and a Modal form with the ShowModal method.

When a form is displayed modally, it is the only form that can accept input from the user. Consequently, when a modal form is on display, the user cannot interact with any other form that may be visible. The modal form must be closed before interaction can continue with any other form. ShowMessage and InputBox are examples of modal forms. The user must click on a button that closes the dialog box before the program can return to the form where the dialog box was called from.

By contrast, when a form is displayed modelessly (with the Show method) all its own operations and all other loaded forms' operations are available. The user can switch freely between any forms on display and activities in different parts of the application can continue in parallel (ie simultaneously).

- To illustrate the difference between modal and modeless, close the application and change the two Show methods to ShowModal.
- Run the application in the example again, going to the Member form.
- Then drag it to one side and without closing it, try to select any item on the menu.
- As you can see, the main form of the application is not available to the user.
- Close the application and change the two ShowModal methods back to Show.
- Save the application.

User interface factors: modal vs modeless

From a user interface design perspective, is it better to use modal or modeless forms? As an example, consider the Microsoft Internet Explorer application. Clicking on File | Internet Options displays a modal form. If you try to click anywhere outside this form within the Internet Explorer window, the user interface beeps at you. On the other hand, if you download a file from a site, a modeless form is used to display the download progress. This means that you can switch back to the main Internet Explorer window to continue browsing while the download is progressing. Imagine how frustrating it would be if the download form was programmed to be modal?

In general, it is preferable to use modeless forms, because it allows the user to switch between forms without having to close one form and open the other (it is therefore more economical). There are situations, however, where an application requires forms to be modal. For example, all dialogs are modal because the application requires a response from the user before continuing.

Using a data module

In this application so far, we need access to the SQLConnection component (one per database) from two different forms. Later, when we add the functionality of issuing and returning books as well as generating reports, we will see that we also need access to the same tables from different forms. So, to eliminate duplication, on which form must we actually keep the data components? The answer is to use a *data module* for centralised handling of all the data components. Figure 16.11 illustrates how the application will use the forms, units and data module.

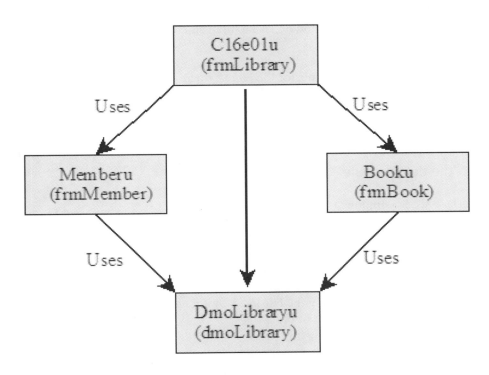

Figure 16.11 Schematic representation of the units, forms and data module in the application

EX 16.1 STEP 7 Create a data module for the Data Access and dbExpress components

- Select File | New Data Module (Delphi 8) or File | New and double-click the Data Module icon in the New Items window (Delphi 6/7). Delphi opens an empty data module.
- Size the data module to make it bigger.
- Change its Name property to dmoLibrary.
- Save the data module's unit file with File | Save As. Use file name dmoLibraryu.

- As we do with forms, we can now add components to the data module by selecting them on the Component/Tool Palette. When a component is selected on the data module, we can edit its properties in the Object Inspector just as we would if the component was on a form.

EX 16.1 STEP 8 Move the dbExpress and Data Access components from frmMember to the data module

We already have the data components that we need on frmMember and frmBook, so we can just cut and paste them from there to the data module.
- Toggle to form frmMember. (If it is not opened yet, open it with View | Forms and select frmMember from the list of forms in the project.)
- Select all the dbExpress and Data Access components on the form (scoMyVPLibrary, sdsMember, dspMember, cdsMember and datMember) (select one component and then hold <Shift> down while clicking on all the others in turn).
- Select the menu sequence Edit | Cut.
- Click on the dmoLibraryu tag to go to the data module, make sure you are in Designer/Form view and select Edit | Paste.

This puts all the dbExpress and Data Access components for the LibraryMember table in the data module and deletes them from form frmMember.
- Position the components on the data module as in figure 16.12.

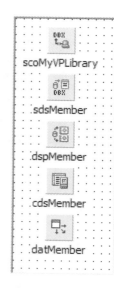

Figure 16.12 The dbExpress & DataAccess components in the data module

EX 16.1 STEP 9 Linking to the data module

Because the dbExpress and Data Access components have moved from frmMember to the data module, the user interface components need to know their new location. The data module is already part of the project, but the components on form frmMember do not have access to it yet.
- Click on the Memberu or frmMember tab in the Code Editor or Designer to make frmMember the active form.
- Add the data module to its uses clause by selecting the File | Use Unit menu sequence and selecting dmoLibraryu from the list of units.
- Click OK.
- Select the DBGrid component on form frmMember and set its DataSource property to dmoLibrary.datMember.

If the Active property of datMember and the Connected property of scoMyVPLibrary is True, the data will be alive again. As we have seen, the DataSource component datMember in data module dmoLibraryu (dmoLibrary.datMember) can now be selected from the drop-down list of the DataSource property in the Object Inspector. This is so, because form frmMember has access to all the components on the data module because it is included in its uses clause.

EX 16.1 STEP 10 Access the data module from frmMember's event handlers

As explained in Chapter 15, the SQLConnection component's Connected property must be set to False when the project is completed (during design time). It must be set to True during run time. We use one connection to the database throughout the execution of the program and so we connect when the main form, frmLibrary, is displayed.

- To make the data module accessible from the main unit, with C16e01u the active unit, select File | Use Unit and select dmoLibraryu to add it to the uses clause in C16e01u.
- Change the code for the OnShow event handler for frmLibrary to set the SQLConnection component's connected property to True:

```
procedure TfrmLibrary.FormShow(Sender: TObject);
begin
    dmoLibrary.scoMyVPLibrary.Connected := True;
end;
```

The event handlers in unit Memberu execute methods of the ClientDataSet, cdsMember, in data module dmoLibrary, so we have to change them accordingly.

- Change the code for the OnShow event handler for the Members form as follows:

```
procedure TfrmMember.FormShow(Sender: TObject);
begin
    dmoLibrary.cdsMember.Open;
end;
```

- Change the code for the OnClose event handler for the Members form as follows:

```
procedure TfrmMember.FormClose(Sender: TObject; var Action: TCloseAction);
begin
    if (dmoLibrary.cdsMember.ChangeCount > 0) then
        dmoLibrary.cdsMember.ApplyUpdates(0);     //MaxErrors parameter: 0
    dmoLibrary.cdsMember.Close;
end;
```

- Change the code for the bmbUndoLastChangeClick event handler for the Members form as follows:

```
procedure TfrmMember.bmbUndoLastChangeClick(Sender: TObject);
begin
    dmoLibrary.cdsMember.UndoLastChange(True);
end;
```

- Save the project with File | Save All or click the Save All SpeedButton.

EX 16.1 STEP 11   Modify frmBook to use the data module

- Toggle to form frmBook. (If it is not opened yet, open it with View | Forms and selecting frmBook from the list of forms in the project.)
- Delete the SQLConnection component, scoMyVPLibrary, from the form. (We already have an SQLConnection component in the data module: we need only one per database.)
- Select all the dbExpress and Data Access components on the form (select one component and hold <Shift> down while clicking on all the others in turn).
- Select the menu sequence Edit | Cut.
- Click on the dmoLibraryu tag to go to the data module, change to Designer | Form view and select Edit | Paste. (This puts all the dbExpress and Data Access components for the LibraryBook table on the data module and deletes them from form frmBook.)
- Position the components on the data module as in figure 16.13.
- Change the SQLConnection property of the SQLDataSet sdsBook to scoMyVPLibrary.

The data module now contains all the components for the LibraryBook table as well as for the LibraryMember table.

Figure 16.13 The dbExpress & Data Access components in the data module

EX 16.1 STEP 12   Linking the DBEdits on frmBook to the data module

The data module is already part of the project, but the components on form frmBook do not have access to it yet.
- Click on the Booku tab in the Code Editor or Designer to make frmBook the active form and add the data module to its uses clause by selecting the File | Use Unit menu sequence and selecting dmoLibraryu from the list of units.
- Click OK.
- Set the DataSource property of all the DBEdits and the DBNavigator on form frmBook to dmoLibrary.datBook.

As we have seen, the DataSource component datBook on data module dmoLibraryu (dmoLibrary.datBook) can now be selected from the drop-down list of the DataSource property in the Object Inspector. Form frmBook has access to all the components on the data module because it is included in its uses clause.

EX 16.1 STEP 13   Accessing the data module from frmBook's event handlers

Form frmBook's event handlers execute methods of the ClientDataSet, cdsMember, on the data module, so we have to change them accordingly.

- Change the code for the OnShow event handler for the book form as follows:

```
procedure TfrmBook.FormShow(Sender: TObject);
begin
  dmoLibrary.cdsBook.Open;
end;
```

- Change the code for the OnClose event handler for the book form as follows:

```
procedure TfrmBook.FormClose(Sender: TObject; var Action: TCloseAction);
begin
  if (dmoLibrary.cdsBook.ChangeCount > 0) then
    dmoLibrary.cdsBook.ApplyUpdates(0);
  dmoLibrary.cdsBook.Close;
end;
```

- Change the code for the bmbUndoLastChangeClick event handler for the book form as follows:

```
procedure TfrmBook.bmbUndoLastChangeClick(Sender: TObject);
begin
  dmoLibrary.cdsBook.UndoLastChange(True);
end;
```

- If it is not False already, set scoMyVPLibrary's Connected property and sdsBook's Active property to False.
- Save the project with File | Save All and run it to see if you can activate the maintenance forms for the members and books.

The application with its forms, units and data module as it is now, is represented schematically in figure 16.11.

EXAMPLE 16.2 Library acquisitions: using an SQL statement and adding records programmatically

A library may have more than one copy of the same title and needs to keep track of which copy is issued to whom. So we use a table (LibraryAcquisition) with two fields: a unique acquisition number and the ISBN number.

Each title already has an ISBN number, but we need to generate a unique acquisition number for each copy of a title (each book in the library).

There is no general algorithm for generating such a number. Various libraries have different ways of doing this. We will use the following method: for each book, we use the year in which it is acquired and concatenate to it an incremental number. For example, say we acquired our first book in 2004, it will have the acquisition number 20040001, the second one will have acquisition number 20040002, the third 20040003 and so on. If we acquire 87 books in 2004, the first book that we acquire in 2005 will have the acquisition number 20050088.

In this example, we write the code to maintain the book acquisitions.

EX 16.2   Planning

We create the LibraryAcquisition table and then write an application that handles the acquisition of new books for the library. The application explores:

○ using a DBLookupComboBox component to search for a specific record;

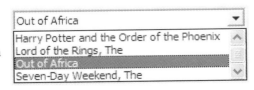

Figure 16.14 Selecting a title from a drop-down list of available titles

- using an SQL statement;
- adding and changing records in a data table programmatically.

The application works as follows: A new book arrives in the library

1. If this is the first copy of this title, the title details are added to the LibraryBook table using Database maintenance | Book table (figure 16.5);
2. The new book is then given a unique acquisition number using Database maintenance | Acquisition table (figure 16.15).

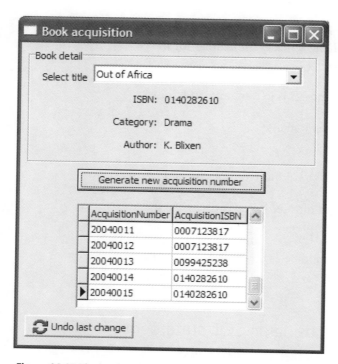

Figure 16.15 The book acquisition form

To enter a new book acquisition the user selects the new book's title (it is easier to search a title than an ISBN number) from a drop-down list of available titles as shown in figure 16.14. As the drop-down list closes up, the corresponding ISBN, Category and Author are displayed in the Book detail GroupBox.

When the user clicks the Generate new acquisition number button (figure 16.15), the application generates a new acquisition number and adds a new acquisition record to the LibraryAcquisition table. These additions are shown in the grid at the bottom of the form.

EX 16.2 STEP 1 Create table LibraryAcquisition in database MyVPLibrary

- Run the MySQL Control Center.
- Similarly to how we created all the other tables, create a new table in MyVPLibrary for all the book acquisitions in the library.
- Specify the table structure and field lengths as in figure 16.16.
- Specify field AcquisitionNumber as the primary key.
- Save the new table.

Field	Type	Null	Key	Default
AcquisitionNumber	varchar(10)		PRI	
AcquisitionISBN	varchar(13)			

Figure 16.16 Structure of the LibraryAcquisition table

- Enter LibraryAcquisition as the name of the new table and click OK.
- Close the MySQL Control Center.

EX 16.2 STEP 2 Add the dbExpress and Data Access components for LibraryAcquisition to the data module

- If it is not already open, open the data module dmoLibrary in Designer | Form View.
- Add the components in the table below. This adds the components we need for the LibraryAquisition table to those for the LibraryBook table and LibraryMember table that are already on the data module.

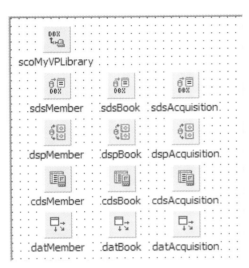

Component	Property	Value
SQLDataSet (dbExpress tab)	Name SQLConnection CommandType CommandText	sdsAcquisition scoMyVPLibrary ctTable LibraryAcquisition
DataSetProvider (Data Access tab)	Name DataSet	dspAcquisition sdsAcquisition
ClientDataSet (Data Access tab)	Name ProviderName	cdsAcquisition dspAcquisition
DataSource (Data Access tab)	Name DataSet	datAcquisition cdsAcquisition

Figure 16.17 The data module

Data module dmoVPLibrary now resembles figure 16.17.
- Save the unit file.

EX 16.2 STEP 3 Create the new form and activate it from the main form

- Still working in project C16e01p, with File | New VCL Form (not VCL application) (Delphi 8) or File | New Form (Delphi 6/7) create a new form.
- Make data module dmoLibraryu accessible to this new form with File | Use Unit and selecting it from the list.
- Add the components as in the table below to resemble figure 16.15.

This new form, frmAcquisition, uses data from two different tables, the LibraryBook table and the LibraryAcquisition table. The DataSources of both of these are on the data module. So, in the property table below, the DBLookupComboBox and the DBTexts use dmoLibrary.datBook as their data sources, while the DBGrid uses dmoLibrary.datAcquisition as its data source.

Component	Property	Value
Form1	Name	frmAcquisition
	Caption	Book acquisition
GroupBox1	Name	gpbBookDetail
	Caption	Book detail
DBLookupComboBox1	Name	dlcTitle
(DataControls tab	ListSource	dmoLibrary.datBook
in GroupBox1)	ListField	BookTitle
	KeyField	BookISBN
Label1	Name, Caption	lblPrompt, Select title
(in GroupBox1)		
Label2	Name, Caption	lblISBN, ISBN:
(in GroupBox1)		
Label3	Name, Caption	lblCategory, Category:
(in GroupBox1)		
Label4	Name, Caption	lblAuthor, Author:
(DataControls tab		
in GroupBox1)		
DBText1 .. DBText3	DataSource	dmoLibrary.datBook
(DataControls tab		
in GroupBox1)		
DBText1	Name	dbtISBN
	DataField	BookISBN
DBText2	Name	dbtCategory
	Datafield	BookCategory
DBText3	Name	dbtAuthor
	Datafield	BookAuthor
Button1	Name	btnGenerateAcqNumber
	Caption	Generate new acquisition number
BitBtn1	Name	bmbUndoLastChange
	Kind	btRetry
	Caption	Undo last change
DBGrid	Name	dbgAcquisition
	DataSource	dmoLibrary.datAcquisition

- Save the unit as AcquireBooku. (We deviate from our project naming convention: although this example and all those that follow have different numbers, we will keep working on the same project, C16e01p.)
- To enable the main form (frmLibrary) to show form frmBookAcquisition, click on the C16e01u tab in the designer or CodeEditor to make it the active unit and Using File | Use Unit, select unit AcquireBooku.
- Click OK. This adds AcquireBooku to the uses clause in C16e01u.
- Enter the event handler for the Database maintenance | Acquisition table... menu sequence as follows:

```
procedure TfrmLibrary.Acquisitiontable1Click(Sender: TObject);
begin
   frmAcquisition.Show;
end;
```

- Save unit C16e01u.
- Without adding any event handlers for the acquisition form, run the application, select the Database maintenance | Acquisition table menu sequence, and see how the dbLookupComboBox works. (We create the event handlers in the next step.)

Notice that the titles are not sorted alphabetically and with a very long list of titles in the drop-down list, it might be difficult to find the title that you are looking for. The primary key of the LibraryBook table is the BookISBN field, so the table is ordered by default according to this field. To make this example worth while, we need the table to be sorted according to the BookTitle field. We order the titles using an SQL statement in the OnShow event handler in the next step.

The DBLookupComboBox component

Here we use a DBLookupComboBox to find a specific record: as the user selects the title of a book in the drop-down list, that title's record becomes active and all its field values are shown in the DBText components. The ListField property refers to the specific field (BookTitle) in the data source (specified in the ListSource property (datBook)) whose values must appear in the drop-down list.

This is only part of the DBComboBox's functionality. It can also associate a set of field values in one data set with a corresponding set of values from another data set. (We explain this in the NEW DELPHI FEATURES section at the end of this chapter.)

The DBText component

We use the DBText component to display the contents of a field in the current active record of a data set on a form. Field values displayed by DBText controls cannot be modified by the user. To allow the user to edit the field value, use DBEdit.

EX 16.2 STEP 4 Create event handlers FormClose, UndoLastChange and FormShow

- If it is not already included, add the Borland.Vcl.SqlExpr namespace (Delphi 8) or SqlExpr unit (Delphi 6 & 7) by including it in the uses statement below the interface part of the unit, Aquirebooku.
- Enter the event handlers given below:

```
1  procedure TfrmAcquisition.FormClose(Sender: TObject;
2                                        var Action: TCloseAction);
3  begin
4    if (dmoLibrary.cdsAcquisition.ChangeCount > 0) then
5      dmoLibrary.cdsAcquisition.ApplyUpdates(0);
6    dmoLibrary.cdsAcquisition.Close;
7    dmoLibrary.cdsBook.Close;
8  end;

9  procedure TfrmAcquisition.bmbUndoLastChangeClick(Sender: TObject);
10 begin
11   dmoLibrary.cdsAcquisition.UndoLastChange(True);
12 end;
```

```
13 procedure TfrmAcquisition.FormShow(Sender: TObject);
14 begin
15   dmoLibrary.cdsBook.close;       //Close the data set before making changes
16   //Setting up the SQLDataSet component as a query
17   dmoLibrary.sdsBook.CommandType := ctQuery;
18   dmoLibrary.sdsBook.CommandText :=
19                         'SELECT * from librarybook ORDER BY BookTitle';
20   dmoLibrary.cdsBook.Open;
21   dmoLibrary.cdsAcquisition.Open;
22   dmoLibrary.cdsBook.Refresh;
23 end;
```

- Save all the files and run the program. Select Database Maintenance | Acquisition table… and notice how the titles in the ComboBox are now ordered alphabetically.

SQL's SELECT statement

SQL's command for retrieving records from a table or tables is SELECT. The SELECT statement has the following general structure:

```
SELECT column1, column2, ...
FROM table1, table2, ...
WHERE selection_criteria
```

The SELECT clause specifies the columns you want to see. The FROM clause specifies the tables to get the data from. The WHERE clause (optional) can contain a wide variety of criteria that identify which rows you want to retrieve. An asterisk (*) is used to retrieve all the columns (fields) in a table in the order in which they are defined. The implications of the different settings of the CommandType property of an SQLDataSet are explained below:

- CommandType: ctTable
  In the examples in Chapter 15, we set the CommandType property to ctTable indicating that we need the SQLDataSet to retrieve all the records in the database table specified in property CommandText (for example LibraryMember). The SQL statement generated automatically during run time by the SQLDataSet is SELECT * FROM LibraryMember (without a WHERE clause).

- CommandType: ctQuery
  We set CommandType to ctQuery if we want to retrieve only a subset of the records in a table or only selected columns (fields) (as in TfrmAcquisition. FormShow, line 17) and we then have to specify the SQL query in the CommandText property (lines 18 & 19). If we only want to see the data of all the members with surname 'Jones', we would use the SQL statement:

```
SELECT * FROM LibraryMember
WHERE LibraryMember.Surname = 'Jones'
```

If we only want to see the initials and email addresses of all the Jones members, we would use the SQL statement:

```
SELECT LibraryMember.MemberInitials,LibraryMember.MemberEmail
FROM LibraryMember
WHERE LibraryMember.Surname = 'Jones'
```

- CommandType: ctStoredProc
  We set the CommandType property to ctStoredProc if we want to retrieve only a
  subset of the records from a table or tables by executing an SQL statement stored
  in a procedure. The CommandText property then needs to be set to the name of a
  stored procedure. (Stored procedures are beyond the scope of this book.)

The SQL query in TfrmAcquisition.FormShow

In this example, we set the CommandType property to ctQuery (line 17) indicating
that we want to specify our own SQL statement to retrieve data from the database
table. Although we retrieve all the records in the LibraryBook table, we use the SQL
statement to order them according to the BookTitle field (lines 18 & 19). (By
default, it is ordered according to the primary key, which is the BookISBN field.)

It is important to note (from lines 18 & 19) that the SQL statement is
enclosed in quotes as the CommandText property takes only string values. If
there is a mistake in the SQL statement, we will get a run time error.

Another example of an SQL query statement is:

```
SELECT * from librarybook
WHERE BookCategory = 'Fantasy'
ORDER BY BookTitle
```

This SQL query will retrieve only the books in the 'Fantasy' category.

- To extend our understanding of queries, include a WHERE clause in the SQL
  statement above in `TfrmAcquisition.FormShow` by changing it as follows:

```
dmoLibrary.sdsBook.CommandText := 'SELECT * from librarybook '+
                                  'WHERE BookCategory = ''Fantasy'''+
                                  'ORDER BY BookTitle';
```

Since the CommandText property requires values of type string, we need to
replace each single quote inside the SQL statement with a pair of single quotes.

- Run the program to see the effect of using this SQL statement.

Selecting the Database maintenance | Acquisition table... menu sequence will
now only show the titles of the books in the Fantasy category in the library.

- Now close the Book acquisition form (not the application) and select the
  Database Maintenance | Book table... menu sequence.

Now only the records of the books in the Fantasy category are available for
maintenance. If you think carefully, this is not surprising at all! In the OnShow
event handler that executed when we selected the Database maintenance |
Acquisition table menu sequence earlier, we specify the SQLDataSet (in sdsBook's
CommandText property) to extract only the fantasy books from the database into
the ClientDataSet (cdsBook). Because this program is event-driven the user can
select menu sequences in any order that we cannot predict, so we have to reset
sdsBook and refresh cdsBook so that we can have all the book records available
again for maintenance. We do this in frmBook's OnShow event handler.

EX 16.2 STEP 5   Refreshing the ClientDataSet for the books

- Change TfrmBook.FormShow as follows:

```
procedure TfrmBook.FormShow(Sender: TObject);
begin
  dmoLibrary.sdsBook.CommandType := ctTable;
  dmoLibrary.sdsBook.CommandText := 'LibraryBook';
  dmoLibrary.cdsBook.Open;
  dmoLibrary.cdsBook.Refresh;
end;
```

- Run the program with the Database Maintenance | Book table... and Database maintenance | Acquisition... table sequences again to see the effect of the change.
- Now change the SQL statement in TfrmAcquisition.FormShow back to lines 18 and 19 in STEP 4 again.
- Save the unit as AquireBooku.

The ClientDataSet's Refresh method

TfrmBook.FormShow and TfrmAcquisition.FormShow call the cdsBook ClientDataSet's Refresh method to ensure that it has the latest data from the database. We do this here because if the ClientDataSet previously contained the result of a query, it should be Refreshed to display all records in the data set, not just those that used to meet the query condition.

EX 16.2 STEP 6   Using DateUtils

- To be able to use Delphi's standard routines for the manipulation of dates (values of type TDateTime) to generate the acquisition numbers, we need to add the Borland.Vcl.DateUtils namespace (Delphi 8) or DateUtils unit (Delphi 6 & 7) by including it in the uses statement below the interface part of the unit. The uses statements must now be: (The changes are shown in bold.)

```
uses   //Delphi 8
       Windows, Messages, SysUtils, Variants, Classes, Graphics, Controls,
       Forms,Dialogs, DBXpress, FMTBcd, Borland.Vcl.Db, Borland.Vcl.DBClient,
       Borland.Vcl.Provider,System.ComponentModel, Borland.Vcl.Grids,
       Borland.Vcl.DBGrids, Borland.Vcl.ExtCtrls, Borland.Vcl.DBCtrls,
       Borland.Vcl.StdCtrls, Borland.Vcl.Buttons, Borland.Vcl.Mask,
       Borland.Vcl.SqlExpr, Borland.Vcl.DateUtils;

uses   //Delphi 6 & 7
       Windows, Messages, SysUtils, Variants, Classes, Graphics, Controls,
       Forms, Dialogs, Grids, DBGrids, Buttons, StdCtrls, DBCtrls,
       SqlExpr, DateUtils;
```

EX 16.2 STEP 7   The Generate new acquisition number event handler

- Enter the `btnGenerateAcqNumberClick` event handler shown below:

```
1 procedure TfrmAcquisition.btnGenerateAcqNumberClick(Sender: TObject);
2 Var ThisYear,Acq: Integer;
3     ThisDay: TDateTime;  //Today's date
4     AcqStr,AcqNumber: string;
5 begin
6   ThisDay := Date;
7   ThisYear := YearOf(ThisDay); //Get the year part of today's date

8   Acq := dmoLibrary.cdsAcquisition.RecordCount + 1; //1st Acq number
9   //Pad the number with zeros
10  Case Acq of
11       1..9: AcqStr := '000' + IntToStr(Acq);
12     10..99: AcqStr := '00' + IntToStr(Acq);
13   100..999: AcqStr := '0' + IntToStr (Acq);
14 1000..9999: AcqStr := IntToStr (Acq);
15  else
16    begin
17      ShowMessage ('Library full.');
18    end;
19  end; //Case
20  AcqNumber := IntToStr(ThisYear) + AcqStr;

21  //Adding record to acquisition table
22  dmoLibrary.cdsAcquisition.Insert;   //Inserting new empty record

23  dmoLibrary.cdsAcquisition.FieldByName('AcquisitionNumber').AsString
24                                                    := AcqNumber;
25  dmoLibrary.cdsAcquisition.FieldByName('AcquisitionISBN').AsString
26           := dmoLibrary.cdsBook.FieldByName('BookISBN').AsString;
27  dmoLibrary.cdsAcquisition.Post;       //Saving new record

28 end;
```

- Save the unit and run the application. Add a few acquisitions. HINT: If `DateUtils` (Delphi 6/7) or `Borland.Vcl.DateUtils` (Delphi 8) has not been included in the Uses clause, then the function Date will give an error.

Date operations

In the `btnGenerateAcqNumberClick` event handler, we declare variable `ThisDay` of type TDateTime (line 3). TDateTime is a type that maps to a Double. The integral part of a Delphi TDateTime value is the number of days that have passed since 30/12/1899. The fractional part of the TDateTime value is fraction of a 24 hour day that has elapsed. The table below shows examples of TDateTime values and their corresponding dates and times:

TDateTime value	Date	Time
0	30/12/1899	12:00 am
2.75	1/1/1900	6:00 pm
−1.25	29/12/1899	6:00 am
35065	1/1/1996	12:00 am

To find the fractional number of days between two dates, we simply subtract the two values, unless one of the TDateTime values is negative (before 30/12/1899). Similarly, to increment a date and time value by a certain fractional number of days, we add the fractional number to the date and time value if the TDateTime value is positive (on or after 30/12/1899).

Date (line 6) is a standard Delphi function that returns a TDateTime value with the date portion set to the current date and the time portion set to 0. (Remember we added the DateUtils unit (Delphi 6/7) or Borland.Vcl.DateUtils namespace (Delphi 8) above? These date manipulation routines are in there.)

YearOf (line 7) obtains the year represented by a specified TDateTime value. YearOf returns a value between 1 and 9999.

Working with the ClientDataSet

In line 8 we access ClientDataSet cdsAcquisition's RecordCount property to determine the number of records in the data set. Lines 23–26,

```
dmoLibrary.cdsAcquisition.FieldByName('AcquisitionNumber').AsString
          := AcqNumber;
dmoLibrary.cdsAcquisition.FieldByName('AcquisitionISBN').AsString
          := dmoLibrary.cdsBook.FieldByName('BookISBN').AsString;
```

put values into the AcquisitionNumber and AcquisitionISBN fields of the current record (the newly inserted record) of the cdsAcquisition ClientDataSet. Of special interest is the second statement which takes the value of field BookISBN of the current record in ClientDataSet cdsBook, and assigns it to field AcquisitionISBN of the active record in ClientDataSet cdsAcquisition.

It is important to note that if the specified field does not exist, FieldByName raises an EDatabaseError exception.

We can also get values from (or put values into) fields of types other than String for example with:

AsFloat   To read the value of an active record's Double field or to assign a Double value to the contents of the field.

AsInteger   To read the value of the active record's Integer field or to assign an Integer value to the contents of the field.

AsBoolean   To read the value of the active record's Boolean field or to assign a Boolean value to the contents of the field.

AsDateTime To read the value of the active record's DateTime field or to assign a DateTime value to the contents of the field.

In line 22, the `Insert` method inserts a new, empty record in the data set (cdsAcquisition here) and makes it the current record. After a call to `Insert`, an application can put data in the fields of the record or allow users to enter data in the fields of the record, and then post those changes to the database.

We subsequently apply the updates to the database by calling `ApplyUpdates` in the OnClose event handler of the form.

Line 27 calls `Post` to commit (save) the changes to the current record (the newly inserted one) in the cdsAcquisition ClientDataSet (the changes still need to be applied to the database with the `ApplyUpdates` method). The ClientDataSet's methods that change the data set state (such as `Edit`, `Insert`, or `Append`, or that move from one record to another, such as `First`, `Last`, `Next`, and `Prior`) automatically call the `Post` method. (See the discussion of the DBNavigator in Chapter 15.)

EXAMPLE 16.3 Library loans | Issue book...

In this example, we write the event handler for the Book loans | Issue book... menu sequence (figure 16.18). This will create a new book loan record. (We will write the event handler for the Return/Renew book... menu item in the next example.)

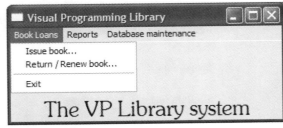

Figure 16.18 Issuing, returning or renewing a book

Clicking the Issue book... menu item

When the user clicks the Issue book... menu item, the form in figure 16.21 appears. The user selects a specific acquisition number from the drop-down list, selects a surname from the surname drop-down list and clicks the Issue book BitButton.

EX 16.3 Planning: What does issuing a book involve?

First, we have to decide what exactly a book issue involves. For every book issued, a record needs to be added to the LibraryLoan table (a new table that we still have to create). Each loan record will contain the acquisition number of the book (not the ISBN because we can have more than one copy with the same ISBN), the date that the book is due back and the ID number of the library member borrowing the book. This form therefore interacts with the LibraryMember, LibraryAcquisition and LibraryLoan tables.

EX 16.3 STEP 1 Create the LibraryLoan table

- Using the MySQL Control Center, create a new table with the fields shown in figure 16.19.
- Save the table as LibraryLoan in database MyVPLibrary.

Field	Type	Null	Key	Default
🔑 LoanAcquisitionNumber	varchar(8)		PRI	
LoanMemberID	varchar(13)			
LoanDueDate	date			0000-00-00

Figure 16.19 The structure of the LibraryLoan table

EX 16.3 STEP 2 Add LibraryLoan to the data module

- If project C16e01p is not open, open it.
- Using File | Open and double-clicking on dmoLibraryu (or View | Forms and selecting dmoLibrary) open the data module in Designer | Form View and add the components below. These are the components we need for the new LibraryLoan table.

Component	Property	Value
SQLDataSet1	Name	sdsLoan
	SQLConnection	scoMyVPLibrary
	CommandType	ctTable
	CommandText	LibraryLoan
DataSetProvider1	Name	dspLoan
	DataSet	sdsLoan
ClientDataSet1	Name	cdsLoan
	ProviderName	dspLoan
	Active	True
Datasource1	Name	datLoan
	DataSet	cdsLoan

The data module now resembles figure 16.20.
- Save it.

What happens when a book is issued

Libraries usually use scanners to read the acquisition number of each book taken to the loan counter. In our system the acquisition number is selected by the librarian at the loan counter. We therefore have to accommodate human error as best we can.

The form that we use for issuing books is shown in figure 16.21. Initially, the Issue book BitButton is disabled. As soon as an acquisition number as well as a surname are selected from the respective drop-down lists, the Issue book BitButton becomes enabled. The librarian can then issue the selected book to the selected member.

A specific copy of a book can be borrowed by only one member. So, as the librarian clicks the Issue book button, the program searches the LibraryLoan table to ensure that the book is not already on loan (possible if librarian selects wrong acquisition number). If the specific record is not found in the table, we know that the book is available and the book can be issued. Books can be borrowed for 14 days at a time.

If it is established that the book can be issued, an empty record is inserted into the LibraryLoan table, the LoanAcquisitionNumber, LoanMemberID and LoanDueDate fields are set and the record is saved. The rest of this example takes us through the steps needed to perform these operations.

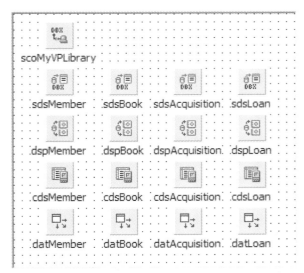

Figure 16.20 The data module with all the dbExpress and Data Access components

EX 16.3 STEP 3 Creating the form for issuing a book

- Create a new form with File | New VCL Form (Delphi 8) or File | New Form (Delphi 6/7).
- Before we can create the user interface, we need to make the data module accessible to this form, so that it can refer to the LibraryMember and LibraryBook tables.
- Ensure that Form1 is the active form and with File | Use Unit, select dmoLibraryu and click OK.
- Now create the user interface (figure 16.21). We use the components below to access, display and update the relevant data.

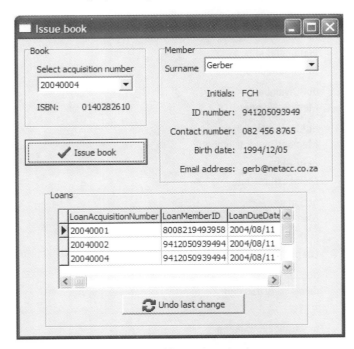

Figure 16.21 The interface used for issuing a book

Component	Property	Value
Form1	Name	frmIssueBook
	Caption	Issue book
GroupBox1	Name	gpbBook
	Caption	Book
Label1	Name	lblAck
(in GroupBox1)	Caption	Select acquisition number
DBLookupComboBox1	Name	dlcAcqNumber
(in GroupBox1)	ListSource	dmoLibrary.datAcquisition
	ListField	AcquisitionNumber
	KeyField	AcquisitionNumber
Label2	Name	lblISBN
(in GroupBox1)	Caption	ISBN:
DBText1	Name	dbtISBN
(in GroupBox1)	DataSource	dmoLibrary.datAcquisition
	Datafield	dmoLibrary.AcquisitionISBN
BitButton1	Name	bmbIssueBook
	Kind	bkOk
	Caption	Issue book
	Enabled	False
Groupbox2	Name	gpbMember
	Caption	Member
Label3, Label4 ... Label8	Caption	Surname, Initials, ID number,
(in Groupbox2)		Contact number, Birth date,
		Email address (respectively)
DBLookupComboBox2	Name	dlcSurname
(in Groupbox2)	ListSource	dmoLibrary.datMember
	ListField	MemberSurname
	KeyField	MemberNumber
DBText2 .. DBText6	Datasource	dmoLibrary.datMember
(in Groupbox2)		
DBText2	Name	dbtInitials
	DataField	MemberInitials
DBText3	Name	dbtIDNumber
	DataField	MemberNumber
DBText4	Name	dbtContactNumber
	DataField	MemberContactNumber
DBText5	Name	dbtBirthDate
	DataField	MemberBirthDate
DBText6	Name	dbtEmail
	DataField	MemberEmail
GroupBox3	Name	gpbLoans
	Caption	Loans
DBGrid1	Name	dbgLoan
(in GroupBox3)	DataSource	dmoLibrary.datLoan
	ReadOnly	True
BitButton2	Name	bmbUndoLastChange
(inGroupBox3)	Kind	bkRetry
	Caption	Undo last change

- Save the unit as IssueBooku.

EX 16.3 STEP 4 Make unit IssueBooku accessible from C16e01u

- Click on the C16e01u tab in the code editor or designer and with the File | Use Unit menu sequence, select IssueBooku to include it in C16e01u's uses statement.
- Enable the Book loans... menu item by setting its Enabled property to True.
- Save unit C16e01u.
- Enter frmLibrary.Issuebook1Click below that shows the Book issue form from the Book Loans | Issue book... menu selection:

```
procedure TfrmLibrary.Issuebook1Click(Sender: TObject);
begin
  frmIssueBook.Show;
end;
```

EX 16.3 STEP 5 The event handlers for frmIssueBook

- Enter the OnShow event handler given below for form frmIssuebook

```
procedure TfrmIssuebook.FormShow(Sender: TObject);
begin
  dmoLibrary.cdsAcquisition.Open;
  dmoLibrary.cdsMember.Open;
  dmoLibrary.cdsLoan.Open;
  dmoLibrary.cdsAcquisition.Refresh;
  dmoLibrary.cdsMember.Refresh;
  dmoLibrary.cdsLoan.Refresh;
end;
```

- Enter the OnClose event handler given below for form frmIssueBook

```
procedure TfrmIssuebook.FormClose(Sender: Tobject; var Action: TCloseAction);
begin
  if (dmoLibrary.cdsLoan.ChangeCount > 0) then
    dmoLibrary.cdsLoan.ApplyUpdates(0);    //MaxErrors parameter: 0
  dmoLibrary.cdsAcquisition.Close;
  dmoLibrary.cdsMember.Close;
  dmoLibrary.cdsLoan.Close;
end;
```

- Enter the OnClick event handler given below for the Undo last change button.

```
procedure TfrmIssuebook.bmbUndoLastChangeClick(Sender: Tobject);
begin
  dmoLibrary.cdsLoan.UndoLastChange(True);
end;
```

To allow for human error, we include the OnCloseUp event handlers for the two DBLookupComboBoxes respectively, so that the Issue book button only becomes enabled when the user has selected an acquisition number and a member surname:

```
procedure TfrmIssuebook.dlcAcqNumberCloseUp(Sender: TObject);
begin
  If (dlcSurname.Text <> '') and (dlcAcqNumber.Text <> '') then
    bmbIssueBook.Enabled := True;
end;


procedure TfrmIssuebook.dlcSurnameCloseUp(Sender: TObject);
begin
  If (dlcSurname.Text <> '') and (dlcAcqNumber.Text <> '') then
    bmbIssueBook.Enabled := True;
end;
```

- Enter the OnClick event handler given below for the Issue book button.

```
1  procedure TfrmIssuebook.bmbIssueBookClick(Sender: TObject);
2  var MemberID, Acquisition: string;
3      DueDate : DateTime;
4  begin
5    MemberID := dmoLibrary.cdsMember.FieldByName('MemberNumber').AsString;
6    Acquisition := dmoLibrary.cdsAcquisition.FieldByName('AcquisitionNumber').AsString;

7    //Is book available?
8    If dmoLibrary.cdsLoan.FindKey([Acquisition]) then
9      //Record exists, so book already out
10     ShowMessage('Book not available')

11   else       //Record not in LibraryLoan table, so book is available
12   begin
13     //Add new empty Loan record
14     dmoLibrary.cdsLoan.Insert;
15     //Put the values in the fields
16     DueDate := Date + 14;      //14 days after today
17     dmoLibrary.cdsLoan.FieldByName('LoanAcquisitionNumber').AsString := Acquisition;
18     dmoLibrary.cdsLoan.FieldByName('LoanMemberID').AsString := MemberID;
19     dmoLibrary.cdsLoan.FieldByName('LoanDueDate').AsDateTime := DueDate;

20     //Save the new record;
21     dmoLibrary.cdsLoan.Post;
22     ShowMessage ('Book issued');
23     bmbIssueBook.Enabled := False;
24   end;
25
26 end;
```

- Save the unit, run it and issue a few books.

Searching for a specific record using the FindKey method

The FindKey method searches the data set (in this case the LibraryLoan data table) for a record whose key field(s) match the list of values it receives as arguments. In our example, there is only one key field, so there is only one value in the list. If there is more than one key value, say for example LoanISBN and LoanMemberID, these will be a set and are given in square brackets separated by commas. FindKey searches for the record and if a matching record is found, it makes it the active (current) record and returns True. If a matching record is not found, the current record does not change, and it returns False. So, if the FindKey method returns True, we report in line 10 that the book is already on loan because it exists in the LibraryLoan table.

As another example, the FindKey method call

```
dmoLibrary.cdsLoan.FindKey([dlcISBN.Text])
```

searches the cdsLoan ClientDataSet, in module dmoLibraryu, for a record with the LoanISBN field corresponding to the value of dlcISBN.Text. Note that we put this value in square brackets - even if the key in this case consists of only one value, it must still be in square brackets since it is a set.

If the primary key of the table consists of more than one field, values for all these fields need to be included as parameters in the order specified in the SortFieldNames property of the SQLDataSet. For example, if a key consists of the `ResortName`, `RoomNumber` and `Date` fields the call would be:

```
cdsReservation.FindKey([ResortNameValue, RoomNumberValue, DateValue])
```

Problem 16.1 explores this further.

Date routines

Date is a standard Delphi function that obtains the current local date as a TDateTime value. The time portion of the value is 0 (midnight). In line 16 we set a date 14 days from today (the period for which a book can be on loan).

Although we do not use them in this example, there are other useful date routines for presenting dates in more user friendly formats.

Getting values from and entering values into the fields of the new record

In lines 5 and 6 we use the statements,

```
MemberID := dmoLibrary.cdsMember.FieldByName('MemberNumber').AsString;
Acquisition := dmoLibrary.cdsAcquisition.FieldByName('AcquisitionNumber').AsString;
```

to get values from the fields in the active records of the cdsMember and cdsAcquisition ClientDataSets respectively.

We also use the statements (lines 17–19),

```
dmoLibrary.cdsLoan.FieldByName('LoanAcquisitionNumber').AsString := Acquisition;
dmoLibrary.cdsLoan.FieldByName('LoanMemberID').AsString := MemberID;
dmoLibrary.cdsLoan.FieldByName('LoanDueDate').AsDateTime := DueDate;
```

to enter values in the LoanISBN, LoanMemberID and LoanDueDate fields of the active record in the cdsLoan ClientDataSet.

Data sets have many other useful methods (as explained in Delphi's Help), and we list some at the end of this chapter.

EXAMPLE 16.4) Returning or renewing a book

In this example (figure 16.22), we handle the Book loans | Return/Renew book... menu sequence. For late books, the member pays a fine of R1.50 per book per day.

When a book is returned, the fine is calculated and displayed (if necessary) (see figure 16.24) and the record is deleted from the LibraryLoan table.

When a book is renewed, the record is located in the LibraryLoan table, the fine is calculated and displayed (if necessary) and the due date is moved on by another 14 days.

Before each return and renewal confirmation message dialogs are displayed as shown in figure 16.23.

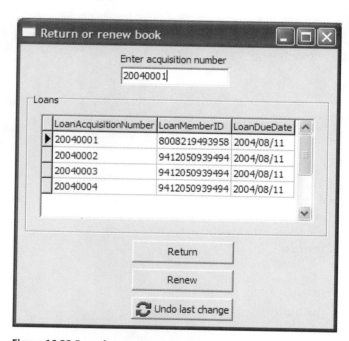

Figure 16.22 Form for returning/renewing a book

EX 16.4 STEP 1 Create the Return / Renew book form

- Open project C16e01p.
- Make sure that the data module is opened, so that you can set the data controls' DataSource properties on the new form. (Use the menu sequence View | Units, then select dmoLibraryu from the list.)
- With File | New VCL Form (Delphi 8) or File | New Form (Delphi 6/7) create a new form.

- Save the new unit as ReturnBooku
- Make data module dmoLibraryu accessible from the form with File | Use Unit and select dmoLibraryu from the list.
- Create the user interface as in figure 16.22. The components and their property values are shown in the table below.

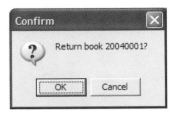

Figure 16.23 Confirmation message

Figure 16.24 Displaying the fine for a specific book

Component	Property	Value
Form1	Name	frmReturnBook
	Caption	Return or renew book
Label1	Name	lblAcqNumber
	Caption	Enter acquisition number
Edit1	Name	edtAcqNumber
	Text	<Blank>
GroupBox1	Name	gpbLoans
	Caption	Loans
DBGrid1	Name	dbgLoans
(GroupBox1)	Datasource	dmoLibrary.datLoan
	ReadOnly	True
Button1	Name	btnReturn
	Caption	Return
Button2	Name	btnRenew
	Caption	Renew
BitBtn1	Name	bmbUndoLastChange
	Kind	bkRetry
	Caption	Undo Last Change

EX 16.4 STEP 2 Displaying the form from the main menu

- Toggle to frmLibrary and enter the click event handler for menu item Return / Renew book ...

```
procedure TfrmLibrary.ReturnRenewbook1Click(Sender: TObject);
begin
  frmReturnBook.Show;
end;
```

- With File | Use Unit, include ReturnBooku in C16e01u's uses clause.

EX 16.4 STEP 3 The event handlers and method

- Toggle to form frmReturnBook and enter the form's OnShow, OnClose and Undo last change event handlers as before:

```
procedure TfrmReturnBook.FormShow(Sender: TObject);
begin
  dmoLibrary.cdsLoan.Open;
  dmoLibrary.cdsLoan.Refresh;
end;


procedure TfrmReturnBook.FormClose(Sender: Tobject; var Action: TCloseAction);
begin
  if (dmoLibrary.cdsLoan.ChangeCount > 0) then
       dmoLibrary.cdsLoan.ApplyUpdates(0); //MaxErrors parameter: 0
  dmoLibrary.cdsLoan.Close;
end;


procedure TfrmReturnBook.bmbUndoLastChangeClick(Sender: TObject);
begin
  dmoLibrary.cdsLoan.UndoLastChange(True);
end;
```

- Enter the OnChange event handler for the edtAcqNumber component.

```
procedure TfrmReturnBook.edtAcqNumberChange(Sender: TObject);
begin
  dmoLibrary.cdsLoan.FindNearest([edtAcqNumber.Text]);
end;
```

- In the ReturnBooku unit, enter the procedure below to determine and show
  the fine (remember to also add the method declaration to the private
  section of the class declaration).

```
1  procedure TfrmReturnBook.DetermineAndShowFine (DueDate : TDateTime);
2  const FinePerDay = 1.50;
3  var ThisDay: TDateTime;
4      Fine: double;
5      FineStr: string;
6  begin
7    //Is the book late?
8    ThisDay := Date;
9    If (ThisDay > DueDate) then
10   begin
11     //Book is late
12     //Calculate fine at R1.50 per day late
13     Fine := (ThisDay - DueDate) * FinePerDay;
14     FineStr := FloatToStrF (Fine,ffCurrency,10,2);
15     ShowMessage ('Late book fine: '+ FineStr);
16   end;
17 end;
```

- Create the following event handlers for the Return and Renew buttons:

```
18 procedure TfrmReturnBook.btnReturnClick(Sender: TObject);
19 var DueDate   : TDateTime;
20     AcqNumber : string;
21 begin
22   AcqNumber :=dmoLibrary.cdsLoan.FieldByName('LoanAcquisitionNumber').AsString;
```

```
23
24    if (MessageDlg('Return book '+ AcqNumber+'?',
25                mtConfirmation,[mbOK,mbCancel],0)= mrOK) then
26    begin
27      //Is the book late?
28      DueDate := dmoLibrary.cdsLoan.FieldByName('LoanDueDate').AsDateTime;
29      DetermineAndShowFine (DueDate);
30      dmoLibrary.cdsLoan.Delete;
31      ShowMessage ('Book returned');
32    end;
33 end;

34 procedure TfrmReturnBook.btnRenewClick(Sender: TObject);
35 var DueDate, NewDueDate : TDateTime;
36      AcqNumber: string;
37 begin
38    AcqNumber :=dmoLibrary.cdsLoan.FieldByName('LoanAcquisitionNumber').AsString;
39
40    if (MessageDlg('Renew book '+ AcqNumber+'?',
41                mtConfirmation,[mbOK,mbCancel],0)= mrOK) then
42    begin
43      //Is the book late?
44      DueDate := dmoLibrary.cdsLoan.FieldByName('LoanDueDate').AsDateTime;
45      DetermineAndShowFine(DueDate);
46      //To renew: Set the LoanDueDate field  to 14 days from today
47      NewDueDate := Date() + 14;
48      //Change the loan record to reflect the new due date
49      dmoLibrary.cdsLoan.Edit;                        //Puts data set in Edit mode
50      dmoLibrary.cdsLoan.FieldByName('LoanDueDate').AsDateTime := NewDueDate;
51      dmoLibrary.cdsLoan.Post;                              //Save record
52      ShowMessage ('Book renewed');
53    end;
54 end;
```

- Save the unit, run it and return and renew a few books. HINT: If DateUtils (Delphi 7) or Borland.Vcl.DateUtils (Delphi 8) has not been included in the Uses clause, then the function Date will give an error.

- To test your program thoroughly, you may want to issue a few books. Using MySQL Control Center, change some of the due dates in the LibraryLoan table to be before today's date. Then return to your program and renew or return some of these late books.

Note that there is duplication in the code above. For the sake of simplicity we have left it in. The duplication can be eliminated using one event handler for both the btnReturn and btnRenew click events and using the Sender parameter in an if statement to determine which button was clicked.

The ClientDataSet's FindNearest method

In the edtAcqNumberChange event handler we call cdsLoan's FindNearest method to move the cursor to a specific record in a data set, or to the first record in the data set that is greater than the acquisition number as it is with each character that the user adds. The reason why we use this method in the OnChange event handler is as follows: When the table containing the loans is very big and the acquisition number is a long number, moving closer to the required record with each digit that we enter, results in us finding the record quicker.

The application now

Schematically, the application (and its forms, units and data module), as it is now, can be represented in the figure below.

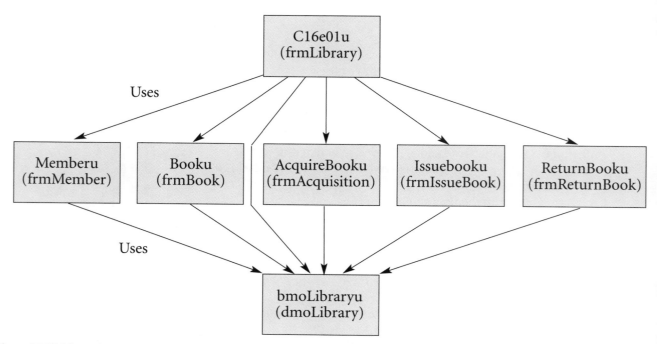

Figure 16.25 Schematic representation of the units, forms and data module in the application

Exception handling

As the application is now, it lets Delphi handle any exceptions that might be raised. For example, FieldByName raises an exception if the specified field does not exist. (This can happen when a table used by an application is restructured (for example field names changed) after the application was written.) Since the default exception handling is sufficient for this example, we won't add any of our own exception handling.

The DateTimePicker component

Although we did not use it in the examples here, it often happens that we want the user to enter dates or times. The DateTimePicker is a visual component designed specially for entering dates or times. In dmComboBox date mode (see the DateMode property) it resembles a ComboBox, except that the drop-down list is replaced with a calendar illustration (figure 16.26) from which users can select a date.

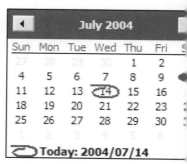

Figure 16.26 A calendar on which the user selects a date

The DateTimePicker component can be found in the Win32 tab of the Component/Tool Palette.

Delphi has handy DateTime routines that one can use in the manipulation of DateTime values, such as function DayOfTheWeek that accepts a value of type TDateTime and returns the day of the week represented by the specified TDateTime value. DayOfTheWeek returns a value between 1 and 7, where 1 indicates Monday and 7 indicates Sunday. So DayOfTheWeek considers Monday as the first day of the week, and Sunday as the last day of the week.

See DateUtils in the Delphi Help for a complete list of these DateTime routines.

REVIEW

In this chapter we wrote a database application that uses a data module and multiple forms.

We used a data module to handle all the data components centrally.

We displayed forms in one of two ways: modelessly (Show method) and modally (ShowModal method). When a form is displayed modelessly, all its own operations and all the other loaded forms' operations are available. When a form is displayed modally, it is the only form that can accept input from the user.

We used the SQLDataSet to represent a table from the database and as a query with an SQL statement.

We used the FindKey and FindNearest functions to search for a specific record in a data set.

We used program code to add, delete and change records. To add a new record, we used the ClientDataSet's Insert method to add an empty record. We then made changes to the value of each individual field of the new record using the ClientDataSet's FieldByName method and called the ClientDataSet's Post method to save the changes to the local ClientDataSet.

We used the ClientDataSet's ApplyUpdates method to apply the updates to the physical database and its UndoLastChange method to cancel the last change made to the local data set.

NEW DELPHI FEATURES

Data module

A data module holds non-visual components such as the SQLConnection, SQLDataSet, DataSetProvider, ClientDataSet and DataSource components. A data module is a specialized Delphi class for centralised handling of any non-visual component in an application. A data module is used for all the data manipulation ie to connect to a database, retrieve records and update records.

Date routines

DayOfTheWeek	This function returns the day of the week of a specific date as an integer between 1 and 7, where Monday is the first day of the week and Sunday is the seventh.
YearOf	This function returns the year represented by a specified TDateTime value. YearOf returns a value between 1 and 9999.

TClientDataSet

Method	Close	Close sets the Active property of a data set to false. When Active is false, the data set is closed; it cannot read or write data and data-aware controls can't use it to fetch data or post edits.
	Delete	Delete removes the active record from the database. If the data set is inactive, Delete raises an exception.
	Edit	Edit permits editing of the active record in the data set.
	FieldByName	FieldByName retrieves field information for a field given its name. If the specified field does not exist, FieldByName raises an EDatabaseError exception.FindNearestCalling the FindNearest method moves the cursor to a specific record in a data set or to the first record in the data set that matches or is greater than the values specified in the data set as (a) key(s). If there are no records that match or exceed the specified criteria, FindNearest positions the cursor on the last record in the table. FindNearest works only with string data types.
	FindKey	FindKey searches for a specific record in a data set. The key values are provided in a comma-delimited array of field values, called a key. If the search is successful, the matching record becomes the current (active) record and FindKey returns True. Otherwise the previously current record stays the active one, and FindKey returns False.
	First	First makes the first record in the data set the active (or current) record. InsertInsert opens a new, empty record in the data set and sets the active record to the new record.
	IsEmpty	The IsEmpty method determines if a data set has records. IsEmpty returns true if the data set does not contain any records. Otherwise it returns false.LastLast makes the last record in the data set active. NextNext moves to the next record in the data set, making it the active record. Next posts any changes to the active record and sets the Bof and Eof properties to false.
	Open	Open sets the Active property for the data set to true. When Active is true, data sets can be populated with data. It can read data from a database or other source.
	Prior	Prior moves to the previous record in the data set, making it the active record. Prior posts any changes to the active record and sets the Bof and Eof properties to false.
	Refresh	The Refresh method ensures that an application has the latest data from a database.

TDateTimePicker

Property	DateTime	We use DateTime to get or set the date (and, if relevant, the time) marked on the calendar. The value of DateTime must lie within the range specified by MaxDate and MinDate.
	DateMode	In dmComboBox date mode it resembles a ComboBox, except that the drop-down list is replaced by a calendar illustration from which users can select a date.
Prefix	dtp	
Use	The DateTimePicker is a visual component specifically for entering dates or times.	

TDBLookupComboBox

Property	DataSource	The DataSource property specifies the DataSource component that identifies the data set the lookup component represents. If the lookup component is used to edit data, the field that actually gets changed is the one in the DataSource.
	DataField	Identifies the field whose value is represented by the DBLookupComboBox. It binds the component to a field in the data set specified by the DataSource property. The DataField is the field whose value can be set by the DBLookupComboBox, not the field which supplies the lookup values displayed in the drop-down list.
	ListSource	The ListSource links the DBLookupComboBox to the lookup table that holds the field actually displayed in the drop-down list.
	ListField	Identifies the field or fields whose values are displayed in the drop-down list of the DBLookupComboBox.
	Keyfield	Identifies the field in the ListSource data set that must match the value of the DataField property.
Event	onCloseUp	Occurs when the combobox list is closed
Prefix	dlc	
Use		The DBLookupComboBox provides the user with a drop-down list of items for filling in fields that require data from another data set.

TDBText

Property	DataSource	The DataSource property links the database text control to a data set in which the data can be found. To specify a database field for the control fully, both the data set and a field within that data set must be defined.
	Datafield	The DataField property specifies the particular field within the data set specified by the DataSource property.
Prefix	dbt	
Use		We use TDBText to display the contents of a field in the current (active) record of a data set on a form. Field values displayed by database text controls cannot be modified by the user using the text control.

TForm

Method	Show	We use the Show method to set the form's Visible property to true and to bring the form to the front of other forms on the screen.
	ShowModal	We use the ShowModal method to show a form modally. A modal form is one where the rest of the application can't continue to run until the form is closed. Thus ShowModal does not return until the form closes.

PROBLEMS

PROBLEM 16.1 Accommodation

The *Home away from home*, central reservation company, needs a computer system to help them administrate the reservations for several accommodation establishments. To simplify the application, we allow reservations for full one-week periods only, from Saturday to Friday.

a   Create a database called Accommodation containing the following tables:
    i AccommodationEstablishment table

Field	Type	Null	Key	Default	Extra
⚷ EstablishmentName	varchar(20)		PRI		
EstablishmentTelephone	varchar(15)				
EstablishmentOwnerID	varchar(13)				
EstablishmentCategory	varchar(20)				
EstablishmentProvince	varchar(20)				

Figure 16.27 Structure of the AccommodationEstablishment

This table contains data about the various establishments registered with the *Home away from home* central reservation company. The various categories (EstablishmentCategory field) in which the establishments can be registered are:

        Self-catering
        Bed and breakfast
        Guest house
        Lodge
        Country house
        Hotel

The province (EstablishmentProvince field) in which an establishment is situated, can be one of the following:

        Eastern Cape
        Free State
        Gauteng
        KwaZulu Natal
        Limpopo Province
        Mpumalanga
        Northern Cape
        North West Province
        Western Cape

    ii AccommodationOwner table

Field	Type	Null	Key	Default	Extra
⚷ OwnerID	varchar(13)		PRI		
OwnerSurname	varchar(20)				
OwnerAddress	varchar(30)				

Figure 16.28 Structure of the AccommodationOwner table

This table contains data about the owners of the establishments registered with the *Home away from home* central reservation company.

iii   AccommodationRoom table

Field	Type	Null	Key	Default	Extra
🔑 RoomEstablishmentName	varchar(20)		PRI		
🔑 RoomNumber	int(11)		PRI	0	
RoomNoOfPersons	int(11)			0	
RoomPrice	double			0	

Figure 16.29 Structure of the AccommodationRoom table

Notice that the first two fields together form the unique key.

iv AccommodationReservation table

Field	Type	Null	Key	Default	Extra
🔑 ReservationEstablishmentName	varchar(20)		PRI		
🔑 ReservationRoomNumber	int(11)		PRI	0	
🔑 ReservationDate	date		PRI	0000-00-00	
ReservationGuest	varchar(20)				
ReservationGuestTel	varchar(30)				

Figure 16.30 Structure of the AccommodationReservation table

Notice that the first three fields together form the unique key.

b   Write the database application using the Accommodation database created in (a) that enables the *Home away from home* company to administrate the reservations for the registered establishments. The main form is shown in figures 16.31 and 16.32.

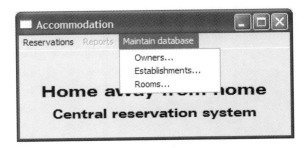

Figure 16.31 The main form of the application: the Maintain database menu item

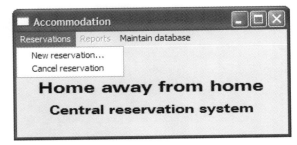

Figure 16.32 The main form of the application: the Reservations menu item

Use the form in figure 16.33 to maintain the AccommodationOwner table. You need to populate this table with data first.

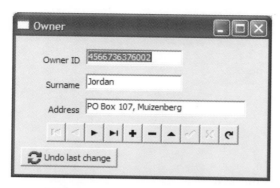

Figure 16.33 The form to maintain the AccommodationOwner table

To maintain the AccommodationEstablishment table, use the form in figure 16.34. It uses DBComboBoxes for the AccommodationCategory and AccommodationProvince fields and a DBLookupComboBox for the AccommodationOwnerID field. (As the user selects a valid owner ID number from the drop-down list, the corresponding owner's detail are displayed in the Owner GroupBox, and the AccommodationOwnerID field is set with the Owner ID selected.)

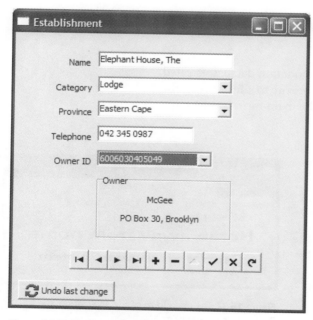

Figure 16.34 The form to maintain the AccommodationEstablishment table

Use the form in figure 16.35 to maintain the AccommodationRoom data table. Notice that the Establishment's name is selected from a DBLookupComboBox, populated with the EstablishmentName field values of the AccommodationEstablishment.

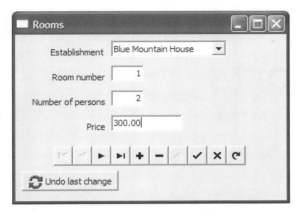

Figure 16.35 The form used to maintain the AccommodationRoom table

The form used for adding reservations is shown in figure 16.36.

For every reservation, a record needs to be added to the AccommodationReservation data table. When the user has selected an establishment, a date (which falls on a Saturday, day 6) and a specific room in the grid, the Check room availability BitButton becomes enabled.

When the user clicks the Check room availability BitButton, the application checks whether the specific room in the specified establishment is available for the one-week period starting on the specified date. If it is available, the user can enter the guest information and make the reservation. If it is not available (a record with the specified keys already exist) an appropriate message is displayed and the user can select another establishment, room and/or date.

Figure 16.36 The form for making reservations

CHAPTER 17

Reporting: using Rave reports

PURPOSE OF THIS CHAPTER

In this chapter we convert the data in the database to *information* through the generation of *reports*. Data and information are not the same thing. Data refers to facts about a specific record, such as an employee's name, surname or date of birth. Information on the other hand, can be described as data that has been rearranged into a useful format, for example, we consider the individual fields within an employee record as data. However, a list of employees working in a specific department is information that has been produced from the data about individual employees.

In the database applications that we have written up to now, we were interested in all the records in the underlying data tables. What if, for the purpose of a specific report, we are interested only in a subset of the records? For example, what if we want only to see the loan detail of the books that are late? Or only the loan detail of the books with a specific title?

The ability to ask questions such as these, and to see the answers is provided through the use of SQL queries. Queries let us see the data we want in the sequence we want it. They let us select specific records from a table (or from several tables) and show some or all of the fields for the selected records. We discussed queries briefly in Chapter 16. In this chapter we use queries to generate reports.

In example 17.1 we generate a notice that is viewed (or printed) when a member returns or renews a late book. We use parameters to send values from the application to be displayed or printed in the report.

In example 17.2 we create the report generated when the user selects the Reports | List of titles menu sequence (figure 17.1). This report shows all the records in the LibraryBook data table.

In example 17.3 we create the report generated when the user selects the Reports | Late books menu sequence. This report shows those records in the LibraryLoan data table whose LoanDueDate field is earlier than the current date.

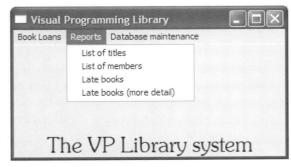

Figure 17.1 The Reports menu

In example 17.4 we create the report generated when the user selects the Reports | Late books (more detail) menu sequence. This report shows selected fields from records from the LibraryLoan, LibraryBook and LibraryMember data tables.

In example 17.5 we neaten the application.

Rave reports

Delphi 7 has included Rave Reports as the default reporting solution replacing Quick Reports. It can be used with Delphi 4 and later versions, and is compatible with the Kylix version of Rave for Linux. Rave has its own report designer, and saves a designed report using the file format .rav. This means that your reports can be made 'standalone' and can be used or updated independently of your application. The report can even be made available in an intranet or the internet using Nevrons's Rave Report Server. You can also save the report in a form's .dfm.

EXAMPLE 17.1 Introducing Rave: printing/viewing late return notices

In this example, we continue the application started in Chapter 16 and introduce Rave reports by changing the code for book returns or renewals so that it generates a simple fine notice for books that are returned or renewed late. The notice that we generate is shown in figure 17.2. It shows the Rave Report Preview window from which the user can preview and print the report.

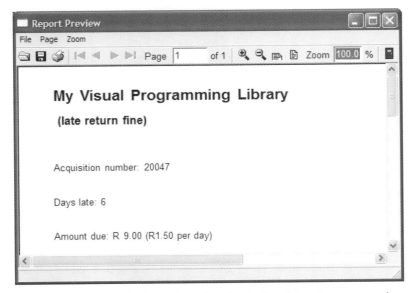

Figure 17.2 A report in the form of a notice of a fine for a late return or renewal

EX 17.1 STEP 1   Change the due dates in some records for testing purposes

For each book loan record, application C16e01p generates a due date fourteen days after the day the loan was made. So it is possible that the data in the loan table won't enable you to test this report as there might not be any late books yet. For testing purposes we therefore edit the LibraryLoan table using the MySQL Control Center to make sure that some of the books are late.

- Run MySQLcc, right-click on table LibraryLoan and select Open Table | Return all rows.
- Double-click on one (or more) of the LoanDueDate field values and change it to a date earlier than the current date, forcing the book(s) to be late.
- Close the table and close MySQL Control Center.

EX 17.1 STEP 2   TrvProject and TrvSystem components

If you have installed Rave reports (see Appendix 4 for details on how to do this), there will be a Rave tab on Delphi's Component/Tool Palette.

- In Delphi, open project C16e01p and go to data module dmoLibraryu.
- In designer/Form view drop a TRvProject and a TRvSystem component from the Rave tab of the Component/Tool Palette on data module dmoLibrary.
- Change their property values as shown below.

Component	Property	Value
RvSystem1	Name	rvsLibrary
RvProject1	Name	rvpLibrary
	Engine	rvsLibrary

The RvProject and RvSystem components

The RvProject component is the link from your application to the reports you develop. The RvSystem is the object responsible for the general configuration of the reports (eg the printer, the margins and the number of pages).

EX 17.1 STEP 3   The Rave Visual Designer

- To start a new report project, double-click on component rvpLibrary (on the data module) or select Rave Visual Designer from its pop-up menu or select the Tools | Rave Reports Designer menu sequence.

The Rave Visual Designer is shown in figure 17.3. (Rave Reports 5.0 for Delphi 7 does not have the Data Viewer tab.)

The top of this designer contains the menu, the toolbar and the Component Palette that contains the components that can be used in the reports. (If you cannot see the tabs in the Component Palette, maximise the Rave screen.) On the left-hand side is the Object Inspector which we will use to adjust the properties of the components on the report. The Page Designer, Event Editor and Data Viewer tabs (Rave 5.5) are in the middle. The Project TreeView is on the right-hand side.

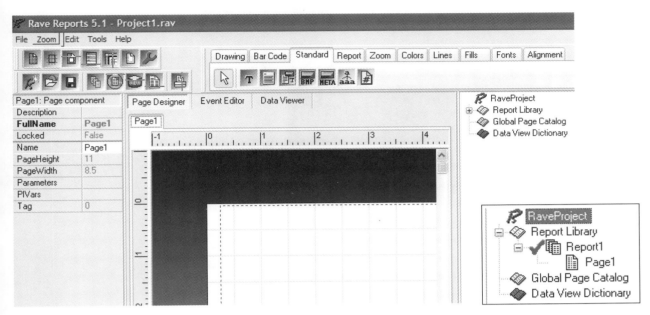

Figure 17.3 The Rave Visual Designer

Figure 17.4 Project TreeView

The Project TreeView

The Project TreeView provides a way to visually manage all the reports in your project. It shows the structure of the Rave project and the types of components contained on each page with icons that are the same as the component buttons on the component palette.

- Expand the Report Library node of the Project TreeView (figure 17.4). The Project TreeView shows the current selection (green check mark). You can select components by clicking on the component on the Page in the Visual Designer or on the Project Tree.
- Double-click on Report1. Its properties will show in the Object Inspector and its first page will show in the Page Designer window.
- Change Report1's Name property to repFineNotice. (Make sure that you change the report's name and not the page's.)
- Add two Text components from the Standard tab of the component palette.
- Change their properties as shown below:

Component	Property	Value
Report1	Name	repFineNotice
Text1	Name	txtReportTitle1
	Text	My Visual Programming Library
	Font	Arial,16,Bold (use the font editor)
Text2	Name	txtReportTitle2
	Text	(late return fine)
	Font	Arial,12,Bold (use the font editor)

- Size and position the components as in figure 17.5.
- Save the project with File | Save As, and name the project LibraryReports.rav.

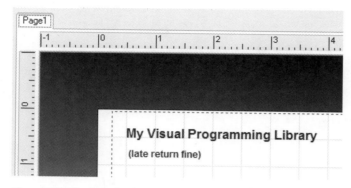

Figure 17.5 The Page Designer with the Text components

We now have a Rave project saved in a file called LibraryReports.rav and containing one report called repFineNotice.

- You can preview the result of this simple report in the designer, by pressing <F9> (or selecting File | Execute Report or pressing the Execute Report speed button).
- You can specify the report to be printed, previewed or copied to a file by selecting the Printer, Preview or File radio buttons respectively in the Report Destination group box (figure 17.6).
- Select Preview and click OK to preview the report as it is so far.
- Close the Report Preview window.

EX 17.1 STEP 4 Executing the report from the application

- Go back to project C16e01p in Delphi. (You don't have to close Rave, just minimise it.)
- In dmoLibrary, set the ProjectFile property of the RvProject component, rvpLibrary, to the .rav project file that you saved in step 3. (Include the

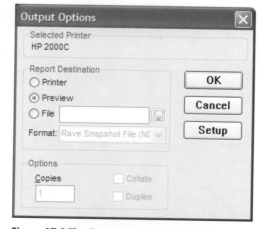

Figure 17.6 The Output Options window

complete path using the Select Rave Project File dialog, for example
c:/Delphi 2005/Programs/LibraryReports.rav.)

- View form frmReturnBook.
- Change procedure `TfrmReturnBook.DetermineAndShowFine` as shown below.

The changes are shown in bold in lines 17–19.

```
1  procedure TfrmReturnBook.DetermineAndShowFine (DueDate : TDateTime);
2
3  const FinePerDay = 1.50;
4  Var ThisDay : TDateTime;
5      Fine    : double;
6      FineStr : string;
7  begin
8    //Is the book late?
9    ThisDay := Date;
10   if (ThisDay > DueDate) then
11   begin
12     //Book is late
13     //Calculate fine at R1.50 per day late
14     Fine := (ThisDay - DueDate) * FinePerDay;
15     //ShowMessage ('Late book fine: '+ FineStr);     //Fine message taken out
16     //Generate fine notice
17     dmoLibrary.rvpLibrary.Open;                       //Open the Rave project
18     dmoLibrary.rvpLibrary.Execute;                  //Execute the Rave project
19     dmoLibrary.rvpLibrary.Close;                       //Close Rave project
20   end;
21 end;
```

- Save the unit.
- Returning a book deletes the corresponding record from the LibraryLoan table (after procedure `DetermineAndShowFine` is called), so you may want to make sure that there exists at least one loan record with a late due date by changing the event handler `TfrmReturnBook.btnReturnClick` by commenting out the statement that deletes the record:
  `//dmoLibrary.cdsLoan.Delete;`
- Run the application.
- Return a late book to ensure that the application generates the report.
- Preview the report. (Except for the heading, the report does not contain any useful information yet.)

EX 17.1 STEP 5 Interact with the Rave project using parameters

To complete the rest of the report (as shown in figure 17.2) we need the following values from the application: the acquisition number, number of days late, and the amount of the fine. We define them as parameters inside the Rave Visual designer using the Parameters property of the report. (We can also define parameters for the project or page.)

It is important to know that you can only select the Project and Report through the Project TreeView. A page, however, can be selected using the Project TreeView or clicking on its title tab above the page designer.

To see how parameters work:
- Go back to Rave (don't close Delphi, just maximise Rave).
- Keep the report repFineNotice as the selected report.
- Click on the dots next to the Parameter property.
- Enter the parameter names in the Strings Editor as in figure 17.7.

All the parameters of the project must be listed here, each on a separate line.

Parameters are printed or previewed using DataText components (available from the Report tab of the Component Palette) so:
- Add three DataText components to the Page Designer.
- Set their Name properties as in the table below:

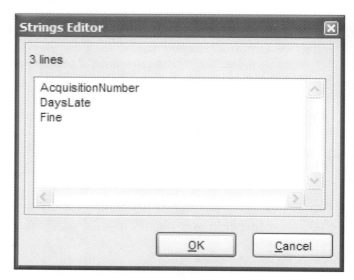

Figure 17.7 Entering the parameter names

Component	Property	Value
DataText1	Name	dtxAcqNumber
DataText2	Name	dtxDaysLate
DataText3	Name	dtxFine

- Position the DataText components as in figure 17.2. The rest of the text will be added in the next step.

EX 17.1 STEP 6 Setting the DataField properties of the DataText components

- Click on dtxAcqNumber.
- Go to the DataField property.
- Click on the dots to open the Data Text Editor.
- To set the Data Text value (as shown in figure 17.8) type in the first part: 'Acquisition number: ' + .
- Choose parameter AcquisitionNumber from the Project Parameters drop-down combo box.
- Click the Insert Parameter button to the right of it. (You can also just enter the text as it appears in figure 17.8.)
- Click OK to close the Data Text Editor.
- Similarly set the DataText properties of dtxDaysLate and dtxFine (as in figures 17.9 and 17.10 respectively).
- Execute the report as before.
- Note that the parameter values are not shown since the parameters have not been set in the application yet.
- Save your Rave project.
- Minimize Rave and return to Delphi.

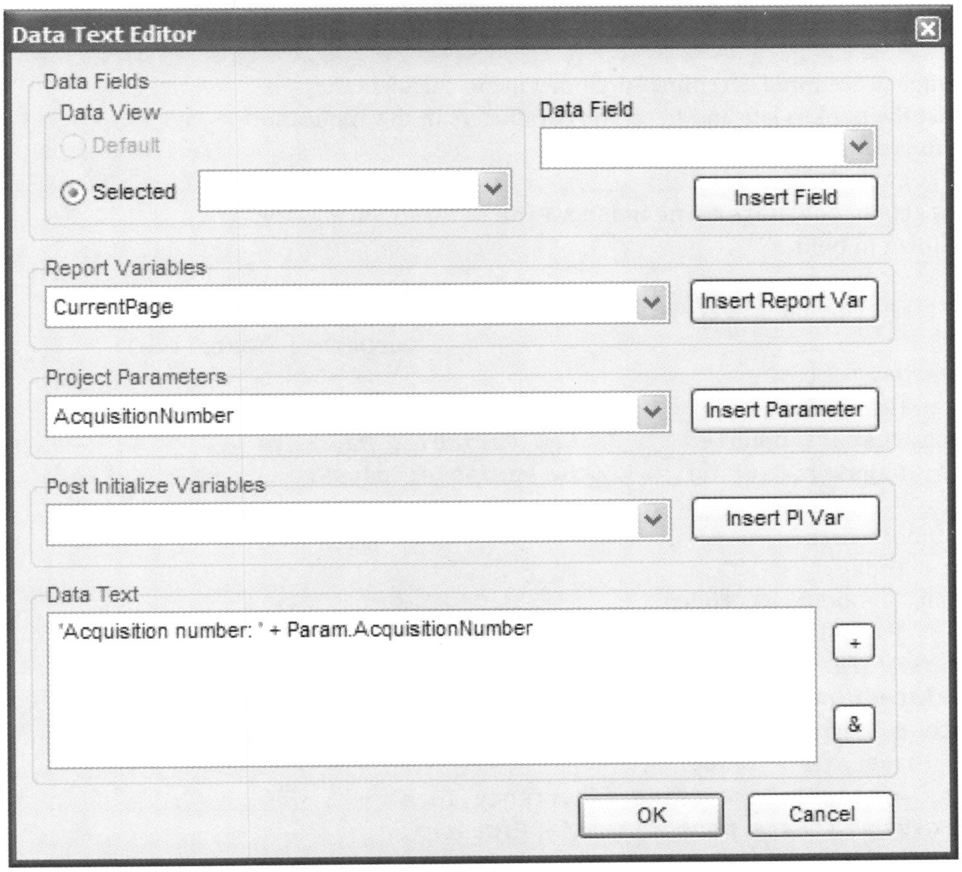

Data Text Editor

Data Fields

Data View

○ Default
◉ Selected [▾]

Data Field
[▾]

[Insert Field]

Report Variables
[CurrentPage   ▾] [Insert Report Var]

Project Parameters
[AcquisitionNumber   ▾] [Insert Parameter]

Post Initialize Variables
[▾] [Insert PI Var]

Data Text

'Acquisition number: ' + Param.AcquisitionNumber

[+]
[&]

[OK]   [Cancel]

Figure 17.8 The Data Text Editor

Data Text

'Days late: ' + Param.DaysLate

[+]
[&]

Figure 17.9 Setting the DataField property of the dtxDaysLate DataText component

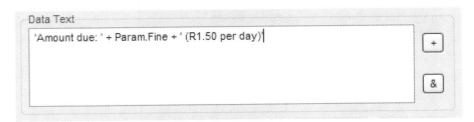

Data Text

'Amount due: ' + Param.Fine + ' (R1.50 per day)'

[+]
[&]

Figure 17.10 Setting the DataField property of the dtxFine DataText component

EX 17.1 STEP 7   Set the parameter values in the application

In this step we change procedure DetermineAndShowFine to calculate the number of days that the book is late and to set the parameters in the application before generating the report.

- Change TfrmReturnBook.DetermineAndShowFine to the following (the changes are shown in bold):

```
1  procedure TfrmReturnBook.DetermineAndShowFine (AcqNumber : string;
2                                                 DueDate : TDateTime);
3  const FinePerDay = 1.50;
4  var ThisDay: TDateTime;
5      Fine, DaysLate : double;      // New variable: DaysLate
6      FineStr, DaysStr: string;     //New variable: DaysStr
7  begin
8    //Is the book late?
9    ThisDay := Today;
10   If (ThisDay > DueDate) then
11   begin
12     //Book is late
13     //Calculate fine at R1.50 per day late
14     DaysLate := ThisDay - DueDate;     //Calculating number of days late
15     Fine := DaysLate * 1.50;
16     FineStr := FloatToStrF (Fine,ffCurrency,10,2);
17     //ShowMessage ('Late book fine: '+ FineStr);
18     //Generate fine notice
19     dmoLibrary.rvpLibrary.Open;
20
21     //Setting the parameters
22     dmoLibrary.rvpLibrary.SetParam('AcquisitionNumber',AcqNumber);
23     DaysStr := FloatToStrF(DaysLate,ffFixed,10,0);
24     dmoLibrary.rvpLibrary.SetParam('DaysLate',DaysStr);
25     dmoLibrary.rvpLibrary.SetParam('Fine',FineStr);
26
27     dmoLibrary.rvpLibrary.Execute;
28     dmoLibrary.rvpLibrary.Close;
29   end;
30 end;
```

- Save the unit and run the application.

If you followed all the steps, the report should now resemble figure 17.2. (Hint: you may need to increase the width of the DataTexts to ensure that all the data is displayed.)

Project Parameters

Project parameters are custom variables that you create and initialize from your Delphi application. Project Parameters can be used for items such as user defined report titles, printing the current user name or other custom information. In this application we used project parameters for the late book's acquisition number, the number of days that the book is late and the amount of the fine.

EX 17.1 STEP 8   Select a specific report

There is only one report in our Rave project at the moment, but we will add more reports in the examples that follow, and then we will need to select the specific report before we can execute it.

- To select report repFineNotice, insert the following statement between lines 19 and 20 in procedure `TfrmReturnBook.DetermineAndShowFine`:

  ```
  dmoLibrary.rvpLibrary.SelectReport('repFineNotice',False);
  ```

- Save the unit and run it again to make sure that it still works.

Global pages

We may require the same header on more than one report in a project. We can put headers on a global page to be shared between the reports. For this example we require the name of our library, the date and time that the report is generated, the current page and the number of pages of the report, as a header on each of our reports.

EX 17.1 STEP 9   Add a common header to our reports

- Back in the Rave Visual Designer, use File | New Global Page to add a global page to the project.
- On this page, add a Section component from the Standard tab of the Component Palette. (Sections group components logically, so that they can easily be moved around the report.)
- Cut and paste the library name (My Visual Programming Library) from Page1 to the Section component on the Global page.
- Add two DataText components (from the Report tab).
- To set the DataField property of the first DataText: select the Report Variables DateLong and TimeShort from the drop-down combo box, click Insert Report Var in the Data Text Editor. Add the + ' ' + between them (figure 17.11).
- Similarly use the CurrentPage and TotalPages Report Variables to set the DataField property of the second DataText component (figure 17.11).
- Set the FontJustify property of the second DataText to pjRight.

Figure 17.11 The Section on the Global Page

The property values of the two DataText components are shown below.

Component	Property	Value
DataText1	DataField	Report.DateLong + ' ' + Report.TimeShort
DataText2	DataField FontJustify	'Page' + Report.CurrentPage + ' of ' + Report.TotalPages pjRight

- Go back to Page1 of the Page Designer by clicking on the Page1 tab.
- If necessary, select all the components on the page and move these down to make space for a new section.
- Add a DataMirrorSection (from the Report tab) to Page1 of report repFineNotice.
- Set the section's DataMirrors property to GlobalPage1. Section1 using the Data Mirror Editor (figure 17.12). (If the components on this editor are disabled, click the Add button.)
- Save the project, go to Delphi and run the application. Test it by returning a book again.

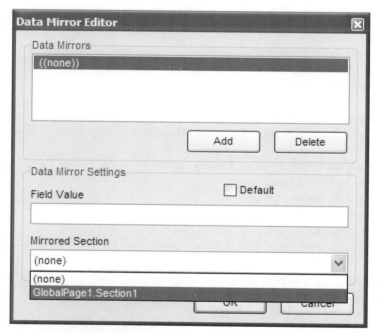

Figure 17.12 The Data Mirror Editor

You should now see a copy of the header you created in the global page.

Mirroring

When a component is set to mirror another, it assumes the appearance and properties of the component it is mirroring. The two components can be on the same page, across pages within the same report or on a global page as we have it here. This is the primary purpose of a global page. You can think of it as a central location to store reporting items that you want accessible to more than one report. When the original component changes, all mirroring components will also change.

Report Variables

Report variables are items such as total pages or current date and time in a variety of formats.

EXAMPLE 17.2) Create a Data Aware report using Bands

In this example, we use the data aware capabilities of Rave to generate a list of all the records in the LibraryBook data table (figure 17.13) for the menu sequence Reports | List of titles. We use the connection established by our application C16e01p, fetching records from the data sets that exist in data module dmoLibrary.

EX 17.2 STEP 1   Add a RvDataSetConnection component

- In Delphi, drop a RvDataSetConnection component from the Rave tab in the Component/Tool Palette on data module dmoLibrary.

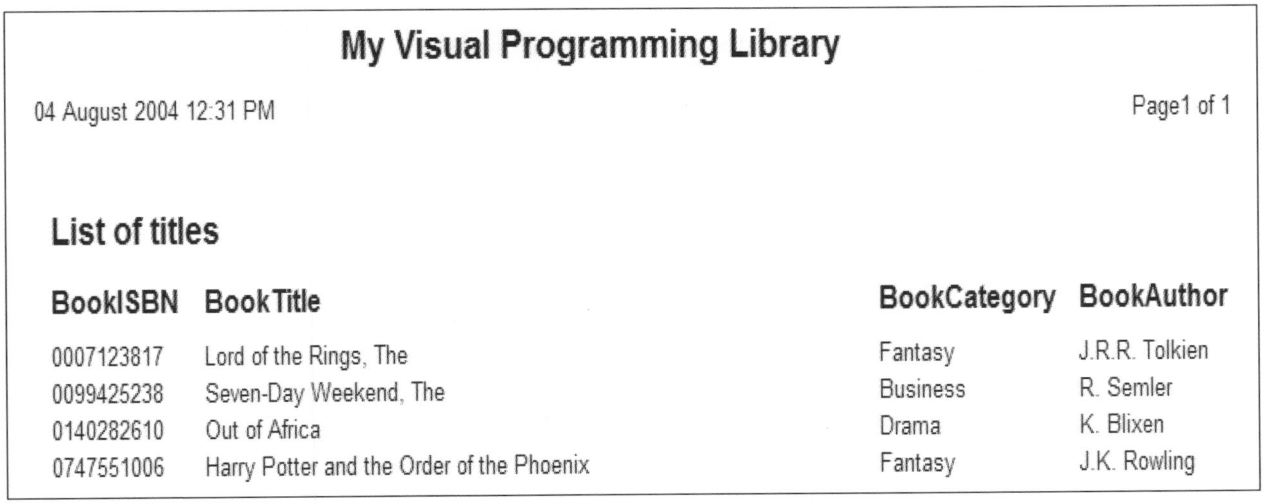

My Visual Programming Library

04 August 2004 12:31 PM   Page1 of 1

List of titles

BookISBN	BookTitle	BookCategory	BookAuthor
0007123817	Lord of the Rings, The	Fantasy	J.R.R. Tolkien
0099425238	Seven-Day Weekend, The	Business	R. Semler
0140282610	Out of Africa	Drama	K. Blixen
0747551006	Harry Potter and the Order of the Phoenix	Fantasy	J.K. Rowling

---

Figure 17.13 Report listing the titles

- Set the properties as below:

Component	Property	Value
RvDataSetConnection1	Name	dscBook
	DataSet	cdsBook

The RvDataSetConnection component provides a bridge between the data in the application and the Rave visual components and so has a similar function to the DataSet components we have used previously.

- Save the unit.
- Go to Rave. (If it isn't running, double-click on rvpLibrary on the data module or select Tools | Rave Reports Designer.)

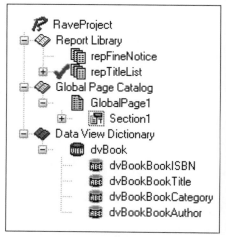

Figure 17.14 The Project TreeView

EX 17.2 STEP 2 Design a new report in Rave project LibraryReports.rav

- If it is not open, open Rave project LibraryReports.rav.
- Create a new report with File | New Report.
- Change its Name property to repTitleList.
- With File | New Data Object, select Direct Data View.
- You should see the RvDataSetConnection (dscBook) you added to the data module in the previous step.
- Select dscBook.
- Click Finish to create a DataView.
- Expand the DataView Dictionary in the Project TreeView.
- Double-click on DataView1 and change its Name property to dvBook.

In the Project TreeView, you now see the fields under the newly created Data View dvBook (figure 17.14).

The Data Viewer (Delphi 8)

- Click on the Data Viewer tab to see the values of the fields of the selected DataView (figure 17.15).

Page Designer	Event Editor	Data Viewer

dvBook

Record #	BookISBN	BookTitle
1	0007123817	Lord of the Rings, The
2	0099425238	Seven-Day Weekend, The
3	0140282610	Out of Africa
4	0747551006	Harry Potter and the Order of the Phoenix
EOF		

Figure 17.15 The Data Viewer viewing dvBook

EX 17.2 STEP 3 Add the global header from GlobalPage1

- Go back to the Page Designer by clicking the corresponding tab.
- Add a DataMirrorSection as in ex 17.1 step 9.
- Set the DataMirrorSection's DataMirrors property to GlobalPage1.Section1

using the Data Mirror Editor (figure 17.12). (If the components on this editor are disabled, click the Add button.)

EX 17.2 STEP 4 Create the report title, the Region and the Bands

- Add a Text component (Standard tab) underneath the DataMirrorSection.
- Add a Region component (Report tab) to Page1 covering its whole area from below the DataMirrorSection.
- For the column headers, add a Band (Report tab) inside the region.
- To print the book data, add a DataBand (Report tab).
- Change the component properties on the Page Designer as in the table below.

Component	Property	Value	
Text1	Name	txtReportTitle	
	Text	List of titles	
	Font	Arial,14,Bold	
Band1	Name	Header	
	ControllerBand	BookData	
DataBand1	Name	BookData	
	DataView	dvBook	(select from drop-down list)

If you want a report footer on every page, you can add another Band. (We won't use a footer here.) Page1 in the Page Designer should now resemble the one in figure 17.16.

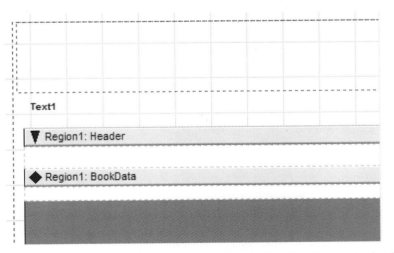

Figure 17.16 The Page Designer with a DataMirrorSection, Text, Region, Band and DataBand

Bands and Regions

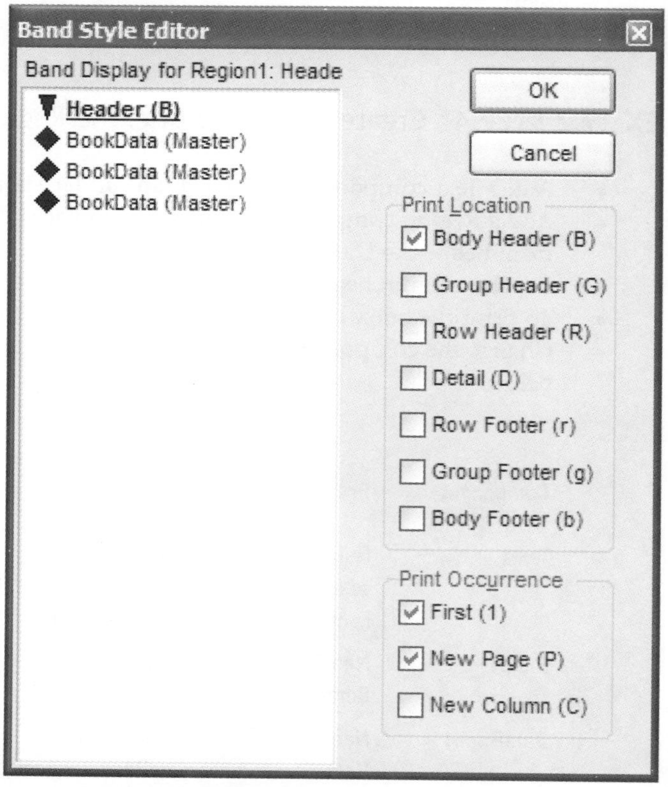

Report components that should be printed in a fixed position on every page, like headers and footers can be put directly onto the page, but components whose position are dependant on previously printed items, such as record field values, should be put in bands. DataBands (from the Report tab) are printed once for every record in the linked DataView while Bands (from the Standard tab) are only printed once. Both these bands can contain data-aware components (such as DataText) or other components.

Bands (both types) are put inside Regions, which delimit the width of the bands. Regions also determine the maximum height that bands can use before starting a new page. One page can consist of many regions and one region of many bands.

(If you want to change the ordering of the bands on the report, you can use the Move Forward and Move Behind buttons in the Alignment toolbar.)

Figure 17.17 The BandStyle Editor

- Run the Band Style Editor by clicking on the three dots next to the BandStyle property of band Header in the Object Inspector.
- Set the Print Location to Body Header (B) (figure 17.17).
- Check the New Page (P) option in the Print Occurrence GroupBox to set the header to be printed on other pages in case the listing spans more than one page.

(The Band Style Editor gives an indication of how the report is going to be printed. It shows iterating bands repeated three times, BookData (Master), and the header band, Header (B), only once.)

EX 17.2 STEP 5 Add the column headers and fields

- To add the column headers as Text components on the Header Band (as in figure 17.18), <Alt>+Drag the fields from the DataView in the Project TreeView. (Press and hold the <Alt> key in while dragging the fields from the Project TreeView onto the Header Band.)

(If you do it this way, the field names are used as column headers. You can also set the headers to whatever you need using Text components.)

- To add the fields as DataText components on the BookData DataBand (as in figure 17.18), <Ctrl>+Drag them from the DataView in the Project TreeView. (Press and hold the <Ctrl> key in while dragging the fields from the Project Treeview onto the BookData DataBand.)
- Change the font size of the header Text to be slightly bigger than the

DataText components. (You can also make them bold as in figure 17.18.)

- Execute the report with File | Execute Report or <F9>, or the Execute Report speed button. Check to see if the layout of your report is correct.
- If you don't see all the records, check that the Region is big enough. If it is too small, there is only space for one or two records. (You can modify the Height attribute of the region or size the region to fill the complete page.)
- Close the preview window and save the Rave project.

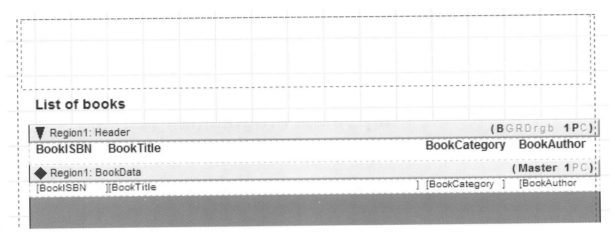

Figure 17.18 The Page Designer with the column headings and the data fields

EX 17.2 STEP 6   Generate the report from the application

- Go back to Delphi and create the event handler shown below for when the user selects the Reports | List of titles menu sequence.

```
1  procedure TfrmLibrary.Listoftitles1Click(Sender: TObject);
2  begin
3    dmoLibrary.cdsBook.Open;
4    dmoLibrary.cdsBook.Refresh;

5    //Generate the report
6    dmoLibrary.rvpLibrary.Open;                              //Open Rave project
7    dmoLibrary.rvpLibrary.SelectReport('repTitleList',False);   //Select report
8    dmoLibrary.rvpLibrary.Execute;                        //Execute Rave project
9    dmoLibrary.rvpLibrary.Close;                            //Close Rave project

10   //Close the ClientDataSet
11   dmoLibrary.cdsBook.Close;
12 end;
```

The event handler is similar to the one that we used for the fine report in example 17.2, except that this one does not set any report parameters.

- Save the Delphi project and run it. When you select the Reports | List of titles menu item, the report shown in figure 17.13 should be generated.

The Member list report is similar to the Title list report and needs to be generated in problem 17.1.

EXAMPLE 17.3 Create a data aware report using an SQL query

In this example we create the report showing all the books that are late. This report is generated when the Reports | Late books menu sequence is selected. The report is shown in figure 17.19. It shows the fields in the LibraryLoan table of all the books that are late (ie all the records where the value of field LoanDueDate is earlier than the current date).

In example 17.4 we add more detail to the report using a more complicated SQL statement that retrieves data from more than one table to generate a similar report showing the late books. This report includes the title of each late book and the surname and contact telephone number of the member who borrowed the book.

My Visual Programming Library

12 August 2004 07:40 PM

Page1 of

Late books

LoanAcquisitionNumber	LoanMemberID	LoanDueDate
20040011	6006030034988	2004/07/23
20040012	9412050939494	2004/07/20
20040013	8008219493958	2004/07/15
20040003	9412050939494	2004/07/20
20040004	9412050939494	2004/08/11
20040002	9412050939494	2004/08/11
20040001	8008219493958	2004/08/11

Figure 17.19 Report with the records in the loan table of the books that are late

EX 17.3 STEP 1 Add the dbExpress, Data Access and Rave components

- Add the following components to the data module and set the properties as shown.

Component	Property	Value
SQLDataSet1 (dbExpress tab)	Name	sdsLateBooks
	SQLConnection	scoMyVPLibrary
	Commandtype	ctQuery
	CommandText	SELECT * FROM libraryloan WHERE libraryloan.LoanDueDate <CURRENT_DATE
DataSetProvider1 (Data Access tab)	Name	dspLateBooks
	DataSet	sdsLateBooks

ClientDataSet1	Name	cdsLateBooks
(Data Access tab)	ProviderName	dspLateBooks
	ReadOnly	True
RvDataSetConnection1	Name	dscLateBooks
(Rave tab)	DataSet	cdsLateBooks

- Save the unit.

Notice that we set the ReadOnly property of the ClientDataSet toTrue because we use it only to generate a report and not to update data (as in Chapter 16).

EX 17.3 STEP 2   Define the new report in Rave

- Go to Rave (double-click on rvpLibrary on the data module if it is not running).
- Create a new report with File | New Report and change the new report's Name property to repLateBooks.
- Select File | New Data Object and choose Direct Data View.
- Select dscLateBooks.
- Click Finish to create a new Data View.
- Expand the Data View Dictionary in the Project TreeView.
- Double-click on DataView1 and change its Name property to dvLateBooks.

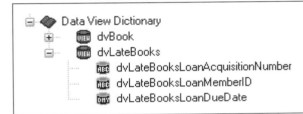

Figure 17.20 The Data View Dictionary

The fields under the newly created Data View dvLateBooks are shown in figure 17.20.

- To add the common report header, add a DataMirrorSection (Report tab).
- Set the DataMirrorSection's DataMirrors property to GlobalPage1.Section1 using the Data Mirror Editor.
- Add a Text component (Standard tab) for this report's header.
- Add a Region component (Report tab) to the page covering its whole area from below the Text component.
- Add a Band (Report tab) for the column headers inside the region.
- Add a DataBand (Report tab).
- Set the component properties on the Page Designer as below.

Component	Property	Value	
DataMirrorSection1	DataMirors	GlobalPage1.Section1	
Text1	Name	txtReportTitle	
	Text	Late books	
	Font	Arial,14,bold	
Band1	Name	Header	
(On Region1)	ControllerBand	LateBooks	
DataBand1	Name	LateBooks	
(On Region1)	DataView	dvLateBooks	(select from drop-down list)

- Run the Band Style Editor by clicking on the three dots next to the BandStyle property of band Header in the Object Inspector as in ex 17.2 step 4.
- Set the Print Location to Body Header (B).
- Check the New Page option in the Print Occurrence GroupBox to set the header to be printed on other pages in case the listing spans more than one page.
- Add the column headers.
- Add the fields.
- Save the Rave project.

EX 17.3 STEP 3 Create the event handler

- Go back to Delphi and create the event handler shown below for when the user selects the Reports | Late books menu sequence

```
1  procedure TfrmLibrary.Latebooks1Click(Sender: TObject);
2  begin
3    dmoLibrary.cdsLateBooks.Open;
4    dmoLibrary.cdsLateBooks.Refresh;

5    //Generate the report
6    dmoLibrary.rvpLibrary.Open;                              //Open Rave project
7    dmoLibrary.rvpLibrary.SelectReport('repLateBooks',False);  //Select report
8    dmoLibrary.rvpLibrary.Execute;                           //Execute Rave project
9    dmoLibrary.rvpLibrary.Close;

10   //Close the ClientDataSet
11   dmoLibrary.cdsLateBooks.Close;
12 end;
```

- Set cdsLateBooks's Active property to False.
- Save the application and run it to check that it functions correctly.
- If you get a compilation error indicating that ctQuery is an undefined identifier, add unit SqlExpr (Delphi 6/7) or namespace Borland.Vcl.SqlExpr (Delphi 8) to C16e01u's uses clause in the interface section and run the application again.
- When you select the Reports | Late books menu item, the report shown in figure 17.19 should be generated.

When testing this report, you must first ensure that there are late books. The report will only show data if late books exist otherwise, there is nothing to show and the report cannot be tested.

EXAMPLE 17.4 More detail through a more sophisticated SQL

In this example we change the layout of repLateBooks in Rave and use an SQL query statement that retrieves data from more than one table to generate the report in figure 17.21.

My Visual Programming Library

12 August 2004 07:38 PM

Page1 of 1

Late books detail

Acquisition	Due date	Title	Member	Contact number
20040011	2004/07/23	Lord of the Rings, The	McGee	083 544 8475
20040013	2004/07/15	Seven-Day Weekend, The	Manamela	074 354 0092
20040001	2004/08/11	Lord of the Rings, The	Manamela	074 354 0092
20040012	2004/07/20	Lord of the Rings, The	Gerber	082 456 8765
20040003	2004/07/20	Seven-Day Weekend, The	Gerber	082 456 8765
20040004	2004/08/11	Out of Africa	Gerber	082 456 8765
20040002	2004/08/11	Lord of the Rings, The	Gerber	082 456 8765

Figure 17.21 The report showing more detail of the late books

EX 17.4 STEP 1 Develop and test the SQL query in MySQL Control Center

The SQL query that we use here is more complicated than the one in example 17.3. It is always a good idea to develop and test an SQL query incrementally before including it in the program code. We will develop and test it in MySQLcc to see if the syntax and the logic of the statement are correct.

- Enter the SQL query below in a Notepad document.

```
SELECT  libraryloan.LoanAcquisitionNumber,
        librarybook.BookTitle
FROM    libraryloan, libraryacquisition, librarybook
WHERE   libraryloan.LoanAcquisitionNumber = libraryacquisition.AcquisitionNumber AND
        libraryacquisition.AcquisitionISBN = librarybook.BookISBN AND
        libraryloan.LoanDueDate < CURRENT_DATE
```

- Save the Notepad document in a file called SQLQuery.txt.
- RunMySQLcc and click on the SQL Speedbutton (the hint says Query <Ctrl>+Q) to open the Query Window.
- Copy the SQL statement from the Notepad document and paste it in the Query Window.
- To execute the query click the ! Speedbutton (or Execute <Ctrl>+E).
- If the you entered the SQL query statement as given, the result of the SELECT statement will be shown in the Query Window as in figure 17.22. (Your data might differ. If you have no late books in your LibraryLoan table, then the result will be empty.)

As you can see, we have combined data fields from three of the tables to obtain a result set showing the acquisition numbers and titles of the late books. We now develop the SQL query further to include the due dates of the books and the surnames and contact numbers of the members that have them.

REPORTING **473**

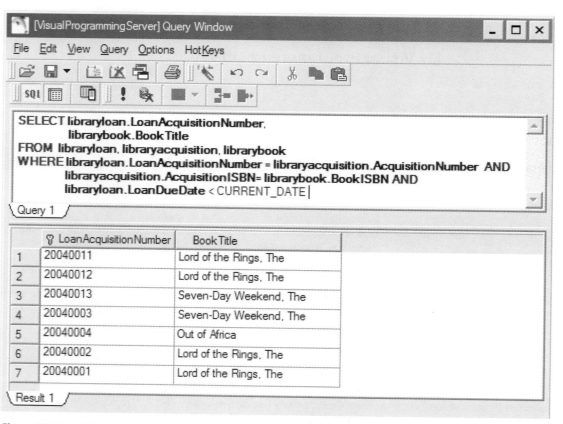

Figure 17.22 MySQL Control Center's Query Window with Query 1 and Result 1

- Change the query in the Notepad document to the following:

```
SELECT    libraryloan.LoanAcquisitionNumber,
          libraryloan.LoanDueDate,
          librarybook.BookTitle,
          librarymember.MemberSurname,
          librarymember.MemberContactNumber
FROM libraryacquisition, librarybook,  libraryloan, librarymember
WHERE    libraryacquisition.AcquisitionNumber= libraryloan.LoanAcquisitionNumber AND
         libraryacquisition.AcquisitionISBN= librarybook.BookISBN AND
         libraryloan.LoanMemberID= librarymember.MemberNumber AND
         libraryloan.LoanDueDate < CURRENT_DATE
```

- Save the Notepad document.
- In MySQL Control Center, select the File | New Tab menu sequence to create a new Query Window for Query 2.
- Copy the SQL query from the Notepad document and paste it in the Query Window for Query 2.
- Execute the query by clicking the ! speed button.

The result is shown in figure 17.23.

We have combined data fields from all four tables to obtain a result showing the acquisition numbers, due dates and titles of the late books as well as the surnames and contact numbers of the members that have them. This result cannot be generated using only one table.

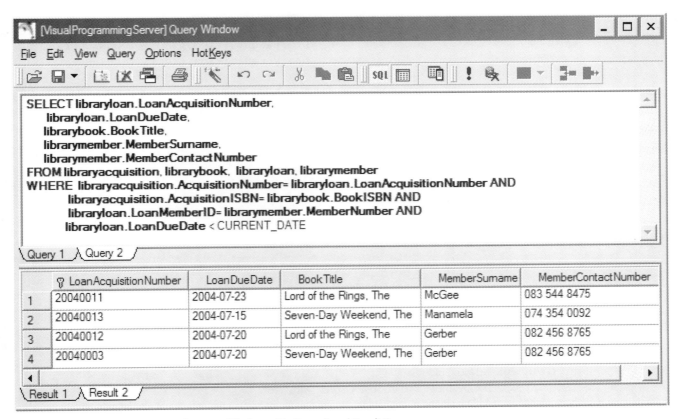

Figure 17.23 MySQL Control Center's Query Window with Query 2 and Result 2

In the steps that follow, we will use this SQL query in our Delphi application to generate the report shown above programmatically.

EX 17.4 STEP 2 Add dbExpress and Data Access components to provide the correct Data View for the report

- In Delphi, add the following components to the data module and set the properties as shown. Copy the second version of the SQL query from Notepad into the DataSet's CommandText property.

Component	Property	Value
SQLDataSet1 (dbExpress tab)	Name	sdsLateBooksDetail
	SQLConnecion	scoMyVPLibrary
	CommandType	ctQuery
	CommandText	SELECT libraryloan.LoanAcquisitionNumber, libraryloan.LoanDueDate, librarybook.BookTitle, librarymember.MemberSurname, librarymember.MemberContactNumber FROM libraryloan, libraryacquisition, librarybook, librarymember

```
WHERE libraryloan.LoanAcquisitionNumber =
              libraryacquisition.AcquisitionNumber
AND    libraryacquisition.AcquisitionISBN=
              librarybook.BookISBN AND
       libraryloan.LoanMemberID=
              librarymember.MemberNumber
```

DataSetProvider1	Name	dspLateBooksDetail
(Data Access tab)	DataSet	sdsLateBooksDetail
ClientDataSet1	Name	cdsLateBooksDetail
(Data Access tab)	ProviderName	dspLateBooksDetail
	ReadOnly	True
RvDataSetConnection1	Name	dscLateBooksDetail
(Rave tab)	DataSet	cdsLateBooksDetail

EX 17.4 STEP 3   Define the new report in Rave

- Go to Rave (double-click on rvpLibrary on the data module if it is not running).
- Create a new report with File | New Report and change the new report's Name property to repLateBooksDetail.
- Select File | New Data Object and choose Direct Data View.
- Select dscLateBooksDetail (figure 17.24).
- Click Finish to create a new Data View.
- Expand the Data View Dictionary in the Project TreeView.
- Double-click on DataView1 and change its Name property to dvLateBooksDetail.

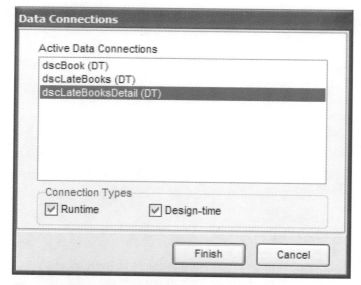

Figure 17.24 Selecting a new Data Object

The fields under the newly created Data View dvLateBooksDetail are shown in figure 17.25.

- To add the common report header, add a DataMirrorSection.
- Set the DataMirrorSection's DataMirrors property to GlobalPage1.Section1 using the Data Mirror Editor.

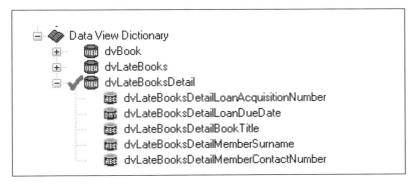

Figure 17.25 The fields in dvLateBooksDetail

- Add a Text property for the report title.
- Add a Region component to the page covering its whole area from below the DataMirrorSection.
- Add a Band for the column headers.
- Add a DataBand for the field values.
- Change the component properties on the Page Designer as shown below.

Component	Property	Value	
Text1	Name	txtReportTitle	
	Text	Late books detail	
	Font	Arial,14,Bold	
DataBand1	Name	LateBooksDetail	
	DataView	dvLateBooksDetail	(select from drop-down list)
Band1	Name	Header	
	ControllerBand	LateBooksDetailData	

- Run the Band Style Editor by clicking on the three dots next to the BandStyle property of Band1 (Header) in the Object Inspector.
- Set the Print Location to Body Header (B).
- Check the New Page option in the Print Occurrence GroupBox to set the header to be printed on other pages in case the listing spans more than one page.
- Using the fields in Data View dvLateBooksDetail, add the column headers.
- Using the fields in Data View dvLateBooksDetail, add the field values.
- Change the column headers as shown below.

Component	Property	Value
Text2	Text	Acquisition
Text3	Text	Due date
Text4	Text	Title
Text5	Text	Member
Text5	Text	Contact number

- Save the Rave project.

- Execute the report to see if it generates the report structure shown in figure 17.21.
- Close Rave.

EX 17.4 STEP 4   The event handler

- Go back to Delphi and create the event handler shown below for when the user selects the Reports | Late books (more detail) menu sequence.

```
procedure TfrmLibrary.Latebooksmoredetail1Click(Sender: TObject);
begin
  dmoLibrary.cdsLateBooksDetail.Open;
  dmoLibrary.cdsLateBooksDetail.Refresh;

  //Generate the report
  dmoLibrary.rvpLibrary.Open;                            //Open Rave project
  //Select report
  dmoLibrary.rvpLibrary.SelectReport('repLateBooksDetail',False);
  dmoLibrary.rvpLibrary.Execute;                         //Execute Rave project
  dmoLibrary.rvpLibrary.Close;

  //Close the ClientDataSet
  dmoLibrary.cdsLateBooksDetail.Close;
end;
```

- Save the application and run it.
- When you select the Reports | Late books (more detail) menu item, the report shown in figure 17.21 should be generated.

EXAMPLE 17.5) Neaten up the application

The main unit of the application as it stands now contains duplication. Consider the event handlers for generating the List of titles (example 17.2), Late books (example 17.3) and Late books detail reports (example 17.4). Note that the code looks the same except for the name of the ClientDataSet that is used and the name of the report that is selected. In each case the following happens:
- the ClientDataSet is opened and refreshed;
- the Rave project is opened;
- a specific report in the project is selected;
- the Rave project is executed;
- the Rave project is closed, and,
- the ClientDataSet is closed.

(The event handlers are repeated below.)

```
procedure TfrmLibrary.Listoftitles1Click(Sender: TObject);
begin
  dmoLibrary.cdsBook.Open;
  dmoLibrary.cdsBook.Refresh;
```

```
   //Generate the report
   dmoLibrary.rvpLibrary.Open;                        //Open Rave project
   //Select report
   dmoLibrary.rvpLibrary.SelectReport('repTitleList',False);
   dmoLibrary.rvpLibrary.Execute;                     //Execute Rave project
   dmoLibrary.rvpLibrary.Close;                       //Close Rave project

   //Close the ClientDataSet
   dmoLibrary.cdsBook.Close;
end;


procedure TfrmLibrary.Latebooks1Click(Sender: TObject);
begin
   dmoLibrary.cdsLateBooks.Open;
   dmoLibrary.cdsLateBooks.Refresh;

   //Generate the report
   dmoLibrary.rvpLibrary.Open;                        //Open Rave project
   //Select report
   dmoLibrary.rvpLibrary.SelectReport('repLateBooks',False);
   dmoLibrary.rvpLibrary.Execute;                     //Execute Rave project
   dmoLibrary.rvpLibrary.Close;

   //Close the ClientDataSet
   dmoLibrary.cdsLateBooks.Close;
end;

procedure TfrmLibrary.Latebooksmoredetail1Click(Sender: TObject);
begin
   dmoLibrary.cdsLateBooksDetail.Open;
   dmoLibrary.cdsLateBooksDetail.Refresh;

   //Generate the report
   dmoLibrary.rvpLibrary.Open;      //Open Rave project
   //Select report
   dmoLibrary.rvpLibrary.SelectReport('repLateBooksDetail',False);
   dmoLibrary.rvpLibrary.Execute; //Execute Rave project
   dmoLibrary.rvpLibrary.Close;

   //Close the ClientDataSet
   dmoLibrary.cdsLateBooksDetail.Close;
end;
```

We now eliminate the duplication by introducing a procedure.

EX 17.5 STEP 1 Create the procedure

- Create the procedure shown below.

```
procedure TfrmLibrary.GenerateReport(CDS: TClientDataSet;
                                     ReportName: String);
```

```
begin
  CDS.Open;
  CDS.Refresh;

  //Generate the report
  dmoLibrary.rvpLibrary.Open;                          //Open Rave project
  dmoLibrary.rvpLibrary.SelectReport(ReportName,False); //Select report
  dmoLibrary.rvpLibrary.Execute;                        //Execute Rave project
  dmoLibrary.rvpLibrary.Close;

  //Close the ClientDataSet
  CDS.Close;
end;
```

- Remember to also add the declaration to the private section of the class TfrmLibrary as below:

```
private
procedure GenerateReport(CDS: TClientDataSet;ReportName: String);
```

EX 17.5 STEP 2 Change the event handlers

- Change the event handlers to call the procedure created above as shown below.

```
procedure TfrmLibrary.Listoftitles1Click(Sender: TObject);
begin
  GenerateReport (dmoLibrary.cdsBook,'repTitleList');
end;

procedure TfrmLibrary.Latebooks1Click(Sender: TObject);
begin
  GenerateReport (dmoLibrary.cdsLateBooks,'repLateBooks');
end;

procedure TfrmLibrary.Latebooksmoredetail1Click(Sender: TObject);
begin
  GenerateReport (dmoLibrary.cdsLateBooksDetail,'repLateBooksDetail');
end;
```

- Save the application, run it and generate the reports to see if they still work.
- If you have a compilation error stating that TClientDataSet is undefined, add the namespace Borland.Vcl.DBClient (Delphi 8) or the unit DBClient (Delphi 6/7) to unit C16e01u's uses clause under the interface section.

As you can see, we have eliminated the duplication and the code is now much more elegant.

REVIEW

We generated reports in this chapter by creating a Rave project and defining the layout of various reports within the Rave project. We introduced three new Delphi components: TRvProject, TRvSystem and TRvDataSetConnection. The TRvProject component is the link between the application and the reports in the Rave project while TRvSystem is responsible for the general configuration of the reports for the printer, margins, number of pages and so on. The TRvDataSetConnection component provides a bridge between the data in our application and the Rave data aware components.

Reports are built up of regions containing bands with printable components on them.

Static text such as headlines, titles and column headers are usually printed with the Text component. We set the text in the Text component's Text property. Dynamic text such as record field values are printed using the DataText component. Associated with a band containing DataTexts is a data view that is used to associate DataText components with field names of a specific data set. We specify the data set in the DataBand's DataView property and the data field in the DataText's DataField property.

To preview a report in design mode, we click the Execute speed button, <F9>, or select the File | Execute Report menu sequence. To activate the report at run time, we

- open and refresh the ClientDataSet (if it is a data aware report);
- open the Rave project with the TrvProject's Open method;
- select a specific report in the project with the TrvProject's SelectReport method;
- execute the Rave project with the TrvProject's Execute method;
- close the Rave project with the TrvProject's Close method and
- close the ClientDataSet.

IMPORTANT CONCEPTS

Rave reports

Data aware report: A report is data aware if it uses data from a database.
Data View: Refers to the TRvDataSetConnection component linking the data aware components in the Rave project to the fields in the corresponding data set in the application. Data Views provide a link to the data in your application.
Data View Dictionary: The Data View Dictionary is shown in the Project TreeView and it shows all the Data Views in the Rave project as well as all the fields in each view.
Data viewer: The Data viewer is used to view the data live in the Rave project.
Global Page: When we want the same header (for example with the company name, the date and time that the report is generated and the page number) for more than one report, we put it in a Global Page so that it can be shared between the reports. Global Pages can then be added to the DataMirrorSections of reports via the DataMirrors property. This is the primary purpose of a global page. It is like as a central location for you to store reporting items that you want accessible to more than one report.
Global Page Catalog: The Global Page Catalog is shown in the Project TreeView and it shows all the Global Pages in the Rave project.

Mirroring: When a component is set to mirror another, it assumes the appearance and properties of the component it is mirroring. The two components can be on the same page, across pages within the same report or on a global page. This is the primary purpose of a global page. You can almost think of it like an Object Repository, a central location for you to store reporting items that you want accessible to more than one report. If the component is a container control like TRaveSection (similar to Delphi's TPanel), all child components are mirrored as well. When the original component changes, all mirroring components will also change. While the mirrored component cannot change it properties, you can add additional components if it is a container control.

Project TreeView: Shows all the objects in the Rave project. There are three main sections in the Project Tree: the Report Library, the Global Page Catalog, and the Data View Dictionary. Reports can contain any number of page definitions. Global Pages are used to hold items that you want accessible to multiple reports.

Rave Visual Designer: Used to design the layout of reports in a Rave project. It enables the use of printable components with properties that can be set using the Object Inspector.

Report Library: The Report Library is shown in the Project TreeView and it shows all the reports with all the components that they consist of.

Report Variables: Items such as total pages or current date and time in a variety of formats.

Project Parameters: Custom variables that you create and initialize from your Delphi application. Project Parameters can be used for items such as user defined report titles, printing the current user name or other custom information.

NEW DELPHI FEATURES

TRvDataSetConnection		
Properties	DataSet	Points to the data set to which the connection provides access.
Prefix	dsc	
Use		Rave uses data from your application. This is done with a data connection component such as TRvDataSetConnection providing a bridge between the data in your application and the Rave visual components.

TRvProject		
Properties	ProjectFile	This property defines the report project file that your application uses to hold the report definitions. This file will have an extension of .rav and it can contain as many report definitions as you need.
	Engine	This property allows you to define an alternate output engine to be used. This allows you to output Rave reports through the Text, RTF or HTML filer components or to define custom setup and preview screens through the TRvSystem component.
Methods	Open	This method loads this report project file into memory to prepare for printing or end-user design changes.

	SelectReport	This method accepts two parameters, ReportName and FullName. The method will select the report specified by parameter ReportName. If FullName is true, the function will search the report whose full name matches, otherwise it will search the short names.
	SetParam	SetParam enables the application to pass project parameters to the currently loaded Rave project. These parameters can be used to control dynamic layouts, SQL parameters or other items to print in a visually designed report.
	Execute	This method will generate the currently selected Rave report.
	Close	This method is called when you no longer need the report project or before you close your application.
Prefix	rvp	
Use		This component provides access to the visual reports you create with Rave. Normally you will have a single TRvProject component in your application, although you can have more if necessary.

TRvSystem

Properties	DefaultDest	This is where the report will be sent if no setup screen is used or is the default during setup. Can be rdFile, rdPreview or rdPrinter.
Prefix	rvs	
Use		This component can send a report to the printer or a preview screen and can display a setup and status screen as well.

RAVE FEATURES

Band component

Properties	ControllerBand	Defines the band that determines when this band prints. In other words, this band acts as a header or footer band for the Controller band depending on the BandStyle property. This relationship is shown visually in the Page Designer with a coloured arrow that points towards the ControllerBand which contains a diamond shape of the same colour.
	BandStyle	Defines the positions and occurrences where the band will print. The current band's style setting is visible on the right hand side of the band header in the PageDesigner. The Band Style Editor displays a virtual layout of all of your bands for the given print locations of each band or data band. You can also control the Print Occurrence for a Band, having it continue on a new page or column or any combination of occurrence settings.
Prefix	bnd	
Use		A Band component can only be created within a region. You can create as many Bands as you like and a Band may print in multiple locations if the report design requires it. So for example, if you want a solid horizontal line to appear above and below a detail body, you could create a single band and set it to print on both the Body Header and Body Footer via the Band Style Editor.

DataBand component

Property	DataView	Defines the data view this band will print from. The data band cycles through the records of the data view until it reaches the last record.
Prefix	dbn	
Use		The DataBand component is similar to a band component except that it is tied to a particular DataView and iterates across the rows in the DataView. DataBands are printed once for every record in the DataView. DataBands can contain data-aware components (such as DataText) or other components. DataBands are put inside Regions, which delimit the width of the bands.

DataText component

Properties	Datafield	Defines the data field to print. Using the Data Text Editor, any combination of data fields, report variables, project parameters or string constants can be defined.
	DataView	Defines the default data view that will be used for the DataField property.
Prefix	dtx	
Use		The DataText component is the primary means to output fields from your database. You can select a specific DataView and DataField or use the Data Text Editor to create any combination of string constants, data fields, report variables or project parameters.

DataMirrorSection component

Properties	DataMirrors	Defines combinations of field values and section components. These are used to determine which section will be mirrored when this component is printed. A default data mirror can be defined that will be used if no other match is found.
Prefix	dms	
Use		Similar to Rave's section component with one difference, it will dynamically mirror another section depending upon the value of a DataField. (We use it here without setting the DataField property.) You configure the data mirror section using the Data Mirror Editor. This component is useful for printing out data that has different formats depending upon the type of data.

Region component

Prefix	rgn	
Use		Regions determines the maximum height that bands can use before starting a new page. One page can consist of many regions and one region of many bands.
		Acts as a container for Band and DataBand components. To create a composite or sub-report, simply drop more than one region on a page and add the appropriate bands to each.

Section component

Prefix	sec	
Use		Acts as a container for other components, in other words it helps you to group components together.

Text component			
Property	Text		The text to be printed.
Prefix	txt		
Use		To display fixed text on reports for items such as column headers or report titles.	

PROBLEMS

PROBLEM 17.1) Generate the Members list report

Change the application C16e01p to include the Member list report generated by
the Reports | Member list menu sequence.

PROBLEM 17.2)

Define the reports and write the event handlers for the items in the Reports
menu of the accommodation application written in problem 16.1.

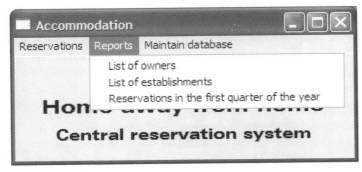

Figure 17.26 The Reports menu

CHAPTER 18

Investigating objects

PURPOSE OF THIS CHAPTER

Object-oriented (OO) programming has become important because it is one of the best approaches available for dealing with many of the problems facing software developers. Since the 1980s, when computer scientists began to realize what an important influence object orientation could have on software development, more and more object-oriented development tools have become available. We are now at the point where understanding what 'object orientation' means is important for many systems analysts, designers and programmers.

Delphi is a practical example of an object-oriented programming language, and we have been using objects informally until now. Full object orientation, however, goes a lot further. Space constraints prevent us going into detail, so we will use this chapter to look at some basic characteristics.

Depending on your background, these object concepts may be comparatively easy to understand or may be confusing at first. You do not have to understand absolutely everything in this chapter the first time you work through it, and you should plan to work through it a few times. It may also be useful occasionally to page backwards and reread previous sections to remind yourself of the concepts that have gone before.

EXAMPLE 18.1) The basic 'unit' file

Just about every 'thing' you can think of in Delphi is an object. A form is an object and the various components we place on a form are also objects. We'll start investigating object orientation by looking at the classes and objects that Delphi creates for us automatically.

- Open a new application and look at the code for Unit1. (You may need to click on the code tab at the bottom of the screen, or to press <F12>, to display the code listing.) It will be something like this:

```
1 unit Unit1;

2 interface

3 uses
4    Windows, Messages, SysUtils, Variants, Classes, Graphics,
5    Controls, Forms, Dialogs;

6 type
7    TForm1 = class(TForm)
8    private
9       { Private declarations }
10   public
11      { Public declarations }
12   end;

13 var
14    Form1: TForm1;

15 implementation

16 {$R *.DFM}

17 end.
```

We write our Delphi programs in a unit file. As we saw briefly in Chapter 12 the basic structure of a unit file comprises three sections, the *unit name* (as in line 1 above), the *interface section* (lines 2-14) and the *implementation section* (lines 15-17). Most of the programs in this book consist of a single unit file, though large Delphi programs have many units.

The unit name

The default unit name is Unit1 (line 1) or Unit2, Unit3 and so on if we have more than one unit. Delphi changes the unit's name when we save the file under a new name (with the File | Save As ... menu sequence) and maintains a cross-reference to this file in the project (.dpr or .bdsproj) file. This cross-referencing is the reason we change the unit's name through File | Save As .... If we edit the name directly in the editor, we must also make the corresponding change in the .dpr file, and it's easy to make a mistake.

The interface section

The *interface section* (lines 2-14) provides the link between a particular unit and other units. Briefly, if we have unit A, other units know only as much about unit A as it reveals in the public parts of the interface section. The interface section consists of several subsections: the *uses clause* (lines 3-5), the *type declarations* (lines 6-12) and the *global variable declarations* (lines 13-14). (Global constant declarations take a similar form.)

The *uses clause* (lines 3-5): In order to run, a Delphi program needs a lot of background information, such as how to interact with the operating system and how to create forms and components such as buttons. This information is contained in various unit files that are a standard part of Delphi. For instance, the file 'SysUtils' (line 4) gives information about the string handling routines (eg StrToInt) and the date and time routines (eg TimeToStr), among others. If this were not in the list, we would not be able to do any of the string operations. To make this information available to our program Delphi automatically lists these additional units under the uses clause. (If you are curious to find out more about any of these units, highlight its name in the editor and then press <F1> for Help.) Different versions of Delphi list slightly different files in the uses clause so your list may differ a bit from ours.

The *type declaration* (lines 6-12): In object-oriented programming languages, a *type* or *class** is a template we use to create an object. In the next example we'll see how Delphi generates the form's class declaration as we add components and event handlers. Later in this chapter we'll write our own class declarations.

Focusing first on the code shown above, line 6 notifies the compiler that the type declarations follow. In this program we declare only one type, TForm1, but if necessary we can declare additional types as well (as we'll see later).

Line 7 states that we are going to derive a new class, called TForm1, *from* TForm. TForm is a standard part of Delphi and is the template for the blank form that appears when we start a new application. The standard TForm class has a lot of capability built into it. For instance, it 'knows' (through its methods) how to create itself and how to show itself on the screen. It also has properties such as a Caption, a Height and a Width. Because of line 7 we *inherit* all this capability from TForm as a starting point for our own form, TForm1. When we add components and event handlers Delphi automatically adds these objects and methods to the type declaration of TForm1.

The *var (variable) declaration*: Lines 13 and 14 give the var (or variable) declarations. The previous subsection, the type declaration, provides the additional classes (or types) that are available in our program in addition to the standard types that Delphi provides. However, a class or type is a template *only* and not an object. In this section, the var declaration, we declare what objects we will create from the available types. The only variable so far is the Form object that Delphi creates automatically when we start a new project. It is called Form1, and is of type TForm1. To help us keep the distinction between the type and the object, Delphi has the convention of starting type names with a 'T'. Therefore, TForm1 is the type and Form1 is the object.

The implementation section

The third part of a unit is the implementation section. This is where we write our program code. Because we have not written any procedures or functions yet, the implementation section is empty except for the compiler directive in line 16 (*{$R *.DFM}* up to Delphi 7, *{$R *.nfm}* in Delphi 8). At first glance,

---

* In this context in Delphi, 'type' and 'class' mean the same thing and Delphi uses both these words as reserved words in the type declaration, as we'll see in a moment.

the curly brackets make this compiler directive look like a comment, and so presumably we should be able to delete it. But don't be fooled! The opening symbol here is the compound symbol {$, which means that it is *not* a conventional comment but is instead a special instruction to the compiler. *{$R *.DFM}* and *{$R *.nfm}* are resource directives that tell the compiler to include the Form file (the .dfm or .nfm file) in the application. So *do not delete* this line.

Unlike the interface section that makes communication with other units possible, the implementation section is *private to the unit* and describes the inner workings of all the types declared in the type declaration.

Although not shown here, the implementation section can also contain a unit level uses clause and, as we have seen in previous chapters, unit level constant and variable declarations before the method definitions.

Example 18.1 summary: The unit file has a name for identifying itself, an interface section for communicating with other units and an implementation section giving the private details of the unit's functioning. The interface section contains the global uses clause, the type declarations, and the global constant and variable declarations.

EXAMPLE 18.2) Extending the basic application

In this example we create a small Delphi program and then look at the unit's listing again to see the changes that Delphi introduces.
- Starting with a new application, add two buttons.
- Set the following properties and create the buttons' OnClick event handlers (lines 21-28 below).
- Then save the unit and project as C18e02u and C18e02p.

Component	Property	Value
Form1	Name	frmStructureDemo
	Caption	Demo of a Form's Structure
Button1	Name	btnYellow
	Caption	&Yellow
Button2	Name	btnPurple
	Caption	&Purple

```
1 unit C18e02u;

2 interface

3 uses
4    Windows, Messages, SysUtils, Classes, Graphics, Controls, Forms,
5    Dialogs, StdCtrls;

6 type
7    TfrmStructureDemo = class(TForm)
8       btnYellow: TButton;
9       btnPurple: TButton;
10      procedure btnYellowClick(Sender: TObject);
11      procedure btnPurpleClick(Sender: TObject);
```

```
12    private
13      { Private declarations }
14    public
15      { Public declarations }
16    end;

17 var
18    frmStructureDemo: TfrmStructureDemo;

19 implementation

20 {$R *.DFM}

21 procedure TfrmStructureDemo.btnYellowClick(Sender: TObject);
22 begin
23    Color := clYellow;
24 end;

25 procedure TfrmStructureDemo.btnPurpleClick(Sender: TObject);
26 begin
27    Color := clPurple;
28 end;

29 end.
```

We have made several changes in comparison to example 18.1. In addition to changing the unit's name (line 1), we have changed the form's name (and Caption), added two buttons to the form and written an OnClick event handler for each button. Let's look at the effects these changes have had on the program listing.

Changing the form's name

In the Object Inspector we changed the form's name to frmStructureDemo. Using this as a basis, Delphi changed the name of the new form *type* to TfrmStructureDemo, which is still derived from TForm (line 7). (Remember the convention of a 'T' prefix to indicate a type.) Delphi then declared the form *object* as frmStructureDemo (without the 'T' prefix) to be of type TfrmStructureDemo (with the 'T' prefix) (line 18).

Adding buttons

We added two buttons to the form and called them btnYellow and btnPurple. On this basis, Delphi automatically inserted these as part of the TfrmStructureDemo type declaration. Line 8 states that the TfrmStructureDemo class contains an object btnYellow of type TButton, which is Delphi's standard class for buttons. Line 9 states that TfrmStructureDemo contains a second object, btnPurple, also of type TButton. These objects are now part of the new type TfrmStructureDemo. They are reflected in the Object TreeView (up to Delphi 7) or the Model View (Delphi 8), though you may have to expand the hierarchy to see them.

Here we see that a class, in this case TfrmStructureDemo, can be *composed* of other objects, in this case btnYellow and btnPurple. To add each button to the form, we simply clicked on the icon for the TButton class on the Component/Tool palette and then positioned the button object on the form. Delphi automatically inserted the necessary code into the type declaration (lines 8-9). Since TButton, like TForm, is a standard Delphi class, we *automatically gain all of the capability that is part of TButton* (such as the button's Caption and its OnClick event handler) when we include it in our form.

Adding event handlers

We added an event handler for each button. Delphi automatically incorporates these as *methods of TfrmStructureDemo* by declaring these procedures in the type structure (lines 10 and 11). These declarations do not define what the procedures do, so Delphi also created the skeletons for these event-handlers in the implementation section (lines 21-28), leaving us to fill in the appropriate programming statements (lines 23 and 27). In Delphi Pascal, although methods can be either procedures or functions, event handlers are always procedures. Along with all the methods available from the TForm and TButton types, these event handlers are now also methods belonging to the TfrmStructureDemo class.

A method declaration, as in line 10, is sometimes referred to as a *method signature* since it gives the method name (btnYellowClick), the type of subroutine (a procedure) and the parameter list (`Sender: TObject`).

EXAMPLE 18.3) Creating our own classes and objects

Now that we have seen how Delphi sets up classes and objects we are ready to start creating our own classes and objects. While working through the rest of this chapter, remember that these examples, like all the examples in this book, are highly simplified in order to emphasize particular points of interest.

Jolly Joe's Flying Circus is a small airline that links a few provincial towns. It needs a small computer program to total up all the units of luggage that are loaded onto a particular aircraft.

To do this, we could write a small Delphi program along the lines of the other programs in this book. It would need a unit level variable to keep track of the total units of luggage. An alternative approach is to create an *object*, rather than a unit level variable, to store the number of units already checked in and to add the numbers of new units as needed.

We'll call our new class TCounter. It'll have an integer data field to record the total and four methods, two procedures and two functions. One procedure will add a given number to the total and the other will clear the total. The functions return an integer and a string representation of the current value of the total.

Because object orientation (OO) is about encapsulation and keeping data and the inner workings of classes private, we'll create this new class in a separate unit. In the database chapters we became familiar with multiple forms, each with its own unit. In this example we have a single form but two units.

Unit 1, the unit accompanying Form1, will contain the user interface and will manipulate the Counter object. The other unit, Unit2, will contain the definition of the TCounter class.

EX 18.3 STEP 1   The overall framework

- To start, open a new application.
- On the form (frmUnits) place a SpinEdit, two buttons and a Label (figure 18.1). Button1 (btnAdd) will call the Counter's 'Add' method, passing the value in the SpinEdit (sedNewUnits) as a parameter. The Counter object will add this value to the total. Button2 (btnClear) will call the Counter's 'Clear' method. In each case the updated value appears in the Label (lblTotalUnits).

We mentioned that the TCounter class will be defined in Unit2.

- To add Unit2 to the project, select File | New | Unit from the menu.* A second tab, labelled Unit2, appears in the edit window. Because it has no accompanying form, this unit is very simple. It provides only the unit name and the skeleton for the interface and implementation sections:

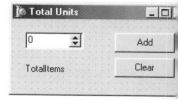

Figure 18.1 Form with SpinEdit, two buttons and Label

```
unit Unit2;

interface

implementation

end.
```

When adding an additional unit like this we must insert the program code defining classes, methods, and so on manually. Fortunately we can base what we do on the structure Delphi creates automatically for a form as discussed in example 18.2. So we will be adding TCounter's type declaration in the `interface` section and its four methods, procedures Add and Clear, and functions GetTotal and GetTotalStr, to the `implementation` section. But before doing that, let's look at the project file.

- Select View | Units and double-click on `Project1`. When it appears in the editor, we can see that it lists both `Unit1` and `Unit2` in the uses section and indicates that `Form1` is part of `Unit1`. (To support the .NET environment the Delphi 8 project file carries more information than is shown below, but for our purposes we can ignore the other code.)

```
program Project1;

uses
  Forms,
  Unit1 in 'Unit1.pas' {Form1},
  Unit2 in 'Unit2.pas';

{$R *.RES}

begin
  Application.Initialize;
  Application.CreateForm(TForm1, Form1);
  Application.Run;
end.
```

- Let's rename and save what we have done so far. With Unit2 displayed in the edit window, select File | Save as ... and save Unit2 as CounterU.
- Now click on the Unit1 tab in the edit window and save it as DemoU.
- Finally, using File | Save Project As ..., save the project file as C18e03p.

If we look at the project file now, we'll see all three of these name changes reflected there:

---

* The sequence for adding a unit varies slightly between different versions of Delphi.

```
program C18e03p;

uses
  Forms,
  DemoU in 'DemoU.pas' {Form1},
  CounterU in 'CounterU.pas';
  ...
```

EX 18.3 STEP 2   The TCounter class

- Now click on the CounterU tab in the edit window and enter the code for the TCounter class as follows:

```
1 unit CounterU;

2 interface

3 type
4   TCounter = class(TObject)        // set up class inheritance
5   private              // private, so only this unit has access
6     FTotal: Integer;
7   public                           // public, any code can use these
8     procedure Add (Number: Integer);
9     procedure Clear;
10    function GetTotal: integer;
11    function GetTotalStr: string;
12  end; // end TCounter = class(TObject)

13 implementation

14 uses
15   SysUtils;                       // Add for IntToStr below

16 procedure TCounter.Add (Number: Integer);
17 begin
18   FTotal := FTotal + Number;
19 end; // end procedure TCounter.Add

20 procedure TCounter.Clear;
21 begin
22   FTotal := 0;
23 end; // end procedure TCounter.Clear

24 function TCounter.GetTotal: integer;
25 begin
26   Result := FTotal;
27 end; // end function TCounter.GetTotal

28 function TCounter.GetTotalStr: string;
29 begin
30   Result := IntToStr (FTotal);
31 end; // end function TCounter.GetTotalStr

32 end. // end unit CounterU
```

Let's start by looking at the type declaration (lines 3-12). It is much like Delphi's automatic form declaration (example 18.2). Line 4 states that we are defining a new class, of type TCounter, which is derived from TObject, Delphi's base class. TCounter will have one data item, FTotal, of type integer (line 6) which we are making private to this unit (line 5). TCounter has four methods, all of which are public (line 7) and so are available to other units in this project. Line 8 informs the compiler that TCounter has a procedure type method called Add that accepts an integer parameter. Line 9 declares another procedure type method, Clear, that has no incoming parameters. Lines 10 and 11 declare function type methods that have no incoming parameters. One supplies an integer value and one a string value.

The methods themselves are defined in the implementation section (lines 13-32). Because procedure Add is one of TCounter's methods, and so is part of TCounter, we use dot notation to include the TCounter relationship in the procedure header (line 16). Line 18 adds the value of the incoming parameter (`Number`) to the `FTotal` variable declared in line 6 and then assigns this new value to `FTotal`.

The Clear method (lines 20-23) is similar. It has no incoming parameters and sets the value of `FTotal` to 0. Note that `FTotal` is *not* declared as a local variable in either method. It is declared as part of class TCounter in line 6 and both methods manipulate this value. However, because `FTotal` is declared as `private` (lines 5-6), no other units have access to `FTotal`.

The third method, function GetTotal, returns the value of `FTotal`, formatted as an integer, through the (automatic) `Result` variable (line 26). The fourth method, funtion GetTotalStr, returns the value of `FTotal` formatted as a string (line 30) and uses the `IntToStr` system function. `IntToStr` is declared in the `SysUtils` unit and so we must list `SysUtils` in the uses clause (lines 14-15). (To find out where `IntToStr` is declared, place the cursor on it in the editor and then press <F1> for Help.)

The Code Explorer

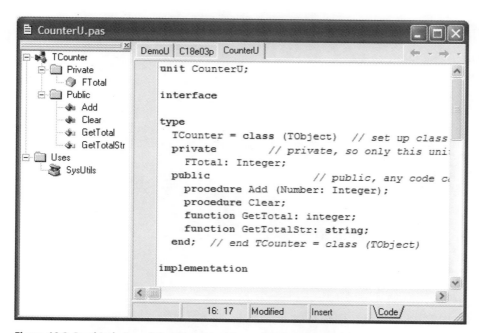

Figure 18.2 Graphical view of the TCounter object using the Code Explorer in Delphi 7

A window that we have not yet looked at is the Code Explorer. In Delphi 7 and earlier versions it is docked to the left of the editor. In Delphi 8 use the sequence View | Code Explorer. The Code Explorer window displays a tree diagram showing, among other things, the types, classes and methods defined in the unit displayed in the editor. If we expand the tree by clicking the little plus signs at each node, the Code Explorer gives a useful graphical view of the TCounter class we have just defined, showing the private data field, FTotal, and the public methods, Add, Clear, GetTotal and GetTotalStr (figure 18.2).

EX 18.3 STEP 3   Using the class

Having defined the TCounter class, let's now use it to total up the number of units of luggage. In the unit associated with the form, DemoU.pas, we'll create an object of type TCounter and then manipulate it through event handlers attached to the buttons.

- Select the DemoU tab within the edit window to display unit Demo.pas.

We need to:
o   Add a reference to the other unit (CounterU, line 6 below) after the standard Delphi list* because this unit uses a class (Tcounter) that is defined in unit CounterU.pas.
o   Declare the object we are going to create (Units, line 17 below) as being of type TCounter.
o   Create the object in the form's OnCreate event handler (lines 25-28 below). When we use components such as a form and buttons, Delphi creates the objects automatically. However, if we define a class ourselves, like TCounter, we must ourselves create an object of this type before we can use it. Here it is convenient to create this object (Units) in the form's OnCreate event handler so that it exists by the time the form appears. To do this we use the Create method which TCounter *inherits* from TObject (line 27).
o   Use the object in the two OnClick event handlers through calls to its methods. Depending on the operation we need we call either the Add method (line 31) or the Clear method (line 38). We then use the GetTotalStr method, which supplies a string, to build up the Caption strings in the event handlers (lines 32 and 39).

- Enter this code, remembering to create the event handler skeletons by double-clicking on the form and on each button in turn or in the Events tab of the Object Inspector.

```
1 unit DemoU;

2 interface

3 uses
4   Windows, Messages, SysUtils, Classes, Graphics, Controls, Forms,
5   Dialogs, StdCtrls, Spin,          // standard Delphi units
6   CounterU;                         // add reference to our own unit

7 type
8   TfrmUnits = class(TForm)
9     sedNewUnits: TSpinEdit;
10    btnAdd: TButton;
11    btnClear: TButton;
```

*   The standard Delphi list in the uses clause varies slightly in different versions of Delphi, so your list (lines 4 and 5) may differ. The important thing is to add 'CounterU' to the uses list Delphi creates somewhere before the terminating semicolon. (Line 5 now ends on a comma and so the uses clause extends to line 6.)

```
12      lblTotalUnits: TLabel;
13      procedure FormCreate(Sender: TObject);
14      procedure btnAddClick(Sender: TObject);
15      procedure btnClearClick(Sender: TObject);
16    private
17      Units: TCounter;                    // declare our own object
18    public
19      { Public declarations }
20    end;


21 var
22    frmUnits: TfrmUnits;


23 implementation


24 {$R *.DFM}


25 procedure TfrmUnits.FormCreate(Sender: TObject);
26 begin
27    Units := TCounter.Create;
28 end; // end procedure TfrmUnits.FormCreate


29 procedure TfrmUnits.btnAddClick(Sender: TObject);
30 begin
31    Units.Add (sedNewUnits.Value);
32    lblTotalUnits.Caption := Units.GetTotalStr+ ' units of luggage';
33    sedNewUnits.Value := 0;
34    sedNewUnits.SetFocus;
35 end; // end procedure TfrmUnits.btnAddClick


36 procedure TfrmUnits.btnClearClick(Sender: TObject);
37 begin
38    Units.Clear;
39    lblTotalUnits.Caption := Units.GetTotalStr + ' units of luggage';
40    sedNewUnits.SetFocus;
41 end; // end procedure TfrmUnits.btnClearClick


42 end. // end unit DemoU
```

Notice that we create (instantiate) an object from a class. So when creating an object we call the *class's* Create method (TCounter.Create in line 27) and assign that to the object name declared in the class declaration (line 17). When using an object, once it has been created, the method calls are to that *object* (Units.Add(…) in line 31, Units.Clear in line 38 and Units.GetTotalStr in lines 32 and 39).

- Use File | Save All to save the code you have entered under the file names chosen in step 1. Then run and test the program.
- If you are unsure of what is happening in this program:
  - Return to the editor and place breakpoints in the bodies of the OnClick event handlers (lines 31 and 38 in unit DemoU).
  - Run the program again, click on the Add button and step through the program line by line by using <F7>. Notice how execution moves between units.

Clicking on the Add button calls its OnClick event handler (lines 29-35 in unit DemoU). This calls the object's Add method, passing it the value entered in the

SpinEdit (line 31). The object's Add method (lines 16-19 in unit CounterU) adds the value of the incoming parameter to the object's data field (FTotal). Line 32 above then requests the updated value and uses it to build up the Caption for the Label before resetting the interface. The Clear button's event handler is similar.

EXAMPLE 18.4) Extending TCounter

An important advantage claimed for object orientation is that it encourages re-use and extention. Continuing from example 18.3, we are going to create a hockey or soccer scoreboard application. We'll start with the TCounter class and extend it by deriving a TSoccerScore class from TCounter. Through inheritance, TSoccerScore will be able to re-use all of TCounter's existing methods. It will implement only those additional methods it needs that are not already part of TCounter.

EX 18.4 STEP 1   Inheriting from TCounter

- Start by creating a new application. In this new application we want to re-use the Counter.pas unit from the previous example.
- To do this, select Project | Add to Project and select CounterU. (You may have to navigate to the directory where you stored the unit and project files from example 18.3.)
- Now, in a different directory, save Unit1 as ScoreBrdU, CounterU as CounterU in this different directory and the project as C18e04p.
- If you would like to see the project file, select View | Units and click on C18e04p. It lists both ScoreBrdU and CounterU in the uses section. We show the Delphi 7 project file. The Delphi 8 has this listing and the .NET support:

```
program C18e04p;

uses
  Forms,
  ScoreBrdU in 'ScoreBrdU.pas' {Form1},
  CounterU in 'CounterU.pas';

{$R *.RES}

begin
  Application.Initialize;
  Application.CreateForm(TForm1, Form1);
  Application.Run;
end.
```

- Modify unit CounterU to derive a TSoccerScore class from TCounter (lines 14–17, 21–22 and 39–42 below). (Notice the slight change to TCounter in line 7).

```
1 unit CounterU;

2 interface
```

```
 3 type
 4   TCounter = class (TObject)                    // set up class inheritance
 5   private                        // private, so only this unit has access
 6     FTotal : Integer;
 7   protected                  // protected, only this unit and subclasses
 8     procedure Add (Number: Integer);
 9   public                                 // public, any code can use these
10     procedure Clear;
11     function GetTotal: integer;
12     function GetTotalStr: string;
13   end; // end TCounter = class (TObject)

14   TSoccerScore = class (TCounter)          // subclass of our own class
15   public
16     procedure AddGoal;                             // a subclass method
17   end; // end TSoccerScore = class (TCounter)

18 implementation

19 uses
20   SysUtils;                                // Add for IntToStr below
21 const
22   Goal = 1;

23 procedure TCounter.Add (Number : integer);
24 begin
25   FTotal := FTotal + Number;
26 end; // end procedure TCounter.Add

27 procedure TCounter.Clear;
28 begin
29   FTotal := 0;
30 end; // end procedure TCounter.Add

31 function TCounter.GetTotal: integer;
32 begin
33   Result := FTotal;
34 end; // end function TCounter.GetTotal

35 function TCounter.GetTotalStr: string;
36 begin
37   Result := IntToStr (FTotal);
38 end; // end function TCounter.GetTotalStr

39 procedure TSoccerScore.AddGoal;                  // derived class's method
40 begin
41   Add (Goal);                             // Use Add inherited from TCounter
42 end; // end procedure TSoccerScore.AddGoal

43 end. // end unit CounterU
```

Here, in addition to the TCounter definition (lines 4-13) that we had previously, we define a new type called TSoccerScore (lines 14-17). While TCounter is derived from TObject (line 4), TSoccerScore is derived from TCounter (line 14).

This means that *TSoccerScore is a subclass of TCounter* and so inherits all the data fields and methods that TCounter has. In this way all the functionality of TCounter is available in TSoccerScore without rewriting any of the code. TSoccerScore also has its own method, the procedure AddGoal declared in line 16.

In the implementation section (lines 18-43) TCounter's methods Add (lines 23-26), Clear (lines 27-30), GetTotal (lines 31-34) and GetTotalStr (lines 35-38) remain as before. Lines 39-42 define TSoccerScore's method AddGoal. The dot notation for the name in the header (line 39) shows clearly that AddGoal is part of TSoccerScore. Since a goal in soccer or hockey is always worth only 1 point, AddGoal calls TCounter's Add method, passing the constant Goal, declared in lines 21-22, as a parameter.

In this example we have introduced the *protected* visibility specifier (lines 7–8). Its scope lies between the private and public specifiers. Anything that is protected can be accessed only by that class and its subclasses (even if the subclasses are in separate units) or by other classes specified in the same unit. With private, a subclass can access a superclass's private fields only if it is defined in the same unit. With public, access is open to all. Here we have decided that we want the subclass to be able to use the superclass's Add method, but no-one else, and so we have declared it as protected. Delphi 8 also has the *strict protected* specifier that limits visibility to the class and its subclasses only (whether they are in the same or different units).

Although methods for both TCounter and TSoccerScore appear in the implementation section of this unit, we can tell them apart by their headers since the class appears before the dot in their names. Through inheritance, all of TCounter's methods and data are also available to TSoccerScore. For example, since clearing the value is the same for both classes, we don't re-implement Clear for TSoccerScore but simply rely on the inherited Clear. TSoccerScore.AddGoal uses TCounter's Add method. Being able to re-use pieces of code so easily rather than rewriting them is one of the great benefits of object orientation.

The TSoccerScore subclass has a method of its own but no extra data. Since inheritance works only in one direction, TSoccerScore can use TCounter's data and methods but TCounter cannot use the method AddGoal declared in TSoccerScore.

EX 18.4 STEP 2 Using the new class

Now we come to the actual application. As (nearly) always with small GUI applications, let's start with the user interface (figure 18.3).

Figure 18.3 The complete user interface for the scoreboard application

- First place a GroupBox on the form. Inside this GroupBox place a button and Label (figure 18.4). You should not be able to drag the button or Label out of the GroupBox.

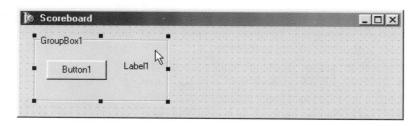

Figure 18.4 The first GroupBox placed on the form

- If you can drag the button or Label out of the GroupBox, delete the wrongly placed component, click inside the GroupBox with the left mouse button (or select the GroupBox in the Object Inspector), then once again add the button or Label.
- We could now place a second, corresponding GroupBox, button and Label on the form to get a layout to match figure 18.3, but it would be interesting to explore Delphi's copy-and-paste capabilities.
- Click *inside* the GroupBox but not on either of the other two components (or select the GroupBox in the Object Inspector). The sizing handles appear around the GroupBox (figure 18.4). Copy this GroupBox through the Edit | Copy sequence. Because the GroupBox is a container component (Chapter 2), you will also copy the button and Label it contains.
- Now click on the form *outside* the GroupBox and then select Edit | Paste. A copy of the GroupBox and its contents appears, overlapping the original (figure 18.5).

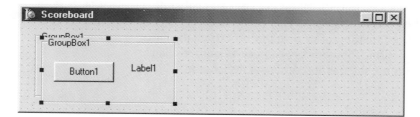

Figure 18.5 The copy of the GroupBox, overlapping the original

- Click the mouse inside the copied GroupBox, avoiding the other components, and drag the copy to the right of the original. You can also position this GroupBox through its Top and Left properties by using the Object Inspector.
- Add a button between the GroupBoxes to match figure 18.3.
- Set the following properties:

Component	Property	Value
Form1	Name	frmScoreboard
	Caption	Scoreboard
GroupBox1	Name	gpbTeam1
	Caption	Team 1
Label1	Name	lblScore1
(in gpbTeam1)	Caption	<Blank>

Button1	Name	btnAddGoal1
(in gpbTeam1)	Caption	Add Goal
GroupBox2	Name	gpbTeam2
	Caption	Team 2
Label2	Name	lblScore2
(in gpbTeam2)	Caption	<Blank>
Button2	Name	btnAddGoal2
(in gpbTeam2)	Caption	Add Goal
Button3	Name	btnClearScores
	Caption	Clear Scores

- Create the following program in unit ScoreBrdU. Delphi creates most of this program, but we must add CounterU to the uses clause (line 6), declare the two objects we will be creating (line 21), and fill in the event handler skeletons (lines 31-32, 36-37, 41-42, 46-49):

```
1 unit ScoreBrdU;

2 interface

3 uses
4   Windows, Messages, SysUtils, Classes, Graphics, Controls, Forms,
5   Dialogs, StdCtrls, Buttons,
6   CounterU;                        // our unit containing TCounter

7 type
8   TfrmScoreboard = class(TForm)
9     gpbTeam1: TGroupBox;
10    btnAddGoal1: TButton;
11    lblScore1: TLabel;
12    gpbTeam2: TGroupBox;
13    lblScore2: TLabel;
14    btnAddGoal2: TButton;
15    btnClearScores: TButton;
16    procedure FormCreate(Sender: TObject);
17    procedure btnAddGoal1Click(Sender: TObject);
18    procedure btnAddGoal2Click(Sender: TObject);
19    procedure btnClearScoresClick(Sender: TObject);
20  private
21    Score1, Score2: TSoccerScore;   // Need two TSoccerScore objects
22  public
23    { Public declarations }
24  end;

25 var
26   frmScoreboard: TfrmScoreboard;

27 implementation

28 {$R *.DFM}
```

```
29 procedure TfrmScoreboard.FormCreate(Sender: TObject);
30 begin                                                // Create both objects
31    Score1 := TSoccerScore.Create;
32    Score2 := TSoccerScore.Create;
33 end; // end procedure TfrmScoreboard.FormCreate


34 procedure TfrmScoreboard.btnAddGoal1Click(Sender: TObject);
35 begin
36    Score1.AddGoal;
37    lblScore1.Caption := Score1.GetTotalStr;
38 end; // end procedure TfrmScoreboard.btnAddGoal1Click


39 procedure TfrmScoreboard.btnAddGoal2Click(Sender: TObject);
40 begin
41    Score2.AddGoal;
42    lblScore2.Caption := Score2.GetTotalStr;
43 end; // end procedure TfrmScoreboard.btnAddGoal2Click


44 procedure TfrmScoreboard.btnClearScoresClick(Sender: TObject);
45 begin
46    Score1.Clear;
47    lblScore1.Caption := Score1.GetTotalStr;
48    Score2.Clear;
49    lblScore2.Caption := Score2.GetTotalStr;
50 end; // end procedure TfrmScoreboard.btnClearScoresClick


51 end. // end unit ScoreBrdU
```

There are a few things to notice here.

o   We have two teams, each with its own score, and so we declare two
    TSoccerScore objects, Score1 and Score2, both of type TSoccerScore (line
    21). We then create both these objects in the form's OnCreate event handler
    (lines 31-32). (TSoccerScore's Create method is inherited from TObject via
    TCounter.)

o   To add a goal for either team, we use the dot notation to combine the
    object's name with the AddGoal method that is part of the TSoccerScore
    class (lines 36, 41). To clear the scores we use the Clear method (lines 46,
    48), again linked to the objects' names. To get the display value, we use the
    GetTotalStr method (lines 37, 42, 47, 49). The Clear and GetTotalStr meth-
    ods are actually part of TCounter, but the TSoccerScore objects automati-
    cally reuse all TCounter's methods through inheritance. Notice that here the
    method calls could be mistaken for property references but they are method
    (function or procedure) calls without any parameters.

•   Save all, and then run and test this program.

Example 18.4 summary: There are three steps to the process of creating and
using classes and objects:

1   First we create our own type (or class) by *declaring* the class and defining
    the *implementation* of the methods (eg example 18.4 step 1). (As a guide to
    doing this we can imitate the way Delphi defines the form in a unit file.)

2   We must declare a reference to the object. Here we declare it in the private
    section of TfrmScoreboard (eg example 18.4 step 2 line 21).

3   We must actively instruct Delphi to create the object before we can use it in
    our program (eg example 18.4 step 2 lines 31 and 32).

After completing these steps we can then go ahead and use the object through its method calls (eg example 18.4 step 2 lines 36-37, 41-42 and 46-49). These use the standard dot notation with the object name followed by the method name and any parameters that may be needed.

Navigating through the Code Explorer

Let's go back to the Code Explorer briefly. (In Delphi 8 use the menu sequence View | Code Explorer if necessary.)

- Click on the CounterU tab in the edit window. Notice that the Code Explorer now shows both classes, TCounter and TSoccerScore, declared in this unit.
- Expand the tree by clicking on the small plus signs in the tree. We can navigate through the program code using this tree.
- Double-click on Clear in the TCounter tree and the editor automatically displays the implementation for the Clear method (figure 18.6).
- Double-click on TCounter in the Code Explorer and the editor automatically displays TCounter's declaration, and so on.

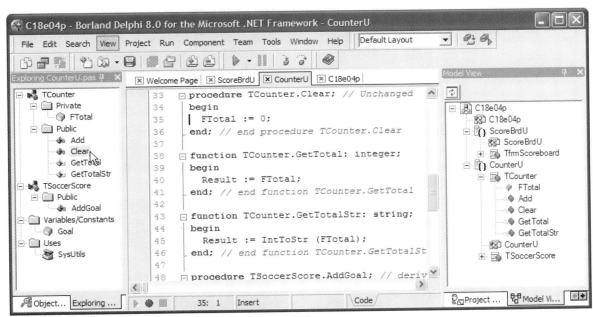

Figure 18.6 Navigating through code using the Code Explorer (Delphi 8)

The Project Browser

While this example is still on the screen, it is worth looking at Delphi's Project Browser, available at View | Browser in versions 7 and earlier. (The project loaded must have run in the current session before the Browser option becomes available.) The Project Browser gives a more detailed display than either the Object TreeView or the Code Explorer. Here we are exploring the classes we have created in this project along with their inheritance structure (figure 18.7). We see TObject is the root class with TCounter derived from TObject and TSoccerScore derived in turn from TCounter. It also shows that the form we have created,

TfrmScoreboard, is derived from TForm, which in turn is derived from a series of other objects all the way back to TObject.

If we select TCounter in the left pane, in the right pane we see that TCounter has a private data field FTotal, a protected method Add and three public methods, Clear, GetTotal and GetTotalStr (figure 18.7). If we select TSoccerScore in the left panel we'll see these as inherited data and methods along with its own public method AddGoal and all the methods inherited from TObject.

The Project Browser has many more capabilities. For more information, press <F1> while the Browser is the active window.

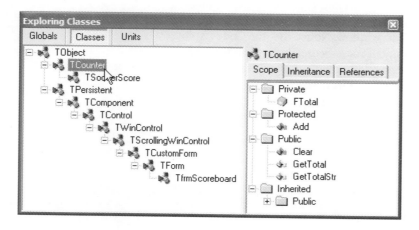

Figure 18.7 Classes and their inheritance structure displayed in the Project Browser (Delphi 7 and earlier)

Simple object orientation (OO)

Object-oriented and traditional procedural programming share a common set of programming fundamentals:

o   sequential execution of program statements
o   variables, expressions and assignment
o   structured constructs such as conditional evaluation (eg If, Case) and iteration (eg While, Repeat, For)
o   input and output management
o   subroutines, and
o   addressing, indexing, pointers.

This book mainly emphasizes these fundamental concepts that are essential for both object-oriented and procedural approaches. However, since Delphi Pascal is an object-oriented language, we have also been exposed to a number of object-oriented principles, mainly through using components.

Basic object-orientation principles

An object is a *self-contained entity* that has *state* and *behaviour* through its attributes, methods and properties. There are several fundamental characteristics of OO that are supported directly in a full object-oriented language:

- *Encapsulation.* An object is a distinct entity that has its own data (for Delphi components, properties such as Top and Left) and behaviour (determined by its methods). An object 'owns' this data and behaviour and other objects do not have direct access to them. Consequently, when one object requires another object to do something, it passes a message to that object requesting the appropriate action.
- *Inheritance.* Objects lower down the hierarchy inherit data and behaviour from their ancestors higher up the hierarchy.
- *Polymorphism.* An object can operate interchangeably with an ancestor in relation to the attributes and methods it inherits from the ancestor.

A number of other concepts are also commonly associated with OO – for example, composition, which is the principle by which we can compose an object out of several sub-objects.

Classes and objects

In our programming, we happily use all sorts of components: buttons, Labels, Edits, and so on. But how does a button know how to be a button? How does a form know what to do in order to be a form that we can use to develop our programs?

The answer lies in the important distinction between *classes* and *objects*. A *class* can be seen as a template for making something. An everyday example would be a pattern for making a shirt. We cannot use a class directly, just as we do not wear the shirt pattern. Instead, the class has the necessary knowledge to make something that we can use. For example, Delphi's TButton class 'knows' how to create a button that can be clicked, have a position and size, have a Caption and Name, and so on.

The Component/Tool palette lists a large number of components that we can use in our program. Each component icon is like a type or class – it represents a set of instructions for creating an object. When we double-click on an icon on the Component palette, Delphi creates an object of that type on the form. We can double-click repeatedly on that icon to create however many objects (or 'instances') of that type we need. Each object (instance) we create on the form is a unique individual with its own set of properties, such as Name, Caption and Width, that we set either statically through the Object Inspector or dynamically through code.

To summarise, when we double-click on the button symbol on the Component palette and put a button on the form, Delphi uses the TButton class as a pattern to create a specific, individual button. This specific button, which we can see and use, is a button *object*. An object is sometimes also called an *instance* (of a class). Once we have instantiated (ie created) an object from a class, we can set the object's properties and its behaviour. In example 18.2 we have two buttons, btnYellow and btnPurple. They share many similar characteristics because they are both of the TButton class. But they are also distinct, separate objects with their own positions, Captions and Names. If we change one object's characteristics, for instance changing btnYellow's Caption from Yellow to Bright Yellow, we do not affect the other object, btnPurple, in any way. However, if we were to change the TButton class, all the objects we instantiate from that class will include the changes we have made (to the class).

Let's return to the shirt pattern example. The pattern, remember, is like the *class* – we cannot wear it! But we can use it to make a whole lot of shirt *objects* that we can wear. Each shirt object can be slightly different – we can have a spotted shirt and a striped shirt, a shirt with small wooden buttons or large silver buttons, and so on.

In a programming language such as Delphi, the language designers provide a library of standard classes, such as TForm, TButton, TBitBtn and TLabel. (The T at the beginning of each class name stands for Type, the word Delphi also uses to mean 'class'.) As programmers, we use these different classes to create objects that we customize and adapt to create the programs we need.

Encapsulation

An object is a self-contained entity that encapsulates its own data and methods. It has control over the way in which other objects can access its data and methods, and can hide anything that it wants to keep private from other objects. Usually, objects hide their data and the inner working of their methods.

An object declaration, such as that in example 18.4, appears in the interface section of the unit. Within the interface section, we usually declare data and helper methods to be private and access methods to be public so that objects have access only to other objects' access methods and not to any data or helper methods. Chapters 12 and 13 have examples of helper methods and the GetTotal and GetTotalStr methods of examples 18.3 and 18.4 are examples of access methods.

The actual bodies of the methods, ie the methods' inner workings, appear in the implementation section along with the unit level variables and constants. The implementation section is always private, ensuring that an object cannot go fiddling around, either accidentally or on purpose, with any other object's inner workings.

To summarise the basics of encapsulation, a unit has a name, an interface section and an implementation section. The name and those parts of the interface section that are marked 'public' are available to others. The rest is private. Usually, the data and helper methods are private and access methods are public.

Efficiency, reliability and re-use through inheritance

Looking at the available components*, we notice that they have varying degrees of similarity and difference. If we compare a TButton and a TLabel, we see that there are some similarities between them. For one thing, they are both visible on a form at a specific position. But clearly there are also major differences between them. If we compare a TButton and a TBitBtn, we see that the similarities between them are much greater. How do we accommodate varying degrees of similarity and difference effectively?

It makes sense to use the same set of instructions for creating whatever is the same between components and use new instructions only for the *differences* between components. This is exactly what happens in object-oriented systems through the class hierarchy and inheritance. Figure 18.8 shows a *highly* simplified representation of Delphi's class hierarchy.

All Delphi classes must be able to create and destroy instances of themselves, and so TObject, which is the root of Delphi's inheritance hierarchy, has these abilities. Some Delphi types are components and so the TComponent type appears below TObject in the hierarchy. It introduces the ability to appear

* In this book we look at Delphi's VCL or Visual Component Library. From version 6 onwards, Delphi also has the CLX library for Linux. From version 8 onwards, Delphi includes libraries for .NET.

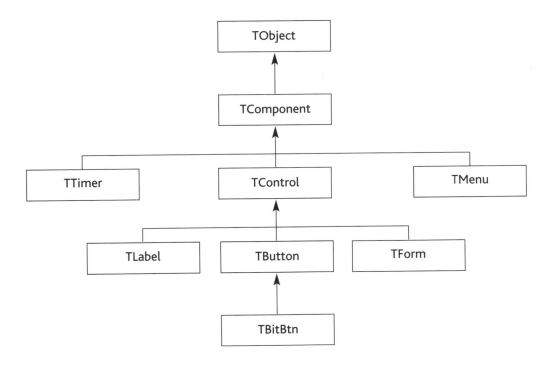

Figure 18.8 A highly simplified diagram of part of Delphi's VCL class hierarchy

on the Component/Tool palette, to be manipulated in the Form Designer, and a number of properties such as Name. From TObject higher up the hierarchy it also *inherits* the ability to create and destroy objects.

Some components are visual and others, like TTimer, are not. Visual components are visible at run time and so they need additional abilities such as Left and Top to give their position on the form, the pop-up hints and the ability to respond to mouse actions. These abilities are packaged in TControl.

Going further down the hierarchy, we finally reach the actual components that we use in our programs, such as TLabel and TButton. These inherit all the abilities available in TControl, which in turn inherits all the TComponent abilities, which in turn inherits all the TObject abilities.

Inheritance means that all the common abilities are coded only once, higher up the hierarchy; and each new level in the hierarchy needs to code only *additional* abilities and does not need to repeat what is available from higher up. So general characteristics are coded high up the hierarchy while the more specialized characteristics are coded lower down.

Because TObject introduces the ability to create and destroy instances, and because all Delphi's classes descend from TObject, all the Delphi classes have create and destroy abilities. As we saw, TControl introduces properties for Left and Top, and so it and its descendants have the Left and Top property. So, referring to figure 18.8, we see that TControl, TLabel, TButton, TForm and TBitBtn all have the Left and Top properties. However, TMenu, TComponent and TObject, which are not descendants of TControl, do not inherit the Left and Top properties.

A class hierarchy provides enormous savings through re-use. When we add a new class at the bottom of the hierarchy we don't need to recode the methods it inherits from classes higher up the hierarchy and so we can concentrate on coding and testing the additional methods.

In brief, inheritance is one of the most important concepts in OO, introducing significant benefits in terms of efficiency, reliability and re-use.

Composition – combining objects

Often a group of objects are combined to create a 'super-object'. A car, for instance, is made of wheels, an engine, seats, and so on. Similarly, software classes can be composed of other objects. In example 18.3, for instance, the user interface (class TfrmStructureDemo) is *derived* from the TForm type and *composed* of two buttons. It also has two methods, which in this case are event handlers. We can see this by looking at the type declaration in that program:

```
type
  TfrmStructureDemo = class(TForm)        // inheritance
    btnYellow: TButton;                   // composition
    btnPurple: TButton;                   // composition
    procedure btnYellowClick(Sender: TObject);
    procedure btnPurpleClick(Sender: TObject);
  private
    { Private declarations }
  public
    { Public declarations }
  end;
```

Here the objects btnYellow and btnPurple are actually part of the TfrmStructureDemo class.

In OO, building an object from other objects is called *composition*. The aim behind composition is similar to inheritance – to be able to re-use existing objects and classes and so to write code only for additional characteristics. In OO, composition and inheritance are two major tools for creating new classes.

Example 18.5 The Sender parameter in event handlers

In the examples in this chapter we have been looking at inheritance and the class hierarchy. Lower levels in the hierarchy inherit characteristics from the higher levels and then add characteristics of their own. A consequence of this is that a subclass object can often behave as though it were a superclass object. This ability is called *substitution*. We won't go into it in much detail here, but to get a flavour of it we will look at the Sender parameter that appears in the parameter list for all event handlers.

To start, let's look at some typical event handler headers:

```
procedure TfrmShow.pnlShowMouseMove(Sender: TObject;
        Shift: TShiftState; X, Y: Integer);

procedure TfrmSystemTime.tmrSysTimeTimer(Sender: TObject);

procedure TfrmSystemTime.FormMouseDown(Sender: TObject;
        Button: TMouseButton; Shift: TShiftState; X, Y: Integer);

procedure TfrmFormEvents.FormShow(Sender: TObject);
```

As this list suggests, different events have different parameter lists but the first in the list for all the different events attached to the different components is Sender, which identifies the component that initiated the event. It can be helpful to know which object has initiated an event, but this is not completely straightforward. The difficulty is that every parameter must have a type, and so Sender must be declared as a specific type. But what type should it be? Every component is different. In the list above, the first Sender is a TPanel, the second is a TTimer, and the third and fourth are TForms.

As we'll see in the example below, Delphi uses the Sender parameter and the inheritance hierarchy to solve this problem. We also use this example to look at the Align and Position properties that some components possess.

EX 18.5 STEP 1   Static design (user interface)

We'll begin our exploration of the Sender: TObject parameter by using the interface in figure 18.9.
- Start a new application and add two TPanels to the form from the Standard tab.
- Using the Object Inspector, set the following properties:

Figure 18.9 User interface for example 18.5

Component	Property	Value
Form1	Name	frmSender
	Caption	Sender parameter demo
	Position	poScreenCenter
Panel1	Name	pnlControl
	Align	alTop
	Caption	<Blank>
Panel2	Name	pnlReport
	Align	alBottom
	Caption	<Blank>

We have not used a form's Position property before. Its effect is not obvious at design time, but when we run the project 'poScreenCenter' positions the form in the centre of the screen.

TPanel, in common with several other components, has an Align property which orients the component relative to its container (in this case, the form). This effect is visible at design time and here the Panels are aligned along the top and the bottom of the form.

Like TGroupBox, TPanel is also a container component. We will place six SpeedButtons inside the top Panel as shown in figure 18.9.
- First select pnlControl by clicking inside it with the mouse (or select it in the Object Inspector).
- From the Additional tab place six evenly spaced SpeedButtons inside pnlControl as in figure 18.9.
- Set the properties as follows, noting that the six buttons do not all have the same properties:

Component	Property	Value
SpeedButton1	Name	spdOne
	Caption	1
SpeedButton2	Name	spdTwo
	Caption	2
SpeedButton3	Name	spdThree
	Caption	3
	GroupIndex	1
	Down	True
SpeedButton4	Name	spdFour
	Caption	4
	GroupIndex	1
SpeedButton5	Name	spdFive
	Caption	5
	GroupIndex	2
SpeedButton6	Name	spdSix
	Caption	6
	GroupIndex	2
spdFive & spdSix	AllowAllUp	True
	Flat	True

EX 18.5 STEP 2   The OnClick event handler (version 1)

Now we'll start adding some simple code and then gradually, in the following steps, develop the complete program.
*   Create an OnClick event handler for spdOne to display the value of spdOne's Caption.

```
procedure TfrmSender.spdOneClick(Sender: TObject);
begin
  pnlReport.Caption := 'You clicked on ' + spdOne.Name;
end; // procedure TfrmSender.spdOneClick
```

*   Save the unit and project files as C18e05u and C18e05p and then test this first version of the program.
*   Check that spdOne's OnClick event handler works correctly and play around with the SpeedButtons to see the effects of the different values for the properties. (Refer to Chapter 12 for a description of these properties.)

EX 18.5 STEP 3   Using the Sender parameter

The goal of this program is to display an appropriate message in response to a click on any of the buttons, the Panels or the form. One way of doing this would be to write another eight event handlers, like the one in step 2, only changing spdOne to spdTwo, spdThree and so on in each of them.

But this leads to a lot of effort and, worse, repeated code with a chance of errors creeping in in the future if any changes ever need to be made. What would be better would be to write just one procedure, to route all the OnClick events through this code, and then somehow to generate the appropriate message using the Sender parameter to display which component has been clicked.

First we'll modify the existing event handler to use the Sender parameter. When we have got that working we can then route all the other buttons' OnClick events through it.

So let's start by modifying the existing spdOneClick to use the Sender parameter. Perhaps you would like to try doing this before going any further.

One possibility is to change spdOne in the assignment statement of step 2 to Sender:

```
1 procedure TfrmSender.spdOneClick(Sender: TObject);
2 begin
3   pnlReport.Caption := 'You clicked on ' + Sender.Name;
4 end;
```

If you tried this, well done – it's a good try – but you'll know that it does not work. The compiler returns an 'Undeclared identifier' error. Why? In the parameter list in the header of this OnClick event handler, and all other event handlers, Sender's type is defined as the root class of the hierarchy, TObject, and not as TSpeedButton (line 1). But the TObject class does not have a Name property and so, when the compiler reaches Sender.Name in line 3, it generates an error.

This means that we have to instruct Delphi to treat Sender as a TSpeedButton - in other words, we must *typecast Sender as a TSpeedButton*. There are different ways to do this. Here we use the 'as' class operator as follows (line 4):

```
1 procedure TfrmSender.spdOneClick(Sender: TObject);
2 begin
3   pnlReport.Caption := 'You clicked on ' +
4                        (Sender as TSpeedButton).Name;
5 end;
```

If you test this now by running this version of the program, you will see that clicking spdOne gives the right message, so we seem to be using the Sender parameter correctly.

How does this work? The expression (Sender as TSpeedButton) tells Delphi that although Sender is declared in the parameter list as a TObject, because it could be any one of a number of different classes, in this particular case Delphi must treat it as a TSpeedButton.

EX 18.5 STEP 4   Linking in the other SpeedButtons

None of the other buttons display a message yet and so we must now pay attention to linking them in.
- If the program is still running, close it.
- Select spdOne and then select the Events tab in the Object Inspector.
- To make things less confusing, change the name of the OnClick handler from spdOneClick to GeneralClick. Delphi will now automatically make this change in the program code. (Don't change the program directly.)

Figure 18.10 Linking the different components to the same event handler

The final part of this step is to link the other SpeedButtons to this event handler.

- Selecting each button in turn, select 'GeneralClick' from the drop-down box alongside OnClick on the Events tab of the Object Inspector (figure 18.10). Thus we are routing each SpeedButton's event to the single 'GeneralClick' event handler.
- Save this version of the program and run it.
- Check that the text in the Panel gives the correct name for each button that you click.

EX 18.5 STEP 5   Testing the Sender parameter

What happens if an event handler can receive an event from more than one type of component? For instance, what if we link the event handler GeneralClick to respond to clicks on the Panels or the form as well as to clicks on the buttons? How do we then decide whether to typecast the Sender parameter as a TSpeedButton, as a TPanel or as a TForm?

As you can see in the next version of the GeneralClick procedure, Delphi has a special operator, the is class operator, to determine what *type* of component Sender refers to.

- Change the GeneralClick procedure to the following:

```
procedure TfrmSender.GeneralClick(Sender: TObject);
begin
  if Sender is TSpeedButton then
    pnlReport.Caption := 'You clicked on ' +
                         (Sender as TSpeedButton).Name

  else if Sender is TForm then
    pnlReport.Caption := 'You clicked on ' + (Sender as TForm).Name

  else if Sender is TPanel then
    pnlReport.Caption := 'You clicked on ' + (Sender as TPanel).Name;
end; // end TfrmSender.GeneralClick
```

- Using the Events tab of the Object Inspector, link the OnClick events for pnlControl, pnlReport and frmSender to the GeneralClick event handler.
- Run and test this version of the program and check that it responds correctly to clicks on the Panels and the form. (Notice that we use a conditional test even in the last else clause to ensure that it will respond only to TPanels.)

EX 18.5 STEP 6   Substitution

The program in step 5 above is very interesting. Being able to use Sender as a parameter of type TObject shows us that variables of various types, in this case TSpeedButton, TForm or TPanel, can function as if they were their ancestors.

We can even take this concept one step further and in the process reduce the number of If statements from three to one. Remember, when we were discussing the concept of class hierarchy a little earlier, we mentioned that TComponent introduces the Name property. TSpeedButton, TForm and TPanel are all descendants of TComponent, that's why they all have the Name property. In addition, TComponent is in turn a descendant of TObject. We can take advantage of this in our program by working with TComponent instead of the individual classes (lines 3 and 5 below).

```
1 procedure TfrmSender.GeneralClick(Sender: TObject);
2 begin
3   if Sender is TComponent then
4     pnlReport.Caption := 'You clicked on ' +
5                               (Sender as TComponent).Name
6 end; // end TfrmSender.GeneralClick
```

- Save and run this version of the program. It gives the required message whether we click on a SpeedButton, a Panel or the form, just as step 5 did.

Here we see the benefit of *substitution* in the inheritance hierarchy. Because TSpeedButton, TPanel and TForm are all descendants of TComponent, and because TComponent has a Name property, we can test for TComponent (line 3) and cast as TComponent (line 5) instead of testing and casting for each one separately as we did in step 5.

Where we are using a property that a group of child classes inherit from a parent, we can work with the parent class instead of each child class individually. This substitution saves programming. We don't have to cater separately for each child class and so we can avoid situations such as step 5, where we had a separate If statement for each child class. It also means that if in future we introduce a further child class, we don't have to search through the entire program to cater specifically for it.

To summarise: Sender is of type TObject. TObject is an ancestor of TComponent. TComponent, in turn, is an ancestor of the other objects used here (TSpeedButton, TPanel and TForm). These objects all inherit the Name property from their TComponent ancestor, and so casting Sender to a TComponent allows us to work with all its descendants as a group rather than needing to work with each one individually.

EX 18.5 STEP 7 An alternative typecasting operator

The as operator is part of Delphi Pascal but was not part of the original Pascal. as has the advantage of doing strict error-checking and throwing an exception if one tries to typecast wrongly. Originally Pascal typecast through brackets, and Delphi recognizes this too. So we can change line 5 of the program above to:

```
1 procedure TfrmSender.GeneralClick(Sender: TObject);
2 begin
3   if Sender is TComponent then
4     pnlReport.Caption := 'You clicked on ' +
5                               TComponent(Sender).Name
6 end; // end TfrmSender.GeneralClick
```

The bracket notation looks a bit like a subroutine call and does not perform any error-checking. So, although it is slightly less efficient, many programmers would stick to the as operator for typecasting since it is more robust and is easier to read.

So far we have used the Sender parameter with the is and as *class* operators. is determines what *class* or *type* Sender represents and often forms the conditional part of an If statement. If we want to find out which specific *component* or *object* Sender represents, we can use the equality operator =. For example, let's assume that the form's colour should be aqua if spdFive is clicked and green if any other component is clicked. We can do this as follows (lines 6 to 9):

```
 1 procedure TfrmSender.GeneralClick(Sender: TObject);
 2 begin
 3   if Sender is TComponent then
 4     pnlReport.Caption := 'You clicked on ' +
 5                             (Sender as TComponent).Name;
 6   if Sender = spdFive then
 7     Color := clAqua
 8   else
 9     Color := clGreen;
10 end; // end TfrmSender.GeneralClick
```

Example 18.5 summary: A parameter is a mechanism for passing a value from one part of a program to another part. The Sender parameter, which is part of every event, tells the event handler which component initiated the event. Many different components can initiate events and so the Sender parameter is of type TObject, the most general type of object that there is in Delphi. The is and the = operators allow us to test whether Sender represents either a particular class or a particular object. We often need to typecast the Sender parameter to a specific class and we can use either as (with error checking) or () (without checking) for the typecasting. Sender is of type TObject, which is the root object from which all other Delphi objects are derived. In step 5 of this example we see that TSpeedButton, TForm and TPanel can all behave as a TObject since the Sender parameter is of class TObject. In step 6 we see that all three of these can also function as TComponents.

REVIEW

An object is a distinct entity that has a *unique name*, its own *state* or *data* (for Delphi components, values for properties such as 'Top' and 'Left') and *behaviour* (determined by its procedures and functions, together known as methods). An object 'owns' (or encapsulates) this data and behaviour, and controls the kind of access other objects (even other objects of the same class) have to its data and behaviour. Consequently, when one object requires another object to do something, it passes a message to that object requesting the appropriate action and does not directly manipulate the inner workings of the object.

Classes are arranged in *hierarchies*. Classes lower down the hierarchy *inherit* data and behaviour from their ancestors higher up. Thus, if we have a method available for an ancestor object, we save programming effort since we don't have to recode the same method for each descendant. This has an advantage for maintainability too: if we improve an ancestor method without reducing its functionality, these improvements are automatically available to all the descendants.

We have seen *composition* from the start of this book in the way forms are composed of other objects (components). Together, inheritance and composition form the basic ways of creating the classes and objects that specific programs need and of reusing existing classes.

There are three steps in creating and using our own objects:

1 We create our own class (or type) by declaring the class and defining the implementation of the methods. (As a guide to doing this we can imitate the way Delphi defines the Form in a unit file.)

2 We declare a reference to an object by specifying a name and a class.

3 We instruct Delphi to create the object so that we can use it in our program.

After completing these steps we can then go ahead and use the object through its method calls. These use the standard dot notation with the object name followed by the method name and any parameters that may be needed.

All events have at least the Sender parameter and so, using the principle of substitution, Sender is of the most general class available in Delphi (TObject). Here we see again that objects can be used as parameters. To use Sender requires the various typecasting operators. Learning to use Sender provides a brief introduction to *substitution*, which is the ability of object oriented languages to treat an object as though it belongs to an ancestor class.

We also explored further IDE features: navigating through code with the Code Explorer, viewing class inheritance with the Project Browser for Delphi 7 and earlier, and cutting and pasting a container component along with its children.

IMPORTANT CONCEPTS

Fundamental programming concepts

Classes and objects: Classes (or types) provide a template from which we instantiate (or create) objects (or instances).

Composition: A new class can contain objects, providing an alternative means to inheritance of building on existing classes. Thus a user interface form is derived from the TForm class (inheritance) and is composed of all the components placed on the form (eg buttons, Labels).

Creating and using an object: Before an object can be used, it must be declared as belonging to a particular type and it must then be created.

Declaring a class: A class is declared through a type declaration that specifies the class name, its direct ancestor and its constituent data and methods along with their visibility (eg private or public).

Encapsulation: Delphi classes have both *public* interfaces and *private* sections. The public section provides the communication path to other objects and declares *what* a class's capabilities are. The private implementation section describes *how* the class performs these capabilities by defining the procedures and functions that make up the *methods*.

Inheritance/Subclassing: Every new class is defined as a descendant of an existing class, with TObject being the root Delphi class. Descendants inherit the data and behaviour of their ancestors and so the more general characteristics are defined in classes higher up the hierarchy and the more specialized characteristics lower down the hierarchy.

Re-use: Object orientation supports re-use in several ways. Once a class has been defined, it represents a unit of functionality that can be re-used in other programs. It can be re-used as it stands, as a parent for a new class (inheritance) or as a constituent of another class (composition). To facilitate re-use, classes should be declared in one or more separate units and not as part of the user interface unit that contains the form definition.

Subclass: Any descendant of a class.

Superclass: Any ancestor of a class.

Substitution: Where an object acts interchangeably for an ancestor.

Typecasting: Because Sender can be any one of a number of different classes, Delphi declares it in the parameter list as a TObject. Before using Sender we typecast it to the appropriate class. Without this typecasting it is not possible to use any of the methods or data fields that are declared at levels below TObject. (The `is` operator is useful for testing what class it is.)

Programming environment

Code Explorer: Provides a graphical tree structure for seeing the structure of classes and for navigating through individual units.

Cut and paste for container components: If a container component is copied or cut using the edit functions, any child components are also copied.

Project Browser: A detailed display showing, among other things, the inheritance structure and structure of each class.

Writing a program

Program structure: A Delphi program consists of a project file (.dpr or .bdsproj) along with the units (.pas) that it specifies. User interface windows (forms) are specified in the units with the initialization values in the form description file (.dfm or .nfm). Also see Appendix 2.

Project file: The project file ties together all the separate files that make up a Delphi program and launches the Delphi application on startup.

Unit structure: A Delphi unit consists of three main sections: name, interface and implementation. The name supplies the unit's identity. The interface lists the other units that this unit refers to and declares the different classes and variables that the unit defines and uses. It can be divided into public or private parts. The implementation describes the internal working of each method and is private.

NEW DELPHI FEATURES

Additional common property	
Align	The set of values [alNone, alTop, alBottom, alLeft, alRight, alClient] that determines how the control aligns within its container, used here for TPanels.

Additional TForm property	
Position	The set of values [poDesigned, poDefault, poDefaultPosOnly, poDefaultSizeOnly, poScreenCenter, poDesktopCenter, poMainFormCenter, poOwnerFormCenter] to get or set the position and placement of a form on the screen.

Additional TSpeedButton property	
Flat	If Flat is True, the button does *not* have a 3D border that provides a raised or lowered look.

Operators/Keywords	
as	Typecasts an object reference to a different class type *with* error checking.
equality [=]	Checks for equality and returns Boolean True or False (eg in If statements). Used here to check whether an object is a particular object. (It tests for a specific *object* and not a class.)
is	Tests whether an object is of a particular *class* or descended from that class.
typecast [()]	Converts an object reference to a different class *without* error checking.

PROBLEMS

PROBLEM 18.1 The expanding airline

JJ's Flying Circus is expanding.

- Enhance the program of example 18.3 to display and process three flights at the same time using the interface shown (figure 18.11). Jolly Joe wants the SpinEdit cleared each time the corresponding Add button is clicked and he wants the Focus placed on the related SpinEdit whenever the corresponding Clear button is clicked.

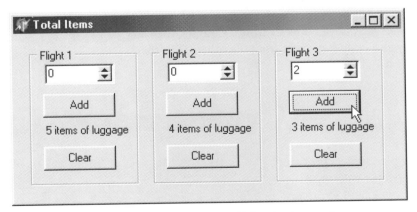

Figure 18.11 User interface for displaying three flights simultaneously

a   Draw up a set of test cases for this program.
b   Write the program, testing it against the test cases and correcting any errors that exist.

Rugby scoreboard

In example 18.4 we extended the TCounter class to create a scoreboard for soccer or hockey. Now we need a scoreboard for rugby.

- Use object-oriented principles to create one, re-using whatever is useful from the soccer scoreboard. In other words, use inheritance to provide whatever is similar between the two applications and write special code only for the differences. (In object-oriented jargon, we can talk about *coding for differences*.) The main difference here is that Rugby scores add up in steps other than 1.

- So, using TSoccerScore as a guide, create TRugbyScore at the same level. Its type definition would appear in CounterU.pas and would be something like this:

```
TRugbyScore = class (TCounter)       // another subclass of Tcounter
public
  procedure AddConversion;                 // Rugby conversion is +2
  procedure AddDropGoal;                   // Rugby dropgoal is +3
  procedure AddGoal;         // Rugby goal is a try plus a conversion
  procedure AddPenalty;                    // Rugby penalty is +3
  procedure AddTry;                        // Rugby try is +5
end; // end TRugbyScore = class (TCounter)
```

TRugbyScore's AddConversion method would be something like this:

```
procedure TRugbyScore.AddConversion;
begin
  Add(RugbyConversion);
end; // end procedure TRugbyScore.AddConversion
```

TRugbyScore's other methods are similar.

- Write them and then modify ScoreBrdU.pas by adding additional buttons for a Try (5 points), a Conversion (2 points), a Goal (which is a try plus a conversion), a DropGoal (3 points) and a Penalty (3 points) that call these new methods.

(TRugbyScore's AddGoal method and TSoccerScore's AddGoal method are different. Because both these classes are derived directly from TCounter, they are at the same level of the hierarchy and neither inherits from the other. Thus their AddGoal methods are independent.)

PROBLEM 18.3 Up and down count

- Using object-oriented principles, write a program that records the number of people entering a museum and the number leaving, and so displays clearly the number of visitors still inside the museum (figure 18.12).

Figure 18.12 User interface displaying the movement of visitors in and out of the museum

PROBLEM 18.4 Time-operated light

The program below controls a simple time-operated light (figure 18.13). The On and Off buttons switch the light on and off (for the sake of this example, they change the colour of a Shape object between yellow and black). If the light is not switched off first, there is a Timer that switches the light off automatically five seconds after the On button was last clicked. The program consists of two event handlers. The On button's OnClick event activates the LightOn procedure. The Off button's OnClick event and the OnTimer event *both* activate the LightOff procedure.

Figure 18.13 User interface for time-operated light

Component	Property	Value
Form1	Name	frmAutoLight
	Caption	Auto Light
Shape1	Name	shpLight
	Brush.Color	clBlack
	Shape	stRoundSquare
Button1, 2	Name	btnOn, btnOff
	Caption	On, Off
Timer1	Name	tmrOff
	Enabled	False
	Interval	5000

```
procedure TfrmAutoLight.LightOn(Sender: TObject);
begin
   shpLight.Brush.Color := clYellow;
   tmrOff.Enabled := False; // restart the timer
   tmrOff.Enabled := True;
end; // end procedure TfrmAutoLight.LightOn

procedure TfrmAutoLight.LightOff(Sender: TObject);
begin
   shpLight.Brush.Color := clBlack;
   tmrOff.Enabled := False; // reset the timer
end; // end procedure TfrmAutoLight.LightOff
```

- Extend this program. Increase the height of the form and add a Panel along the bottom. When the light is switched on or off through clicking on a button, the Panel displays the message 'Button operated'. If the light switches off because of the Timer, the Panel displays the message 'Timer operated'.

PROBLEM 18.5) Using the Sender parameter (1)

In this problem we extend example 18.5.

- Change the program so that the message identifies the Caption and the GroupIndex of the button that is clicked. If the Panels or form are clicked, the message remains as previously (figure 18.14).

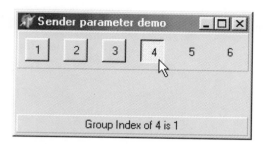

Figure 18.14 Sender parameter demo, button 4 clicked

PROBLEM 18.6) Using the Sender parameter (2)

Here we also extend example 18.5.

- Place a Label, lblSubstitution, on the form. Its Caption is 'Substitution Demo'.

a   Starting with example 18.5 step 5, add the code needed to identify the Label in the message on the lower Panel (figure 18.15).

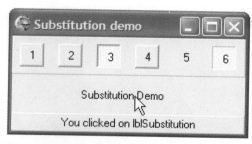

Figure 18.15 Substitution demo, after clicking on the label

b   Repeat the functionality of the previous step, but start with example 18.5 step 6.

c   Comment on the differences between parts (a) and (b).

APPENDIX 1

Deployment

In this appendix we tell you about InstallShield Express Limited Edition, a tool for creating a disk that contains an application in installable format. Since the InstallShield Express is quite a comprehensive software package, we cannot cover or discuss it fully in an appendix, but we will help you to get started with the deployment process.

What is deployment?

When you compile a Delphi program, it creates an executable file (with extension .exe) for your application. This .exe file will have the same name as your project file (ie the .dpr file). The .exe file makes it possible to run your program from Windows, without starting up Delphi first. For simple Delphi programs such as those that we've written in Chapters 1 to 14 of this book, the .exe file is all you need to run the program on any computer with Windows as the operating system. This will, however, work only if the program does not use any external files, such as graphic images or database files.

Programs that involve more than just the unit and project files need to be deployed in a way which ensures that, when the user installs the program on his or her computer, all the required files will be copied. With a database application, for example, all the data tables must be installed, as well as the drivers and dynamic link libraries (.dll files) required by the specific type of database the application uses. This means the user will have to go through an installation process similar to that when you loaded the Delphi software on your computer before he or she can run the application.

Why InstallShield Express?

There are a variety of products available for deploying Windows applications, one of which is InstallShield Express. We have chosen to discuss Borland's limited edition of InstallShield Express because it is included in the Delphi software package. Different versions of Delphi come packaged with different versions of InstallShield Express. In this appendix, we discuss how to get started with InstallShield Express – Borland Limited Edition (Version 3.03) and InstallShield Express 4 – Borland Free Edition.

The limited edition of InstallShield Express builds installations using tools specifically for Delphi developers. It provides the basic InstallShield Express functions for creating installations that support any Windows platform. On the other hand, the standard edition of InstallShield Express provides more comprehensive functionality, but the features provided by the limited edition are sufficient to deploy most Delphi applications.

Installing InstallShield Express

InstallShield Express is not automatically installed when you install Delphi: you have to install it from the Delphi CD-ROM before you can use it. After installing it, you can activate it using the Windows Start | Programs | InstallShield | InstallShield Express menu sequence. Depending on the version of InstallShield Express you have, work through one of the following sections on how to get started.

Getting started with InstallShield Express – Borland Limited Edition

When you start InstallShield Express – Borland Limited Edition, the window illustrated in figure A1.1 is displayed:

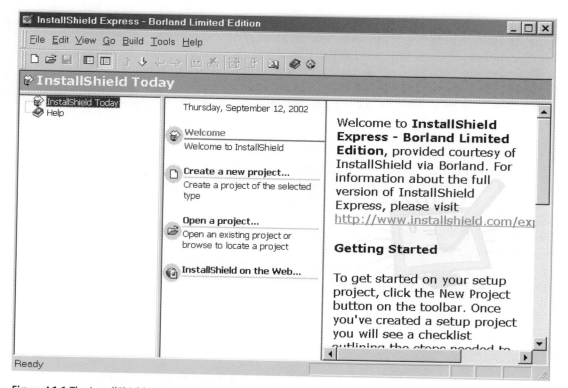

Figure A1.1 The InstallShield Express – Borland Limited Edition opening screen

In the left pane there are two options: InstallShield today and Help. Before you try to create your first installation, select Help (note that there is a difference between the Help in the left pane and Help on the main menu bar). The screen changes as shown in figure A1.2:

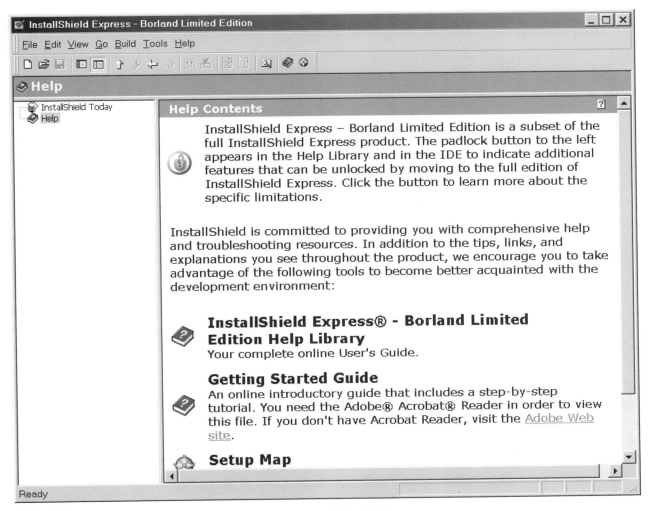

Figure A1.2 The contents of InstallShield Express – Borland Limited Edition's Help

We suggest that you select the Getting Started Guide option to open an online guide. This guide includes a tutorial that takes you through the steps to create an installation project for a sample project included in the InstallShield software. We strongly recommend that you work through this tutorial (which shouldn't take more than 30 minutes) before you attempt to create your own InstallShield project.

The other two Help topics are also very useful. The Setup Map briefly describes each step in the process of creating an InstallShield project, whereas the Help Library provides more comprehensive information on specific InstallShield topics.

When you return to the InstallShield Today option in the left pane, you will see that the last option in the middle pane is InstallShield on the Web.... If you have an Internet connection, you can use this option to go to the InstallShield website, where you will find all the additional information you need to be able to use the software to best advantage.

Getting started with InstallShield Express 4 – Borland Free Edition

When you start InstallShield Express 4 – Borland Free Edition, the window shown in figure A1.3 is displayed. Before you attempt to create your own project, we strongly recommend that you work through the Help provided. The following instructions will guide you through the process of getting started with the Help facility.

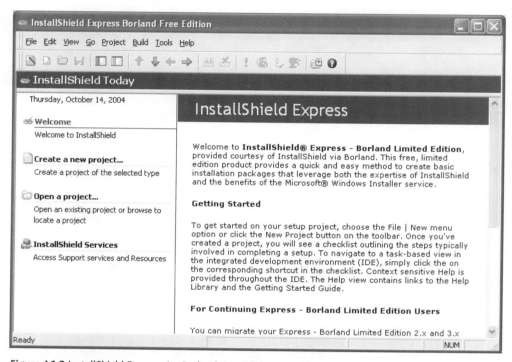

Figure A1.3 InstallShield Express 4 – Borland Free Edition opening screen

- Using the main menu, select Help | Contents.
- On the left pane, expand 'InstallShield Express Help Library'.
- To understand the basics of InstallShield Express, work through the topics of 'Express Concepts' and 'Express Procedures and Tasks'.
- In the left tab, expand 'Express Tutorials' and click on 'Basic Tutorial' (figure A1.4). This tutorial takes you through the steps to create an installation project for a sample project included in the InstallShield Express folders.

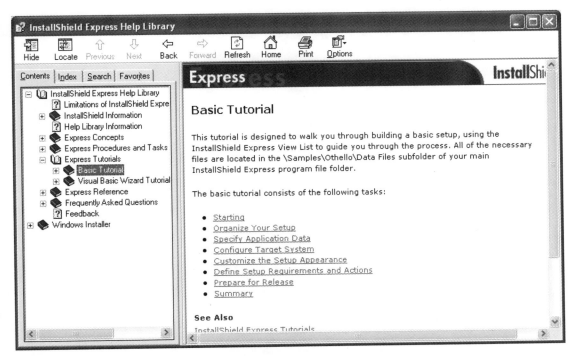

Figure A1.4 Finding the Basic Tutorial in InstallShield Express 4 – Borland Free Edition

For further help, consult the other help topics or click on 'InstallShield Services' on the opening screen (figure A1.3) to access further resources on the Web.

APPENDIX 2

File types

When you create a new application, Delphi creates the necessary files. These are the main files that Delphi uses for simple applications such as the ones we write in this book. Some of these files only apply to particular versions of Delphi.

Extension	Description
.bdsproj	Borland Developer Studio project file (Delphi 8). This is an XML file containing information needed to build the project.
.cfg	The project configuration file (command line compiler).
.dcu	A compiled (unit binary object) file. Allows others to use your code in their programs without giving them access to your source code.
.dcuil	Delphi compiled unit file (Delphi 8)
.dfm	The form description file, which is an essential file. (You can see this in the Delphi editor by pressing <Alt+F12> or by right-clicking on the form and selecting View as Text from the pop-up menu. Return to viewing the form by pressing <Alt+F12> or via the pop-up menu.)
.dof	The project options file.
.dpr	Standard Delphi project file. An essential file.
.dsk	The project desktop file.
.exe	The final executable file. For simple Delphi programs, such as those in this book excluding the database programs, this is the only file needed to run a program.
.nfm	Delphi Form file (Delphi 8). Similar in function to the .dfm file for earlier versions of Delphi.
.pas	The Delphi Pascal source file, the unit file, which is an essential file.
.pdb	Program database file (Delphi 8). Holds debugging and project state information.
.res	The compiled (Windows) binary resource file.

Delphi's files

The source code for even a simple Delphi program consists of several files. The three essential file types are:

- the unit file (.pas), where we do our coding (for larger projects there may be more than one unit file);
- the project file (.dpr), the main program file that Delphi creates for us automatically (Delphi 8 regenerates the .bdsproj file if the .dpr file is present);
- the form description file (.dfm or optionally .nfm in Delphi 8), which specifies the form. Delphi also creates this file automatically, largely on the basis of the objects we place on the form and the values we enter in the Object Inspector. A .dfm file exists for each form used in the program, so there may be more than one .dfm file in a project. Delphi 8 creates a .nfm file, but can use either a .nfm or a. dfm file.

If you want to back up your programs, or compile them on another computer, these are the three essential file types to copy (as well as any resource files you may be using). Delphi will regenerate the other files when it loads and compiles the program. You should test for compatibility if you are moving files from one version of Delphi to another.

APPENDIX 3

....

Component naming conventions

From Chapter 2 onwards, we use a standard naming convention throughout the book based on a three-letter prefix. The prefixes for the commoner components appear in the table below. In some situations there is a 'T' in front of the component name to emphasize the Type (or class). Button becomes TButton, for example. On the other hand, in the code we are naming specific objects and so the T does not form part of the abbreviation.

This convention of using a lowercase three-letter prefix followed by a descriptive capitalized Name was introduced by a Hungarian, Charles Simonyi, and so it is sometimes loosely called the 'Hungarian Naming Convention'. Several different sets of abbreviations have arisen in Delphi and so other books and programmers may use different ones. Whatever abbreviation one uses is not that important, provided one uses it consistently.

Using standard prefixes with good descriptive names is a good habit to adopt and helps significantly, particularly as the program size increases. By looking at program code we should know what type of objects we are dealing with and, if the descriptive part of the name is carefully chosen, what the component's role is in the program.

The following table provides a quick reference to chapters in which particular components are discussed and their characteristics presented. Some of these components are also used in subsequent chapters. The table also specifies the name of the tab in the Component/Tool palette where the component can be found.

Component	Naming	Information	Tab in Component/Tool palette
Action	act...	Chapter 9	(create in ActionList editor)
ActionList	acl...	Chapter 9	Standard
Band	bnd...	Chapter 17	Rave Reports: Report tab
BitBtn	bmb...	Chapter 2, 13	Additional
Button	btn...	Chapter 1, 2, 10	Standard
CheckBox	chk...	Chapter 6	Standard

ClientDataSet	cds...	Chapter 15	DataAccess
ColorDialog	cdl...	Chapter 9	Dialogs
ComboBox	cbo...	Chapter 8	Standard
DataBand	dbn...	Chapter 17	Rave Reports: Report tab
DataMirrorSection	dms...	Chapter 17	Rave Reports: Report tab
DataSetProvider	dsp...	Chapter 15	Data Access
DataSource	dat...	Chapter 15	Data Access
DataText	dtx...	Chapter 17	Rave Reports: Report tab
DateTimePicker	dtp...	Chapter 16	Win32
DBComboBox	dbc...	Chapter 15	Data Controls
DBEdit	dbe...	Chapter 15	Data Controls
DBGrid	dbg...	Chapter 15	Data Controls
DBLookupComboBox	dlc...	Chapter 16	Data Controls
DBNavigator	nav...	Chapter 15	Data Controls
DBText	dbt...	Chapter 16	Data Controls
Edit	edt...	Chapter 2	Standard
FontDialog	fod...	Chapter 5	Dialogs
Form	frm...	Chapter 1, 2, 8, 16, 18	(create using Delphi's File menu)
GroupBox	gpb...	Chapter 2	Standard
Label	lbl...	Chapter 2	Standard
ListBox	lst...	Chapter 3, 8	Standard
Memo	mem...	Chapter 5, 7, 11	Standard
MainMenu	mnu...	Chapter 9	Standard
OpenDialog	opd...	Chapter 5	Dialogs
Panel	pnl...	Chapter 10	Standard
PopupMenu	pum...	Chapter 9	Standard
RadioButton	rad...	Chapter 2	Standard
RadioGroup	rgp...	Chapter 8	Standard
Region	rgn...	Chapter 17	Rave Reports: Report tab
Report	rep...	Chapter 17	(create using file menu of Rave Reports)
RvDataSetConnection	dsc..	Chapter 17	Rave
RvProject	rvp...	Chapter 17	Rave
RvSystem	rvs...	Chapter 17	Rave
SaveDialog	svd...	Chapter 5	Dialogs
Section	sec...	Chapter 17	Rave Reports: Standard tab
Shape	shp	Chapter 18	Additional
SpeedButton	spd...	Chapter 12, 18	Additional
SpinEdit	sed...	Chapter 4	Samples
SQLConnection	sco...	Chapter 15	dbExpress
SQLDataSet	sds...	Chapter 15	dbExpress
Text	txt...	Chapter 17	Rave Reports: Standard tab
Timer	tmr...	Chapter 10	System

APPENDIX 4

Installation notes

To work through all the chapters in this book, there are a number of different programs and components that you need to install. Some of these only apply to certain versions of Delphi and to certain chapters of the book. Glance through all the sections in this appendix to find out which are applicable to you.

Which version of Delphi should I use?

This book covers Delphi from version 4 to version 8. Delphi 4 to 7 are similar in most respects for the topics in this book. Delphi 8 is sometimes called Delphi for .NET. It looks different and in some ways behaves differently to the earlier versions. We discuss these differences where they are significant and so all the examples in Chapters 1 to 14 and Chapter 18 can be done in any of the versions. However, because of the differences in the databases, Chapters 15 and 16 need Delphi 6, 7 or 8. Chapter 17 uses Nevrona Rave Reports. Rave Reports is provided on the Delphi 8 installation disks and can be installed to work with Delphi 8 or previous versions of Delphi.

At the time of writing (October 2004), Borland bundles Delphi 7 with Delphi 8. So if you buy Delphi 8, you receive the installation disks for both Delphi 7 and Delphi 8. The installation and registration of Delphi 8 is more complicated than previous versions (see below), so you may prefer to install Delphi 7 (or earlier versions) at least in the initial stages of learning to program.

Borland have also just announced Delphi 2005 which combines Delphi 7.1, Delphi for .NET and C#. We have not been able to test this yet, but either of these versions should be fully compatible with the examples and presentation in this book.

Installing Delphi 4 to 7

This is a straightforward process. Insert the install disk. If it does not install automatically, run the install.exe file.

Installing Delphi 8

To install Delphi 8 you need Windows 2000 or XP or a later version and at least 600 MB hard disk space.

Because of the need to build a suitable .NET environment on the computer, and depending on your current computer configuration, installing Delphi 8 can take some time. We recommend you set aside approximately 1 – 1.5 hours to complete the installation process. To start the installation, insert Delphi 8 Disk 1 of 2 and follow the instructions. You may need to install particular Windows service packs before you can continue with the installation. The installation program will check your system and tell you what you need to install. At times during the various steps of the installation it may seem as if nothing is happening, but be patient. You will need to respond fairly regularly to various questions. In general it is safest to stick to the default options and settings at each step.

After installing Delphi 8, you need to register the product. Delphi 8 will run unregistered for 30 days after which it will stop working. The registration wizard (which runs every time you run Delphi 8 until it is registered) provides you with a number of different ways of registering. If you run into problems registering Delphi 8, phone your nearest Borland office for help. They will require your licence key number and authorization code as well as a registration key (this is generated if you specify in the registration wizard that you wish to register later using the phone or web page).

To avoid a number of potential problems and frustrations we recommend you install the Delphi 8 update pack (described below).

Installing Samples tab for Delphi 8

From Chapter 4 onwards we use a component called a SpinEdit. The SpinEdit component appears in the Samples tab of the Component/Tool palette. The Samples tab is automatically included in versions of Delphi prior to Delphi 8. If you are using Delphi 8 you need to install the Samples tab yourself. The following steps guide you through this process:

- Run Delphi 8 and, using the main menu, select File | Close all.
- Select File | Open. Navigate to the following directory:
  c:\Program Files\Borland\BDS\2.0\Demos\VCL\Samples\
  Now select file Borland.Vcl.Samples.bdsproj and click on Open (figure A4.1).
- Click on Project | Options... and select Directories/Conditionals in the left pane (figure A4.2).
- Type the following into the Output directory box (or browse to the folder using the ... button):
  C:\Program Files\Borland\BDS\2.0\Bin
- Click OK to close the Project Options window.
- Select Project | Compile Borland.Vcl.Samples.
- Select File | Close All (click Yes to save the project).
- Select Component | Installed .NET Components (this may take a long time to respond).
- In the window that (eventually) appears, click on the .NET VCL Components tab.
- Click on Add, browse to the following file
  C:\Program Files\Borland\BDS\2.0\Bin\Borland.VCL.Samples.dll
  and click on Open.

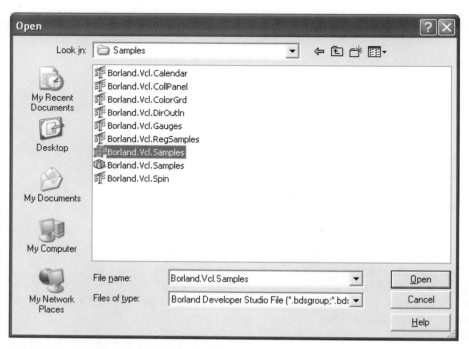

Figure A4.1 Opening Borland.Vcl.Samples.bdsproj

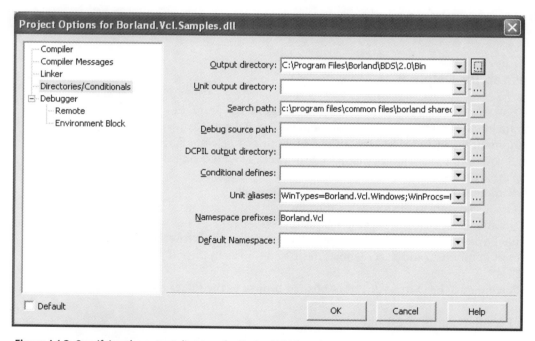

Figure A4.2 Specifying the output directory for Borland.Vcl.Samples

- Click on OK to close the Installed .NET Components window.

The next time you create a new VCL Forms Application the Sample tab, which includes the SpinEdit component, will be in the Tool palette.

Installing Delphi 8 Update Pack

If you are using Delphi 8 prior to the Delphi 2005 release we highly recommend that you install the latest update pack as follows:
- Go to the Borland web site: www.borland.com.
- Using the Downloads link, select 'Delphi for .NET'.
- Scroll down to the table titled 'Registered Users' and click on 'General Update 2'(this is the latest Update version that was available at the time of going to press – if there is a later version, select the later version).
- If necessary log in using your Borland Community username/email address and password.
- Check which particular version of Delphi 8 you have (Architect, Enterprise or Professional) and download the associated file (the particular version will be printed on your installation disks).
- When the download is complete run the .exe file that you downloaded and follow the instructions.

Installing Delphi 6 Update Pack

If you are using Delphi 6, you need to install the Delphi 6 Update Pack before working through the Database chapters (Chapters 15,16 and 17). This Update Pack includes the dbExpress driver for MySQL:
- Go to the Borland web site: www.borland.com.
- Using the Downloads link, select 'Delphi'.
- Scroll down to the table titled 'Registered Users' and click on 'Updates' for Windows version 6.
- You will need to log in using your Borland Community username/email address and password.
- Agree to the terms of licence.
- Scroll down until you see a heading 'General Update 2'.
- Check on your installation disk which particular version of Delphi 6 you have (Enterprise, Professional or Personal) and download the associated file.
- When the download is complete run the .exe file that you downloaded and follow the instructions.

Installing MySQL and MySQL Control Center

Chapters 15 to 17 cover database programming in Delphi. In this edition we use an external database called MySQL. If you plan to work through these chapters, you need to install MySQL as well as MySQL Control Center. MySQL is a database system that is widely used and is free under the GNU General Public Licence model. MySQL Control Center is a visual interface to MySQL, which we use to create and manipulate databases. MySQL and MySQL Control Center are available for download from the MySQL Developer Zone website (http://dev.mysql.com/) by following the Downloads link.

If you are using Delphi 6 or 7, then do the following:
- On the Dowloads page, under the heading 'MySQL database server & standard clients' click on 'Older releases'.
- Click on 'MySQL Database Server 3.23'.

- Click on '3.23.58 (44 files)'.
- Find the link that corresponds to the file mysql-3.23.58-win.zip and download the file.

If you are using Delphi 8, then do the following:
- On the Dowloads page, under the heading 'MySQL database server & standard clients' click on 'Older releases'.
- Click on 'MySQL Database Server 4.0.18 (106 files)'.
- Find the link that corresponds to the file mysql-4.0.18-win.zip and download the file.

After you have downloaded the applicable zip file for MySQL, install it as follows:
- Create a new folder on your hard drive, say c:\DBInstallationFiles (not c:\mysql).
- Copy the applicable zip file to this new folder.
- Double-click on the zip file and extract all the files from the zip archive into the new folder.
- Once the files have been extracted, double-click on Setup.exe. This will install MySQL on your computer. The default location is c:\mysql. We recommend that you use this default setting.

Once you have installed MySQL, a program called WinMySQLAdmin will be placed automatically in Windows Startup. This means that every time you start Windows WinMySQLAdmin will run in the background (as explained in Chapter 15, this is the traffic light icon that appears in the Windows Taskbar). When WinMySQLAdmin runs for the first time a window titled 'WinMySQLadmin Quick Setup' appears. Type in any user name and password and click OK. When WinMySQLAdmin runs a window may briefly appear, but it should automatically hide itself after a few seconds. Do not close this window, otherwise the MySQL server will no longer be running. If the window does not hide itself, click the 'Hide me' button on the bottom left corner.

To download and install MySQL Control Center, do the following:
- On the MySQL Downloads page, under the heading 'Graphical Clients' click on 'MySQL Control Center'.
- Pick a suitable link and download the file mysqlcc-0.9.4-win32.zip.
- After the file has downloaded, create a new folder, say c:\CCInstallationFiles and copy the mysqlcc-0.9.4-win32.zip to this new folder.
- Extract all the files from the zip archive to this folder.
- Run Setup.exe to install MySQLcc in c:\Program Files\mysqlcc.

You are now ready to use the MySQL software as the database for your Delphi programming as described in Chapters 15 to 17.

Installing Rave Reports

To work through Chapter 17 you need to install Rave Reports. Rave Reports is available on the Delphi 8 installation disks. To install Rave Reports, insert Delphi 8 installation disk 1, click on Install Products and select 'Rave Reports Borland Edition for the Microsoft(R) .NET Framework'. Insert disk 2 and follow the instructions. When you next run Delphi an additional Tab called Rave will appear in your Component / Tool palette.

INDEX